Human Resource Management in Public Service

3 EDITION

Human Resource Management in Public Service

Paradoxes, Processes, and Problems

3

EDITION

Evan M. Berman
National Chengchi University

James S. Bowman
Florida State University

Jonathan P. West
University of Miami

Montgomery R. Van Wart
California State University at San Bernardino

Los Angeles | London | New Delhi
Singapore | Washington DC

For information:

SAGE Publications, Inc.
2455 Teller Road
Thousand Oaks, California 91320
E-mail: order@sagepub.com

SAGE Publications Ltd.
1 Oliver's Yard
55 City Road
London EC1Y 1SP
United Kingdom

SAGE Publications India Pvt. Ltd.
B 1/I 1 Mohan Cooperative Industrial Area
Mathura Road, New Delhi 110 044
India

SAGE Publications Asia-Pacific Pte. Ltd.
33 Pekin Street #02-01
Far East Square
Singapore 048763

Printed in the United States of America

Library of Congress Cataloging-in-Publication Data

Human resource management in public service: Paradoxes, processes, and problems/Evan M. Berman . . . [et al.]. — 3rd ed.
    p. cm.
Includes bibliographical references and index.
ISBN 978-1-4129-6743-3 (cloth)
   1. Civil service—Personnel management. I. Berman, Evan M.

JF1601.H86 2010
352.6—dc22   2008050782

Printed on acid-free paper.

09 10 11 12 13   10 9 8 7 6 5 4 3 2 1

Acquiring Editor:	Lisa Cuevas Shaw
Editorial Assistant:	MaryAnn Vail
Production Editor:	Sarah K. Quesenberry
Copy Editor:	Alison Hope
Proofreader:	Vicki Reed-Castro
Indexer:	Wendy Allex
Typesetter:	C&M Digitals (P) Ltd.
Cover Designer:	Edgar Abarca
Marketing Manager:	Jennifer Reed Banando

Contents

PREFACE

*H*uman Resource Management in Public Service: Paradoxes, Processes, and Problems introduces managers and aspiring managers to this personally relevant and professionally exciting field. Not only do all people encounter human capital processes, but these issues frequently are found in headline news reports. Execrable or exemplary, such cases make this an unusually interesting one to study. Whether the topic is genetic testing in the recruitment and selection function, pay reform initiatives in compensation, employee and management competencies in training and development, novel ways to evaluate individuals in the appraisal process, or the right to strike in labor-management relations there is no shortage of controversy. The worldwide economic downturn of 2008 and 2009, in fact, made human resource management more difficult and critical as managers are faced with hiring freezes, layoffs, frustrations of too few to do too much, challenges to civil service safeguards, and union activism, to mention only just a few of the likely impacts.

This third edition retains many essential qualities and purposes of earlier editions while incorporating numerous revisions, updates, and refinements. Specifically, because employees and managers alike regularly confront human resource problems, the book probes such issues from both employee and managerial viewpoints. It discusses these problems, explains how they arise, and suggests what can be done about them. It continues to offer paradoxical perspectives about the inherent challenges as well as the unique political and legal context of the public sector management within which they take place.

Furthermore, this edition offers

- a thoroughly revised and accessible chapter on legal rights and responsibilities, contributed by labor law expert, Sally Gertz;
- a new chapter on employee motivation;
- an updated and expanded treatment on many issues;
- new sections on the German public service, the New Millennials (also called Generation-Y, or Gen-Y), sexual orientation and gender diversity, contract personnel, civil service reform in the United States and Ukraine, the "clockless" office, breast-feeding at work, elder care, child care in Denmark, workplace violence, Chinese performance appraisal, ethics training, succession planning, exit interviews and terminations, public sector strikes in France; and
- additional skill-building exercises and revised exercises.

In short, our team—combining more than 100 years of professional and academic experience (we are much too young to be that old!)—has crafted a volume that

- assumes that readers are or will be generalist line managers,
- presents a comprehensive range of topics and issues,
- illustrates these discussions with a blend of examples from local, state, and federal jurisdictions, and
- encourages students not merely to peruse the material, but also to apply it.

As long-time members of the American Society of Public Administration, who have widely published in the field (see About the Authors), we believe that what shapes an agency, commission, department, or government enterprise is its people and how they are managed. That belief motivated us to write the type of text described below.

The Introduction, after articulating the importance of human resource management, sets out the book's provocative theme that paradoxes pervade the field; it then shows how those paradoxes can be explored and addressed. The chapters that follow feature learning objectives, essential knowledge and skills, pertinent editorial exhibits, key terms, telling endnotes, and management exercises. The intent is to make the material user-friendly and accessible by highlighting dilemmas, challenging readers to resolve them, and enticing them to go beyond the text to discover and confront other dilemmas. The idea is not to stuff but rather to stretch minds.

Part I: Context and Challenges, showcases two topic areas. Chapter 1, the heritage of public service, takes an unusual approach: it examines the normative and ethical underpinnings of the field by discussing reform movements from past generations to the present day. Knowledge of what has gone before is helpful for understanding contemporary issues and for avoiding repetition of past mistakes—which themselves were often reincarnations of earlier errors. Paradoxes abound. Today, for example, both the "thickening" of "top" government and the "hollowing" of "big" government (the increase in political appointees, the decrease of career public servants) are occurring at the same time. Since much of human resource management is framed by law, Chapter 2 introduces legal obligations that agencies and their employees must recognize—not merely to conform with the law, but also to grasp its spirit. Thus what is legal may not be ethical and vice versa: law represents minimally acceptable behavior but ethics inspires exemplary action.

With these foundations in hand, attention turns to the core management functions in Part II: Processes and Skills. Rife with ironies, these chapters are sequenced, reflecting the stages of employment, from start to finish. Thus employees encounter recruitment and selection first, followed by being placed into the organization, motivated, compensated, trained, and evaluated. In the process, they face issues such as

- the quasi-science of employee selection;
- the oftentimes unrecognized importance of position management—and why it may be absorbed into cyberspace;
- the enigma of human motivation;
- the difficulty of knowing how much someone should be paid;
- the important yet uncertain nature of "employee-friendly" policies, policies which can be quite unfriendly;

- the challenges involved in creating training and development policies; and
- the contradictions of personnel evaluation.

The critical approach found in these chapters—stalking, contesting, and seeking resolution to paradoxes—is a distinctive feature of this work.

The final chapter explores labor-management relations as the capstone of human resource management. That is, both the foundations of the field as well as its functions have been—and will be—affected by the relationship between public employers and their employees. The key conundrum: the framework undergirding this relationship actually undermines it, a fact that is largely unrecognized. The volume closes with conclusions and provocations about emergent technologies, human competencies, and the drama of personal excellence. A glossary and indices will assist inquisitive readers in exploring the material and discovering new resources. In so doing, we hope that they will contact us with suggestions for further improvements in the book.

Welcome to human resource management in a text that is, paradoxically, both conventional and unconventional in its coverage of issues affecting the future of all readers in their careers.

Evan M. Berman
James S. Bowman
Jonathan P. West
Montgomery R. Van Wart

ACKNOWLEDGMENTS

The authors are pleased to recognize the many individuals who helped us in this work. We thank Al Bruckner and MaryAnn Vail at SAGE as well as colleagues in the American Society for Public Administration for their encouragement and support. We are grateful to Barbara Moore and Christine Ulrich of the International City/County Management Association as well as The Council of State Governments, the AFL-CIO, the International Personnel Management Association, the American Society for Public Administration, the Families and Work Institute, and the National Academy of Public Administration. In addition, the following provided helpful advice: Ms. Doris Jui, the University of Miami, School of Business Administration Librarian; Clint Davis; Iowa Department of Personnel; Polk County Department of Personnel; City of Des Moines Personnel Department; City of Ames Personnel Department; the Iowa State University Department of Human Resources; and Riverside County, California. All of us have benefited from our students and graduate assistants, with special appreciation to Marcia A. Beck, Kristan Brown, Susan Spice, Victor Munoz, Shane Markowitz, Martha Medina, David J. Miller, Michael Kennedy, and Adrian Buckland. Finally, but not least, we want to thank the anonymous reviewers for their dedication to this project, as well as numerous colleagues and students who, through their feedback and adoption decisions, have helped make this book successful.

INTRODUCTION

If there are two courses of action, you should always pick the third.

—Proverb

There are two questions virtually everyone asks: "Why is managing people so hard?" and "Why do people dislike management so much?" The answers to both questions are about *paradoxes*—seemingly incompatible ideas and practices that have to be made to work well together in organizations. Working well means that they are, on the one hand, efficient and effective at achieving their intended purposes and, on the other, that they are the kinds of places where people would like to be. This book, written for current and future public managers, not personnel technicians, highlights paradoxes in human resource management and invites you to join the search to improve work life in organizations. While human resource management may start with identifying workplace problems—the subject of scathing criticism over the past century and the "Dilbert" cartoons of today—the purpose is ultimately to find ways to make life better for employees and to enhance performance of public institutions as a whole.

In so doing, this text seeks to both "build in" (Latin: *instruere*) and "draw out" (*educare*). That is, most people benefit from an integrated, structured knowledge base more so than disconnected facts and ideas. Yet learning is not simply instruction: it is also an unpredictable process of exploring and questioning, a process that draws out the best in the human mind. Accordingly, truly "own" this publication by annotating these pages with *your* ideas, disputes, satisfactions, discomforts, experiences, comparisons, applications, inventions, and paradoxes. Then interact with other readers in a live or virtual classroom to stretch your thinking about the management of work. The way to get the most *out* of the book is to get *into* it! Ask more of yourself than anyone can ever ask of you; that way you will always be ready for anything. Nothing is as exhausting as underachieving. Become knowledgeable, for without knowledge progress is doomed; be prepared to contribute, because giving ensures growth.

▐▐ MANAGING PEOPLE

What, then, is *human resource management?* If an organization can be defined as a group of people working toward a goal, and management can be defined as the process of accomplishing these goals through other people, then the subject of this volume is the development of policies for effective utilization of human resources in an organization. Stated differently, all decisions affecting the relationship between the individual and the organization can be seen as dimensions of human resource management. Psychological and productivity goals are pivotal to this relationship. That is, the work performed must be meaningful to employees as well as to the institution. Not surprisingly, these two goals are interactive, reciprocal—and sometimes contradictory.

Human resource management, then, is a titanic force that shapes the conditions in which people find themselves. Its daily practice is an area that administrators are responsible for and can have a genuine impact on. Human resource management *matters*. Indeed, the most important job of an administrator is to help her organization use its most valuable asset— people—productively. From deciding how individuals will be recruited to how they are then compensated, trained, and evaluated, human resource administration has a significant, even definitive, effect on the careers of all employees. Legislative officials and chief executives may have authority to design new programs and approve budgets, but it is managers who hire, place, pay, develop, and appraise subordinates. They will spend more time on managing people than on anything else. Nothing is of more consequence; nothing is more difficult.

And it is not going to get easier. Not only have personnel specialists in many jurisdictions been "downsized," but also they are experimenting with entirely new approaches to human resource management, including far-reaching civil service reform (e.g., the states of Florida, Georgia, and South Carolina, as well as selected federal agencies such as the departments of Homeland Security and Defense). Managers are being required to do more with less, despite the fact that human resource issues are becoming—as this text demonstrates—more numerous and complicated. Clearly, a supervisor who regards personnel concerns as a nuisance to be endured will be overwhelmed by additional responsibilities and the need to deal with them. As one wise official stated, "Put human resource management first because it is the most important." The unimpeachable fact is that a leader that does not take care of her people will have no one to lead. Fail to honor people, and they will fail to honor you. The tragedy: few are trained to manage employees.

■■ THE PARADOX PUZZLE

An inexorable element of the world is that it evolves and becomes more complex, making management of organizations more difficult. Rapid and spastic change spawns confusing, contradictory **paradoxes** (from the Greek *para* or beyond and *doxa* or belief). Existing in a twilight zone between the rational and irrational, they are anomalous juxtapositions of incongruous, incredible contentions. Seeming absurdities, such tantalizing riddles contradict oversimplifications and overrationalizations in conventional thinking. In so doing, they produce humility, vitality, and surprise; the beginning of wisdom is the realization of ignorance. These gnarly predicaments jolt the brain, alternatively puzzling and inspiring people to wring further understanding from understanding by making the unknown known (Rescher, 2001). This creates a deeper comprehension of the principles behind the paradoxes, furnishes valuable insights, and provides unexpected solutions to thinking about people and institutions. Indeed, the recognition of ambiguities, equivocations, and unstated assumptions inherent in paradoxes has led to significant advances in science, philosophy, mathematics, and other fields over the years. "The true test of a first-rate mind," F. Scott Fitzgerald said, "is the ability to hold two contradictory ideas at the same time and still function." Some of the best-led organizations, likewise, are those that achieve a balance between seemingly contradictory opposites.

Full of paradoxes, the management of human capital embodies clashes between apparent truths that sow confusion and tax the ability of administrators. Paradoxes lurk and mock both study and practice. Everyone agrees in principle that people are essential, for example, but often they are taken for granted in organizations. One key conundrum, as obvious as it is ignored, is the **paradox of democracy**. Citizens have many civil rights in the conduct of public affairs (e.g., the freedoms of speech, elections, and assembly), but employees experience precious few such rights in organizations (e.g., subordinates seldom choose superiors). One part of American culture stresses individualism, diversity, equality, participation, and a suspicious attitude toward power, but another emphasizes conformity, uniformity, inequality, and submission to authority. In fact, the unity of opposites revealed by paradoxes is at the heart of the human condition—birth and death, night and day, happiness and misery, good and evil as each defines the other.

People may value freedom very highly, but in the end they work in organizations that significantly reduce it. As Rousseau observed, "Man is free, but everywhere he is in chains." Political democracy lies uneasily along side economic authoritarianism. While "we the people" mandates sovereignty over political and economic life, political power has been democratized to serve the many, but economic power nonetheless serves the few (Kelly, 2001)—which includes relentless pressures to turn concerned citizens into mindless consumers. "We stress the advantages of the free enterprise system," Robert E. Wood, former chief executive of Sears is quoted as saying, "but in our individual organizations, we have created more or less a totalitarian system." Because capitalism and democracy are mutually exclusive concepts, the manner in which this contradiction is resolved greatly affects quality of life. Does the economy exist for society—or vice versa? Does America belong to citizens or to corporations? In a democratic society, should there be an arbitrary distinction between having a voice in political decisions but not in economic decisions?

A related fundamental riddle is the **paradox of needs**—individuals and organizations need one another, but human happiness and organizational rationality are as likely to conflict as they are to coincide. Many institutions today remain predicated on the machine model of yesteryear; indeed, the vast majority of them were born in the Machine Age of the industrial era. A top-down, command-and-control approach, revealed by the hierarchical organization chart, seeks to impose static predictability, demand efficiency, and expect self-sacrifice—the hallmarks of bureaucratization. But human beings, by definition, are not premised on a mechanical model, but rather on an organic one. They are everything machines are not: dynamic, growing, spontaneous problem solvers. Thus not only do people surrender their democratic liberties, but they also give them up to work in organizations quite unlike themselves. Human flourishing is no mean task in such conditions.

The cardinal human resource management problem is this: "Do organizational processes and procedures help or hinder the resolution of these two grand, bittersweet paradoxes in democratic and work life?" To put it bluntly, what difference does it make if people function efficiently in a schizophrenic civic culture and in dysfunctional work organizations? Such issues cannot be left unaddressed by institutions whose stated purpose is to champion public, not private, interests—ultimately, government by, for, and of the people. Human resource management in democracy is simply too important to be left to those who would see it as a technical problem. Public administration has always been about governance, not merely management. Unmasking the false clarity found in taken-for-granted operational assumptions can bring about a broader view of the role of citizens in society and organizations.

"There is," then, "nothing like a paradox to take the scum off your mind" (Justice Holmes, as quoted in Vaill, 1991, p. 83). Starting with a "clean sheet" (Exhibit 0.1) is a vital position from which to reconcile points of view that often seem, and sometimes are, irreconcilable. In fact, dealing with contradictions defines much of a manager's job. Nonetheless, contemplating ironic, ambivalent, inconsistent, poisonous paradoxes is something few employees and managers relish; attempting to make sense out of what seems wholly illogical is generally avoided.

Exhibit 0.1   "Close Enough for Government Work": A Linguistic Hijacking

There is much to be said for forcing people to rethink the basic assumptions of how they run their operations by starting with a clean slate. We all "know," however, certain things that may not be true. Some are all too willing to chuckle after some imperfection is found and say, "Close enough for government work." The phrase originated with government contractors who were making uniforms for the military 150 years ago. Because government standards for uniforms were so high at that time, saying that something was "close enough" meant that it was genuinely first-rate quality. How far we've come! It's all too easy to let the "can't do" types in the office beat down our optimism and desire for change. Starting with a clean slate challenges assumptions about how work is done and how it might be changed.

Source: Adapted from Linden, 1994, p. 155.

Yet it is precisely because paradoxes reveal the tensions in operating assumptions that exciting opportunities for investigation, discovery, insight, and innovation exist in managing organizations. Using paradoxes as a way to think about human resource administration is hardly a panacea, however. What it will provide is an occasion for reflection on and questioning of perplexing organizational routines. The right queries can provoke interesting, different, and—sometimes—quite suitable answers. If nothing else, a deeper understanding of dilemmas will be achieved, which is, of course, the first step toward their resolution. Ways to embrace paradoxes include inquiring into the bases of clashing perspectives, identifying and appreciating the best of different viewpoints, and striving to create new viewpoints that incorporate a balance of divergent opinions.

In other words, systematic, **dialectic** reasoning juxtaposes contradictory opposing ideas (theses and antitheses) and seeks to resolve them by creating new syntheses. A dialectic, then, is a method of reasoning that compares opposing viewpoints in order to seek a reconciliation that integrates the best of both. There can be unity in diversity. Jazz, for instance, "beautifully expresses the dialectic between hope and despair," the tension between individual freedom, and the greater good (Hertsgaard, 2002, p. 59). Leaving your "comfort zone" to engage in this mode of thinking should be as challenging as it is rewarding; change is inevitable, growth is optional. "You cannot solve the problem," Einstein once said, "with the same kind of thinking that created the problem."

Developing a capacity to manage—and even thrive on—paradoxes is important because they will only multiply in the years ahead with the emergence of the information superhighway, the virtual workplace, and a demographically diverse workforce. Make no mistake about it: any changes in how people are managed are unlikely to be effective without recognition of the paradoxes born in the 21st century (Heller, 2003). Know, too, the paradox that embodies all such paradoxes: as contradictions proliferate, the expectations to resolve them become increasingly intense.

■■ CHALLENGES AHEAD: CARPE DIEM

Reading is a commitment to the future, an odyssey characterized by the unexpected. To facilitate the journey, this text includes critical questions for you and your organization, be it a governmental agency, nonprofit organization, or educational institution. It reveals logical inconsistencies and conflicting assumptions in human capital management; in so doing, intriguing occasions arise to position problems in quite different ways. The charge is to recognize and use this fact—i.e., to manage conflicts for mutual benefit. *Human Resource Management: Paradoxes, Processes, and Problems* is a reality check on management and the workplace to enrich the organization's human capital.

Louis Pasteur once said, "Chance favors the prepared mind." Since the trends discussed in this volume will change you whether or not you read it, an authentic opportunity now presents itself to "seize the day" and think creatively about managing people. To do this, use the text as a springboard, and expand on the example of Leonardo da Vinci (Exhibit 0.2) by developing your own techniques of discovery. The analysis here will spark but seldom settle discussions about how to "do" human resource management. Revealing useful insights does not necessarily lead to easy answers. Reader learning, instead, will develop as much, we hope more, from personal reflection as from pedagogical suggestion.

Indeed, we hope to change you from thinking as you normally do, but fall far short of telling you what to think. The book is peppered with a precipitous, pernicious, persnickety, pugnacious, perfidious paradoxes designed to propel you toward reflection on and resolution of work-life puzzles. Complete escape from paradoxes, however, is unlikely because pathways through them, ironically, may generate new problems. But paradoxes also create unique opportunities and, together with the tools and strategies presented here, a chance to achieve democratic freedom in organizations and a matching of individual and institutional needs. "The best way out," wrote Robert Frost, "is always through."

And now for the adventure!

Exhibit 0.2   Da Vinci's Parachute

"There is no use in trying," said Alice; "one can't believe impossible things."

"I dare say you haven't had much practice," said the Queen. "When I was your age, I always did it for half an hour a day. Why, sometimes I've believed as many as six impossible things before breakfast."

—Lewis Carroll, *Through the Looking Glass*

The example of Leonardo da Vinci—an accomplished painter, inventor, sculptor, engineer, architect, botanist, and physicist—has inspired people for hundreds of years to tap their creativity (Gelb, 1998). Thus, for instance, by studying the science of art, his masterpiece, the *Mona Lisa,* reveals how many different truths can be held, and enjoyed, simultaneously. Conversely, by studying the art of science, he invented a perfectly designed parachute—centuries before the airplane. To wit, as long as you are going to think anyway, you may as well think big!

In doing so, resist your first impulse, as jumping to conclusions stifles creativity. "I don't know," is often one of the wisest things that can be said as a prelude to contemplation. A mind is like da Vinci's parachute (it can only function when it is open), and paradoxes will never be adequately addressed without the creativity of a nimble mind. Ask yourself, for instance, "What would I attempt to do if I knew I could not fail." "If the obvious ways to deal with a problem did not exist, then what would I do?" Answers may not be immediate, specific actions but rather may evolve from a different perspective, a changed basis for choices, or an alternative way of thinking. As John Lennon once said, "Reality leaves a lot to the imagination."

The act of discovery, in short, consists not of finding new lands but in seeing with new eyes. (For instance, what color are apples? White, of course, once you get inside.) To nurture this capacity to think "outside the box," do at least one of the following every day:

- Take a 5-minute "imagination break."
- Look into a kaleidoscope.
- Pretend to be the secretary of a major government agency.
- Make odd friends.
- Develop a new hobby.
- Talk to someone from a different walk of life about a challenging problem.
- Use healthy snacks (chocolate, some claim, is not a vegetable) as imaginary "brain pills."
- Form a team and use the "25 in 10" brainstorming approach: aim for 25 ideas to solve a problem in 10 minutes.

It is no surprise, for instance, that Japanese workers are encouraged to learn flower arranging, practice the highly ritualized tea ceremony, and play team sports to appreciate the value of beauty, precision, and cooperation in producing goods and services.

KEY TERMS

Dialectic	Paradox of democracy
Paradox	Paradox of needs

REFERENCES

Gelb, M. J. (1998). *How to think like Leonardo da Vinci.* New York: Delacorte Publishing.

Heller, R. (2003). *The fusion manager.* London: Profile Books.

Hertsgaard, M. (2002). *The eagle's shadow: Why America fascinates and infuriates the world.* New York: Farrar, Strauss, and Giroux.

Kelly, M. (2001). *The divine right of capital: Dethroning the corporate aristocracy.* San Francisco: Berrett-Koehler.

Linden, R. M. (1994). *Seamless government.* San Francisco: Jossey-Bass.

Rescher, N. (2001). *Paradoxes: Their roots, range, and resolution.* Chicago: Open Court.

Vaill, P. B. (1991). *Managing as a performing art.* San Francisco: Jossey-Bass.

Part I

Context and Challenges

Chapter 1

The Public Service Heritage

Context, Continuity, and Change

When government has the right people, and the right system, and the right intentions, many good things are possible. The trick is knowing which ones they are.

—Alan Ehrenhalt (1998, p. 11)

After studying this chapter, you should be able to

- understand the changing environment, key principles, and operating characteristics of public human resource management;
- distinguish the various tides of reform that are part of the public service heritage;
- identify the paradoxes and contradictions in public service history;
- recognize how legacies from the past affect human resource management in the present;
- assess the contributions of recent reforms to effective management;
- show how values influence managers in addressing human resource issues; and
- describe ethical judgments required in human resource management and use guiding questions to making such decisions.

Concern about good government has deep roots in America. It has long been recognized that for government to be effective, good people must be hired, trained, and rewarded. There is also a well-established tradition that a properly designed system for managing people is critical to good government. Indeed, two schools of thought have emerged over time: one argues that breakdown in government performance is an "incompetent people" problem and another argues that it is an "evil system" problem (Ehrenhalt, 1998). Others have pointed to an "ethics" problem that demands attention if confidence in government is to be restored (West & Berman,

2004). As the above quotation suggests, good intentions and the ethical actions that ideally result from them are critical to the creation of a high-performance workplace.

These three things in combination—good people, good systems, and good intentions—are the focus for this chapter. Good people are needed to manage government's most important resource—its employees. A few work in the human resource department, but the vast majority is line and staff managers. Their abilities are critical to the performance and achievement of public purpose. The system in which these people operate is also crucial to the achievement of results. Managing human resources has taken many forms over time and involves activities such as recruitment, compensation, classification, and training. The third component, intentions, refers to the tasks one proposes to accomplish and the values guiding the effort. Intentions of employees and managers, informed by individual and organizational values and ethics, guide their actions for good or ill. Admirable intentions are crucial to government performance, especially given today's emphasis on citizen service.

The discussion begins by identifying various important human resource management functions. This is done from the perspective of a municipal human resource official who faces "people management" problems that must be addressed cooperatively with line administrators. Managing people in government requires knowledge of the organizational context, key operating principles, the history of reform "tides" affecting the public service, and the institutional environment. Following a discussion of these topics, this chapter shifts attention to more-contemporary developments: initiatives to introduce change by reforming government and the role of values and ethics in providing continuity to human resource management. Throughout, there is no shortage of paradoxes.[1] Knowledge of the public sector heritage provides a foundation for more specialized chapters to follow.

▪▪ A DAY IN THE LIFE OF MARIA HERNANDEZ

Maria Hernandez is the human resource director of a large southeastern city. She heads a department organized into five divisions—Examinations, Development and Training, Classification, Employee Relations, and Compensation and Benefits. Like most large-city human resource directors, Ms. Hernandez faces a thorny set of issues that pose challenges, threats, and opportunities to her and to city government. Her work life is complicated by a rapidly changing workforce, an increasingly cumbersome legal and regulatory environment, declining budgets, heightened citizen complaints, pressures for higher productivity, outsourcing, restive unions, and pending layoffs. In addition, she faces the frequent turnover of political leadership, the increasing impact of technology, and the visible and public way in which government decisions are made. Hernandez earned her MPA degree with a concentration in personnel management more than 20 years ago. She has been working for the city since that time, progressing up the ranks to human resource director, a position she has held for the past 10 years.

After rising at 6:00 AM, Hernandez is dressed and having morning coffee when she hears a local TV news brief reporting an increase in the area's unemployment rate. This development will increase the number of people seeking work with the city, and pending municipal layoffs will add to the unemployment problem. These upcoming layoffs are linked to the city's decision to contract with the private sector for services in two areas: transportation, and tree trimming and planting. Many of the city department heads have contacted her about the best way to deal with the people issues that arise from privatization. Several department heads are especially concerned about avoiding litigation that might arise from layoffs.

Hernandez also reads in the paper that the mayor is rejecting demands from the city's sanitation workers for salary hikes and changes in work rules. The unions, in turn, are reluctant to endorse the city manager's proposal for productivity improvements and further privatization efforts. Labor unrest among the city's sanitation workers could spill over and affect other unionized employees who are still at the bargaining table hammering out next year's agreement. Hernandez is meeting later today with the city's negotiating team to get an update and to strategize in hopes of averting a strike. The department heads expect that she will help resolve this problem.

In addition, the newspaper contains a story in the local section detailing some of the facts involved in a lawsuit filed against a city supervisor who is charged with sexually harassing one of his employees. This is not the first time this particular supervisor has run into difficulties of this type; Hernandez is concerned about the potential fallout from this case. Her office has been conducting sexual harassment training in most departments during the past year. Although this helps reduce the city's legal exposure, she must still be on top of potentially litigious situations. She has made it her policy to investigate promptly every rumor about possible sexual harassment.

Hernandez arrives at work by 7:30 AM, having dropped her children at school and carpooled to work with fellow city workers. The carpool conversation reveals concerns among dual-career couples who have youngsters and the need for on-site child care as well as more-flexible working conditions. This is an issue Hernandez has tried to address by proposing to the city manager a set of employee-friendly initiatives for consideration. Action on this item has been slow and piecemeal, but many employees and a newly elected city councilperson have been pushing for it. Some managers have also told her that it would make the city more competitive in its recruitment.

Hernandez reviews her day's schedule (see Exhibit 1.1). Many of these topics can move the city forward and help its employees and managers to be more productive. Although her day is tightly structured around a series of meetings, she tries to set aside a block of time each day to consider the longer range initiatives she is pushing, including a new plan to implement performance measurement in key departments, incentive pay for selected workers, online access to human resource policies and procedures, and a cafeteria-style employee benefit plan. She also hopes to start a preretirement training program for all city employees over age 55, and to broaden the description of job classes. Nevertheless, human resource issues are sometimes unpredictable, and she knows that she will be interrupted many times as managers and employees ask her opinion on ways to deal with them. When she leaves the office at 6:30 PM, Hernandez picks up her children at the childcare center. After dinner, she reviews two reports on subjects that will occupy her attention at work early the next morning.

Hernandez's day shows the broad range of issues that might be encountered by today's human resource director. These include coping first hand with worker unrest, labor shortages, productivity and performance measurement, and errant employees. They also involve crafting employee responsive policies, dealing with the insecurities of those employees vulnerable to layoffs, and feeling the pressures for greater efficiency. Managers must hire, promote, discipline, and fire employees. They have to respond to grievances, evaluate performance, recommend pay rates, approve job reclassifications, and motivate workers. The constitutional rights of employees must be respected, and managers must be careful not to run afoul of legal requirements (e.g., those dealing with affirmative action; sexual harassment; and age, gender, or handicap status).

Exhibit 1.1	Maria Hernandez's Monday Schedule
8:00	Staff meeting with human resource professionals
9:00	Conduct employee orientation for new hires
10:00	Department heads—implementing new performance measurement program
11:30	Assistant city manager, budget officer, and department reps (discuss recruitment plan)
12:00	Lunch with legal counsel—review status of pending lawsuits and sexual harassment charge
1:45	Labor negotiating team—update on bargaining issues and impasses
2:30	Media briefing—tout elements of family-friendly policy initiative for city employees
4:00	University contractors—review design of training program regarding computer network
5:30	Administrative assistant—review plans for updating all job descriptions

These challenges suggest the range of activities that fall within the purview of **human resource management**—challenges that seek to increase the ways that people contribute to public organizations from the initial hiring through development, motivation, and maintenance of human resources. Strategic human resource management has evolved from what was previously called **personnel administration**. Whereas traditional personnel administration was concerned primarily with internal processes—recruitment, compensation, discipline—and the application of the rules and procedures of the civil service system, human resource management embraces a broader, more strategic, and "people-focused" definition of the management of human capital with an eye to the kind of workforce needed. As noted in the Introduction, it encompasses all decisions affecting the relationship between the individual and the organization. This includes employee and organizational development, organizational design, performance management, reward systems and benefits, productivity improvement, staffing, employee-employer relations, and health and safety (Abramson & Gardner, 2002). **Civil service** refers to the branches of public service, excluding legislative, judicial, or military: positions typically are filled based on competitive examinations, and a professional career public service exists with protection against political influence and patronage.

The next section reviews the changing work environment and the principles and operating characteristics of human resource management. The historical and institutional context is then examined to better understand the origins and impacts of administrative reforms affecting the public service. Next, recent efforts to reform government and improve its performance are explored. Finally, the role of values and ethics in government and some ways to manage ethics are explored.

▪▪ A DYNAMIC ENVIRONMENT AND KEY PRINCIPLES

Work Environment

Managers today need to be mindful of several trends in the government environment. These trends are important because they provide the context in which decisions are made. The bulleted items below highlight significant developments for human resource management in the foreseeable future.

- *Changing workforce.* The workforce has become, paradoxically, both grayer and younger. On the one hand, as the Baby Boomer generation is nearing retirement the average age of many seasoned employees and managers is rising. There is an obvious need for those who can immediately fill their shoes, but such a workforce is often lacking. Demographically, **Generation X** (Gen-X) workers (those born between 1960 and 1980) who might replace them are fewer in number, which has caused a graying of the workforce in past decades. On the other hand, the very large cohort of **New Millennials** (those born after 1980) has now begun to enter the workforce; they are the latest job entrants. In a few years, they will experience increasing job opportunities. These new entrants reduce the average age of the workforce. At the same time, many authors also comment on how the career and working styles of Gen-X and New Millennials are different from Baby Boomers and other preceding generations: the newer generations are more likely to change careers and sectors often, demonstrate less loyalty to their employer, be comfortable with new technology, be more independent, be more comfortable working on multiple projects, and seek balance between their work and personal lives (Marston, 2007). Exhibit 1.2 provides some reasons why young people choose public service work. Beyond this, the workforce is also increasingly composed of more women and minorities than in previous years (Condrey, 2005).
- *Declining confidence in government.* In spite of a brief spike in 2001 after 9/11, opinion polls since the 1960s have shown a steady erosion in confidence and trust in government at all levels. In the early 1960s, six out of ten Americans claimed to trust the federal government most of the time. By 1994, only one in five made that claim, and since then trust has improved somewhat but remains well short of the levels of the early 1960s (Edwards, Wattenberg, & Lineberry, 2004). According to Gallup polling, 43% of Americans said they trusted the executive branch in 2007 and only 50% said they trusted the legislative branch. These numbers compare to Watergate-era polling in 1974 that showed 40% and 68%, respectively, of Americans trusted these branches of government. Although trust in state and local government is higher than for federal, declining confidence is evident at those levels as well. This can erode the morale of the public service and impede performance. Rebuilding trust is an important challenge facing the public sector at all levels.
- *Declining budgets.* A combination of tax limitation measures, budget cuts, and political pressures to curb future expenditures has occurred at all levels of government.

Exhibit 1.2   Reasons Young People Choose Public Service
- To make a difference in a wide variety of leadership positions in the nonprofit and for-profit sectors; different branches of local, state, regional, and federal governments; and the international arena - To become engaged intellectually in the challenges facing their communities - To establish career and personal development skills that they can use throughout their lives - To build a better future for the world and to solve big problems - To establish communication links within and between different communities - To gain a sense of responsibility for others and the causes they care about

Sources: Education Development Center, 2002; Light, 2008a.

- *Contract or alternative work arrangements.* Government policy makers, mindful of the impending exodus of Baby Boomers, and to help keep costs down, are paying increased attention to alternative work arrangements. One variant, noted by J. Thompson and Mastracci (2005) and Barr (2005), involves use of the core-ring staffing model with the core comprising full-time workers in permanent jobs and the ring comprising employees in contingent or alternative arrangements (e.g., contractors, temporary workers, and part-time employees). Paul Light (1999) estimated that there are about 8 million nonfederal workers supported by contracts and grants, many times larger than the 1.8 million federal civilian employees. Exhibit 1.3 provides examples of such a blended workforce in various U.S. governmental settings. Exhibit 1.4 expands the focus to 20 high-income countries in comparison to the United States that enable alternative work arrangements to achieve more broadly defined purposes. Note that, unlike the United States, most of these countries have statutes authorizing a range of flexible arrangements enabling employees to alter how many hours they work, and when and where they work at their current job.

Exhibit 1.3   Blended Workforces in U.S. Government Settings

Naval Research Lab

The Naval Research Lab has established contractual arrangements that provide for flexibility in the workforce for various special research projects. In this system, the hiring and firing of employees and layoff procedures are left to the contractor; they take place outside the federal personnel system, allowing for quick downsizing if necessary. Other advantages to the system include the ability to evaluate contract workers and hire the best-performing ones for long-term employment. The Naval Research Lab has also taken advantage of part-time work arrangements to create a family-friendly work environment, which has reduced the turnover rate in the workforce. In addition, they have created student positions with the goal of transitioning students into permanent employment.

Transportation Security Administration

With the need to respond quickly to the requirements in the Aviation and Transportation Security Act of 2001 after the 9/11 attacks, the Transportation Security Administration pursued flexible policies in hiring and maintaining its workforce. It has taken advantage of indirect-hire arrangements with contractors that has allowed the agency to use workers for specific purposes when those needs are required. The Transportation Security Administration has also made part-time work a priority, with 16% of its workforce serving in this role in 2004. Part-time work allows the agency to schedule workers when they are most needed, particularly peak flight times in the morning and afternoon, and allows administration to screen for exceptional workers to become permanent full-time employees in the future.

National Aeronautics and Space Administration

NASA has focused extensively on creating flexible arrangements for employees who seek to use them. The Glenn Research Center, for example, has allowed full-time employees to change to part-time status as a result of health, family, education, or other reasons. Administration has used term appointments to hire workers for defined periods of time, most particularly for work on special research projects. NASA has also used student employment programs to allow students to transition into long-term employment, with 80% of students remaining with NASA after program completion.

Sources: Adapted from Barr, 2005; J. Thompson & Mastracci, 2005.

Exhibit 1.4 Overview of Statutes Enabling Alternative Work Arrangements (AWAs), 2007

Nation	Universal right to reduced hours[1]	Gradual return to work	Parental Rights			Care for Adults	Training and Education	Older Education
			Parental leave on part-time basis	Reduced hours and other AWA	Refuse overtime/ shift patterns	Reduced hours and other AWA	Reduced hours and other AWA	Reduced hours with partial pension
Australia				■2	■2	■2		■
Austria		■		■				■
Belgium	■	■	■			■	■	
Canada								
Denmark		■						■
Finland	■3	■	■				■	■
France	■	■					■	■
Germany	■	■					■4	■
Greece			5					
Ireland								
Italy			6			6		
Luxembourg	■	■					■	■
Netherlands	■	■	■				■	■
New Zealand				■7		■7		
Norway		■	■	■	■		■	8
Portugal		■	■	■			■	
Spain		■	■	■	■	■	■	■
Sweden			■	■	■		■	■
Switzerland								
United Kingdom		9		■		■		
United States	★							

Sources: Adapted from Institute for Women's Policy Research, 2008; Light, *The Tides of Reform: Making Government Work* (1997), Exhibit 1.4. Yale University Press.

Notes:

1. Statues in this category include changes in numbers of hours and/or scheduling, not homework or flextime. Flextime is widely available via collective agreements in many countries.
2. Australia: Provided indirectly, as part of protection against family caregiver discrimination.
3. Finland: The statue governs conditions for reduced hours with wage replacement, subject to hiring an unemployed person for the vacated hours.
4. Germany: No national law, state laws provide one to two weeks annual leave for training and education.
5. Ireland: Parental leave may be divided into several blocks; daily reduced hours option is not specified.
6. Italy: A basic commitment to provide preferential access to reduced hours for those who are caring for fully disabled person, parents of children under thirteen or with a disability, or a relative of a seriously ill person has been passed into law in Dec. 2007, with a mandate to introduce specific legislation by end of 2008.
7. New Zealand: Law will come into force July 2008.
8. Norway: No statute but binding collective agreements in most sectors.
9. United Kingdom: Might be negotiated as part of flexible working rights for parents of young children.
★ United States: Draft legislation currently before Congress.

Note: For full description of the statutes, including the year of implementation; tenure requirements; and small employer exemptions, see http://agingandwork.bc.edu/globalpolicy. This information is correct, to the best of the authors' knowledge, up to December 2007.

- *Downsizing and upsizing.* The size of the federal civilian workforce was cut by 258,000 (to 2.7 million) between 1994 and 2003 (U.S. Office of Personnel Management [OPM], 2005); buyouts and early retirements were preferred over disruptive layoffs. Staff in human resource offices have been especially hard hit by layoffs at all levels, with reductions at the federal level averaging more than 20% from 1992 to early 1999 (Hornestay, 1999). This has left line managers with additional, burdensome administrative tasks. The combination of federal downsizing, scandal, and the war on waste led Paul Light (1999, 2000, 2008b) to warn of a looming brain drain and to predict further decreases in government-centered public service with a corresponding increase in multisectored service. By contrast, the size of the state and local government workforce increased by 2,159,211 (to 15,602,141 full-time equivalents) from 1993 to 2002 (U.S. Bureau of the Census [Census], 1993, 2002). Despite this, many individual jurisdictions have experienced workforce reductions. These reductions are often linked to privatization, deregulation, budget or service cuts, and program terminations—trends that are likely to continue well into the future.

- *Demands for productivity.* Jurisdictions at all levels are under pressure to improve performance without raising costs. A survey by the U.S. Merit Systems Protection Board of 9,700 managers and employees found that three of four supervisors assumed additional responsibilities, but only one in five detected any new flexibility in taking personnel actions (Hornestay, 1999), although more recently this has begun to change (Bowman & West, 2007a; J. Thompson, 2007). The federal Human Capital Survey reported that just 30% of employees believe awards programs offer an incentive to do their best (U.S. Office of Management and Budget [OMB], 2004).

- *Emerging virtual workplace and virtual government.* With the advent of new information technologies, innovative organizations are replacing some traditional nine-to-five workplaces with fixed central office locations with more flexible arrangements (telecommuting, flexi-place). This development alters relationships between employers and employees and raises questions about how human resource professionals give support to the variety of work arrangements in a virtual workplace (Jones, 1998; West & Berman, 2001). In addition, virtual workplaces alter the relationship between citizens and government. Numerous federal government initiatives begun in the mid-1990s enable citizen transactions to be conducted electronically. Indeed, the 1998 Government Paperwork Elimination Act states that federal agencies must allow people the option of submitting information or transacting electronically. These are just a few ways that new information technology can influence the public workplace (discussed further in Chapter 8). Key Web sites of government agencies and professional associations are included in Exhibit 1.5.

- *Reforming and reengineering initiatives.* New approaches to the delivery of goods and services are being proposed and implemented with increasing frequency. (This will be discussed later in this chapter.)

- *Centralization and decentralization of human resource activities.* At federal, state, and local levels, there has been a reallocation of responsibilities from centralized staff agencies (e.g., **U.S. Office of Personnel Management [OPM]**) to line agencies and managers. Administrators at the operational level now have greater flexibility and discretion in the acquisition, development, motivation, and maintenance of human resources.

- *Increased managerial flexibility.* Recent civil service reforms at all levels of government have loosened restrictions and increased managerial discretion over matters of pay, hiring, discipline, and termination. At the federal level, this is evident in reforms under way at the U.S. Department of Homeland Security (DHS) and the U.S. Department of Defense (DOD); at the state and local levels, it is reflected in New Public Management reforms and the move in some jurisdictions toward at-will employment (Bowman & West, 2007a).

Exhibit 1.5	Key Web Sites of Government Agencies and Professional Associations
Government Agencies	
Bureau of Labor Statistics	www.stats.bls.gov
Federal Labor Relations Authority	www.flra.gov
U.S. Merit Systems Protection Board	www.mspb.gov
National Labor Relations Board	www.nlrb.gov
U.S. Office of Personnel Management	www.opm.gov
Professional Associations	
American Society for Public Administration	www.aspanet.org
Council of State Governments	www.csg.org
Ethics Section, American Society for Public Administration	www.aspaonline.org
International City/County Management Association	www.icma.org
National Academy of Public Administration	www.napawash.org
National Association of Counties	www.naco.org

These trends influence the way officials carry out their functions; each trend has important implications for human resource management; their relevance is considered in detail in this book.

■■ HUMAN RESOURCE MANAGEMENT PRINCIPLES

Managers need to be mindful not only of the changing environment, but also of several principles of human resource management. Nine tenets, in particular, should be in the forefront of managerial thinking. These are further explored in this and subsequent chapters:

- *Many roles of public service.* Stakeholders expect civil servants to do many different things (ensure effective government performance, implement controversial social policies, respond to political imperatives, and others). Often civil servants are called on to respond to conflicting pressures simultaneously, but managers need to provide leadership in reconciling competing demands (e.g., designing layoffs to balance the budget and simultaneously addressing other factors, such as adhering to the principle of seniority, complying with EEO and AA requirements, meeting performance standards, and maintaining ethical principles). The overriding priority has been and will continue to be organizational effectiveness.

- *Values that matter.* **Neutral competence** of the public service has been stressed since the beginning of the **merit system** in the late 1800s, but *neutrality* (noninvolvement of employees in partisan political activities) should not suggest that values of the work-force are irrelevant. Managers recruit and reward employees who are competent *and* those who exhibit integrity: ethics is consistent with higher performance and fewer legal troubles (Berman & West, 1998; Bowman, West, & Beck, 2010). In addition, pub-lic sector values are changing. Exhibit 1.6 compares traditional system and values with the newer, competing system and values. Managers need to assess systems and values in their jurisdictions and adjust their leadership styles as appropriate.

Exhibit 1.6	Shifting From a Traditional Public Sector System to a System for the 21st Century
Traditional Public Sector System	*Public Service for the 21st Century*
1. Single system in theory; in reality, multiple systems not developed strategically	1. Recognize multiple systems, be strategic about system development, define and include core values
2. Merit definition that had the outcome of protecting people and equated fairness as sameness	2. Merit definition that has the outcome of encouraging better performance and allows differentiation between different talent
3. Emphasis on process and rules	3. Emphasis on performance and results
4. Hiring/promotion of talent based on technical expertise	4. Hire, nurture, and promote talent to the right places
5. Treating personnel as a cost	5. Treating human resources as an asset and an investment
6. Job for life/lifelong commitment	6. Inners and outers who share core values
7. Protection justifies tenure	7. Employee performance and employer need justifies retention
8. Performance appraisal based on individual activities	8. Performance appraisal based on demonstrated individual contribution to organizational goals
9. Labor-management relationship based on conflicting goals, antagonistic relationship, and ex post disputes and arbitration on individual cases	9. Labor-management partnership based on mutual goals of successful organization and employee satisfaction, ex ante involvement in work design
10. Central agency that fulfilled the personnel function for agencies	10. Central agency that enables agencies, especially managers, to fulfill the personnel function for themselves

Source: Adapted from Patricia Ingraham, Sally Selden, and Donald Moynihan, 2000. People and Performance: Challenges for the Future Public Service: The Report From the Wye River Conference, in *Public Administration Review 60(1)*, p. 58. Reprinted with permission of the American Society for Public Administration (ASPA), 1120 G Street NW, Suite 700, Washington, DC 20005.

- *Understanding the rationale for a personnel system.* The public workforce is subject to different personnel systems (e.g., elected officials; appointed officials; federal, state, city, county, and special-purpose district employees). Each has its unique rationale and operating limitations. Effective managers understand their system's rationale and find ways to deal with its limitations.
- *Alternatives to civil service.* Public services historically have been delivered by civil service employees; however, alternative mechanisms have emerged (e.g., purchase of service agreements, privatization, franchise agreements, subsidy arrangements, vouchers, volunteers, self-help, regulatory and tax incentives). These arrangements affect managers by redefining relationships with service providers, altering control structures, and reshaping administrative roles (Klingner & Lynn, 2005).
- *Rule of law.* Public sector personnel systems, processes, and rules are often based on legal requirements. The complexity of this government environment is a fundamental difference between the public and private sectors, and these elaborate structural characteristics influence how human resources are managed. For example, legal requirements establish minimum standards of conduct and specify the missions of the public workforce. Law is important, and limiting liability is a legitimate managerial concern, but administrators need to be more than compliance officers. Merely conforming to legal strictures does not ensure high performance.
- *Performance.* Human resource management seeks optimal contributions to an organization by acquiring, developing, motivating, and retaining people. This challenge requires an understanding of human relations and what motivates workers. Monetary incentives alone are insufficient motivators. Managers must be aware of the available tools and the ways to use them to ensure high performance.
- *Public accountability and access.* Another distinguishing feature of human resource management is that government decisions are subject to intense public visibility and scrutiny. This influences how work is done, how resources are managed, how decisions are made, and how systems are developed. Unlike the business sector where decisions usually are made in private (because the Freedom of Information Act does not apply), public sector decisions typically require greater citizen access and input. Officials must remember that they are accountable to the populace, but they often face tension between their primary responsibility to all citizens and loyalty to their organizational superiors or their own consciences.
- *Transparency.* Related to accountability, the principle of transparency is fundamental to effective and ethical government. Open-meeting and open-records laws help to advance the ideas of government transparency and increase citizen trust in policy implementation. Those in public service should be as open as possible about all decisions and actions, providing a rationale for their decisions and restricting information only when it would jeopardize the broader public interest.
- *Human resource management leadership.* Given the labor-intensive characteristics of public organizations, the effective and efficient use of human capital is of paramount importance. Leadership from human resource professionals is a crucial ingredient for achieving the goals and advancing the public service mission of government. Human resource managers must partner with top management in guiding organizational change initiatives. Professionals in human resources should promote and support the above principles by leadership and example.

With this brief introduction to environmental considerations and operating principles, attention is turned to the past for some historical perspectives on key issues and reforms, as well as institutional arrangements that affect human resource management.

■■ HISTORICAL AND INSTITUTIONAL CONTEXT

Tides of Reform

A useful framework for considering the history of reform efforts is provided by Paul Light (1997) in *The Tides of Reform*. He identified four reform philosophies, each of which has its own goals, implementation efforts, and outcomes: scientific management, war on waste, watchful eye, and liberation management. Although Light's analysis focuses on these four tides as they influence the overall performance of government, Light's framework is borrowed here to examine briefly the implications of these four philosophies for human resource management.

Scientific Management

The first tide is **scientific management**. Here the focus is on hierarchy, microdivision of labor, specialization, and well-defined chains of command. This philosophy, usually associated with Frederick Taylor, is manifest in the bureaucratic organizational form with its emphasis on structure, rules, and search for "the one best way." Technical experts in this environment apply the "scientific" principles of administration (e.g., unity of command and **POSDCORB**—planning, organizing, staffing, directing, coordinating, reporting, and budgeting). The scientific management approach is evident in recommendations from two presidential commissions: the Brownlow Committee (1936–1937, changing the administrative management and government structure to improve efficiency) and the first Hoover Commission (1947–1949, reorganizing agencies around an integrated purpose and eliminating overlapping services). Herbert Hoover is the "patron saint" of scientific management, and the National Academy of Public Administration's Standing Panel on Executive Organization is a patron organization. Light also provides examples of defining legislation (1939 Reorganization Act establishing the Executive Office of the President), expressions (1990 Chief Financial Officers Act centralizing control over financial affairs), and contradictions (1994 **National Partnership for Reinventing Government** initiative for improving government performance). The latter is a contradiction, because its employee empowerment initiatives weakened rather than strengthened top-level unified command.

Scientific management has implications for human resources. It emphasizes conformity and predictability of employees' contributions to the organization (machine model), and it sees human relationships as subject to management control. Hallmarks of scientific management such as job design (characterized by standard procedures, narrow span of control, and specific job descriptions instituted to improve efficiency) may actually impede achievement of quality performance in today's organizations where customization, innovation, autonomous work teams, and empowerment are required. Similarly, various human resource actions mirroring scientific management differ from avant-garde practices. For example, training is changing from an emphasis on functional, technical, job-related competencies to a broader range of skills, cross-functional training, and diagnostic, problem-solving capabilities. Performance measurement and evaluation has been shifting from individual goals and supervisory review to team goals and multiple reviewers (customer, peer, supervisory). Rewards have been moving from individually based merit increases to team- or group-based rewards—both financial and nonfinancial. Nevertheless, current emphasis on productivity measurement, financial incentives, and efficiency reflects the continuing influence of scientific management.

War on Waste

The second reform tide is the **war on waste**, which emphasizes economy. Auditors, investigators, and inspectors general are used to pursue this goal. Congressional hearings on welfare fraud are a defining moment in this tide, and the **Inspector General Act of 1978** is defining legislation. The 1992 Federal Housing Enterprises Financial Safety and Soundness Act is an expression of the war on waste with its provisions to fight internal corruption. The 1993 Hatch Act Reform Amendments are a contradiction to this tide because they relaxed (rather than tightened) limits on the political activities of federal employees. The "patron saints" for the war on waste are W. R. Grace, who headed President Reagan's task force (1982–1984) to determine how government could be operated for less; Jack Anderson, the crusading journalist who put the spotlight on government boondoggles; and Senator William Proxmire, who originated the Golden Fleece Award. Citizens Against Government Waste, founded in 1984 by the late Jack Anderson and the late J. Peter Grace, is the patron organization for the fight to achieve economy in government.

The implications of the war on waste for human resource management are plentiful. Preoccupation with waste leads to increases in internal controls, oversight and regulations, managerial directives, tight supervision, and concerns about accountability. It can result in a proliferation of detailed rules, processes, procedures, and multiple reviews that are characteristic of government bureaucracy and that influence personnel management. Critics who detect waste and attribute it to maladministration of public resources or unneeded spending may focus on the deficiencies of employees. Fearful workers seek cover from criticism when they do things strictly by the book. Managers concerned with controlling waste try to minimize idle time, avoid bottlenecks, install time clocks, audit travel vouchers and long distance phone records, inventory office supplies, and monitor attendance and punctuality. Use of temporary rather than permanent staff and service privatization may be ways to contain costs while maintaining performance standards. Clearly, contemporary human resource practices are linked to the heritage of the war on waste.

Watchful Eye

The third tide of reform, the **watchful eye**, emphasizes fairness and openness. Whistleblowers, the media, interest groups, and the public need access to information to ensure that rights and the general interest are protected. Congress and the courts become the institutional champions seeking to ensure fairness. The need for the watchful eye and government that is more open became apparent after abuses of the Watergate scandal (watchful eye: the Woodward and Bernstein *Washington Post* investigation) and U.S. expanded involvement in Vietnam (watchful eye: publication of the Pentagon Papers). The "guerilla government" discussed by Rosemary O'Leary (2006, pp. 5–6) describes those in public service whose watchful eyes might help to uncover and document fraud and abuse and whose tactics might involve working behind the scenes, cultivating allies, sharing data, and occasionally even sabotaging agency activities for reasons both commendable and disturbing.

The 1946 Administrative Procedure Act is the defining statute for this reform tide, and the 1989 **Ethics Reform Act** is its most recent expression. The former was important because it established procedural standards regarding how government agencies must operate. Specific provisions of the latter are efforts to curb lobbying influence and promote ethics in government. Two pieces of legislation are contradictions to the watchful-eye philosophy: the 1990 Administrative Dispute Resolution Act (authorizing federal agencies to use a wide range of administrative dispute resolution procedures to save money and avoid litigation) and the 1990 Negotiated Rulemaking Act (authorizing negotiated rulemaking by federal agencies to resolve disputes more quickly, more satisfactorily, and less expensively). Both of these consensus-seeking laws run counter to the adversarial processes of the 1947 Administrative Procedure Act. John Gardner and Common Cause and Ralph Nader and Public Citizen provide examples of the "patron saints" and patron organizations linked to the watchful eye.

Human resource implications from this philosophy can be identified as well. Concern about ethical conduct of employees leads to greater scrutiny in the hiring process to ensure integrity, as well as job-related competence, of new recruits. Attentiveness to ethics also minimizes the illegitimate use of hiring criteria such as sex, race, age, and handicap status. Such scrutiny should minimize arbitrary decisions to fire employees. Creating an organizational culture of openness, transparency, careful record keeping, and compliance with full disclosure and sunshine requirements is consistent with the watchful-eye philosophy. Adoptions of minimum standards of conduct or codes of ethics along with ethics training are other examples. Union stewards are likely to cast their watchful eyes on negotiated contract violations and to blow the whistle when they occur. Professional employees will be alert to actions that conflict with ethics codes in a watchful environment. Managers should seek congruence between the standards espoused by the organization and the behavior of public workers. Calls for integrity at all levels of government reflect the contemporary influence of the watchful-eye mentality.

Liberation Management

The final tide of reform is called **liberation management**. Its goal is higher performance in government. Buzzwords like *evaluations, outcomes,* and *results* are associated with this tide. Achieving high-performance goals falls to frontline employees, teams, and evaluators. At the national level, the impetus for liberation management is generally the president. The most visible participant, however, was former Vice President Al Gore and his National Performance Review initiatives. The 1993 Government Performance and Results Act is the defining statute and expression of this philosophy, and its most recent contradictions are the 1989 **Whistleblower Protection Act** and the 1994 Independent Counsel Reauthorization, which expired in 1999. The latter two are contradictions because they promote vigilant monitoring to detect wrongdoing. Al Gore and Richard Nixon (because of his interest in reorganization) are identified as patron saints of this tide; the Alliance for Redesigning Government is the patron organization.

Liberation management also holds implications for managing people in government. Public administration trends toward employee empowerment, reengineering, work teams, continuous improvement, customer service, flattened hierarchies, and self-directed employees reflect the breakdown of the bureaucratic machine model and the move toward liberation. Belief in harmonious relations between employees and management increases the prospects for productive partnerships. Decentralization of personnel management expands authority and discretion of line agencies and gives managers freedom to achieve provable results. Before these strategies are implemented, it is necessary to determine the readiness of employees and units to assume new responsibilities, forge new relationships, and increase outputs. Line administrators can facilitate this state of readiness by identifying likely candidates for training and development and by tailoring incentives to the particular motivational needs of individual employees. Although the public sector will not banish bureaucracy, greater flexibility is evident at all levels of government and is likely to increase in the future.

Tide Philosophies in Legislation

Two landmark pieces of legislation affecting federal human resource management can be assessed using Light's framework: the 1883 **Pendleton Act** introducing the merit system to the federal government, and the 1978 **Civil Service Reform Act** (CSRA) refining the merit system and modifying the institutions by which it operates. The Pendleton Act is "a signal moment in the march of scientific management, but it also involved a war on waste, a bit of watchful eye, and an ultimate hope for liberation management" (Light, 1997, p. 18). The CSRA manifests each of the four tides, as noted by Light:

[A] Senior Executive Service (SES) to strengthen the presidential chain of command (scientific management), a cap on total federal employment to save money (war on waste), whistleblower protection to assure truth telling from the inside (watchful eye), and pay for performance to reward employees for doing something more than just show up for work (liberation management). (p. 71)

Understanding the **tides of reform** helps to appreciate the public service heritage by highlighting recurring themes that characterize such changes (Exhibits 1.7 and 1.8). Paradoxes are also apparent: Two of the reform tides—war on waste and watchful eye—are based on mistrust and cynicism regarding government; the two other tides—scientific management and liberation management—reflect trust and confidence in government. The paradox is that reform reflects both trust and distrust in government, and it may cause both as well. As the Pendleton Act and CSRA demonstrate, however, these conflicting impulses are embedded in these two landmark laws dealing with human resource management (and many other statutes as well).

Institutional structures and procedures are important because managers must operate through them to achieve their objectives. These institutional arrangements have evolved over time, and understanding their purposes, functions, and limitations helps managers to think strategically about the threats and opportunities in their human resource environment and how to cope with them. Next, we examine the goals and characteristics of these institutions.

Exhibit 1.7	Tides of Reform			
Key Characteristics	*Scientific Management*	*War on Waste*	*Watchful Eye*	*Liberation Management*
Goal	Efficiency	Economy	Fairness	Higher performance
Key input(s)	Principles of administration	Generally accepted practices	Rights	Standards, evaluations
Key product(s)	Structure, rules	Findings (audits, investigations)	Information	Outcomes, results
Key participants	Experts	Inspectors general, the media	Whistleblowers, interest groups, the media, the public	Frontline employees, teams, evaluators
Institutional champion(s)	The presidency	Congress	Congress and the courts	The presidency
Defining moment(s)	Brownlow Committee, First Hoover Commission	Welfare fraud hearings	Vietnam, Watergate	Gore National Performance Review
Defining statute	1939 Reorganization Act	1978 Inspector General Act	1946 Administrative Procedure Act	1993 Government Performance and Results Act
Most recent expression	1990 Financial Officers Act	1992 Federal Housing Enterprises Financial Safety and Soundness Act	1989 Ethics Reform Act	1993 Government Performance and Results Act
Most recent contradiction(s)	1994 Reinventing Government Package	1993 Hatch Act Reform Amendments	1990 Administrative Dispute Resolution Act, 1990 Negotiated Rulemaking Act	1989 Whistle-blower Protection Act, 1994 Independent Counsel Reauthorization
Patron saint(s)	Herbert Hoover	W. R. Grace, Jack Anderson	John Gardner, Ralph Nader	Richard Nixon, Al Gore
Patron organization(s)	National Academy of Public Administration (Standing Panel on Executive Organization)	Citizens Against Government Waste	Common Cause, Public Citizen	Alliance for Redesigning Government

Source: Adapted from P. C. Light, *The Tides of Reform: Making Government Work 1945–1995* (New Haven, CT: Yale University Press), pp. 21, 26, 32, and 37. © Copyright 1997 by Yale University Press. Reprinted with permission.

Exhibit 1.8	Historical Periods and Tides of Reform: Characterization, Implications, and Tools

Name	Characterization	Human Resource Management Implications	Human Resource Management Tools
Aristocracy 1776–1826	Government small and led by affluent gentlemen	Much leeway, potential for corruption and ineptitude	Appointment based on "fitness" of character, geographic representation, and input from congressional representatives
Spoils System 1826–1886	Large-scale hiring of political supporters, limited competency	Large-scale concerns of incompetence and corruption, resulting murder of Garfield 1881	Appointments are at will, and based on patronage and, at times, graft
Reform period 1886–1905	Move to merit: Pendleton Act of 1883	Balance political responsiveness and professional and neutral competence	1. competitive entry exams; 2. neutral and competent civil service; 3. tenure; 4. prohibition of mandatory campaign contributions; 5. civil service commission–created rules; 6. entry at any level permitted; 7. employees maintain high standards of integrity

Four Tides of Reform

MERIT SYSTEM	Name	Characterization	Human Resource Management Implications	Human Resource Management Tools
	Scientific management 1905–	Rational production, ensure chain of command	Conformity and predictability of employees	Job descriptions, rational and merit-based selection procedures and appraisal, rule of three
	War on Waste 1945–	Increase economy	Cut costs (benefits, travel, above-market salaries)	Regulations and detailed justifications required for expenses, hiring
	Watchful Eye 1960–	Increase fairness and openness	Integrity in personnel actions and inclusiveness	Enforcement of antidiscrimination statutes, diversity, ethics laws
	Liberation Management 1980–	Improve outcomes by reducing controls and increasing accountability	Alignment of personnel with needs of the organization	Cut red tape in hiring, above-market salaries for exceptional staff, decentralized decision making, faster termination, real recognition and rewards, broadband

Institutional Context

As noted above, the Pendleton Act of 1883 and the CSRA of 1978 established the institutional framework for federal human resource management. The Pendleton Act created a bipartisan **Civil Service Commission** as a protective buffer against the partisan pressures from the executive and legislative branches. It also served as a model for use by reformers seeking change in subnational governments. The merit system was established as a result of this act, but its coverage was initially limited to one in ten federal workers. Competitive practical exams were introduced, and a neutral (nonpartisan), competent, career civil service with legally mandated tenure was expected to carry out the business of government. Entry into the civil service was permitted at any level in the hierarchy, unlike systems where new recruits were required to start at the entry level and work their way up.

The reform movement that led to the Pendleton Act was clear about what it was against but less clear about what it favored. This has led some observers to describe the reformers' efforts as essentially negative. They wanted to get rid of the **spoils system** (appointments based on political favor) and the evils (graft, corruption, waste, incompetence) associated with it. Separating politics from administration was key to accomplishing this objective. Using moralistic arguments, reformers campaigned against what was "bad" in the civil service (politics and spoils) and, to a lesser extent, campaigned for what was "good" (merit and administration) government and improved efficiency. (See Chapter 4 for further discussion of this topic.)

Although 95 years of experience with the Pendleton Act's institutional arrangements showed mixed results, by the mid- to late-1970s it was clear that the existing federal personnel system aimed at efficiency was, paradoxically, often inefficient. Among the problems were entrenched civil servants hindering executive initiatives, difficulty getting rid of incompetent employees, ease of circumventing merit system requirements, managerial frustration at cumbersome rules and red tape, and conflict in the roles of the Civil Service Commission. President Jimmy Carter proposed reforms to address these problems.

The CSRA of 1978 is built on the Pendleton Act and altered the institutional arrangement for federal personnel management. In place of the Civil Service Commission, two new institutions were created: the U.S. Office of Personnel Management (OPM) and the **U.S. Merit Systems Protection Board (MSPB)**. The OPM is charged with the "doing" side of human resource management—coordinating the federal government's personnel program. The director is appointed or removed by the president and functions as the president's principal advisor on personnel matters. The MSPB is the adjudicatory side, hearing employee appeals and investigating merit system violations. Two other important provisions in the CSRA were the creation of the **Federal Labor Relations Authority (FLRA)** and the establishment of the **Senior Executive Service (SES)**. The FLRA functions as the federal sector counterpart to the private sector's National Labor Relations Board. It is charged with overseeing, investigating, announcing, and enforcing rules pertaining to labor-management relations. The SES comprises top-level administrators—mostly career civil servants and a lesser number of political appointees. It sought (but failed to achieve) a European-like professional administrative class of senior executives who may be assigned or reassigned based on performance and ability. The structures created by the CSRA for human resource management are depicted in Exhibit 1.9.

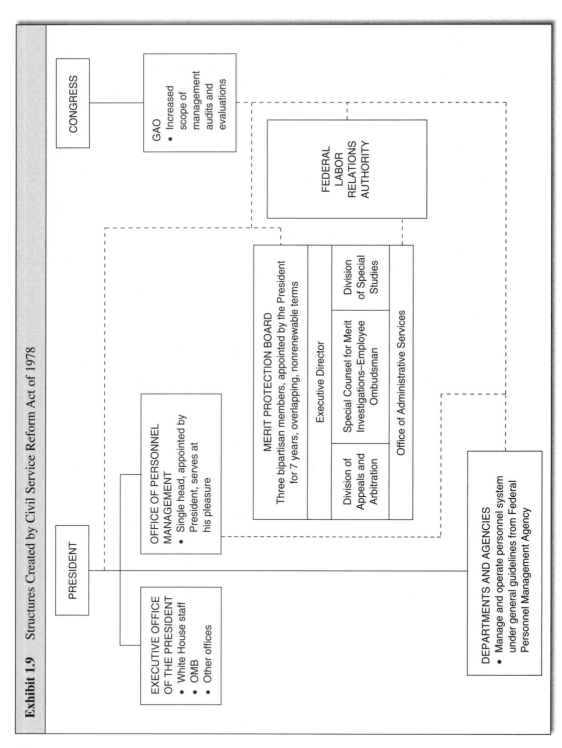

Exhibit 1.9 Structures Created by Civil Service Reform Act of 1978

CONGRESS

GAO
• Increased scope of management audits and evaluations

FEDERAL LABOR RELATIONS AUTHORITY

PRESIDENT

EXECUTIVE OFFICE OF THE PRESIDENT
• White House staff
• OMB
• Other offices

OFFICE OF PERSONNEL MANAGEMENT
• Single head, appointed by President, serves at his pleasure

MERIT PROTECTION BOARD
Three bipartisan members, appointed by the President for 7 years, overlapping, nonrenewable terms

Executive Director

Special Counsel for Merit Investigations–Employee Ombudsman

Division of Special Studies

Division of Appeals and Arbitration

Office of Administrative Services

DEPARTMENTS AND AGENCIES
• Manage and operate personnel system under general guidelines from Federal Personnel Management Agency

Source: Final Staff Report, 1977, p. 244.

State and local jurisdictions have varied institutional arrangements, but in many cases, these governments have patterned their structures after those at the federal level. In some instances, state and local governments provided a model for federal human resource management reforms. Parallelism between federal and subnational governments is seen in the existence of civil service commissions, guardian appeals boards protecting the merit system, executive personnel systems, and employee relations boards, among other features. **Civil service reform** refers to efforts undertaken by groups or individuals to alter the nature of government service. The CSRA and its state and local counterparts have been the subject of recent criticism from those who wish to reform policies and practices. The next section briefly addresses reformer's actions and proposals.

▪▪ REFORMING GOVERNMENT IN THE CLINTON AND BUSH YEARS: IMPLICATIONS FOR THE NEW ADMINISTRATION

Federal Level

Administrative change has been a recurring item on the public agenda for the past 15 years. Spurred by David Osborne and Ted Gaebler's (1992) book, *Reinventing Government,* reforms at the federal level started in 1993 with the Clinton administration's National Performance Review (NPR; later renamed National Partnership for Reinventing Government). The goal was to achieve government that "works better, costs less, and gets results Americans care about" (Kamensky, 1999). In Light's framework, the National Partnership for Reinventing Government is an illustration of the liberation management tide of reform, although it also contains elements of Hamiltonian activism and scientific management. The key features of reinvention and NPR were to achieve government that is catalytic, empowering, enterprising, competitive, mission and customer driven, anticipatory, results oriented, decentralized, and market oriented.

Reformers identified the link between performance improvement and the personnel system. In general, they detected flaws in the system rather than in the individual civil servants, and harshly criticized the counterproductive civil service system that they viewed as beyond redemption. Bilmes and Neal (2003, pp. 115–116) summarized problems facing civil service systems:

[H]iring, firing, promotion, organizational structure, lack of lateral opportunities, insufficient training, poor compensation, limited awards and recognition, few fringe benefits, lack of career development, legalistic dispute resolution, inflexibility, poor performance measurement and evaluation, use of contractors for mission-critical activities, antiquated information technology, and unhealthy, unsanitary office facilities.

Academics and professional groups proposed administrative changes in response to such problems (see, e.g., Donahue & Nye, 2003; National Academy of Public Administration, 2004). Some of these reform proposals echoed past calls for government-wide reorganization (e.g., the 1989 National Commission on the Public Service or the Volcker Commission) and anticipated more recent reform recommendations as well (e.g., the 2003 Volcker Commission;

see Exhibit 1.10). The earlier report identifies the so-called quiet crisis facing civil service, and recommends several familiar changes, including increased salaries, performance-based pay, simplified hiring, fewer political appointees, improved training, and so forth. The latter report follows characterizations of the federal civil service as a system at risk (Blunt, 2002; Lane, Wolf, & Woodard, 2003). Indeed, in 2001 U.S. Comptroller General David Walker elevated human capital to the U.S. Government Accountability Office's (GAO's) list of "high-risk government operations" (a designation recently renewed), stating that agencies are vulnerable to mission failure when they lack a focus on human capital development.

Exhibit 1.10   Recommendations From the National Commission on the Public Service

Organization

- Reorganize the executive branch into a limited number of mission-related departments.
- Select agency managers based on their operational skills and give them authority to develop management and personnel systems appropriate to missions.
- Give the president expedited authority to recommend agency and departmental reorganization.
- Realign congressional committees to match mission-driven reorganization of executive branch.

Leadership

- Streamline and speed up the presidential appointment process.
- Reduce executive branch political positions.
- Divide Senior Executive Service into management corps and professional and technical corps.
- Examine employee ethics regulations and modify those with little public benefit.
- Increase judicial, executive, and legislative salaries to be comparable with other professions.
- Break the statutory link tying the salaries of judges and senior political appointees to those of congressional members.

Operations

- Develop more flexible personnel management systems.
- Continue efforts to simplify and accelerate employee recruitment.
- Allow agencies to set compensation related to current market conditions.
- Set outsourcing standards and goals that advance the public interest and do not undermine core government functions.

Source: National Commission on the Public Service, 2003.

A retrospective on civil service reform over the years argues that the 1990s witnessed the disaggregation of the federal civil service. This little-noticed phenomenon resulted in slightly fewer than half of all executive branch employees becoming part of the excepted service, thereby relinquishing traditional civil service protections. In the quest for hyperflexibility, the Clinton administration pursued a three-prong strategy: (a) authorizing personnel demonstration projects, (b) creating "performance based organizations," and [c] constructing modified personnel systems for malfunctioning agencies (J. Thompson, 2001, p. 91).

The George W. Bush administration (2001–2009) had its own management reform agenda to address management dysfunctions. Five key areas were highlighted: human capital, competitive sourcing, financial performance, E-government, and budget-performance integration.

The first two areas are most relevant to human resource management. The administration's initiatives address people-related problems, giving greatest attention to the need for organizational restructuring, performance measurement, performance-based pay, hiring and development plans to fill key skill gaps, competitive sourcing, and information technology. For example, the 2001 Freedom to Manage Initiative and Managerial Flexibility Act sought to "eliminate legal barriers to effective management," just as Clinton's NPR reinvention reforms sought to move "from red tape to results." The Federal Activities Inventory Reform Act required agencies to assess the susceptibility to competition of the activities performed by their workforce in anticipation of placing federal workers in competition with the private sector. In the words of one analyst, these reforms "contain the excesses of Madisonian protection" and "promote the opportunity for Hamiltonian performance" (Behn, 2003, p. 199).

The Bush administration stressed the need for strategic management of human capital by obtaining the talent to get the job done, seeking continuity of competent leadership, and creating a results-oriented performance culture (OMB, 2004). To monitor implementation of the agenda, the administration developed a simple grading system—red, yellow, and green. Key federal agencies are assessed regarding achievement of standards for success. Exhibit 1.11 reports the scorecard for 26 agencies during the quarter ending on March 31, 2007 (latest available) on the dimensions of human capital and competitive sourcing. A green designation indicates progress in implementing the president's management agenda. This is more evident on human capital than it is on competitive sourcing. Although a green designation is evident for many agencies on the progress dimension, no agency has yet to receive such a designation on the current status dimension for either human capital or competitive sourcing.

Recent reforms have been the target of critics. For example, the second report from the Volcker Commission was opposed by the American Federation of Government Employees and the National Treasury Employees Unions, the two largest federal employee unions, but was warmly received by the Bush administration, which favored the increased flexibility resulting from restructuring (Kauffman, 2003a). Similarly, the Bush administration's outsourcing initiative, which seeks to subject as many of the government's approximately 850,000 commercial jobs as possible to privatization, has been opposed by the American Federation of Government Employees, other unions, and some lawmakers. Opponents claim the privatization or contracting-out agenda would diminish service quality in search for the lowest price (Phinney, 2003a). They protest the designation of certain positions as "commercial jobs" and seek to shield selected jobs from privatization (Phinney, 2003b).

Some of the proposed and adopted reforms have been particularly contentious, including the increased flexibility of personnel policies in DHS and DOD, the overhaul of pay for the SES, performance-based contracting, alteration of the number of political appointees, withdrawal of collective bargaining rights for selected groups of public employees, weakening of the merit system, and the requirement for competitive sourcing (Bowman & West, 2007a; Kauffman, 2003a, 2003b, 2003c; Phinney, 2003a, 2003b; Robb, 2003; J. Thompson, 2007). The history and rationale behind the personnel reforms in DHS and DOD have been summarized by Brook and King (2008), who pointed out that these reforms were claimed to be justified on the basis of national security and that increasing managerial power and flexibility were to deal with the threat from terrorist attacks. A recent analysis by Underhill and Oman (2007) provides a summary and assessment of possible impacts of the civil service reforms in DHS and DOD (Exhibit 1.12).

Exhibit 1.11   Executive Branch Management Scorecard

Agency	Current status as of March 31, 2008		Progress in implementing President's management agenda	
	Human Capital	Competitive Sourcing	Human Capital	Competitive Sourcing
Agriculture	Green	Yellow	Yellow	Yellow
Commerce	Green	Yellow	Green	Green
Defense	Yellow	Yellow	Green	Green
Education	Yellow	Yellow	Green	Yellow
Energy	Green	Red	Red	Yellow
EPA	Green	Green	Green	Green
HHS	Green	Green	Green	Green
Homeland	Yellow	Yellow	Green	Yellow
HUD	Yellow	Red	Green	Yellow
Interior	Green	Green	Green	Yellow
Justice	Green	Green	Green	Green
Labor	Green	Green	Green	Green
State	Green	Yellow	Green	Green
DOT	Green	Yellow	Green	Green
Treasury	Green	Yellow	Green	Yellow
VA	Green	Red	Green	Yellow
AID	Yellow	Yellow	Green	Green
Corps	Green	Yellow	Green	Green
GSA	Green	Yellow	Green	Yellow
NASA	Green	Green	Green	Green
NSF	Yellow	Red	Red	Red
OMB	Yellow	Yellow	Green	Green
OPM	Green	Green	Green	Green
SBA	Yellow	Yellow	Green	Yellow
Smithsonian	Yellow	Red	Green	Green
SSA	Green	Green	Green	Green

Source: OMB, 2008.

Exhibit 1.12 Summary and Critique of Proposed Civil Service Reforms

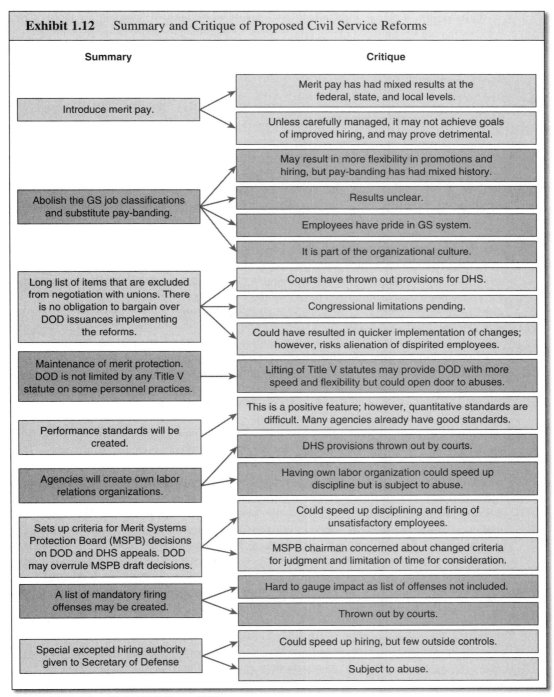

Summary	Critique
Introduce merit pay.	Merit pay has had mixed results at the federal, state, and local levels.
	Unless carefully managed, it may not achieve goals of improved hiring, and may prove detrimental.
Abolish the GS job classifications and substitute pay-banding.	May result in more flexibility in promotions and hiring, but pay-banding has had mixed history.
	Results unclear.
	Employees have pride in GS system.
	It is part of the organizational culture.
Long list of items that are excluded from negotiation with unions. There is no obligation to bargain over DOD issuances implementing the reforms.	Courts have thrown out provisions for DHS.
	Congressional limitations pending.
	Could have resulted in quicker implementation of changes; however, risks alienation of dispirited employees.
Maintenance of merit protection. DOD is not limited by any Title V statute on some personnel practices.	Lifting of Title V statutes may provide DOD with more speed and flexibility but could open door to abuses.
Performance standards will be created.	This is a positive feature; however, quantitative standards are difficult. Many agencies already have good standards.
	DHS provisions thrown out by courts.
Agencies will create own labor relations organizations.	Having own labor organization could speed up discipline but is subject to abuse.
Sets up criteria for Merit Systems Protection Board (MSPB) decisions on DOD and DHS appeals. DOD may overrule MSPB draft decisions.	Could speed up disciplining and firing of unsatisfactory employees.
	MSPB chairman concerned about changed criteria for judgment and limitation of time for consideration.
A list of mandatory firing offenses may be created.	Hard to gauge impact as list of offenses not included.
	Thrown out by courts.
Special excepted hiring authority given to Secretary of Defense	Could speed up hiring, but few outside controls.
	Subject to abuse.

Source: Adapted from Underhill & Oman, 2007.

Note: GS = General Schedule; DHS = U.S. Department of Homeland Security; DOD = U.S. Department of Defense; MSPB = U.S. Merit Systems Protection Board.

While reform trends in the United States involve weakening or dismantling civil service systems in order to enhance managerial control of the bureaucracy, reformers in some other parts of the world such as Ukraine are seeking to strengthen the civil service system (see Exhibit 1.13). Civil service reforms in Germany parallel some of the changes in the United States (see Exhibit 1.14).

State and Local Levels

The National Commission on the State and Local Public Service report (National Commission on the State and Local Public Service [Winter Commission], 1993) outlines an agenda that targets, among other institutions, civil service systems. The human resource portion of this report diagnoses *civil service paralysis* as a problem, and prescribes deregulation of government's personnel system. Favoring a more flexible and less rule-bound system, the commission's recommendations includes the following:

- More decentralization of the merit system
- Less reliance on written tests
- Rejection of the rule of three and other requirements that severely restrict managerial discretion in selecting from a pool of eligible applicants
- Less weight given to seniority and veteran's preference
- Fewer job classifications
- Less-cumbersome procedures for removing employees from positions
- More-portable pensions enabling government-to-government mobility
- More flexibility to provide financial incentives to exemplary performance by work teams

These recommendations for increased managerial flexibility echoed earlier suggestions from the National Commissions on the Public Service (1989, 2003) and resembled parallel observations from the Clinton administration's National Performance Review and the Bush administration's Management Agenda (F. Thompson, 1994; J. Thompson, 2007). The recommendations of these National Commissions on the Public Service continue to be relevant, as they continue to guide jurisdictions in shaping human resource management policies.

Subnational reforms have included significant changes to the civil service system. Indeed, one state, Georgia, undertook radical reform—withdrawing merit protection for all new state employees beginning in 1996. Florida's 2001 radical reform withdrew civil service protection from more than 16,000 managers, making them at-will employees who could be terminated for any or no reason not contrary to law (West & Bowman, 2004). Six other states have experienced notable reforms (Massachusetts, Minnesota, New Jersey, Ohio, Oklahoma, and South Carolina). Reforms are most common in classification (reducing or increasing the number of job classifications; consolidating or broad-banding classifications), compensation (pay for performance, noncash incentives, bonuses, incentive-based pay), and performance evaluation (performance plans and standards). Managers' abilities to complete their tasks successfully depends, in large measure, on their ability to attract, develop, motivate, and retain top-quality employees—the essential functions of human resource management. Reform efforts are designed to help meet these responsibilities.

The prognosis for reform efforts is more mixed than might be suggested from the emerging consensus that formed in the mid- to late-2000s. Efforts to reform human resource

Exhibit 1.13   Civil Service Form: Different in the United States and in Ukraine

While much of the recent New Public Management reform literature from the West advocates streamlining, dismantling, or weakening civil service systems to "let managers manage," those familiar with management reforms in the nascent democracy of post-Soviet Ukraine suggest the opposite: a strong civil service is key to the sustained development and legitimacy of Ukrainian governmental structures. Unlike U.S. reforms prompted "from above" by the regime in power, reform in Ukraine is initiated "from within" the professional bureaucracy itself. The civil service in Ukraine since 2005 has been working to reduce corrupt bureaucratic behavior (Spector, Winbourne, O'Brien, & Budenshiold, 2006).

Ukraine's Law on Civil Service (of November 2007) is broad. It extends civil service protection to high bureaucratic levels but excludes cabinet members, the judiciary, and the military. Article 3 of the proposed law articulates the "main principles of civil service: rule of law, conformance with the constitution, legality, professionalism, patriotism, integrity, political neutrality, loyalty, transparency, stability, objectivity, glasnost, responsibility, and equal access to civil service" (2007, pp. 2–3). From the above listing, it is apparent that Ukraine views civil service as important and as undergirding bureaucratic legitimacy and authority. The exhibit figure presents a heuristic model for the civil service reform and development.

Heuristic Model for the Development and Reform of Civil Service Systems

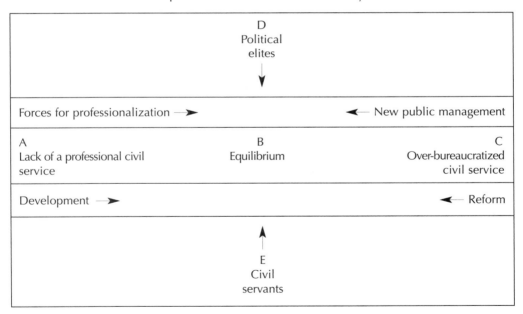

The figure shows the tension between forces for professionalization and the counter forces of New Public Management that seek to empower managers, even if in opposition to traditional tenets of civil service. The model also demonstrates the inherent tension between political elites and civil servants in seeking a harmonious balance between political influence and professionalism. The overall concept is that there is no "one best way" to engender bureaucratic reform and professional government. Additionally, the model suggests that the Anglo-American-English model of management reform focus may not cure what ails post-Soviet governmental bureaucracies.

Source: Adapted from Condrey, Battaglio, Slava, & Palinchak, 2008; Condrey, Purvis, & Slava, 2001.

Exhibit 1.14   Germany's Civil Service: Prestige or Performance?

The German civil service is based on the concept of the *Rechtsstaat*—the "rule-of-law state" that transcends divisive political divisions and acts in the name of all citizens on the basis of administrative law. After World War II, the system was decentralized to put the focus on regional and local civil service. The German federal bureaucracy is thus relatively small, with the bulk of civil servants working in the 16 *Länder* (states) and local governments.

The system is complex, with three categories of public servants (career civil servants, public employees, and public workers) and five administrative divisions within each category. The foundations of the German service are designed to make public service the most highly respected of all professions (Dahrendorf, 1969, pp. 235–241), since civil servants act in the name of the state and reinforce constitutional principles. Most teachers and educators, including university professors, are civil servants; a large proportion are lawyers, a group constituting 63% of employees in federal ministries as of the early 2000s (Kuhlmann & Roeber, 2004, p. 8). Although this proportion is decreasing at the federal level, the high numbers still prevail in the 16 states (Zuem, 2003, p. 9). As of the late 1990s, there was an "overabundance of candidates for a small number of positions" in German public administration, leading to "a rise in the number of higher educational degrees and thus to an oversupply of highly-qualified persons" (Rothenbacher, 1997, ¶ 34), due largely, no doubt, to the traditionally high status, pay, and benefits that accompanied public service careers in Germany. Government leaders have been attempting to change what has been considered to be an overly bureaucratic civil service system since the 1970s.

After the incorporation of the former East Germany into the Federal Republic of Germany and the consequent financial crises at all levels of government after 1990, reformers in government managed to initiate a series of personnel management reforms in 1997, when the German parliament passed the *Civil Service Reform Law*. The goal was to introduce more flexibility and improve performance through the following measures:

- Increased employee productivity in the context of reduced costs and personnel downsizing
- Performance measures and employee evaluations based on results, not process
- The ongoing motivation of employees to excel
- Promotion and pay based on performance, not seniority
- Increased flextime and part-time work
- Probationary periods for promoted employees, with the option of denying the promotion
- Integrated personnel management to enhance employee productivity and satisfaction
- Soft management techniques to improve organizational culture and leadership development
- Outsourcing of public services to commercial and nonprofit organizations

The personal, political, and structural resistance to personnel management reforms was great. Civil servants used to generous salaries and benefits, as well as clear guidelines about promotion and pay, rebelled against performance-based outcomes and probationary periods, and the elimination of their traditional "thirteenth month" paycheck and reduction in pensions (Zagelmeyer, 1997, pp. 2–3). Germany's public service trade unions, more influential than those in the United States, for example, strongly resisted the reforms that reduced the benefits or job security of civil servants. A system based on codified administrative law does not easily adapt to management reforms that emphasize autonomy and creativity in the middle layers of the bureaucracy. Administrative managers tended to view personnel strategies in terms of cost rather than productivity (Kuhlmann & Roeber, 2004, p. 21). Supervisors hesitated to implement pay-for-performance reforms or offer performance bonuses (see Chapter 7 Compensation) out of concern that this would introduce tension and resentment in the workplace; many civil servants suspected that the reforms were simply an excuse to downsize and reduce pay and benefits (Kuhlmann & Roeber, 2004, pp. 19, 21).

Analysts agreed that the 1997 law was only a first step toward meaningful reform of the German civil service (Kuhlmann & Roeber, 2004; Zagelmeyer, 1997). An important second step came when Germany's Federal Ministry of the Interior built on the 1997 law through its Modern State–Modern Administration program in 2005, designed to modernize administrative management (Federal Republic of Germany, 2005). This government program envisions a sweeping overhaul of the civil service based on increasing efficiency and responsiveness, emphasizing motivation of and competency development in employees, improving effectiveness through strategic partnerships and privatization of services, and encouraging a more customer-oriented (i.e., citizen-oriented) civil service (Federal Republic of Germany, 2005, p. 2). The privatization of the railway system and the post office and the introduction of E-Government have been big steps in this direction.

The German example is complicated by reunification, cultural predispositions, political complexities, and the legal system. Government reformers hope that the features that rendered German civil service the proudest of professions in the past will not hinder new reforms designed to make performance as important as the profession itself.

---

management were not without their critics and skeptics (Bowman, 2002; Bowman & West, 2007a; Bowman, West, & Gertz, 2006; Elling & Thompson, 2007; Hays & Kearney, 1999; Hays & Sowa, 2007; Kearney & Hays, 1998). A sampling of some criticisms and shortcomings include the following:

- The role of public servants (e.g., privatization, downsizing) is undermined.
- Results fail to meet expectations (e.g., pay for performance).
- Too few people with the necessary skills (e.g., contract negotiating and auditing) are attracted to public service.
- Performance rewards (bonuses) are underfunded.
- Oversight of the public service (decentralization, deregulation, outsourcing) is reduced, inviting corruption.
- In-service training for continuous learning and planning is frequently inadequate.
- Pursuit of quick successes via downsizing too often takes precedence over improving performance.
- Ideas borrowed from the private sector and accepted blindly often create more problems than solutions.
- Empowerment initiatives frequently are uneven.

Overall, civil service reform efforts have experienced a combination of successes, failures, and something in between (Ban & Riccucci, 1994; Bowman, Gertz, Gertz, & Williams, 2003; Bowman & West, 2007a; Cohen & Eimicke, 1994; Condrey & Maranto, 2001; Kellough & Nigro, 2006; Perry, Wise, & Martin, 1994; Pfiffner & Brook, 2000; Stein, 1994; Suleiman, 2003; Wechsler, 1994; West, 2002). One lesson is that when change advocates leave office, reform quickly loses salience as an issue. This result is likely to occur in regard to reform initiatives from the White House, state house, or city hall.

The impetus to improve performance and reduce costs, stated goals of the Clinton and Bush administrations and implied objectives of the Winter Commission, will continue even if the strategies for achieving such goals change. Similarly, it is likely that experimentation in some form with new approaches to human resource management also will continue. These reform tides are part of the public service heritage and contain strains from earlier eras—scientific management, war on waste, watchful eye, and liberation management. Nevertheless, changing social, economic, technological, and political forces are likely to introduce new tides as well.

The final section of this chapter shifts attention from administrative reforms to the normative issues of values and ethics, and ways to manage ethics. This focus on values is important because managers need a clear understanding of the values of their community, government, and employee groups. Values serve as decision criteria when managers face choices among competing alternatives. They shape perceptions and interpretations about issues like downsizing and managing diversity. They also limit available choices by leading administrators to exclude certain alternatives because they are not viable. Finally, values help define the inducements (positive or negative) that managers may apply to actions of employees. Ethics helps address the question, "What should I do?" when confronting issues of right and wrong behavior. Although officials might feel that values and ethics are beyond their proper domain, they play an important, though not always obvious, role in virtually every decision of management.

▪▪ VALUES, ETHICS, AND MANAGEMENT

Values

Public managers walk a tightrope seeking to balance the jurisdiction's basic values, the needs of workers, and the organization's financial resources. When there is uncertainty about fundamental values, managers lack guidance and direction in dealing with workplace issues.

To address this matter, some jurisdictions and agencies have adopted a statement of values. For example, the Miami Department of Veterans Administration Medical Center has developed mission, vision, value, and pledge statements (Exhibit 1.15). Such statements have relevance because they typically contain content regarding managing the public service. The following are some important values of modern human resource management:

- Valuing employee talents
- Encouraging professional growth
- Promoting fairness
- Providing productive work environments
- Increasing efficiency
- Developing teamwork
- Demonstrating concern for others
- Fostering openness
- Maintaining ethical principles
- Ensuring high-quality service
- Meeting customer needs

Prominent among these values are the goals of various prior reform tides that constitute the public service heritage—efficiency, economy, fairness, and high performance, among others. Managers and employees need to be conscious of such values as guides to behavior.

Clarification of basic values is important, but it requires education about values. There is considerable variation among employees regarding the degree of individual or organizational value consciousness. Van Wart (1998) divided value consciousness into three levels:

Exhibit 1.15	Mission, Vision, Values, and Pledge of the Miami Department of Veterans Administration Medical Center

Mission

To provide timely, quality health care, individualized to meet the specific needs of our veterans and military patients. The mission is supported by our committed efforts to

Customer satisfaction

Advancements in research and education

Respect for all

Excellence

Vision

We will become a center of excellence in comprehensive, compassionate health care, continuing graduate education, and healthcare research

Values

Customer satisfaction

Continuous improvement

Quality care

Teamwork and partnership

I pledge to

Smile and be courteous, kind, caring, and compassionate

Go beyond the limits of my job to find solutions

Have a positive attitude

Have respect for all

Make a difference!

Please ask ME!

Our core values

Trust

Respect

Commitment

Compassion

Excellence

Source: Adapted from materials used by the Miami Department of Veterans Administration Medical Center. Copyright by Miami Department of Veterans Administration Medical Center. Reprinted with permission.

Note: Miami VAMC employees wear the above information on plastic cards attached to their identification badges.

(a) unconsciousness, (b) elementary consciousness, and (c) advanced consciousness. Administrators at Level 1—values unconsciousness—lack understanding or basic awareness of agency values, missions, or standard operating procedures, and they may knowingly or unconsciously take inappropriate or illegal actions. At Level 2—elementary values consciousness—managers have a basic grasp of the mission, laws, and rules, and they focus on conforming in order to avoid legal violations or inappropriate actions. Managers at Level 3—advanced values consciousness—have a thorough understanding of their unit's mission, values, and mandate. They can take actions that reflect the ideals associated with good government, such as efficiency, economy, ethics, fairness, and the public good.

The distinctions between various levels of values consciousness have important implications. If employees lack awareness of agency values, missions, laws, or standard operating procedures, managers need to educate them. For example, ignorance of sexual harassment laws, affirmative action requirements, or workplace safety procedures (Level 1) can be very costly to an organization; managers must not tolerate such ignorance. Furthermore, mere conformity to laws, rules, and standard operating procedures (Level 2) puts managers in the role of compliance officers who spend their time detecting and correcting wrongdoing. This is an important role for them, but it should not be their exclusive activity. A more expansive perspective is found at Level 3, where managers are fully conversant with agency values, missions, and requirements and view human resources as a precious resource for improving governmental performance.

Conflicts among fundamental values create dilemmas once values are applied. For instance, Americans value both liberty and equality. Nevertheless, programs such as affirmative action may promote equality by preventing discrimination, but infringe on the liberty of managers to hire or promote whomever they prefer. Other administrative values are also in tension: change and continuity, unfettered flexibility and unbending centralized control, and responsiveness to elected officials and respecting institutional memory (Smith, 1998). Seeking the proper balance among competing values is a major challenge. For example, timeliness and openness are competing values in hiring that are particularly intractable: It is difficult to hire quickly when jurisdictions require that all citizens have access to jobs. An additional example of conflicts is filling a vacancy quickly when a qualified candidate is already known but laws and organizational values require public announcement, open competition, and recruiting to ensure a diverse talent pool.

Ethics

Clarifying values, raising consciousness of values, and balancing conflicting values must be accompanied by an emphasis on ethics. Ethics involves behavior that is concerned with doing the right thing or acting on the right values.

Here, too, managers have a difficult task: discretion must be exercised in addressing specific ethical issues. Ethical judgment is required of managers facing complex issues such as the following:

- Responding to instructions to fire a public health nurse for refusing on religious grounds to distribute birth control (e.g., condoms or birth control pills) to unmarried individuals
- Honoring a request to refuse to consider female job applicants age 30 or older
- Censuring a military officer for publicly opposing a ban on gays in the military

- Investigating a report by a third party that an employee was abusing legal substances (prescription drugs or alcohol) at work
- Reporting to coworkers who accidentally discovered information about pending layoffs
- Resolving a struggle between the benefits administration and the medical department over the length of time an employee can be absent from work following a surgical procedure
- Disciplining an employee for going on a fiscal binge of purchasing activity at the end of the fiscal year
- Reprimanding those who shirk distasteful responsibilities or scapegoat personal failures
- Reporting to supervisors observations of loafing and loitering
- Coping with pressure to fire newly hired minority supervisors because they do not "appear to fit" the prevailing organizational culture
- Questioning the high pay levels and job security given to core staff when employees on the periphery are paid low wages and offered minimal job security (Brumback, 1991; Grensing-Pophal, 1998; Legge, 1996; Theedom, 1995).

In dealing with the above issues of legality, ethics, and fairness, managers are indeed required to weigh competing pressures. They are often squeezed from above and below in resolving such matters. Officials are also expected to conform to the organization's stated values and ethics codes. At a minimum, they must communicate the organization's policies and codes to employees (Level 1). Ideally, such policies or codes should be brief, be clear, and provide practical guidance to help managers and employees deal with problems. Typical provisions might include conflict of interest, gift giving or receiving, confidentiality, sexual harassment, political activity, equal employment opportunities, and moonlighting (Pickard, 1995; Van Wart, 2003; West & Berman, 2006; West, Berman, & Cava, 1993). If policies or codes are adopted, they need to be observed so that there is no gap between expectations and behavior. Exhibit 1.16 reports the extent to which various ethics management strategies are used in city government, and the changes in their use. It is paradoxical that ethical behavior is expected of municipal employees and stressed by their professional associations (e.g., the American Society for Public Administration and the International City/County Management Association), but ethics management strategies are generally underdeveloped in local government: most jurisdictions have no ethics training programs (West & Berman, 2004; West, Berman, Bonczek, & Keller, 1998).

A valuable decision-making tool, the "ethics triangle" (Svara, 2007) can be used to think through and resolve ethical dilemmas by drawing on three schools of thought based on (1) expected results of action (consequentialism or teleology), (2) application of pertinent rules (duty ethics or deontology), and (3) personal integrity or character (virtue ethics). The first two approaches to resolving ethical dilemmas view matters of right and wrong as a cognitive function. By contrast, the third approach views moral intuition rather than intellect as the critical faculty (see Exhibit 1.17). Used in combination, the triangle illustrates that both cognition without virtue and virtue without cognition are inadequate. Svara (1997, 2007) applied this tool to a plethora of managerial decisions and Bowman and West (2007b, 2009) used it to analyze such salient issues as at-will employment and reform of the federal Hatch Act (legislation passed in 1939 to restrict the political activities of federal employees). Thus, the tool can help to provide an ethically justifiable decision derived from consideration of results, rules, and virtues. It is useful for analytical purposes and in judging proposed actions from a normative perspective (see Exhibit 1.17).

Exhibit 1.16   Use of Ethics Management Strategies, 1992 and 2002

	(N = 427) 1992 (A)	(N = 129) 2002 (B)	Change from 1992 to 2002
Exemplary moral leadership by senior management	73%	81.3%	8.3%
Adopting a standard of conduct	41	68.2	27.2
Exemplary moral leadership by elected officials	57	62.5	5.5
Adopting a code of ethics	41	60.0	19.0
Requiring financial disclosure	53	55.9	2.9
Monitoring adherence to a code of ethics	29	55.5	26.5
Requiring approval of outside activities	56	53.9	−2.1
Required familiarity with code of ethics	29	53.5	24.5
Regular communication to employees about ethics	29	50.4	21.4
Using ethics as a criterion in hiring and promotion	27	48.4	21.4
Voluntary ethics training for employees	41	43.5	2.5
Making counselors available for ethical issues	22	37.2	15.2
Mandatory ethics training for all employees	29	37.2	8.2
Mandatory ethics training for violators	6	25.3	19.3
Surveying opinions about ethics issues	7	14.6	7.6
Establishing an ethics hotline	3	11.6	8.6

Source: Adapted from West & Berman, 2004.

Exhibit 1.17   The Ethics Triangle: Key Elements and Central Ideals

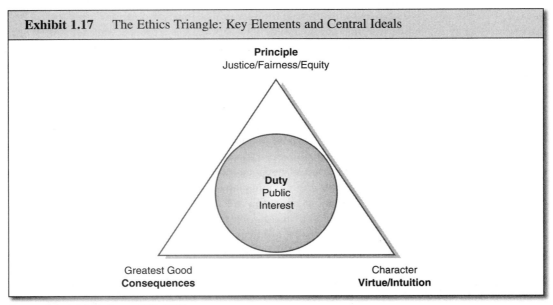

Source: Adapted from Svara, 1997, 2007.

Management

Ethics in human resource management can be further considered by focusing on two key subsystems: (a) selection, socialization, and performance and (b) appraisal, reward, recognition, or incentive, and development. Most administrators are involved in selection, socialization, and performance management of their employees. The joining-up process in a Level 1 work culture would be managed differently from the joining-up process in a Level 2 or Level 3 culture. When workers lack basic consciousness about values and appropriate ethical conduct, then ethics and integrity are often managed using fear, threats, and punishment. At Level 2, there is an effort to have employees conform to work processes and comply with externally mandated standards. When employees and managers have a well-developed sense of ethics and the reasoning behind such standards (Level 3), there is an emphasis on democratic participation and collective responsibility for setting moral standards.

Similar observations can be made about the second subsystem—appraisal, rewards, and development. In a Level 1 culture, responses are nonexistent, selective, or reactive. Managers disregard or are slow to punish (reward) unethical (exemplary) conduct. Such an environment is characterized by the absence of any career guidance (no feedback, career ladder, or organizational development efforts) and by the absence of empowerment or other initiatives to develop intrinsic motivation in workers. In a Level 2 culture, this subsystem is characterized by policies to appraise, reward, and develop employees. Conformity to conventional standards and legal compliance is commended and hailed as superior ethical behavior. The work environment provides occasional career guidance and fosters some empowerment and intrinsic motivation. Level 3 work cultures take into account ethical behavior in individual and group appraisal and in allocating rewards and recognition. Career development systems are pervasive and fair, and exceed legal requirements. Moral exemplars are praised and ethical wrongdoers are criticized. Performance feedback, empowerment, and intrinsic motivation are found throughout the workplace (Petrick & Quinn, 1997).

Understanding the work culture and the ethical imperatives of public service is crucial. Cultures vary from agency to agency and government to government, but the ethical imperatives remain constant and provide continuity. Managers are expected to help their units develop from Level 1 to Level 3 consciousness. Doing so increases ethical awareness, which may reduce ethical shortfalls as well as create a positive climate for professional development. The strategies for ensuring integrity at work might differ from setting to setting and from one subsystem to another, but ethics management is an important responsibility for administrators. The following approaches to ethics management are repeatedly suggested in the personnel literature (Lewis & Gilman, 2005; Menzel, 2007; Richter & Burke, 2007; Svara, 2007; West & Berman, 2006):

1. Modeling exemplary moral leadership to top officials

2. Adopting an organizational credo that promotes aspirational values

3. Developing and enforcing a code of ethics

4. Conducting an ethics audit

5. Using ethics as a criterion in hiring and promotion

6. Including ethics in employee and management training programs

7. Factoring ethics into performance appraisal

Finally, those with responsibilities for human resource and ethics management need to bear in mind three misconceptions identified by D. Thompson (1992) as "paradoxes of government ethics." First, *because other issues are more important than ethics, ethics are more important than any issue.* Here, he highlights the relative importance of government ethics as a precondition for good government, a way to restore confidence in government, and a guideline to maintain focus on policies and practices rather than disputes about wrongdoing. Second, *private virtue is not public virtue.* In this paradox, Thompson is making key distinctions: Personal morality is different from political ethics. Restrictive standards of behavior are required for those in public life (e.g., avoid giving preference to close friends, observe postemployment practices, disclose financial holdings, comply with conflict-of-interest provisions). Third, *appearing to do wrong while doing right is really wrong.* Although the appearance-of-impropriety standard may seem subjective, Thompson reminds us that it is important to recognize that, in ethics as in politics, appearances matter. Those who serve in government and manage employees need to heed the messages. Ethics is of central importance, adhering to restrictive ethics standards is expected, and appearances count. These lessons are not learned intuitively, and the seven approaches will help to reinforce them. Those with human resource responsibilities must push for their implementation.

■ SUMMARY AND CONCLUSION

Managers need to be prepared for the challenges that will confront them. Human resource issues involve improving the ways people contribute to organizations and concern such values as efficiency, economy, fairness, and high performance. The recognition that many issues and the alternatives for addressing them are not new but rather are recurring manifestations of problems and solutions from earlier historic periods is fundamental. The tides from the past—scientific management, war on waste, watchful eye, and liberation management—provide lessons for the present and future. Good managers will heed these lessons and pursue best practices. Failure to do so will be costly. As Franklin D. Roosevelt observed, "A government without good management is a house built on sand."

As they seek to improve performance and rebuild a firm foundation of public trust, government managers need to hark back to the basic principles of reformers from years past and reexamine the heritage of public service. They must continue to exhibit professionalism, promote merit, ensure accountability to political leaders, and avoid partisan bias. Beyond this, managers should also work to reduce waste, demonstrate vigilance in pursuit of the public interest, reconcile competing demands for flexibility and consistency, and advance a strong sense of public service ethics. Reformers of today are still searching for ways to improve the system by which people are managed; this, too, requires continued creative effort. These are tall tasks, but Alan Ehrenhalt has it right in the quotation that opened this chapter. As he put it, good things are possible "when government has the right people, and the right system, and the right intentions" (1998, p. 11). A vision for the future of the public service emerged from the Wye River Conference, which points to a shift from a traditional public sector system to a system for this century (see Exhibit 1.6).

Effective human resource problem solving also requires that managers combine right intentions with personal integrity and that they engage in careful values assessment. Defining core values and being guided by bedrock principles helps administrators make the critical ethical judgments often required in resolving nettlesome human resource issues. Public values are continuously changing, and managers must recognize and guide that change process. Thomas Jefferson said, "In matters of style, swim with the current; in matters of principle, stand like a rock."[2] Managers must decide, amid the turbulence in the public sector environment, when to swim with the current and when to stand against it, not succumbing to pressures that would compromise core values and ethical principles.

Changes are also occurring in the way government does business and the way the public service is managed. Reforms at all levels of government are being proposed and implemented at a dizzying pace. These reforms influence the ability of administrators to do their jobs— favorably or unfavorably—so it is incumbent on them to keep abreast of new developments and guide this change process as well. The chapters that follow will highlight best practices, paradoxes, problems, and solutions to the tricky human resource challenges facing managers as change agents in the 21st century.

KEY TERMS

Civil service

Civil Service Commission

Civil service reform

Civil Service Reform Act (CSRA) of 1978

Ethics Reform Act of 1989

Federal Labor Relations Authority (FLRA)

Generation X

Human resource management

Inspector General Act of 1978

Liberation management

Merit system

National Partnership for Reinventing Government

Neutral competence

New Millennials

Pendleton Act of 1883

Personnel administration

POSDCORB

Scientific management

Senior Executive Service

Spoils system

Tides of reform

U.S. Merit Systems Protection Board (MSPB)

U.S. Office of Personnel Management (OPM)

War on waste

Watchful eye

Whistleblower Protection Act of 1989

EXERCISES

Class Discussion

1. Do you think Maria Hernandez is an example of a good human resource director? Why? What advice would you give her? Explain.

2. Identify and discuss some paradoxes and contradictions in the public service heritage. Why are they significant? To what extent do they reflect the two underlying paradoxes discussed in the Introduction?

3. What are some fundamental differences between the public and private sectors that influence how human resources are managed?

4. Use da Vinci's parachute (Exhibit 0.2) as inspiration. Now answer these questions: Which trends in the government environment are likely to continue in the future? Why? How will future trends influence human resource management?

5. Identify the tides of reform. What are the implications of these four philosophies for human resource management? Evaluate the tides. Which do you consider to be the most valuable philosophy for human resource management?

Team Activities

6. Employing the "25 in 10" technique (Exhibit 0.2), brainstorm the types of ethical dilemmas related to human resource management you think line and staff managers are likely to encounter at work.

7. Discuss the lessons from each of the four historical tides of reform and how they can influence human resource management decisions today.

8. What are the human resource management consequences of different levels of value consciousness?

9. Which ethics management strategies do you think are most effective? Why?

10. Evaluate the Miami Department of Veterans Administration Medical Center values statement. Does it communicate the values of the government or department adequately? How would you modify the statements to improve them?

Individual Assignments

11. Identify several trends that affect managers and show how the listed principles of human resource management might influence the way you respond to each trend.

12. What is the purpose of the value statement? How does it further the goals of an organization?

13. Interview a public manager and ask him to describe the most difficult human resource issues he has had to deal with. What areas of human resource management do they fall into? How were they handled?

14. Has the public service been significantly affected by civil service reform initiatives? How? Why?

15. Select one of the four tides of reform and (a) identify a public organization that demonstrates the characteristics of this reform philosophy, and (b) describe these characteristics and their consequences for government performance.

NOTES

1. For example, reforms that simultaneously reflect and cause distrust in government, national policies that contradict reform tides, restructuring themes embedded in the same statute.
2. Thomas Jefferson, as quoted on the World Wide Web: http://www.quotationspage.com/quote/27616.html

REFERENCES

Abramson, M., & Gardner, N. (2002). *Human capital 2002*. Lanham, MD: Rowman & Littlefield.
Ban, C., & Riccucci, N. (1994). New York State: Civil service reform in a complex political environment. *Review of Public Personnel Administration, 14*(2), 28–39.
Barr, S. (2005, June 8). Government should consider temporary workers, professors say. *The Washington Post.*

Behn, R. (2003). Creating leadership capacity for the twenty-first century: Not another technical fix. In J. Donahue & J. Nye (Eds.), *For the people: Can we fix public service?* (pp. 191–224). Washington, DC: Brookings Institution Press.

Berman, E., & West, J. (1998). Responsible risk taking. *Public Administration Review, 58*(4), 346–352.

Bilmes, L., & Neal, J. (2003). The people factor: Human resources reform in government. In J. Donahue and J. Nye (Eds.), *For the people: Can we fix public service?* (pp. 113–133). Washington, DC: Brookings.

Blunt, R. (2002). Organizations growing leaders: Best practices and principles in the public service. In M. Abramson & N. Gardner (Eds.), *Human capital* (pp. 111–162). Lanham, MD: Rowman & Littlefield.

Bowman, J. (2002). At-will employment in Florida: A naked formula to corrupt public service. *WorkingUSA, 6*(2), 90–102.

Bowman, J., Gertz, S., Gertz, M., & Williams, R. (2003). Civil service reform in Florida state government: Employee attitudes 1 year later. *Review of Public Personnel Administration, 23*(4), 286–304.

Bowman, J., & West, J. (2007a). *American public service: Radical reform and the merit system.* New York: Taylor & Francis.

Bowman, J., & West, J. (2007b). Lord Acton and employment doctrines: Absolute power and the spread of at-will employment. *Journal of Business Ethics, 74,* 119–130.

Bowman, J., & West, J. (2009). To "re-Hatch" public employees or not? An ethical analysis of the relaxation of restrictions on political activities in civil service. *Public Administration Review, 69*(1), 52–63.

Bowman, J., West, J., & Beck, M. (2010). *Achieving competencies in public service: The professional edge.* New York: M. E. Sharpe.

Bowman, J., West, J., & Gertz, S. (2006). Florida's "service first": Radical reform in the sunshine state. In E. Kellough & L. Nigro (Eds.), *Civil service reform in the states* (pp. 145–170). Albany: SUNY Press.

Brook, D., & King, C. (2008). Federal personnel management reform. *Review of Public Personnel Administration, 28*(3), 205–221.

Brumback, G. (1991). Institutionalizing ethics in government. *Public Personnel Management, 20*(3), 353–363.

Cohen, S., & Eimicke, W. (1994). The overregulated civil service. *Review of Public Personnel Administration, 14*(2), 10–27.

Condrey, S. (2005). *Handbook of human resource management in government* (2nd ed.). San Francisco: Jossey-Bass.

Condrey, S., Battaglio, P., Slava, S., & Palinchak, M. (2008, March 7–10). *Ukrainian public management and the Orange revolution: Topdown or bottom-up reform?* Unpublished paper presented at the American Society for Public Administration annual conference, Dallas, TX.

Condrey, S., & Maranto, R. (Eds.). (2001). *Radical reform of the civil service.* Lanham, MD: Lexington.

Condrey, S., Purvis, K., & Slava, S. (2001). Public management reform under stress: The Ukrainian civil service experience. *Public Management Review, 67*(3), 425–436.

Dahrendorf, R. (1969). *Society and democracy in Germany.* New York: Doubleday & Co.

Donahue, J., & Nye, J. (2003). *For the people: Can we fix public service?* Washington, DC: Brookings Institution Press.

Education Development Center. (2002). *Service-learning satisfies young people's desire for public service.* Retrieved June 24, 2008, from http://main.edc.org/newsroom/features/LID_report.asp

Edwards, G., Wattenberg, M., & Lineberry, R. (2004). *Government in America: People, politics, and policy.* New York: Longman.

Ehrenhalt, A. (1998, May). Why governments don't work. *Governing,* pp. 7–11.

Elling, R., & Thompson, L. (2007). Dissin' the deadwood or coddling the incompetents? Patterns and issues in employee discipline and dismissal in the states. In J. Bowman & J. West (Eds.), *American public service: Radical reform and the merits system* (pp. 195–217). New York: Taylor & Francis.

Federal Republic of Germany, Ministry of the Interior. (2005, June). *Progress Report 2005 of the government programme modern state–modern administration in the field of modern administrative management.* Retrieved November 25, 2008, from http://www.bmi.bund.de/Internet/Content/ Common/Anlagen/Broschueren/2005/Fortschrittsbericht_2005_en,templateId=raw,property=public ationFile.pdf/Fortschrittsbericht_2005_en.pdf

Final Staff Report. (1977). *Personnel management project.* Washington, DC: Government Printing Office.

Grensing-Pophal, L. (1998). Walking the tightrope, balancing risks and gains. *HRMagazine, 11*(43), 112–118.

Hays, S., & Kearney, R. (1999). A brief rejoinder: Saving the civil service. *Review of Public Personnel Administration, 19*(1), 77–79.

Hays, S., & Sowa, J. (2007). Changes in state civil service systems: A national survey. In J. Bowman & J. West (Eds.), *American public service: Radical reform and the merit system* (pp. 3–21). New York: Taylor & Francis.

Hornestay, D. (1999, February 14). The human factor. *Government Executive,* pp. 1–10. Retrieved November 25, 2008, from www.govexec.com/gpp/0299hr.htm

Ingraham, P., Selden, S., & Moynihan, D. (2000). People and performance: Challenges for the future public service: The report from the Wye River Conference. *Public Administration Review, 60*(1), 54–60.

Institute for Women's Policy Research. (2008). *Statutory routes to workplace flexibility in cross-national perspective.* Washington, DC: Author. Retrieved June 23, 2008, from www.iwpr.org/pdf/B258work placeflex.pdf

Jones, J. (1998). *Virtual HR.* Menlo Park, CA: Crisp.

Kamensky, J. (1999). *National Partnership for Reinventing Government: A brief history.* http://govinfo .library.unt.edu/npr/whoweare/history2.html

Kauffman, T. (2003a, January 13). Volcker's radical Rx. *Federal Times,* pp. 1, 6.

Kauffman, T. (2003b, April 7). The new reform agenda: Congress takes up bills to overhaul pay, personnel rules. *Federal Times,* pp. 1, 6.

Kauffman, T. (2003c, April 21). Overhaul at defense: Sweeping personnel authorities proposed for DOD secretary. *Federal Times,* pp. 1, 11.

Kearney, R., & Hays, S. (1998, Fall). Reinventing government: The new public management and civil service systems in international perspective. *Review of Public Personnel Administration, 18,* 38–54.

Kellough, J. E., & Nigro, L. (Eds.). (2006). *Civil service reform in the states.* Albany: State University of New York Press.

Klingner, D., & Lynn, D. (2005). Beyond civil service: The politics of the emergent paradigms. In S. Condrey (Ed.), *Handbook of human resource management in government* (2nd ed., pp. 37–57). San Francisco: Jossey-Bass.

Kuhlmann, S., & Roeber, M. (2004). *Civil service in Germany: Characteristics of public employment and modernization of public personnel management.* Paper presented at the meeting Modernization of State and Administration in Europe: A France-Germany Comparison, May 14–15, Goethe Institute, Bordeaux, France. Retrieved November 25, 2008, from http://www.unikonstanz.de/bogumil/ kuhlmann/Download/KuhlmannRoeber1.pdf

Lane, L., Wolf, J., & Woodard, C. (2003). Reassessing the human resource crisis in the public service, 1987–2002. *American Review of Public Administration, 33*(2), 123–145.

Legge, K. (1996). Morality bound: Ethics in human resource management. *People Management, 25*(2), 34–39.

Lewis, C., & Gilman, S. (2005). *The ethics challenge in public service.* San Francisco: Jossey-Bass.

Light, P. C. (1997). *Tides of reform: Making government work 1945–1995.* New Haven, CT: Yale University Press.

Light, P. C. (1999). *The new public service.* Washington, DC: Brookings Institution Press.

Light, P. C. (2000). The empty government talent pool. *Brookings Review, 18*(1), 20–23.

Light, P. C. (2008a, June 09). Ask not what graduates can do for the nation. *The Christian Science Monitor.* Retrieved November 25, 2008, from http://www.csmonitor.com/2008/0609/p09s 01-coop.html

Light, P. C. (2008b). *A government ill executed: The decline of the federal service and how to reverse it.* Cambridge, MA: Harvard University Press.

Marston, C. (2007). *Motivating the "What's in it for me?" workforce.* Hoboken, NJ: John Wiley & Sons, Inc.

Menzel, D. (2007). *Ethics management for public administrators: Building organizations of integrity.* Amonk, NY: M. E. Sharpe.

National Academy of Public Administration. (2004). *Conversations on public service: Performance-based pay in the federal government.* Washington, DC: Author.

National Commission on the Public Service (Volcker Commission). (1989). *Leadership for America: Rebuilding the public service.* Washington, DC: Author.

National Commission on the Public Service (Volcker Commission). (2003). *Urgent business for America: Revitalizing the federal government for the 21st century.* Washington, DC: Brookings Institution Press.

National Commission on the State and Local Public Service (Winter Commission). (1993). *Hard truths/tough choices: An agenda for state and local reform.* Albany, NY: Rockefeller Institute of Government.

O'Leary, R. (2006). *The ethics of dissent: Managing guerrilla government.* Washington, DC: CQ Press.

Osborne, D., & Gaebler, T. (1992). *Reinventing government: How the entrepreneurial spirit is transforming the public sector.* New York: Penguin.

Perry, J., Wise, L., & Martin, M. (1994). Breaking the civil service mold: The case of Indianapolis. *Review of Public Personnel Administration, 14*(2), 40–54.

Petrick, J. A., & Quinn, J. F. (1997). *Management ethics: Integrity at work.* Thousand Oaks, CA: Sage.

Phinney, D. (2003a, June 16). Employees step up resistance to outsourcing efforts. *Federal Times,* pp. 1, 6.

Phinney, D. (2003b, September 22). Opposition to outsourcing builds in Congress. *Federal Times,* pp. 6, 7.

Pfiffner, J., & Brook, D. (Eds.). (2000). *The future of merit: Twenty years after the civil service reform act.* Baltimore: Johns Hopkins University Press.

Pickard, J. (1995). Prepare to make a moral judgment. *People Management, 9*(1), 22–31.

Richter, W., & Burke, F. (Eds.). (2007). *Combating corruption, encouraging ethics: A practical guide to management ethics* (2nd ed). Lanham, MD: Rowman & Littlefield.

Robb, K. (2003, October 27). Still micromanaging: Managers slow to embrace performance-based contracting. *Federal Times,* pp. 1, 4.

Rothenbacher, F. (1997). Public sector employment in Europe: Where will the decline end? University of Mannheim, Mannheim Centre for European Social Research, EURODATA, Mannheim, Germany. Retrieved November 25, 2008, from http://www.mzes.uni-mannheim.de/eurodata/newsletter/ n06/feature.html

Smith, C. (1998). Reinventing our understanding of merit. *Administration & Society, 20*(6), 620–623.

Spector, B., Winbourne, S., O'Brien, J., & Budenshiold, E. (2006). *Corruption assessment: Ukraine (final report). No. DFD-I-0203–00144, Task Order 02.* Washington, DC: U.S. Agency on International Development (USAID).

Stein, L. (1994). Personnel rules and reforms in an unreformed setting. *Review of Public Personnel Administration, 14*(2), 55–63.

Suleiman, E. (2003). *Dismantling democratic states.* Princeton, NJ: Princeton University Press.

Svara, J. H. (1997). The ethical triangle: Synthesizing the bases of administrative ethics. *Public integrity annual 1997* (pp. 33–41). Lexington, KY: Council of State Governments.

Svara, J. H. (2007). *The ethics primer for public administrators in government and nonprofit organizations.* Boston: Jones and Bartlett.

Theedom, R. (1995). Employee recognition and a code of ethics in the public service. *Optimum, 25*(4), 38–40.

Thompson, D. (1992). Paradoxes of government ethics. *Public Administration Review, 52*(2), 255–256.

Thompson, F. (1994). Deregulation and public personnel administration: The Winter Commission. *Review of Public Personnel Administration, 14*(2), 5–10.

Thompson, J. (2001). The civil service under Clinton: The institutional consequences of disaggregation. *Review of Public Personnel Administration, 21*(2), 87–113.

Thompson, J. (2007). Federal labor management relations under George W. Bush: Enlightened management or political retribution? In J. Bowman & J. West (Eds.), *American public service: Radical reform and the merit system* (pp. 233–255). New York: Taylor & Francis.

Thompson, J., & Mastracci, S. (2005). *The blended workforce: Maximizing agility through nonstandard work arrangements.* Washington, DC: IBM Center for the Business of Government. Retrieved June 25, 2007, from http://www.businessofgovernment.org/pdfs/MastracciReport.pdf

Ukraine's Law on Civil Service. (November 2007).

Underhill, J., & Oman, R. (2007). A critical review of the sweeping federal civil service changes: The case of the Departments of Homeland Security and Defense. *Review of Public Personnel Administration, 27*(4), 401–420.

U.S. Bureau of the Census (Census). (1993). *Public employee data.* Retrieved November 25, 2008, from www.census.gov/govs/apes/93stlus.txt

U.S. Bureau of the Census (Census). (2002). *Public employee data.* Retrieved November 25, 2008, from www.census.gov/govs/apes/02stlus.txt

U.S. Office of Management and Budget (OMB). (2004). *Progress implementing the president's management agenda.* Retrieved December 3, 2008, from www.whitehouse.gov/omb/budget/fy2004/progress.html+"federal+human+capital+survey"+OMB

U.S. Office of Management and Budget (OMB). (2008). *Progress implementing the president's management agenda.* Retrieved June 5, 2008, from www.whitehouse.gov/results/agenda/FY8Q2.SCORECARD.pdf

U.S. Office of Personnel Management (OPM). (2005). *Factbook 2005.* Retrieved November 25, 2008, from http://www.opm.gov/feddata/factbook/2005/factbook2005.pdf

Van Wart, M. (1998). *Changing public sector values.* New York: Garland.

Van Wart, M. (2003). Codes of ethics as living documents: The case of the American society for public administration. *Public Integrity, 5*(4), 331–346.

Wechsler, B. (1994). Reinventing Florida's civil service system: The failure of reform. *Review of Public Personnel Administration, 14*(2), 64–76.

West, J. (2002). Georgia on the mind of radical civil service reformers. *Review of Public Personnel Administration, 21*(2), 79–93.

West, J., & Berman, E. (2001). From traditional to virtual HR: Is the transition occurring in local government? *Review of Public Personnel Administration, 21*(1), 38–64.

West, J., & Berman, E. (2004). Ethics training in U.S. cities: Content, pedagogy, and impact. *Public Integrity, 6*(3), 189–206.

West, J., & Berman, E. (2006). *The ethics edge.* Washington, DC: International City/County Management Association.

West, J., Berman, E., Bonczek, S., & Keller, E. (1998). Frontiers of ethics training. *Public Management, 80*(6), 4–9.

West, J., Berman, E., & Cava, A. (1993). Ethics in the municipal workplace. In *Municipal Yearbook* (pp. 3–16). Washington, DC: International City/County Management Association.

West, J., & Bowman, J. (2004). Stakeholder analysis of civil service reform in Florida: A descriptive, instrumental, normative human resource management perspective. *State and Local Government Review, 36*(1), 20–34.

Zagelmeyer, S. (1997). Civil service law reform comes into force on 1 July 1997.

Zuem, M. (2003). Mission Statement of the Academic Director of the Hertie School of Government HSoG Series, Paper #2, 2003. Retrieved November 25, 2008, from http://www.hertie-school.org/binaries/addon/239_hertie_paper_zuern_eng.pdf

Chapter 2

Legal Rights and Responsibilities

Laws Governing the Workplace

Sally Gertz

No man is above the law and no man is below it.

—Theodore Roosevelt

After studying this chapter, you should be able to

- explain the sources of human resource management law,
- describe the structure of the federal and state court systems,
- distinguish between a binding and persuasive judicial decision,
- identify the main laws that create the framework for human resource management and explain each law's purpose and basic requirements,
- recognize employment practices that raise legal concerns, and
- identify situations when a human resource professional or lawyer should be contacted.

People do not have the same rights to liberty on their jobs that they have as citizens. Employees must arrive on time, follow orders, accept limited freedom of speech, and conform to a host of regulations. Broadly conceived, the ultimate paradox presented by employment is this: to get something (money, opportunity to make a difference), employees must give up something (liberty, time).

Many obligations and restraints that people experience at the workplace are grounded in the law. If they are to manage individuals effectively, agency leaders must be familiar with basic legal principles and processes and be able to explain them clearly to others. They also need to know the law to stay out of trouble. Although workplace laws give supervisors wide discretion in many matters, the rights of employees cannot be trampled without fear of legal repercussions. Avoiding liability is not the only concern here. A manager who acquires a reputation for embroiling the agency in lawsuits, even lawsuits that eventually are won, will see his career suffer. Litigation consumes enormous amounts of time and imposes high psychological costs on all involved. No organization wants a manager who repeatedly causes it to go to court. Hence, another paradox is this: managers must embrace the law to avoid the law. They must learn the intricacies of the law to ensure they do not spend their careers entangled in legal controversies.

No matter how complex employment law on a particular topic appears to be, it is typically grounded in the balance of three often-competing interests: (1) the need of employers to manage their workforce and operations in efficient ways; (2) the rights that employees have in their jobs, privacy, and other matters; and (3) the interest of governments to pursue social objectives through public policy. The balance struck varies from situation to situation and changes dynamically over time. Indeed, as attitudes, social norms, and economic conditions change, previously resolved issues resurface (e.g., health insurance benefits for family members may extend to same-sex partners) and new areas of contention arise (e.g., privacy policies for employees with AIDS).

For managers, one of the frustrations of the law is its uncertainty. A constitutional provision, statute, rule, or case may contain only a general principle. Consider, for example, the admonition in the Americans with Disabilities Act (ADA) to provide "reasonable accommodation" to disabled workers. It does not prescribe actions to take or proscribe practices to avoid. Does this mean that department heads must constantly call the organization's human resource professional or attorney with specific questions? Of course, legal experts will be available and should be consulted regularly, but contacting them for every decision is not feasible. Managers must make choices daily about how work is to be performed and often there is no time for input from others. A basic understanding of the law, which this chapter begins to provide, will help them make those decisions and recognize when not to make a decision until a legal expert can be consulted.

There are other reasons to become acquainted with the law. One is to assist in implementing important social objectives. Equality, fairness, dignity, economic well-being, strong familial relationships, and healthfulness are all goals employment laws seek to further by regulating the employer-employee relationship. In many instances, the government, the largest employer in the nation, has led the way in complying with new workplace laws and modeling socially desirable employer behavior. An example is the government's leadership in providing equality of opportunity for women, minorities, and the disabled. By delving into the law and comprehending policy objectives, administrators can implement both the spirit and letter of workplace initiatives.

A final reason to know the law is to gain the confidence to make difficult managerial decisions, such as when to discipline or discharge an employee. These emotion-laden judgment calls are hard enough to make without fearing a lawsuit will result. Wariness is especially likely when the employee in question possesses a legally protected characteristic (e.g., race, color, religion, sex, national origin, age, or disability) or has engaged in legally protected conduct (e.g., organized a union, filed a workers' compensation claim, complained of harassment) because managers realize there are "added" legal protections in place in these circumstances. Indeed, sometimes employees brandish these legal protections like a shield to deflect scrutiny of their performance. But employment laws do not shield workers from discipline when it is warranted and supervisors should not yield to the temptation to avoid lawsuits by inaction (or by not hiring women and minorities). Failure to take disciplinary action when necessary creates problems as well. It is much better to master the law and confidently apply workplace rules uniformly and objectively.

Challenges and paradoxes are plentiful in the legal arena, including five commonly occurring ones:

1. Those in charge are expected to uphold the law in their decisions, but the complexities of constitutional, statutory, administrative, and common law make compliance difficult.

2. Legal requirements and interpretations of them are voluminous and dynamic, so managers sometimes have the experience that "the more you know, the less you know." Once they become familiar with some laws, they realize how much more information about them there is to learn.

3. Supervisors may contact legal counsel for assistance, but formal opinions may take considerable time to obtain, and legal staff may be unwilling to stand behind initial, informal opinions.

4. Using case law is difficult because cases are decided on specific facts, but managers seldom confront identical facts, so they must determine whether minor factual distinctions matter.

5. Legal requirements may be crosscutting so that compliance with one directive conflicts with another. For example, antidiscrimination laws require swift action to stop harassment, but civil service laws require time-consuming and fairness-ensuring procedures to be followed before discipline is taken.

This chapter deals primarily with the rights and responsibilities of individual employees—in other words, *employment law*. Chapter 11 discusses *labor law*—the collective rights of employees to organize and bargain in public sector workplaces. Since 1960, the trend has been toward more direct government intervention into employees' individual relationships with employers, and the result has been a proliferation of employment law statutes and court decisions. Still, in America, union membership in the public sector is high compared with the private sector. So frequently, the "rules" applied to workplace issues are in collective bargaining agreements, not in the law. When this is the case, disputes are resolved through grievance procedures, not lawsuits in courts. This chapter's focus on legal processes also means that alternative dispute resolution methods such as mediation receive little attention. Yet the fact is that most employment disputes are resolved before they reach judicial venues. Of the complaints that are formally filed in judicial forums, more than 90% are resolved before trial. For managers, learning alternative dispute resolution skills is at least as valuable as learning the law.

This chapter begins with some basic legal principles to lay the groundwork for understanding the broad topic of employment law. The remainder of the chapter focuses on particular employee activities and employer practices. It covers a diverse array of topics, including disciplinary procedures, speech and political activity, compensation, health and safety, and the individual liability of employees for violations of law. It also examines searches, drug and alcohol testing, and preemployment investigation of applicants. The last part of the chapter explains how antidiscrimination laws affect the employment relationship. For each activity addressed, the applicable constitutional provisions, statutes, local laws, and judicial decisions are considered. Thus, at the conclusion of this chapter students should be able to identify an employment condition, such as a dress code, explain the legal provisions that apply to it, and determine what workplace policies are permissible. Checking agency decisions against current regulations to ensure they are lawful is an ongoing process. Exhibit 2.1 discusses strategies for staying up to date. Exhibit 2.2 lists the main federal human resource management statutes and their purposes.

Exhibit 2.1   Keeping Abreast

How do administrators stay up to date with legal changes? Most managers prefer to await policy directives from their organizations. This approach works well most of the time, but sometimes employers are behind the curve and managers need current information. A proactive strategy may be the better approach.

The human resource department is usually a good source for legal knowledge. Singular situations for line managers are routine events for human resource managers, who have access to networks of personnel specialists and lawyers and usually subscribe to specialized publications.

Still, it pays to develop an independent perspective. Professional association newsletters and conferences are ideal for learning about the latest trends. The International Public Management Association (IPMA), for example, publishes a manager-friendly newsletter that covers legal issues. Leading newspapers follow legal developments. Legal resources abound on the Internet. Particularly noteworthy is the Catherwood Library at the Cornell University School of Industrial and Labor Relations, which has a vast collection of labor and employment law materials and a user-friendly subject guide (http://www.ilr.cornell.edu/library).

Exhibit 2.2   Overview of Selected Federal Employment Laws

42 U.S.C. § 1981 (Civil Rights Act of 1866)	Section 1981 was the first major antidiscrimination employment statute. The Act prohibits intentional employment discrimination based on race and ethnicity.
42 U.S.C. § 1983 (Civil Rights Act of 1871)	Allows individuals to sue state actors in state or federal courts for civil rights violations. It prohibits public sector employment discrimination based on race, color, religion, sex, and national origin. It is the exclusive tool for challenging discharge due to exercising freedom of expression.
42 U.S.C. § 1985	Prohibits conspiracies to deprive citizens of equal protection of the law or equal privileges and immunities under the law. Can be used to challenge public sector employment discrimination with §§ 1981 and 1983.
Age Discrimination in Employment Act	Protects workers age 40 and over in hiring, promotion, and termination decisions.
Americans with Disabilities Act	Prohibits employment discrimination against qualified individuals with disabilities. After the Supreme Court issued several decisions narrowing the Act's scope, Congress amended the Act in 2008 and broadened its application.
Civil Rights Act of 1964, Title VII	Prohibits employers from discriminating against employees in hiring, promotion, and termination decisions based on race, color, religion, sex, or national origin.

Civil Rights Act of 1991	For discrimination claims, provides the right to trial by jury and emotional distress damages.
Consolidated Omnibus Budget Reconciliation Act of 1985	Mandates an insurance program giving some employees the ability to continue health insurance coverage after leaving employment.
Consumer Credit Protection Act	Regulates the use of credit reports by employers. Limits the amount of an employee's earning that may be garnished, and protects employees from being discharged because their wages have been garnished.
Employee Polygraph Protection Act	Limits the uses of lie detectors by private employers with respect to employees and job applicants. The Act does not apply to governmental employers.
Employee Retirement Income Security Act	Establishes minimum standards for pension plans in private industry.
Equal Pay Act	Makes it illegal to pay men and women different wage rates for equal work on jobs that require equal skill, effort, and responsibility and are performed under similar working conditions.
Fair Labor Standards Act	Sets minimum wage and overtime pay standards, and record keeping for child labor laws.
Family and Medical Leave Act	Requires employers of 50 of more employees and all public agencies to provide up to 12 weeks of unpaid leave to eligible employees for the birth and care of a child, adoption and placement of a child, or serious illness of the employee or immediate family member.
Genetic Information Nondiscrimination Act of 2008	Prohibits employers from discriminating on the basis of genetic information, requiring genetic testing, purchasing or collecting genetic information, and disclosing genetic information.
Health Insurance Portability and Accountability Act	Protects the security and privacy of health data.
Immigration Reform and Control Act	Makes it illegal to knowingly hire or recruit immigrants who do not possess lawful work authorization.
Occupational Safety and Health Act	Regulates safety and health conditions, including exposure to a variety of health hazards.
Pregnancy Discrimination Act	An amendment to Title VII that prohibits discrimination on the basis of pregnancy, childbirth, or related medical conditions.
Rehabilitation Act of 1973, Sections 501 and 505	The first civil rights statute for workers with disabilities.
Uniformed Services Employment and Reemployment Rights Act	Protects the employment rights of National Guard and Reserve members called up to active duty.

■ THE FOUNDATIONS OF EMPLOYMENT LAW

The United States is a **common law system**. Most "rules" are not written down in statutes or codes, but are in the form of judicial opinions in previously decided cases. "The law" is built up case by case by judges, and therefore the law is found in their published opinions. In contrast, **civil law systems** place their primary emphasis on legislation. There are comprehensive statutes or codes enacted by a legislative body on every subject. While still useful, these distinctions are not as true as they once were. This is an "age of statutes." Increasingly in America, specialized federal and state statutes provide comprehensive legal rules on many issues. Nonetheless, even when there are statutes on a topic, the legislature leaves many gaps for courts to fill by applying the statute to individual circumstances, so judicial interpretations remain important in developing and memorializing the law.

But not all judicial decisions are equal. To determine the legal force of a court's decision, one must understand the court's place in the judicial structure. The United States has a federal judiciary, 50 independent state court systems, and countless administrative and quasi-judicial bodies. In general, the federal and state court systems have a pyramid structure. In the federal system, the 90 federal district courts (trial courts) are at the base. The 12 federal circuit courts (appellate courts) make up the middle, and the Supreme Court of the United States sits at the pinnacle. For a court's opinion to be a *controlling precedent* or *binding precedent,* it must have been written by a court directly up the pyramid from the lower court. Accordingly, the Supreme Court's interpretation of federal law is controlling in all the circuit courts and district courts. But each circuit court's opinion binds only the district courts directly below it. When reading a court's opinion it should be determined whether it is controlling or *persuasive precedent.* The latter term refers to a court decision that does not control but that may be followed voluntarily by another court because the facts are comparable and the reasoning strong.

Statutes and court opinions are not the best sources for answers to fact-specific questions about federal employment laws. If a federal agency enforces or administers a statute, the agency's regulations, compliance manuals, and guidances explain how to apply it. The **Equal Employment Opportunity Commission (EEOC)** and U.S. Department of Labor are responsible for most federal employment laws and their publications provide detailed explanations about the laws within their purview. State agencies, such as state civil service commissions and civil rights commissions, enforce and administer state employment laws, but they seldom provide the comprehensive guidance that federal agencies do. An agency's interpretation of a statute is not binding on a court, but it receives deference because of the agency's expertise.

As noted, not all employment laws are national laws. State constitutions and statutes and local ordinances impact the employer-employee relationship as well. States, for instance, have created civil service systems, raised the minimum wage above the national minimum, and passed antidiscrimination and antiretaliation laws, often with broader protections than national laws for employees. Many local governments, too, have civil service systems, antidiscrimination and antiretaliation ordinances, and "living wage" ordinances that raise the minimum wage above the federal minimum for businesses that receive assistance or have contracts with the regional government. (Some cities, such as San Francisco, California, and Santa Fe, New Mexico, have minimum wage provisions that are even more wide reaching.)

Not surprisingly, sometimes the laws of different governmental bodies conflict and courts must decide which prevails. A question frequently addressed is whether one law *preempts* another. The term generally refers to the displacing effect that federal law has on a conflicting or inconsistent state law under the Supremacy Clause of the U.S. Constitution (Article VI, section 2), but it also refers to the displacing effect state laws have on conflicting local government ordinances. Problems also arise when Congress attempts to abrogate *sovereign immunity* by passing laws purportedly giving state employees the right to sue state employers. The Eleventh Amendment to the U.S. Constitution creates a federal system in which each state is a sovereign entity that can be sued only if it consents to be sued. Congress can abrogate sovereign immunity if it unequivocally expresses its intent to do so and if the remedy is congruent and proportional to the wrong addressed. In recent years, the Supreme Court surprised many by holding that the Americans with Disabilities Act (ADA; Title I, Employment), Age Discrimination in Employment Act (ADEA), and the 1938 Fair Labor Standards Act (FLSA) did not pass this test, which means state employees may not use these acts to sue state employers in federal courts for money damages. Only states, not other political subdivisions, are immune from suits for damages under the Eleventh Amendment.

Each legal claim comes with procedural requirements (preconditions to suit, jurisdictional thresholds, filing deadlines) and substantive law (elements, defenses, remedies). *Remedies* represent the agency's risk for violating a law—essential information for managers weighing personnel options. Violating a state tort law can be costly, but improperly terminating a civil servant may simply mean reinstating her (and enduring the civil service appeal process). Remedies are determined by the legal claim and the litigant's losses, but in the employment law realm the possibilities include hiring, reinstatement, retroactive seniority, reasonable accommodation, back pay, front pay, declaratory statements, injunctions, court-ordered affirmative action, compensation for emotional distress, punitive damages, attorney's fees, expert witness fees, and litigation costs. When confronting a legal claim, a manager should always know what remedy a court will order if the agency loses.

■■ THE EMPLOYMENT RELATIONSHIP

At-will employment is the predominant employment relationship in American businesses. It means that, unless the parties have previously agreed to a specific duration of employment, either party may terminate employment at any time, without notice, for any lawful reason. The arrangement is justified as a fair balance of interests between employers and employees because either party is free to sever the relationship. But the truth is many workers need their jobs more than their employers need them, so it opens the door to abuse. It permits employers to refuse to hire disfavored groups, to engage in opportunistic firings, and to punish employees for behaving in socially desirable ways. The many countries that disallow employment at will also decry its impact on families: it subjects them to uncertainty and hardship based on employers' whims. To ameliorate some of these effects, American lawmakers and courts have carved out numerous *exceptions* to at-will employment. These exceptions make it unlawful to take adverse action against employees for specific bad reasons. The civil rights laws are the most well-known exception, but two doctrines have evolved in the public sector that impose restraints solely on government employers.

First, the Supreme Court ruled that when a public employer takes adverse personnel action against employees it is "state action," so federal and state constitutional protections apply. As a result, employees who exercise freedom of speech, freedom of association, or assert the right to privacy at work cannot be punished if their conduct falls within the ambit of constitutional protections. Second, public educational institutions created tenure systems and governments created civil service systems that promised employees they would only be discharged "for cause." The Supreme Court ruled that when a law, rule, or understanding creates an expectation of continued employment in a government job, then employees possess a property interest that cannot be taken away without due process of law. These two developments fashioned significant exceptions to the employment at will doctrine in the public sector and created a model that more equitably balances the interests of employees, employers, and the government.

■ BALANCING EMPLOYER, EMPLOYEE, AND SOCIETAL INTERESTS

This section examines the attempt to balance employer interests, employee rights, and social objectives in six different areas: furnishing due process, taking adverse personnel action, safeguarding free speech and political activity, providing compensation, protecting health and safety, and holding employees individually liable.

Procedural Due Process

The Fifth Amendment (applicable to the federal government) and the Fourteenth Amendment (applicable to the states) forbid the taking of "life, liberty, or property without due process of law." Odd as it may seem semantically, the right to continued public employment sometimes falls within the meaning of the word "property" as it is used in these amendments. When an employee has a *property interest* in his job, he also has **due process rights**: he may not be terminated unless procedures designed to guarantee fairness are followed. Managers (and courts) frequently grapple with two questions that flow from this proposition: (1) How is a property interest created? (2) What type of process is due before a property interest can be taken away?

In *Board of Regents v. Roth* (1972), the Supreme Court explained the conditions that raise government employment to the level of a property interest. The employee must have a legitimate claim of entitlement to continued employment based on codified rules or explicitly agreed-upon contract terms. Generally, academic employees with tenure, and classified civil servants with permanent (nonprobationary) status and the statutory right to be discharged only "for cause," fit this description.

In *Cleveland Board of Education v. Loudermill* (1985), the Supreme Court elaborated on the process that is due when a property interest in employment is jeopardized. The case involved a security guard—a civil servant who could only be dismissed for cause—who was fired because he lied on his job application. As required by Ohio state statutes, Loudermill received a full, evidentiary, *posttermination hearing* before an unbiased decision maker, but the Supreme Court ruled that the posttermination hearing alone was not enough to satisfy the constitutional requirement of procedural due process; Loudermill *also* had to be provided a pretermination hearing because that is when employers are more likely to exercise discretion. The pretermination hearing should provide notice of the charges, an explanation of the employer's evidence, and an opportunity for the employee to present his side of the story. A *Loudermill pretermination hearing* is an initial check against mistaken decisions and should establish "whether there are reasonable grounds to believe the charges against the employee are true and support the proposed action" (*Cleveland Board of Education v. Loudermill,* 1985). Currently, procedures for these hearings are spelled out in statutes, rules, and collective bargaining agreements. In rare situations, when an employer must act quickly and a satisfactory posttermination process is in place, a pretermination hearing may not be required. In practice, employers rarely alter their decision at the pretermination hearing. Instead, they routinely use it to offer employees the option to resign and avoid being discharged.[1]

The Due Process Clause also prohibits governments from depriving citizens of their *liberty* without a fair process. When a public employer discharges an employee for stigmatizing reasons (e.g., immoral acts) and the allegations become publicly known, the employee, on request, must be provided an evidentiary hearing to allow him to clear his name. Otherwise, his future job prospects are unjustly compromised. In practice, this means that sometimes employees who do not have a property interest in their jobs (i.e., probationary or exempt civil servants), still must be provided a posttermination hearing. If the employee prevails, the discipline is nullified, but he is not reinstated; his remedy is his liberty to seek other jobs with a clean record.

Adverse Action

Formal discipline of an employee (covered in Chapter 10) is referred to as **adverse action.** Suspensions, salary reductions, demotions, and terminations typically activate the right to a hearing. Employees may believe that other measures adversely affect them (e.g., reprimands, transfers, alteration of duties, changes in schedule, denial of promotion), but these normally do not trigger the right to a hearing. The legal right to challenge adverse action has been created chiefly by statute; it is a critical component of civil service systems designed to ensure discipline and hiring decisions are based on merit, not patronage. Civil servants in classified (covered) positions have this right. Probationary employees and individuals in unclassified (uncovered or exempt) positions do not, so they are "at will." Staff members who initially have the right to challenge adverse action may lose it by being promoted to an exempt position or by having their position reclassified as exempt, a practice utilized extensively by some states in recent years (Bowman & West, 2007). Although adverse action rights are created by statute, they also provide constitutionally required procedural due process.

Adverse action may be prompted by an employee's unsatisfactory performance or misconduct. The process differs depending on which is involved. The probationary period is the best time to weed out employees who are unable to do their jobs. Once they become permanent, prior to adverse action for unsatisfactory performance, employees typically must be notified of deficiencies, provided with an explanation of them, given remedial assistance if necessary, and allowed time to improve. The purpose of the process is to improve deficiencies. Written performance evaluations (Chapter 10) are critical—both to show initial deficiencies and improvement or lack thereof.

The process used to punish misconduct is often quicker. Low-level discipline, such as a reprimand, may be handled by the immediate supervisor, but more-serious discipline usually involves a high-level manager, a representative from the personnel department, and one of the agency's attorneys. This group reviews the supervisor's recommendation for discipline and, if necessary, requests an investigator to interview witnesses, review documents and physical evidence, and prepare a report. After reviewing the information gathered, the group determines whether the employee's conduct appears to violate agency standards—the *cause* question. If it does, they select a penalty.

The posttermination hearings available to employees in adverse actions are unlike trials in courts in many ways. Most governments have created quasi-judicial administrative agencies with jurisdiction to hear these disputes, such as the U.S. Merit Systems Protection Board and state civil service commissions. An administrative law judge usually hears the case. As in courts, parties have the right to call witnesses, cross-examine the opposing party's witnesses, and introduce documents. The administrative law judge determines what happened, whether there is cause for discipline, and whether the penalty is fair. Her decision is reviewed by a panel of politically appointed decision makers—the board or commission. Prehearing discovery is limited (e.g., depositions), and there are few pretrial motions (e.g., summary judgment). The judge uses relaxed evidentiary rules (hearsay is allowed), a low standard of proof (preponderance of evidence), and expedited timelines (e.g., a hearing within 30 days of discipline). Employees often represent themselves, without attorneys. If the employee prevails, her remedy is reinstatement or reduction of the discipline and perhaps back pay and attorney's fees—but no other monetary damages. Many organizations offer employees the choice of challenging adverse action through an administrative hearing or through the grievance procedure in the collective bargaining agreement, but personnel who grieve discipline may have to pay the costs of arbitration.

Typically, a civil service statute or rule lists offenses that constitute cause for discipline. Florida's statute, for example, prohibits "poor performance, negligence, inefficiency or inability to perform assigned duties, insubordination, violation of the provisions of law or agency rules, conduct unbecoming a public employee, misconduct, habitual drug abuse, or conviction of any crime" (Florida Statutes, 2008). Agencies maximize their discretion by making lists open-ended (e.g., "misconduct includes, but is not limited to") and by referencing additional standards not listed (i.e., "violation of the provisions of law or agency rules" incorporates all rules, directives, policies, regulations, and internal operating procedures promulgated by the agency and its subdivisions). Agency "cause" standards should be clear enough to apprise employees of what is prohibited and prevent unbridled agency discretion (Gertz, 2001).

Public employees may sometimes be disciplined for off-duty conduct. Usually the standard violated is "conduct unbecoming a public employee" or "conviction of any crime." Law enforcement officers and teachers, especially, are held to high standards, but all government leaders worry about their agencies' reputations being sullied by off-duty behavior. Generally, to discipline someone for off-duty conduct there must be a demonstrable connection, or a *nexus,* to job or agency performance. For example, a school employee likely could be terminated for any off-duty misconduct involving illegal drugs due to the government's strong interest in drug-free schools.

On a related matter, individuals who are terminated may seek partial, temporary replacement wages while they look for a new job by filing for **unemployment compensation**. This federal-state insurance program is funded by employers through a tax on payrolls. Employers with repeated claims pay a higher tax rate. An employer may prevent a former employee from obtaining benefits (and raising its rates) by appearing at an unemployment compensation hearing and proving that an employee voluntarily resigned or was discharged "for cause." Consequently, these administrative hearings often cover the same issues and involve the same parties as adverse action hearings.

Freedom of Speech

Citizens do not relinquish their **free speech rights** when they enter government employment, but they do accept restrictions on them. The First Amendment protects a government employee's right, in limited circumstances, to speak out as a citizen on matters of public concern. In *Pickering v. Board of Education* (1968), the Supreme Court weighed the need for workplace efficiency against free speech rights. The case concerned a teacher who was dismissed for disloyalty and insubordination after the local newspaper published a letter he wrote to it criticizing the school board's funding priorities. The Court found that the letter addressed a matter of public concern and had not unduly disrupted operation of the school district. As a result, it held that the Board could not fire Pickering for writing the letter. Out of this decision grew the two-part *Pickering balancing test*. To determine whether an employer can take adverse action against an employee for her speech, courts ask (a) whether the employee has spoken on a matter of public concern, and (b) whether the disruptive nature of the speech justifies the adverse personnel action. To enforce their First Amendment rights, employees may file actions in courts and seek money damages.

Trying to determine what constitutes a matter of public concern proved confusing for managers. The Supreme Court sought to clarify the issue in a 1983 decision, stating that the speech must relate to a "political, social or other concern of the community" (*Connick v. Myers,* 1983). A district attorney's questionnaire to coworkers soliciting their opinions about office management did not qualify because it primarily concerned matters of personal grievance, not public policy. Many similar decisions followed, which held that frustrated, disgruntled staff members who vented their personal disagreements were not speaking about matters of public concern.

The teacher in *Pickering* had no responsibility for monitoring the budget or communicating with the press, so the case did not discuss a worker's right to speak about a matter of public concern while performing his job duties. In *Garcetti v. Ceballos* (2006a), the Supreme Court issued a controversial decision giving public employers wide discretion to take adverse action against those who voice criticisms while fulfilling job responsibilities. Ceballos, a district attorney, wrote a memo to his superiors questioning the veracity of a sheriff's affidavit used to secure a search warrant and recommending that the case not be prosecuted. Ceballos claimed he was moved to a less desirable position, transferred to a different courthouse, and denied promotion as a result. The Court held there was no violation of First Amendment rights because an employee's expression "made pursuant to official responsibilities" is not protected (*Garcetti v. Ceballos,* 2006b). For supervisors attempting to implement this decision, there is now a preliminary question to ask before applying the *Pickering* balancing test: was the speech made pursuant to the employee's official responsibilities? If the answer is yes, it is exempt from First Amendment protection and no further analysis is necessary.

Critics of *Garcetti* claim the decision will increase the public's and government leaders' ignorance about organizational problems because it will deter employees from reporting their concerns. And, critics assert, **whistleblower statutes** will not overcome this reticence (Gertz, 2007). Almost all jurisdictions have enacted legislation protecting personnel from retaliatory adverse action when, in good faith, they object to agency misconduct. But safeguards are limited. For example, the Whistleblower Protection Act of 1989 encompasses only federal employees' disclosures of gross mismanagement or waste of funds, illegal acts, misuse of funds, and danger to the public safety or health. Employees initially must seek assistance from the U.S. Office of Special Counsel, an agency charged with protecting federal employees and applicants from prohibited personnel practices. If unsatisfied, they may request a hearing before the U.S. Merit Systems Protection Board, but *employees* have the burden to prove that the adverse action was retaliatory. (In routine adverse action cases, *employers* must prove that employees committed misconduct.) Employees may not initiate private actions for money damages in courts. State whistleblower statutes vary, but they likewise protect a narrow range of speech, offer weak remedies, and impose burdensome procedures.

Political Activity and Affiliation

During the 19th century, public employees routinely campaigned and raised funds for the political party or executive who appointed them. Now, government workers are limited in the political activity in which they may engage by the federal **Hatch Act of 1939** and state and local little Hatch Acts. These acts restrict the First Amendment right to political expression, but they pass muster with courts because they reduce political coercion of the bureaucracy and promote a nonpartisan, efficient government workforce.

The Hatch Act of 1939 prohibited federal employees from taking an active part in political campaigns. The second Hatch Act of 1940 extended these provisions to state and local personnel in functions that receive federal funding, and barred them from being candidates for elective political office, soliciting or handling political contributions, speaking at political meetings, being officers in political organizations, and electioneering. Amendments in 1993 proscribed political activity while on duty or in uniform (even if off duty) or on government property, soliciting financial or manpower contributions from any political organization or candidate, campaigning for partisan positions in government, distributing campaign literature in the workplace, or using authority to influence or interfere with election results.

Congress retreated from some initial restrictions because it feared that denying so many Americans their right to engage in political activity was negatively affecting the quality of democracy. The Federal Elections Campaign Act of 1974 removed some of the limitations for state and local employees. The Federal Employees Political Activities Act of 1993 allowed federal employees to raise funds, manage campaigns, and hold office in political parties. The effect of this liberalizing, in particular whether it is repoliticizing the bureaucracy, remains unclear (Bloch, 2005; Bowman & West, 2009).

What happens when new leaders from a different political party take office and want to replace current civil servants with loyal party supporters? Classified civil servants cannot be discharged without cause, but can exempt civil servants be ousted for this purpose? Even though exempt civil servants are at-will employees, they cannot be discharged for certain prohibited reasons. Here, the First Amendment potentially bars the way because it forbids adverse action based on beliefs as well as on speech. In *Elrod v. Burns* (1976), the Supreme Court held that *patronage dismissals* of this type are allowed only in policy-making and confidential positions. In *Branti v. Finkel* (1980) the Court clarified that, regardless of whether the "policy maker" or "confidential" label fits, the ultimate question is whether party affiliation is necessary for effective performance of the job. Finally, in *Rutan v. Republican Party of Illinois* (1990), the Court extended this logic to hirings, promotions, transfers, and recalls.

Compensation

If a work site is organized, the collective bargaining agreement likely addresses the matter of wages. The primary statute covering the right to compensation is the **1938 Fair Labor Standards Act** (FLSA), which mandates that a minimum wage be paid and requires that overtime be paid, at time-and-a-half of the regular rate, for hours more than 40 per week. State and local governments may substitute compensatory time off, at the rate of time and a half, for mandatory overtime. The FLSA applies to federal, state, and local employees, but actions against states by private litigants are barred by Eleventh Amendment sovereign immunity. (The U.S. Department of Labor, however, may file a suit against a state.) The U.S. Department of Labor is the federal agency responsible for enforcing the FLSA. Many states and localities mandate a minimum wage higher than the one in the FLSA. The constitutionality of the City of Berkeley's minimum wage requirement was challenged and upheld by the Ninth Circuit in 2004.

Some FLSA requirements are frequently the subject of disputes; an example is the *white-collar exemption.* Employees who are engaged in an executive, administrative, or professional capacity, which includes many government workers, are exempt from both minimum wage and overtime requirements. Since 2004, to be classified in one of these categories, an individual must be paid on a salary basis, earn at least $455 per week, and meet the duties test of the category. Conflict also occurs over whether *idle time* is compensable work time. Waiting time, on-call time, sleep time, travel time, and rest and meal periods all raise this question and require managers to examine the precise facts and to look for specific rules and guidances from the U.S. Department of Labor. The FLSA has complicated overtime exemptions for firefighters and law enforcement personnel; agencies with these positions will have an expert who is familiar with them.

The 1963 Equal Pay Act, an amendment to the FLSA, requires employers to pay men and women equal wages for equal work, unless the employer can justify the differential by seniority, merit, piecework, or any other factor other than sex. The "equal work" standard is often the battleground. Equal work means that the skill, effort, responsibility, and working conditions are equal. The work need not be identical, but significant portions of it should be. A plaintiff must find one opposite sex "comparator" who is doing equal work at a higher rate and may use statistical evidence of gender-based disparity to buttress a claim. An employer found guilty can only comply with the Equal Pay Act by raising the rate of a lower-paid employee; it may not reduce the wages of higher-paid individuals. (Chapters 7 and 8 cover pay and benefit programs.)

Public sector pensions are highly prized compensation. There is no public sector counterpart to the Employee Retirement Income Security Act, the main law governing private sector pensions, so state constitutions, statutes, and court decisions rooted in contract law determine individuals' rights. In general, employees acquire unalterable, "vested" contractual rights in the pension plan existing at the inception of employment. Reductions in benefits typically are not permitted, either during employment or after retirement, although changes substituting equal benefits may be permitted. Privatization raises difficult legal issues about pension rights that are beyond this short summary (Ravitch & Lawther, 1999). Pensions may be lost by bad conduct. Forfeiture laws in at least 13 states allow public employers to withhold pensions from employees for misbehavior. Depending on the state, misbehavior may be defined as a felony conviction, administrative misconduct, or conviction of a particular crime. The contractual right to a pension is meaningless if there is no money available, but public employees have limited ability to ensure governments adequately fund plans. The Pension Protection Act of 2006 addressed problems associated with underfunded private pensions, but not public ones. Public employees have filed suits in courts trying to block officials from raiding retirement funds to pay other debts, but seldom with success.

Health and Safety

In 2006, there were 501 fatal occupational injuries to government workers. They occurred most often in police protection (128, or 25%); construction (56, or 11.23%); trade, transportation, and utilities (52, or 10.4%); national security (51, or 10.2%); and education (49, or 9.8%; Bureau of Labor Statistics, 2007). The number of nonfatal public sector injures is unavailable. People suffer harm on the job when employers create dangerous conditions, employees fail to use reasonable care, individuals commit violent acts, or nature intervenes. Workplace violence (Chapters 7 and 8) is more prevalent at government sites than in private industry but the homicidal reputation of postal workers is exaggerated (Bureau of Labor Statistics, 2006).

The Occupational Safety and Health (OSH) Act of 1970 is the main federal statute protecting employees from unsafe working conditions. Section 19 contains special provisions for federal employees; the Act does not apply to state or local personnel. Twenty-three states have adopted their own OSH acts for public and private employees, and a few states have plans that cover only public employees (the Workplace Fairness Web site has a comprehensive chart of state OSH acts). In general, federal and state OSH acts mandate standards and enforce them through inspections, fines, and closures. They do not give employees the right to sue.

The remedies available to injured personnel generally are those provided in **workers' compensation** acts. In 1908, Congress passed the Federal Employees Compensation Act. Subsequently, each state passed workers' compensation laws covering almost all public and private employees. These laws require both employers and employees to sacrifice rights to ensure that all injured workers receive health care and lost wages. Employees relinquish the right to sue employers in civil court for on-the-job injuries, which, in some instances, means giving up large damage awards. Employers forfeit the right to deny benefits to employees whose own negligence caused or contributed to the injury; these plans are "no fault." Employers finance these systems through insurance premiums, or by being self-insured and paying claims themselves. Disputes are resolved through an administrative system. Benefits include partial replacement income, medical expenses and, if an injury is fatal, survivors' benefits. Permanently injured employees who are unable to work at all also may be eligible for social security disability benefits and early pension benefits.[2]

Are public employers legally obligated to provide health insurance to employees? The answer is yes. Private sector employment-based health benefits are voluntary, but public-sector plans are created by laws. The main federal statute regulating health insurance plans is the Employee Retirement Income Security Act, but government employers are exempt from it. The result of this regulatory scheme is widespread coverage of employees and payment of most of the cost of plans by employers. All employed and retired federal employees have access to the Federal Employees Health Benefits Program. In 2007, about 85% of those eligible were enrolled. The federal government paid 72% of the average premium across all plans, but no more than 75% of any particular plan's premium (U.S. Government Accountability Office [GAO], 2007). In the same year, 94% of state workers and 85% of local government workers had access to plans. Their employers paid 90% of the cost of single coverage, and 74% of the cost of family coverage (Bureau of Labor Statistics, 2008).

The Employee Retirement Income Security Act does not apply to government employers, but two amendments to it—the Consolidated Omnibus Budget Reconciliation Act of 1985 (COBRA) and the Health Insurance Portability and Accountability Act (HIPPA)—do apply. COBRA requires employers who offer health benefits to offer continued coverage to most former employees for 18 to 36 months or until coverage of another plan begins. Employers may not charge more than 102% of their cost. HIPPA curtails the use of exclusions for preexisting conditions, pregnancy, newborns, or adopted children. Genetic information may not be treated as a preexisting condition. Individuals may not be discriminated against in eligibility, enrollment, or premiums due to health status or risky activity. The best-known part of HIPAA is its Privacy Rule—employers must safeguard the privacy and security of personally identifiable health information through a panoply of measures spelled out in the Act and its accompanying rules.

Two groups, retirees and same-sex domestic partners, have captured headlines recently for health insurance–related reasons. Most public employers offer health insurance coverage to retirees, and many subsidize the premium. Financing these benefits is a growing challenge, especially as large numbers of workers under age 65 and not yet eligible for Medicare retire.[3] Same-sex partners may add further to the strain on health insurance rolls. In 2005, the Alaska Supreme Court held that the state constitution's Equal Protection Clause prohibited a public employer from denying health coverage to same-sex domestic partners if it offered coverage to spouses, but the decision may be anomalous. In 2007, a New Jersey midlevel appellate court reached an opposite conclusion and the New Jersey Supreme Court declined to review it.

In addition to insurance, employees need time off for health problems. The **Family and Medical Leave Act (FMLA)** covers local, state, and federal government agencies and provides eligible workers with up to twelve weeks of *unpaid* leave, during any twelve-month period, for childbirth or adoption, illness of a family member, or illness of an employee. In 2008, the U.S. Department of Labor issued new rules on several contentious issues, including the definition of a "serious health condition," the use of unscheduled and intermittent leave, and the medical certification process. To enforce the Act, employees may file suit in court, or request the secretary of labor to bring suit on their behalf. The remedies available include back pay, money damages, and attorney's fees. In 2003, the Supreme Court departed from what seemed to be its "states' rights" trend and held that Congress could abrogate sovereign immunity and give employees the right to sue state employers using this Act. In addition to this federal law, approximately half the states have their own family and medical leave laws. Collective bargaining about workplace safety, health, and leave is common. (Chapter 8 examines the effects of health and safety policies.)

Individual Liability

Generally, employees prefer to sue their deep-pocketed employers, but sometimes they sue officials in their individual capacities, seeking to hold them personally liable for constitutional, statutory, and common law violations. This could include, for instance, claims based on incursions of privacy due to unreasonable searches, the infliction of cruel and unusual punishment, denial of due process, deprivation of civil rights, and defamation.

Official immunity is a common law doctrine that shields government employees from individual liability. It is based on the belief that government actors should not be made hesitant in carrying out their responsibilities by threats of lawsuits, and should not be diverted from their duties by litigation. A few officials, such as judges and legislators, have *absolute immunity* for actions performed in furtherance of judicial or legislative functions. But most officials have *qualified immunity*. Under this concept, government actors are immune from liability for discretionary acts in the scope of their duties if they act in good faith (without malice) and reasonably. To act reasonably, they must not violate clearly established rights of employees.

In reality, public employees are shielded from most lawsuits. The Federal Employees Liability Reform and Tort Compensation Act of 1988 gives federal personnel the right to request that suits against them be converted into suits against the government. Many states shield their personnel from liability, as well. Of course, this does not make officials unaccountable: they still may be disciplined by their agencies for misconduct.

▪▪ PRIVACY ISSUES

Searches

Conflicts arise when employees feel that managers invade their private life or private work spaces. These invisible barriers may be breached in the regular course of business, such as when a supervisor calls a subordinate at home or searches through her briefcase to retrieve job-related material. The Fourth Amendment, which limits government's ability to conduct **"unreasonable searches** and seizures," is the main restriction on workplace searches by government employers.

In the leading case of *O'Connor v. Ortega* (1987), the Supreme Court held that Fourth Amendment protection depends initially on whether the area is one in which the employee has a *reasonable expectation of privacy*. Ortega, a physician, had a reasonable expectation of privacy in his desk and file cabinets because he was the only one who used the office, he stored only personal materials there, and his hospital-employer never had discouraged him from keeping personal items at work.

But the analysis does not end there: even if there is a reasonable expectation of privacy, the search may be lawful if it is reasonable under the circumstances. A reasonable search must balance the governmental interest in the efficient and proper operation of the workplace with the employee's privacy interests. "Reasonableness" does not require an employer to obtain a warrant or even to give an employee prior notice. In *Ortega,* the hospital's need to retrieve job-relevant material overrode the doctor's privacy rights, so it was permissible. In the end, the reasonableness of an employee's privacy expectations and the reasonableness of a search are determined on a case-by-case basis.

Employers can reduce expectations of privacy by eliminating personal work spaces and adopting policies authorizing searches. (Paradoxically, such measures may erode employee-supervisor trust and impede effective managing.) According to courts, employees do not have privacy expectations in their email or in their use of the Internet, so it is permissible to examine both. Agencies also may conduct video and telephone surveillance if these policies are communicated in advance to eliminate privacy expectations. In sum, there are few restrictions on the rights of organizations to monitor personnel at work.[4]

Testing for Alcohol or Drug Use

In 1986, President Reagan issued Executive Order 12,564, requiring executive agencies to test federal employees in "sensitive positions" for illegal drug use. Because the term is defined broadly, about half the nation's 2 million federal employees occupy a "sensitive position." The Order authorizes drug testing in four circumstances: (1) where there is a reasonable suspicion of illegal drug use, (2) in a postaccident investigation, (3) as part of counseling or rehabilitation for drug use through an employee assistance program, and (4) to screen any job applicant. Congress also passed two laws affecting large numbers of private sector employees. The Drug-Free Workplace Act of 1988 covers federal government contractors and grant recipients. And the Omnibus Transportation Employee Testing Act of 1991 requires drug and alcohol testing of 6 million workers in transportation industries. Numerous states and localities have followed the federal government's lead and passed drug-testing laws.

Drug testing of public employees (Chapter 4) has been challenged on a variety of constitutional grounds. In *National Treasury Employees Union v. Von Raab* (1989), the Supreme Court ruled that urine analysis, the most common drug-testing method, is a search and seizure under the Fourth Amendment.[5] Whether it is a reasonable search, and therefore lawful, depends on a number of factors.

The timing of the test (preemployment, periodic, random, promotion) is important to constitutional analysis, as is the nature of the job. Testing at the preemployment stage is more liberally allowed. Postapplication but preplacement testing also generally is permitted. For current staff, whether testing is constitutional depends on whether a person's duties impact public safety; courts largely defer to employers' determinations on that question. For *safety-sensitive* and *security-sensitive* positions, suspicionless, *random testing* is allowed. Hence, a federal court allowed the suspicionless testing of the Army's civilian air traffic controllers, mechanics, police, guards, and drug counselors. Another court permitted random testing of the Navy's civilian employees with top security clearance. At the state and local level, police officers and firefighters may be tested randomly. More surprisingly, a court allowed a broad group of school staff (principals, assistant principals, teachers, aides, substitute teachers, secretaries, and bus drivers) to be tested without suspicion. On the other hand, courts disallowed the random testing of all federal prison employees, all Army civilian lab workers, and a city sanitation worker.

Current employees in positions that do not impact safety may be tested only with *reasonable suspicion.* Reasonable suspicion means information which would lead a reasonable person to suspect on-the-job drug use, possession, or impairment. Return to work testing after an accident, periodic testing with advance notice, and testing upon promotion are less intrusive because employees expect these tests. Still, if they involve people in positions that do not impact safety, reasonable suspicion may be required.

Grooming and Dress Codes

One should pity the poor manager forced to grapple with **dress and grooming codes** in today's workplace. The landscape is fascinating—bejeweled faces, exposed undergarments, colorful tattoos, plunging necklines, dirty toenails, and stubbly cheeks will captivate the most sober bureaucrat. But legal and interpersonal land mines await. Employees deeply resent bosses who interfere with their personal appearance. And in the legal arena, grooming and dress codes may be unconstitutional and discriminatory. This is an area where administrators should ask human resource professionals for help.

Constitutional Law

Grooming requirements have been challenged using the First Amendment (free expression, free exercise of religion) and the Fourteenth Amendment (equal protection, due process). In general, courts will uphold an employer's rules if they are *rationally related* to a legitimate interest. In the leading case of *Kelley v. Johnson* (1976), a police officer challenged a county policy limiting the length of male officers' hair. The court concluded that the regulation was rationally related to safety because it provided a disciplined and easily recognizable police force. Bans on mustaches, goatees, and beards for police also have been upheld because they promote an esprit de corps. Prohibitions on beards for firefighters and on mustaches and beards for emergency medical technicians have been upheld for safety reasons.

Grooming regulations have survived constitutional challenges based on the free exercise of religion, but caution is warranted. The Fourth Circuit upheld a rule preventing correctional officers from wearing dreadlocks due to safety concerns, even though the hairstyle was required by the employee's religion. The result was different when a Muslim police officer who desired to wear a beard for religious reasons challenged a police department rule that prohibited beards, but allowed an exemption for medical reasons. The Third Circuit applied the rigorous *strict scrutiny* standard, which requires a measure to be narrowly tailored and further a compelling governmental interest, and struck down the rule. By allowing an exemption for a secular but not a religious purpose, the county discriminated against those with religious motivations.

Dress codes raise similar constitutional issues. The leading dress code case is *Goldman v. Weinberger* (1986), involving the Free Exercise Clause. The Air Force's dress code prevented an Orthodox Jew from wearing a yarmulke (skullcap) while on duty. The Supreme Court determined the dress code was lawful because it served the legitimate purpose of encouraging "the subordination of personal preferences and identities in favor of the overall group mission" (*Goldman v. Weinberger*). In 2003, the Third Circuit upheld a county's requirement that all van drivers wear pants against an employee's claim that her religious beliefs required her to wear a skirt. The court applied a rational basis standard and accepted the county's explanation that skirts posed a risk to safety. On the other hand, in 2005 a District Court in Kentucky held that a public library violated an employee's free exercise rights by prohibiting her from wearing a necklace with a cross on it.

Antidiscrimination Statutes

Title VII of the Civil Rights Act of 1964 (Title VII) forbids employers from discriminating in terms and conditions of employment based on race, color, religion, sex, or national origin. State and local discrimination statutes often prohibit discrimination based on additional characteristics.[6] Grooming policies and dress codes are "terms and conditions of employment" and they have been challenged as gender, race, and religious discrimination.

The grooming policies attacked as gender discrimination primarily have been different hair length requirements for men and women. Courts routinely uphold such standards if they reflect cultural norms and do not treat one sex more harshly than another. The grooming rules challenged as race discrimination mainly have been no-beard rules. About 25% of black men (compared with less than 1% of white men) suffer from a skin disorder caused by clean shaving, so no-beard rules have a disparate negative impact on black men. (Disparate impact is discussed in the Discrimination section of this chapter.) Some courts have upheld no-beard rules while others have pronounced them unlawful.

Dress codes that treat the sexes differently, such as rules that require men to wear ties and forbid them from wearing earrings, are lawful if they do not favor one gender over the other. On the other hand, rules that require only women to wear revealing or physically uncomfortable uniforms, facial makeup, or contacts instead of glasses have been invalidated as discriminatory. (The employers sued for mandating these "sexually appealing" uniforms were not governments.)

Dress codes that limit an individual's ability to observe religious customs have been attacked as religious discrimination. In 1990, the Third Circuit ruled that a Muslim public school teacher could be prohibited from wearing a religious head covering by a state statute that forbade teaching in religious garb. Likewise, in 2007, the City of Philadelphia's rule prohibiting a Muslim police officer from wearing a head covering was upheld. In both cases, the courts found that requiring accommodation would impose undue hardship. (The duty of public employers not only to refrain from discriminating, but also to accommodate employees' religious beliefs, is discussed in the Discrimination section of this chapter.) But in 2008, the New York State Department of Corrections settled a high-profile Title VII case by agreeing to determine case by case whether to grant religious exemptions from uniform and grooming requirements. The Department also agreed to allow personnel to wear close-fitting, solid dark blue or black religious skullcaps, provided no undue hardship was posed. (Exhibit 2.3 considers the need for dress and grooming codes in the government workplace.)

Preemployment Investigations: Truth, Personality, Health, Credit, and Criminal Records

The cardinal rule for **preemployment investigations**, including interviews, questionnaires, and record checks, is that they must be job related. To illustrate, employers should not inquire about personal matters, such as sexual orientation, marital status, or even the willingness of a working spouse to relocate. The latter question is not germane to the candidate's ability to perform the job. Instead, the interviewer should ask whether there are any barriers to relocation, which solicits the information the organization actually needs to know. Likewise, an interviewer should not ask women of childbearing age if they intend to have children, but should ask parents with children if they have adequate child care. (Chapter 4 reviews the hiring process in detail.)

How can employers ascertain if applicants are providing truthful answers to their inquiries? "Scientific" tests are alluring, but the Employee Polygraph Protection Act of 1988 limits the use of *polygraph tests* due to concerns about the technology's accuracy. In private

Exhibit 2.3   Dress and Grooming Regulations in the Public Service

Clothes make the man. Naked people have little or no influence in society.

—Mark Twain

Written and unwritten dress and grooming codes are common in the private and public sectors because a suitably attired and groomed workforce is an integral part of a professional, productive organization. As vital mediators in social relations, clothing and hairstyle choices can reflect complex feelings about power, money, autonomy, and gender, feelings that often have significant interpersonal consequences. Although few would deny the obvious superiority of character and values as bases for judgment, too much credence may be given to glib assertions that images are without moment; empirical evidence demonstrates that people readily form opinions—right or wrong—about the social and professional desirability of individuals based largely on their appearance.

The government is a highly visible employer; its employment relations practices are observed and emulated. One reason dress and grooming practices matter to public employers is because they have subtle and obvious implications for management philosophies (e.g., participative management), task organization (employee teams), personnel functions (selection, placement, evaluation), quality of work life (self-confidence, mutual respect), and constitutional issues (freedom of speech, equal treatment, sex discrimination). In government, dress and grooming can also represent the mantle of state authority.

Managers also should be aware of the instrumental role played by dress and grooming in communicating personal and organizational credibility and responsibility. In one national sample of state managers, a majority of respondents thought "well-dressed and groomed people are often perceived as more intelligent, hardworking, and socially acceptable than those with a more casual appearance." They rejected the contention that "an employee's appearance is unimportant to the organization." Given this consensus, it is not surprising that an Oklahoma agency dress code codifies these attitudes and affirms that "All employees . . . are representatives of the State . . . and shall dress accordingly, in a manner that presents a good image."

These data suggest that certain norms, or formal and informal dress rules, are part of the fabric of most agency cultures. Ignoring commonly held standards of neatness, demonstrating an inability to adapt to the work environment, and showing insensitivity to one's milieu could affect job performance. For example, an employee of the Equal Employment Opportunity Commission would likely encounter difficulties in rendering service to the public if he or she wore Nazi or Ku Klux Klan insignia to work.

A current social trend is body art and ornamentation. According to the American Academy of Dermatology (2008), 24% of the population has at least one tattoo compared with 1% a generation ago. As with dress and grooming standards, employers have wide latitude in developing appearance regulations to address skin decoration, but rules must be justifiable, consistently enforced, nondiscriminatory, and flexible enough to allow for reasonable accommodation of religious beliefs and disabilities. (These legal requirements are discussed in the Grooming and Dress Codes section of this chapter.) To illustrate, the state has a right to promote a disciplined, identifiable, and professional police force by maintaining its uniform as a symbol of impartiality; accordingly, the state can require tattoos that are offensive or disruptive to be covered.

A clear, one-size-fits-all standard of dress and grooming is not recommended here. Given wide variations of occupations and agencies, not only would such a code be difficult to promulgate, but it also would be contrary to the agency-initiated, participative management approach needed to develop useful standards. A contingency approach seems warranted.

Sources: American Academy of Dermatology, 2008; Bowman, 1992, pp. 35–51.

businesses, testing is lawful only in limited situations. Public agencies are exempt from the Act, but the Act does not preempt state or local regulation, so about half the states have antipolygraph statutes; 11 of those prohibit state governments from using polygraphs. Even when testing is not prohibited, it has been challenged in court with success. The Texas Supreme Court held that a state agency's use of mandatory polygraph testing violated the state constitution's right to privacy. And the Montana Supreme Court determined that a state law allowing polygraph testing of law enforcement personnel, but not other government employees, violated the state constitution's Equal Protection Clause (the Washington Supreme Court reached a contrary result). If used, questions about characteristics protected by antidiscrimination laws should be avoided because they suggest that hiring decisions will be based on those prohibited factors.

Some organizations seek to refine the hiring process by using personality and psychological tests, such as the Myers-Briggs Type Indicator, which provides information about decision-making styles and interpersonal interactions, and the Minnesota Multiphasic Personality Inventory (MMPI), which tests for some adult psychopathologies. If the test is a "medical exam" under the ADA, which some courts have found the MMPI to be, it may not be administered until after a conditional offer of employment. And, if a disability is revealed, such as an alcoholic tendency, ADA requirements must be followed. Some states, for example Massachusetts, prohibit the use of any written exam used to assess honesty, which includes the MMPI. In general, psychological and personality exams should be used for public sector applicants only when state laws allow it and when the tests are job related, such as when public safety is involved. Employers should ensure that tests are given at the right point in time, tests are valid, results are interpreted and used lawfully, and confidentiality is maintained. Agencies may be required to give individuals access to their own test results under state laws mandating disclosure of medical records.

Medical testing of public sector applicants is usually done to detect drug and alcohol use or the presence of communicable diseases. Under the ADA, preoffer applicants may not be required to answer medical questionnaires or to take medical tests. Postoffer but preplacement medical exams are permissible and need not be job related. Medical testing of current employees must be job related. For example, an AIDS test may be administered if transmission of the HIV virus is a demonstrable risk. Return-to-work medical exams after disability leave also are lawful. The results of tests should be kept confidential and used in a nondiscriminatory way. An emerging concern is the use of genetic testing for illnesses that might affect job performance, such as Alzheimer's disease. The Genetic Information Nondiscrimination Act of 2008 (covered in greater detail in Chapter 4) prohibits employers from discriminating on the basis of genetic information, requiring genetic testing, purchasing or collecting genetic information, and disclosing genetic information. Some 35 states also have laws against genetic discrimination in employment, but the laws vary widely and the federal law may preempt them.

Do applicants' personal finances reveal whether they will be dependable, trustworthy employees? Perhaps, but the Fair Credit Reporting Act of 1970, as amended in 2003, was enacted in part to protect consumers from inaccurate or arbitrary information being used against them by employers. To obtain a credit report, an employer must disclose to the applicant that a report will be obtained and the applicant must authorize one. Before taking adverse action based on a report, the employer must provide the applicant with a copy and advise her of her legal rights. About one-third of the states also have laws regulating the use of consumer reports, but the Fair Credit Reporting Act may preempt them. The federal Bankruptcy Act prohibits public and private organizations from denying or terminating employment because an individual declared bankruptcy. *Garnishment* of wages for child support or other reasons places unwanted administrative burdens on employers, but many states forbid adverse action due to garnishment and, if the adverse action has a disparate impact (discussed later in this chapter) it may violate Title VII.

Criminal records, understandably, are of great moment to employers. Many laws mandate preemployment criminal record reviews for applicants seeking positions with access to vulnerable persons (children, the elderly, patients, and prisoners) and positions of great trust (the lottery, nuclear power facilities, and law enforcement). In a second group are laws that allow but do not require these checks. And a third group of laws restrict access to or use of criminal records or allow applicants to withhold this information. Deciding what to do with the information revealed is a separate policy choice. Governments may disqualify persons convicted of certain offenses (e.g., felonies) for certain jobs, either permanently or for a set period, or they may consider each applicant's situation individually. In an attempt to forestall the unemployment of America's estimated 12 million ex-felons, a few states prohibit discrimination against applicants with criminal records. Even in states without laws of this type, constitutional law and Title VII provide some protection for ex-felons. For example, a state law prohibiting the hiring of all convicted felons for civil service positions was held to violate the federal Equal Protection Clause, and an agency's refusal to hire individuals with arrest records violated the state constitution. In another case, the blanket rejection of all convicted felons was disparate impact race discrimination (discussed later in this chapter) under Title VII. Criminal record checks are necessary for many public sector positions, but managers should pay attention to state law, the relationship between the crime and the position, and the time elapsed since the conviction. They also should base restrictions on convictions, not arrests.

Postemployment References

Should an employer be able to blackball a former employee by providing a negative reference? Generally, the law recognizes that open communication about employees in the job market is desirable, but that protection from **defamation** is needed. A job reference is defamatory if it contains a false statement that injures an individual's work reputation. Written defamation is libel; spoken defamation is slander. References with *unfounded* allegations of misconduct, incompetence, poor performance, criminal or other illegal conduct, dishonesty, or falsification of records all would be defamatory because they impugn the employee's ability or fitness for her job. Employers who provide job references enjoy a common law *privilege* that protects them from liability. But they lose the privilege if they abuse it by providing information they know is false, by acting in reckless disregard for the truth or falsity of the information, by communicating the statements to persons who are not within the purpose of the privilege, or by excessive publication. In addition to this common law shield, approximately 36 states have crafted legislative shields, protecting employers who in good faith provide job-related information in references. Still, some organizations take the "name, rank, and serial number" approach, and provide only abbreviated references (job title, dates of employment, and salary history), due to fear of litigation (Cooper, 2001). If an agency allows supervisors to give references, training on how to compose lawful references should be provided.

▪▪ DISCRIMINATION

Antidiscrimination Laws

The "big three" federal antidiscrimination statutes—Title VII of the Civil Rights Act of 1964, the **Age Discrimination in Employment Act**, and the **Americans with Disabilities Act**—are discussed below. The result of these laws is that governments may not discriminate against employees on the basis of race, color, national origin, religion, sex (gender), age (40 years and older), and disability. A host of other federal laws[7] and myriad state and local laws forbid discrimination based on additional criteria, such as sexual orientation, gender identity, marital status, familial status, medical condition, political affiliation, military discharge status, weight, height, and physical appearance.

In public employment, an oft-cited goal of antidiscrimination laws and affirmative action initiatives is a representative bureaucracy. Has this objective been accomplished? A study using data from 2000 found that the federal government employed a higher proportion of African Americans, Asians, Natives and Others, and a lower proportion of Hispanics than would be expected based on the labor pool, leading the author to conclude that affirmative action programs have increased the overall representation of minorities, but benefited certain groups at the expense of others (Kogut & Short, 2007). Another scholar noted that, as of 2000, women were still grossly underrepresented in high-level positions (Hsieh & Winslow, 2006). More generally, critics contend that current antidiscrimination law is out-of-date because it addresses only conscious prejudice, not unconscious bias, which persists (Cunningham, Preacher, & Banaji, 2001). The demographic changes in America's workforce, the legal erosions of affirmative action, and new understandings derived from psychological and sociological research pose challenges to those devising future *diversity* efforts, a topic covered in Chapters 3 and 4. (Exhibit 2.4 explains how antidiscrimination laws are enforced in the public sector.)

Intentional Discrimination

Title VII, the ADEA, and the ADA make it unlawful for an employer to make an adverse employment decision because of an individual's race, color, religion, sex, national origin, age, or disability. The most straightforward claim is one alleging **disparate treatment**, or intentional or invidious discrimination. Under this theory of liability, the bad motivation of the employer is key. But proving an employer's state of mind is difficult; it cannot be observed, so it must be inferred from statements and actions. One way plaintiffs can prove discriminatory motivation is with **direct evidence**. In this approach, plaintiffs rely on statements that demonstrate mental bias by the decision maker at the time of an adverse employment decision. An example would be a supervisor calling an employee a "black radical" while firing him. A stray remark expressing a personal opinion and not reflecting a discriminatory intent to limit employment opportunities is not sufficient proof. For example, a supervisor's remark that all Italians are "mobsters and goombahs," uttered to a coworker months before the plaintiff's discharge was not adequate to prove anti-Italian bias toward the plaintiff at the time of his discharge.

Another way to prove intentional discrimination is to use **indirect evidence**. Here, the employee relies on actions by the employer to support an inference of unlawful motive. In the

---

Exhibit 2.4   Government Employers

Private sector employees seeking to enforce Title VII must initially file complaints with the Equal Employment Opportunity Commission (EEOC) or a state gate-keeping agency, or both. These agencies investigate discrimination and retaliation claims, determine whether they have merit, and try to conciliate disputes. In some instances, these agencies may prosecute the complaints themselves. Eventually, plaintiffs with meritorious complaints may file them in courts. Undesirable employer conduct is punished and deterred by damage awards, including attorneys' fees and, if the discrimination was intentional, compensatory damages (emotional pain and suffering) and punitive damages (although these are capped). In the public sector, alternative enforcement models seek to resolve disputes at the lowest level possible, to prevent lengthy litigation, and to limit the governments' financial exposure. For example, no punitive damages are available against governments.

Federal employees enjoy the protections of Title VII, the Rehabilitation Act of 1973 (which, like the American with Disabilities Act of 1990 [ADA], prohibits discrimination due to disability), and the Age Discrimination in Employment Act of 1967 (ADEA). But Title VII and the Rehabilitation Act contain unique enforcement procedures for federal workers designed to promote interagency resolution. Each agency has an equal employment opportunity counselor; individuals must submit complaints to this counselor first. If the counselor cannot resolve the matter, the agency investigates, holds a hearing if requested, and issues a decision. Only then may unsatisfied parties file with the EEOC and then with a court. Federal personnel may file ADEA complaints directly with the EEOC.

The Congressional Accountability Act of 1995 applied the protections of 11 employment laws, including Title VII, to Congress, but created special procedures and remedies for its employees. Following suit, the Judicial Conference of the United States adopted the Model Employment Dispute Resolution Plan (Model EDR Plan), which recommends that employees in the federal court system have rights comparable to those in the legislative branch. Subsequently, numerous federal courts approved the plan.

State and local government employers are covered by Title VII if they have 15 or more employees, but personal staff, legal advisors, and policy-making assistants have special procedures and minimal remedies. When these employees are involved, the EEOC is the final decision maker, subject to limited judicial review. If a local enforcing agency has authority to remedy the conduct, the EEOC must give it 60 days to act. State governments cannot be sued by private litigants with the ADEA or ADA due to sovereign immunity, but the EEOC, acting in its prosecutorial role, may bring claims against states.

---

first stage, the plaintiff must present evidence that he was treated differently based on a forbidden criterion. In a hiring case alleging race discrimination, the Supreme Court said the plaintiff could do this by proving four elements: (1) that he belongs to a racial minority; (2) that he applied for and was qualified for a job for which the employer was seeking applicants; (3) that, despite his qualifications, he was rejected; and (4) that after his rejection, the position remained open and the employer continued to seek applicants from persons of complainant's qualifications. These elements are flexible and can be adapted to fit promotion, discharge, and other adverse action claims. In the second stage, the employer can defeat the plaintiff's claim by presenting evidence that it had a *legitimate business reason* for its action. In the third stage, the plaintiff can introduce evidence to show that the employer's stated business reason is a *pretext* to hide its discriminatory motive. This framework, known as the ***McDonnel /Douglas* burden-shifting**

approach, was announced by the Supreme Court in *McDonnell Douglas Corp. v. Green* (1973). The plaintiff's overall burden is to persuade the fact-finder that it is more likely than not that the employer's actions were motivated by a forbidden consideration.

A *mixed motive* case is one in which adverse employment action was motivated by an unlawful criterion *and* a legitimate business factor. In the Civil Rights Act of 1991, Congress amended Title VII to provide an employer with a partial defense if it proves that, although it had a mixed motive, it would have made the same decision without the illegal factor. When an employer proves a mixed motive, the plaintiff's remedies are limited to declaratory relief and attorney's fees. In cases under the ADEA and ADA, a mixed motive is an absolute defense.

Title VII and the ADEA prevent employers from segregating workers in positions on the basis of a protected dimension. For example, employers may not limit job applicants for a position to those under 40. But these Acts specifically allow segregation in the rare circumstances where it is a *bona fide occupational qualification* (BFOQ). An example would be auditioning only female actors for a female role. Race is not listed in Title VII as a permissible BFOQ defense, so it never is one. Today, BFOQs are seldom utilized because they are difficult to defend. Thus, a men's prison may not make "being male" a job qualification for guards unless it can show that, for job-related reasons, females must be excluded. (Exhibit 2.5 discusses the need to prohibit employers from making decisions based on sexual orientation and gender identity.)

Retaliation

Title VII, the ADEA, and the ADA make it unlawful to discriminate against an individual because of *opposition* to a prohibited employment practice or because of *participation* in an investigation, proceeding, or hearing. To prevail, a plaintiff must prove that she engaged in a protected activity, that adverse action was taken against her, and that there was a causal relationship between the two. An example of this type of case is an employee who is fired after she reports that she was sexually harassed. Retaliatory motive may be proven with direct evidence or with indirect evidence using the *McDonnell Douglas* burden-shifting approach. In 2007, **retaliation** claims accounted for approximately 30% of all charges filed with the EEOC. Strategically, they offer plaintiffs the advantage of having to prove only retaliation, not discrimination. From the employer's perspective, these claims are a disincentive to discipline individuals who have engaged in protected activity, especially those who have done so recently, because the time sequence suggests a cause-and-effect relationship. Courts have tried to bolster the confidence of employers by assuring them that "temporal proximity" alone is not sufficient evidence of retaliatory motive. Besides Title VII, the ADA, and the ADEA, many other laws, including the FLSA, the Family and Medical Leave Act, 42 U.S.C. 1981, whistleblower acts, civil rights acts, and workers' compensation acts protect employees from retaliation.

Harassment

In *Harris v. Forklift Systems* (1993), the Supreme Court held that Title VII makes it unlawful for an employee to be subjected, on the basis of a protected criterion, to unwelcome **harassment** that is severe or pervasive enough to create an objectively hostile or abusive work environment. Many people associate harassment claims with gender discrimination (i.e., sexual harassment),

---

Exhibit 2.5   Inclusive Nondiscrimination Policies: Sexual Orientation and Gender Diversity, by Kristin M. Brown, MSW, MPA

Every year thousands of workers experience unfair failure-to-hire, denial of promotion, hostile workplaces, and even unfair termination simply because they don't meet someone else's idea of a "real man" or a "real woman."

—Gender Public Advocacy Coalition (2007)

Feminine males and masculine females are more likely to face employment discrimination than persons with a traditional gender presentation (Flynn, 2001). Although nontraditional gender presentation may be more common in nonheterosexual populations, some heterosexual people also have a nontraditional gender presentation. Among those with nontraditional gender presentation are people whose inner sense of gender identity differs from the gender designated at birth, known as transgender people. Transgender people may choose to transition their physical body to match their inner sense of gender, following a standardized medical process, and they may be heterosexual or nonheterosexual.

Federal statutes prohibit job-related discrimination on the basis of race, color, religion, sex, national origin, age, and disability. Executive Order 13087 outlawed discrimination related to "sexual orientation" in federal civilian employment, but many areas in the United States still lack policies prohibiting differential workplace treatment on this basis. Protection of "gender identity and expression" is even rarer.

Currently, 20 states and 282 local governments prohibit discrimination based on "sexual orientation." Twelve of these states and 98 of these local governments also prohibit discrimination based on "gender identity" (Human Rights Campaign [HRC], 2008). Furthermore, 2,035 private sector companies and 571 universities and colleges include "sexual orientation" as a protected category in their nondiscrimination policies; 447 of these private sector companies and approximately 87 of these universities and colleges also include "gender identity" as a protected category (HRC, 2008). Some of the policies also include "gender expression."

Policies that prohibit discrimination due to anatomical "sex" and "sexual orientation" do not adequately protect all people from discrimination. Flynn (2001) explained that, at its core, much discrimination involves "hostility based on failure to conform to conventional gender norms" (p. 392), which is not protected by either of these two categories. In order to protect all people from discrimination related to actual or perceived gender and sexual orientation, it is necessary to include "gender identity and expression."

In addition to examining nondiscrimination statements, managers should examine other workplace and employee policies. Many health insurance policies specifically exclude medical procedures and prescriptions for transgender employees' health care. San Francisco County found that providing medical coverage for transgender employees did not increase employer costs (Colvin, 2007). The Human Rights Campaign (www.hrc.org) provides information for employers and employees on inclusive policy implementation.

---

but a claim is viable if an employee is harassed due to any characteristic listed in Title VII, the ADEA, or the ADA. Sexual harassment claims may be brought by men, but the reason for the harassment must be gender, not sexual orientation. Typically, it is the behavior of supervisors, coworkers, and others at the workplace that creates a **hostile environment**.

Whether objectionable conduct is severe or pervasive enough to be unlawful is often the pivotal question. These laws are not "general civility codes," and do not provide redress for behavior that is simply rude, abrasive, unkind, or insensitive. Courts look at the gravity, frequency, duration, character, and threatening nature of the conduct. Occasional racial or ethic slurs are seldom enough to create a hostile environment, but a six-month period of being called "ayatollah" and "camel jockey" was sufficient to support an Iraqi employee's claim. In another case, a female employee who acquiesced to her supervisor's ongoing unwelcome sexual conduct established a claim. And non-English-speaking workers forced to abide by an employer's English-only rules also have been successful.

Employers in hostile environment harassment cases have a defense, the ***Ellerth/Faragher affirmative defense***, if they exercise reasonable care to prevent and correct harassment, and if an employee unreasonably fails to use an employer's remedial procedures. An organization may reasonably prevent harassment by adopting adequate policies and procedures, ensuring that all staff members receive the policies, and training supervisors to properly handle complaints. The Virginia Department of Corrections is a good example of an employer who avoided liability by quickly correcting harassment. A supervisor distributed a memo to prison personnel about dress codes and identified the plaintiff as someone who wore attire that was too revealing. After the memo was distributed, she was subjected to crude jokes. Managers at the prison prevented public posting of the memo, counseled the supervisor who wrote and distributed it, admonished the employees who made the remarks, and stopped the harassment. When nonsupervisory coworkers or nonemployees, such as customers, contractors, or individuals sharing the work site, create a hostile work environment, the agency is responsible if it was negligent, meaning if it knew or should have known of the harassment and failed to take prompt and appropriate corrective action.

Sexual harassment victims may base their claims on a hostile environment or on a **tangible employment action**—a significant change in employment status, such as hiring, firing, failing to promote, reassignment with significantly different responsibilities, or a decision causing a significant change in benefits. The plaintiff must prove that an employment benefit was conditioned on a sexual favor. An example would be an administrative assistant who resists a boss's sexual demands and is given less-desirable work assignments, or who is promoted if she acquiesces. This category includes the well-known *quid pro quo* (this for that) harassment. If a supervisor takes tangible employment action against a victim based on unwelcome sexual conduct, the employer faces a tough legal battle; the employer cannot use the *Ellerth/Faragher* affirmative defense.

Affirmative Action

Employers may voluntarily choose to adopt **affirmative action** programs to increase the number of employees from groups historically excluded from their workplaces. Firms seeking contracts from the government usually adopt plans to comply with agency rules requiring vendors to have them. These plans use various means to achieve a more representative workforce, including targeted recruitment and training programs, numerical goals and timetables, and special preferences in hiring and promotion. Beginning in the early 1960s, many government employers began voluntarily adopting affirmative action plans, but court decisions in the 1980s and 1990s raised doubts about their lawfulness, so most were modified or suspended. A public employer's plan must not run afoul of Title VII or the Equal Protection Clause of the 14th Amendment. Even when affirmative action programs are legal, they tend to foment controversy.

Title VII requires voluntary affirmative action programs to be put in a plan. A plan must remedy conspicuous racial imbalances in traditionally segregated job categories, it must be temporary, its purpose must be to remedy underrepresentation (not to maintain gender or racial balances indefinitely), and it must not unduly trammel the rights of the majority. Title VII protects all groups, including majority groups, from discrimination. As a result, white employees, for example, who have been treated disparately on the basis or race due to affirmative action plans may use Title VII to bring actions for *reverse discrimination.*

Under the Equal Protection Clause, government affirmative action programs based on race and ethnicity are reviewed using the exacting strict scrutiny standard. They are constitutional only if they are narrowly tailored to further a compelling governmental interest. To date, only the goal of remedying past discrimination has been compelling enough for the Supreme Court to approve a plan. Furthermore, the government must provide convincing proof of its past discrimination.[8] If an affirmative action program is based on gender rather than on race or ethnicity, it receives less-rigorous intermediate judicial scrutiny; it will be approved if it has a substantial relationship to an important governmental interest.

In 2003, the Supreme Court decided *Grutter v. Bollinger* (2003) and held that the University of Michigan Law School could constitutionally use a race-conscious admissions policy because the law school had a compelling interest in attaining a diverse student body. The impact of this decision in the public employment context is the subject of much speculation. Prior to *Grutter,* it was widely accepted that attaining workforce diversity was not a sufficiently compelling reason for a race-based program. But after *Grutter,* the Seventh Circuit concluded that the City of Chicago had a compelling interest in attaining diversity among its sergeants in order to set the proper tone in the department and to earn the trust of the community, which in turn would increase police effectiveness. This is an area where caution and expert advice is necessary. A plan that seeks cultural diversity risks being denounced as unlawful racial or ethnic balancing.

In rare cases, affirmative action plans may be involuntarily imposed on employers by courts to remedy past discrimination. In 1987, for example, after years of litigation, a federal court ordered the Alabama Department of Public Safety to use quotas to increase the number of minority state troopers. The Supreme Court approved the plan because of the department's history of overt and defiant racism.

Unintentional Discrimination

In addition to intentional discrimination, Title VII and the ADA prohibit neutral practices that inadvertently produce a disproportionate or **disparate impact** on a protected group. It is unclear whether the disparate impact rubric may be used for claims under the ADEA. The Supreme Court first accepted the theory in *Griggs v. Duke Power Co.* (1971), and it was codified in the Civil Rights Act of 1991. Disparate impact claims most frequently challenge hiring and promotion devices, but the theory can be used for layoffs and other employment practices. To aid enforcement, the EEOC requires employers to maintain records of all hiring, promotion, and firing by race, sex, and national origin. Hiring and promotion test scores also must be kept.

To prove disparate impact, employees must show that a specific selection device had an exclusionary effect. In *Griggs,* a high school graduation requirement and a battery of aptitude tests disproportionately excluded blacks from being hired. There is no "bright line" rule stating how much disparity is unlawful, but the EEOC uses an 80% or four-fifths "rule of thumb." If qualification rates of protected groups are less than 80% of the highest group, then the selection device is suspect. The Supreme Court has disparaged the EEOC's *80% rule* and stated that a "case-by-case" approach is necessary because "statistics come in a variety and their usefulness depends on all the surrounding facts and circumstances" (*Watson v. Fort Worth Bank & Trust,* 1988). Still, since the EEOC investigates and determines the merit of claims, and sometimes prosecutes them, agencies should use the 80% rule as a guide.

Employers can defend against disparate impact claims by showing a challenged practice is job related and a business necessity. This defense can be used for subjective procedures, such as interviews, and objective procedures, such as tests. To defend tests as job related, agencies must prove their validity. The EEOC adopted *Uniform Guidelines on Employee Selection Procedures* to assist organizations with this endeavor. If a test is proven to have predictive validity, content validity, or construct validity under the *Guidelines,* then it is job related and its use is justified even if it has a disparate impact. (Chapter 4 explains these validation methods in detail.)

Rather than validate tests, some employers have sought to avoid a disparate impact by using scores creatively. For example, one agency adopted a cutoff score, above which test performance was irrelevant; but the court ruled the cutoff score had to be validated. Another minimized the relative weight of the exam in the selection process; the court found the practice to be an unlawful affirmative action plan. Others took the top scores in each racial and gender group, a practice known as **race norming** that is now prohibited by the Civil Rights Act of 1991. Still others, including the City and County of San Francisco, the City of New Orleans, and the City of Bridgeport, have used **banding**, meaning they treat applicants within a certain range as having identical scores. So far, this process has not been found unlawful, but certain aspects (such as bandwidth) may need to be validated.

Age

The ADEA is the main federal statute prohibiting age discrimination. It forbids discrimination against those at least 40 years old, on the basis of age, in the terms and conditions of employment. There is no claim for reverse discrimination by the young. Involuntary retirement generally may not be required, but mandatory retirement in public safety and executive policy-making positions is permissible. Voluntary early retirement incentives are permitted. The Act provides a defense for the use of a bona fide seniority system and for a BFOQ, but BFOQs are difficult to justify. Employers cannot rely on stereotyped assumptions about older workers' strength, endurance, or speed. The courts have struck down rules that limited flight engineers to those under age 60 and bus drivers to those under 65.

Disability

The ADA prohibits discrimination against qualified persons with a physical or mental impairment that substantially limits a major life activity. It also protects those with a record of impairment, those regarded as impaired, and those who associate with impaired persons. Employers must provide qualified disabled persons with **reasonable accommodation**. The terms "qualified person," "substantially limits," and "major life activity" have spawned considerable litigation. When it was enacted, the ADA was hailed as a major step toward eradicating disability discrimination, but the Supreme Court issued several decisions that sharply limited the scope of the statute (Selmi, 2008). In response, Congress amended the ADA in 2008. The amendment rejected numerous Supreme Court decisions and EEOC regulations narrowing the Act's coverage, and emphasized that the definition of "disability" should be interpreted broadly.

When an employee requests to be accommodated, managers should make an individualized assessment, with the assistance of the human resources and legal departments, to determine if the person meets threshold conditions to be covered by the Act. (Of course, an employer may voluntarily provide accommodation even when it is not legally required.) For qualified persons, accommodations likewise should be determined through an individualized assessment. These might include, for example, reserved parking, special equipment, personal aides, part-time or flextime work schedules, and building renovations. Accommodations that cause *undue hardship* to employers are not required. At interviews, administrators should not ask job applicants if they have a disability or need an accommodation, but they should ask candidates if they are able to do job-related tasks, such as climbing a ladder. The ADA prohibits preoffer medical tests and questionnaires.

Religion

Religious employees may request time off for sacred holidays, schedules omitting work on the Sabbath, breaks during the workday to pray and a place to do so, and exceptions to dress and grooming codes. Title VII does more than simply prohibit religious discrimination. It requires employers to make reasonable accommodation for religious beliefs and practices that do not impose undue hardship. Reasonable accommodation means that which is minimally necessary for the individual to fulfill his or her religious obligation or conscience. It is an undue hardship for an employer to provide more than the least burdensome accommodation. Organizations are not required to compensate workers for time off the job fulfilling religious duties, nor are they *required* to alter work schedules or duty assignments. According to the EEOC, the most common methods of accommodation are (a) flexible scheduling, (b) *voluntary* substitutes or swaps of shifts and assignments, (c) lateral transfer or change of job assignment, and (d) modifying workplace practices, policies, or procedures (EEOC, 2008). The Free Exercise Clause of the First Amendment (as balanced by the Establishment Clause) may expand a public employer's duty to accommodate religiously motivated requests, but the law is unclear. The impact of the Religious Freedom Restoration Act of 1993 on the duty to accommodate also is uncertain. Managers need not accept an employee's suggestions for accommodation, but if offered, they should be considered. The Religious Discrimination section of the *EEOC Compliance Manual* is available online and is a helpful resource for managers responding to accommodation requests (EEOC, 2008).

How can managers prevent discrimination and retaliation claims from occurring and successfully defend those that do arise? Agencies should *have* and be able to *prove* legitimate business reasons for the actions they take. Some basic strategies enable managers to do this. First, agency leaders should not act rashly, but should carefully investigate and review all relevant information before making personnel decisions. Job-related criteria should be consciously articulated and used. Deliberation with other professionals makes decisions sounder and more defensible. Collective decisions are less likely to have been influenced by any one individual's bad motive. Communication with employees also is essential. Open, two-way communication eliminates surprises, reduces the likelihood of suit, and increases the odds of winning. This should include regular, timely performance evaluations, with positive and negative feedback, and articulation of organizational expectations. When problems arise, supervisors should promptly discuss them with staff members. Documenting this communication contemporaneously not only underscores management's seriousness, it also provides credible evidence. Business records are deemed more reliable than the self-serving testimony of litigants. Finally, supervisors and managers should treat all complaints of discrimination and retaliation seriously, regardless of whether complaints are made formally or informally.

■■ SUMMARY AND CONCLUSION

Workplace laws reflect a balance among three competing objectives: managerial efficiency, employee rights, and social aspirations of the law. This balance is not fixed. Rather, it changes to reflect lawmaking and decision making over time. At present, a trend exists to interpret laws in favor of managerial efficiency. Employee rights are becoming ever more narrowly defined.

For example, staff members have few privacy rights at work. "Reasonable" searches of their offices, computers, phones, and excretory fluids are permitted, as is surveillance of their movements. Workers may be required to alter their dress and grooming habits. Applicants for certain jobs may be investigated extensively. Employees must be careful what they say at work. The First Amendment does not prevent employers from punishing workers for disruptive speech, or for pointing out agency problems as they carry out their duties. Greater numbers of government jobs are being made "at will," so that the people in them can be fired without cause, notice, or explanation.

Still, certain rights remain intact. If an employee has a property interest in employment, he cannot be discharged except for cause and he must be provided with due process before adverse action can be taken. Certain reasons for taking adverse action remain clearly prohibited: an employer may not discipline an employee for speaking about a matter of public concern in a nondisruptive way, for "blowing the whistle" in a manner protected by a whistleblower statute, or for being a member of the "wrong" political party after an election (unless party membership is necessary for the job). An employer cannot retaliate against an individual for participating in a proceeding to enforce a law or for opposing violation of a law. Antidiscrimination laws forbid an employer from intentionally or unintentionally making an employment decision based on a proscribed dimension (and in some areas of the country the list of proscribed dimensions is expanding). Employees must be paid at least a minimum wage and time and a half for overtime (unless they are exempt), must be paid the same as members of the other gender, and must be awarded the pensions they earn. OSH Acts require work sites to meet safety standards, and workers' compensation, health insurance, and FMLA leave provisions provide a safety net for those who become hurt or sick. Public employees are rarely held individually responsible for violating a law.

Of course each "law" above has conditions, exceptions, and grey areas. Managers who expect the law to provide an exhaustive, well-defined set of prohibited behaviors will be disappointed. Statutes are broad and vague—they usually lack precise standards capable of ready application. Court decisions analyze specific conduct under specific conditions, but situations exactly like the ones that have been litigated seldom arise.

What are administrators to do when the law and their own employers fail to provide definitive guidance? They must form their own judgment. The basis for judgment is the intent of the law—the values that underlie the cases and statutes discussed in this chapter. For example, if supervisors must respect employees' privacy, then it follows that they should ask permission when they think privacy expectations might be violated, even if they are unclear whether a "right" exists. If employees refuse to cooperate, resolution should be attempted through collaboration, perhaps with assistance from other managers. Cases and laws seldom provide clear-cut answers, but they do provide guideposts to use to ensure that actions are consistent with the spirit and aims of legislation and court decisions.

KEY TERMS

Adverse action

Affirmative action

Age Discrimination in Employment Act

Americans with Disabilities Act

At-will employment

Banding

Civil law system

Common law system

Defamation

Direct evidence

Disparate impact

Disparate treatment

Dress and grooming codes

Due process rights

Ellerth/Faragher affirmative defense

Equal Employment Opportunity Commission

Fair Labor Standards Act (FLSA)

Family and Medical Leave Act

Free speech rights

Harassment

Hatch Act

Hostile environment

Indirect evidence

McDonnell Douglas burden-shifting approach

Official immunity

Preemployment investigation

Race norming

Reasonable accommodation

Retaliation

Tangible employment action

Title VII of the Civil Rights Act of 1964

Unemployment compensation

Unreasonable search

Whistleblower statutes

Workers' compensation

EXERCISES

Class Discussion

1. Some departments in universities believe that their faculty should mirror the demographic composition of the student body and that faculty recruitment should use "diversity" policies to pursue this objective. Assess the merits of this proposition. What laws does it implicate?

2. Many people are increasingly conducting part of their work at home through telecommuting. Which privacy rights and responsibilities, if any, might this activity raise, and how might managers deal with them?

3. Identify a controversial workplace topic, and then use the test of balancing employee, employer, and society's interests to develop a range of possible policies addressing it.

4. A person with a mobility disability applies for a job in your office. Which interview questions can be asked about this disability without violating ADA provisions? Which questions should not be asked? How does this problem exemplify the *paradox of needs* discussed in the book's Introduction?

5. Consider the steps of the hiring process. How can a manager prove that she did not discriminate in hiring based on a forbidden criteria but had a legitimate business reason for her choice? What witnesses and documents are available?

Team Activities

6. Design a work group seminar to inform employees about their rights and limits when using email and the Internet. What paradoxes protrude, and how can they be dealt with?

7. A coworker informs you, in confidence, that she feels attracted to another coworker in your office. What legal or policy advice would you give her? If she supervises the person she is attracted to, would that change your advice?

8. An employee requests a leave of absence to observe a religious event. He is important to the success of an effort that you are undertaking as a manager, and the employee's leave is likely to cause some delay and cost. What do you do?

9. Develop a policy for increasing workplace diversity that meets legal standards.

10. An abuse investigator at the state agency responsible for child protection tells you that he is going to write a letter to the governor and to the newspaper stating that the heavy caseloads of investigators are endangering children. How would you advise this coworker?

Individual Assignments

11. Explain the free speech rights of employees. Are there any limits?

12. For what unlawful actions can public employees be held individually responsible?

13. Define and explain the 80% rule.

14. What substantial interests do public employees have in their jobs?

15. What accommodations must employers make for disabled persons?

16. Based on your experience, give an example of either the *paradox of democracy* or the *paradox of needs* using one of the issues raised in this chapter. Both paradoxes are discussed in the book's Introduction.

17. What restrictions are imposed by the various Hatch Acts?

18. Roman playwright and carpenter Plautus (254–184 BCE) advised that you should "Practice what you preach." Do you agree with this advice? Explain your answer using issues from this chapter.

NOTES

1. After *Loudermill,* the Supreme Court ruled that a law enforcement officer who was suspended, rather than discharged, was not entitled to a predeprivation hearing because the postdeprivation hearing

was prompt and the loss of income relatively insignificant. To avoid having to engage in this hair-splitting, many organizations provide *Loudermill* pretermination hearings for all adverse actions.

2. Disagreements arise over whether a condition was preexisting, a treatment is medically necessary, or a treatment is experimental, but most often parties disagree about whether an injury-related disability is permanent and how much will adequately compensate for it.

3. Government Accounting Standards Board Statements 43 and 45, effective in 2006 and 2007, require public sector employers to report net present liability for future retiree benefits on an accrual basis. A similar accounting change for private sector employers was blamed for a decline in private-sector retiree healthcare coverage. Whether public employers will reduce benefits for retirees remains to be seen.

4. Strip searches are in a different category. Employees with public safety duties have a diminished expectation of privacy, but strip searches are so intrusive they must meet a higher standard to be reasonable. The Eighth Circuit adopted a "reasonable suspicion" standard for strip searches of correctional officers, which means there must be specific objective facts and rational inferences supporting the belief that the employee has contraband hidden on her person.

5. The privacy intrusion is fourfold: it forces individuals to hand over bodily fluids they normally do not share with others, requires overseers to listen to or watch employees urinate to ensure samples are unadulterated, forces individuals to disclose confidential information about medications they are taking (Viagra, antidepressants, HIV-related drugs) to explain possible cross reactions, and allows employers to monitor off-duty conduct because trace amounts of drugs stay in the body for days.

6. The District of Columbia has one of the broadest dress code and grooming statutes. The law prohibits discrimination based on "the outward appearance of any person, irrespective of sex, with regard to bodily condition or characteristics, manner or style of dress, and manner or style of personal grooming, including, but not limited to, hair style and beards" (District of Columbia Human Rights Act, 2008). An employer violated this statute by discharging a receptionist who had disheveled hair and wore low-cut, tight blouses.

7. For example, the Equal Pay Act, the Rehabilitation Act, the Family Medical Leave Act, Title IX, the Nineteenth Century Civil Rights Acts (§§ 1981, 1983, 1985), the Genetic Information Non-discrimination Law, the Uniformed Services Employment and Reemployment Act, and the Black Lung Act also prohibit discrimination.

8. Two cases demonstrate how this is possible. In 2003, seven Caucasian police officers sued the city of Boston alleging that their rights were violated when the police department promoted three African American officers with identical test scores instead of them. The First Circuit found that the department's history of discrimination was well documented by past litigation and records, and the city's evidence of disparity in the promotion of officers to sergeant was strong. In 2007, the Seventh Circuit approved the disadvantaged business enterprises program of the state transportation agency of Illinois, which included goal setting. The state relied on the federal government's compelling interest in remedying the effects of past discrimination in the national construction market.

REFERENCES

American Academy of Dermatology. (2008). Retrieved on March 20, 2008 from http://www.aad.org

Bloch, S. (2005, Winter). The judgment of history: Faction, political machines, and the Hatch Act. *University of Pennsylvania Journal of Labor & Employment Law, 7,* 255–277.

Board of Regents v. Roth, 408 U.S. 564 (1972).

Bowman, J. (1992). Dress standards in government: A national survey of state administrators. *Review of Public Personnel Administration, 12,* 35–51.

Bowman, J., & West, J. (Eds.). (2007). *American public service: Radical reform and the merit system.* Boca Raton, FL: Taylor & Francis.

Bowman, J., & West, J. (2009, January/February). To "re-Hatch" public employees or not? An ethical analysis of the relaxation of restrictions on political activities in civil service. *Public Administration Review, 68,* 52–62.

Branti v. Finkel, 445 U.S. 507 (1980).

Bureau of Labor Statistics, U.S. Department of Labor. (2006). *Survey of workplace violence prevention, 2005.* Retrieved July 20, 2008, from http://www.bls.gov/iif/oshwc/osnr0026.pdf

Bureau of Labor Statistics, U.S. Department of Labor. (2007). *Census of fatal occupational injuries (CFOI): Current and revised data.* Retrieved July 20, 2008, from http://www.bls.gov/iif/oshcfoi1.htm

Bureau of Labor Statistics, U.S. Department of Labor. (2008). *National compensation survey: Employee benefits in state and local governments in the United States, September 2007.* Retrieved July 20, 2008, from http://www.bls.gov/ncs/ebs/sp/ebsm0007.pdf

Cleveland Board of Educ. v. Loudermill, 470 U.S. 532 (1985).

Colvin, R. A. (2007). The rise of transgender-inclusive laws. *Review of Public Personnel Administration, 27*(4), 336–360.

Connick v. Myers, 461 U.S. 138 (1983).

Cooper, M. (2001, Fall). Job reference immunity statutes: Prevalent but irrelevant. *Cornell Journal of Law and Public Policy, 11*, 1–68.

Cunningham, W., Preacher, K. J., & Banaji, M. R. (2001). Implicit attitude measures: Consistency, stability, and convergent validity. *Psychological Science, 12*(2), 163–170.

District of Columbia Human Rights Act, D.C. Code § 2–1401.02 (22), (2008).

Elrod v. Burns, 427 U.S. 347 (1976).

Equal Employment Opportunity Commission (EEOC). (2008). Section 12: Religious discrimination. In *EEOC compliance manual.* Retrieved July 25, 2008, from http://www.eeoc.gov/policy/docs/religion.html

Florida Statutes, § 110.227(1) (2008).

Flynn, T. (2001). Transforming the debate: Why we need to include transgender rights in the struggles for sex and sexual orientation equality. *Columbia Law Review, 101*(2), 392–420.

Garcetti v. Ceballos, 126 U.S. 1951 (2006a).

Garcetti v. Ceballos, 547 U.S. 410, 424 (2006b).

Gender Public Advocacy Coalition. (2007). Home page. Retrieved July 9, 2007, from http://www.gpac.org/newweb/workplace/

Gertz, S. (2001). Florida's Civil Service appeal process: How "protective" is it? *The Justice System Journal, 22*(2), 117–135.

Gertz, S. (2007). At-will employment: Origins, applications, exceptions, and expansions in public service. In J. Bowman & J. West (Eds.), *American public service: Radical reform and the merit system* (pp. 47–74). Boca Raton, FL: Taylor & Francis.

Goldman v. Weinberger, 475 U.S. 503 (1986).

Griggs v. Duke Power Co., 401 U.S. 424 (1971).

Grutter v. Bollinger, 539 U.S. 306 (2003).

Harris v. Forklift Systems, 510 U.S. 17 (1993).

Hsieh, C., & Winslow, E. (2006, September). Gender representation in the federal workforce: A comparison among groups. *Review of Public Personnel Administration, 26*(3), 276–294.

Human Rights Campaign Foundation. (2008). Organizational website. http://www.hrc.org/issues/workplace.asp

Kelley v. Johnson, 425 U.S. 347 (1976).

Kogut, C., & Short, L. (2007, Fall). Affirmative action in federal employment: Good intentions run amuck? *Public Personnel Management, 36*(3), 197–206.

McDonnell Douglas Corp. v. Green, 411 U.S. 792 (1973).

National Treasury Employees Union v. Von Raab, 489 U.S. 656 (1989).

O'Connor v. Ortega, 480 U.S. 709 (1987).

Pickering v. Board of Educ., 391 U.S. 563 (1968).

Ravitch, F., & Lawther, W. (1999, Winter). Privatization and public employee pension rights: Treading in unexplored territory. *Review of Public Personnel Administration, 19*(1), 41–58.

Rutan v. Republican Party of Illinois, 497 U.S. 62 (1990).

Selmi, M. (2008). Interpreting the Americans with Disabilities Act: Why the Supreme Court rewrote the statute, and why Congress did not care. *George Washington Law Review, 76*, 522–575.

U.S. Government Accountability Office (GAO). (2007). *Federal Employees Health Benefits Program: Premiums continue to rise, but rate of growth has recently slowed.* Retrieved August 6, 2008, from http://www.gao.gov/new.items/d07873t.pdf

Watson v. Fort Worth Bank & Trust, 487 U.S. 977, 995 (1988).

Part II

Processes and Skills
From Start to Finish

Chapter 3

Recruitment

From Passive Posting to Headhunting

Your recruiting process should say to the candidate, "How'd you like to be part of our community, do neat things together, grow individually and with your peers?"

—Tom Peters

After studying this chapter, you should be able to

- identify the key paradoxes and challenges in recruitment from an organizational viewpoint,
- explain the steps in the civil service staffing process,
- pose preliminary questions such as whether to hire internally or externally and whether to duplicate the previous recruitment process or to restructure the position,
- write a customized job announcement,
- spot the strengths and weaknesses of various strategies and be able to determine an effective mix for specific staffing situations,
- describe some of the "do's and don'ts" of the recruitment process from an applicant's standpoint, and enhance it with effective networking skills, and
- incorporate tactics for enhancing diversity.

Having examined human resource management's context and challenges—the civil service heritage and the legal environment—we now explore the essential functions of human resource management, beginning with recruitment, arguably the most important function of all. From an applicant's perspective, recruitment is often daunting and esoteric. Ultimately, it can be life changing, as the applicant must navigate through what is sometimes a bewildering variety of procedures. From the organization's perspective, recruitment is a process of soliciting the most talented and motivated applicants, and as such it is a bedrock function. Only with highly skilled staff—**human capital**—do organizations have the opportunity to thrive in an era in which work tends to be complex, customized, and rapidly changing. This chapter, then, discusses an array of concerns that agencies and applicants encounter and explains why the public sector confronts unique challenges.

One paradox is that procurement strategies and techniques, despite their importance, may seem relatively insignificant compared with the American sociopolitical environment within which this function takes place. That is, three cultural forces—the historical recruitment philosophy, the social status of public employment, and political leadership—form a powerful context within which government seeks employees. Historically, recruitment has been passive; until the 1950s, it was not legal for the federal government to advertise in newspapers. Recruitment has also been highly negative and legalistic, often "turning off" would-be job applicants and contributing to the perception of excessive red tape (U.S. Merit Systems Protection Board [MSPB], 2000). Furthermore, the loss of prestige of the public service from its high-water mark in the 1930s and 1940s is a constant concern (Lewis & Frank, 2002). Finally, politicians may make public employment harder by both "bashing the bureaucracy" (which they are in charge of) and starving it of resources needed for high-quality recruitment (such as pay and adequate signing bonuses for hard-to-fill classifications).

For the job seeker, another stark paradox is the seeming abundance of employment opportunities but scarcity of desirable positions (or **fast-track positions**). There are several reasons for this. Not only is there a tendency to increase the span of control and eliminate whole layers of middle management, but also there is a propensity to reduce the number of specialists who have management rank and perquisites; as a result, positions with attractive professional opportunities can easily elicit scores of qualified candidates.

Applicants also often are perplexed by the mixed messages. Is recruitment a politically neutral, skill-based process, as it purports to be, or is it frequently a personalistic, "underground" hiring system with "wired" jobs subject to subtle, modern-day patronage? As discussed below, the public service was once largely based on patronage; even today, patronage positions are among the most influential in government. The bulk of those senior positions, however, are supposed to be based strictly on technical merit; nonetheless, the influence of "political" or personal factors is common. Below the policy level, however, personal factors cannot be discounted. Local government has always prided itself on a balanced approach using technical merit and a "good fit." Even at the federal level, entry-level job applicants hear about a job more frequently from friends and relatives than from any other source (MSPB, 2008a), and internal promotions are affected by personal factors (MSPB, 2001). Thus, paradoxically, depending on the position, both perspectives can be true, and the wise applicant is open to the dualistic nature of recruiting. (That is, luck, "fit," and connections are often as important as competence.)

In addition, should management aspirants prepare themselves as specialists or as generalists? Paradoxically, the answer is sometimes "yes." That is, applicants for better positions must be both. Until recently, the American tradition has largely favored specialists. The best case workers in social service agencies would often be promoted to supervisors, the best engineers in transportation agencies would be appointed as managers, and good researchers in state universities would become administrators. Advanced positions seldom required either generalist management training or experience in rotational assignments to gain broad experience. Although organizations seem to appreciate generalist training, it is usually on top of specialist training—for those few who are advanced in today's flatter hierarchies.

Generalist training, however, is critical for managers who deal with diverse functions and who rarely have the time to maintain specialist expertise.

Paradoxes and challenges also exist from an organizational perspective. They start with the notion that recruitment is the most compelling human resource function, but it is generally acknowledged to be the weakest in most organizations (U.S. Government Accountability Office [GAO], 2003). It is pivotal because if recruitment is done poorly, then all subsequent human resource functions will be negatively affected. It is often weakest because when done properly, it is a time-consuming, expensive process that busy administrators may try to circumvent. A challenge, given the contemporary demand for well-paying jobs, is that **staffing** practices may not consistently produce "the best and the brightest." Perceptions of lower pay and lower job quality haunt the public sector even though those perceptions are often untrue (MSPB, 2008b). Therefore, recruitment must not depend on pay comparability, which sometimes outstrips regional pay in rural areas but rarely keeps pace in urban and executive positions. Best-practice organizations, however, realize that success in a competitive environment cannot occur without first starting with entrepreneurial recruitment practices, such as better hiring efficiency and test flexibility (Lavigna, 2002), as is afforded through the use of the Internet in disseminating information and gathering and evaluating applicant data (Kauffman & Robb, 2003).

Another challenge is the focus of recruitment: should it be on current skills or future potential? Traditionally, procuring personnel emphasized technical skills and longevity.[1] More and more, however, organizations are interested in employee potential. The ability to adapt to new responsibilities and positions is critical as agencies reorganize and decentralize decision making. Detecting future ability and identifying flexible employees takes a staffing process that seeks a different set of skills than was commonly the case (Redman & Mathews, 1997).

Next is the paradox of balancing competing values: the need for timely recruitment—generally the biggest single concern of applicants and hiring supervisors alike—while maintaining lengthy processes in the name of fairness and openness. Although on-the-spot hiring occurs in government (see noncompetitive recruitment strategies below), months can elapse between the **job (position) announcement** and an offer of employment (GAO, 2003).

Another paradox is what to emphasize in the recruitment process. Which of the following are most significant: (a) knowledge, skills, and abilities; (b) motivation; (c) diversity and broad representation of minority and protected classes in the workforce; or (d) loyalty? Certainly technical skills are important, but it is quite possible to hire an employee who is well qualified yet who is poorly motivated, contributes to a racial or gender imbalance, and is not loyal. Nontechnical emphases have several challenges as well. Motivation is hard to predict, although it can transform a workplace. Diversity has an important management and ethical dimension, although it is rarely allowed to be more than a "plus" factor in recruiting. Organizations that lack employee loyalty likely lack trust, innovation, or dedication as well. Similarly, there is the dilemma of whether to use open recruitment, which encourages a broader pool and fresh ideas, or closed recruitment limited to the organization, which rewards service and loyalty. Closed recruitment is also generally faster.

Finally, what responsibility does the organization have to the applicant? Job seekers spend a great deal of energy and time on the process. For example, is it ethical to use open recruitment to fulfill a perceived legal requirement when a candidate, usually internal, has implicitly been selected for the position? **Sham recruitment** processes are infuriating for the candidate and a drain on the resources of the organization. Is it fair to ask for job references in the initial job application process when only those of the most highly ranked candidates will be read?

Such paradoxes illustrate the rich and complex factors that go into a seemingly simple process. Although there are few definitive answers across all situations, an examination of context and proven recruitment principles does lead to numerous best practices, which will be discussed in this chapter. The chapter first identifies the overarching factors affecting recruiting success and then introduces specific steps in the **recruitment process**. Then, three steps—planning and approval, position announcements, and **recruitment strategies**—are probed in more detail. Additional discussions include recruitment and diversity, the division of recruitment responsibilities, and job seeker advice. The chapter closes with a summary and concluding recommendations.

■■ FACTORS IN RECRUITMENT: EMPLOYER AND APPLICANT PERSPECTIVES

Recruitment can be seen from two perspectives. What are the factors that affect success for the organization? And, just as important, what are applicants' perspectives on what a quality process is, even if they are not selected?

High-Quality Recruitment: An Employer's Perspective

At least five major elements influence the effectiveness of recruitment: (1) the breadth and quality of the process, (2) the size of the labor pool and the location of jobs, (3) pay and benefits (discussed in Chapters 7 and 8), (4) job quality, and (5) organizational image.

Having a sound recruitment philosophy means asking the right and wise questions from the outset (Breaugh & Starke, 2000). Is the entire procedure well conceived so that it fully embodies vital organization goals? Are enough—and the correct—strategies used to reach a broad range of those who might be qualified and interested? Is the process aggressive enough to encourage the best candidates to apply? Is it clear and nonbureaucratic so that would-be employees will not be discouraged? Is the process free from legal challenges yet not excessively legalistic or stultifying? Do applicants feel good about the recruitment process? Finally, is the overall procedure cost-effective for the position being considered and the recruitment environment, both of which vary enormously (GAO, 2008a)? The bulk of this chapter is devoted to this pragmatic element: providing an excellent recruitment process.

Although the size of the labor pool and the location of jobs, pay and benefits, job quality, and organizational image are not emphasized in this chapter, they have influence on the context within which the technical process operates. Labor pool size and job location play a role in recruitment (Smith, 2000). For instance, in the last generation, thousands of public sector jobs have been privatized, with the result that they have gone to private domestic and overseas contractors. Economic boom or bust cycles also affect recruitment. For school districts, for example, this means that sometimes human resource offices may be inundated with high-quality candidates. In times of shortages, though, districts may travel out of state to job fairs and offer signing bonuses and moving allowances to fill vacancies. Good economic times generally mean that few professionals of all types—lawyers, accountants, doctors, engineers, and others—may be available to apply for an open position; when the economy is weak, employee supply expands to the advantage of employers.

Pay and benefits are often the first factor that potential applicants review and consider. Public sector pay generally varies from being uncompetitive to moderately competitive, depending on the agency, location, and position. Public sector benefits are generally perceived as on par with to substantially better than the private sector on average and thus a recruiting strength. The nonprofit sector often suffers from a substantially lower pay scale and more limited benefits than either the private or public sectors, and thus must make up for these weaknesses in the intrinsic job quality elements.

Job quality may or may not be an element that applicants are immediately aware of, but top candidates invariably become proficient analysts of the organization they are considering. The best ones investigate with a critical eye such aspects as job security, advancement potential, interesting work, working conditions, and professional perquisites such as travel and training. For example, in a recent survey of federal employment, the most important factors that influenced those accepting employment were job security (28%), advancement opportunities (12%), and challenging and interesting work (10%), with only 10% identifying pay as the key factor (MSPB, 2008a, p. 37). Although much of the candidate's understanding of job quality is sought and verified in the selection process (Chapter 4), it begins with recruitment. Challenging and interesting work leads among factors in the nonprofit sector (Nickson, Warhurst, Dutton, & Hurrell, 2008).

Finally, organizational status plays a significant role (Gatehouse, Gowan, & Lautenschlager, 1993). Being an auditor in a social service agency beleaguered with a series of child protective service and welfare scandals may not be as appealing as working as an auditor in a large accounting firm. When the pay differential is factored in as well, it means that one organization may have Ivy League graduates competing for interviews, whereas the other does not. Laudable as the public service ethic may be, it can wear people out if agencies do not contribute to employee welfare in important ways.

To illustrate, although most public defender offices pay poorly and overwork assistant public defenders, some have fine candidates because the training afforded is excellent and the work is as exciting as it is challenging. Furthermore, because of a short-term surge in popularity of a strong service ethic after the 9/11 terrorist attacks, interest in public employment increased (Kauffman, 2004). Also, there has been increased attention on polishing agencies' images—called branding—which is often done in tandem with recruiting (Bailes, 2002; Davidson, Lepeak, & Newman, 2007). A related trend is organizational ranking, such as The Best Places to Work in the Federal Government data, which highlights top agencies by size, improvement, class, demographics, and so on (Partnership for Public Service, 2007).

High-Quality Recruitment: An Applicant's Perspective

According to recruitment expert Sara Rynes (1993), too often employers neglect to think of the applicant's perspective in the recruitment process. Instead of candidates being impressed by the organization whether they are hired or not, most feel resentment because of cold, unthoughtful, or dilatory treatment. In addition to an efficient and clear process,

Rynes offers four suggestions for employers who want people to have a good impression of the agency:

1. Time recruitment steps to minimize anxiety. Good candidates expect recruitment processes to result in timely notification of being in contention, prompt follow-ups, and enough time to make a reasonable choice among offers.

2. Provide feedback to optimize scarce job search resources. "Withholding of negative feedback is often interpreted as 'stringing applicants along' to preserve complete freedom of organizational decision making" (Rynes, 1993, p. 31). In other words, as soon as agencies have eliminated applicants by narrowing the field to a short list, they should consider notifying candidates rather than wait until the final person has been selected.

3. Offer information that makes distinctions. People prefer to have information that is detailed enough to allow realistic assumptions about the specific job content rather than the single sentence descriptions common in many announcements. In the interview process, candidates appreciate a realistic job preview because they understand Malcolm Forbes's view, "If you have a job without aggravation, you don't have a job."

4. Use enthusiastic, informative, and credible representatives. In the initial recruitment process, applicants respond much better to warm and enthusiastic recruiters. In the interview process, candidates not only notice whether they meet top organizational leaders and coworkers, but also are sensitive to how their time is used. Dead time in the schedule or a casual interview schedule is seen as a negative factor from the candidate's perspective.

Overall, treat applicants as customers, and manage the recruitment process in a professional manner. With the backdrop of these recruitment factors and applicant preferences, attention now turns to the technical processes.

■■ RECRUITMENT STEPS

Recruitment provides information about available positions and encourages qualified candidates to apply. It has three stages: (1) planning and approval of the position, (2) preparation of the position announcement, and (3) selection and use of specific strategies. The recruitment process should be seamlessly connected with the selection process (Chapter 4). Together these processes are known as staffing (the receipt of applications and the closing date of the position signal the end of recruitment and the beginning of the selection process). The procedure is highlighted in Exhibit 3.1.

Generalizations are necessary but difficult, because substantial variations in the recruitment process exist.[2] Thus, the process for an entry-level position may be quite different from that used for a midlevel manager, which in turn may be unlike that for an administrative head. Furthermore, recruitment in small and large organizations will vary considerably. Even large agencies will range between centralized and decentralized practices. Finally, departments often rotate between **individual recruitment** for a particular position and **institutional** or **pool recruitment** to procure many people for a job classification such as entry-level secretaries, accountants, laborers, forest rangers, or caseworkers.

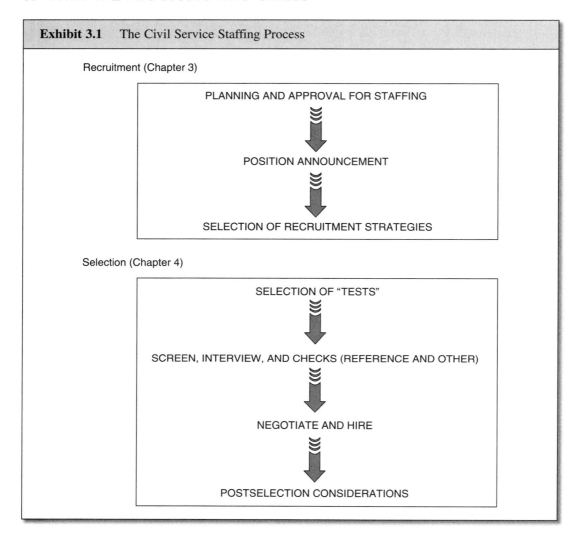

Exhibit 3.1   The Civil Service Staffing Process

Recruitment (Chapter 3)

PLANNING AND APPROVAL FOR STAFFING

POSITION ANNOUNCEMENT

SELECTION OF RECRUITMENT STRATEGIES

Selection (Chapter 4)

SELECTION OF "TESTS"

SCREEN, INTERVIEW, AND CHECKS (REFERENCE AND OTHER)

NEGOTIATE AND HIRE

POSTSELECTION CONSIDERATIONS

An important long-term trend in the last century was **proceduralism** (or red tape). It connotes processes that have become excessively detailed, complicated, protracted, or impersonal (e.g., filling out different forms requesting the same information, having to go to multiple locations, or lengthy procedures that could be accomplished in a short time). Ever since the widespread use of civil service systems, the ideal has been to be as neutral as possible to make the process fair and unbiased. To accommodate numerous applicant requests for a large range of positions, centralized systems emerged in the federal government in the 1920s and elsewhere thereafter (Hamman & Desai, 1995, p. 90). Certainly, this was sensible, helping to combat excessive political cronyism and managerial personalism and to overcome a lack of hiring expertise dispersed among various units. It led, however, to rigidity and formalism as well. Adding to proceduralism in the mid-1960s was the interest in providing greater employment accessibility for minorities, women, and other protected classes.[3]

The trend today seeks to ease the effects of proceduralism by decentralizing to allow hiring managers more control and the opportunity to try innovative methods to compete in the new employment environment. Recent government reform initiatives have affected staffing in three ways:

(1) There has been a strong drive to decentralize staffing activities in the largest organizations where extreme centralization historically has been the norm. To the extent feasible, line managers are being provided with greater influence in recruitment and selection efforts. This trend has been particularly evident at the federal and state levels because of their size, but much less so with local governments and the not-for-profit sector in which extreme centralization has not been so widespread.

(2) Government appears to be making a sincere effort to simplify and invigorate intake functions. Better agencies are spending more time on selling themselves to prospective workers, and they are spending more attention at easing new employees' passage into the workforce. However, there is clear evidence that agencies' practices are diverging widely based on both the much more constrained resources of some agencies as well as an organizational interest, or lack thereof, in this critical function (Davidson et al., 2007).

(3) Many human resource offices (with legislative approval) are demonstrating a willingness to experiment with new staffing strategies such as on-the-spot hiring, fully online applications, and electronic scaling of applications.

▪▪ PLANNING AND APPROVAL

At least two different types of planning occur in well-managed organizations (Mintzberg, 1994). First, they engage in strategic thinking about the future needs, challenges, and opportunities of their incoming workforce. True strategic planning requires research, original thinking, and a willingness to change. Second, agencies operationalize strategic plans as concrete positions become available. In other words, preliminary, vital questions should be rigorously asked about available positions before the actual recruitment process takes place (Lavelle, 2007).

Strategic Planning and Management of Vacancies

A plan for staffing begins with a **labor market survey** or specific position parity studies that compare agency job clusters. What are trends in terms of availability, salaries, and education levels? Statistics and information regarding the national labor force can be obtained at the Bureau of Labor Statistics home page (www.bls.gov); a useful occupational outlook handbook can be found online (Bureau of Labor Statistics, 2008). Local and regional data can be gathered from each state's bureau of labor as well as from some of the larger jurisdictions. Local job parity studies are often performed by local agencies engaging in job evaluation (see Chapter 5) or groups of organizations that jointly commission regular studies to benchmark pay trends. Many agencies do not want to be uncompetitive, while others want to be highly competitive. Public organizations often suffer most in tight labor markets because of the difficulty of implementing flexible pay policies to compete for workers.

In addition to a market analysis, a needs assessment should be done. What does the organization anticipate its requirements will be for new positions, restructured positions, and eliminated positions? Some of these issues may crosscut the entire organization while others primarily affect a series of jobs.

- An issue facing organizations today is the retirement of the large Baby Boomer generation (and the last of the traditionalists), as well as the integration of the Generation Xers and New Millennials. Mass retirements always provide challenges, but can offer opportunities for renewal if well planned. One important issue frequently raised relates to **succession planning**, which refers to an organization's ability to replace its executive and senior management ranks with high-quality talent (GAO, 2008a). Other related issues are the differences among the generations and their varying needs and the preferences of newer generations (Crumpacker & Crumpacker, 2007), as well as the need to retain or rehire some mature workers past retirement, and hire new older workers who may want a reduced schedule through job sharing or part-time work (Armstrong-Stassen & Templer, 2006; Dychtwald & Baxter, 2007; GAO, 2008b).
- If an agency is required to strengthen its educative or facilitative role and decrease its regulative role (such as occurred at the U.S. Department of Housing and Urban Development in the 1990s, for instance), then it will need new skills and even different types of staff.
- The rapid shift in the responsibilities—from a traditional war-fighting operation in Desert Storm and the initial invasion in Iraq in 2003, to counterinsurgency and nation building after the fall of Baghdad—has caused an enormous strain on an unprepared service.
- An example at the local level is the housing boom after 2000, and the housing bust beginning in 2007, which has led to dramatic shifts in staffing in code enforcement, building services, and the types of economic development initiatives undertaken. Additionally, dropping home prices have led to automatic tax reductions, and thus lowered public sector revenues (hence widespread hiring freezes and even reductions-in-force in some cases), even as the demand for public services is increasing (especially unemployment benefits, job counseling and training, and welfare benefits).
- Given the rapid growth of law enforcement concerns after 9/11 and increasing demand for heightened border security, an enormous wave of federal hiring has made retaining and hiring public safety personnel dramatically more difficult at the state and local levels. It is nevertheless customary to find workforces lacking the requisite technical, interpersonal, and problem-solving skills. Such mission transitions are common today. Although the decentralization of human resource functions overall has made planning at the systems level more difficult for states and cities, it has made such planning more flexible at the department and unit levels. (See U.S. Office of Personnel Management [OPM], 2006, Chap. 2, for a guide to strategic workforce planning and an analytic tool to manage this process.)

Planning can take a number of different forms. Organizations can make sure that the staff intake function is properly funded. They can work on institutional image to positively affect recruitment. Agencies can enhance job quality by offering flexible schedules, family support policies like child care, comparable pay, and technology upgrades. Such planning and action take place long before any particular position is advertised. A final aspect of planning is to make sure that the process is timely and user friendly.

Ultimately, each position that opens may have special problems and opportunities. Administrators need to be able to assess whether a routine protocol is best or whether closer examination is necessary. If any of the following red flags are present, the hiring manager should probably give special attention to a new or customized process:

- Applicants for recent positions have been poorly qualified.
- Supervisors complain that new workers do not fit well into the department.
- The best candidates do not apply.
- Better applicants have already found jobs by the time the position is offered.

When strategic issues are involved, it is time to consult with the human resources department and colleagues in the agency and other organizations, as well as to consult professional trade journals. Systemic concerns should trigger the use of decision-making tools such as cause-and-effect charts, statistical analysis, and Delphi techniques (i.e., the pooling of expert opinions on a problem or issue) so that solutions can be found.

An example of a strategic problem comes from a midlevel information technology manager arguing with his supervisor about whether to hire an underqualified but high-potential candidate. The supervisor's view was that such employees take at least three months to have marginal utility and six months to perform at standard. Furthermore, some never come up to speed but rather plateau at a low performance level. The midlevel manager's position was that the unit had five open positions, was struggling to keep up with a rapidly expanding workload, and found that fully qualified personnel were simply not applying, despite a new, higher pay level.

By discussing the systemic problem with human resource experts, however, the manager and supervisor uncovered a strategic opportunity. Why not hire five technically underqualified but high-potential candidates (who were relatively plentiful) and offer a special training class? This would be worth the effort because its size would justify a full-time trainer, which, in turn, would ensure higher-quality training than the ad hoc on-the-job training provided to single hires. Furthermore, furnishing a trainer would reduce the demands on the already overworked personnel in the unit for whom training new employees was generally a distraction.

Only with a clear sense of the demographics and competition of the job market, as well as the general direction of the organization, can one focus with confidence on a specific position.

Preliminary Decisions About a Specific Position

Before the recruitment for a position begins, some thought must be given to staffing fundamentals. Is it advisable to fill the position at all? Sometimes it is better to leave one position unfilled so that the spare capacity can be used elsewhere in the unit or organization. Another question is whether the position needs to be restructured or if expectations need to be adjusted (see also Chapter 5 on classification). Has the position become over- or underclassified? Is it too narrowly or too broadly defined? Have fundamental job skills shifted because of technology or program maturation? Sometimes one or two vacancies provide a good opportunity to raise such questions.

If the position is not entry level, should it be filled from candidates internal to the organization only or should it be filled from outside applicants? In very large systems, a third option is outside the agency but within the same governmental system (e.g., federal, state, county, or city). Morale, it is generally argued, is improved by **inside (internal) recruitment**, whereas depth and diversity are improved by **outside (external) recruitment**. Generally, "inside only" decisions are used by departments that rely on rank classification (such as the military and public safety organizations) and by strong union agencies in which priority application provisions for existing employees are tantamount to property rights. Whereas government tended to have a preference for internal promotion in the past, even at the federal level new flexibilities ("hiring authorities") are making greater use of external candidates (Kauffman, 2003).

The type of recruitment process is another issue: individual versus pool or institutional recruitment. At the federal level, these categories are "case examining" versus "standing inventories." Broad, entry-level classifications in moderately large organizations generally use pool hiring. For example, a personnel department may generically advertise for numerous entry-level secretaries, computer programmers, and accountants to be placed on a standing certified list to be used by numerous state agencies in the selection process. The advantages are increased efficiency, low cost, and multiple considerations of qualified applications; disadvantages are primarily the difficulties of keeping the list up to date. Common or hard-to-fill positions may be on a continuous list in order to constantly replenish candidates. Individual recruitment is used for most positions above the entry level, jobs in smaller organizations, and less-common classifications.

A critical decision is the breadth of involvement of those in hiring and related units. Sometimes, typically for entry-level slots, the supervisor is the sole decision maker and works exclusively with the personnel authority. At the other extreme—commonly in senior level and professional positions—is a search committee that selects the finalists for an interview and recommends a best candidate to the hiring supervisor. A midpoint is often struck for middle management jobs in which input is solicited from the affected subordinates and colleagues, but the final decision is still primarily the domain of the supervisor.

For many positions, especially those involved in first-line management, the question of the generalist versus the specialist arises. Of course, there is no definitive answer; it depends on the needs of the position. Specialists may relate to line workers well and understand technical issues; however, as the philosopher Shunryu Suzuki noted, "In the generalist's mind there are many opportunities; in an expert's mind there are few." Generalists tend to have a broader perspective that is valuable in management positions. On the whole, they can see both the forest and the trees, have superior people skills, and are easier to cross-train. Specialists, on the other hand, can be more efficient because of their technical background, are easier to justify in the budget in frontline supervisory positions, and require relatively little training for the production work that many supervisors today continue to do. The challenge is that frontline positions need specialist abilities, but when those same people are promoted, their new management responsibilities tend to focus on generalist competencies. In the 21st century, it may be less important what one knows and more important what one has in the way of potential to respond to unknown challenges.

The final preliminary issue is getting authority for hiring and approval for any job adjustments that may be needed. Positions are a carefully guarded resource, with hiring freezes instituted directly by presidents, governors, county commissioners, and mayors. Paperwork must be carefully completed, adjustments must be documented, and acquiring formal union approval or informal approval by colleagues is prudent. Hiring supervisors who are sloppy or impatient with the process or inarticulate with their rationale may find their hiring opportunities hamstrung by human resource specialists or stymied by superiors. As often as not, managers who demand expedited processes have simply neglected to plan properly or learn long-established procedures.

In summary, recruitment begins before a position becomes available. An agency that wants to appeal to the best candidates will make sure that it is competitive in terms of pay, reputation, working conditions, and collegiality and that its personnel procurement process has resources to identify and attract the finest people available. As positions become available, proper planning requires a series of preliminary questions related to job currency and restructuring, inside versus outside recruitment, pool versus individual hiring, scope of involvement, specialist-generalist characteristics, and timeliness. This planning occurs prior to designing the job announcement, discussed next.

∷ POSITION ANNOUNCEMENTS

Because there are no standard legal requirements about minimum information in job (position) announcements, they vary from jurisdiction to jurisdiction, from entry level to professional recruitment, and from source to source. For example, one jurisdiction may routinely include information about its benefits package, whereas another may not. Or a professional-level announcement in a national trade journal may insert a promotional paragraph about the agency or its jurisdiction that would rarely appear in an entry-level announcement in a local newspaper. Many agencies use advertisements that have relatively little detail, that are aimed at notifying applicants of opportunities that can be more fully explored by requesting more information. A cost-effective compromise may be to post an ad in a national job search Web site (job board) like Monster.com or Careerpaths.com; such ads include a series of questions that screen qualified prospective applicants as they read them. In any event, the announcement should be designed initially using a full format, which subsequently can be modified (see Exhibit 3.2).

Style and tone matter more in announcements today than in the past because of a tight labor market and the difficulty of getting well-qualified people. Although announcements were once expected to be solemn, standardized, and neutral, now they must, at least to some degree, be inviting and interesting (Zeidner, 2001). In an in-depth analysis of vacancy announcements, the MSPB criticized federal recruitment in this area:

> Our systematic review of a random sample of vacancy announcements found that at least half of them are poorly written and that they make little or no attempt to sell the government, the agency, or the positions to be filled. Far too often vacancy announcements are difficult to understand and use threatening and insulting language, characteristics that are more likely to drive applicants away than attract them. (MSPB, 2003, p. 7)

Some of the recommendations from that study that apply to all public sector organizations include the following:

- Greatly reduce the length of vacancy announcements.
- Reduce the use of negative, threatening, and legalistic language.

Exhibit 3.2   The Elements of a Job Announcement

The following types of information are relatively standard in a full announcement:

1. *Title and agency/organization affiliation.* This can include the official title and/or the working title. The agency/division affiliation is mentioned except when recruitment is being conducted on a centralized basis (e.g., statewide or citywide).

2. *Salary range.* The range generally indicates the starting salary as well as its ceiling. Professional and executive positions may simply state that a "competitive salary" is offered depending on experience and credentials.

3. *Description of job duties and responsibilities.* This is essentially a short job description. What will the incumbent actually do and be responsible for? Supervisory responsibilities, financial duties, and program responsibilities are especially useful in nonentry positions. Work hours are also standard information, although sometimes omitted when conventional.

4. *Minimum qualifications.* What education, skills, and experience are required, as a minimum, to qualify for the job? Education requirements could be a degree in select fields or a specialized certification. Skills could be as specific as typing speed or as general as communication facility. Many positions require specific experiences such as at least 3 years as a planner or 7 years in positions with progressively more responsibility (e.g., managerial). Minimum qualifications must be job related; employers should not arbitrarily raise such qualifications just to reduce the number of job applicants.

5. *Special conditions.* These often signal applicants to aspects of the job that some people (but not necessarily all) may find unappealing. Common special conditions include travel requirements, being stationed at outlying locations, a harsh or dangerous work environment, requirements for background checks, unusual hours, and residency requirements.

6. *Application procedures.* What exam method will be used? If there is a specific test, when is it administered? Or is examination done by rating the education and experience of candidates? To whom and where does one apply, and with what exact materials? A closing date for the recruitment period is necessary, although sometimes positions "remain open until filled" after the closing date. Re-advertised positions may "begin interviewing immediately." Otherwise, most jurisdictions require 3 weeks or more to close the recruitment period. Minimum periods for advertising are often in the legal code or statute and should be scrupulously followed. Emergency and temporary hiring practices are always possible but generally require exceptional justification and authorization.

7. *Equal Opportunity Employment.* Standard phrases are used to indicate the organization's commitment to equal opportunity employment and affirmative action.

Beyond these standard types of information, some other kinds are not routine but are nevertheless common.

1. *Classification.* The specific ranking of the position in the organizational system (grade level) is often not included in external postings because it may confuse outsiders. When it is relatively easy to understand, such as the federal General Schedule, it should be listed. Grade level is invariably of interest to organizational members, so internal postings should always include this more technical data.

2. *Career potential.* A good job posting should discourage poorly qualified applicants, but it should also encourage those who are well qualified. Candidates often are looking at not only the position but its career potential. Mentioning career potential generally helps recruit better and more ambitious applicants. Examples include opportunities for promotion, training and education, and special experience.

3. *Special benefits.* Some positions have special benefits. Examples might be seasonal vacations (such as summers for teachers and faculty), opportunities for extra pay, availability to work with distinguished people, or exceptional retirement programs (such as the military and paramilitary organizations).

- Design a message to sell the job and the agency and, to the extent possible, to present the agency as the employer of choice.
- Clearly and realistically describe the job and its requirements.
- Require the least amount of information needed to make basic qualification determinations and then request more information as needed later in the process.
- Give straightforward instructions on how to apply.

Finally, announcements should always be reviewed carefully for both accuracy and currency because misstatements become legally binding and errors make the organization look unprofessional. Of course, they should tie directly to the official job description, which in turn often is based on a formal job analysis (see Chapter 5). Although conceptually job analyses and descriptions precede announcements, it is not unheard of that preparation of an announcement sparks changes in a description or causes a new job analysis. Once an announcement is completed and authorized, the department can focus on an appropriate set of recruitment strategies.

▪▪ RECRUITMENT STRATEGIES

There are numerous recruitment strategies—methods of contacting and informing potential applicants—but seldom are they all used. Of course, it is not the sheer number that determines a quality intake process but the choice of an appropriate combination. Unfortunately, governments historically have eschewed aggressive recruitment practices. There is a new activism today (MSPB, 2006), which means that agencies are using more approaches and trying to do so with more effect. Ten strategies are discussed here, each of which has strengths and weaknesses and, therefore, various utilization patterns. Four major factors (relative ease of use, effectiveness, cost, and common usage) will be identified for each strategy.

1. **Job posting** was originally the placing of the announcement on walls in prominent places such as post offices or city halls. Many civil service systems still require physical posting in a minimum number of public places. Today it also refers to listing jobs with in-house job bulletins, newspapers, or standard communications. Posting is considered the most basic of all recruitment strategies; it is easy to do because the entire announcement can be used without modification.

Its effectiveness is largely limited to organization members and aggressive job seekers who come to the agency's employment office. For a job that must be filled internally, say a fire lieutenant's position, posting alone can be sufficient. Many positions, however, are recruited outside the organization and traditional posting is unlikely to be effective. As Eleanor Trice (1999) of the International Personnel Management Association said, "The days when government organizations could recruit by simply posting a vacancy announcement, then sitting back and assuming that enough qualified applicants would apply, are gone" (p. 10).

2. Today posting also refers to **electronic posting**—listing jobs on agency Web sites or Web sites exclusively dedicated to job seekers. The Internet is an enormously important recruitment tool whose cost is minimal. Some examples are the following:

- U.S. federal jobs (www.usajobs.gov)
- Federal Web site directory (www.fedworld.gov)
- *Federal Times,* under career information (www.federaltimes.com)
- Jobs in government (www.JobsInGovernment.com)
- International City/County Management Association (http://jobs.icma.org)
- All government (www.govtjobs.com/jobopp)
- California state government (www.spb.ca.gov)
- Arizona state government (www.secure.azstatejobs.gov)
- Suffolk County, NY (www.co.suffolk.ny.us/Home/departments/civilservice)
- City of Philadelphia (www.phila.gov/personnel/announce)
- City of Las Vegas (www.lasvegasnevada.gov)
- True Careers (www.truecareers.com)

Electronic posting is now required by law for federal positions that are competitively recruited and is the baseline for all but the most specialized jobs or the smallest agencies. The ease of placing job advertisements has become a substantial advantage, as has the ability to reach an enormous pool at minimal cost. The interlinking of job board data makes dissemination relatively easy. Federal data show that electronic posting is the second most important method after friends or relatives (MSPB, 2008a, 2008b). Very importantly, now more than 50% of all initial applications for government positions can be done completely online (Davidson et al., 2007, p. 9), a percentage that has been climbing swiftly in recent years. Despite its growth and popularity as the recruitment tool, there are indications that human resource personnel are already overly relying on electronic posting. The MSPB (2003) cautioned against overreliance on electronic methods because of concerns about universal digital access.

3. Newspaper recruitment focuses on local or regional openings. The employment section of the largest local Sunday paper is the most common vehicle for job announcements, but some jurisdictions use daily employment sections as well. Smaller papers may be ideal for a local job, especially those that are entry level, low paying, or part time. Despite cost, newspapers can be relatively effective in external recruitment.

4. Trade journals are the newsletters and magazines that inform members of professions about activities on a regular basis (e.g., *PA Times, ICMA Newsletter,* and *IPMA Newsletter*). The audience is narrower than that of a newspaper in terms of professional range but broader in terms of national scope. Trade journals are used extensively for professional and senior management positions in which high levels of specialized expertise are desired and generally available only on the national market. If a federal agency is looking for a senior math statistician,

a state agency is seeking a director for its lottery department, or a municipality is searching for a city manager, they are all likely to list these positions in relevant journals where candidates can easily scan the entire job market. To the degree that appointive positions use open procedures, trade journals are also a strategy of choice, despite the associated cost.

5. **Mail (and email) recruitment** (custom mailing) is a highly personalized approach in which individuals are encouraged by letter to apply. Aggressive private sector corporations use this strategy to contact students who are in the top few deciles of a handful of institutions identified as sources of exceptional candidates. Even more targeted-recruitment occurs when a search committee identifies a select number of individuals who are exceedingly qualified and then personally encourages them. Such an approach "seeds" the recruitment pool with candidates who may not otherwise apply. It is rarely used in the public sector but is a mainstay strategy for Fortune 500 companies. Both sectors use search firms that rely on such personalized approaches. In addition, email provides an inexpensive, informal, and rapid outreach technique.

6. Other mass communications (excluding the print and electronic methods already mentioned) include dedicated phone lines, government access TV, radio, institutional advertising, and positive public relations stories. Dedicated phone lines are used by centralized personnel agencies to accommodate the standardized information needs of applicants who can call about jobs 24 hours a day. Government-access TV is frequently used by cities and counties that have a controlled-access government station provided by the authorized cable company. It is common for these stations to list available jobs at various times throughout the day. Some organizations (e.g., state universities) use institutional advertising, especially when they have a service to sell. This advertising increases awareness and prestige, even though it does not target select positions. Positive media coverage can have a similar effect on recruitment efforts. As important for many organizations as institutional advertising is maintaining a state-of-the-art Web site that is detailed and interactive (Cober, Brown, Keeping, & Levy, 2004).

7. **Personal contact recruitment** occurs when recruiters, managers, or search panel members attend job fairs, conduct on-campus recruiting, or individually contact top candidates for positions. Recruiters generally travel to such events, perhaps across town but sometimes to other states, or make targeted calls to potential candidates who have not applied. Such tactics are routine for some corporations, professional sports teams, and elite law firms, but are less common for all but the largest government agencies. Job fairs provide candidates a chance to talk to prospective employers and provide the organization an opportunity to increase its visibility and scout for suitable talent. The practice of managers personally contacting executive candidates is typical in business; it is less typical in the public sector, which is considered vulnerable to accusations of cronyism and bias. Nonetheless, job fairs are reported as being more important than www.usajobs.gov to those under 30, while older job seekers relied far more heavily on both www.usajobs.gov and the agency's Web site (MSPB, 2008a).

8. **Internship recruitment** programs are a usual practice in many midsized and large jurisdictions (see Exhibit 3.3 for two examples). Elite organizations screen interns nearly as closely as job applicants because of program cost and subsequent high hiring rates. Consequently, such opportunities are a standard element of almost all master's of public administration (MPA) curricula. Program quality in these internships can be quite high. Organizations that make large-scale and effective use of this strategy report that the benefits in terms of training, acculturation, job preview, and job longevity are unequaled by other methods.

Exhibit 3.3   Examples of Internship Recruiting

MANAGEMENT INTERNSHIP

City of Phoenix, Arizona

ABOUT THE PROGRAM

The City of Phoenix Management Intern Program has been attracting outstanding individuals to government service since 1950. If you are interested in a career in public administration, this one-year, full-time program is an excellent opportunity to experience a variety of innovative management systems; gain exposure to many of the issues facing a large, well-run city government; and develop important professional skills. Our program is one of the most respected local government training programs in the United States. It is designed to attract, develop, and retain innovative people in local government.

A Wide Range of Experiences

If selected, you will work in the City Manager's Office, the Budget and Research Department, and a department that provides direct service to the community. You will also work on a wide array of projects and assignments that will develop and refine your professional skills. Past completed projects include

- researching and coordinating outreach activities to increase the diversity of community leaders on public arts boards,
- analyzing best practices to implement a pilot program to apprehend graffiti vandals, and
- developing a department budget.

Professional Development

This program gives you the opportunity to observe first hand the efforts of a large city government to resolve some of its most pressing issues. You will staff administrative and community committees and attend city council and management policy meetings. You will be able to network with the city's top officials and managers through one-on-one meetings. You also will have the opportunity to attend local and regional professional conferences during the year where you can meet and network with government professionals from throughout the southwest.

Salary and Benefits

While the salary schedule for the 2008–09 fiscal year is not in place, the present salary range is $35,318–$52,603 annually. City employees who are in a higher salary range would remain at their current rate of pay throughout the program.

- The city's comprehensive benefits package includes medical and dental insurance, city-sponsored training, and seminar/tuition reimbursement. For more information, please visit phoenix.gov/JOBSPECS/bene007.html.

PRESIDENTIAL MANAGEMENT FELLOWSHIP

ABOUT THE PROGRAM

Since 1977, the Presidential Management Fellows (PMF) Program and its predecessor, the Presidential Management Intern (PMI) Program, have been attracting outstanding graduate, law, and doctoral students to the federal service. The PMF Program is your passport to a unique and rewarding career experience with the federal government. It provides you with an opportunity to apply the knowledge you acquired from graduate study. As a PMF, your assignments may involve public policy and administration; domestic or international issues; information technology; human resources; engineering, health, and medical sciences; law; financial management; and many other fields in support of public service programs.

Eligibility Graduate students from all academic disciplines who expect to complete an advanced degree (master's, law, or doctoral-level degree) from a qualifying college or university during the current academic year are eligible to be nominated by their schools if they demonstrate the following: breadth and quality of accomplishments, capacity for leadership, and a commitment to excellence in the leadership and management of public policies and programs.

Application Period The PMF application will be available via a vacancy announcement on USAJOBS (www.usajobs.gov) and via a link on the "PMF Application" webpage. Specific dates for the application period will be announced in the vacancy announcement. (Applications are always accepted in the fall.) Eligible applicants are those students who will meet graduate degree requirements before the end of the academic year corresponding to that year's application period. For example, students meeting graduate degree requirements between September 1, 2008, and August 31, 2009, would apply in the fall of 2008 for acceptance to the PMF class of 2009.

Source: City of Phoenix Web site; OPM Web site.

The federal government has well-known initiatives such as the Presidential Management Fellowship (formerly the Presidential Management Internship program), Federal Career Intern Program (now the largest by far), Outstanding Scholar AmeriCorps, National Health Service Corps, and Reserve Officer Training Corps (ROTC), including high school junior ROTC. Cooperative education programs are endorsed by the federal government as well (called the Student Educational Employment Program). In such programs, agencies employ students while they are completing a degree program without going through a competitive process. Approximately half of all professional and administrative hires by the federal government now come through various internship programs (MSPB, 2008a). Federal law permits conversion of these positions to regular positions if the agency is so inclined, but this is currently being challenged. States and cities have set up similar undertakings. Ties between MPA programs and local or regional agencies enhance academic curricula and are appreciated by both students and agencies.

Internship and shadowing programs at the high school level are a long-term recruitment strategy. They can make strong impressions while providing a useful service component for the host agency. Fellowships, which can be extremely competitive, are generally aimed at top graduates from masters programs and mid- to senior-level professional candidates interested in new or broader professional experiences.

9. **Headhunting**, or external recruitment, occurs when the staffing function is farmed out to a third party that makes the initial contact or even provides the hiring contract. Ironically, it is used most for both the lowest and highest, but not the middle positions in government. Public agencies contract employment firms, especially in a tight labor market, for basic labor, clerical, and temporary positions (generally en masse). At the top end of the spectrum, private sector organizations have long relied on headhunting strategies to fill executive and senior management

positions. This strategy is less prevalent in government, which places a premium on open processes from beginning to end. Executive headhunting is on the upswing as an expanded practice in state governments; it has always been common for city and county management positions. Large public agencies may also have a specialized internal executive recruiter who will actively seek out high-quality candidates. The executive recruiter for the County of Riverside handles only searches for deputy director level and up. Departments are required to do job analyses that are more thorough, candidates get more "red carpet" treatment, and the pool normally is seeded with some applicants who have been personally recruited to apply by phone or email.

10. **Noncompetitive recruitment** means that a single official completes the process without a formal comparison of candidates (also called direct or one-day hiring). Therefore, recruitment may be "open" for certain jobs or types of applicants. Sometimes it means that immediate hiring is allowed if candidates meet certain standards; at other times the decision maker simply has the authority to select those people deemed appropriate. An illustration of the first instance is when local government recruiters are authorized to hire hard-to-fill categories on the spot, or when the federal government allows its campus recruiters to hire students immediately if they meet certain grade point standards (e.g., the Outstanding Scholar Program). An example of the second instance is the process of appointing confidential staff: elected and senior appointed officials can hire advisers, deputies, and personal assistants without either a formal merit or legislative consent process (known as Schedule B appointments at the federal level, which do not require a competitive examination). Of course, a noncompetitive process is easier and less costly than other methods. The practice is effective in a limited number of cases such as hard-to-fill positions where meeting a given standard is sufficient for hiring, or where political and personal loyalty is an appropriate factor. However, since it is open to abuse and violates merit principles, it is generally highly restricted and monitored.

Which strategies are best for which jobs? For management positions in police, fire, and paramilitary organizations with strong seniority policies, there is little reason to go much beyond physical and virtual posting. Organizational members wait for these opportunities, and internal recruitment is usually sufficient. The situation is quite different elsewhere, when competition for high-quality candidates can often be fierce. The question is not which but how many strategies to use, given financial and personnel resources. Following its strategic plan, the U.S. State Department uses both cutting-edge technology and interpersonal relations. By integrating traditional marketing, outreach techniques, and public relations with Web-based technology, its Diplomatic Readiness Initiative made the department's recruitment program a model (Pearson, 2004).

The strengths of public sector recruitment have been in notification strategies—job posting, electronic posting, newspapers, trade journals, and some mass communication methods. Traditional weaknesses have been the lack of expensive, proactive strategies—well-paid internship programs (with the notable exception of internships with the federal government), systematic personal contacts, mail recruitment, headhunting, and noncompetitive hiring. Future innovations are more likely to be in these latter strategies (see Exhibit 3.4). Current innovations cluster around increasing timeliness, in general, and flexibility where positions are hard to fill (see Exhibit 3.5). In 2004, for instance, OPM developed Recruitment One-Stop, an integrated, government-wide online recruitment system. A critical aspect in selecting recruitment strategies is determining whom they target and whether they encourage diversity in the organization; promoting diversity in recruitment is examined below.

Exhibit 3.4   Just How Aggressive Should Public Sector Organizations Become?

Government is often urged to act more like business. Should it adopt private sector strategies about recruitment? For example, should it abandon competitive hiring (comparing multiple candidates) for selected "hot" fields and substitute minimum standards coupled with on-the-spot hiring in order to make timely offers? Should it use signing bonuses, common in the private sector for difficult-to-hire positions? Although there was a time when this strategy was unheard of, it is now used by school districts desperate to fill positions and by agencies hiring for information technology positions. Should government follow the example of those corporations that target select institutions where the graduates are known to be superior, often tracking specific students during the latter part of their academic study? Should agencies actively hire specific high-performing employees away from other organizations, even though they have not applied for positions? Corporate raiding of employees is common practice, often with public sector employees being the target. Is it appropriate and ethical for public agencies to use such an approach? Finally, should the inducements for outstanding candidates be enhanced by special contracts promising advantageous opportunities? An example might include rotational fast-track assignments for junior applicants (this has always been done to some degree in the military with academy officers). Instances of these proactive strategies exist in the government, but they are all unusual. How common should they be? Just how aggressive should public organizations become?

Exhibit 3.5   Becoming More Aggressive to Increase Quality: Same-Day Hiring in Riverside County, California

Some of the most important innovations in recruitment have to do with hard-to-fill jobs and getting high-quality applicants to apply for positions that are slow to fill. The Human Resource Department in Riverside is an example of a department that uses One-Day Hiring Events every other month or so to overcome these barriers for hard-to-fill entry clerical and accounting positions, making more than 50 same-day offers annually. Although large numbers of applicants are in the pool at any given time, the highest-quality prospects have many opportunities and frequently are unwilling to tolerate a dilatory process. Therefore, many of the positions are filled by weaker candidates or remain open.

The county advertises its One-Day Hiring Event as an expedited process providing high-quality applicants with a minimum of three interviews. Prospects are initially screened by filling in an application and taking a proctored or unproctored knowledge and skill test. The top "band" is invited to the event where they are provided an orientation about the departments with which they can select to interview. At the event, each department may extend a contingent offer immediately or wait until later in the day. Time is set aside at the end of the day for those to whom offers are made to take a (confirming) proctored version of the knowledge and skill test if they previously took an unproctored test, an on-site background check, and have a time set up for their preemployment physical within a week. They can also tentatively schedule their first day of work. The county has found that the format brings out much higher candidates who are more motivated because they know that they will have multiple interviews immediately if they choose to attend the event. Departments fill their vacancies in a third the time it normally takes, and with better applicants.

Although the human resource recruitment team must carefully manage the recruitment, testing, departments, and follow-up, it is highly efficient because so many applicants can be handled in a concentrated time frame.

Source: Loi, 2008.

A major strength of recruiting for many not-for-profit organizations has been the passion that many people have for the "doing good" aspect that is intrinsic to much of the sector. These agencies often have a humanitarian basis over areas such as arts and culture; education; the environment; animals; health; human services; international affairs; public affairs; social benefits; religious-oriented and funded by religions; science and technology; and social sciences. Not-for-profits also cover advocacy groups such as professional associations and political interest groups. While the larger and better-funded nonprofits mirror the practices of most public sector organizations very closely, many of the tens of thousands of smaller ones find it difficult to do so because of funding and other resource constraints. Nonetheless, they often find that they are competing in the same pool for staff and must follow public sector rules because of the obligations required by their government contracts, or to maintain their tax status. These challenges are illustrated in Exhibit 3.6.

Promoting Diversity in Recruitment

Even though affirmative action has been deemphasized in recent years, a diverse workforce is both ethical and a management necessity. There are three factors to consider. First, does the agency provide an environment compatible for diversity through its promotion processes and organizational culture? A department that insists on standard working hours, does not provide childcare assistance, and subtly penalizes leaves of absence for family reasons does not create a suitable atmosphere for employee-parents. Such issues might be subtle but are critical if a diverse environment is to be created and to be optimally productive.

An illustration of providing a hospitable environment is the creation of spousal assistance programs. Spousal assistance may be offered to help reduce the trauma of relocating families. Such plans are more conventional in the private sphere (28%), especially in large corporations (52%), than in the public sector (Mercer, 1996). For dual-career couples, a transfer or relocation of one spouse is highly disruptive to the other's career plans. This has led to refusals to accept jobs, promotions, or transfers to avoid such disruptions. Research highlights the need for such assistance: More than one-third of formerly employed spouses lacked opportunities three months after relocating, one out of five dual-career spouses was assisted by the employee's firm, and eight out of ten desired such assistance in a future relocation (Rukeyser, 1996). Organizations that do not provide spousal assistance may find themselves accepting less-than-ideal candidates for positions because their preferred candidate declined to relocate.

Second, is there a conscious attempt to maintain a well-rounded workforce so that no group, including white males, has a legitimate complaint? Are resources made available to minority members in the organization? All things being equal, qualified women and minorities should be given priority if they are clearly underrepresented in proportion to the available, eligible workforce. Research indicates that minorities are highly sensitive to the presence of role models in the recruitment process and to the comparative level of resources available (Gilbert, 2000). Although the public sector has generally done better than business in this regard, there are many workplaces that are still negligent in promoting diversity. Examples include not hiring women in paramilitary agencies, lower employment of Hispanics in the federal workforce (GAO, 2006), and a low representation of African Americans in senior management positions across all levels of government (MSPB, 2008c).

Third, there should be awareness that where and how recruitment takes place will have an effect (Thaler-Carter, 2001). Sometimes procurement practices need to target locations where

Exhibit 3.6   Staffing Realities in a Not-for-Profit Organization: Getting the Right Person at the Right Time

BYLINE FROM AN MPA STUDENT

It goes without saying that one of the best ways to prevent high turnover is to hire the right person for the right job at the right time. There are several challenges that managers face in trying to achieve this balance, however. For example, recruitment of the "right" person may not be possible unless the position is available, there is funding for it, and, in some cases, legislative authority to hire for it. Large agencies have a greater pool in which to fish, either for employees to promote, employees seeking lateral transfers, or individuals wanting to join the agency. Public sector recruitment is constrained by specific regulations on when jobs can be posted and how long the posting must remain open; nonprofits may have the same constraints if they provide governmental services.

Getting the recruitment process "right" suggests that there is a strategy to be employed. This implies that the agency knows that a vacancy will occur, when it will happen, and that there will be sufficient time and money to recruit the ideal candidate. The reality is that many agencies do not become aware of a pending vacancy until the outgoing employee turns in her two-week notice of intent to leave. This leaves the manager scrambling to get the job advertised and interviews completed in a timely manner. It also leaves the position's supervisor hoping that at least one qualified, desirable potential employee will respond to the posting in time and, if interviewed early in the process, will be willing to wait until the position closes before being offered the job.

This was an issue, especially with the nursing staff, at the not-for-profit organization (NPO) where I worked from 1998 to 2006. The staff consisted of 13 nurses who provided case management for approximately 8,000 children in north Florida receiving public assistance or who had chronic health problems, four secretaries, and five administrative personnel. On rare occasions, a nurse's departure was expected, usually so she could accompany her husband to his new job in another town. More often than not, the supervisor would learn about an employee's intent to leave when she handed in her resignation.

The administrative assistant generally posted the job announcement within 24–48 hours of being told of the imminent departure. As a state-contracted service provider, the agency followed state human resources policies. Because of this, announcements had to remain open for at least one month from initial posting. Thus, the challenge was to find a replacement interested in working with pediatric case management, who had sufficient qualifications (a BS degree in nursing was required), could receive background and fingerprint clearance, and was interested in working with our client base. Strategic planning and headhunting were not viable options because we never knew when positions would become available.

There were similar issues with the secretaries, although it was considerably easier to replace them because of the difference in skill level required. Unfortunately, being an NPO meant salaries were not high. This, and the physical nature of the work (filing hundreds of client charts a day), limited the pool of individuals interested in working with us to young women in their early 20s. However, recent changes in the structure of the "secretarial pool" have radically decreased turnover. Originally four positions, the pool was cut to three with the fourth salary (and workload) shared between the remaining employees. This raised their salaries to a level where they could support themselves, which reduced turnover. Their increased workload actually raised morale because the remaining secretaries felt more valued and appreciated.

In a perfect world, all employees would have those same feelings of worth and value. Governmental managers would not only be able to recruit the right personnel, but also would actively headhunt for the best. Likewise, NPOs would have sufficient funds to pay competitive salaries and the right person would always be available at the right time and salary. Unfortunately, the reality is usually that managers have to "satisfice" and recruit the best they can with the resources available.

Source: Spice, 2008.

diverse candidates are more likely to congregate (perhaps particular schools or job fairs) and sources that such individuals are likely to read (such as ethnically oriented newspapers and newsletters).

Dividing Responsibilities

There is no hard-and-fast rule about who is responsible for what aspects of recruitment. As discussed in the Wye River Conference (see Exhibit 1.11 in Chapter 1), the central agency should enable individual units and managers to better perform the human resource function. In large government agencies, the responsibility has been divided among three entities: (1) the centralized human resource office, (2) full-time human resource experts in agencies and departments, and (3) local managers and supervisors. The centralized human resource office is often responsible for (a) overseeing diversity plans, (b) providing a comprehensive listing of recruitment sources, (c) supplying coordination of institutional recruitment (such as mass entry-level positions) and personal procurement (such as job fairs and college recruitment), and (d) furnishing a centralized recruitment source when departments elect not to handle recruitment on their own. These offices function as expert sources of assistance for departments. A second approach is that agencies have either full-time human resource experts or coordinators with personnel responsibilities. These specialists provide support to operational units and monitor hiring practices. Finally, organizations may conduct much of their recruitment directly, especially for midlevel and senior positions. This has the advantage of increased buy-in and involvement from departments in the entire process; it also may mean that there is an opportunity for inappropriate practices if hiring units do not take the responsibility seriously or plan for it properly. Increasingly, line managers are mandated to attend training before being allowed to participate in the hiring process in order to ensure that organizational and legal requirements are met.

∷ ENHANCING RECRUITMENT PROSPECTS: THE SEEKER'S PERSPECTIVE

The basics of job seeking may be widely known but are not necessarily commonly practiced.

- The first suggestion is to *know the recruitment process* and *know what resources are available.* Reading this chapter accomplishes the first aspect. Learning where recruitment occurs in a targeted profession includes consulting with practicing professionals who can identify the standard trade journals, knowing the newspapers that carry the appropriate advertisements, and exploring to find additional sources through the Internet and elsewhere. Developing personal contacts—networking—can make an enormous difference in discovering good prospects (Exhibit 3.7).
- Take the time to *envision the types of jobs, organizations, and career paths you might be interested in.* For those without public sector experience, this may mean a review of lesser-known agencies in order to expand horizons.
- Next, *carefully screen jobs before applying.* Although it may cost little to send out 100 résumés, it is discouraging to hear nothing from so many, which is likely to happen with a shotgun approach. If one does not already bring some appropriate expertise or some

| **Exhibit 3.7** | Recruitment for Job Seekers: Networking |

The mantra for any job seeker is networking, networking, networking. Professional acquaintances help job seekers by giving them advanced notice of upcoming openings and agency needs. They can also act as advocates for those they would like to see fill positions in their agency or department or serve as references who can vouch for the job experience, performance, and personal attributes of job seekers. It is well known that jobs may have been wired for others; these people often had a network of advocates working for them. Most professionals belong to several networks. On the national level, for example, you may belong to a national association in your specific line of work. Other networks are statewide or regional associations for more in-depth or frequent interaction with other professionals in your field. And still others are local groups of all types, formal and informal.

Networks are not built overnight. They are often the result of attending professional conferences for several years and building ties with similar professionals in other agencies. Such ties often are formed among those with similar professional interests, commitments, and values. Indeed, a basic, prerequisite skill for any professional is the ability to articulate these in a relatively concise and coherent fashion: People need to know what others stand for. How else do humans form enduring bonds?

It is unclear how large a professional network needs to be in order to be effective, but most professionals who feel part of a network would know about 30 to 60 people fairly well and probably know a couple hundred by face or name. How do people get to know so many people? First, most individuals know more people than they realize and even more people who could introduce them to others if only they were asked to do so. Second, a large network requires a commitment to go to venues such as conferences where people meet others. Attending a conference once may lead to knowing only a very few others, but attending for 4 years may lead to knowing half the attendees. Maintaining a professional network requires an investment of time to keep others informed of your professional self. Third, another great way to network is to volunteer. Often people at lower levels in the organizations know what they want to do, but their job or boss does not provide for that. Volunteering for a nonprofit is a great way to gain experience and meet people. Doing good, professional work outside the scope of employment might even get back to a current employer who then may consider the volunteer "management material" because of the extra commitment shown.

Having a strong network, and helping others in the network, brings numerous rewards. Networking is also helpful for other purposes such as to increase professional resources for doing one's job (getting advice, help with a problem). Through networking, job seekers also learn about employers: Are they really as good as they claim? Are others happy working there? Or is the department a snake pit, best to be avoided? People in a network often have information about these matters. Find out where people who have similar interests go. Join with them. It will be worth the cost.

special experience to a job, there is little likelihood of being a finalist. If necessary experience is lacking, there may be a need to either get more experience in an internship or take a lower-level position.

- *Make sure that all the information about the job is available.* Short newspaper and trade journal advertisements are generally reduced versions of the full announcements. Contact the appropriate source to see if there is additional information available.
- *Take the time to write a customized, flawless cover letter.* A letter that is simply "good" will not be noticed. A substantive one is highly focused, responding to the exact points covered in the job announcement. Although all the elements indicated in the announcement may be in the résumé, be sure that they are spelled out in the sequence requested in the cover letter. Failure to do so indicates a lack of seriousness.

- *Write a carefully crafted résumé.* Certainly, you must not make things up, but be sure the résumé has all the relevant experience and that the presentation is professional in content. Résumé writing is an art, and those making distinctions at the reviewing end quickly become master critics. Many "how-to" guides are available online and in bookstores. Generally, they discuss variations of two types of résumés (the chronological and the functional), as well as presentation styles. You should always have your résumé reviewed by an expert. Be sure to have an electronic copy that can be altered for specific jobs. Use the term curriculum vitae (Latin for "course of life") if the job has a research or academic component.
- *When selected as a finalist,* immediately do research on the organization via the Web and via information provided by the initial point of contact, friends, and any other sources (discussed in Chapter 4).

Advancing From Job Seeking to Career Development

Midcareer professionals (including most completing MPA degrees) are beyond such basics. They have had one or more positions and perhaps have been a part of the hiring process themselves. Those retooling their skills and looking at entry-level positions are seeking jobs whose career potential is exceptional. They understand that the competition for good management and technical jobs is generally quite intense. For example, in one study of public sector hiring practices, 85% of the hiring managers reported that they use the quality of the candidate's application itself to a great or moderate extent in selection (MSPB, 2003). For the ambitious midcareer professional, by necessity, job seeking needs to evolve into carefully planned career development.

- In addition to passively hunting for positions, the midcareer professional needs to *envision the ideal position.* Such a process requires the candidate to distinguish critical job characteristics from those that are unimportant. It also helps the career developer focus on the most appropriate prospects.
- At the same time, individuals need to *assess their strengths and weaknesses candidly.* Of course, the initial question is rating one's own technical competence and experience. Technical competence and experience are only part of what employers seek, however (Hicks, 1998). Frequently, the single most desired characteristic is communication skills (written, oral, listening, persuasiveness). Does the candidate have basic computer literacy skills such as competence in word processing, spreadsheet programs, Internet usage, and the standard programs utilized in the field? Also high on employers' lists are team skills, facility with interpersonal relations, and the ability to be creative and innovative. Those seriously developing their career today need to make sure that they have not only developed these skills, but also have examples to demonstrate competency.
- A rigorous self-assessment should lead one *to enhance the ability to demonstrate one's strengths.* One of the best ways is to develop a portfolio of materials, examples, and references. Copies of successful projects, job evaluations, photographs where visual representations are useful, and letters of reference are examples of the types of materials to be collected and shared as needed.
- The self-assessment should also lead a career developer to *improve weaknesses.* Deficiencies can be improved by self-study and reading, by training inside or outside

the organization, and by formal education. Strengthening weaknesses takes considerable self-discipline because it is easier to ignore or hide them; yet not addressing them damages both job prospects and performance. In a competitive market, lack of exceptional or unusual knowledge, skills, and abilities may be a weakness because basic qualifications are assumed. For instance, although police chiefs (and senior police commanders) in large municipal, county, and state law enforcement agencies may not technically be required to have master's degrees, management and executive training at the FBI and national command schools, and areas of extraordinary competence, the reality is that such jobs are inundated with exceptional candidates who do possess all these characteristics.

- Better jobs always include a substantial interview process in which the position is often won or lost. *There is no substitute for practice.* When practiced, difficult questions offer a chance to shine. When unpracticed, these questions are just tough and cause elimination.
- Finally, even before the actual recruitment process begins, those seeking better positions must *be realistic, practical, and disciplined.* Preparation for the position should begin long before the recruitment process. The procedure itself is generally a protracted effort, requiring a long-term devotion of personal resources, numerous attempts, and self-discipline in the face of challenges and disappointments.

▪▪ SUMMARY AND CONCLUSION

Finding talented workers for the public sector organization is a function involving five elements, of which the quality of the recruitment process per se is only one. Pay, labor pool size, organizational image, and job quality are also important. A first-class intake process can optimize or minimize these other factors substantially. Historically, recruitment has not been a strength in many organizations. Of the seven staffing steps, the first three constituting recruitment often have been the more passively administered, whereas those that constitute selection have been the more rigorously pursued. If competitive candidates are not in the pool, however, then the value of a neutral and precise selection process is limited.

What steps can be taken to ensure that appropriate applicants are attracted? First, quality recruitment is affected by planning. This involves asking and answering key questions, in advance of hiring, so that the recruitment and selection processes do not waste time and resources. Errors include not anticipating vacancies and labor shortages, not providing proper funding for recruitment, not mitigating negative factors, and not effectively identifying agency strengths. Competent planning involves asking pertinent questions about the position, such as whether (a) it is needed at all, (b) it should be hired from within, or (c) it should be restructured, as well as (d) who should be involved in the process and whether necessary forethought has been devoted to the authorization process. The announcement should always be written out fully. It is unwise to rush an advertisement to press before it is carefully crafted and endorsed. The final consideration is which recruitment methods to use in combination, with the goal of producing a customized applicant pool. Strategies include physical posting, electronic posting, newspapers, trade journals, custom mailings, other mass communication methods, personal contact, internship programs, headhunting, and noncompetitive recruiting. The variety of methods and the need for a diverse workforce place a major responsibility on the line manager, who is increasingly responsible for organizing and implementing the recruitment process.

Clearly, the recruitment of high-quality human capital is an area that is particularly susceptible to reform for those agencies serious about being "world-class organizations." Traditional passivity must give way to more-aggressive strategies in which quality candidates are actively sought. There must be an insistence that most recruitment pools include truly exceptional, rather than just acceptable, candidates. This implies that organizations must devote more resources and energy to recruitment, just as the armed forces did when converting from a draft to a volunteer system in the 1970s. The business example of senior managers going on annual recruiting trips is unusual in the public sector but should be practiced more frequently.[4] Finally, it is critical that unit supervisors and employees take seriously their increased responsibilities in decentralized recruiting systems, because they directly affect the quality of the future workforce.

KEY TERMS

Electronic posting

Fast-track positions

Headhunting

Human capital

Individual vs. "pool" or institutional recruitment

Inside (internal) vs. outside (external) recruitment

Internship recruitment

Job (position) announcements

Job posting

Labor market survey

Mail (and email) recruitment

Noncompetitive recruitment

Personal contact recruitment

Proceduralism

Recruitment process

Recruitment strategies

Sham recruitment

Staffing

Succession planning

EXERCISES

Class Exercises

1. In your area, identify some of the factors affecting recruitment, *excluding the recruitment process itself*. That is, discuss the labor pool, pay and benefits, images of public sector organizations, and perceptions of jobs in government as they affect local agencies' recruitment capacity.

2. How broadly should members of the hiring unit participate in the staffing process? Does the nature of the position (entry vs. midlevel, technical master's administrative) make a difference? When should a hiring unit vote on the best candidate (such as is common for state university faculty positions)?

3. What examples have class members witnessed, if any, of shoddy or inappropriate recruitment practices? How should those practices be modified or improved?

4. What internships are available in the state, county, and cities in your area? Which are paid? How does one apply? Are there any fellowship programs?

5. What is the typical size of the applicant pool for jobs in your organization (be it a public agency, university, or nonprofit organization)? Typically, how many applicants are minimally qualified? Well qualified? Are job searches ever canceled for lack of qualified applicants?

6. Divide the Web sites listed on page 94. Which ones are the most helpful in thinking about recruitment? Which provide the best links to other sites?

Team Exercises

7. To what extent would you emphasize future potential over current skills in each of the following jobs: office manager, police recruit, division director, and agency director (appointive but nominated by a committee)?

8. Find out from group members what recruitment strategies they have personally experienced, as well as their perceptions of those sources (e.g. posting vs. newspapers vs. the Internet).

9. According to your group members, what would agencies have to do to attract the most outstanding university students?

10. Identify and discuss some paradoxes from your own recruitment experience.

Individual Assignments

11. Rate each of the following factors, by percentage, in terms of importance in recruiting a social service case management supervisor. The unit is predominantly white females, characterized by lower pay, low morale, and high turnover.

    Knowledge, skills, and abilities ___%

    Motivation ___%

    Diversity ___%

    Loyalty ___%

12. In the previous example, if you believed that there was only one well-qualified internal candidate who happened to be the only white male in the unit, would you recruit internally or externally? What would your goal be? How would you use recruitment to achieve that goal? How would you publicize that goal to the hiring unit?

13. Clip or print some job advertisements for public sector jobs from several sources, including the local paper. What are the variations in format and style that you notice? How might the advertisements be improved?

NOTES

1. See the discussion on rank-in-job versus rank-in-person systems in Chapter 5. Rank-in-job positions have been the most common and emphasize technical skills. Rank-in-person systems (such as the military) emphasize employee development potential.

2. In true patronage positions, elected officials can select whomever they please without review. These often include staff positions. Appointive positions such as department heads and their chief

deputies arguably are not true patronage positions because they are reviewed by the appropriate legislative body for confirmation. Of course, recruitment in elective positions is generally through the democratic process of primaries.

3. Employment statistics indicate that government has generally been a leader in hiring a diverse workforce. Meeting the requirements and documenting compliance with equal opportunity, affirmative action, age discrimination, and disability accommodation, however, has added to proceduralism.

4. Some examples do exist, of course. For years, GAO has assigned senior executives to do annual campus visits (Walker, 2007).

REFERENCES

Armstrong-Stassen, M., & Templer, A. J. (2006). The response of Canadian public and private sector human resource professionals to the challenge of the aging workforce. *Public Personnel Management, 35*(3), 247–260.

Bailes, A. L. (2002, Spring). Who says it can't be done? Recruiting the next generation of public servants. *Business of Government,* pp. 51–55. www.businessofgovernment.org/pdfs/EBG_Spring02.pdf

Breaugh, J. A., & Starke, M. (2000). Research on employee recruitment: So many studies, so many remaining questions. *Journal of Management, 26*(3), 405–435.

Bureau of Labor Statistics, U.S. Department of Labor. (2008). *Occupational outlook handbook, 2008–09 edition.* http://www.bls.gov/OCO/

Cober, R. T., Brown, D. J., Keeping, L. M., & Levy, P. E. (2004). Recruitment on the Net: How do organizational Website characteristics influence applicant attraction? *Journal of Management, 30*(5), 623–646.

Crumpacker, M., & Crumpacker, J. (2007). Succession planning and generational stereotypes: Should HR consider age-based values and attitudes a relevant factor or a passing fad? *Public Personnel Management, 36*(4), 349–369.

Davidson, G., Lepeak, S., & Newman, E. (2007). *Recruiting and staffing in the public sector: Results from the IPMA-HR research series.* Alexandria, VA: International Public Management Association for Human Resources. www.ipma-hr.org

Dychtwald, K., & Baxter, D. (2007). Capitalizing on the new mature workforce. *Public Personnel Management, 36*(4), 325–334.

Gatehouse, R. D., Gowan, M. A., & Lautenschlager, G. J. (1993). Corporate image, recruitment image, and initial job choice decisions. *Academy of Management Journal, 36*(2), 414–428.

Gilbert, J. A. (2000). An empirical examination of resources in a diverse environment. *Public Personnel Management, 29*(2), 175–184.

Hamman, J. A., & Desai, U. (1995). Current issues and challenges in recruitment and selection. In S. Hays & R. Kearney (Eds.), *Public personnel administration: Problems and prospects* (3rd ed., pp. 89–104). Englewood Cliffs, NJ: Prentice Hall.

Hicks, L. (1998, September 27). Central Iowa labor crisis looms. *Des Moines Sunday Register,* pp. 1G–2G.

Kauffman, T. (2003, June 16). OPM expands hiring, early retirement authorities. *Federal Times.*

Kauffman, T. (2004, July 2). Job seekers favor government, OPM surveys find. *Federal Times.*

Kauffman, T., & Robb, K. (2003, July 14). Online recruitment: New system promises more choice, faster hires. *Federal Times.*

Lavelle, J. (2007). On workforce architecture, employment relationships and lifecycles: Expanding the purview of workforce planning and management. *Public Personnel Management, 36*(4), 371–385.

Lavigna, R. J. (2002). Best practices in public-sector human resources: Wisconsin state government. *Human Resource Management, 41*(3), 369–384.

Lewis, G. B., & Frank, S. A. (2002). Who wants to work for government? *Public Administration Review, 62*(4), 395–404.

Loi, J. (2008). Human Resources Services Manager, County of Riverside. Personal communication.

Mercer, W. M. (1996). *Mercer work/life and diversity initiatives.* Retrieved January 15, 2004, from www.dcclifecare.com/mercer/mercer-c.html

Mintzberg, H. (1994, January/February). The fall and rise of strategic planning. *Harvard Business Review,* pp. 107–114.

Nickson, D., Warhurst, C., Dutton, E., & Hurrell, S. (2008). A job to believe in: Recruitment in the Scottish voluntary sector. *Human Resource Management Journal, 18*(1), 20–35.

Partnership for Public Service. (2007). *The best places to work in the federal government.* http://bestplacestowork.org/BPTW/about/

Pearson, R. (2004, July 12). Technology helps state recruit the best. *Federal Times,* p. 21.

Redman, T., & Mathews, B. P. (1997). What do recruiters want in a public sector manager? *Public Personnel Management, 26*(2), 245–256.

Rukeyser, W. (1996, January 18). *Relocation brings anxiety to two-career families.* Retrieved January 15, 2004, from www.cnnfn.com/mymoney/9601/18/relocation/index.html

Rynes, S. L. (1993). When recruitment fails to attract: Individual expectations meet organizational realities in recruitment. In H. Schuler, J. L. Farr, & M. Smith (Eds.), *Personnel selection and assessment: Individual and organizational perspectives* (pp. 27–40). Hillsdale, NJ: Lawrence Erlbaum.

Smith, M. (2000, March). Innovative personnel recruitment/changing workforce demographics. *IPMA News,* pp. 12–14.

Spice. Susan. (2008) MPA student at University of South Florida. Personal communication.

Thaler-Carter, R. E. (2001, June). Diversify your recruitment advertising. *HRMagazine,* pp. 92–100.

Trice, E. (1999, June). Timely hiring: Making your agency a best practice. *IPMA News,* pp. 10–11.

U.S. Government Accountability Office (GAO). (2003). *Human capital: Opportunities to improve executive agencies' hiring processes.* Washington, DC: Author.

U.S. Government Accountability Office (GAO). (2006). *The federal workforce: Additional insights could enhance agency efforts related to Hispanic representation.* Washington, DC: Author.

U.S. Government Accountability Office (GAO). (2008a). *Federal workforce challenges in the 21st century.* Washington, DC: Author.

U.S. Government Accountability Office (GAO). (2008b). *Older workers: Federal agencies face challenges, but have opportunities to hire and retain experienced employees.* Washington, DC: Author.

U.S. Merit Systems Protection Board (MSPB). (2000). *Competing for federal jobs: Job search experiences of new hires.* Washington, DC: Author.

U.S. Merit Systems Protection Board (MSPB). (2001). *Attracting quality graduates to the federal government: A view of college recruiting.* Washington, DC: Author.

U.S. Merit Systems Protection Board (MSPB). (2003). *Help wanted: A review of federal vacancy announcements.* Washington, DC: Author.

U.S. Merit Systems Protection Board (MSPB). (2006). *Reforming federal hiring: Beyond faster and cheaper.* Washington, DC: Author.

U.S. Merit Systems Protection Board (MSPB). (2008a). *Attracting the next generation: A look at federal entry-level new hires.* Washington, DC: Author.

U.S. Merit Systems Protection Board (MSPB). (2008b). *In search of highly skilled workers: A study of the hiring of upper level employees from outside the federal government.* Washington, DC: Author.

U.S. Merit Systems Protection Board (MSPB). (2008c). *Workforce diversity governmentwide and at the Department of Homeland Security.* Washington, DC: Author.

U.S. Office of Personnel Management (OPM). (2006). *Career patterns: A 21st century approach to attracting talent* (A guide for agencies). Washington, DC: Author.

Walker, D. M. (2007). GAO and human capital reform: Leading by example. *Public Personnel Management, 36*(4), 317–323.

Zeidner, R. (2001, October 1). Do-it-yourself hiring process. *Federal Times.*

Chapter 4

Selection

From Civil Service Commissions to Decentralized Decision Making

First-rate people hire first-rate people; second-rate people hire third-rate people.

—Leo Rosten

After studying this chapter, you should be able to

- recognize and seek to resolve paradoxical dimensions in the selection process,
- articulate the different philosophical bases of selection,
- understand the history of civil service commissions and how they continue to affect thinking in employee selection despite their reduced roles,
- distinguish historical eras and the current trends in selection,
- discuss the "ideal" stages of the selection process,
- choose appropriate examination methods ("tests") for different selection stages and job search needs,
- understand the different types of validity related to selection processes,
- avoid illegal questions in the interview and reference check process, and
- determine who will make hiring decisions and how they will be made and documented.

Selection technically starts when applications have been received. Which of the applicants will be chosen, by what process, and by whom? Certainly the public sector is far stronger for having outgrown the excesses of 19th century patronage, which permeated jobs at all levels of government and resulted in widespread corruption and graft such as vote racketeering and kickbacks (Mosher, 1982). During the 20th century, merit principles replaced patronage as the most common—but by no means the sole—selection criterion. Today, patronage excesses are relatively rare—far less common than in the private sector—and they constitute little problem for the bulk of positions in government (a position that has been strengthened in Supreme Court cases such as *Branti v. Finkel,* 1980; *Elrod v. Burns,* 1976; and *Rutan v. Republican Party of Illinois,* 1990).[1] Even when mayors, governors, and presidents have strong appointive power and loyalty may initially be a legitimate factor in selection, excessive patronage considerations can get them in trouble as it did for President Bill Clinton when he replaced long-time White House travel specialists with Arkansas friends (a scandal known as "Travelgate"), and President George W. Bush when he appointed Michael Brown director of FEMA because of his close connections to his former campaign director, even though Brown lacked any knowledge of emergency management whatsoever.

One challenge in selection is that political appointment—a form of patronage—is the primary selection method for most senior government positions. Appointees are often selected as much based on party and personal affiliations as on technical merit. The U.S. president selects not only all the agency and department heads, but also thousands of second- and third-layer executives as well, including up to 10% of the senior executive service. Governors generally have hundreds of appointive positions in their control. "Strong" mayors and county boards of supervisors also have extensive appointive responsibilities that lend themselves to patronage. Nor is it unheard of for high appointees and elected officials to provide "character references," wherein career supervisors are "encouraged" to hire campaign workers and friends for low-level positions. This paradox—merit systems run by dilettantes—often contributes to cynicism by career employees who view political appointees as transitory, poorly trained, and inexperienced. Without that occasional fresh administrative leadership, however, the public service might become unresponsive, rigid, and self-serving, just as the private sector increasingly turns to "outside" CEOs in times of industry transition or organizational decline.

Another irony is that although public sector selection is primarily an open application of merit principles, selection for many positions is determined largely by **internally based hiring.** Such hiring is said to boost internal morale, increase loyalty, reduce training time, and provide recruiting incentives for strong candidates. Nonetheless, such practice reduces full competition and the introduction of outside skills and insights (Grensing-Pophal, 2006). For example, agency policy or union contracts often require a strict ordering in selection rights that results in most of the better jobs being labeled "promotional" and therefore not available to "outside" candidates. Many entry-level and nearly all midlevel vacancies are filled internally. For example, the U.S. Merit Systems Protection Board (MSPB) reported that supervisors filled vacancies with current agency personnel 46% of the time, and with other federal employees 25% of the time. Only 29% of the time did they select from outside the government (MSPB, 2001a). This trend is more severe at the senior levels at which only 15% are externally hired (MSPB, 2008b).

Yet another paradox, or tension, is promoting merit principles with robust testing, and introducing more flexibility in testing, sometimes at the expense of thoroughness (Ingraham, Selden, & Moynihan, 2000). Increased rigor can mean better assessment and higher-quality selection; however, it can also mean more time, expense, and applicant aggravation, leading to reduced applicant levels and the loss of some of the best applicants to faster moving competing organizations. Even as the federal government becomes increasingly interested in a competency-based hiring or promotional model, it is more willing to expand the hiring discretion of agencies and their managers. Such discretion can also mean that they may abuse it out of haste or ignorance (MSPB, 2006). State governments are increasing flexibility in many cases, too, which opens them up to reducing the rigor of merit (full competition) and even the prospect of illegal practices due to reduced oversight of fragmented systems (Condrey & Maranto, 2001).

Although the selection process has always been a significant role for managers and supervisors, that role has taken on far greater responsibility with the dramatic downsizing of human resource departments throughout government. For example, the U.S. Office of Personnel Management (OPM) was downsized by more than 50% as it was being reinvented in the 1990s (MSPB, 2001b). Therefore, today it is important to recognize that human resource management skills are critical generalist competencies for *all* managers. The challenge for managers is that the scope and depth of responsibilities has grown in the last generation, making the prospect of a "quick and dirty" hiring process more likely.

Other important tensions were alluded to in the last chapter about whom to recruit; those tensions now resurface in this chapter about how candidates are selected and who it emphasizes. Should the selection process emphasize the potential of newly graduated students or the ability of older candidates? How do you encourage diversity in selection while balancing merit principles? In selection, everyone puts his best foot forward, but average performance on the job may be more important. For example, a talented, brilliant, and charming individual may be highly distractible, lazy, or emotionally temperamental. How does the selection process capture and evaluate the difference between typical and maximal performance?

It is interesting to note that international trends in recruitment and selection are similar, and seem to be converging. All emphasize person-job fit and person-unit fit and use remarkably similar methods discussed here. As one might expect, Australia, Europe, New Zealand, and the United States show the most in common emphasizing results, decentralization, and past performance in employees. Some Asian countries (e.g., Japan and Taiwan) emphasize potential more than past performance. Many Latin American countries still emphasize family and personal connections (Anderson & Witvliet, 2008; Werbel, Song, & Yan, 2008; Wolf & Jenkins, 2006).

This chapter begins with a broad discussion of the criteria used in a selection process and how different principles have taken precedence in civil service positions in various historical eras. The majority of the chapter focuses on prominent technical aspects of selection related to application review, testing, interviewing, reference checks, the hiring decision, and posthiring issues. It concludes by reaffirming that this important human resource function is as easy to understand as it is difficult to carry out. Predicting human behavior, a goal in the selection process, is no easy task, as illustrated by the fact that former professional basketball superstar Michael Jordan was cut from his high school basketball team because he lacked potential.

▪▪ THE BASES AND ORIGIN OF SELECTION

Selection Criteria

Selection is arguably the most momentous, politically sensitive aspect of human resource activities (Ployhart, 2006). Indeed, historical eras of human resource management are largely defined by the underlying philosophy of selection. There are essentially six possible criteria that can be used, separately or in combination, to provide the basis for the decision: (1) **electoral popularity**, (2) **social class selection**, (3) **patronage**, (4) **merit selection**, (5) **seniority**, and (6) **representativeness**. All except for social class are explicitly used in various arenas of the public sector. Although the terms *civil service* and *merit* are often used as synonyms, in common practice *civil service* is a broader term because it embraces elements of seniority and representativeness, as well as merit.

1. Electoral Popularity

Electoral popularity is the basis of representative democracy. Citizens vote for those who they think will do or are doing a good job. What types of positions are reserved for the electoral popularity model? First and foremost, they are policy-making jobs that craft laws and the broad administrative missions of national, state, and local governments. Such officials occupy the legislative bodies at all levels of government—Congress, state legislatures, county boards of supervisors, city councils, and boards of townships, school districts, and other special units. To a substantially lesser degree, but still common, is the election of judicial personnel: examples are judges, state attorneys general, county attorneys, and local justices of the peace.

Of course, elected executives such as presidents, governors, and mayors are significant and visible in the American democratic system. Although they share a policy role with legislators, they also have a critical administrative role in managing the agencies and departments of government. It should be noted, however, that some elected officials were intended to be primarily administrative and are so to this day (e.g., state-level secretaries of state, education, and treasury; and county-level sheriffs, treasurers, clerks of court, auditors, and recorders). For instance, in small jurisdictions the full-time elected official may come to the counter to assist in busy periods. Of course, the bulk of all elected officials serve on school boards and town councils with little or no pay. The strength of the electoral selection philosophy is its support of democratic theory through popular involvement as well as popular accountability. The limits of this strategy are also clear: Voters have natural limitations of knowledge, time, and interest. As the number of those who run for election increases and as the issues involved become more technical and complex, the attention of citizens becomes diluted and turnout declines. The highly fragmented structure of most county governments is a prime example of the accountability problem.

2. Social Class

Social class selection, the antithesis of democratic selection, is generally illegal as an explicit selection philosophy in the United States. In many societies, however, the administrative classes were "bred" so that they would have the requisite education to fulfill administrative functions. This remains evident in many European democracies and is one of the distinctive features of some rank-based systems (discussed in Chapter 5). In the United States during the Federalist period, education was more limited, and a strong upper and upper-middle class bias existed in administrative roles. In contemporary advanced democracies, with their high literacy rates and widespread access to universities, this philosophical base has limited virtue, although minorities and women often argue that the dominant culture still subtly guides the selection process itself. For example, prestigious educational institutions sometimes become proxies for social class, with classic cases being the U.S. State Department's historical preference for select eastern universities at the federal level, and state governments giving preference to their flagship university at that level.

3. Patronage

Patronage applies to a broad class of selection decisions in which a single person is responsible for designating officials or employees without a requirement for a formalized application process. Such appointments may or may not be subject to a confirmation process. As a process, it tends to have a negative connotation because it assumes that loyalty will be to the patron or person making the selection rather than to the government at large. This is not always true, however, and it sometimes is not a negative feature. Supreme Court justices are often picked because of their political leanings and personal connections to presidents, yet they sometimes become remarkably independent. A different case is the political adviser who is hired on the public payroll by a political executive for personal loyalty and party-based affinity and whose ideological bias is expected. Ultimately, those using such appointments employ three criteria: (1) political loyalty, (2) personal acquaintance, and (3) technical competence or merit. In the ideal case for a political executive, the pool of possible candidates can be narrowed to those who are of the same party or who have the same political preferences. The executive can identify people she has known or worked with in the past and then select people who are still highly experienced in the targeted area and competent for the duties to be assigned.

Problems occur when the first two principles are met, but the third is not. For instance, well-connected policy generalists are sometimes installed as directors of large agencies when they lack either the in-depth policy background or the administrative experience to cope with their new responsibilities (e.g., a former Playboy bunny, with no relevant expertise, was appointed to run a large agency in a southern state in the late 1990s). To reduce the political and personal nature of many executive appointments at the city and county levels, professional manager systems have been installed so that competence rather than patronage becomes the primary factor for department heads.

4. Merit

Merit-based systems emphasize technical qualifications using processes that analyze job competencies and require open application procedures.[2] These systems require "tests," but they may consist of an education and experience review, performance evaluations, or licensure, as well as written tests. Merit selection is the primary philosophy for civil service systems that dominate nonexecutive employment. The strengths of merit selection are its fairness to candidates, its availability to scrutiny, and its assurance of minimum competencies and qualifications. It also fits well with notions of democratic access and accountability.

Merit, however, does not always live up to its promise. Selection is often so mechanical and technical that the best candidates never apply, diversity of experience is inhibited, there is an excessive emphasis on tangible skills over future potential, and the time required to process an enormous pool of candidates becomes onerous. As the discussion here will highlight, the pursuit of precise and valid indicators of merit is challenging when considering what tests to use and how much weight to give to them. This has led to a decrease in some jurisdictions in the number of "true" merit positions in which a formal competitive process is required. For example, the state of Maryland moved 1,400 management positions from merit to "noncompetitive" and changed their termination rights from "just cause" to "for any reason" (see Exhibit 4.1). Likewise, the entire state middle management corps in Florida was also converted in 2001.

Exhibit 4.1   Personnel Reform in Maryland

In 1996, the Maryland General Assembly passed legislation that resulted in a restructuring of the State Government Management System. Prior to that time, the majority of positions were covered by the classified service merit system. The law diminished the number of those covered by the classified service and established four services for employees, as follows:

(1) *Skilled service.* Positions are competitively selected, and termination must be for just cause. There are approximately 37,000 positions in the skilled service at this time, most of which were previously in the classified service.

(2) *Professional service.* Positions are selected competitively, and termination must be for just cause. These require a professional license or an advanced degree. There are some 4,500 positions in the professional service, most of which were previously in the classified service.

(3) *Management service.* Positions are selected noncompetitively, and termination may be for any reason not prohibited by law. They must have direct responsibility for management of a program, including responsibility for personnel and financial resources. There are roughly 1,900 positions in the management service, most of which were previously in the classified service.

(4) *Executive service.* Positions are selected noncompetitively, and employees may be terminated for any reason not prohibited by law. These positions include cabinet secretaries, deputy cabinet secretaries, assistant secretaries, and other officials of equivalent rank. There are approximately 190 executive service employees. These positions worked under similar nonmerit rules prior to reform.

A fifth category is strictly patronage based.

(5) *Special appointments.* Positions are noncompetitively selected, and termination may be for any reason not prohibited by law. These include jobs that have a direct reporting relationship to an employee in the executive service or that have substantial responsibility for developing and recommending high-level agency policies. The majority of these 4,700 positions were in the unclassified service in which they did not have merit protection.

The impact of the new personnel reform changes, especially in relationship to the management service, has yet to be determined because there has not been a change in political parties or the state's fiscal condition since the legislation was passed.

Source: Martin Smith, Personnel Services Administration, Maryland Department of Health and Mental Hygiene (personal communication, 2006).

5. Seniority

Seniority is also a crucial selection principle in civil service systems. Philosophically, it asserts that those already employed in the agency (a) have already been through the merit process once,

(b) have been screened in probationary periods and evaluation processes, and (c) have superior organizational insight and loyalty because of their history of employment. Systems that emphasize seniority either limit many job searches to internal candidates or give internal candidates substantial advantages in the process, such as points for years of service or opportunities to fill positions prior to advertisement outside the agency. The effects are that civil service employment occurs primarily in selected entry positions and that external hiring is unusual at the supervisory level and above. This is particularly noticeable in highly unionized environments and in paramilitary occupations such as those concerned with public safety. Very few organizations follow strict **seniority-based selection** (following the exact date of hiring) in promoton, but strict seniority often prevails in the case of layoffs and the accompanying "bumping rights" that are sometimes authorized.

Seniority systems ensure that organizations provide a sense of loyalty to their staff as well as career development paths; however, such systems also tend to lock employees into a single governmental system (often just their own division and unit) for career growth. Organizationally, seniority systems can lead to "inbreeding" and "groupthink," and they can prevent fresh management insights, which are a prime motivation for lateral hiring. Even more insidious is that strong seniority systems can provide a milieu in which the "Peter principle" operates.[3]

6. Representativeness

The final principle of selection is representativeness. This principle can be interpreted in numerous ways such as by geography, social class, gender, racial or ethnic groups, prior military service, and disability. The Constitution supports geography in electoral issues through its federal system. President Andrew Jackson and his supporters believed too many federal jobs went to easterners and the social elite, and they therefore emphasized appointments to those from western states (of that day) and from less-privileged classes. A contemporary debate is selection (or more generally nonselection) based on sexual orientation. Because veterans are taken out of the labor force and might have a liability in seeking employment upon leaving the military, they receive a preference in civil service systems. **Veterans' points** are used by the federal government (such as in the Veterans' Preference Act of 1944 and the Veterans' Employment Opportunity Act of 1998) and are also used in many states. Typically, veterans serving during wars are eligible for extra points in ratings systems, and wounded veterans may be eligible for additional points.

In the past half century, there has been an emphasis on gender and racial representativeness, as evidenced by military integration (both African Americans and women), equal opportunity legislation, affirmative action plans, and, more recently, diversity programs. Generally speaking, affirmative action tries to encourage women and minorities to seek positions for which they are qualified, especially where the targeted rate of employment is low. Ceteris paribus—all things being equal—the targeted groups should be offered positions in areas of underrepresentation.

That is to say, affirmative action generally has upheld merit as the premier value but has given representativeness a strong second-place consideration when merit principles are followed. In terms of implementation, affirmative action programs also require extensive analysis of **disparate impact** on women and minorities so that applicant pools can be restructured where underrepresentation appears to be a problem. Although numerically based goal systems are rarely allowed (except in extreme cases as short-term fixes), chronic underrepresentation of some groups remains an important and legitimate consideration; this is especially true in many formerly male- and white-dominated organizations where occupational segregation has merely given way to tokenism. Representativeness remains a legally appropriate consideration on a case-by-case basis as long as there is equivalent merit and documented imbalance. In more recent diversity programs, numerical representativeness has been replaced by an emphasis on a supportive environment that welcomes employment of different groups and embraces their heterogeneity.

The History of Selection: Six Eras

Selection philosophies—except for elected positions—have varied over time (Mosher, 1982; Van Riper, 1958); note that the later timeframes overlap.

Administration by Gentility: 1789–1829

From President Washington until President Jackson, patronage (appointment based on connections and political views) was the primary system for selection. It was muted, however, by the ethic of "fitness of character" and genteel education (social class). President Washington was a strong force in shaping a tradition that balanced competence and political neutrality. Although he avoided appointing those openly hostile to his political views, he was careful in selecting candidates from among all the states and from a range of political perspectives. He generally gave preference to those of education—hence those of a higher social class— although he only appointed those known for integrity and public spirit. He also did sometimes give preference to Revolutionary War military officers. With the evolution of political parties, Jefferson was faced with replacing enough Federalists to ensure responsiveness to his Democratic Republican Party. During the presidencies of James Madison, James Monroe, and John Quincy Adams, the ethic of fitness of character and political neutrality generally held sway but increasingly came under pressure as the party ruling Congress urged for more political determination of administrative posts at all levels of government.

Selection by Spoils: 1829–1883

President Jackson insisted on better representation of all social classes and of those from the west, and thought that rotation of government positions was healthy. He advocated keeping government jobs as simple as possible so that those with modest education could be eligible. He argued that greater political responsiveness would reduce corruption and complacency. Although he replaced only 20% of the federal workforce (a proportion not substantially greater than that replaced by Jefferson) and was himself not really an advocate of a **spoils system** (appointment of jobs as spoils of victory to those active in the victorious campaign, despite lack of qualifications), he did create the philosophical basis for widespread abuses in the following decades (Van Riper, 1958, p. 42).

Several problems with a solely patronage-based civil service became increasingly clear over the next 50 years, starting in 1829. First, appointments were often assigned with little regard for experience, knowledge, or abilities. Second, inequities in pay were frequent:

compensation was as much a function of connection to a political patron as to specific job responsibilities. Third, it became common to require government workers to campaign for the reelection of politicians in office and to relinquish a portion of their pay to the party in power. Furthermore, spoils appointments often included jobs for those who did not work full time (or at all), despite receiving a paycheck.

Rampant corruption spawned a public-driven government reform movement after the Civil War that lasted nearly 50 years. One of the early, if brief, successes was during the administration of President Ulysses S. Grant: he signed a bill authorizing competitive examinations for some federal positions. It lapsed only two years later for lack of funding because of congressional fears of curbs on patronage opportunities. Many cities that had rampant political patronage and corruption saw the development of civil service reform associations at the municipal level. The pressure continued to build as governmental incompetence and abuse became more blatant and government responsibilities expanded.

Technical Merit Systems: 1883–1912

The **Pendleton Act** of 1883 signaled a new era in personnel management, although it was more than 50 years before the system evolved into one that was comprehensive in the federal government, widely adopted across other levels of government, and generally rigorously applied. Although the act was prompted by the assassination of President James Garfield by a disappointed job seeker in 1881, it responded to the growing perception that the functions of government had become too large, complex, and important to be handled entirely by a patronage system. The new system incorporated the following:

- Open, competitive examinations based on technical qualifications
- Lists of those eligible or "certified" to the hiring authority
- Rules against politicians intervening in civil service selection, coercing civil servants to work in political campaigns, or requiring employees to provide kickbacks for civil government employment
- An independent **Civil Service Commission**, which administered practical competitive examinations (essentially a central job register) and acted as a judicial review board for abuses

This new model required bipartisan and independent selection of employees by a commission for covered (or civil service) positions—that is, for those over which the commission had jurisdiction. Initially, only 10% of federal employees were covered (Van Riper, 1958). The proportion gradually increased to around 48% in 1900. By mid-century and continuing today, more than 90% were included in civil service positions, broadly construed.

As Merit Principles Expands, So Do Employee Rights and Seniority: 1912–1978

Although a few city and state governments were quick to replicate the new reform model, the increase in civil service systems was slow. To facilitate acceptance of civil service models, the federal government conditioned some financial assistance to other levels of government on the use of merit-based employment systems. Especially in this regard effective was the Social Security Act of 1935. Other programs continued this requirement, which led to the institution of at least partial or modified civil service systems in all the states, most municipalities, and many counties. The depoliticization of the personnel process was further enhanced by the Hatch Act of 1939 (amended and relaxed in 1993), strongly prohibiting most political activity by federal workers. Subsequently, "little" Hatch Acts, modeled on the federal legislation, were enacted by most states (Bowman & West, 2009).

As civil service systems grew in number and size, so too did employee rights. Although the Pendleton Act prohibited political removals at the federal level, it was frequently circumvented. Through an executive order, President William McKinley prohibited removal from the competitive service except for just cause and for reasons given in writing. Furthermore, the person being discharged had to have the basic due process right to respond in writing. This important principle and process was placed into permanent legislation in the Lloyd-LaFollette Act of 1912.

Once in the system and protected from political and arbitrary firing, employee seniority was substantially enhanced. As the legal footing of the seniority principle grew, those outside the service would have access to fewer jobs, and those inside the service would have greater access to promotional selections. With the growth of public sector unions, starting in the 1950s, some areas such as public safety frequently eliminated lateral selection from outside the agency.

Expansion of Access: 1964–1990

The era of equal opportunity, which began in the early 1960s, did not replace merit but modified its execution and made hiring more complicated (Chapter 2). The Civil Rights Act of 1964 addressed discrimination based on race, color, religion, gender, or national origin. The Equal Employment Opportunity Act of 1972 expanded these rights to state and local governments and promoted equal employment opportunity through affirmative action. Other major applicant and employee rights that were enhanced during this period were age (Age Discrimination in Employment Act of 1967, and amended in 1974) and disability (Rehabilitation Act of 1973) discrimination for federal employees. At the federal level, the 1978 Civil Service Reform Act (CSRA) established the **80% rule** to provide selection "floors" for protected classes. That is, selection processes should not result in qualification rates of protected groups that are less than 80% of the highest group.

The burst of attention to representativeness in the 1960s and 1970s, symbolized by widespread use of affirmative action programs to correct imbalances, certainly continued into the 1980s as an organizational way of life. Perhaps the final great push for representation was the Americans with Disabilities Act of 1990 in which reasonable accommodations were required in the selection process for those with allowable disabilities.

The tide turned in the 1990s when bellwether legal cases generally required more-tailored and narrowly defined remedies for representational problems. For example, race norming was disallowed by the Civil Rights Act of 1991 (see Chapter 2). Quotas have always been illegal except when court ordered in response to egregious cases. Although equal opportunity continued to be strongly encouraged, it was increasingly through diversity programs rather than through affirmative action.

Contemporary Selection Trends: 1978–Present

The potential excesses of the civil service system started to emerge as early as the 1930s when the administration of President Franklin Delano Roosevelt toyed with the idea of major civil service reform. Complaints about the civil service system included the following:

- rigidity (e.g., restricting interviews and selection to three top candidates based on technical qualifications)
- proceduralism, or "red tape" (e.g., difficulties in hiring rapidly in an applicant's market)
- isolation from the executive branch (e.g., independent centralized testing agencies apart from the hiring agencies)
- inadequate accountability (e.g., difficulties in severing employees who perform poorly)

Contemporary trends have emphasized flexibility, speed, integration of the selection function with other management responsibilities, and increased employee accountability for productivity. At the federal level, the CSRA of 1978 reintegrated selection functions into the executive branch through the OPM. It also provided for more managerial latitude. Initially, personnel responsibilities were tightly held by OPM, but the reinventing government initiative begun in 1992 probably had a greater effect on OPM than on any other agency. By 1996, OPM was required to decentralize most of its responsibilities to other agencies (called "delegated examination authority"). Civil service commissions today (e.g., the MSPB) often function as policy and review boards, although in some jurisdictions even these responsibilities have passed to the agencies.

In an important trend, a growing number of agencies or bureaus in agencies were able to opt out of the traditional ("competitive") civil service system. This parallel system (the "excepted service" or noncompetitive service) is still required to follow the broad traditions of merit: notification of open positions, reliance on technical merit through minimum established standards, and due process for employees. It allows, however, far more management flexibility and control over selection and employee appraisal. The largest example of an entirely excepted service agency is the U.S. Department of Homeland Security. Approximately one-half of all federal new hires are made through excepted service provisions (MSPB, 2008a). The U.S. Department of Defense began to follow suit in 2006, but has reduced the scope somewhat due to court and congressional challenges.

At the state and local levels, the move to more flexible, nimble, integrated, and accountable civil service systems mirrored the federal experience, but this trend was far from uniform. Many progressive cities such as Phoenix, Arizona, and Madison, Wisconsin, never suffered the same degree of rigidity and were quick to enhance managerial rationality. Some cities and counties that had traditionally allowed more managerial and political responsiveness found themselves in vogue. However, some school districts, such as Washington, DC's, have found themselves taken over in order to have strong city intervention or outright privatization leading to radical personnel reforms. Most states had followed the traditional federal pattern but have undergone change in recent years (Bowman & West, 2007; Kellough & Nigro, 2006). Some states, such as Florida and Georgia, have been more radical in their reform efforts (Condrey & Maranto, 2001), whereas others, such as Maryland, South Carolina, and Washington, have implemented more modest changes. Several states that have attempted major personnel reform, such as California and Rhode Island, have failed to do so.

The long-time values of civil service systems (technical merit and seniority) seem to have experienced countervailing pressures expanding managerial accountability and flexibility. Some states have abolished or weakened their civil service systems. In relation to selection, the ability to contract out has increased (e.g., the state of Washington). Also, the use of **temporary employees** (those without contracts, tenure rights, and usually without benefits) rose in significance during the 1990s (Hays & Kearney, 1999), but because the Internal Revenue Service insisted that long-term, temporary employees are de facto regular employees ("permatemps"), a new tendency is the use of **term employees.** For example, the federal government is making widespread use of term appointments for two to four years, with a contract and benefits but without tenure rights. Although such practices allow organizations considerable flexibility, they undermine employee security and increase opportunities for politicization of the civil service. The enormous downturn in the economy and constrained budgets starting in 2008 make personnel change much more politically feasible than it was before.

There has also been an increasing interest in finding opportunities for older workers, many of whom are receiving retirement benefits from one or more sources. These people bring experience and flexibility in that their services can be more targeted to specific needs. Often they want part-time or job-sharing positions, and may be more interested in the benefits package than remuneration per se. Older employees may be rehired annuitants, or workers from outside the hiring agency (Partnership for Public Service, 2008b).

Technology has also been a major trend in selection in two ways. First, not only has Web-based recruitment become a dominant tool, but also Web-based testing has taken a firm hold, and is increasingly accepted by researchers as valid (Nye, Do, Drasgow, & Fine, 2008; Potosky & Bobko, 2004) and by applicants as fair (Dineen, Noe, & Wang, 2004). Furthermore, automated screening has become commonplace as a "first-cut" method wherever large numbers of individuals are applying for positions, from temporary to supervisory (Buckley, Minette, Joy, & Michaels, 2004). Automated screening programs cull either applications or résumés for key phrases, sorting eligibles from ineligibles. If candidates are interested in specific positions, they are wise to ensure that in their application or résumé as many of the key desired elements are listed in language as similar to the job vacancy posting as possible. Because the contemporary preference in many of these software programs is to use an application format as the initial screening mechanism, and to use the résumé attachment as data for in-depth review by human resource specialists or the hiring unit after the first cut, applicants are also wise not to use "see attached" on applications unless directed to do so.

Selection, then, potentially is shared by three areas: a civil service commission, a human resources department, and the hiring department. Up through the 1970s, the most usual model was for the civil service commission to "test" and provide formal review, the personnel department to provide technical assistance such as benefits and salary information, and the hiring department to initiate actions for hiring and to make final selections from short lists of certified applicants. In the 1980s, the most typical model was for personnel departments to provide **certified lists** to hiring units and for the civil service commission to act as administrative judge in disputed cases. By the end of the 1990s, an increasingly common model was for hiring departments to recruit and select applicants directly, following merit principles but having wider discretion in testing practices and interview choices. Human resource departments then provided technical assistance and oversight of legal compliance issues and statistical records, as well as administrative review when necessary. The new model has some definite strengths: greater control and ownership by hiring agencies, greater flexibility, and less perceived red tape by candidates, who often are interested in specific agencies and positions. Inevitably, there are also weaknesses: increased fragmentation of selection practices and less use of economies of scale, less consistency, and more potential for abuse of discretion.

In sum, the eras are defined by their emphasis and deemphasis of values related to selection: social class, patronage (political responsiveness), merit (technical qualifications, performance criteria), seniority (employee protections and expanded privileges), and representativeness. Although all the values (except social class) have been explicit in each of the eras, some values have been emphasized at the expense of others. Below is a rough gauge of the dominant values in each period:

- Administration by gentility: political responsiveness, social class, technical qualifications (fitness of character and education)
- Selection by spoils: political responsiveness, performance (though impressionistically defined and evaluated), representativeness
- Early technical merit: technical qualifications
- Expanded merit: technical qualifications, employee protections, and expanded seniority
- Expansion of access: representativeness via affirmative action (superimposed on technical qualifications and seniority)
- Contemporary trends: performance criteria (flexibility in hiring, employee accountability), representativeness via diversity, technological efficiency via Web- and electronic-screening methods

▪▪ SELECTION: FOUR SCREENING PHASES

Selection processes can be divided into four phases of screening, although sometimes these phases are combined for convenience or necessity. In Phase 1, the procedure emphasizes discriminating between the qualified and the unqualified. Applicant pools typically have a substantial number of individuals who do not meet basic qualifications and whose applications can be put aside. In order to eliminate candidates, the initial qualifications need to be carefully identified, both from the general job description and from those special needs identified for the position in the job posting. Did the applicant provide a complete packet in the required timeline? Does the person have the required education, job-related experience, licensing, or test score (e.g., of the 25 original applicants for a position, five may have incomplete applications, three may have insufficient educational background, and half a dozen may not have the required experience)? Sometimes the screening at this point is done by staff or computer.

In Phase 2, the most highly qualified people are identified and screened. If the initial screening ranked all candidates, it is a simple matter to choose those with the highest scores. In **unassembled tests,** candidates are only ranked on those items that can be submitted by mail or email—applications, résumés, written **work samples**, letters of recommendation, and possibly online or written self-reported assessments. In **assembled tests,** applicants are required to come to a central location or locations to take general aptitude tests (a general mental ability test) or specific work tests (e.g., a typing test), or provide live work samples in a proctored setting. The idea is to narrow the pool to a number that is practical to interview or test in-depth. In the example, 11 candidates were qualified in Phase 1, but five were identified to interview in Phase 2. Until one is chosen and has accepted the position, the others are not barred from later consideration.

Invariably, the interview is the centerpiece of this process. Of course, when the **rule of three** applies, the finalists are limited to the top three candidates. In some cases, however, the finalists may be numerous, especially when multiple openings exist. In some unusual cases, the finalists may be limited to one or two clearly exceptional candidates. This is a good time to require live samples of work and to check references.

Phase 3 results in a single candidate to offer the position to, as well as backup applicants should the individual turn down the offer. Choosing the first choice from the array of candidates may be easy, or in some cases it may be difficult because the top candidates seem equally qualified or bring different types of human assets to the position. Negotiation may be mechanical in the case of front-line positions in which the terms of employment are relatively rigid, or quite flexible in the case of many senior positions or hard-to-recruit specialist jobs.

Phase 4 confirms the qualifications and ability of the candidate after the offer. Many offers are conditional on successful drug tests, medical exams, or even background checks. This phase may also include the first period of employment in which the candidate has probationary status and can be terminated without cause. The probationary period is especially warranted in cases where extensive or rigorous schooling is required and some new hires "wash out."

The four-phased approach allows for better review of applicants and less waste of time on unselected candidates. However, in some limited cases it may be too slow in responding to a dynamic applicant pool or too costly for the agency. A reduced or consolidated selection process may sometimes be appropriate, such as the hiring of term employees or entry-level staff workers, or in the event of a situation where hiring must be done as an emergency action.

■■ INITIAL REVIEWING AND TESTING

Critical for all review and test procedures is their relationship to job-related competencies (Connerley et al., 2001). How does the procedure specifically relate to the essential job functions? On the one hand, it is important to get good indicators of skills and likely performance. On the other, it is neither appropriate nor legal to pile on job requirements as a screening mechanism. Because of affirmative action cases, courts have insisted that all hiring practices, especially written tests, have verifiable connections to *core* responsibilities and be appropriate predictors of success—that is, that they be "valid" (see Exhibit 4.2 for a discussion of **test validity**). It is not possible to provide high levels of validity without job analysis, a topic covered in Chapter 5.

A wide variety of reviewing and testing mechanisms is available. The cost to organizations and the burden to applicants, however, require restraint in the use of these procedures. Most initial tests (in Phases 1 and 2) are **education and experience evaluations**, letters of recommendation, self-reported assessments, general aptitude and trait tests, and **performance tests** for specific job qualifications.

Education and Experience Evaluations

Education and experience evaluations include application forms, cover letters, and résumés (Carlson, 2003). Video résumés have fans among some applicants, but have yet to

Exhibit 4.2   Three Types of Test Validity

The *Uniform Guidelines on Employee Selection Procedures* established three acceptable validation strategies: content, construct, and criterion. Because of concerns about disparate impact on minorities and women in the 1970s and 1980s, and about applicants with disabilities in the 1990s, test validation has become an important concern in the selection process. For example, the guidelines assert that employers should regularly validate all selection procedures. Where possible, valid selection procedures having less adverse impact on underrepresented groups should be used over those that have more adverse impact. Finally, employers should keep records of all those who applied and were accepted in order to ascertain whether adverse impact occurs, which is generally defined as a selection rate of less than 80% of the group with the highest selection rate.

Content validity requires demonstrating a direct relationship of the test to actual job duties or responsibilities. It is generally the easiest to verify and is the most common validation procedure. Validity is documented through conducting a thorough job analysis of the position and connecting those elements to concrete items in the test. Examples are typing tests for clerical positions; written tests that assess specific knowledge needed, such as mathematical skills customarily used by accountants; and actual work samples such as error analysis of social work cases for supervisory positions. A subsequent issue to content validity is proportionality; for example, a typing test is appropriate for a clerical position but is only a portion of the content that is important in the position. Content validity is easiest to conduct on jobs with definable and measurable skills requiring concrete behaviors and knowledge. It is readily customized to individual positions; however, it is relatively difficult to conduct with complex jobs involving extensive discretion, abstraction, and interpersonal skills as well as identifying types of people more innately suited to certain types of work.

Criterion validity involves correlating high test scores (the predictor) with good job performance (the criterion) by those taking the test. For example, perhaps the applicants need few job skills and knowledge prior to employment because subsequent training will provide that information (and therefore content validation is inappropriate). How does one predict and select those who will be most suitable? This is the case in entry-level public safety and corrections positions. Criterion validity generally examines aptitudes or cognitive skills for learning and performing well in a given job environment—for example, the aptitude to learn language, remember key data, or use logical reasoning.

The problems with demonstrating this type of predictive ability are twofold. First, how can a sample be obtained with both high and low scorers, given that the agency wants to hire only high scorers? Second, how can it be known that performance ratings are accurate, given that they are often said to be of low reliability and validity (see Chapter 9)? Documenting criterion-related validity that is predictive generally requires experimental designs that are costly and prone to methodological challenges.

A more common strategy to prove criterion validity is to use a concurrent approach. That is, incumbent employees (rather than applicants) are tested to demonstrate a statistical relationship between high scorers and high performers. Again, the quality of performance ratings becomes a significant hurdle to overcome. Because criterion validation is difficult and expensive, it is generally used only for high-volume, entry-level positions or for systemwide generic tests that look at clusters of jobs using related skills such as math, language, spatial ability, and abstract thinking. For example, the federal government formerly used six different general-entry, administrative tests (Administrative Careers With America), such as the health-safety-environment exam, for occupational clusters. It is also used for management tests that employ generalized assessment centers because concrete skills are difficult to define. The job analysis should determine what general types of skills and aptitudes are necessary for success, and the assessment center should provide opportunities to look for these generalized abilities.

Construct validity documents the relationship of select abstract personal traits and characteristics (such as intelligence, integrity, creativity, aggressiveness, industriousness, and anxiety) to job performance. Tests with high construct validity accurately predict future job performance by examining the characteristics of successful job incumbents and judging whether applicants have those characteristics. Construct validation is used for psychological tests that screen candidates based on trait/attitude profiles. Despite the concerns with construct validity expressed in the Uniform Federal Guidelines and by some researchers because of the tenuous connection between personal traits and job performance, tests relying on construct validity are selectively used in some areas such as law enforcement for identifying traits like aggressiveness and hostility. There is also an increase in testing for integrity. Testing for the "big five" personality dimensions (extraversion, emotional stability, agreeableness, conscientiousness, and openness to experience) has been shown to have validity in some occupations.

Documenting validity ensures that tests are job related and legally nondiscriminatory. It should not deter organizations from trying to gather as much information as possible about candidates in their efforts in appraising the best qualified and the most likely to succeed. Well-constructed tests can provide an excellent method of identifying and eliminating those without minimum competencies or weak in aptitude or predisposition so that other methods can focus on selecting the best qualified from a smaller pool. It may be a mistake for organizations not to use tests simply because of a disinclination to document test validity. Various types of data help provide different perspectives about job suitability. In fact, when integrated with education and experience evaluations, interviews, and reference checks so that a broad "basket" of indicators is established, content-, criterion-, and construct-based tests can provide a solid base of information on which to make selections.

Source: Uniform Guidelines on Employee Selection Procedures, 1978.

catch on in the organizational world, especially in the public sector (Jesdanun, 2007). Forms generally run from one to three pages for job- or agency-specific applications to five or six pages for the "general purpose" forms used by many state governments or large agencies. They generally include requests for biographical data, education, job experiences (asking for organization, address, title, supervisor, and duties), the job title or titles for which the applicant is applying, work location preference (in state systems), work limitations (such as availability), and special qualifications. They also normally have additional information about such topics as reasonable accommodation, **diversity policies,** and veterans' points. Finally, applications invariably have certification and authorization statements to be signed. Such statements notify candidates of the consequences of false information, inform them that applications are available for public inspection, and authorize background checks. Occasionally, applications are customized for specific positions, and applicants are requested to provide biographical answers to fit specific job-related questions regarding their achievements, education, training, conscientiousness, and work experience.

Not all jobs require application forms. Some substitute a cover letter and a résumé, especially for management and executive jobs. Although forms have the benefit of uniformity and provide standard preemployment waivers, they give little insight into the career development, management style, and unique abilities or experiences of candidates. Cover letters provide an opportunity for respondents to explain why they feel they are qualified for an advertised position, and the résumé generally provides more-specific information about job experience than would fit in an application form. Typically, applicants are asked to provide references—addresses and telephone numbers or sometimes completed letters of recommendation (see below under Letters of Recommendation). Cover letters and résumés create more work for both the applicant and reviewers, but they generally are more informative. Also, sometimes work samples are requested such as a written work product or visual image of a completed project. Whenever the cover letter and résumé is substituted for the application, the selected candidate is generally required to fill out the form later in the process.

A number of jobs require a specific license, certificate, or endorsement. These include many medical positions (such as doctors, nurses, and anesthesiologists), engineering and technician positions, teaching positions, legal positions (such as lawyers), jobs requiring special driver's permits (commercial, chauffeur's), and positions in architecture and hazardous material handling. In such cases, licensure is generally the minimum requirement for consideration for hiring. In some cases, certification is required for the position but is provided by the employer as training. In those cases, it is a selection method only to the degree that some candidates drop out or fail the certification process. (A prime example is for positions requiring certified peace officer status or select military occupational programs.)

Although licensure is useful for its definitiveness, it does raise the issue of private control over the process in many occupational settings, sometimes leading to excessive occupational selectivity, which in turn creates a market bottleneck and inflates salaries. Some jurisdictions use emergency and temporary certificates to remedy this situation when it becomes acute.

Letters of Recommendation

Letters take considerable effort on the part of candidates and those recommending them, and time to read on the part of the reviewers. Therefore, they should be solicited with forethought. Letters of recommendation are generally most appropriate for those seeking jobs of high potential such as entry-level professional positions or management posts. Although letters are most easily included in the original job posting, increasingly employers are deferring their requests until the finalists have been selected in midlevel and senior positions. Because better jobs require customized letters of recommendation, some highly qualified applicants may choose not to waste a scarce resource on questionable competitions. By postponing this request, the hiring authority often widens its pool. In general, the most useful letters of recommendation are from former employers. The same is true for those called as references. They can speak to abilities, work effectiveness, and work habits most directly.

Self-Assessments

Because past performance is the best predictor of future performance, one effective assessment technique is to ask candidates to provide detailed examples about themselves on the important accomplishment dimensions (i.e., competencies) of the job. The self-reported assessment technique is called the behavioral consistency method (OPM, 1999). Ideally, candidates are asked to report information about five to ten accomplishment dimensions on which they are rated. Critical competencies for a frontline employee might be examples of mastering new skills, work accuracy, work speed, cooperation with colleagues, innovation, perseverance, and commitment. A supervisory position, in contrast, might include monitoring work, operations planning, delegating work, clarifying and informing, developing staff, motivating staff, building teams, managing conflict, and stimulating creativity. Prior to judging the self-reports, the evaluators should have anchored rating scales. If the competencies are valid and the rating scale is carefully designed, this can be one of the most statistically valid of all selection methods (Schmidt & Hunter, 1998, p. 268). Shortcuts in this method, however, lower the validity significantly, even where the method is encouraged (MSPB, 2006). Behaviorally anchored questioning (relating specific experience to current job competencies) can be integrated into customized applications, requested as a complementary tool to the biographically oriented résumé, or become the basis of a **structured interview**.

General Aptitude and Trait Tests

There are at least three types of aptitude and trait tests: (1) psychological, (2) general skills, and (3) general physical ability.

1. **Psychological tests** examine the personality traits and compare them to the job requirements (Corcoran, 2005; Lievens, Highhouse, & De Corte, 2005). For instance, research has shown that, compared with others with equal knowledge and skill, people who have a low sense of efficacy shy away from difficult tasks, have low aspirations and weak commitment to goals, and give up quickly in the face of difficulties. For example, the military forces sometimes use psychological hardiness tests to predict resiliency under stress (Bartone, Roland, Picano, & Williams, 2008). The challenge is that providing the validity necessary for specific positions is difficult, given the standards of correlation that the courts have demanded (Exhibit 4.2, above). Such tests are common only in public safety positions—law enforcement, corrections, emergency services—where job structure and stress justify the research and expense. Noncognitive abilities found to be critical are also assessed, such as motivation, attitude toward people, and sense of responsibility. Although not as prevalent, integrity and civil virtue tests (Viswesvaran, Deller, & Ones, 2007) are sometimes used (and seem to be on the rise) to screen out those with attitudes poorly suited to public sector ideals and the particularly high ethical standards required.[4] Very broad psychological constructs such as intelligence might be useful (Rae & Earles, 1994) but generally have been considered to fall far short of contemporary validity requirements. There is a good deal of debate over the use of personality, integrity, and civic virtue tests for selection in both the practitioner and research communities (see, for example, Morgeson et al., 2007; Ones, Dilchert, Viswesvaran, & Judge, 2007).

2. **General skills tests** provide information about abilities or aptitudes in areas such as reading, mathematics, abstract thinking, spelling, language usage, general problem solving, judgment, proofreading, and memory (Ryan & Tippins, 2004). These tests are common for entry-level positions where commercial vendors have a wide variety of products from which to choose, or where large agencies can create their own tests for large job classes. The measurement of general cognitive skill is used in educational selection in tests such as the SAT, the ACT, and the GRE. In a common case, a 100-item police officer general skills test covers learning and applying police information, remembering details, verbal aptitude, following directions, and using judgment and logic. Although such tests are most often used for broad

classification series at the lower end of the administrative hierarchy, they can be purchased or developed for more-senior professional positions that justify the expense and effort, such as air traffic controllers (Ackerman & Kanfer, 1993), general skills for middle managers, and for various police and fire commanders. For example, for many years the Immigration and Naturalization Service (INS) had a problem with their border patrol–training program because more than 10% were unable to complete the language component successfully. The INS designed and implemented an artificial language test as a selection screen that assessed ability to learn a new language. Subsequently, the failure rate fell 76% and produced a $6.5 million savings over five years (MSPB, 2002, p. 9).

3. When general physical ability is a major part of the job, as it is for public safety personnel, tests of physical ability (e.g., strength, agility, eyesight) may be part of a battery of tests used to determine initial job qualification (Arvey, Nutting, & Landon, 1992; Hogan, 1991). Generally, however, medical, physical, and eyesight examinations—when incidental but necessary—are done after extending an offer but before employment (see Postoffer and Hiring Issues below).

Performance Tests for Specific Jobs

Performance tests directly assess the skills necessary for specific jobs.[5] Although tests based on single-factor performance models are somewhat useful and dominated early personnel research and practice, the multifactor nature of performance is better appreciated today (Campbell, 2001). Some jobs have specific physical skills such as typing (or keyboarding) or equipment operation that can be tested. Many job-related knowledge tests use multiple-choice, true-false, and short-answer formats. Sometimes tests use video versions. Occasionally, an essay or oral format is analyzed in the first screening. Knowledge-based tests also commonly are utilized in promotional hiring in public safety and technical positions.

Job-related skills can be tested through work samples or job simulations: those applicants tested are required to produce a sample of the work or demonstrate their skills in a series of simulated activities, generally known as **assessment centers.** Examples include requiring trainers to conduct a short workshop, operators to demonstrate telephone skills, or management applicants to complete a series of activities requiring them to write memoranda, give directions (in writing), and decide on actions to take. Work samples and assessment centers generally are quite effective but are not often used as initial screening devices because of the substantial time and cost involved for customized screening. They are used more commonly as a part of the process to review the narrowed pool that goes through an interview process or for promotional purposes.

Other Considerations Regarding Reviewing and Testing

Licensure, general aptitude, and performance tests have proliferated over the years. For example, a civilian detention officer position in an Iowa county sheriff's office listed seven tests, excluding the interview: (a) written exam, (b) physical ability test, (c) polygraph exam, (d) psychological test, (e) medical exam, (f) drug test, and (g) residency requirement. Undoubtedly, more testing methods and higher-quality testing methods substantially increase the likelihood of successful hires. Many critics, however, have called for more selection flexibility and a greater reliance on background education and experience reviews than on aptitude and performance tests (Gore, 1993; MSPB, 2004). The reasons are easy to discern. Lengthy testing protocols are expensive to administer and discourage some qualified job seekers from applying. Testing often slows the employment process as applicants wait for test dates and organizations wait for test scores. This is particularly true in a low-unemployment economy. However, the advent of online testing has provided flexibility in this regard. Unproctored versions may be subject to proctored retesting as a postoffer requirement. Also, vendors provide convenient composite tests for job classes that include language, knowledge, aptitude, and attitude questions in a variety of formats, sometimes with performance elements built into them. An example is testing for the ability to multitask by asking applicants to respond to "requests" during the test itself.

Another challenge in using standardized tests is the changing nature of contemporary work (Howard, 1995). Jobs in general tend to be broader, change more frequently, possess more interpersonal and team skills, need more creativity and self-initiative, and have more demanding performance standards, with broader skill sets required (Jordan-Nowe, 2007; Van Wart & Berman, 1999). This scenario suggests the need for an increased use of examinations and tests that look for the more abstract characteristics of the job in the applicant. Even with this new need—and although the ability to screen for these skills has increased because of research in affective behavior, general aptitude, and attitude testing—concerns about cost, time, and validity have dampened usage. Thus, there continues to be strong countervailing trends to use more tests to increase the rigor in many cases. In others, there is a tendency to reduce the numbers of exams and avoid testing for abstract constructs.

There is no simple rule of thumb for which or how many tests to use. For example, see Exhibit 4.3, which indicates that although some methods have greater validity, several are necessary at a minimum to provide the degree of assurance appropriate for such an important decision. Factors that lend themselves to larger test batteries include sizable applicant pools and criticality of candidate suitability because of training cost or public safety. Factors that lend themselves to reduced test procedures include difficulties with travel and test administration, the need to move candidates through selection quickly (MSPB, 2006), and the ability to screen a manageable number of top applicants through interviewing and reference checks (see Phase 2 discussion, below).

Exhibit 4.3   Validity Scores of Selected Assessment Methods

Assessment Procedure	Validity Score
Work sample tests	.54
Structure interviews	.51
General mental ability tests	.51
Job knowledge tests	.48
Training and experience (behavioral consistency model)	.45
Job try-out procedure	.44
Unstructured interviews	.38
Biographical data measures	.35
Reference checks	.26
Grade point average	.20
Years of job experience	.18
Training and experience (point method)	.11
Years of education	.10

Source: MSPB, 2008a, p. 24.

■■ INTERVIEWING AND REFERENCE CHECKS: REDUCING THE POOL

For candidates, a selection interview means that they have made "the cut." Interviewees should anticipate one to three other strong candidates, so doing well in the process is key (see Exhibit 4.4).

Exhibit 4.4   How Well Do You Interview?

Management candidates are expected to interview well. Some of the common errors include the following:

Not practicing: To a large degree, interviews are performances, and performances take practice. It is not acceptable answers that get jobs; it is highly articulate responses. Make up a handful of easy questions and another group of difficult ones. Write out the answers and rehearse them. Although these exact questions may not be asked, similar ones will be.

Not knowing the organization and its employees in advance: Read as much about the agency as possible; certainly the Internet has made this easier. Find out about people on the interview committee and in the hiring unit (generally information will be sent in advance of an interview; if not, ask for it).

Not listening: Candidates are "selling" themselves and talking a lot, but as good salespeople know, it is listening that makes the sale. Good listening shows courtesy, makes others feel satisfied with the interaction, and ensures that you do not miss subtle cues. People can tell the difference between active and passive listening, so do not mistake listening for being quiet without paying attention to others' ideas.

Not balancing technical and nontechnical aspects: Reviewing the technical aspects of a job is certainly key, yet just as important are your work philosophy, leadership style, and work-related goals. Do not forget to address the "big picture" while reviewing the details in preparation for an interview.

Not dressing the part: As obvious as it may seem (see Exhibit 2.5), appropriate dress and grooming can make a difference, yet many people "make do" in the critical interview. Clothes should be well fitted and relatively new so that they still have crispness.

Interviewing and reference checks are major responsibilities for the hiring manager and involve discretion. Although this discretion is important, unstructured interviews and haphazard reference checks frequently result in low validity, wasted resources, frustrated candidates, and illegal practices (MSPB, 2003). Generally speaking, only structured interviews (described below) have high validity. (For a general discussion of validity issues related to interviewing see Ryan & Tippins, 2004; Schmidt & Hunter, 1998.) It is especially important to conduct high-quality interviews and reference checks, given the trend toward decreasing use of tests.

The first issue is deciding who will conduct the interviews. The four options are (a) the supervisor, (b) the human resource department or a third party, (c) a panel or committee, or (d) a series of interviewers who may include the immediate supervisor, higher-level supervisors, a committee, a colleague forum, and clients.[6] Nonprofessional entry positions often have a supervisor conduct the interview; in the case of "no minimum education or experience" requirements in which there is high turnover (laundry workers, aides, receptionists, and drivers), professional interviewers in the human resource department conduct the interview. Entry-level professional positions (such as caseworkers, law enforcement officers, correctional service officers, technicians, engineers, and lawyers) frequently use a selection panel to enhance the diversity of opinions about candidates. Frequently, candidates vying for senior or professional positions have separate interviews with an advisory selection panel and with the hiring supervisor who makes a final selection. High positions may also require more resources by having candidates talk to a variety of parties in addition to the selection committee and hiring supervisor.

A second critical question is that of whom to interview (Carlson, 2003). Public sector employment involves two different approaches. The less common approach is to interview all candidates who meet minimum qualifications, but this is time consuming for the reviewers and may unnecessarily inflate the hopes of candidates. Where the applicant pool is small, multiple positions are open, or where the time of interviewers is available, however, such an option may make sense. In another case, the candidate pool may lack exceptional candidates so that more-extensive interviewing may be logical in trying to discover hidden talent.

By far the most common approach, however, is to interview only the most qualified people. At one time, the rule of three was common (promulgated by civil service commissions); it restricted hiring authorities to interviewing the top three candidates who were "certified." This practice was used to keep much lower ranked "eligibles" from being selected because of fears of political interference or managerial cronyism. This injunction is still in place in many federal agencies, although it is much criticized (U.S. Government Accounting Office, 2003). In many civil service systems, the allowable number to be certified is often expanded to a rule of four, five, or six, or sometimes to the top "tier." Today, the tendency is to give the hiring authority discretion to interview any number it wishes of those deemed to meet the minimum qualifications, making the "eligible" and "certified" lists identical. Nonetheless, there are practical reasons to restrict interviewing. In most cases, the top three or four candidates are obvious, and to interview more is unlikely to be productive.

Where interview discretion exists, hiring authorities can consider alternate models. Online or telephone interviews, or both, can rapidly provide a good deal of information and answer many preliminary questions. Likewise, two-way videoconferencing can precede on-site interviews and winnow down the applicant field. Reference checks can be done before the interview process to gather information to help select the most desirable candidates to invite.

General Considerations for Those Conducting Interviews

A good procedure takes preparation, knowledge of the position, and awareness of the various interviewer biases that may occur. Steps to consider in preparing for a structured interview are as follows:

1. Plan how it should proceed. Who will meet the applicants? Where will people wait if they do not proceed directly to the interview? Who will explain the general process to be used? If there is more than one interviewer, who will ask which questions?

2. Explain basic facts about the position to the candidate: which department, what division or unit, and the supervisor. Review the job responsibilities.

3. Use the position description and advertisement as guides to ensure that the focus is on essential job functions. In addition, include some of the job challenges and opportunities as part of a realistic preview.

4. Set up interviews in a private setting in which distractions are unlikely.

5. Concentrate on listening to an applicant's answers; take notes. Also, be sure that the candidate has opportunities to ask questions during the interview. If only one such opportunity exists and is at the end of the interview, then the candidate may feel rushed if the interview used up most of the allotted time.

6. Be sure that there is a specific list of written questions asked of all candidates. This should not keep the interviewer from asking follow-up questions. Ensure that the questions have a logical sequence. They should always be reviewed in advance and circulated to relevant parties to ensure balance and appropriateness. In many cases, questions must be approved by the human resource department in advance.

7. Use behaviorally anchored questions relating past experience to the current position, situational judgment questions to probe thinking processes, or work samples to see mini-demonstrations as a part of the process. Illustrations of behaviorally anchored questions (Krajewski, Goffin, McCarthy, Rothstein, & Johnston, 2006) follow.

   • "Tell us about working with a hostile customer and how you resolved the situation." "Can you describe a difficult project that you were required to handle?" "Would you please describe leading groups in different circumstances, such as when you were the formal leader and when you were not."
   • "We have all had to deal with difficult employees. Can you describe one such situation and how you worked with the employee?"

"Tell us how you deal with repeated interruptions and concurrent projects. In other words, how are you at multi-tasking?" Situational judgment questions ask the candidate to speculate about how to solve problems that might be encountered on the job (Lievens, Peeters, & Schollaert, 2008; McDaniel, Hartman, Whetzel, & Grubb, 2007). Examples of situational judgment questions follow:

   • Critique or evaluate something (a program, policy, procedure, or a report's recommendations, conclusions, decision, or viewpoint).
   • Define a relevant problem, identify its causes, develop alternative solutions, decide what to do, and outline an implementation plan.
   • Lay out a plan or steps for conducting a study, researching an issue, or reaching a goal.
   • Prioritize a number of issues, problems, or activities.
   • Solve a hypothetical supervisory problem concerning planning, organizing, assigning, directing, motivating, evaluating, or facilitating the work of others.
   • Persuade or convince a hypothetical client or audience of something.
   • Respond to a hypothetical complaint or hostile person.
   • Role-play a hypothetical work situation.

Cases of work knowledge or samples (which may be done outside the interview with trained raters but in a proximal time frame) could include the following:

   • Perform tasks relevant to the position:
     ○ Demonstrate administration of CPR with a resuscitation dummy.
     ○ Demonstrate map-reading skills.
     ○ Troubleshoot a mechanical problem.

       ○ Write a short business letter.
       ○ Follow a set of directions.
- Write or edit written material that is specifically job related.
- What is the relevant code (statute, or regulation) for . . . ?
- What are the standard steps in . . . ?
- Who are the primary experts on . . . ?
- Deliver an oral presentation (based on information that the candidate is given time to review and prepare, assuming that such presentations are a part of the job).

Although research generally supports behavioral ranking and work samples as having higher validity with job performance, ceteris paribus (Poe, 2003), they are all useful and can be integrated without much difficulty.

8. Be careful that no oral commitments or suggestions about employment prospects are made. Be prepared to give candidates an estimate of when they will receive feedback.

9. Complete the evaluation notes while impressions are fresh, preferably immediately after the interview. Use a predetermined rating system for the questions.

10. To comply with the Americans with Disabilities Act, be prepared to make accommodations for applicants on request. Even if applicants do not request an accommodation for the interview, it is best to ask all individuals: "Can you perform the essential functions of this position with or without a reasonable accommodation?" If accommodation is needed, then consult with human resources specialists. Having to provide accommodation is not an acceptable reason for declining to offer employment.

Finally, it is important that interviewers keep questions focused on the job. Appropriate questions include past work experiences (both paid and volunteer), military experience, education and training, authorization to work in the United States, and personal characteristics related to performing essential functions of the job. Topics to avoid include age, race and ethnicity, disability, national origin, marital status and children, religion, gender (because some jobs are dominated by one gender or the other), arrest record (but not conviction record), credit references, garnishment record, types of military discharges, childcare arrangements, height and weight, transportation not explicitly job related, and past workers' compensation claims. Exhibit 4.5 provides a guide for nondiscriminatory interviewing.

Reference Checks

References can be verified at different times during the process and in various ways; for example, letters of recommendation are a type of reference check. Although perhaps convenient for the search panel, obtaining letters of recommendation can produce dozens of letters that may not be carefully examined, is a nuisance to applicants, and requires candidates to divulge their interest in positions before they may be serious candidates. Telephone reference checking can be done prior to interviews, after interviews, and before hiring, or after selection but in advance of the offer (MSPB, 2005; Taylor, Pajo, Cheung, & Stringfield, 2004). In most cases, it is best to conduct these checks just prior to or after interviews so that the information may add to the selection decision. Where more

Exhibit 4.5   Guide to Nondiscriminatory Hiring

Guide to Preemployment Inquiries

	Acceptable	*Unacceptable*
Arrest records	No questions acceptable. (For convictions see below. Positions in law enforcement may be an exception.)	Unacceptable are inquiries about number of and reasons for arrests.
Availability for work on weekends or evenings	Acceptable if asked of all applicants and it is a business necessity for the person to be available to work weekends or evenings, or both.	Unacceptable are any inquiries about the candidate's religious observance.
Child care	No questions acceptable.	Unacceptable are any inquiries about childcare arrangements if asked of only one gender of applicants.
Citizenship, birthplace, and national origin	The only legitimate concern here is whether the applicant is eligible to work in the United States under terms of the Immigration Reform and Control Act of 1986. There is a fair and advisable way to obtain this information. The best approach is to ask, Are you either a U.S. citizen or an alien authorized to work in the United States? The "Yes" or "No" answer that follows provides all needed information while not disclosing which (citizen or alien) the applicant is.	Unacceptable are questions on birthplace, national origin, ancestry, or lineage of applicant, applicant's parents, or applicant's spouse.
Conviction records	Inquiries into convictions if job related are acceptable.	Unacceptable are any inquiries about conviction unrelated to job requirements.
Creed or religion	No questions acceptable, except where religion is a bona fide occupational qualification.	Unacceptable are any inquiries about applicant's religious affiliation, church, parish, or religious holidays observed.
Credit records	The interviewer must follow the Fair Credit Reporting Act. This act requires notification of applicants if the interviewer uses outside sources to provide information to make adverse decisions about applicants.	Unacceptable is not informing applicants when interviewer uses information gained from sources outside the hiring organization.
Disability	It is acceptable to ask whether the applicant can perform essential functions of the job in question.	Unacceptable are any inquiries that ask applicant to list or describe any disability.
Family status	Acceptable are inquiries as to whether applicants have responsibilities or commitments which will prevent meeting work schedules, if they are asked of all applicants, regardless of sex.	Unacceptable are any inquiries about marital status, number and age of children, or spouse's job.

Guide to Preemployment Inquiries

	Acceptable	Unacceptable
Height and weight	No questions acceptable, unless clearly job related.	Unacceptable are any inquiries unrelated to job requirements.
Language	It is acceptable to ask what language or languages applicant speaks or writes fluently, if job related.	Unacceptable are any inquiries about applicant's native tongue, language used by applicant at home, or how applicant acquired the ability to read, write, or speak a second language.
Marital status	No questions acceptable.	Unacceptable are any inquiries about whether applicant is married, single, divorced, separated, engaged, or widowed.
Military service	Questions on military experience or training are acceptable.	Unacceptable are any inquiries about type or condition of discharge.
Name	Questions on whether applicant has worked under a different name are acceptable.	Unacceptable are any inquiries about the original name of an applicant whose name has been legally changed, or about the national origin of an applicant's name.
Organizations	Questions about applicant's membership in professional organizations, if job related, are acceptable.	Unacceptable are any inquiries about clubs, social fraternities, societies, lodges, or organizations to which applicant belongs.
Photographs	No questions acceptable except after hiring.	Unacceptable are any photographs with application or after interview, but before hiring.
Pregnancy	No questions acceptable.	Unacceptable are any inquiries into applicant's pregnancy, medical history of pregnancy, or family plans.
Race or color	No questions acceptable.	Unacceptable are any inquiries about applicant's race or color of applicant's skin.
References	Asking for names of work references is acceptable.	It is unacceptable to ask for references from applicant's pastor or religious leader.
Relatives or friends	It is acceptable to ask for names of applicant's relatives already employed by the organization or a competitor. Interviewer may not give preference if women and minorities are underrepresented in the workforce, however.	Unacceptable are inquiries about names of friends working for the company or of relatives other than those working for the company.

Source: State of Iowa, 2006, pp. 135–137.

thorough—and expensive—background investigations are necessary for reasons of public safety (e.g., education, air traffic control, transportation, law enforcement, corrections, child care, elder care), preliminary checking may be appropriate. Failure to do so could result in **negligent hiring** lawsuits against the agency should the person hired engage in wrongdoing (Connerley & Bernardy, 2001; Walter, 1992).

Telephone reference checks should be planned as carefully as interviews, especially in the current environment in which employers are increasingly reluctant to provide detailed reference information. Four useful issues to address include (a) verification of employment dates and responsibilities, (b) general assessments of strengths and weaknesses, (c) examples of candidate abilities, and (d) whether the individual was given added responsibilities, was a candidate for advancement, and, most importantly, would be eligible for rehire. Straying beyond documented facts when providing negative information can expose the employer to defamation suits from the former employee. Despite the more constrained environment for reference checks of former employers, they can be useful, especially if the applicant waives his rights to see the letters. Verifying basic information is a requirement of good management. Questions about strengths, successes, and additional responsibilities provide depth in the candidate's abilities. Even muted responses to questions may provide "red flags" to investigate.

Whereas the above focuses on what organizations can do, the Appendix for this chapter discusses what job seekers can do to make themselves more attractive to prospective employers and to improve their communications with them. The Appendix discusses the professional commitment statement (PCS), a tool for improved communication and focus of one's aspirations. Students who develop their PCSs often report improved networking and interviewing success.

∎∎ CHOOSING AND NEGOTIATION

Who determines who the final candidate will be? What if a clear candidate does not emerge from the interviews? How should the offer be made? What documentation is necessary in making the offer?

The final selection is most frequently made by the supervisor for the position. Often she has a ranked list from a search committee for professional or competitive positions. Supervisors should not overturn search committee recommendations lightly. Although these committees (or whole departments) never technically hire candidates, their decisions may be definitive. For some positions requiring minimum or no qualifications, or where competition for qualified staff is particularly fierce, the hiring authority may essentially be delegated to the human resources department so that immediate selection may take place. In some promotional hiring cases with strong seniority systems and an established testing regimen, the decision may be formulaic: the person with the highest score on the required tests gets the position.

Sometimes the interview procedure leaves the supervisor or the search committee bewildered about the best candidate; in such cases, a second round of interviewing may be a solution. If the supervisor or committee is confident that the applicant pool is weak, then the search can be continued by re-advertising and interviewing a second pool, or the search can be closed entirely, to be opened at a later date. The situation is different, however, if two or three people look highly qualified but bring different strengths to the position. In such a case, the person doing the hiring should simply make the decision. Delaying decisions with competitive candidates means that they may not be available when needed.

The actual hiring normally begins with an informal phone call. Is the person still interested? Do they understand what the salary is? Do they have any final questions? For entry-level positions, there is usually little ability to negotiate salary or working conditions; senior-level and competitive positions may provide flexibility. Both the organization and the candidate should have a clear idea of how long the agency is willing to wait for a decision; a period of at least several days is reasonable. Once the candidate orally accepts the position, a letter to confirm the offer (**letter of intent**) likely will follow. The person is then generally asked to report to the work site to complete employment forms. This is also done when the starting date of employment is not immediate because of funds availability or because the applicant must give notice at another job. In very senior positions, the letter of intent dictates the special conditions of employment, including retreat rights (to other positions), special travel or equipment allowances, and so on. Only when the organization is confident that the position has been filled are letters (or calls) made to those interviewed but not selected to inform them that the position has been filled.

One significant variation exists when a physical exam or drug test is a part of the hiring process but is conducted after the offer; an offer of employment is then **contingent**. This must be clearly stipulated. Other contingencies exist such as funding availability, job freezes, or completion of training. It is also useful to point out that in the probationary period job termination can normally occur without the need to show either cause or reason.

The final part of the hiring process is the documentation of the process itself. Generally, the human resource department or affirmative action office will want a form filled out that confirms who the eligible individuals were and the reasons for selection and nonselection. This process is made much easier, and is less subject to challenge, if the hiring authority has done a thorough job of defining essential position functions and then scoring all eligible candidates on the job-related functions.

■■ POSTOFFER AND HIRING ISSUES

Some "tests," as mentioned, occur after the offer, with employment conditional on successfully passing them. They are sometimes allowed or required for security purposes or public safety. Although drug testing is generally illegal for most positions, it is legal for those conveying passengers and involved in public safety positions (e.g., peace officers, corrections, emergency services; Drug-Free Workplace Act, 1988; Omnibus Transportation Employees Testing Act, 1991). Law enforcement and corrections positions also frequently require extensive background checks and sometimes polygraph examinations, although the questions asked must be carefully screened for job relevance (as stipulated in the Employee Polygraph Protection Act of 1988). Generally, these tests are conducted after an offer but before employment is finalized. It is also legal for governments to impose residency requirements for select positions (*McCarthy v. Philadelphia Civil Service Commission,* 1976), a condition that generally has been modified to distance-from-work requirements for appropriate public safety, public works, and other employees with emergency responsibilities. The Genetic Information Nondiscrimination Act of 2008, the first civil rights law of the new century, protects workers from having to provide genetic information prior to employment or enrollment in health insurance plans.

Even after the person has accepted the position and documentation on the hiring process has been filed, the selection process is not over. All candidates interviewed or, in some senior level cases, all persons who applied should to be informed that a decision has been made.

Just as important, the supervisor needs to begin to get ready for the new applicant's arrival and integration to the organization. This process is called **onboarding** (Partnership for Public Service, 2008a). It begins with a review of what the new employee will need to be successful and to feel like a valued member of the organization. For example, anticipating any office and equipment needs for the new person helps with a smooth transition.

Next, what are the plans for orientation and training? Orientation includes sessions that inform the new person of general policies and benefits packages and provides familiarization with facilities. Training provides specific instruction on job-related processes and equipment. The workload of new employees should be reduced initially whenever possible; they should be informed accordingly. Will the training be conducted by a training department and be part of an established program, or will it be done by the supervisor or an in-house instructor? Although on-the-job training has the virtues of relevance and immediacy when done properly, it is frequently completed in an excessively casual manner that really could be called "you-are-on-your-own" training (Van Wart, Cayer, & Cook, 1993; also see Chapter 9, this volume).

A related option to consider is a mentor. Who will make sure that the new employee is introduced to people after the first day, answer questions about the job and culture of the organization, and simply take a special interest in the new person's well-being? The initial period is the most critical in preventing early turnover as well as in establishing a positive bond between the employee and the agency. Those who realize that the necessary training and support are not provided are wise to ask for it. Lack of training is generally a simple oversight; even in resource-poor organizations, additional assistance is likely to go to those who ask for it.

Finally, the probationary period itself, where it exists, can be a key part of the selection function. Most are for six months or a year, although the Canadian government allows up to 36 months in some fields of employment. Generally, termination during probation is difficult to challenge as long as it is for nondiscriminatory reasons; mediocre performance is usually grounds for dismissal, and standards of proof may be minimal. That means that supervisors have an exceptional opportunity, although some let probation lapse as the candidate "gets up to speed." Setting tough standards for probationary employees as an extension of a rigorous selection process may avoid future performance problems. Federal data indicate that discharges during probation have increased from 4% to 6% in recent years and that challenges to termination are extraordinarily low (MSPB, 2002). Overall, the paradox of probation is that it may be the best selection technique but that it may not be taken seriously by some employers for a variety of practical reasons. When done well, however, it can resolve the paradox of needs.

■■ SUMMARY AND CONCLUSION

Although almost everyone agrees that the single most important class of management decisions is hiring the "right" people, there is much less consensus on the basis for deciding who is right. In fact, democracies require fundamentally different selection processes for different public sector positions. Presidents, governors, and mayors do not take civil service examinations, and midlevel managers are not elected. Technical merit, the focus of this chapter, may be the heart of the civil service system, but most systems pay attention to internal considerations and representativeness as well. Even where merit principles apply—hiring technically qualified candidates through an open process that scrutinizes the essential job functions and applicants' special knowledge, skills, and abilities—there are different models of implementation. Coming out of an era of excessive patronage, civil service systems originally removed all but the final selection from executive branch agencies to prevent political or managerial tampering. Today, with crass political patronage for nonexecutive jobs relatively uncommon, public sector systems have moved selection functions to agency human resource departments or into the hiring units themselves. Line managers have greater responsibilities. Certification lists are being lengthened to give greater discretion, or are sometimes being changed to qualified lists.

Test selection includes many possibilities from education and experience evaluations to licensure, to general aptitude and trait examinations, and to performance tests for specific job qualifications. The current tendency has been for fewer aptitude and performance tests in an environment emphasizing speed and managerial flexibility. However, a stronger employer market provides opportunities to scrutinize more extensively without fear of losing many good candidates. Exhibit 4.6 summarizes when various selection tests are used. Interviewing is a complex event with legal pitfalls, yet when it is planned carefully even candidates who

Exhibit 4.6	When Various Selection Tests Are Most Commonly Used			
Type of Selection Test	**Phase One** *Select All Those Eligible*	**Phase Two** *Select the High-Quality Group*	**Phase Three** *Select the Final Candidate for the Job Offer*	**Phase Four** *Confirm Contingency Qualifications and on-the-Job Ability*
Education and experience	X (general review)	X (detailed matching and point system)		
Letters of recommendation	X (part of job application)	X (supplemental request)		
Self-reported assessments	X	X	X	
General aptitude and trait tests	X	X		
Work samples and assessment centers	X (e.g., examples of written work)	X (live samples)	X (live samples)	
Interviews		X	X	
Reference checks		X	X	
Special tests				X
Probationary period				X

are not selected appreciate the opportunity to have been interviewed. The actual hiring decision, also, is made much easier by careful planning, which includes contingency planning should the initial round of interviewing not produce a clear choice. Following through on posthiring issues ensures that the candidate is oriented, trained, and supported so that she can pass successfully through the probationary period and become productive.

Increased demands on organizations to be productive, flexible, and responsive—often while only maintaining staff or even losing employees—make selecting the best people critical. More than ever before, line managers need to be informed about and involved in the selection process.

KEY TERMS

80% rule

Assembled tests

Assessment center

Certified lists

Civil service commission

Contingent hiring

Disparate impact

Education and experience evaluations

Electoral popularity

General skills tests

Internally based hiring

Letter of intent

Merit selection

Negligent hiring

Onboarding

Patronage

Pendleton Act

Performance tests

Psychological tests

Representativeness

Rule of three

Seniority

Seniority-based selection

Social class selection

Spoils system

Structured interviews

Temporary employees

Term employees

Test validity

Unassembled tests

Veterans' points

Work samples

EXERCISES

Class Discussion

1. The paradox of freedom (see the Introduction) looms over the selection function, most notably in such areas as drug, lie, and genetic testing. Using dialectic reasoning, stalk this paradox using Einstein's famous dictum: "You cannot solve the problem with the same kind of thinking that created it."

2. What is the "best" balance of selection strategies? Should all civil service jobs be purely merit? Should seniority be a major factor in promotional hiring? Should representativeness (both affirmative action and veterans' points) be phased out? Should the number of patronage appointments be decreased or increased?

3. Has anyone in class taken a civil service examination? What was it like?

4. Who in the class has conducted interviews? What were some of the interviewee "mistakes"? Among the finalists, what was the determining factor: technical competence or interpersonal skills?

Team Activities

5. Discuss what you would do if, in an interview for a merit position, you were asked your party affiliation? What would you do if later you were asked when you graduated from college? If you refused to answer either of these questions and subsequently were not hired, would you do anything about it? How can the selection process be like a chess match?

6. Assume that you are on the search committee for a new management intern program. It has been determined that interns will be paid between $25,000 and $30,000, will have one-year appointments, and may apply for permanent positions if they receive good evaluations. The recruitment is to be announced nationally, but no travel money will be available; therefore, it is expected that the bulk of the candidates will be local. Design the selection process.

7. You are on the search committee for a public information officer (this is a non–civil service, exempt position in the organization). The last incumbent, although a friend of the agency director and a former reporter, was a disaster. Most of the time, people did not know what he did; when he did organize press conferences he sometimes became more controversial than the issue being discussed. Having learned her lesson, the director has asked you to nominate a slate of three ranked candidates. Design the selection process.

8. If selection techniques for a new or small organization did not exist, what rules would you set up if you had the authority?

9. Team members should investigate three organizations to determine the virtual nature of their recruitment and selection process. Compare as well as contrast your findings, and report them to the entire class.

Individual Assignment

10. You are the hiring supervisor for a junior management position in the city manager's office. The position would largely be responsible for special projects—both analysis (requiring strong quantitative skills) and implementation (mandating interpersonal and coordination skills). The three candidates interviewed all have recent MPA degrees. Set up a matrix of no more than five factors, give weights to the factors, and score and rank the candidates:

Jill Owens: Good interpersonal skills, pleasant personality, very talkative. Sometimes did not seem to listen very well, mediocre quantitative skills, highly energetic, one internship and one summer job in another city government, the second-best grades of the three, excellent references, and good appearance, manners, and understanding of city government. Former supervisors in the city were quite supportive of her candidacy but admitted that she was not exceptional.

Bruce Hughes: Mediocre interpersonal skills, pleasant personality, quiet but extremely attentive, superb quantitative skills, low energy, one internship in this city, the best grades of the group, below average appearance, acceptable manners, and unsure about his understanding of city government. Has a rave reference from the supervisor about a program evaluation project completed in his internship that resulted in highly successful changes.

Mary Washington: Excellent interpersonal skills, charming personality, very good listener, weak quantitative skills, high energy, no city experience but a year's experience in state government in a clerical function prior to finishing her graduate degree, the third-best grades among the candidates but still high, quite satisfactory references, very good manners, and little understanding of city government. Talked about her project management skills, using examples from church and volunteer work. She is the only "diversity" candidate.

11. Select a prospective job, perhaps one that you are interested in. Make sure that you have identified a position description (via a vacancy announcement or an organizational job classification description) first. Your task is to design a set of interview questions and include biographical, situational judgment, behaviorally anchored, and work knowledge items. The actual interview will be 45 minutes long. Also, decide if a work performance sample outside the interview setting is useful or critical for a high-quality selection process.

APPENDIX

The Professional Commitment Statement for Job Seekers

Just as recruitment for agencies must design a message to sell the job to prospective employees, so applicants need to design a message that sells their abilities to organizations and to their network. Job candidates have to give people arguments to help them; if they want others to make a job offer or introduce us to others, then they have to have reasons why they should do so. This is the central point: what matters is not what we want, but rather what others want and whether we can give it to them.

Degrees and accomplishments are not enough to get a job. Every year, many people from top universities end up without jobs. Why? Because people do not make hiring decisions based on résumés alone. Individuals are hired because others believe that they can help them in some way. This is the central idea that needs to be expressed—the idea that we have something important and useful to offer. Just like we chose this or that item in a store because it promises to be better than the next one, so someone will hire or recommend us because we promise to be better or more helpful than someone else. The job market is a market, after all. We need to sell ourselves. Ask this: "If you can't sell yourself, then who can?"

But people and organizations are not very good at job selection (i.e., hiring others). Of all of the skills in human resource management, this may be the least effective one; some people think that hiring is akin to flipping a coin with a 50–50 chance of selecting the best one. With so many opportunities to select the wrong person, the process is in part structured around *reducing the risk of making a bad hiring decision*.

Here are four ways organizations reduce the risk:

(1) Ensuring that the person has a strong and demonstrated commitment to the service area (e.g., economic development or social services. You do not want someone who after six months or the slightest setback would leave you).

(2) Ensuring that the individual has a past record of accomplishment. (That is, that the individual is someone who actually get things done—not merely someone who talks a good game.)

(3) Ensuring that the hired person has a record of getting along with others. (No matter how good a person's skills or accomplishments, people must have this quality.)

(4) Verifying that the candidate has the necessary (minimum) qualifications for the job.

A professional commitment statement (PCS) is designed to help job seekers address these points. When written, people often use parts of it in job interviews and with their networks. A PCS consists of three to four paragraphs that address the following questions:

- What difference do you seek to make for an organization? How do you want to make its stakeholders better off?
- What specific kinds of activities would you like to be involved in now, and in a few years?
- How are your answers to these questions consistent with your present or past experiences and commitments? State these experiences and commitments, which can be either professional and personal in nature.
- How did you come to embrace your commitments? Give some pertinent facts about yourself that others should know.
- What are some of the most important accomplishments and successes in your life? How do these relate to your commitments?
- What are some strengths that are required for being successful in that line of work? Show which ones of these you have, and the evidence for this claim. Also, state what you are currently doing to further improve the skills you need to succeed in your area.

Addressing these issues can make for a compelling and nice story about yourself. Consider this adapted example:[7]

I would like to utilize my background in economics, along with the managerial and analytical skills obtained by my current coursework in public administration, to aid in the delivery of quality healthcare services to individuals of all ages and income levels. In my concentration courses in healthcare administration, I wish to develop the skills necessary to meaningfully contribute to the efficiency and effectiveness of an organization aiming to provide affordable and accessible healthcare to individuals. I will commit myself to continuous self-education of current healthcare trends and policy issues in order to perform my professional duties as diligently as possible.

I wish to bring the same high levels of leadership and commitment to an organization as I have displayed in previous coursework, past organizational memberships, and past places of employment. In order to get some valuable exposure to and experience within the healthcare field, I have recently accepted an internship at State Hospital. I will be exposed to functional areas of the hospital such as quality management, human resources, accounting, and outpatient services. I will also have the opportunity to work on a project involving state hospital accreditation and will be able to sit in on many internal operational meetings with top administrators in order to gain personal insight into emerging issues facing this hospital as well as many others within the state system.

After completing the internship, I will seek employment either at a hospital or within a different type of healthcare setting, such as an [assisted living facility, home health care service, or state health department]. In order to help me, I will contact some administrators and ask to meet with them for about 15 minutes so more people can know what I seek. I will also ask people who I know to make introductions for me. Additionally, other students, faculty members, or fulltime employees at my current place of employment can let me know of available job opportunities or place me in contact with individuals who may be able to give me further advice about the healthcare field or otherwise direct me in my career path.

Such statements are as unique as the students who write them. The above PCS is of interest because it was initially made by a young graduate student with very little professional experience or background;

nonetheless, his commitment and drive are evident. It shows how past course work can be used to buttress claims of commitment, though some additional past, extracurricular accomplishments might have been mentioned, as well. Most students need a few iterations to get their PCSs right, so that they show a logical thread, substance, and energy. In class, students have the option to share their PCSs, which gives everyone an opportunity to ask questions and learn from feedback. In another class, students post their initial PCSs online, get feedback from at least two or three students, and then repost a final PCS a few weeks later.

A common problem is that some students do not know what difference they want to make; they do not know what career they want. Typically, this means that they have a few different ideas that are attractive, but they have not yet pursued any of them. In that case, we tell them to just choose one and run with it for the sake of this PCS. A follow-up assignment is to network with four people by sharing with them their PCS. This gives further information about the career path and students can then decide whether they in fact want to pursue it. Sometimes the only way to know what to do is by doing it.

A second problem is that some students are pursuing very large and long-term dreams. Some people might want to be a sheriff, governor, or agency director. That is fine, of course, and big dreams are to be encouraged, but the PCSs should focus on next steps, not final destinations. There are also some concerns with sharing dreams. First, you might be telling others that you want to be their boss, and they may not be ready to hear that. Second, you would sound arrogant and project yourself as an overly ambitious career-climber, someone who needs to be watched out for and even guarded against. Third, it suggests that you already know that you will not change your mind as new experiences unfold. That sounds unrealistic and shows poor judgment. So, while everyone should have ambitions, it may be best to keep such far-flung expressions to yourself, perhaps sharing only with those who are very close to you.

How useful is it to have a PCS? It surely helps in developing a good résumé, which needs to reflect and substantiate the PCS. But a PCS also helps with difficult interview questions:

"Tell me about yourself."

"Why do you want to work here?"

"What did you like and dislike about your last job?"

"What is your biggest accomplishment?"

"What is your greatest strength? Your largest weakness?"

"Where do you see yourself in five years?"

While some job candidates struggle with these questions, a good PCS makes them a breeze:

"Tell me about yourself." "I am strongly committed to (whatever is stated in your PCS). . . ."

"Why do you want to work here?" "Because your place offers me an opportunity to pursue my commitment to. . . ."

"What did you like and dislike about your last job?" "I liked (disliked) that it gave me (not enough) opportunity to pursue my commitment to. . . ."

"What is your biggest accomplishment?" "I have several, some of them directly related to my commitment to. . . ."

The PCS is a great basis for succeeding in job interviews. A PCS also helps in networking, providing job seekers with a coherent message and clearly justified reasons for asking others for their support.

Supplying your PCS to members of your network for comments provides insights and job leads. Some questions are, "What kind of jobs are available for what I want to do?" "What advice does the interviewee offer for someone pursuing this career?" "What are the ideal qualifications and experiences for these jobs?" "How can I best get these jobs?" Job seekers can proactively contact managers in departments where they would like to work, thereby expanding their network well before any job interview. Doing so helps job seekers learn about career opportunities; some interviewees may follow up with job seekers later, informing them of opportunities that since have become available.

Developing a PCS is an essential task for every job seeker. Many successful officials do so, even when not stated on paper. In the end, the rationale of a strong PCS was well articulated by President John F. Kennedy in his inauguration address: "Ask not what your country can do for you—ask what you can do for your country." Or, your prospective employer, as the case may be.

NOTES

1. Patronage certainly has not been wiped out, nor is it ever likely to be. For example, it still exists in Schedule C exceptions (confidential staff for federal executives) and overseas appointments at the federal level. Many state systems have uneven coverage and experience covert intrusion, such as moving political appointees to civil service permanent positions by "persuasion" or executive order. Local systems may be merit systems in name only, and very small jurisdictions may be exempted from state civil service requirements entirely.

2. This description refers to "ideal" merit systems. In reality, most have seniority elements infused in them for promotional opportunities. In other words, many merit systems limit promotional hires to agency or governmental personnel, although it is possible that candidates outside the agency might be more meritorious on technical grounds.

3. The "Peter principle" states that people are promoted until they achieve a position in which they are incompetent (Peter & Hull, 1969).

4. Higher degrees of correlation between the integrity factor measured in the new "honesty tests" and one of the "Big Five" personality factors, conscientiousness, have generally been most highly supported (Viswesvaran et al., 2007).

5. Ultimately, there is considerable overlap among performance tests, aptitude tests, and psychological tests, which rely on a continuum ranging from concrete to abstract predictors.

6. An alternative structure is the self-managed team, which embodies characteristics of both a hiring panel and a hiring supervisor. As in any other group activity, the team has the opportunity to provide a substantially rich experience if the members understand their work and do it well.

7. We thank Michael Kennedy, MPA graduate from the Louisiana State University, for allowing us to use this example. We adapted it with minor edits from his original posting in class.

REFERENCES

Ackerman, P. L., & Kanfer, R. (1993). Integrating laboratory and field study for improving selection: Development of a battery to predict air traffic controller success. *Journal of Applied Psychology, 78*(3), 413–432.

Anderson, N., & Witvliet, C. (2008). Fairness reactions to personnel selection methods: An international comparison between the Netherlands, the United States, France, Spain, Portugal, and Singapore. *International Journal of Selection and Assessment, 16*(1), 1–13.

Arvey, R. D., Nutting, S. M., & Landon, T. E. (1992). Validation strategies for physical ability testing in police and fire settings. *Public Personnel Management, 21*(3), 301–312.

Bartone, P. T., Roland, R. R., Picano, J. J., & Williams, T. J. (2008). Psychological hardiness predicts success in US Army Special Force candidates. *International Journal of Selection and Assessment, 16*(1), 78–81.

Bowman, J. S., & West, J. (2007). *American public service: Radical reform and the merit system.* New York: Taylor and Francis.

Bowman, J. S., & West, J. (2009, January/February). To "re-Hatch" public employees or not? An ethical analysis of the relaxation of restrictions on political activities in civil service. *Public Administration Review, 68,* 52–62.

Branti v. Finkel, 445 U.S. 507 (1980).

Buckley, P., Minette, K., Joy, D., & Michaels, J. (2004). The use of an automated employment recruiting and screening system for temporary professional employees: A case study. *Human Resource Management, 43*(2/3), 233–241.

Campbell, J. P. (2001). *Project A: Exploring the limits of performance improvement through personnel selection and classification.* Hillsdale, NJ: Erlbaum.

Carlson, K. D. (2003). The staffing cycles framework: Viewing staffing as a system of decision events. *Journal of Management, 29*(1), 51–78.

Condrey, S. E., & Maranto, R. (2001). *Radical reform of the civil service.* Lanham, MD: Lexington Books.

Connerley, M. L., Arvey, R. D., Gilliland, S. W., Mae, F. A., Paetzold, R. L., & Sackett, P. R. (2001). Selection in the workplace: Whose rights prevail? *Employee Responsibilities and Rights Journal, 13*(1), 1–13.

Connerley, M. L., & Bernardy, M. (2001). Criminal background checks for prospective and current employees: Current practices among municipal agencies. *Public Personnel Management, 30*(2), 173–183.

Corcoran, C. (2005). Psychometric testing: Can it add value to HR? *Accountancy Ireland, 37*(4), 63–65.

Dineen, B. R., Noe, R. A., & Wang, C. (2004). Perceived fairness of Web-based applicant screening procedures: Weighing the rules of justice and the role of individual differences. *Human Resource Management, 43*(2/3), 127–145.

Drug-Free Workplace Act, P.L. 100–6klj90, 102 Stat. 4304 (1988).

Elrod v. Burns, 427 U.S. 347 (1976).

Gore, A. (1993). *Creating a government that works better and costs less: The report of the National Performance Review.* Washington, DC: Government Printing Office.

Grensing-Pophal, L. (2006). Internal solutions. *HRMagazine, 51*(12), 75–79.

Hays, S. W., & Kearney, R. C. (1999). *The transformation of public sector human resource management.* Unpublished manuscript.

Hogan, J. (1991). Structure of physical performance in occupational tasks. *Journal of Applied Psychology, 76*(4), 495–507.

Howard, A. (Ed.). (1995). *The changing nature of work.* San Francisco: Jossey-Bass.

Ingraham, P. W., Selden, S. C., & Moynihan, D. P. (2000). People and performance: Challenges for the future: The report from the Wye River Conference. *Public Administration Review, 60*(1), 54–60.

Jesdanun, A. (2007, May 6). Video résumés gain fans, but many experts skeptical. *Arizona Republic,* Sunday, p. E1.

Jordan-Nowe, A. (2007, July 25). "Soft skills" again treasured. *Arizona Republic,* p. E1.

Kellough, J. E., & Nigro, L. G. (2006). *Civil service reform in the states: Personnel policies and politics at the subnational level.* Albany: SUNY.

Krajewski, H. T., Goffin, R. D., McCarthy, J. M., Rothstein, M. G., & Johnston, N. (2006). Comparing the validity of structured interviews for managerial employees: Should we look to the past or focus on the future? *Journal of Occupational and Organizational Psychology, 79*(3), 411–432.

Lievens, F., Highhouse, S., & De Corte, W. (2005, September). The importance of traits and abilities in supervisors' hirability decisions as a function of method of assessment. *Journal of Occupational and Organizational Psychology, 78,* 453–470.

Lievens, F., Peeters, H., & Schollaert, E. (2008). Situational judgment tests: A review of recent research. *Personnel Review, 37*(4), 426–441.

McCarthy v. Philadelphia Civil Service Commission, 424 U.S. 645 (1976).

McDaniel, M. A., Hartman, N. S., Whetzel, D. L., & Grubb, W. L. (2007). Situational judgment tests, response instructions, and validity: A meta-analysis. *Personnel Psychology, 60*(1), 63–91.

Morgeson, F. P., Campion, M. A., Dipboye, R. L., Hollenbeck, R. L., Murphy, K., & Schmitt, N. (2007). Are we getting fooled again? Coming to terms with limitations in the use of personality tests for personnel selection. *Personnel Psychology, 60*(4), 1029–1049.

Mosher, F. C. (1982). *Democracy and the public service* (2nd ed.). New York: Oxford University Press.

Nye, C. D., Do, B., Drasgow, F., & Fine, S. (2008). Two-step testing in employee selection: Is score inflation a problem? *International Journal of Selection and Assessment, 16*(2), 112–120.

Omnibus Transportation Employees Testing Act, P.L. 102–143, 105 Stat. 952 (1991).

Ones, D. S., Dilchert, S., Viswesvaran, C., & Judge, T. A. (2007). In support of personality assessment in organizational setting. *Personnel Psychology, 69*(4), 995–1027.

Partnership for Public Service. (2008a). *Getting on board.* Washington, DC: Author.

Partnership for Public Service. (2008b). *A golden opportunity: Recruiting Baby Boomers into government.* Washington, DC: Author.

Peter, L. J., & Hull, R. (1969). *The Peter principle.* New York: William Morrison.

Ployhart, R. E. (2006). Staffing in the 21st century: New challenges and strategic opportunities. *Journal of Management, 32*(6), 868–897.

Poe, A. C. (2003). Behavioral interviewing can tell you if an applicant just out of college has traits for the job. *HRMagazine, 48*(10), 95–99.

Potosky, D., & Bobko, P. (2004). Selection testing via the Internet: Practical considerations and exploratory empirical findings. *Personnel Psychology, 57*(4), 1003–1034.

Rae, M. J., & Earles, J. A. (1994). The ubiquitous predictiveness of g. In M. G. Rumsey, C. B. Walker, & J. H. Harris (Eds.), *Personnel selection and classification* (pp. 127–136). Hillsdale, NJ: Lawrence Erlbaum.

Rutan v. Republican Party of Illinois, 497 U.S. 62 (1990).

Ryan, A. M., & Tippins, N. T. (2004). Attracting and selecting: What psychological research tells us. *Human Resource Management, 43*(4), 305–318.

Schmidt, F. L., & Hunter, J. E. (1998). The validity and utility of selection methods in personnel psychology: Practical and theoretical implications of 85 years of research findings. *Psychological Bulletin, 124*(2), 262–275.

State of Iowa, (2006, December). Iowa Department of Administrative Services, Human Resources Enterprise. *Applicant Screening Manual.*

Taylor, P. J., Pajo, K., Cheung, G. W., & Stringfield, P. (2004). Dimensionality and validity of a structured telephone reference check procedure. *Personnel Psychology, 57*(3), 745–772.

Uniform guidelines on employee selection procedures. (1978). Title 29. Chapter XIV, Part 1607.

U.S. Government Accounting Office (GAO). (2003). *Human capital: Opportunities to improve executive agencies' hiring processes.* Washington, DC: Author.

U.S. Merit Systems Protection Board (MSPB). (2001a). *The federal merit promotion program.* Washington, DC: Author.

U.S. Merit Systems Protection Board (MSPB). (2001b). *The U.S. Office of Personnel Management in retrospect.* Washington, DC: Author.

U.S. Merit Systems Protection Board (MSPB). (2002). *Assessing federal job-seekers in a delegated examining environment.* Washington, DC: Author.

U.S. Merit Systems Protection Board (MSPB). (2003). *The federal selection interview: Unrealized potential.* Washington, DC: Author.

U.S. Merit Systems Protection Board (MSPB). (2004). *Managing federal recruitment: Issues, insights, and illustrations.* Washington, DC: Author.

U.S. Merit Systems Protection Board (MSPB). (2005). *Reference checking in federal hiring: Making the call.* Washington, DC: Author.

U.S. Merit Systems Protection Board (MSPB). (2006). *Reforming federal hiring: Beyond faster and cheaper.* Washington, DC: Author.

U.S. Merit Systems Protection Board (MSPB). (2008a). *Attracting the next generation: A look at federal entry-level new hires.* Washington, DC: Author.

U.S. Merit Systems Protection Board (MSPB). (2008b). *In search of highly skilled workers: A study on the hiring of upper-level employees from outside the federal government.* Washington, DC: Author.

U.S. Office of Personnel Management (OPM). (1999). *Delegated examining operations handbook: A guide for federal agency examining offices.* Washington, DC: Author.

Van Riper, P. (1958). *History of the United States civil service.* New York: Harper & Row.

Van Wart, M., & Berman, E. (1999). Contemporary public sector productivity values: Narrower scope, tougher standards, and new rules of the game. *Public Productivity & Management Review, 22*(3), 326–347.

Van Wart, M., Cayer, N. J., & Cook, S. (1993). *Handbook of training and development for the public sector.* San Francisco: Jossey-Bass.

Viswesvaran, C., Deller, J., & Ones, D. S. (2007). Personality measures in personnel selection: Some new contributions. *International Journal of Selection and Assessment, 15*(3), 354–358.

Walter, R. J. (1992). Public employers' potential liability from negligence in employment decisions. *Public Administration Review, 52,* 491–495.

Werbel, J. D., Song, L. J., & Yan, S. (2008). The influence of external recruitment practices on job search practices across domestic labor markets: A comparison of the United States and China. *International Journal of Selection and Assessment, 16*(2), 93–101.

Wolf, A., & Jenkins, A. (2006). Explaining greater test use for selection: The role of HR professionals in a world of expanding regulation. *Human Resource Management Journal, 16*(2), 193–213.

Chapter 5

Position Management

Judicious Plan or Jigsaw Puzzle?

The right people in the right jobs.

—Otto von Bismarck, Speech to the North German Reichstag, 1875

After studying this chapter, you should be able to

- identify the profound trends and paradoxical tensions affecting traditional classification strategies that may remake position management systems in the 21st century,
- differentiate among the three overarching types of personnel systems that are found—generally in layers—in most public sphere organizations,
- write a job description,
- conduct informal job analyses and understand when and how more-rigorous methods are used,
- understand the different uses of position classification and understand how jobs are grouped together in theory and in practice, and
- distinguish between job analysis and job evaluation.

Position management is generally thought to be a dry science of little interest to anyone but a few specialists in human resource departments. Such a notion is full of irony and paradoxes, if not outright misconceptions. First, position classification is as much an art as a science: it is actually composed of different systems, each with distinctly different value biases. Furthermore, the biases of each system shift over time. The art, then, is understanding the different values that exist in various systems; the science is the rational implementation of that set of values. Unfortunately, when system values become too rigid and when classification and compensation issues are treated as laws based on hard science, an unbalanced character- ization of position management exists.[1] This tendency was well expressed in a classic essay by Wallace Sayre (1948): "The Triumph of Technique Over Purpose."

Second, the rational order conveyed by classification systems is generally overstated. Most systems of large organizations are quite fragmented, and sometimes they are haphazard because competing stresses such as politics, market forces, merit, social equity, and union influence distort them over time. The classification systems of most small organizations (which make up the vast majority of American governments) are actually **piecemeal personnel systems** rather than ideal classification systems.

Third, although formal methods of **job analysis** and **job evaluation** are often preached in management texts and elsewhere, they are not always used in practice. Informal methods are as common, and such skills are equally important for employees and managers. Finally, although classification may seem to be a subject of little utility to those who are not human resource specialists or managers, it is actually a critical source of knowledge and, by extension, source of power in agencies. Understanding the central organizing structures is as important as budgeting or management principles (Condrey, 1998).

Although classification systems generally convey a sense of judiciousness, they are probably more accurately viewed as jigsaw puzzles. One should not be put off by this realization, however. Because of their importance to job aspirants, wage earners, status seekers, career strategists, managers, executives, and legislators, one should consider them fascinating cornerstones in the complex organizational universe. Decisions about position management are very important in all professional lives, as well as in the health of organizations. Mastering a general knowledge of the tools used in classification is a critical competency for today's manager.

▪ THREE TYPES OF PERSONNEL STRATEGIES

The public sector is composed of three personnel strategies, each of which is represented in a layered fashion in human resource systems. Selection is the core principle in each of these strategies, and it equally affects the subsequent classification and management of positions. The three systems are based on (1) election, (2) appointment, or (3) rules (composed of merit, seniority, and representativeness factors).[2] Although discussed in the previous chapter, it is important to review the three types of personnel strategies here in the context of position classification.

First, election as a strategy for policy making in personnel selection is the foundation of democratic states. The people choose who will make and execute the laws and, to some degree, who will interpret them. Electoral systems emphasize values, debate, political responsiveness, and generalized (rather than expert) knowledge of government. Elected officials are selected as the leaders of most public sector systems but are required to serve terms and be reelected periodically if they want a career in government. Two types of elected officials are common. The most visible is the full-time official who serves in a major office and whose salary is sufficient to provide a living. The more frequent type, however, is the "citizen-legislator" who serves part-time and whose salary is modest or inconsequential.[3]

A second personnel strategy is appointment by elected officials. Generally, appointed officials serve at the will of those who select them. The most salient appointed officials are those who run agencies as cabinet-level secretaries, directors, and commissioners, and their chief deputies. These employees also typically include policy-related advisers and confidential staff. Ideally, elected officials select individuals for full-time paid jobs who they believe are competent or meritorious in addition to being in general agreement about their policy positions. Common practice used to allow elected officials to choose appointees in general government service on the spoils principle—either to reward political supporters or to indirectly enhance one's own personal situation (such as through the appointment of family members), without regard to competence. Such practices still occur and produce well-publicized scandals, but the public relations damage (and sometimes legal and electoral consequences) and ethics laws generally act as a restraint. Gross spoils selection at the career level (i.e., **civil service**) is quite rare today, largely because of court action (Hamilton, 1999), although the "thickening" of government (see the Introduction) with numerous high- and midlevel political appointees should not be overlooked. Some of the most common are those who serve as "citizen appointees" on innumerable boards and commissions at all levels of government on a part-time basis for little or no remuneration.

A third strategy is rule-based selection, which affects the bulk of those in the public service and is the primary focus of this chapter. This strategy gives precedence to merit and is based on technical qualifications and competitive selection. Removal from office is often only for cause (see Chapters 2 and 11). Advanced forms of the merit philosophy in organizations evolved in the 19th century. Two fundamental merit strategies exist (see Exhibit 5.1 for a comparison of the two strategies). **Rank-in-job** personnel strategies[4] are the norm in the United States but nearly unknown elsewhere. Rank and salary are determined by the position that one holds. Substantial salary increases and higher status are attained only through a better job (promotion or reclassification), but multiple promotions within an organization are

---

Exhibit 5.1 Job Versus Rank Classification

There are two approaches to merit classification: job and rank. Although neither may be found in pure form (one sees approximations in organizations), there are very real differences in emphasis. The nearest approximation of the job/position (or "open") strategy is the civil service; the best approximation of the rank (or "closed") strategy is the military officer corps. A number of features distinguish the two types.

Job (Open) Merit Strategy	Rank (Closed) Merit Strategy
Focus on work: "Job makes the person"	Focus on individual: "person makes the job"
Entry based on technical qualifications only	Entry based on general qualifications and long-term potential
Lateral entry allowed	Lateral entry discouraged or prohibited
Promotion based on open competition in most cases	Promotion based on evaluation by superiors
Grade level maintained as long as performance is satisfactory	Expectation that rank will increase over time; an "up-or-out" philosophy will screen out incumbents
Career development is largely the responsibility of the incumbent	Career development is largely planned by the organization through specified career paths
Tends to focus on/produce specialists	Tends to focus on/produce generalists

uncommon beyond the predetermined job series, such as City Planner I, II, and III. Career development is the responsibility of the incumbent (jobholder), and promotions are normally open competitions, including **lateral entry** from outside the organization (leading to the term **open personnel system**). Merit selection relies heavily on systems with many grades or levels.

Rank-in-person strategies are unusual in the United States except for the military and paramilitary organizations such as public safety departments, the foreign service, academic departments, some health agencies, and the federal Senior Executive Service. (Exhibit 5.2 provides some typical examples of occupational ranks.) Rank-in-person emphasizes the development of incumbents over time, especially within the organization, and tends to lead to closed systems. **Closed personnel systems** provide few opportunities for lateral entry for those outside the organization. They allow for more position mobility because personnel carry their rank with them no matter what their current assignment. Promotions are prized and are expected over time. Closed personnel systems typically have a strong **up-or-out philosophy** so that those who are not promoted eventually may be terminated. Ranks may number from as few as three to as many as 10 for military officers.

Hybrid or mixed strategies are also possible. In selected cases, public servants are appointed but serve for set terms (such as state public safety directors and university regents), similar to elected officials. Federal judges and some state judges are appointed for life. There

---

Exhibit 5.2   Three Examples of Occupational Ranks

Army Officer Ranks	Fire Department Ranks	University/Faculty Ranks
Quasi-officers:	Recruit	Unranked/untenured:
Cadets	Firefighter	Teaching assistant
Warrant officers	Engineer	Instructor
Company officers:	Medic	Adjunct faculty
Second lieutenant	Lieutenant	Ranked/untenured:
First lieutenant	Captain	Assistant professor
Captain	District fire chief	Ranked/tenured:
Field officers:	Assistant fire chief	Associate professor
Major	Fire marshal	Full professor
Lieutenant colonel	Deputy fire chief	Professor with special status
Colonel	Fire chief	(distinguished, regent's professor, endowed chair)
General or flag officers:		
Brigadier general		
Major general		
Lieutenant general		
General		
5-star general (general of the army)		

is a renewed interest in linking rule-based (merit) selection with termination processes similar to those in appointment strategies—that is, **at-will employment** in which property rights to jobs are severely limited.[5] Although at-will employment is still the exception rather than the rule in the public sector, this chapter will discuss important contemporary examples of the drive to reform the civil service. The conclusion will focus on this and other trends affecting rank-in-position and rank-in-person systems. (For an example of this debate, see Bowman & West, 2007a, 2007b; DeSoto & Castillo, 1995; Somma & Fox, 1997.)

■■ THE ORIGINS OF POSITION CLASSIFICATION AND MANAGEMENT

In the first century of public sector employment in the United States, from 1789 to 1883, position classification did not exist as a rational system. Positions tended to be created and salaried in an ad hoc fashion, largely based on a **patronage system**, social class, and regional representativeness, and only coincidentally by merit. The initial period was relatively elitist and staid, but public service evolved over the 19th century into a tumultuous system. Congress enacted legislation in 1853 establishing four major job classes with salary rates for each of the classes. This legislation was frequently ignored, however, and all levels of government struggled with merit, equity, and consistency considerations (Mosher, 1982; Van Riper, 1958).

The civil service reform movement, which had gained steam by the end of the 19th century, changed the landscape of position classification and management over time. Nevertheless, the importance of reform should not overshadow other influences. At the same time that political influence was being reduced in recruitment, selection, promotion, discipline, and other personnel processes, principles of modern management were being more generally introduced. By the early 1900s, Frederick Taylor's scientific management, whether or not it was truly "scientific," held great sway over the development of position classification processes. Taylor promoted the idea that there was generally "one best way" to accomplish work, a way that could be found by thorough work analysis. This effectively combated the Jacksonian notion that the government work was "so plain and simple that men of intelligence may readily qualify themselves" (President Andrew Jackson, as quoted in Van Riper, 1958, p. 36).

Work analysis provided the means to select superior methods of performance, to identify those who could perform better, and to provide superior training. Systematic **job descriptions** became commonplace, and work relationships became rationalized. Work analysis highlights differences and breaks work into component parts. Because of this, the scientific management movement then started a long-term trend of "pigeonholing" work, breaking it into hundreds and ultimately thousands of different jobs at dozens of different levels. See, for example, the old and now rarely used *Dictionary of Occupational Titles,* or *DOT* (U.S. Department of Labor, 1991), which had 12,741 occupations listed. The contemporary version is the online ONET, which consolidated the occupational titles to 812 in 2006. (See LaPolice, Carter, & Johnson, 2008, for validity.)[6]

The Classification Act of 1923, capturing the new wisdom of scientific management, provided a model of a rational **position management system**. It established that (a) positions and not individuals were to be classified, (b) **job duties** and responsibilities were the distinguishing characteristics of jobs, (c) qualifications were to be a critical factor in determining classification status, and (d) a member of a class would be qualified for all other positions in the class. This act enhanced legislative ability to monitor and control positions in terms of overall employee numbers, grade ceilings, and salary ranges. The Classification Act of 1949 created a separate schedule for white- and blue-collar workers, which is typical of a trend to divide personnel systems into occupational clusters. The proliferation of rank-in-position systems promoted the idea of fitting people to jobs. During this period, managerial efficiency and legislative control were emphasized on the one hand, and employee procedural rights were increasingly enhanced on the other. Jobs tended to become narrower and less flexible.

Equal opportunity substantially changed position management through legislation addressing discrimination based on race, color, religion, gender, national origin, age, and disabilities. Particularly important was the passage of the Equal Pay Act of 1963, which addressed gender discrimination in pay. The notion of equal pay for equal work, regardless of personal characteristics of the job incumbent, was taken to its logical legal extension, as was equal opportunity for employment and advancement. Although unions in the private sector experienced a marked decline by the 1980s, unions in the public sector continued to increase in numbers and power.

Even though both equal opportunity and worker representation have obvious benefits, the excesses of the position management systems initiated after the Pendleton Act had also become apparent: classification rigidity, extreme specialization and pigeonholing, weak results-oriented accountability, and technical complexity. For example, critics complained that promotion from one **job classification** to another had become positively litigious, the 2,500 different job classifications had become excessive, firing nonperforming employees had become a nightmare, and the technical complexity of nearly three dozen pay systems had become byzantine. State and local government systems tended to demonstrate the same symptoms on a smaller scale. By the mid-1990s, equal opportunity began to recede as the dominant concern in personnel systems (Ewoh & Elliott, 1997).

Although the Civil Service Reform Act of 1978 provided an important initial attempt at reform, the most recent human resources era actually starts in the 1990s and continues today with an emphasis on broad employee categories, more procedural flexibility, more rigorous employee accountability, and technical simplification (Hays, 2004).[7] Examples include **broadbanding**, reinventing government, simplification initiatives in personnel policies and manuals, and revisions in the civil service system. Broadbanding occurs when several grades are combined, creating a wide salary range for a position. Formal promotions are not required for pay movement (as is the case with more traditional—and narrow—classification series), although milestone progress is still required and documented. In some versions, people are ranked in a single classification, such as entry level, journeyman, senior, and specialist, but these designations are determined by the unit rather than by a personnel department or civil service commission. Reinventing government and simplification initiatives in the early 1990s tended to decentralize many personnel functions to the field and, concurrently, to streamline procedures so that field staff (such as field offices, individual departments, or units) can implement them. Current civil service reform focuses on enhancing employee accountability to meet moderate or definable performance standards (U.S. Merit Systems Protection Board [MSPB], 1999). The most dramatic examples of this to date are the termination of the civil service system in Georgia in 1996, the creation of more flexible personnel systems for the U.S. Department of Homeland Security and U.S. Department of Defense (2003), and the rise of employment contracts as well as posttenure faculty review processes in state universities

(Isfahani, 1998). Although the federal classification has yet to undergo major changes with respect to the 1949 act, exemptions from it are increasing (Cipolla, 1999), and recommendations for a moderate to radical overhaul seem to be increasing (Nelson, 2004; U.S. Government Accountability Office [GAO], 2003).

A final historical issue is the effort by human resource experts to utilize a single overarching taxonomy of job titles so that they can be compared in and across industries and countries. In practical terms, classification systems ultimately will be customized; the ideal is that they all use a common language and framework, however. That framework is the Standard Occupational Classification. It divides jobs into 23 major groups, 96 minor groups, 449 broad occupations, and 821 detailed occupations (Pollack, Simons, Romero, & Hausser, 2002) and relates closely to the ONET classification system. It is used by federal departments such as the Bureau of Labor Statistics' *Occupational Outlook Handbook* (Bureau of Labor Statistics, 2008), the U.S. Bureau of the Census, and the U.S. Office of Personnel Management's (OPM, n.d.) *Federal Classification and Job Grading Systems*. Although the hope is that other levels of government—as well as the private sector, which uses the products of these agencies—will eventually gravitate toward the revised Standard Occupational Classification, this convergence of systems is slow to occur because of legacy classification systems.

With this historical background related to position management, this chapter now turns to functional aspects: what the basics in designing jobs are and how current jobs are analyzed, how technically competent descriptions are written, and how jobs are organized into systems for effective human resource management.

▪▪ JOB DESIGN AND JOB ANALYSIS

The fundamental importance of **job design** and job analysis cannot be underestimated. Together, job design—creating balanced jobs in the context of the organizational environment, technology, and resource demands—as well as job analysis—ensuring that the functions of jobs are rationally presented for internal and external uses—form the basis of most human resource functions! See Exhibit 5.3 for how these two skills provide the undergirding for many other areas.

Creating or Recreating Jobs

Job design is the specification of job features, primarily the duties, the quantity of work expected, and the level of responsibility (Clegg & Spencer, 2007; Sherwood, 2000). The *duties* include major work functions to be accomplished; a key issue is the breadth of those duties. Just how narrow or broad should they be? The *quantity of work* aspect determines the balance of those duties. In many jobs, a single duty may take up more than half of an incumbent's time, with others duties taking up relatively small amounts of time. In other jobs, the work is evenly distributed among the duties. The *level of responsibility* of the job relates to the independence of the incumbent and to where the position will be placed in the organizational hierarchy. What types of decisions can the incumbent make independently? At what level and how frequently will the incumbent be reviewed? Also, what will be the scope

---

Exhibit 5.3   Common Examples of Job Design and Analysis

Case #1 (job design): A moderate-sized division realizes that a series of functions are being performed at too high a level. The assistant director of the division has come to act as the Web master, information technology (IT) troubleshooter, and public relations officer for the division. These additional roles prevent him from focusing on operations, which is his role according to his job description. Rather than creating a second assistant director to handle the regular operational workload, the division wants to create specialized functions. The division now interacts with the public a great deal through their Web page, which needs daily maintenance and updates; this role is not yet considered a full-time job. The division also needs a local IT troubleshooter to fix easy systems problems and to manage software purchases; complex problems can be referred to the organization's IT department. Furthermore, because of the Web presence, the division wants to be more proactive in providing good public relations stories as well as educational messages to the public. At first, the hope was that all these functions could be performed by the same person who would provide excellent *job enlargement*. However, after talking with people in these positions in other organizations, the job analyst found that the array of skills seemed too different, and was concerned that combining them into one job would diminish *job specialization* too greatly. The division ultimately decided to hire an IT troubleshooter and Webmaster as well as a separate public information officer who would take over a number of community outreach responsibilities. The IT-Webmaster would report to the public information officer, who would in turn report to the assistant director.

Case #2 (job analysis): A fire department has requested that the human resource division review two series—the firefighter series and the emergency management technician (EMT) series. When the fire department expanded into first-responder services in the 1980s, firefighters did not do medical services generally. Personnel were even segregated by vehicles—fire trucks and ambulances. Over time, however, the expectation of new firefighter recruits to be able to perform basic first responder needs had become routine, and the city could not afford to maintain a large presence exclusively for firefighting when less than 10% of the calls were for fire service, most were for EMT, and a sizeable portion was for various types of rescue services and hazardous materials clean-up. After reviewing existing positions, sending questions to all those affected, conducting focus group interviews, and even performing a number of ride-alongs, the human resources department proposed a new joint firefighter-EMT series. The new series would pay better, but increase the training and job requirements substantially. Hiring would cease in the old series until those classifications have no incumbents, at which time they can be eliminated.

---

of the incumbent's decision making? Will the person have subordinates or levels of subordinates? Will the incumbent have responsibility for one or more program areas? Will the individual have fiduciary responsibility or a legal investiture as the "responsible officer"? Other aspects of job design that may or may not be stipulated include when the individual will carry out responsibilities, the order of tasks and how the incumbent will do them, where the individual will carry out the tasks, additional reporting relationships beyond the incumbent's supervisor (if any), competencies the individual will need to perform the job, the training the individual will need to do the job, and so forth.

Job design—and redesign—are important for managers at all levels. It is their responsibility to maximize both productivity and employee satisfaction; the creation and changing of jobs is an indispensable tool in that effort. Small and large examples of job design are plentiful: A subordinate wants a reclassification to a higher level and the manager must decide whether to support the request and to ensure that the incumbent takes on greater responsibility if approved. A department has grown and it is time to have employees move from being generalists to being specialists. A division has received a new mandate and must create a new unit to handle the programmatic responsibility. An agency is forced to downsize and must decide how to accommodate its work with fewer people. A new technology creates an opportunity to reassign or redesign work (Institute of Management & Administration [IOMA], 2003).

Keeping one eye on the efficiency and effectiveness of productivity is a fundamental responsibility in job design; doing so supports the organization's mission and provides the public with high value. The well-know efficiency consideration relates to the narrowness of responsibilities. **Job specialization**—narrowing job responsibilities—tends to promote higher levels of task mastery and thus speed, less training, and simpler incumbent replacement. In many situations, job specialization leads to more manageable jobs and greater professionalization. In other situations, however, job specialization can be perceived as treating employees like replaceable parts who are in deadening assembly-line-type jobs. The effectiveness consideration relates to how positions are grouped together and to overall workflow. **Process management** is the term for ensuring that the flow of work among individuals and units is as rational (smooth and optimal) as possible. Perhaps the workflow has become suboptimal over time, as people and technology have changed. A work flowchart may reveal that there are steps that can be eliminated in a process, tasks that can be reassigned for greater coherence, or a step that needs to be added to ensure a better customer focus. If the changes that need to be made are radical, it is called **process reengineering**.

Productivity is important, to be sure, but job designers must keep one eye on employee satisfaction. Job satisfaction invariably leads to reduced employee problems such as grievances, better retention rates, and sometimes—but not always—better productivity (Kelly, 1992). Some of the classic considerations here are task variety, development, and autonomy. **Job enlargement** increases the scope of a job by extending the range of job duties and responsibilities. It can sometimes be an antidote to jobs that are perceived as too narrow or stifling, or in which the work is too fragmented from either a worker or client perspective. **Job rotation** is a means of developing employees at all levels so that they understand the "big picture" and become cross-trained. **Job enrichment** attempts to motivate employees by giving them more authority or independence for organizing their work and solving problems. (See Exhibit 5.4 for a typical example of job design.) Because of the importance of employee satisfaction and the numerous other factors that affect it, Chapter 6 is devoted entirely to this topic.

Analyzing and Describing Current Jobs

A job analysis is a systematic process of collecting data for determining the knowledge, skills, and abilities (KSAs) required to perform a job successfully and to make numerous

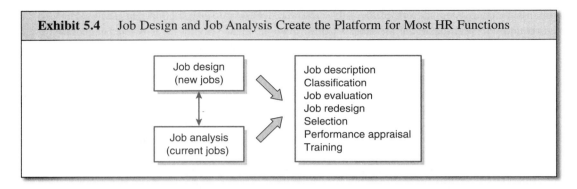

Exhibit 5.4   Job Design and Job Analysis Create the Platform for Most HR Functions

judgments about it (OPM, 2006). It typically is used as a key tool for recruitment, classification, selection, training, employee appraisal, and other functions (Jenkins & Curtin, 2006). In terms of recruitment and position classification, job analysis provides up-to-date information for position announcements and a thorough and rigorous basis for the writing of job descriptions and ranking jobs. For selection, analysis is decisive for determining valid selection criteria that are both practical and legally defensible. For training and development, analysis can be indispensable in identifying and detailing the competencies needed as well as the specific gaps that typically exist between those competencies and incumbent performance. When considering employee appraisal, job analysis can help define concrete standards, and to catalog evaluation criteria. In terms of other human resource functions, job analysis is critical in making reasonable accommodations for disabled persons as well as in redesigning jobs.

Job analysis is a powerful instrument because it offers a unique opportunity for learning about fundamental aspects of the organization as well as an opportunity for thoughtful examination of current practices. Executives can encourage job analyses to make sure that the organizational structure reflects current practices, technology, and work requirements. It is likely that job analyses will discover such inefficiencies as excessive middle management, outdated hardware, absence of appropriate software, and areas of under- and overstaffing. Managers can target problem jobs or clusters of jobs as opportunities for innovation in job redesign or workflow. Employees can study their colleagues' positions for cross-training in informal job analyses or their own positions for better understanding and to recommend changes in their positions. Even students outside the organization can use job analysis methodology as a part of their internship experiences and as a marketable skill, similar to finance management or policy analysis.

Job analyses rely on a combination of four information collection methods: (1) archival data, (2) questionnaires, (3) interviews, and (4) observation (Foster, 1998). The methods chosen tend to depend on the number of jobs to be analyzed, the kind of work being done, and the type of information required. For example, a job analysis of a police sergeant's position intended to develop a selection test for a large urban city would require different strategies than would a job analysis of all the positions in an IT department planning to restructure its operations.

- Use of *archival data* involves a review of job and **position descriptions**, previous job analyses, performance appraisals, training materials, worker manuals and aids, examples of work products, and other artifacts that help describe and define the position. Ideally, these data are employed before other steps, but in practice they often become available as the process evolves. An array of archival data provides a potentially invaluable wealth of contextual and detailed information.

- *Questionnaires* can be either open ended or structured. Open-ended instruments ask incumbents to identify the content of their jobs on their own and quantify the functions by percentage of their time (Exhibit 5.5 provides an example). Those surveys are then reviewed by supervisors. The strengths of this method are its low cost, standard form, and use of the incumbent's knowledge of the position. Unfortunately, questionnaires generally require significant follow-up to fill in gaps and are susceptible to employee embellishment or, in some cases, diffidence. Closed-ended or structured instruments provide task lists from which to select. They provide highly detailed information about the job but require computer-based aggregation and trained staff analysis for effective utilization.
- *Interviews* can be conducted with individuals or groups. The content of jobs can be analyzed through semistructured or wholly structured question protocols of either job incumbents or supervisors. This is a particularly useful method for managerial, technical, and professional positions. Group methods are useful when a class of positions has relatively little variation or when a list of unstructured elements, such as critical incidents, is being elicited. The major drawback of interviews is their time-consuming nature.
- *Observation* involves watching individuals actually perform their jobs. It is particularly effective for analyzing blue-collar positions for which the activities can be observed; it is less useful in analyzing white-collar occupations. It provides the analyst with first-hand experience, which may be enhanced by the analyst performing the functions.

Formal methods are time consuming and expensive. In practice, they are employed in a small number of important cases. First, formal job analysis should always be used when there is an employment test that can be challenged easily on the grounds of validity. Validity challenges (see Chapter 4) are most common for large, entry-level classifications, especially for jobs that are highly sought because of their professional potential, and that require basic knowledge- or skill-based tests. Examples include firefighter and fire lieutenant, police officer and police detective or corporal, sheriff's deputy, FBI agent, IRS investigator, and auditor. Analysis is also important to determine reasonable accommodations for those with disabilities. These types of analyses are conducted by personnel specialists but are frequently subcontracted to specialized consulting firms. Some jurisdictions, especially small ones, use off-the-shelf tests that have been validated by vendors.

Formal job analysis may be used in reclassifications when there is pressure to upgrade the position. Reclassifications generally are formally requested by the incumbent, must be supported by the supervisor, and are administered and approved by the human resource department. It is highly useful for those requesting, supporting, or discouraging reclassifications to understand formal job analysis methodology. (Note that Exhibit 5.5 can be used in reclassifications as well as in the classification of new positions.)

Formal job analysis also may be used as a preliminary step in an evaluation study in which the positions of a division or entire organization are being recalibrated. Such studies normally are subcontracted to consulting firms, if only for the neutrality that external assessors are perceived to possess. Except for relatively consistent (but highly generic) job descriptions, however, formal job analysis may supply information of limited value. Finally, formal job analysis is sometimes used for comprehensive training studies. To summarize, job analysis can

Exhibit 5.5   Position Description Questionnaire

IOWA DEPARTMENT OF PERSONNEL
POSITION DESCRIPTION QUESTIONNAIRE (PDQ)

Read instructions before completing this form.

FOR AGENCY USE ONLY	FOR IDOP USE ONLY PDQ # _____
M-5# _____ ☐ New position ☐ Duties have changed: _____ Position review requested _____ No position review requested ☐ Response to IDOP request	Class Title _____ 18 Digit Position # _____ Personnel Officer _____ Date _____

---

1. Name of employee (if none, write VACANT) 2. Current 18-digit positions # and class title

3. Department, Division, Bureau, Section and Work Address

4. Hours worked (shifts, rotations, travel)   5. ☐ Full-time (40 hours per week)
   ☐ Part-time (list number of hours per week)

6. Have the assigned duties changed since this position was last reviewed for a classification decision? ☐ Yes ☐ No
   If Yes, place an "X" beside each NEW task written below. Also, describe in detail how those tasks are different from those previously assigned.

7. Name and job classification of the immediate supervisor

8. Description of Work: Describe the work in detail. Make the description so clear that the reader can understand each task exactly. In the TIME/% column, enter the percent of time spent on each task during an average work week. List the most important responsibility first. If this is a reclassification request, the previous PDQ must be attached. This PDQ will be returned if any section is incomplete.

TIME/%	WORK PERFORMED
	      (ATTACH ADDITIONAL SHEETS IF NECESSARY)

CFN 552-0094-4   R 4/99

9. Is this position considered to be supervisory? Yes_____ No_____ If Yes, complete a <u>Supervisory Analysis Questionnaire</u> form (CFN 552-0193) and attach it to this form.

10. For what reasons are you requesting that this position be reviewed? Include, if applicable, significant changes or additions to duties, comparison(s) with other positions, etc. Be specific.

I certify that I have read the instructions for the completion of this questionnaire, that the answers are my own, and that they are accurate and complete. I understand that falsification or misrepresentation made in regard to any information submitted may lead to discipline up to and including discharge.

Signed _____ _____
             (Incumbent Employee)   (Date)

If you have not been notified by your department's management of their decision to support or deny this request within 30 days, you may send this request directly to IDOP for review. Address it to: Facilitator, Program Delivery Services, Iowa Department of Personnel, Grimes Building, East 14th & Grand, Des Moines, Iowa 50319-0150.

SUPERVISOR REVIEW OF POSITION DESCRIPTION QUESTIONNAIRE

This section must be completed within 30 days after the PDQ is received from the employee. The employee must be notified of the decision to support or deny the request. Regardless, the request must be forwarded to IDOP. This PDQ will be returned if any section is incomplete.

11. Indicate to what extent, if any, the statements on this form are, in your opinion, not correct or need clarification.

12. Describe the origin of any new duties, i.e., those marked with an "X" in Item 8. If new duties have been added, where were they performed prior to being assigned to this position? Are these duties performed by anyone else? If so, identify the person(s) and the position classification of their positions.

13. What is the basic purpose of this position?

14. Identify the essential functions that must be performed by the incumbent, with or without reasonable accommodation for disabilities. Identify any certifications or licenses that are required. Refer to the instruction sheet and Section 3.15 of the *Managers and Supervisors Manual* for more information on essential functions.

(Continued)

(Continued)

15. Is this position considered to be confidentially or managerially exempt from collective bargaining? Yes_____ No_____ If Yes, complete the <u>Bargaining Exemption Questionnaire</u> (CFN 552-0631) and attach it to this form.

Signed _____   _____   _____
                  (Supervisor)   (Title and Job Classification)   (Date)

APPOINTING AUTHORITY REVIEW OF POSITION DESCRIPTION QUESTIONNAIRE

16. Comments:
    _____
    _____

Signed _____   _____
                  (Appointing Authority)   (Date)

CFN 552-0094-4   R 4/99

Source: Iowa Department of Personnel, 1999.

be utilized not only by human resource departments, but also by managers and employees. Its formal methods tend to be practiced by internal experts or consultants, but informal usage is now considered a generic management skill.[8]

▪▪ JOB AND POSITION DESCRIPTIONS

One of the end products of job design or job analysis is the job description or position description. Although the terms are used nearly interchangeably, with job description being the collective reference, they actually represent different concepts. It is useful to exaggerate the differences for clarity because job and position descriptions are the building blocks of **position classification systems** and management systems. Both are written statements about a job that describe or list the duties, but the focus of the two often varies significantly, as do the uses, writers, and level of specificity.

Job descriptions are statements that codify the typical or average duties (sometimes by using work examples), levels of responsibility, and general competencies and requirements of a job class. They are generally prepared by human resource specialists or personnel consultants. Their primary uses are for systems management (placement of positions in specific classes) and compensation decisions; job descriptions tend to be maintained by the human resource department. The language is usually generic so that a description covers many positions, and the examples used may or may not apply to a specific position. Although the format varies, the underlying structure of job descriptions does not.

Position descriptions are statements that define the exact duties, level of responsibility, and organizational placement of a specific position (or essentially identical group of positions). Although they are sometimes written by personnel specialists, they are generally written by job incumbents or their supervisors. Their primary purposes are for recruitment (where they are modified as vacancy announcements), reclassification (where the duties and responsibilities tend to be compared to the job classification requested), and performance appraisal (where work standards and accomplishments tend to be emphasized). Because of the wide variety of objectives, their format varies considerably. Their maintenance is generally dependent on the specific use of or the culture of the local unit; true position descriptions are rarely centrally maintained. An example of a comparison of job and position descriptions using the class "Equipment Operator 2" is located in the Appendix of this chapter. The job description is for a class with more than 1,000 positions; the position description was used as part of a successful effort to reclassify the position from an Equipment Operator 1 to an Equipment Operator 2.

In practice, small organizations may not maintain job descriptions and may use position descriptions only occasionally, such as when they need to recruit. Small- and medium-size organizations that have overhauled their position classification system within a decade or so often find that they are able to maintain job descriptions that have many characteristics of position descriptions because the number of incumbents is small in each class. In big organizations with many large classes, job descriptions generally are maintained conscientiously (and used for all purposes even if they prove less than ideal for recruitment and appraisal), whereas position descriptions are created selectively for management and human resource purposes.

Finally, it should be noted that traditional and contemporary job and position descriptions vary in two significant regards. The Americans with Disabilities Act of 1990 (ADA) has had a profound effect on job descriptions, position descriptions, and position announcements. Traditionally, jobs were defined as having three to ten major *duties,* each of which might have two or more **job tasks**.[9] Because the ADA prohibits discrimination against an individual with a disability, who with or without reasonable accommodation, can perform the **essential functions** of the employment position, the language more commonly used today is adapted to essential and nonessential functions rather than to duties and tasks. Furthermore, physical, manual, and special requirements are now routinely spelled out in job and position descriptions.[10] Second, the new management emphasis on accountability and results has led to the incorporation of performance standards in some cases. It remains to be seen whether results-oriented job and position descriptions will become the norm.

Writing Job Descriptions

Writing job descriptions is a specific skill that takes study to master. In practice, templates are used, but the style invariably is terse. The simple format furnished here as an example has the following elements or categories: (1) job summary, (2) essential functions, (3) physical and environmental standards required to perform essential functions, and (4) minimum job requirements and qualifications for a town accounts payable or payroll clerk. Most agencies have instructions for writing of job descriptions online (e.g., HR-Guide.com, 2000; U.S. Fish and Wildlife Service, 2008).

The job summary begins with the level of responsibility and identifies the department and level of supervision, if any, followed by a list of major duties.

Example: Under general supervision, this position works in the office of the city administrator. This position is responsible for financial support tasks including payroll processing, accounts receivable, accounts payable, bank deposits and reconciliations, and other general clerical support duties for the administrator and council as assigned.

The second category identifies essential functions, generally those that constitute more than 5% of the incumbent's time and are central to the job. These start with a verb followed by an object and sometimes an explanatory phrase. Ideally, five to seven functions are listed, but there may be as few as three and as many as 10. Long, unorganized task lists once were typical but now are considered poor form. Tasks should be clustered into duty areas and combined where necessary. It is possible to place a performance standard at the end of each statement.

Example: Processes biweekly time sheets and enters payroll information into computer; computes used and accrued sick and vacation time and overtime hours; pays required federal and state taxes; deducts insurance and related payroll costs; prints payroll checks and payroll reports. Extreme accuracy and timeliness is required in performing this critical function.

The third category identifies the physical and environmental standards required to perform essential functions. Physical standards should articulate the exact abilities required to accomplish job tasks as normally constituted, knowing that reasonable accommodation may be necessary for a qualified applicant or incumbent who is disabled. Environmental standards include such conditions as working outdoors, dangerous conditions, and nonstandard working hours. Generally, this section employs a format similar to that used for the essential functions.

Example: Requires the ability to handle a variety of documents and use hands in typing, data entry, using a calculator and related equipment; occasionally lift and carry books, ledgers, reports, and other documents weighing less than 25 pounds. Incumbent will use personal automobile in depositing monies at local banks. Requires visual and hearing ability sufficiently correctable to see clients, hear phones, and operate in an office environment that has limited auxiliary support.

The fourth category identifies minimum requirements and qualifications. Here, required KSAs, as well as special certifications, degrees, and training, are identified. Requirements for excessive credentials should be avoided to ensure consistency with merit principles and equal employment opportunity. Substitutions generally are listed.

Example: Graduation from high school or GED and three years of general accounting or bookkeeping experience; substitution of successful completion of a business or accounting curriculum at a recognized college or school may be made for part of the experience requirement. Must also have good interpersonal skills, and excellent ability to coordinate and balance numerous, sometimes hectic, activities in a calm fashion without letting technical accuracy suffer.

Job design and analysis, then, provide the content of position and job descriptions that are used in a variety of human resource functions from recruiting to appraisal. Now it is time to turn to the way that these individual efforts are assembled into systems.

■■ FROM JOBS TO JOB SYSTEMS

The Two Primary Uses of Classification Systems

Position classification systems can provide the basis for job design and support, as well as the basis to manage, track, and control employment numbers, costs, and position levels. When the function of position classification systems is job design and support, they provide the basis for the division and coordination of work, recruitment efforts, selection methods, training programs, appraisal systems, and other human resource functions through analysis and organization of jobs in the organization.

Position classification systems are also structures that manage, track, and control employment numbers, costs, and levels of positions; in this context they are frequently called position *management* systems. Legislators need to know the number of authorized positions versus the number of filled positions, and to anticipate total personnel costs so that they can curb the number of positions in specific areas and control position grades or ranks. Position management systems typically number positions, assign locations, and determine an exact system of compensation. Positions can be tracked by function, such as transportation, and by specialty, such as engineering. Positions also can be tracked and monitored by grade or rank. For example, the state of Iowa has 57 pay grades and six steps in most grades. A legislator thus can determine how many employees work in what agencies, at what level, and at what cost. A position classification system from this perspective is ultimately a management tool to support compensation systems and control costs.

Grouping Positions

Position systems start with the duties and responsibilities of a single individual, whose job is called a **position**. Clusters of positions with similar characteristics are organized into a job classification, job class, classification, or simply job or class (terms that are used interchangeably). Technically, "jobs" refer to identical positions, whereas "classes" refer to similar positions in which there are equivalent responsibilities and training, although the specific duty assignment may vary. For example, "property appraiser" may be the class, but one individual may be assigned to residential properties and another to commercial. For classification purposes, however, both have generic training with easy rotational opportunities, which is why the concept of job classifications is used (so that excessive numbers of categories will not be created). The number of job classifications varies considerably by organization: The federal government has approximately 2,500, states have anywhere from a high of 4,500 (California) to a low of 550 (South Dakota), and very tiny organizations have just a few classifications (Chi, 1998). Classes that are linked developmentally are grouped into **class series**.[11] For example, the federal government has approximately 450 class series for white-collar workers and another 350 for blue-collar workers. Class series are subsequently grouped into large **occupational families**. Related occupational families, such as all white-collar jobs, are assigned a **pay plan** or schedule in which the grades, steps, and related pay are determined.

As rational as this sounds in theory, practice can produce disorderly systems. The size of the jurisdiction, the number of bargaining units, and the history of the jurisdiction produce very different position classification systems with different sorts of challenges and contradictions. First, systems often have an unnecessary number of pay plans, which are often driven by labor-management negotiations rather than by rational planning. Separate pay plans are created for each major group: blue-collar, public safety, executives, confidential staff, and a variety of professional groups in particular agencies (e.g., health professionals, engineers, lawyers, judges, and so on). Ideally, they would be grouped together.

Second, individuals often change pay plans as they move up the chain of command. Firefighters may be in one plan, fire captains may be in another for midlevel managers in the city, and the fire chief may be in the plan for city executives. The number of plans seems to increase as the jurisdiction size increases (see Exhibit 5.6 for an example of this problem). Although this may increase responsiveness to market factors and enhance comparability, it can lead to a system that is complex and unwieldy. Note that the one system with a moderate number of pay plans (the judicial branch of Iowa) was comprehensively reorganized in the 1980s. Other problems are excessively narrow class definitions (sometimes with only a single job incumbent) and positions that have dual classifications (and different compensation patterns) merely because the identical jobs are found in different organizational or bargaining units of the same government.

Exhibit 5.6   Increase in Number of Pay Plans as Jurisdiction Size Increases (Examples)

	Ames	Iowa Judicial Branch[a]	State of Iowa[b]	United States Federal Government
Number of positions	522	2,200	19,000	5,000,000
Number of classes	224 (average size: 2.3)	132 (average size: 16.7)	850 (average size: 22.4)	2,500 (average size: 2,000)
Number of pay plans or schedules	8	4	15	36

a. This branch of government was rationalized and streamlined in 1986, when the system was converted to a statewide system.

b. The positions do not reflect the 24,000 Regents employees (Iowa State, University of Iowa, and University of Northern Iowa). Regents institutions each have separate classification systems for merit, professional and administrative, faculty, and temporary employees.

Rank-in-person systems reduce the number of job classes through the use of a uniform series of ranks for a multitude of operational positions. "Army captain," "district fire chief," and "assistant professor" are generic job titles for numerous positions identified by a specific army unit, fire district, or department. Systems with rank are normally closed to lateral entry (entry from outside the organization without first completing a junior level or entry position), unlike position systems.

In sum, although many small jurisdictions have, and function acceptably with, piecemeal personnel patterns, large jurisdictions need formal position classification systems. Such systems help them track and control positions as well as support those positions by logical groupings called job classes, class series, occupational families, and pay plans. The special case of classification for pay is considered next.

Analyzing Jobs to Set Pay: Job Evaluation

The two most important tools in position classification and management are job analysis (discussed above) and job evaluation. In theory, a job evaluation is a special type of job analysis, one that attaches a dollar value or worth to the position (Siegel, 1998a, 1998b). In practice, job evaluations are often so specialized that they operate as a different function from job analysis.

Position classification systems provide grades or ranks for all merit positions as well as for nonmerit positions. This allows for rational position management systems that assign **authorized salary ranges** to each grade or rank. In the ideal, all merit jobs are thoroughly analyzed for content and rigorously evaluated for relative worth. Furthermore, the system should provide **internal equity** among organization members and **external equity** with those in similar positions outside the organization (see Chapter 7). The system should also furnish an opportunity to reflect seniority, merit, skill, and other specialized **individual equity** concerns (such as locale and shift differences). In reality, position management systems rarely meet such standards, partly because of the expense and effort in maintaining such ideals and partly because of the competing and inconsistent demands placed on these systems (Chapter 7).

Not all personnel systems are based on formal position classification systems. Piecemeal personnel systems are those that lack grades or ranks and assign salaries on an ad hoc basis. Job relationships may be reflected in an organization chart and brief job descriptions may exist. Detailed job analyses, well-articulated job series, and civil service protections, however, are partial or nonexistent. Piecemeal personnel systems are still common in small governments. Obvious drawbacks include inconsistency; lack of integration of the human resource functions such as hiring, appraisal, and promotion; and the possibility of legal challenge for hiring and promotional validity. These systems, however, do offer flexibility and a level of informality that may suit small organizations fairly well.

Using Factors and Points for Job Evaluation

Historically, jobs were evaluated using a holistic job methodology: What was a particular job thought to be worth in general terms? Despite the flexibility and immediacy of such systems, they are prone to distortions based on personalism, limited information, and excessive focus on the job incumbent. Position classification ushered in an age of factor systems in which job grades or levels were commonly established. Graded systems took into account (often implicitly) such factors as level of responsibility, job requirements, difficulty of work, nature of the relationships, and level of supervision. This led to far more rational and equitable compensation systems. The assignment of points for various factors made these systems still more rigorous.

Today, **point factor methods** are generally used when organizations find that their position classification systems have become too inconsistent and outdated. In the majority of cases, an external consultant conducts the underlying pay study to design the new system because of the time and expertise required to accomplish such a large task.

A point factor system starts with the assumption that factors should be broad enough to apply consistently to all jobs in an organization or schedule. In practice, four to twelve factors generally are selected. For instance, the Federal Evaluation System (FES) uses nine for the General Schedule (GS). Each factor is then weighted by determining a maximum number of points that can be assigned to it (OPM, 1991). In the case of the FES, note the tremendous differences in the weights of the different factors (see Exhibit 5.7).

Exhibit 5.7	Weighting Equivalencies for the Nine Factors Used in the Federal Evaluation System	
Factor	*Maximum Points*	*Evaluation Weight (%)*
Knowledge required	1,850	41.3
Supervisory controls	650	14.5
Guidelines	650	14.5
Complexity	450	10.0
Scope and effect	450	10.0
Personal contacts	110	2.5
Purpose of contacts	220	4.9
Physical demands	50	1.1
Work environment	50	1.1

Source: OPM, 1991.

Next, the factors are defined by levels or standards that are used to determine the actual number of points a job classification will receive. In the Federal Schedule, GS Grade 9 is from 1,855 points to 2,100 points, whereas GS Grade 15 exceeds 4,050 points. Three to five standards interpret the various levels; descriptions are provided of what high, medium, and low levels mean in each factor. Factors may be further subdivided into a number of subfactors. All jobs are then evaluated by individuals, committees, or both. This part of the process should provide internal equity because of the consistency of the process. After all jobs have been evaluated and arranged from lowest to highest, point ranges are selected to determine grade levels. Point factor systems are excellent for internal equity, but do not ensure external equity. External equity is maintained by linking the entire point factor system to compensation comparisons of select jobs outside the organization. A portion of the classifications are chosen as **benchmark jobs**, anchored to general market salary ranges as indicated by reliable compensation survey information.[12] In large organizations, it may be as few as 5% or 10% of the positions; in small organizations it may be as many as 25%. Benchmark jobs are used for each major class series to ensure external equity and that the entire system is in line with market compensation practices.

As a straightforward example, suppose that an organization finds that its position classification system is dated, that most job descriptions do not reflect ADA standards, and that there is an opportunity to modestly increase salaries, which are currently below the market. An external consulting firm is hired that specializes in government compensation studies. The consultant uses four factors: (1) level of responsibility, (2) complexity of problem solving, (3) degree of accountability, and (4) working conditions.[13] Multiple raters examine 7% of the job classes, using the four factors to ensure reliability. This provides reference points (benchmark jobs) in the evaluation of other jobs.

At that point, all classes are analyzed and evaluated using the factors. (As a by-product of the evaluation process, new job descriptions are generated that provide essential and nonessential duties as well as physical requirements and environmental conditions for compatibility with the ADA.) The evaluation assigns a specific point value to each job class.

After all the classes have been arrayed on a point scale from lowest to highest, intervals are selected that determine the grade levels. Those benchmarked jobs are then matched to salary survey data to ensure comparability to market salaries. Throughout the process, the organization has a task force assigned to work with the consultant, which includes the human resource specialist for compensation. After completing the study, the results are forwarded to the entire organization, which has an opportunity to review the analysis and provide further input. The task force presents the study to the governing body, with its recommendations for adoption (or rejection) and for specific changes. Because such studies usually represent salary increase, the governing board may or may not accept the study.

Because comprehensive job evaluations (pay studies) are expensive and time consuming, they occur infrequently.[14] Managers, executives, and legislators need to be aware of how compensation factors were arrived at in the past, how well the compensation system has fared over time, and when a new compensation study and pay plan may be called for, as well as the auxiliary features that such research can produce with planning (see Exhibit 5.8 for a discussion of when to conduct a job evaluation study).

Exhibit 5.8   When to Conduct a Job Evaluation Study

Because organization-wide job evaluation studies are expensive, time-consuming, and often controversial, they should not be used as feasibility studies. If the adoption of the final study (with modifications) is not propitious, it is better not to begin at all. Nor should a comprehensive job evaluation analysis be used if only a few job classifications are at issue; in that event, only those cases or class series should be evaluated.

First, preliminary questions must be asked. How and when were jobs last evaluated (using what methodologies) and by whom? How much controversy does the system seem to generate, and what are its major problems (internal equity such as pay inconsistencies; external equity such as widespread below-market salaries; special problems such as hard-to-recruit and hard-to-retain jobs, excessive job plateauing, inadequate financial incentives)?

Second, the purpose of a proposed study needs to be clearly outlined. Is it for an occupational family, a pay plan, or the entire organization? Would the analysis primarily target internal inequities, overall external inequities such as depressed salaries across the board, more flexible salary plans, merit-based pay systems, or a variety of factors? Who would conduct the evaluation, and how would they be commissioned? What would be the role or input of employee unions? Defining the purposes of the initiative ensures that the organizational or legislative leaders and the evaluators do not have two separate notions of what is to be accomplished (which is not uncommon).

Third, feasibility and political reality must be assessed candidly. If the overall problem with the compensation plan is depressed salaries across the board but government revenues are limited because of economic or financial exigencies (such as a recession or an expensive capital building plan), then a job evaluation study will do little but agitate workers, put executives in an uncomfortable position, and annoy elected officials (who will turn down the plan). Practical questions include the following: Will there be money to both pay for the analysis and increase some or all salaries? Do legislators really understand the underlying need (because the study itself is unlikely to convince them) as well as the general plan of implementation? How can the study be used as a means of enhancing labor-management relations rather than become another bone of contention?

Finally, the jurisdiction needs to be clear if it wants more than just a compensation study conducted. A common outcome desired is job descriptions that have wider human resource utility. Such a by-product must not be assumed and should be carefully spelled out before the process.

For their part, it is essential for employees and managers to understand job evaluation factors to maximize the prospects for success in petitions for reclassification. Too frequently, a good employee is performing well but has weak grounds for a reclassification, which is based on the nature of the position and not on her particular skills or assignments. Unless grounds can be established that the position itself has been fundamentally and permanently altered, a reclassification request is likely to be turned down (although a classification specialist might assist with a market adjustment, special step increase, bonus, or other pay modification suggestion). Because of this type of problem, as well as the perceived rigidity of position management systems in general today, alternative systems such as broadbanding (discussed in Chapter 7) frequently are recommended.

Substituting a Whole Job Methodology for Job Analysis or Job Evaluation

While formal position classification systems generally rely on job analysis and point factor systems, piecemeal classification systems and new positions generally rely on whole job methods, instead. **Whole job analysis** does not systematically break a job down into its constituent parts for purposes of grade and classification but instead relies on past experience and intuition. **Whole job evaluation** methods do not systematically break a job down into its constituent parts for purposes of compensation; rather, they consider the job in its entirety and make summary judgments based on intuition and past experience. Examples are numerous:

- *Whole job analysis:* A supervisor hires a clerical support person from another unit in the organization; this employee clearly has the appropriate skills and already knows the position in general terms. The supervisor needs someone quickly, so no analysis of the position is conducted. Although identified as a "Secretary III" position, the generic job description of the position gives almost no insight into the specific position.
- *Whole job analysis:* A manager hires a special project coordinator for a new position. Although a rough description of the job elements is provided, it is really only suggestive of the types of KSAs that might actually be required.
- *Whole job analysis:* An executive appraises a high-performing manager in general terms, without a detailed knowledge of the specific tasks that the person conducts on a daily basis.
- *Whole job evaluation:* A manager in an organization (that does not have a formal position classification system) intuitively selects a salary for a new position that experience indicates will attract competent candidates.

Whole job methods are simple, summary judgments. Their merits include efficiency and a tendency to honor the decision maker's past experience and wisdom (Van Wart, 2000). The difficulties are that these judgments can be hasty and based on insufficient or inaccurate information. They also may yield little information for various human resource functions and provide inadequate management or legal defense when the decisions are faulty. In systems with large job classifications and typical job valuations, whole job methods are often inappropriate.

▪▪   SUMMARY AND CONCLUSION

Position classification became more of a judicious plan throughout the last century than it ever was before. Outright corruption in the civil service is unusual; rational plans for managing jobs in terms of compensation and other human resource functions exist in all large organizations and are tailored to their needs and histories. In addition, specific tools now exist in this area, such as job analysis and job evaluation, which include both highly sophisticated methodologies and standard methods commonly used by managers. Most small organizations with piecemeal systems follow job analysis and classification methods in spirit, even if they frequently lack the rigor of large agencies.

Nevertheless, the ability to have greater (but not perfect) control, consistency, precision, and rationality (which position classification and management theory and practice have enabled managers to achieve) should not disguise the underlying truth that it is only partially a science and largely an art. The decisions made in position management systems ultimately are founded on value choices, not universal laws (Van Wart, 1998). Many of the values assumed over the last half century are shifting dramatically because of changed economics, politics, and technology. Furthermore, even at its most rational and ideal, the position classification system of large organizations is a combination of at least three fundamentally different personnel systems based on election, appointment, and rule-based criteria. Indeed, rule-based (i.e., merit) criteria are themselves divided between position-based systems and less common rank-based systems, sometimes occurring in the same organization. Finally, the sheer organizational complexity and level of change in organizations today mean that extensive, expensive, difficult-to-maintain position classification systems naturally tend to become less rational, less consistent, and out of date. Paradoxically, then, as much as position classification systems are judicious plans, they are also ever-changing jigsaw puzzles of shifting values, of radically different personnel approaches, and of competing human resource needs to provide management control, on the one hand, and to support and design jobs, on the other (Ingraham & Getha-Taylor, 2005).

The new value changes emanate from elemental transformations in the public sector landscape in terms of what people want public sector organizations to do and how they want them to do it (De Leon & Denhardt, 2000; Yergin & Stanislaw, 1998). Rather than an emphasis on employee rights and internal procedural consistency, there is a far greater interest in placing an emphasis on employee accountability and on concrete achievement translating into an increased reliance on at-will systems (with appointment-based features) and performance standards (Grady & Tax, 1996; MSPB, 2002). This has certainly prompted extensive debate about the advantages and potential liabilities of contemporary civil service reforms. The emphasis on efficiency and effectiveness is in line with the historic tradition of scientific management and can be seen as a logical progression of the art of position management.

Other trends promise to take position management into new domains and configurations. The demand for agencies that are flexible, flatter, and more entrepreneurial requires not only new organizational structures, but also new internal management systems in the United States (Leavitt & Johnson, 1998; Marshall, 1998) and elsewhere in the world (Lodge & Hood, 2005). Such trends will propel institutions to reexamine and simplify their complex systems. Efforts to use broadbanding (fewer classes and enlarged jobs) and work teams are examples, as are attempts to simplify massive management systems. Contemporary initiatives to decentralize responsibility to local managers who will be more accountable for results, but who will also be allowed more flexibility, will also change the landscape. Indeed, some predict the "death of the job" (Crandall & Wallace, 1998; Leonard, 2000) as virtual work designs stretch people beyond narrow, predictable tasks by extending not only their lines of sight (understanding outcomes and how their activities relate to them), but also their lines of impact (confidence stemming from affecting results).

However, whether one comes to view position management systems more as judicious plans or as jigsaw puzzles, they will remain the core of the human resource function that managers, employees, and job aspirants cannot afford to mystify or underutilize.

KEY TERMS

At-will employment	Job specialization
Authorized salary range	Job tasks
Benchmark jobs	Lateral entry
Broadbanding	Occupational families
Civil service	Open personnel system
Class series	Patronage system
Closed personnel systems	Pay plan
Essential function	Piecemeal personnel systems
External equity	Point factor methods
Individual equity	Position
Internal equity	Position classification systems
Job analysis	Position description
Job classification	Position management system
Job description	Process management
Job design	Process reengineering
Job duties	Rank-in-job
Job enlargement	Rank-in-person
Job enrichment	Up-or-out philosophy
Job evaluation	Whole job analysis
Job rotation	Whole job evaluation

EXERCISES

Class Discussion

1. Canvass the class to determine if any members of the class have been a part of a reclassification effort or an organization-wide job evaluation. What happened? Was it successful or not?

2. Ask those in the class who now work or have ever worked in the public sector what position management challenges they have experienced.

3. There is perhaps no better example of the grand paradox of needs (see the Introduction) than position management. Discuss and seek pathways through the paradox as well as subparadoxes found in various position management techniques.

Team Activities

4. Does the position management function help or hinder in resolving the twin paradoxes introduced at the outset of the book?

5. Analyze a public sector organization's classification system. Determine the number of positions, classes, and pay plans. What are the number of elected, appointed, and merit appointees? Does the system "work" and does the checkerboard make sense to those using the system?

6. A large, growing county decides to place a new service center in another city. None of the current employees is interested in relocating. Furthermore, there is some concern that many of the offices are using outdated technology and old-fashioned methods of customer delivery. For example, services related to building permits, licenses, land records, and tax assessment are scattered throughout a variety of buildings in the county seat. The new model of customer service recommends a single, long service counter for related services, with employees who are cross-trained. Almost all the job descriptions are at least a decade old (some are 25 years old!), and nearly all the "training" is on the job. How might a job analysis study be useful? Specifically, what functions might be supported by such a study, and how would they be implemented?

7. As a class, determine which members are currently employed in the public sector and then select some of them to be interviewed in small groups. The small groups are to write a job description. The person interviewed should not do any of the writing, nor should he suggest the format to be used. Compare the results as a class and make friendly suggestions for improvements.

8. You are a manager whose best worker has "topped out"; that is, the employee is at the top step of her pay grade. Furthermore, her job is properly classified. Unfortunately, the government jurisdiction for whom you both work is 20% to 30% below the market in most positions. You know that the person will leave soon if the situation is not altered. You could assign a few people to her to justify a reclassification and pay increase, although it would not make much sense functionally. Take an imagination break (Exhibit 0.2). What would you do? (Teams should compare and justify their recommendations.)

Individual Assignments

9. The reform of civil service will be an important discussion and debate for the next several decades. What are the implications of the civil service reform initiative in Georgia? Do you think that the movement to replace independent civil service commissions with executive branch personnel agencies is a good one? Do you think that job property rights should be abolished in all public sector systems? Will the widespread use of at-will systems lead to patronage problems again, as they did in the 19th century?

10. What are the similarities and dissimilarities between broadbanding and rank-in-person systems?

11. If you were the analyst looking at the position reclassification request in the Appendix (for the Equipment Operator 2), what would the positive and negative points be? Would you grant the request?

APPENDIX

Comparison of a Job and Position Description

Sample Job Description[15]

Equipment Operator 2, Class Code: 08111dy

Definition: Under general supervision, performs specialized and routine roadway and right-of-way maintenance activities including physical laboring activities, the operation of self-propelled mobile equipment, skilled equipment operation, and limited direction of work crews. Performs related work as required.

Work Examples

- Assists a supervisor by performing limited lead work in accordance with set procedures, policies, and standards; and such duties as instructing employees about tasks, answering questions about procedures and policies, and distributing and balancing the workload and checking work. Makes occasional suggestions on appointments, promotions, and reassignments.
- Works on district paint crew in rotation with other paint crew positions.
- Works on the district bridge crew.
- Acts as a maintenance sign crew leader in maintenance areas where work on signs requires a full-time sign crew.
- Acts as a lighting specialist and may be assigned to the state lighting crew to assist that crew in the maintenance and construction of roadway lights.
- Cleans ditches and culverts, excavates soil, straightens drainage channels, and resets culvert ends using a dragline or hydraulic excavator in a residency or districtwide area.
- Operates a mud pump, grout pump, or high reach in a residency or districtwide area.
- Operates the curb-making machine in a residency.
- Performs herbicide spraying operations in right-of-way areas by using a backpack sprayer, by driving a truck, or by operating a pressure sprayer as required.
- Loads and unloads material, demolishes structures, loads debris, and so on, using a small bulldozer. May be required to run a large erosion dozer for erosion control purposes in districtwide or residency-wide areas.

Competencies Required

- Knowledge of specialized highway maintenance equipment, its operation, and use
- Knowledge of highway maintenance procedures and techniques
- Knowledge of highway maintenance terminology
- Ability to work outdoors during inclement weather and to be on call during emergency situations such as snowstorms, pavement blowups, floods, and so on
- Ability to operate a 90-pound jackhammer in the operation of breaking and removing pavement materials
- Ability to lift and load bagged material weighing up to 95 pounds to a truck bed that is 55 inches above ground
- Ability to drive trucks and other vehicles in a safe and conscientious manner
- Ability to understand and carry out written and oral instructions
- Ability to direct the work of and to train crew members
- Ability to meet customer needs in a consistently helpful and courteous manner
- Ability to work cooperatively with others as part of a team

- Ability to apply personal work attitudes such as honesty, responsibility, and trustworthiness to be a productive employee
- Ability to operate specialized highway maintenance equipment that requires hand, foot, and eye coordination

Education, Experience, and Special Requirements

- The equivalency of one-year full-time experience in the operation of heavy equipment, performing highway or other related maintenance functions, or in subprofessional engineering program areas.
- All positions in this job class require applicants to possess a commercial driver's license, class A, at the time of hire. Endorsements may also be required.
- For designated positions, the appointing authority, with Iowa Department of Personnel prior approval, may request applicants to possess a minimum of twelve semester hours of postsecondary education, six months of experience, or a combination of both, or a specific certificate, license, or endorsement in the following areas: air brakes, doubles or triples endorsement, hazardous materials endorsement, or tank vehicles. Applicants wishing to be considered for such designated positions must list applicable course work, experience, certificate, license, or endorsement on the application.

Special Notes

- After accepting an offer of employment, all persons are required to have a physical examination by a doctor of choice verifying the applicant's physical ability to perform the duties described.
- Employees must be available to travel and may be required to stay away from home overnight during assignments.
- Certain designated positions require the employee to be certified by the U.S. Department of Agriculture and Land Stewardship as a Pesticide Applicator.
- Employees must respond to emergency conditions, and so must live within a fifteen-mile distance or be able to report within a 30-minute period of time to their assigned facility.

Sample Position Description (Intended Usage: Reclassification)

Incumbent	John Doe
Agency	Iowa Department of Transportation
Division	Highway Maintenance Division
Unit	District 2
Place of work	Waterloo Maintenance Garage, US 63 and West Ridgeway
Position number and class title of existing position	645 S44 5520 08110 111 Equipment Operator 1
Hours worked	7:00 A.M. through 3:30 P.M., Monday through Friday
Immediate supervisor	Robert Fisck, Highway Supervisor 1
Position requested	Equipment Operator 2

Description of work (List in detail the work you do. List the most important duties first. Indicate the percentage of time or hours in an average work week spent on each duty.)

Time	Work Performed
45%	Grout pump. Operate a grout pump over a districtwide area. Reestablishing pavement support by undersealing. Includes marking and drilling injection holes and injecting a mixture of cement flash grout under low pressure to completely fill any voids under the pavement. Must understand and be able to locate longitudinal subdrains and any other drains located under the pavement to make sure that the drains are not plugged with grout. Must constantly monitor roadway, shoulder, and under the bridge while pumping to make certain not to damage the bridge, shoulder, or roadway in any way. Train and direct a crew of seven to nine operators on the pump and on proper traffic control. Must understand the mechanics of the grout pump so if any problem occurs can take the pump apart and get the grout out of the machine, so as not to have a flash set before a mechanic can get to the job site.
20%	Routine roadway and right-of-way maintenance activities, to include the following: Surfaces: patch spalls, seal/fill joints and cracks, remove bumps, fill depressions, remove and replace damaged pavements Shoulders: fill edge ruts, operate blading equipment to smooth shoulders, patch paved shoulders, and so on Roadsides: pick up litter, cut brush, repair fences, control weeds by mowing and spraying, erect and dismantle snow fences Bridges: clean decks, clean and lubricate working members, spot paint Traffic services: repair guardrails, flag traffic, maintain lighting, erect and maintain signs Drainage: repair and maintain drainage structures and tile lines, clean ditches Performance of these tasks includes the use of physical labor and operation of self-propelled mobile equipment such as dump trucks, front-end loaders, tractors, motor graders, and an array of support equipment and hand tools such as chain saws, pneumatic hammers, hand drills, weed eaters, lawn mowers, and shovels.
20%	Snow removal. Operate snow removal equipment such as single axle dump truck or a tandem-axle dump truck, each of which may be equipped with a tailgate or hopper spreader, a straight blade or V-plow, a wing plow, and underbody ice blade. Procedures include the removal of snow, packed snow, and/or ice by plowing and/or spreading abrasives and de-icing chemicals on the roadway surface.
10%	Equipment maintenance. Service and perform preventive maintenance on all assigned equipment traditionally used in the performance of highway and bridge maintenance.
5%	Other duties. Miscellaneous duties as assigned from time to time.

Source: Iowa Department of Personnel, agency documents.

NOTES

1. Position management and position classification are related—but not identical—concepts. Position classification primarily refers to categorization of positions with a rational set of principles. Position management generally refers to the allocation of positions for budgetary purposes. A position classification system is one of the elements of a position management system, but position classification systems can have nonbudgetary purposes as well, such as the fundamental division and coordination of work, selection, training, and performance appraisal. Position management can have aspects not directly related to classification, such as budget authorization, budget "caps," downsizing, privatization, contracting out, loadshedding, and so on.

2. In the past, hereditary selection was common. It still exists today, even in some advanced democracies.

3. This type includes most city council members, school board members, township trustees, boards, and some locally elected commissions, as well as some county supervisors, among others.

4. Also known as rank-in-position strategies.

5. In at-will jobs, the incumbent must prove that he was removed from the job for an illegal reason such as discrimination based on race, age, or gender. This puts the burden of proof on the job incumbent and provides a narrow scope of appeal. In most civil service positions, the employer must prove "cause" for termination—that is, the incumbent must be documented to be incompetent, to exhibit inappropriate or illegal behavior, or to be unwilling to reform derelict or improper behaviors.

6. The ONET, *Occupational Informational Network on the Internet,* is an online electronic database commonly used by human resource professionals nationally. It has consolidated the occupational listings from the old *DOT* and considerably and more fully analyzes them than in the past.

7. The Civil Service Reform Act of 1978 provided for (a) the bulk of the Civil Service Commission's routine work to be administered by OPM, an executive agency; (b) the creation of the MSPB to be a watchdog of merit employees' rights; (c) a reorganized Federal Labor Relations Authority; (d) the creation of a Senior Executive Service, a quasi-rank-based corps that was more flexible and mobile than the former supergrades (GS grades 16–18); (e) a merit and bonus pay system for GS grades 13–15; and (f) the mandate of performance appraisal systems in the various agencies.

8. Additional online sources include http://www.opm.gov/fedclass/gsadmn.pdf; http://www.hr-guide .com/selection.htm; http://www.job-analysis.net/

9. Job tasks are discrete work activities necessary to performance and that result in an outcome usable to another person. Usage of the term *task* varies. Here it means broad activities such as (with regard to the upcoming example for a payroll clerk) processing time sheets, printing the payroll, and deducting appropriate expenses such as taxes. Another usage (seen in Exhibit 5.4) for the term *task* is as a synonym for "step performed." For example, paying payroll taxes requires the use of different exemptions, distinguishing between salary and reimbursements, and controlling and paying out from a separate tax account. These subtasks are here referred to as "job elements."

10. Depending on the position and the individual, such physical, manual, or special requirements may require a reasonable accommodation.

11. The terms *class series* and *occupational series* are used interchangeably. Both refer to a normal progression pattern that can be followed by employees, sometimes designated by Roman numerals (Secretary I, II, III, IV) and sometimes by a traditional management series (lead worker, supervisor, manager).

12. Because there is a range in the market, the organization must decide whether it wants to be in the middle of the range, at the top, or at the bottom. This is referred to as the "meet, lead, or lag" question (Chapter 7). Because most governments are labor cost–intensive, small differences can be important in terms of budget outlays.

13. These are the general categories for the well-known Hay system.

14. On the other hand, in larger jurisdictions, job evaluation of individual job classes or class series is often constant. This helps with currency but generally leads to inconsistency in the long term in the absence of occasional pay studies to rationalize the overall system.

15. The Work Examples and Competencies listed are for illustrative purposes only and are not intended to be the primary basis for position classification decisions.

REFERENCES

Bowman, J. S., & West, J. P. (Eds.). (2007a). *American public service: Radical reform and the merit system.* New York: Taylor and Francis.

Bowman, J. S., & West, J. P. (2007b). Lord Acton and employment doctrines: Absolute power and the spread of at-will employment. *Journal of Business Ethics, 74,* 119–130.

Bureau of Labor Statistics, U.S. Department of Labor. (2008). *Occupational outlook handbook, 2008–09 ed.* Washington, DC: Author. http://www.bls.gov/OCO/

Chi, K. S. (1998). State civil service systems. In S. E. Condrey (Ed.), *Handbook of human resource management in government* (pp. 35–55). San Francisco: Jossey-Bass.

Cipolla, F. (1999, July 15). Time for the classification system to go. *Federal Times,* p. 15.

Clegg, C., & Spencer, C. (2007). A circular and dynamic model of the process of job design. *Journal of Occupational and Organizational Psychology, 80*(2), 321–339.

Condrey, S. E. (1998). Toward strategic human resource management. In S. E. Condrey (Ed.), *Handbook of human resource management in government* (pp. 1–14). San Francisco: Jossey-Bass.

Crandall, F. N., & Wallace, M. J. (1998). *Work and rewards in the virtual workplace.* New York: AMACOM.

De Leon, L., & Denhardt, R. B. (2000). The political theory of reinvention. *Public Administration Review, 60*(2), 89–97.

DeSoto, W., & Castillo, R. (1995). Police civil service in Texas. *Review of Public Personnel Administration, 15*(1), 98–104.

Ewoh, A. I. E., & Elliott, E. (1997). End of an era? Affirmative action and reaction in the 1990s. *Review of Public Personnel Administration, 17*(4), 38–51.

Foster, M. R. (1998). Effective job analysis methods. In S. E. Condrey (Ed.), *Handbook of human resource management in government* (pp. 322–348). San Francisco: Jossey-Bass.

Grady, D., & Tax, P. C. (1996). Entrepreneurial bureaucrats and democratic accountability: Experience at the state government level. *Review of Public Personnel Administration, 16*(4), 5–14.

Hamilton, D. K. (1999). The continuing judicial assault on patronage. *Public Administration Review, 59*(1), 54–62.

Hays, S. W. (2004). Trends and best practices in state and local human resource management: Lessons to be learned? *Review of Public Personnel Administration, 24*(5), 256–275.

HR-Guide.com. (2000). *HR guide to the Internet: Job analysis: Job descriptions.* http://www.job-analysis.net/G051.htm

Ingraham, P. W., & Getha-Taylor, H. (2005). Common sense, competence, and talent in the public sector in the USA: Finding the right mix in a complex world. *Public Administration, 83*(4), 789–803.

Institute of Management & Administration (IOMA). (2003). Why job descriptions are so necessary for your payroll staff. *IOMA Payroll Manager's Report, 3*(4), 5–8.

Iowa Department of Personnel. (1999). *Position description questionnaire.* Des Moines, IA: Author.

Isfahani, N. (1998). The debate over tenure. *Review of Public Personnel Administration, 18*(1), 80–86.

Jenkins, S. M., & Curtin, P. (2006). Adapting job analysis methodology to improve evaluation practice. *American Journal of Evaluation, 27*(4), 485–494.

Kelly, J. (1992). Does job re-design theory explain job re-design outcomes? *Human Relations, 45*(8), 753–774.

LaPolice, C. C., Carter, G. W., & Johnson, J. W. (2008). Linking ONET descriptions to occupational literacy requirements using job component validation. *Personnel Psychology, 61*(2), 405–441.

Leavitt, W. M., & Johnson, G. (1998). Employee discipline and the post-bureaucratic public organization: A challenge in the change process. *Review of Public Personnel Administration, 18*(2), 73–81.

Leonard, S. (2000). The demise of the job description. *HRMagazine, 45*(8), 184–185.

Lodge, M., & Hood, C. (2005). Symposium introduction: Competency and higher civil servants. *Public Administration, 83*(4), 779–787.

Marshall, G. S. (1998, May/June). Whither (or wither) OPM? *Public Administration Review, 58,* 280–282.

Mosher, F. C. (1982). *Democracy and the public service* (2nd ed.). New York: Oxford University Press.

Nelson, S. (2004). The state of the federal service today: Aching for reform. *Review of Public Personnel Administration, 24*(3), 202–215.

Pollack, L. J., Simons, C., Romero, H., & Hausser, D. (2002). A common language for classifying and describing occupations: The development, structure, and application of the Standard Occupational Classification. *Human Resource Management, 41*(3), 297–307.

Sayre, W. (1948, Spring). The triumph of techniques over purpose. *Public Administration Review, 8,* 134–137.

Sherwood, C. W. (2000). Job design, community policing, and higher education: A tale of two cities. *Police Quarterly, 3*(2), 191–212.

Siegel, G. B. (1998a). Designing and creating an effective compensation plan. In S. E. Condrey (Ed.), *Handbook of human resource management in government* (pp. 608–626). San Francisco: Jossey-Bass.

Siegel, G. B. (1998b). Work management and job evaluation systems in a government environment. In S. E. Condrey (Ed.), *Handbook of human resource management in government* (pp. 586–607). San Francisco: Jossey-Bass.

Somma, M., & Fox, C. J. (1997). It's not civil service, but leadership and communication: Response to DeSoto and Castillo. *Review of Public Personnel Administration, 17*(1), 84–91.

U.S. Department of Labor. (1991). *Dictionary of occupational titles* (4th ed.). Washington, DC: Author. http://www.oalj.dol.gov/libdot.htm

U.S. Fish and Wildlife Service. (2008). http://training.fws.gov/supervisors/supvfaqs/pmclass.htm

U.S. Government Accountability Office (GAO). (2003). *Preliminary observations on DOD's proposed civilian personnel reforms* (Testimony # 03–7171). Washington, DC: Author.

U.S. Merit Systems Protection Board (MSPB). (1999). *Federal supervisors and poor performers.* Washington, DC: Author.

U.S. Merit Systems Protection Board (MSPB). (2002). *Making the public service work: Recommendations for change.* Washington, DC: Author.

U.S. Office of Personnel Management (OPM). (1991). *The classifier's handbook.* http://www.opm.gov/Fedclass/clashnbk.pdf

U.S. Office of Personnel Management (OPM). (2006). *Career patterns: A 21st century approach to attracting talent.* Washington, DC: Author.

U.S. Office of Personnel Management (OPM). (n.d.). *Federal classification and job grading systems.* http://www.opm.gov/fedclass/

Van Riper, P. P. (1958). *History of the United States civil service.* New York: Harper & Row.

Van Wart, M. (1998). *Changing public sector values.* New York: Garland.

Van Wart, M. (2000). The return to simpler methods in job analysis: The case of municipal clerks. *Review of Public Personnel Administration, 20*(3), 5–23.

Yergin, D. A., & Stanislaw, J. (1998). *The commanding heights: The battle between government and the marketplace that is remaking the modern world.* New York: Simon & Schuster.

Chapter 6

Motivation

Possible, Probable, or Impossible?

An employee's motivation is a direct result of the sum of interactions with his or her manager.

—Bob Nelson

After studying this chapter, you should be able to

- understand why human motivation is important,
- know how human motivation varies,
- recognize how human resource management affects motivation,
- discuss personnel strategies for increasing motivation, and
- learn how to deal with difficult employee behaviors.

New employees are often eager to get to work—they are motivated to get started, make a difference, and fit in with their new colleagues. Employees often hope that others will welcome them, and help them to succeed by sharing useful tips and knowledge. They also hope that their boss will help them succeed and support them in their motivation to do well. Motivation is key to employee productivity and performance, and therefore central to human resource management.

Motivation can be defined as the drive or energy that compels people to act, with energy and persistence, toward some goal. To say that someone "has motivation" is to say that that person has substantial energy and drive in pursuit of something. Leaders, managers, and psychologists alike have long pondered how they can better harness and direct people's "psychic energy." Indeed, if human resource management is about the development of policies for effective utilization of human resources in organization, then human resource management is doubly concerned with motivation. First, human resource management cannot ignore the impact that classification, compensation, promotion, training, and other policies have on employee motivation. Second, human resource management involves policies that direct how people interact in organizations. Human resource management can encourage or discourage people from interacting with others in certain ways that affect motivation, often directly.

When people have motivation, they work with energy, enthusiasm, and initiative; when they lack motivation, they accomplish less and seem to need more supervision to do even a basic amount of work and overcome modest challenges. Working managers know this well, and public sector survey data confirm this. Berman and West (2003b) found, for example, that in jurisdictions in which managers have a strong commitment, 77.8% of respondents also agree or strongly agree that "employee productivity is high," compared with only 44.1% in which most managers only have mediocre levels of commitment. While relevant research is sometimes inconclusive, it is difficult to measure performance and motivation; there typically are many intervening factors (e.g., poor supervision and unclear tasks; Wright, 2007). It is fair to state, however, that motivation is widely accepted to be one of several strong influences on performance.

Empirical data also suggest that the level of motivation in the workplace is mixed. Whereas some workers are highly motivated, others are cynical, wary, or only modestly motivated. West and Berman (1997) found in cities with populations of more than 50,000 people that 29.8% of city managers agree or strongly agree with the statement "employees are highly motivated to achieve goals," 48.8% only somewhat agree with this statement, and 21.5% disagree in different degrees with the statement. The heuristic **25–50–25 rule** states that 25% of employees are highly motivated, 50% are fence sitters, and 25% are withdrawn or cynical. Fence sitters are reserved, somewhat motivated, waiting to see whether motivation is warranted. The 25–50–25 rule has not been rigorously validated by scientific research, but many supervisors nevertheless find that it more or less accurately represents their experience. The rule appears to apply here: managers should expect that their workers vary greatly in their level of motivation. That is just how it is.

Motivation matters and varies. Yet, this fact, perhaps oddly, has not always led managers and their organizations to the conclusion that they ought to seek ways to increase employee motivation. Rather, the paradox of democracy, which limits employee rights in the workplace, has sometimes been interpreted as expecting staff to "shut up" at their job. Some supervisors show a less-than-caring attitude about employees' needs and concerns. Their attitude seems to be, if employees do not like it here, they can go elsewhere! Such perspectives certainly do little to make motivation a priority, and are inappropriate and dated (Buckingham & Coffman, 1999). Hence, another paradox is that, while motivation is widely recognized as important, it is sometimes blatantly neglected, as well. However, higher levels of employee motivation are increasingly needed in order to meet expanding workloads and to adapt in positive ways to ongoing change. Increasingly, managers need to be concerned with the motivation and find new ways of ensuring it. A reasonable goal, in an imperfect world, may well be to transform 25–50–25 into 40–50–10!

What can be expected from human resource management? Motivation is a complex but not insurmountable challenge for managers. Various strategies have been discussed in the past, and new strategies often surface. First, this chapter examines the nature of motivation. The phenomenon must be understood, especially the kind of factors that affect it, before attempts are made to shape it. Second, the chapter explores the impact of human resource management policies and strategies on the climate for motivation. Third, the chapter examines managerial strategies for working with individual employees.

▪▪ THEORIES OF MOTIVATION

Motivation is an oft-studied subject, with many different theories. The purpose in this brief space is not to summarize these theories—an entire book alone would scarcely do justice to such a rich topic—but rather to consider some dominant insights that lead to an appropriate appreciation of motivation for managers. Motivation is multifaceted and dynamic. Motivation is shaped by many different factors, and people vary in their susceptibility to them. A central insight is that strategies that treat employees in a one-size-fits-all way are apt to be ineffective; a bit more sophistication is needed.

Motivation theories differ according to what is emphasized. While there is general agreement that motivation is about the drive or energy that compels people to act with energy and persistence toward goals, the question is to know which factors affect this energy. Some theories focus on factors *inherent to individuals,* such as the need for appreciation and achievement and, more recently, also on individuals' mental health (e.g., whether they are depressed or anxious) and physical states (e.g., whether they have adequate energy). The former affect motivation's trigger, whereas the latter two affect the ability of people to be engaged and, hence, motivated. Other theories examine components relating to the *external circumstances* in which people find themselves, such as the effects of work goals, salary, work obstructions, supervision, and leadership. These elements also influence motivation. This diversity of foci brings richness, as well as confusion, to understanding motivation.

This diversity of foci also mirrors the fundamental reality that people are motivated by different things, and that they also vary in their ability to find those things in their job. People do not all want the same thing from their jobs, though there are some commonalities. A key **principle of motivation** is that people are motivated to pursue and satisfy their needs. As President Dwight D. Eisenhower put it, "Motivation is the art of getting people to do what you want them to do because they want to do it." Having a great boss may be relevant to one individual and largely irrelevant to another. Money may be very important to one person, but much less so to someone else. The idea that needs stand central is associated with the work of Abraham Maslow (1954), who developed a "hierarchy of needs," including basic drives around existence such as the ability to pay for food and housing, safety such as job security, belonging such as friendship with peers and supervisors, esteem such as recognition for a job well done, and self-actualization such as the innate pleasures of doing what one likes and finds fulfilling. While later works cast some doubt on the rigid nature of a hierarchy, the notion of needs remain valid.

By focusing on needs, Maslow sought to go beyond some assertions of earlier control-oriented theories, which today are perhaps better known as "Theory X"-type motivation. According to McGregor (1960), **Theory X** holds that all people are inherently lazy, and therefore need a "stick and carrot" approach in order increase motivation. By contrast, **Theory Y** assumes that people are inherently motivated to learn and grow, and therefore the manager's job is to provide developmental opportunities for workers. While both Theory X and Theory Y allow for a broad range of motivational strategies, an important insight is that neither the assumptions of Theory X nor Theory Y are always or necessarily true; some people are more like the assumptions of Theory X, whereas others are closer to Theory Y. Moreover, people are also not always constant in this regard. Sometimes they are slothful, and sometimes they are motivated to learn and grow; we are all like that.

Therefore, many authors focus on actual needs, rather than on assumptions about people's needs. For brevity, these needs can be categorized into eight groups of **motivational needs.**

Group 1: Some needs that people *have concern their physical security.* People need to make enough money to afford food and shelter and, in today's circumstances, to afford health care and make retirement contributions. These latter needs show concern for future physical needs. In recent years, many employers have increased employee benefits for health and retirement needs, and widespread societal discussion in the United States about these expenditures underscores the point that these needs continue to be important today.

Group 2: Some needs that people have are *for acknowledgement and recognition.* Many employees like receiving compliments and recognition for work done well. Sometimes they want to hear words of appreciation, and a salary raise may reinforce this. For some people, being told "thank you" is important, whereas for others it is a less significant need. Because it costs so little to say "thank you," and because managers cannot always know how much being appreciated means to others, managers do well to say "thank you" several times each day. Indeed, managers tend to underestimate the power of appreciation, perhaps because in their own experience they often have to put on a thick skin and receive little of it.

Group 3: Some people have particularly strong *needs for achievement.* Some people really welcome assignments that stretch their skills and abilities, and sometimes also for the sake of a little adrenaline that comes along with it. These people really enjoy work for its own sake (Nadler & Lawler, 1977). In a related vein, path-goal theory suggests that the job of the manager is to lay out clear and doable goals, and to provide a clear path with few obstacles for employees (House, 1971; Locke & Latham, 1990). The achievement need implies that managers should provide challenging goals for those who want them, and help all workers to fulfill their tasks. But again, people surely vary in their need for such goals, and even high achievers sometimes want a day or week off.

Group 4: Other needs that people have are for *making a difference.* A presumed motivation for work in the public sector is wanting to impact the lives of others and the communities in which they live. With this needs comes a desire for power, too, because power is a means to impact the world around them (McClelland, 1985). With power, people can create new programs and develop policies. Various studies show that public employees have a stronger need than their private sector counterparts for such power to make a positive difference in society or their communities (Perry, 2000). Some people are very strongly motivated to make a difference in others, whereas others are less strongly motivated by this need.

Group 5: Many people also have *a need to belong,* to have a sense that they are part of the group, not only in a formal or legal sense, but also in an emotional sense. They have employee relationship needs. People have a need for affiliation—a sense of belonging, trust, and mutual support. It is important for employees to have friends and supportive colleagues at work; they help deal with adversity, make the work experience more fun, often share their knowledge, and help others to do their job better, too.

Group 6: Another group of needs is sometimes called *other, nonwork needs.* For example, many people go to work in order to support their families. The financial rewards of a job make this possible, but having on-site day care and first-rate health insurance helps people with small children satisfy this need even more. Likewise, they want to live in a pleasant environment and have a comfortable home; work makes that possible, too. These requirements go beyond the physical security needs noted earlier, and motivation strategies that only focus on work may miss satisfying these other needs, too, which are often quite important.

Group 7: Almost everyone experiences some *need for predictability and control* over their situation. Individuals need to perceive that they can shape their work experiences in meaningful ways, and to believe the policies and people that affect their job satisfaction and motivation are not subject to anyone's arbitrary whim. There needs to be some control and continuity in an uncertain world.

Group 8: People also have a need to *avoid demotivators* (Herzberg, 1959). Bad rules and regulations demotivate workers when they get in the way of their work and other needs. Good rules and regulations seldom motivate—few people come whistling to work because of their organization's great policies and procedures!—but bad rules surely demotivate. Examples are those that are associated with requiring excessive documentation or that restrict one doing the right thing when needed. Similarly, supervisory relations and peer relations are thought to have more down sides than up sides. Poor supervisory relations and peer relations induce significant stress on workers. Workers may then worry about what might or will happen next, and whether actions and comments are harbingers of bad things to come. Poor peer relations can have similar affects. Smart employees know how to avoid a row (angry dispute) with people around them.

The role of money deserves some special attention, perhaps because it is so universally mentioned and seen as a motivator. In short, when people perceive that they lack sufficient funds (e.g., to buy the lifestyle they desire), the prospect of making more money motivates because it helps them to satisfy more of their needs (e.g., physical security and recognition). Jobs that do not bring enough salary to satisfy basic needs also fail to motivate ("Why work?"); employee turnover in low-paying jobs is often very high. However, studies find that good pay is a far more significant motivator for blue collar workers than for white collar staff (Sanzotta, 1977). Once people are able to satisfy needs that money can buy, money no longer motivates as much. While the prospect of a significant pay increase can spark motivation (it allows for meeting previously unmet needs), once a higher pay level is reached motivation soon returns to where it was before; there are always some unmet needs in life. Thus, the motivational boost of prospective money is only temporary. In short, (a) the lack of money demotivates, (b) the prospect of making more money motivates, but (c) permanent higher salaries are not associated with permanent higher motivation. It might also be noted that for organizations, public and private, permanent salary boosts are an untenable motivation strategy; such moneys are not always available. Other motivational strategies are needed to energize workers.

In conclusion, there are many kinds of needs that motivate people. Exhibit 6.1 considers motivational differences across generations, too. The next section examines how to use this knowledge in practical ways. By the way, how well do you know your needs? Are they constant, or do they change?

▪▪ HUMAN RESOURCE MANAGEMENT AND THE CLIMATE FOR MOTIVATION

Before we explore strategies for motivation, we need to identify several additional realities about the nature of needs. First, motivation follows from personal efforts to fulfill needs, but this does not imply that either managers or employees know their needs well. Needs are

---

Exhibit 6.1 Motivating the New Millennial Generation

Do younger employees differ in the motivations form older workers? Many managers seem to think so, and an emerging literature agrees with them. Cam Marston (2007) in *Motivating the "What's In It For Me?" Generation* argued that older workers, called Baby Boomers and Matures, are motivated to work by making an income, and having identity through their profession and employment by their organization. They are likely to be loyal to their employer in return for increasing growth opportunities. However, he sees younger workers, termed Generation-X and New Millennials, as motivated to make just enough money so that they can enjoy the lifestyle that they seek. They do not see loyalty to employers as a wise strategy, and they are likely to stay with their employer as long as the work is interesting, is educational, and serves their needs. They have loyalty to people, rather than to employers.

So what? The motivations of younger generations are different in some important ways. They are less likely to be persuaded by such concepts as "paying your dues" or "waiting your turn." They are not interested in sticking around when there is no work to be done. Rather, they want a decent income and interesting work (as they see it). When the work is done, well, they're gone! Organizations do not have loyalty to their workers, so why should they? Undoubtedly, as many in public service find opportunities in public, nonprofit, and for-profit organizations, these motivations are apt to be part of the public sector workplace too.

---

dynamic. They change as circumstances change. What is compelling today may be less important in a few years or even a few hours. In addition, people also may be confused about real and imagined needs. Some feel that they ought to be motivated to pursue a career that makes a lot of money or that which makes their parents proud, even though they do not have particularly strong interests in doing those things. Others are not clear about what their goals are. While most people know something about their needs (we all have some self-knowledge), the difficulty of *fully* knowing one's needs becomes obvious when answering the question "What are your needs?," even when limiting this question to the here and now. Second, even when people are clear about some of their needs, communicating these to managers can be dangerous and naïve. For employees, it is akin to giving managers control over their satisfaction. Better that the boss does not know one's real needs, because this information can be used against the employee. Telling someone what is needed or wanted is akin to sharing vulnerabilities, something that requires a good deal of trust between two people.

The implication is that while people are motivated to satisfy their needs, this does not mean as a practical matter that a strategy can be built solely upon directly asking them about their needs. How then can managers shape motivation? Fortunately, the situation is not hopeless. There is a two-part solution to this conundrum. The first part is to ensure that human resource management policies and practices provide for a broad range of conditions that allow employees to satisfy their needs, as they believe them to be. Managers do not need to know the exact needs of each employee, but rather need to implement a broad range of policies and practices through which each employee can find and experience those that help meet their needs, and in sufficient ways to ensure motivation. Nor do employees have to state what satisfies them—they can change their mind as their life or career circumstances shift: they might value on-site child care when raising children, and not value it at all once children are grown. An analogy is of human resource management policies and practices being like a cafeteria or buffet, in which each employee values the selections differently. Most employees will hopefully be satisfied by whatever selection they have made (even if some are mandatory, such as attendance policies!). The term **climate for motivation** is defined as the opportunities for workers to find motivation at work, which, in part, is determined by the range of human resource management policies and practices.

This section examines how human capital strategies shape the climate for motivation in modern organizations. Approaches addressing the motivation conundrum involve managers working one on one with employees. The range of practices accomplish a great deal, but it cannot deal with each personal situation. Since a tailored approach is needed, we examine ideas for motivating individuals.

From the perspective of managers and their organizations, the following constitutes a general climate for worker motivation. When all of these conditions are present, employees will likely find something that motivates them, though some might motivate more than others (Berman, 2006):[1]

1. Competitive salaries

2. Relevant benefits that consider worker needs for economic security (today and in the future) and non-work-related needs (family, vacation)

3. Meaningful rewards and recognition (that are fairly distributed, too)

4. Opportunities for challenging (yet achievable) assignments with further opportunities for learning and skill development

5. Friendly and cooperative workplace relations

6. Assignments that allow workers to make a meaningful contribution to society

7. Feedback that provides both recognition and opportunity for development

8. Meaningful control over employees' work environment

9. Minimization of the demotivating effect of rules and regulations that impede job performance and satisfaction

10. Reduction of negative supervisory relationships

Readers can readily verify that an environment with these conditions is likely to be attractive and motivating. Would you like to work in an organization in which these conditions are present? The factors above are associated with the previously mentioned seven groups of needs, and are affected by human resource management policies and practices. These connections are shown below; many also are explored in other chapters of this book.

1. *Competitive salaries.* At-market compensation helps employees meet needs for physical security; they are also a way for employers to show appreciation and express recognition. Such salaries also further motivation in another way, namely by giving employees a sense that they are receiving a fair return for their efforts. For this reason, it is important that remuneration remains competitive by being periodically adjusted. Compensation is explored in Chapter 7.

2. *Relevant benefits.* Benefits assist workers to meet healthcare, retirement, education, and other needs. In the United States, fewer and fewer of these needs are met through taxes (government programs)—citizens in other developed countries still count on affordable health, education, and retirement plans increasingly unavailable to Americans. People vary in their needs, and many employers offer cafeteria-style menus of benefits. For some workers, retirement contributions, healthcare benefits, and tuition reimbursement plans are key reasons for them to be motivated on the job. Benefits and employee-friendly policies are considered in Chapter 8.

3. *Meaningful rewards and recognition.* People need appreciation, not only expressed by compensation, but also expressed in formal recognition ceremonies and informal thank-you's. As discussed in Chapter 10, in theory agency appraisal systems should, but in practice often fail to provide sufficient appreciation and recognition. Hence, managers must find other ways to acknowledge workers, such as through extra personal time "off," travel for conferences, new computer equipment, small cash awards or gift certificates, and so on. For some employees these things mean little, but for others they are a relevant source of motivation.

4. *Opportunities for challenge and training.* Making the most of other people's strengths and the least of their weaknesses is a surefire formula for managerial success. Some employees have a need for growth and learning (Theory Y), and managers do well to provide these; the lack of meaningful work challenge is a demotivator for productive and creative people. Chapter 9 discusses training and development that can be used to provide growth opportunities.

5. *Friendly and cooperative workplace relations.* Employees prefer to come to a friendly office setting. While this may or may not be associated with increased motivation, an office that is perceived as hostile is a demotivator (Cherniss & Goleman, 2001). For this reason, most organizations make "people skills" a criterion in their hiring and promotion. According to Berman and West (2008), 71.5% of cities agree or strongly agree that they focus on people skills when hiring or promoting managers. A subsequent section of this chapter offers suggestions for how managers can increase friendly and cooperative relations on the job.

6. *Assignments that allow for making meaningful contributions to society.* Most citizens join public and nonprofit organizations because they are motivated to make a difference in society. This is part of the motivation for public service, and it reflects the fundamental achievement need that many people in such organizations have. Needless to say, the task of human resource management is to design jobs that allow for having such impact, and the task of managers is to ensure that in fact they do. Job design and position management are discussed in Chapter 5.

7. *Feedback that provides recognition and opportunity for development.* Feedback is not only part of formal performance appraisal (Chapter 10); the challenges of work require frequent assessment and adjustment. Informal, frequent feedback is a part of the manager's job that is essential to employee performance. The next section in this chapter, on psychological contracts, considers how managers can do that. It also lies at the heart of the "one-minute manager" (Blanchard & Johnson, 1981) who provides frequent and concise feedback to employees.

8. *Meaningful control over the work environment.* Being in control is a source of motivation, as it allows people to tailor their job experience in ways that increase satisfaction, such

as flextime and telecommuting (Chapter 8), or even such things as having plants and choosing wall or cubicle décor or lighting. The lack of such control reduces these sources of satisfaction. Even more important is the extent to which the employee is subject to the whims of others, especially when preferences collide and communication is poor. Exhibit 6.2 looks at one way in which people may benefit from having control over their work (e.g., how and when they take breaks).

Exhibit 6.2   The Effective Manager . . . Takes A Break

Motivation and working hard are not always the same. Indeed, people need a break, too. Berman and West (2008) showed that managers who take a break report themselves as being more effective, with less stress than those who do not take a break. Some managers take breaks during lunch, whereas others take short breaks during the day, often about 10 or 15 minutes each. Doing so clears and restores the mind.

American culture sometimes confuses break taking with slacking off or not being motivated or serious: "[A]ttitudes have not always been very positive about managers taking breaks. Managers experience very busy schedules . . . and they are widely thought to set examples for their workers . . . [T]hey may perceive that taking a break will set a bad example, encouraging workers to work less, thereby feeding negative stereotypes of public sector employees" (Berman & West, 2007).

What can be done? Some avant garde employers provide opportunities for taking a break, such as by supplying quiet spaces, napping pods, or massage chairs. In other instances, managers do well to encourage their subordinates to take breaks as they find it useful to get their work done. It is not the work activity that counts, but the quality of the work that is actually completed.

---

9. *Minimize the demotivating effect of rules and regulations.* The job of the manager is to make it possible for workers to accomplish their tasks, and that includes finding ways of meeting the requirements of rules and regulations, or even working around them when appropriate. While recognizing that many rules and regulations have been adopted for good reason (such as to ensure accountability), the negative side-effects of these rules are recognized, and most organizations aim to meet accountability requirements in other less-burdensome ways.

10. *Reduce negative supervisory relationships.* People need to get along, especially with their bosses. The failure to get along with one's boss can be a source of serious stress and distraction that severely demotivates many employees (Van Wart, 2005). Unfortunately, supervisors really can be nasty and unhelpful; in that case, it usually is necessary for workers to find another job. The cost of supervisory malfunction is high for organizations. Although selection mechanisms are far from perfect, many are making good people skills and professionalism a key requirement for these jobs.

In sum, the above conditions provide for a work environment in which many employee needs can be met. People vary in their needs, and they may be unclear about them and reluctant to disclose them, yet the above practices and conditions are likely to provide satisfaction and motivation for many of them. This is why human resource management is concerned with ensuring that the above practices are in place. The entire set of policies matters, not just one or two that may be emphasized at the expense of others.

▪▪ TWO INDIVIDUALIZED APPROACHES: PSYCHOLOGICAL CONTRACTS AND FEEDBACK

While the above policies and practices set the climate for motivation, managers and employees are likely to find that some tailoring and accommodation are necessary. Managers should recognize, for example, the extent to which any specific worker desires a challenging assignment or seeks to learn a new skill. They need to find out from workers whether they are interested in flextime or telecommuting. Personnel are apt to have to express their desire for a salary raise, and make their case for that (asking never hurts). Administrators cannot read the minds of employees, and they are apt to make errors if they assume that they know what motivates others. More communication can often make both workers and their managers better off.

Psychological Contracts. A tool for increasing productivity and motivation is the psychological contract. It builds on the famous management by objectives (MBO) insight that involvement of workers in goal formation increases buy-in and mutual understanding many times over. However, the MBO focus was on the more formal and documented aspects of joint goal setting (Drucker, 1954). In contrast, a psychological contract is defined as an unwritten understanding about mutual needs, goals, expectations, and procedures. Such agreements go beyond employment contracts that typically include salary, benefits, feedback, and working hours; it can be said that psychological contracts begin where formal employment contracts leave off. Psychological contracts are potentially far reaching (any issue is fair game), but are usually limited to highly valued concerns. Topics could include support in dealing with childcare responsibilities, the frequency and nature of managerial feedback, and opportunities for training. Psychological contracts increase motivation by allowing managers to better understand the needs of individual employees, by helping to provide rewards and conditions that address individual needs, and by ensuring clarity about roles and expectations (Berman, 2006).

Psychological contracts are a relatively new tool. In 2002, a survey of senior local government managers found that 57.3% of them establish psychological contracts with employees, but only about a fifth of these (or 20.7%) said that they fully employ the processes described below. Some administrators refer to them as "informal agreements" or "mutual understandings." What is described below is a bit more comprehensive than most people experience at work, but it is the direction in which things seem to be moving. People who have used contracts say that they work (Berman & West, 2003a; Rousseau, 1995).

Psychological contracts are easy to establish with subordinates. An official can go to an employee and note that it has been some time since their last conversation. The official might say he or she would like to know how things are going, and might ask whether there is anything that might be done to make the employee's work go better. Following the employee's perhaps surprised response, the manager could ask whether the employee has anything he or she would like to achieve or improve or do over the next few months. Then, as items are listed, the manager next discusses them with the employee. The fact that a subordinate wants something does not mean that it can be granted. Thus, an evaluative response is given. The manager explains why (a) something can be done (e.g., training or flextime), or (b) cannot be met (a salary increase over which the manager might not have control), or (c) can be met in a modified form only (the manager might not have control over promotion, but can help through assignments to make the employee more competitive). The job is to help the employee embrace these understandings and facts.

Next, the administrator informs the employee that while the above is a good list, the manager has some job-related needs as well. Perhaps some project needs to be completed, a new strategy pilot tested. In addition, the manager can raise concerns about employee performance or skills. Then the supervisor can suggest a way to resolve the paradox of needs when the employee makes increased commitment to improvement in return for the supervisor assisting the employee to meet some of his or her needs. Perhaps some employee contributions are seen as conditions for the manager helping to meet employee needs. Exhibit 6.3 shows the basic give and take that the psychological contracts entails.

Exhibit 6.3	The Psychological Contract	
Psychological Contract		
	Expect to get	Expect to give
Worker		
Supervisor or other		

Source: As adapted from Osland, Kolb, & Rubin, 2000.

After all the worker's needs and manager's needs have been agreed upon, the manager summarizes the discussion and notes that situations and things do change. The door to communication remains open, especially regarding perceived misunderstandings. Managers should repeat the psychological contract at least twice over the next few weeks. People sometimes "forget" things or don't take them very seriously unless they are repeated. While it is easier for a manager to initiate a psychological contract with a subordinate, sometimes subordinates can initiate such dialogue with their supervisor or with coworkers. Psychological contracts are also easily established within the first few weeks of employment, before routine patterns of communication set in.

Several factors make a psychological contract effective as a motivational tool: (a) It helps bring to light workers' needs that motivate them. (b) It allows the manager to clarify workers' needs, and evaluate the extent to which those needs can be met. (c) It is perceived as fair balance between what the worker wants and what the worker is expected to give. (d) It has a mechanism for following up, ensuring that the agreement is implemented and addressing changes that may occur. The latter are opportunities for further discussion to understanding the extent and nature of the problem, and reach a renewed understanding. Elements of psychological contracts are shown in Exhibit 6.4.

A psychological contract assumes that people can have a rational dialogue and are susceptible to reason. It assumes that employees are able and willing to make expected contributions to the organizations, and that supervisors do have their motivation and welfare at heart. However, there are times when these assumptions are not met. Strategies for addressing these challenging situations are discussed a bit further, as part of feedback and dealing with difficult people.

Exhibit 6.4   Elements of Psychological Contracts

	Respondents Identifying Item(%)
A. Work	
Workload	87.1
Work schedules	75.3
Responsibility or authority	55.9
Quality of work	52.7
Training	39.8
Performance objectives	34.4
Following orders	23.7
Off-site travel	7.5
B. Communication and relationships	
Working relationship with immediate superior	78.5
How and when feedback is given	53.3
Interpersonal relations (general)	45.2
Specific behaviors of employees/managers	35.5
Individually preferred working styles	29.0
Individually preferred communication	28.0
C. Careers and other	
Job security	69.9
Rewards (specific)	59.1
Promotion	58.1
Career development of employees	44.1
Employee/manager influence on what happens to them	41.0
Loyalty	23.0
Rewards (decision-making process)	26.9
Other, please specify: _____	2.2

Source: Berman, E., & J. West. (2003a). Psychological contracts in local government: A preliminary survey. *Review of Public Personnel Administration 23*(4): 267–285.

As noted, a psychological contract is especially (but not only) useful when people begin a new employment relationship. At that point, there is considerable uncertainty, and interaction and communication patterns are still fluid and subject to change. A contract can also be made among group members, or between a group and the group leader. At that time a discussion can take place about what the group wants to get or do, and what the group is willing to give (and give up) in order to get what the members want. The understandings are then written down, distributed, and reviewed a few weeks later. The later review shows commitment to the contract, and allows for dealing with whatever may have come up in the meantime. Establishing psychological contracts is an approach that helps get agreement and alignment among group members, hence, helps motivate workers.

Exhibit 6.5 shows an example of an actual psychological contract between a supervisor and her employee. People who use contracts often report increased communication and satisfaction. The following is an example of such a response by an agency director who used it with a manager; many similar responses are made by supervisors who deal with employees, and sometimes employees who take initiative to make a psychological contract with their superiors.

I am pleased to say that all is going well with the psychological contract entered into with Ms. Johnson, Director of Development. We have continued to meet on a regular basis and discussion continues to be open and fruitful. Our meetings include each of us going over any project we feel the other needs to know about. While my door is always open to any staff member, Gail has taken the initiative to stop in more often just to touch base on pending projects.

Over this past month we have had to deal with some difficult issues, including the postponement of our largest event of the year, due to delays in a major project. She continues to work with a great deal of autonomy that is important to her, and because I see the result of her working within this capacity, I am happy to give her more independence. It has been a good experience, one that will continue. I hope to enter into such contracts with the other five department heads.

Exhibit 6.5   Sample Psychological Contract

What supervisor wants from employee

- Timely arrival at work
- More engagement in oversight of Web maintenance and postings
- Preparation of weekly employment scorecard
- Preparation of weekly updates of orders, account totals, and monetary shortfalls
- Ensurance that orders are processed in compliance with joint forces travel regulations

What employee is willing to give to supervisor

- Greater awareness to punctuality
- More commitment to professional training in department
- More engagement in daily operations and more-frequent updates on account balances and pending orders

What employee wants from supervisor

- Training in new IT program
- Better understanding of use of weekly and monthly products
- Time to finish associates degree

What supervisor is willing to give to employee

- Enrollment in off-site training for IT upgrades
- Greater visibility on internal decision-making processes as well as feedback on internal politics and how they affect products
- Time off work to finish associates degree

Feedback. A related tool is feedback, which is inherent to the psychological contract, but which is used in other situations, too. In the context of human resource management, **feedback** is defined as evaluative information given to employees about their performance or behavior, whose purpose is to influence future performance or behavior. An adage in performance improvement is that feedback should be given frequently and consistently, in a timely and positive way. Feedback loses its effectiveness when it is given sporadically, far removed from the moment of performance or in less than constructive ways. A common error is that managers mistakenly assume that workers receive feedback, such as through others, when in fact they may not.

The **strategy for feedback** is straightforward. Managers should

1. provide a balanced assessment of employee performance (including both positive and negative aspects),
2. emphasize the objective nature of service outcomes (although some facts are indisputable),
3. establish their commitment to helping subordinates achieve positive results,
4. work collaboratively with employees to develop strategies for improving performance (without imposing solutions),
5. help employees develop their perspective that they have the power to affect conditions for success,
6. agree on a timetable for monitoring improvement,
7. provide strategies for support and feedback, and
8. offer future rewards for improvement.

This approach helps minimize problems that occur in practice: (a) workers do not receive sufficient feedback, (b) feedback is given that does not contain adequate information, or (c) feedback is interpreted in ways that do not result in desired changes. The lack of feedback affects motivation among those who need appreciation. Inadequate feedback can be frustrating for those who seek to do better, but who are frustrated by not knowing exactly what is expected or required of them. Feedback that is curt and disrespectful is clearly dysfunctional, especially for those who seek cooperative workplace relations. Moreover, impulsive or emotional outbursts of managers are apt to have negative and demotivating effects. Such outbursts contain nothing that can be construed as being helpful. While they may induce short-term improvement, they can also cause long-term resentment.

People often do less well in giving feedback than what they think. People who need little feedback think that others are just like them, and so they give little feedback, too. Some personnel give their feedback a bit too directly, perhaps with little social tact. It is therefore most helpful that supervisors receive periodic feedback from subordinates; some organizations now require that. For example, one human resource director provided her experience with her subordinates (Berman & West, 2008):

> I was evaluated by the city manager, assistant city manager, department directors, legal department, and other direct reports. Each responded anonymously to about 50 close-ended questions (scale from one to ten) and a half dozen open-ended questions. Some questions dealt with social and communication skills. The summary report by the consultant was 12 to 18 pages, outlining my strengths and weaknesses.

Such detailed feedback is useful for managers, of course, and it is sometimes quite serious when the area of feedback is also the subject of ongoing employee concerns.

Finally, individualized approaches also exist for dealing with unsatisfactory performance. There are instances in which feedback cannot wait until the next formal, annual performance appraisal. Sometimes performance is poor and needs to be corrected quickly. The nature of underlying problems can be highly diverse. A person might be in the wrong position and unable to get the work done well; perhaps the supervisor or organization would do best to find another job for that person. In other instances, though, there are those who, following the 25–50–25 rule, stubbornly refuse to be motivated (Exhibit 6.6). For example, some people are just plain unhappy, and others use being upset as a tool for gaining attention and control over others. Still others bully coworkers and are a destructive influence at work. For managers, all such situations require a response, not only because they affect individual performance, but sometimes also because of their disruptive influences on others and, hence, on the unit's performance.

Exhibit 6.6   Dealing With Difficult People

Some people have ways of behaving toward others that are not only unpleasant, but also counterproductive. Some common patterns are hostility (aggressively criticizing coworkers), incessant complaining, silence and unresponsiveness (providing minimal input and cooperation), being super-agreeable (or "empty good naturedness," being cheerful, but not producing work), negativity (always having reasons why something cannot be done), know-it-all expertness (even when they are dead wrong), and indecisiveness (failing to make decisions that allow a project to go forward). While such behaviors can be taken personally ("Did I do something to provoke such yelling?"), the hidden purpose is usually to gain control over others or the situation.

Recognize that the problem must be addressed before it spirals out of control; if it is not dealt with, then, paradoxically, the victims of "difficult" people may themselves be seen as "difficult." There are a variety of ways to approach the problem, according to Heathfield (2008) including the following:

- Begin with a self-examination to ascertain if the other person's conduct really is the issue, and if your own behavior or attitude is contributing to the problem, or if you are overreacting in some way.
- Discuss your observations and assessment with another person to be sure that you are evaluating the situation correctly.
- Meet with your supervisor, colleagues, or the person in question, focusing on how you can get the problematic behavior to stop. Do not focus on the person, but rather on the conduct. For example, point out that that rudeness will not be tolerated, that the difficult person's opinion is incorrect, that failure with excuses is still failure.
- Follow up after a reasonable interval to assess and reinforce the changed behavior or to determine why the agreement was not effective.

These strategies can often reduce, albeit not fully eliminate, these behaviors. Sometimes, meeting only with the other person is not enough. It may be necessary to let another individual know that you are willing to involve others, and to actually do so. This obviously expands the scope of conflict, so be certain that notes and documentation are available—not on interpersonal issues, but on how the situation negatively affects productivity. If nothing else works, then consider changing jobs—either to another position in the organization or to a new opportunity elsewhere.

Source: Heathfield, 2008.

In short, what is a manager to do when feedback based on rational discourse and spirit of cooperation does not produce the desired result? Limits to rational discourse must be acknowledged. The point of further interaction is to minimize the impact of unsatisfactory behaviors. The basic strategy for **dealing with difficult people** is to arrest patterns of interaction with the difficult person through avoidance, setting boundaries, and confronting each difficult behavior in appropriate and controlling ways (Bramson, 1981; Lubit, 2004). Typically, after several documented interactions, managers do well to contact their human resource director and discuss next steps. One such action is to remove the employee from interaction with mission critical functions until performance and behaviors have improved. A second action is for the manager to stand his or her ground on boundaries, setting limits that are not to be crossed (such as speaking rudely or coming in late). Over time, consistently and immediately responding to such problems can result in a pattern of documented poor performance that can be used in subsequent discipline (Chapter 10).

Unhappily for some supervisors and their organizations, the story seldom ends here. Difficult employees may seek to avoid being disciplined by corrupting, compromising, or blackmailing their supervisors through social or ethical embarrassment. Sometimes people threaten legal action, such as discrimination or harassment lawsuits. The possibility of people gathering "dirt" on others with whom they work over several months or years is very real, of course—everyone has said or done something that another person could try to use to their advantage. The quid pro quo of such silent agreements (or standoffs: "I won't embarrass or sue you if you don't . . .") can allow difficult employees to stay on their job for years. Sometimes, organizations even deal with such people by promoting them out of their current job. While we do not know what percentage of employees are "difficult" employees, most administrators have had some brushes with them, and a reasonable guess is probably about one out of every 20 or 30 employees, depending on how one defines *difficult*. Human resource directors earn their pay not only by creating conditions for motivation, but also by being a confidential aide to managers in dealing with these situations. Dealing with motivation means sometimes dealing with the darker side of human motives.

■■ SUMMARY AND CONCLUSION

Motivating employees is an important management task. When people are motivated, they work with energy, enthusiasm, and initiative. *Motivation* is defined as the drive or energy that compels people to act with energy and persistence toward some goal; it is widely associated with performance. Although important, it varies widely among workers. The 25–50–25 rule states that 25% of employees are highly motivated, 50% are somewhat inspired, and 25% are withdrawn or cynical. While this rule has not been validated by research, many managers feel that it more or less accurately represents their experience.

A key principle is that people are motivated to pursue and satisfy their needs. Individuals vary greatly (different people have different needs), and needs change over time. Some characteristic needs are those relating to physical security, acknowledgement and recognition, achievement, power, personal (nonwork) desires, control and predictability, and the avoidance of demotivators such as poor supervision or obstructive rules and regulations. While money often is mentioned as a motivator, this chapter shows that (a) the lack of money demotivates,

(b) the prospect of making more money may motivate, but (c) permanent, higher salaries are not associated with long-lasting motivation.

Human resource management policies and practices affect motivation by providing (a) a range of conditions that allow employees to satisfy their needs, and (b) individualized strategies that allow workers and supervisors to further tailor or accommodate their needs. Ten conditions that increase the climate for motivation are (1) competitive salaries, (2) relevant benefits, (3) rewards and recognition, (4) opportunities for challenging assignments and learning, (5) friendly workplace relations, (6) making a meaningful contribution to society, (7) feedback, (8) control over the work environment, (9) avoiding negative impacts of rules and regulations, and (10) poor supervisory relationships. Human resource management policies and practices that help shape these conditions affect motivation.

This chapter also discusses psychological contracts and feedback as individualized strategies that further motivation. Such a contract is an *unwritten* understanding about mutual needs, goals, expectations, and procedures. These contracts go beyond employment contracts. Topics are potentially far reaching, and are subject to mutual agreement. Several factors make psychological contracts effective: (a) They help shed light on workers' needs that motivate them. (b) They allow the manager to clarify employee needs, and evaluate the extent to which they can be met. (c) They have a mechanism for following up and addressing any problems.

The chapter also addresses feedback, which is a component of psychological contracts, as well as performance improvement in general. Feedback should be given frequently, and in timely, constructive, and positive ways. The chapter concludes with feedback for situations that involve difficult employees, who may be neither open to rational discourse nor cooperative in nature.

In sum, motivation is an important activity of managers and human resource management. While complex, it is feasible to motivate most workers and thereby improve performance.

KEY TERMS

Climate for motivation

Dealing with difficult people

Feedback

Motivation

Motivational needs

Principle of motivation

Psychological contract

Strategy for feedback

The 25–50–25 rule

Theory X

Theory Y

EXERCISES

Class Discussion

1. Discuss what motivates other students them most in their jobs to verify the statements "people are motivated to pursue and satisfy their needs," and that "people vary in their needs." How can

a manager motivate employees when their needs differ? Is motivation too difficult to accomplish? Is it reasonable to motivate people with "carrots and sticks"?

2. Do other students agree that the 25–50–25 rule exists, based on their experience? What are characteristics of those who are highly motivated? What are characteristics of those who are not highly motivated?

3. Discuss the statement that "difficult employees may seek to avoid being disciplined by corrupting, compromising or blackmailing their supervisors through social, sexual or ethical embarrassment whose purpose is to avoid their supervisors seeking adverse action against them." Can you provide any examples of this? Can you identify any movies that show this theme? What would you do if you were to experience such behaviors?

Team Activities

4. Assume that the members of your group are responsible for a group project, such as a group presentation in this class. Make a psychological contract for the group. Discuss what people need to give and what they expect to receive. Discuss how you would implement the agreement so that it shapes behavior and expectations.

5. Explore some situations that you and others have experienced with difficult bosses and coworkers. What problems did they present for you? How did you respond to these problems? Which strategies worked? Which strategies did not work?

6. Indicate the needs that your team members have at work. What are the most important needs for them? What are the less-important needs? How important is money? Do you agree that permanent, higher salaries are not associated with permanent, higher motivation? If so, how would you deal with motivating workers who already make a good amount of money?

Individual Assignments

7. Identify ways in which your immediate supervisor has knowingly and unknowingly affected your motivation. Which ways increased your motivation? Which ways decreased your motivation? How would you like to be motivated?

8. Make a psychological contract with someone, preferably a work colleague or someone working under you. Discuss what you want from that person, and what that person is willing to give, what that person expects to get from you and what you are willing to give in order to ensure that the understanding works out. Then make the psychological contract and put it in place for a few weeks. See what it does for you. What happens? Was there improvement in any sense? What might you do differently next time?

9. Think of a specific situation in which you gave feedback. What impact did it have? How can you improve the effectiveness of your feedback?

NOTE

1. Adapted from Evan Berman, *Performance Productivity in Public and Nonprofit Organizations,* 2d ed. (Armonk, NY: M. E. Sharpe, 2006): 125–142. Used with permission.

REFERENCES

Berman, E. (2006). *Performance and productivity in public and nonprofit organizations* (2nd ed.) Armonk, NY: M. E. Sharpe.

Berman, E., & West, J. (2003a). Psychological contracts in local government: A preliminary survey. *Review of Public Personnel Administration, 23*(4), 267–285.

Berman, E., & West, J. (2003b, December). What is managerial mediocrity? Definition, prevalence and negative impact (Part 1). *Public Performance & Management Review, 27*(2), 7–27.

Berman, E., & West, J. (2007). The effective manager . . . takes a break. *Review of Public Personnel Administration, 27*(4), 380–400.

Berman, E., & West, J. (2008). Managing emotional intelligence in U.S. cities: A study of public managers. *Public Administration Review, 68*(4), 740–756.

Blanchard, K., & Johnson, S. (1981). *The one minute manager.* New York: William Morrow.

Bramson, R. (1981). *Coping with difficult people.* Garden City, NY: Doubleday.

Buckingham, M., & Coffman, C. (1999). *First, break all the rules: What the world's greatest managers do differently.* New York: Simon & Schuster.

Cherniss, C., & Goleman, D. (2001). *The emotionally intelligent workplace.* San Francisco: Jossey-Bass.

Drucker, P. (1954). *The practice of management.* New York: Harper.

Heathfield, S. M. (2008). *Rise above the fray: Options for dealing with difficult people.* Retrieved July 8, 2008, from http://humanresources.about.com/od/workrelationships/a/difficultpeople.htm

Herzberg, F. (1959). *The motivation to work.* New York: Wiley.

House, R. (1971). *Path-goal theory of leadership.* Seattle: University of Washington.

Locke, E., & Latham, G. (1990). *A theory of goal setting and task performance.* Englewood Cliffs, NJ: Prentice Hall.

Lubit, R. (2004). The tyranny of toxic managers: Applying emotional intelligence to deal with difficult personalities. *Ivey Business Journal, 68*(4), 1–7.

Marston, C. (2007). *Motivating the "What's in it for me?" generation.* New York: John Wiley.

Maslow, A. (1954). *Motivation and personality.* New York: Harper & Row.

McClelland, D. (1985). *Human motivation.* Glenview, IL: Scott, Foresman.

McGregor, D. (1960). *The human side of enterprise.* New York: Wiley & Sons.

Nadler, D., & Lawler, E. (1977). Motivation: A diagnostic approach. In J. Richard Hackman & E. Lawler (Eds.). *Perspectives on behavior in organizations.* New York: McGraw-Hill.

Osland, J., Kolb, D., & Rubin, I. (2000). *Organizational behavior.* Upper Saddle River, NJ: Prentice Hall.

Perry, J. (2000). Bringing society in: Toward a theory of public-service motivation. *Journal of Public Administration Research & Theory, 10*(2), 471–489.

Rousseau, D. (1995). *Psychological contracts in organizations: Understanding written and unwritten agreements.* Thousand Oaks, CA: Sage Publications.

Sanzotta, D. (1977). *Motivational theories and application for managers.* New York: AMACOM.

Van Wart, M. (2005). *Dynamics of leadership: Theory and practice.* Armonk, NY: M. E. Sharpe.

West, J., & Berman, E. (1997). Administrative creativity in local government. *Public Performance & Management Review, 20*(4), 446–458.

Wright, B. (2007). Public sector work motivation: A review of the current literature model and a revised conceptual model. *Journal of Public Administration Research & Theory, 11*(4), 559–587.

Chapter 7

Compensation

Vital, Visible, and Vicious

I may be unappreciated, but at least I'm overworked and underpaid.

—A bureaucrat's lament

After studying this chapter, you should be able to

- recognize that there is no absolute standard used to determine pay—that is, organizations do not pay people what they are worth because they do not know what their employees are worth;
- explain why compensation is a key human resource function, but that pay programs, paradoxically, are not a management system;
- understand that a compensation system is the result of law and policy, labor markets, job evaluation, and personal contribution;
- describe key issues such as pay banding, comparable worth, and gainsharing and their often paradoxical nature;
- design and calculate the essential elements of a salary survey; and
- assess and critique criteria for an ideal compensation system in the context of future trends.

If position classification as well as motivation define the individual-organization relationship (Chapters 5 and 6), then compensation quite literally quantifies it. Earnings affect a person—not only economically, but also socially and psychologically—because they are a concrete indicator of employee value to the institution, purchasing power, social prestige, and, sadly, perhaps even self-worth. Payroll expenses, likewise, represent a substantial investment on the part of the organization; they often constitute the majority of its budget. Labor costs, for example, in the U.S. Department of Defense and the U.S. Postal Service—and most other agencies irrespective of jurisdiction—often amount to more than 80% of outlays.

Accordingly, a compensation system should aim to align individual and organizational objectives, an ideal that may be difficult to achieve when many elected officials—with backgrounds in insurance agencies, real estate offices, law firms, and other small businesses—have little experience in large public organizations.[1] Nevertheless, dilemmas in managing compensation are of paramount importance. Trends in performance accountability and staff reduction suggest that resolution of these issues will be determined by supervisors and employees with human resource management experts serving as consultants, not controllers. It will no longer do to blame controversial decisions on the personnel office.

Organizations have a right to expect staff to be as productive as possible, and individuals have the right to be fairly compensated. Thus, a value-added remuneration system should optimize the balance between institutional constraints and personal expectations by creating value for both the organization and its members. Program goals include attracting new workers, rewarding and retaining existing ones, providing equity, controlling budgets, and supporting the culture that the agency seeks to engender. The design and maintenance of a compensation system is complex and prominent in organizations; other human resource functions are important to some employees, but money is crucial to virtually everyone.

How a jurisdiction handles salaries and **benefits**, then, is vital (for individual sustenance and organizational credibility) and visible (personnel salaries and agency payrolls are a matter of public record), as well as vicious (actual or imagined inequities among workers breed considerable friction in organizations). Competence and performance may be hard to judge (Chapter 10), but pay and benefits are known. For instance, federal bankruptcy judges, excluded from dining and transportation privileges enjoyed by other judges, feel like "second-class citizens."

Despite—or perhaps because of—its importance, the compensation function of human resource management is the one that produces the most displeasure among both public and private sector employees ("Many workers dissatisfied," 2001). There are at least three reasons for discontent. One is that people compare themselves with others: with those doing the same job in the same agency, with those performing different jobs in the agency, and with those holding equivalent positions in other departments. It is not unusual that perceived discrepancies and real discontent emerge as a result of those comparisons.

A second explanation is that remuneration is driven more by political than economic considerations. "It is completely fallacious," contended Risher and Fay (1997, p. 14), "to argue that government pay programs represent a management system." Elected officials typically focus on personnel costs, and compensation policies become pawns in a quest for political advantage. Raising taxes, cutting services, or reallocating budget monies to fund a pay increase are not politically popular. Thus, over time, salaries will be affected more by political opportunism than by objective merit—something not likely to engender confidence in compensation policies.

A final, related reason for concern over pay is that many taxpayers believe civil servants are overpaid and underworked—despite arguably noncompetitive salaries and increased workloads from downsizing. As Risher and Fay (1997, p. 323) observed, "Some people will always think that public pay levels are too high; but it is safe to say that their views have a life of their own independent of the facts." Stated differently, the effectiveness of any compensation reforms is certain to be constrained by the culture in which they are created. These three factors—personal comparisons, political expediency, and public beliefs—tend to reinforce one another in a manner that further exacerbates dissatisfaction. At the root of all these explanations is the fact that most organizations want the most work for the least money, whereas many employees want the most money for the least work. Compensation, in short, is considered crucial by employees, decision makers, and taxpayers alike. Indeed, a problematic model of compensation that emphasizes market data, performance pay, pay banding, and management discretion has emerged in response to claims the traditional approach is antiquated and disintegrating (U.S. Office of Personnel Management [OPM], 2002).

The following pages examine factors that affect the determination of pay: policy and law, **labor markets**, **job evaluation**, and individual contribution. The analysis is framed by equity theory and illustrated with controversial issues including pay banding and **comparable worth**, as well as longevity, merit, skill, and **gainsharing** pay. Having diagnosed problems with compensation programs, the chapter closes with a prescription for an "ideal" program and projections of future trends.

▪▪ EQUITY THEORY

Equity theory—the balance between contributions made by the individual and the rewards received from the organization—provides the basis for most pay programs. Unfortunately, available data suggest that neither "the people who manage the (federal) systems, the managers who use them, [nor] the employee themselves" (Wamsley, 1998, p. 30) hold these programs in high regard. To appreciate the significance of equity theory, the weighing between contributions and rewards, consider the foundations and nature of this balance. Its basis is the presumed link between performance and pay, and its dynamic is how (or whether) this linkage operates. Based on the role of individual perceptions in determining behavior, expectancy theory (Vroom, 1964) offers insights into the choices that people make.

Its tenets are a three-link causal chain:

1. The value ("valence") the employee attaches to a desired result (e.g., higher pay)

2. The person's belief that rewards actually will be provided as a consequence of high performance ("instrumentality")

3. The belief ("expectancy") that the individual can accomplish the task that will lead to reward

Stated differently, the theory assumes that people take action based on their perception of the possible success of that action (expectancy) and the likelihood of achieving outcomes (instrumentality) that they value (valence).

If any of these three links in the chain is weak, then "pay for performance" is called into question. Consider, for instance, that the parole supervisor in a state department of corrections demonstration project has authority to provide productivity **bonuses** to caseworkers who increase the number of interviews with their parolees. These parole officers want the bonus (valence) and understand that it would be awarded if they achieve the improvement objective (instrumentality). They are concerned (expectancy), however, that simply adding the contacts they have with their charges, without a reduction in overall caseload, will result in superficial interviews. They are not convinced that the program is desirable (because it minimizes chances of in-depth information gathering) or feasible (overtime work is not available).

Accordingly, public safety would be put at risk, and employee burnout is likely. In one such case, few sought the bonuses, and the initiative was discontinued.

Consider a more common scenario. Although most people value money (valence), there are often significant constraints in obtaining more of it. When local, state, or national legislative bodies regularly limit pay raises to inconsequential amounts, for example, the importance attached to those amounts is devalued (repeated raises that are below the rate of inflation in effect constitute a pay cut). Suppose instead that substantial monies are provided. Employees must then have confidence that the performance evaluation system (instrumentality) does distribute rewards fairly and accurately. For reasons examined in Chapter 10, such confidence is not often merited. Finally, although many Americans believe that hard work makes a difference (expectation), working smarter also counts. Thus, if training, acceptable working conditions, and up-to-date equipment are not provided, then working harder may make little difference.

As these examples demonstrate, expectancy theory can be an effective diagnostic tool to ensure that the human resource management system is administered in a manner that coherently establishes linkages between valence, instrumentality, and expectancy.

- Are available rewards valued by employees?
- Do employees see a link between the reward and their performance?
- Are employees confident, given their background and organizational climate, that tasks can be accomplished?

Equity and expectancy theories mandate, in other words, that policy makers be concerned about more than the absolute amount of money required to fund public service. They must also focus on comparative levels of pay and how these monies are distributed. Reward systems unconnected to productivity indicators motivate poor workers to stay and high performers to become discouraged and leave. The irony of such a situation is that overall compensation costs rise because more employees are needed to complete tasks that fewer conscientious ones could readily accomplish.

■■ DETERMINATION

With these theoretical—and quite real—considerations in mind, factors affecting pay determination are now explored. Perhaps the most significant goal of any remuneration system is fairness. An organization confronts two types of decisions in the management of compensation to achieve this goal: pay level and pay adjustments. Compensation in any jurisdiction is a product of the following:

- Pay philosophy, as informed by law and policy
- Labor market forces (external competitiveness), as reflected by manipulation of supply and demand
- Job content (internal consistency), as assessed by job evaluation techniques
- Individual contribution, as influenced by longevity, merit, skill, and group pay (Figure 7.1)

Decisions about levels of pay are largely a consequence of philosophy, market, and job evaluation, whereas decisions about pay adjustments emphasize an employee's place in the salary structure. Taken together, these decisions should represent the greater good by aligning the interests of the public and its servants.

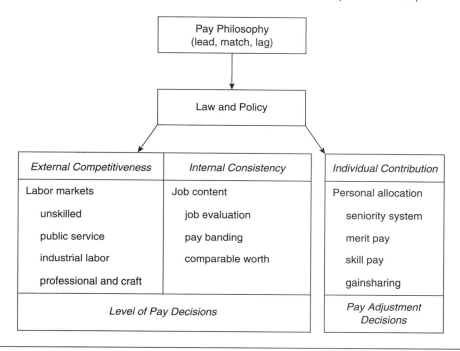

Figure 7.1   Determinants of Compensation

■ PHILOSOPHY

Organizations can lead, match, or lag behind what other employers offer employees (Exhibit 7.1). In sharp contrast to the strategies of many other advanced democracies, the approach in government has been to limit the pool of job candidates to those prepared to accept noncompetitive pay. Compensation is *not* seen as a strategic tool to achieve organizational objectives but rather as a cost to be managed and contained (with the controversial exception of performance pay programs discussed below). At least since the passage of the 1883 Pendleton Act (Chapter 1), public servants have been expected to make financial sacrifices in exchange for an opportunity to serve the citizenry, often in challenging, even unique, ways (e.g., environmental protection, criminal justice, teaching, foreign relations, tax collection). Self-enrichment, after all, was and is not the purpose of service. The idea, unlike the spoils system, was to create a corps of career professionals insulated from political intrigue by providing job security, career progression, and reasonable benefits and working conditions. Also important was the fact that they represented but a tiny proportion of the workforce (less than 1% in 1900); they held little political power or ability to organize themselves into unions, and none at all to strike (Chapter 11).

By the 1960s, however, public employees were far more numerous, had fallen substantially behind in compensation, and had won the right to organize. Beginning with the 1962 Federal Salary Reform Act, attempts were made to establish the principle that federal pay would match that found in the private sector. Codified in the Federal Pay Comparability Act of 1970,

Exhibit 7.1   Pay Policy: Lead, Match, or Lag?

Under the influence either of poverty or of wealth, workmen and their work are equally liable to deteriorate.

—Plato

The paradox of needs (Introduction) indicates that organizational and individual objectives may not coincide. Ideally, business strategy, human resource philosophy, and compensation goals should be aligned in a manner to meet the needs of both the employer and employee.

A wage-lead approach may reflect a belief that by "working smarter" a high-quality, satisfied workforce is a cost-effective, money-saving strategy. That is, total labor costs are not the same as labor rates. It is possible to achieve high productivity from a relatively small workforce if the cost per unit of output is less with a highly efficient, though highly paid workforce. This plan, however, may be seen as counterintuitive and difficult for many cash-strapped public and nonprofit organizations to adopt in the short run.

A wage-competitive policy, second, in effect neutralizes compensation as a factor in human resource management. It does this by paying fairly and accentuating nonmonetary amenities affecting the overall ability to attract and retain employees. These include such time-honored (and timeworn) techniques as "selling scenery" (or the area's weather), believing that the community is "family-friendly," or claiming to be at the seat of power in a political capitol ("Potomac fever" and its subnational equivalents). Many of these tactics, though, are available to organizations using above- and below-market pay policies. Still, a match policy does not necessarily place the organization at a disadvantage in the marketplace.

Last, wage-follower plans may be indicative of: unique characteristics of the occupation (military travel, State Department diplomacy), a philosophy that dictates service is not about making money (Salvation Army), high unemployment in the area, short-time horizons, or simply a "lean and mean" approach to human resources by "working harder" to get the most from as few poorly paid workers as possible (despite counterproductive effects such as low morale, turnover, and training costs). A below-market approach might—arguably—be acceptable for low-skill retailing organizations such as Wal-Mart but clearly is a "penny-wise, pound-foolish" strategy for professionally staffed organizations. For example, the Securities and Exchange Commission and the Federal Bureau of Investigation have substantial difficulty in recruiting and retaining top-caliber personnel because the salaries are a fraction of those available elsewhere.

The selection of an appropriate policy involves a complex set of factors including the types of skills required, job market characteristics, ability to pay, desired institutional image, assumptions about employee work attitudes, and employer ideologies. The strategy chosen likely will competitively position the organization within or across sectors of the economy. Thus, in the public sphere, some Florida cities and counties, for instance, use a wage-lead approach at least when compared with state employment. The federal government, however, is generally superior to many subnational pay policies—but inferior to the approach utilized by major corporations. It should also be noted that different policies may exist within one organization. The compensation package available to public service clerical personnel, for instance, may be better than that found in many small businesses. Such a wage-lead approach is reversed, however, for most public and nonprofit executives within the same agency whose remuneration is the result of a wage-lag strategy.

The paradox of needs may be resolved in good measure by employee self-selection provided that basic economic and noneconomic needs are met. Equity theory suggests, however, that if people do not perceive that a balance exists between their contributions and rewards, then they will try to relieve the tension by reducing productivity, misusing organizational resources, or seeking higher rewards either within the agency or outside it.

Expect these trends to continue as agencies seek pay policies designed to reduce the size of the workforce, evidence less concern with competitive compensation and more with what can be afforded, and attempt incentive programs to make payroll costs more variable than fixed expense. Organizations, in the end, usually get what they are willing to pay for.

the law established a mechanism to provide annual comparability adjustments unless the president directed otherwise—which whoever was in that position did virtually every year for two decades.

In 1989, the first National Commission on the Public Service (the Volcker Commission) called for significant salary increases; the passage of the 1990 **Federal Employees Pay Comparability Act** mandated that the 30% public-private sector pay gap be closed gradually by the end of the century.[2] According to the 2003 Volcker Commission II, the gap is wider than ever because administrations repeatedly cited "severe economic conditions," irrespective of the state of the economy, as a reason to deny employees full pay raises. If the raises promised under the law were enacted in 2008, then according to the Congressional Research Service, they would have been nearly 20% (Davidson, 2008). Although the situation is more varied elsewhere, the difficulties experienced by the national government are manifested in many states and localities.

The problems discussed above are mirrored in different degrees in the distinct pay systems found in most jurisdictions: an executive schedule for political appointees, a General Schedule (GS) for career employees, and, in the federal government, a wage grade schedule for blue-collar workers (using, by law, a match philosophy based on local prevailing rates), as well as various rank-in-person systems (Chapter 5). Many federal white-collar merit positions are in the GS, which has 15 grades and 10 time-in-grade steps in each; many subnational governments have comparable salary structures. Generalizations are hazardous, but government pays below market at entry level, sometimes over market at the middle level, and considerably under market at the top. It is widely understood that the pay gap is most severe for executive, managerial, and professional positions, and less so for managerial and entry-level jobs. One should recognize, however, that in certain jurisdictions or in selected occupations a gap may not exist at all, and in some cases it even might be reversed. Overall, though, "the jobs that show the greatest pay disadvantage for federal workers make up an increasing share of the federal workforce" (Congressional Budget Office, 2002, p. 9).

Paying below-market rates, according to wage efficiency theory, may not be cost effective. The advantages of low compensation are likely to be outweighed by poor morale, citizen service, and job satisfaction, and the resulting high recruitment, training, discipline, and turnover costs. Simply stated, paying more can cost less when productivity, service, and quality are compromised by paying "bottom dollar." It is difficult to see, in any case, how effective organizations, which depend on empowered, high-caliber people, can flourish under these circumstances.

Pay systems, referring again to Figure 7.1, reflect not only law and policy, but also (a) comparisons of similar jobs in different organizations using salary surveys (external competition), (b) comparisons among job content within an agency employing job evaluation techniques (internal consistency), and (c) comparisons among employees in the same job category in the same organization using seniority, merit, skill, or group pay (individual contribution). As each of these equity dimensions is explored below, it is important to note that "there are no absolute measures of job value. . . . For things like temperature and weight, instruments are both reliable and valid. Job value is at best a relative or comparative measure" (Risher & Wise, 1997, p. 99). Instead, what exists in many organizations is an inconsistent mix of fair-pay criteria. A common denominator and underlying assumption shared by all forms of equity, however, is that they implicitly hold a time clock model of work. That is, as examined in Exhibit 7.2, labor is commoditized, to be bought and sold in easily measured time units (hours, days, weeks, months, years). Time is money—or is it?

Exhibit 7.2   How Much Time Do You Owe the Organization?

Time isn't money; money is money.

—Anonymous

In an attempt to curb exploitative work schedules and thereby create jobs during the Great Depression, the 1938 **Fair Labor Standards Act** (FLSA) instituted the 5-day, 40-hour week—a compromise measure agreed to after the Senate passed a 30-hour workweek bill. Since that time, dramatic changes have occurred in the economy (from industrial to service), the workforce (from white male–dominated to diverse female), and lifestyles (from a husband with a stay-at-home wife with children to singles, single parents, and married as well as unmarried dual-career families). Most organizations, however, still structure work hours as if nothing has happened in the intervening decades, a posture that has exacerbated the paradox of needs (Introduction).

This is not to say that there has been no reaction to these changes. Many organizations have experimented with **alternative work schedules**—"the joy of flex"—in the last half century.[1] Variations are nearly infinite (e.g., compressed workweeks currently being used in response to the oil crisis in Utah and elsewhere). The oldest and most common approach, however, alternative schedule consists of a specified bandwidth when the office will be open (e.g., 6:00 A.M. to 8:00 P.M. Monday through Friday) and a set of core hours (perhaps 10:00 A.M. to 2:00 P.M.) around which people can arrange their 8-hour workday (usually on a set schedule rather than permitting daily flexibility). Thus, early risers can come in early and leave at 3:00 P.M., and late risers can come in at 9:00 A.M. and leave late. Typically, everyone completes time sheets. Agencies may also benefit by having offices staffed during a longer workday and by having reduced tardiness and absences.

Advantages should be evident: Employees work when they want to work, with all the personal and organizational benefits that may result from that fact. Drawbacks are of two types: inherent and practical. There is some work that is structured so that it cannot be "flexed," and there are organizations that cannot effectively implement flextime—either because record keeping becomes too burdensome or because managers lose a sense of control over subordinates. When available, flextime is often seen as an individual accommodation that deviates from standard policy instead of a recognition of the changing workforce.

Generally, results are varied, but often flextime improves the quality of work life for people more than it enhances productivity of the organization. **Herzberg's theory of motivation** (Herzberg, Mauser, & Snoplerman, 1959) helps explain this finding. Flextime is a "job context" factor (such extrinsic factors focus on policies, supervision, and working conditions) that, if absent, can create job dissatisfaction. When these factors are available in desired forms, however, they normally are taken for granted. Consider university parking: If convenient, it is unlikely that it would create job satisfaction; if it is a continuous hassle, however, it can create substantial on-the-job morale problems. What really matters in explaining productivity, however, are "job content" factors (these intrinsic elements emphasize challenging work, responsibility, achievement, and the like; see Thomas, 2000). Flextime has nothing to do with the substance of work.

This speaks to the fundamental flaw of all forms of flextime—even if perfectly implemented. It assumes, in a functionally rational mode, that work must be a function of time, instead of the actual task to be performed. Indeed, exempt from FLSA, most professionals of yesteryear[2] and today (managers, surgeons, the clergy, military officers) work until the work is done. They are not paid by the clock but rather for their overall contribution to the organization.

In like manner, Best Buy's Results-Only Work Environment (ROWE) is an unparalleled, *non-time* management program to redefine work from a place to go to something people do. Presence is not defined as productivity at the 4,000 employee corporate headquarters. ROWE's transformational strategy completely alters the way employees work: they decide how, when, and where tasks will be done; they are required to put in only as much time as it takes to do the job; it is flexibility—and accountability—to the maximum. So empowered, surveys reveal that work teams have:

- increased morale and loyalty,
- lower turnover and higher productivity,
- enhanced family-work balance, and
- become more focused and energized about their work as teamwork has improved and the number of meetings has declined (Kiger, 2007).

ROWE, accordingly, appears to resolve the paradox of needs. To the extent that Generation Y rejects traditional workplace routines, the program acknowledges, indeed celebrates, the need for an individualized, accepting, productive workforce. As one employee said, Best Buy "gives you the opportunity to really be an adult" (Kelly & Moen, 2007, p. 497).

Future experimentation and research is needed to determine if the approach produces unintended consequences as employees attempt to set boundaries on work and home commitments. Employee schedule control, for instance, could facilitate higher levels of work. In fact, workplace laws are meant to protect workers from abuses that could occur in a clockless office.

While work/life balance may be the wave of the future, employees at a growing number of other organizations, however, are now expected to sign in at work using biometric identification devices (e.g., palm scanners) that record their arrivals and departures for payroll purposes (Associated Press, 2008).

It is not necessarily maintained that all organizations and jobs could—or should—be reconceptualized in a substantively rational manner. It is suggested, however, that agencies seek a blend of functional and substantive approaches instead of an unquestioning focus on quantity time. A catalytic strategy to accomplish this is an *annual hours program* whereby the number of hours needed during a given year is agreed on and a scheduling format is then designed.

Notes:

1. Indeed, by most accounts, flexible work hours have steadily increased. Although employers may have these opportunities in parts of their organizations, many employees do not participate because they do not know they could; when they do know, most take advantage of them (www.familiesandwork.org).

2. Samurai warriors, who refused to touch money, simply could not understand how it could be used as a substitute for expertise, discipline, and loyalty. The legacy of that feudal tradition remains, as the contemporary Japanese "salaryman" typically has his wife handle family finances.

▪▪ LABOR MARKET FORCES: EXTERNAL COMPETITION

Classical economic theory holds that the "free market" determines salaries based on supply and demand for specific jobs. The obvious, if often overlooked, fact is that pay is not a function of a fanciful, pristine, abstract free market—something that has never existed and never will. Rather, occupations exist in different labor markets, none of which is free. Supply and demand, instead, is affected by public or private political intervention: unskilled labor (congressionally enacted minimum wage), public service (federal, state, or local legislative enactment), industrial labor (labor-management collective bargaining), and professional and craft occupations (interest group lobbying sometimes resulting in public licensure).

Consequently, pay in most organizations is benchmarked using employer-initiated self-salary surveys or surveys published by the Bureau of Labor Statistics (www.bls.gov), state government agencies, industry associations, and consulting firms. The approach taken is to simply ask other organizations what they pay people. For example, universities in the same athletic conference or region of the country may routinely survey one another—a process subject to circumlocution, tautology, and possibly illegal collusion under antitrust laws. Significant technical issues also exist (identifying key jobs and relevant organizations, calculating benefits), but even flawed assessments—in the absence of better data—provide useful information (Exhibit 7.3).[3]

Although salaries form the foundation of most employees' perceptions of pay, accurate estimates of **external equity** cannot focus solely on salary data. Benefits, a trivial "fringe" in most organizations before World War II, now add an average of 41% to the payroll, thus accounting for some 29% of the total employee compensation package. This increase is attributed largely to tax policy (both employers and employees realize tax advantages from certain types of benefits) and the rising costs of health and retirement programs.[4] An interesting paradox nevertheless exists: as the value of benefits increases, employee satisfaction can decrease (see Exhibit 7.4 as well as Chapter 8). Furthermore, the utility of benefits in achieving organizational goals is limited because they are available to all members, irrespective of employee performance.

Historically, low public salaries have been partially offset by benefits (usually untaxed or tax deferred) because their costs can often be put off by lawmakers and are thereby less visible to voters than salary increases. These programs are reputed to be superior to those found in the private domain, as public employees are sometimes covered under more types of plans. When governments are compared with other large white-collar employers, however, such disparities all but disappear, especially because corporate executive perquisites (e.g., stock options, expense accounts, free insurance, no-cost financial and legal counseling, country club memberships, Christmas bonuses, moving expenses, home repairs, clothing allowances, first-class travel, spouse travel, chauffer service, company cars, generous severance pay, estate planning, children's education, vacations) are unusual in other sectors.[5] Indeed, government and nonprofit benefits are often inferior to those in big business, and whatever perceived advantages the public sector has held as a "benefit-rich/salary-poor" employer are being eroded by increasing employee costs and diminishing coverage.

The determination of external equity, in summary, should recognize that conventional free market supply-and-demand theories conceal more than they reveal about labor markets; salary surveys are at once problematic and valuable; benefit programs, although hard to quantify and compare, constitute a significant, often controversial, part of compensation.

▪ JOB CONTENT: INTERNAL CONSISTENCY

Pay decisions are made within the framework of the compensation structure. Some form of job evaluation method is used to systematically assess the value of jobs and assign jobs to salary grades, which in turn are given a range of salaries. This procedure defines an internal

Exhibit 7.3   Projects: Salary Surveys and Asking for Raises

The secret of living is to find people who will pay you money to do what you would pay to do if you had the money.

—Sarah Caldwell, opera conductor

These paired projects—determining organizational pay levels for positions and individual requests for pay increases—both involve planning and preparation, tasks that have been dramatically enhanced by the Internet.

The salary survey exercise below is designed to assist a line manager in determining pay levels. The approach consists of three steps: (1) identify key or benchmark jobs, (2) select comparable organizations, and (3) collect data.

Each step is fraught with problems such as (a) vague job categories (especially in team-based units), (b) difficulties interpreting competitor information (are the jobs truly comparable, and how do you know?), and (c) decisions about how (mail, telephone, and/or interview) and from where (federal or state agencies, professional associations, consulting firms) to gather data.

The process assumes that the questionnaire respondent and the individual interpreting the findings understand the jobs in their respective organizations. The resulting credibility of the information collected is, at best, unknown. Yet reliability and validity are not the only problems, as many jobs are not found in surveys. When no pricing information is available, a technique known as "whole job ranking" is used, a method that Barcellos (2005) said is a "euphemism for guessing" (p. 3).

Recognizing what other organizations are paying is necessary but not sufficient. It is also important to know what those jurisdictions are getting in return for their investment in employees. Even when available, these data are even harder to interpret because they include service quality, workforce quality, citizen satisfaction, and population and employee ratios. Also key are benefits, which are often equally difficult to compare accurately from one jurisdiction to another.

In the light of these problems, and from the perspective of an assistant city manager in a small locality with little human resource management expertise, complete the following:

1. Discuss each of the three steps above with the city manager and compensation specialist in a nearby city.

2. Visit the Web sites for the World at Work: The Professional Association for Compensation, Benefits, and Total Rewards (www.worldatwork.org), a private firm that collects salary data (www.mnemplassoc.com), or the International Personnel Management Association (www.ipma-hr.org) to obtain additional information.

3. Outline how you would conduct a salary survey for your jurisdiction based on the information in (1) and (2). Indicate how you plan to address typical problems found in salary surveys.

Careful study is also needed when employees are seeking raises from their employer. Knowing the agency's pay practices is an obvious first step. (If increases are awarded annually, then asking for one at a different time is problematic; if raises are below the cost of living, then a promotion opportunity may be the only option.) Advance preparation is also essential: using sites such as www.salary.com, www.acinet.org, www.careerjournal.com, www.salarysource.com, and www.lib.gsu.edu can be helpful.

Critically, determine and document how your accomplishments have contributed to departmental goals. During the meeting with the manager, indicate what pay level would be fair and what else needs to be done to become eligible for an increase. And "remember that a difference exists between an employee who is performing the job as expected from a superior performer and an employee who is truly giving the employer superior performance. Pay raises are based on the second" (Heathfield, 2008a).

Exhibit 7.4   Unbeneficial Benefits?

Organizations have generally decided what benefit coverages were needed and that all its members wanted the same mix of programs. Especially in a diverse workforce, however, individual differences in age, sex, marital status, and number of dependents become manifest.

Rigidity, gaps in coverage, and cost shifting to employees have resulted in discontent with employer benefit programs. Some have

- Standardized packages that require participation whether or not benefits are needed (duplicate insurance for two employees in the family) or even desired (inexpensive—and inadequate—group life and disability insurance)
- Considerable omissions in coverage that annoy many participants (e.g., eye and dental care, long-term care policies, legal assistance, child and elder care, domestic partner coverage)
- Cost containment strategies in health care (to the extent that insurance premiums can wipe out pay raises) and retirement plans (changing from employer-paid "defined benefit" programs to employer/employee-paid "defined contribution" programs)

Increasingly popular ways to address such concerns are flexible or "cafeteria" plans, which establish employee accounts or menus equal to the dollar value of benefits. Each person can then choose a combination of appropriate benefits. Administrative barriers may exist in these programs, but they can be overcome (e.g., benefits can be bundled into selected packages to ensure balanced utilization). Such programs can resolve organization-individual conflicts, because employers no longer pay for benefits unwanted by employees—and both can save on taxes. It should be pointed out, however, that flexible programs make it easier for employers to pass cost increases to employees because the individual decides whether to pay more or take less coverage.

More radical than flexible plans would be to simply give employees the cash, and tax, value of their benefits, thus abolishing these programs entirely. Employer-sponsored benefit programs, after all, are largely a result of historical accident; with wage and salary controls during World War II, the only way organizations could keep people from seeking better-paying jobs elsewhere was to add benefits that were not covered by wage and salary restrictions. The logic is straightforward: Even now, desired coverage can be obtained by joining any number of nonemployer group programs that offer rates as low as those provided by employers. Should large organizations terminate their programs, even more, perhaps cheaper, options would be developed by vendors.

value hierarchy based on comparisons of jobs by their contribution to organizational objectives. **Internal equity**, then, rewards jobs of equal value with the same amount and pays jobs of different value according to some set of acceptable differentials.

All systems of job evaluation—the most widely used of which is **point factor analysis** (Chapter 5)—are premised on the need to identify criteria relative to job value (e.g., responsibility, working conditions, skill); jobs are then ranked in the hierarchy on these criteria. Despite its facade of objectivity (and resulting drawbacks), job evaluation retains a measure of face validity and thus remains the basis of internal equity in most organizations. This conventionally staid, arcane aspect of salary determination has been the subject of considerable experimentation and controversy that is sure to continue in the years ahead.

Reform projects have focused on a technique called **pay banding** (or broad or grade banding), made popular by the downsizing and de-layering that characterize many restructured organizations. In this procedure, to make the salary structure more flexible, separate job levels are grouped into broad categories of related jobs; the bands may have broad salary ranges with midpoints and quartiles. This provides considerable discretion in setting pay within these levels.

> Grouping pay ranges. In pay banding, [federal] agencies may collapse the 15 General Schedule grades into a smaller number of pay ranges or bands. For example, an agency could establish four bands encompassing GS 1–5, the GS 6–11, the GS 12–13, and the GS 14–15 levels.... At today's rates, for instance the second band . . . would allow managers . . . to set pay anywhere from $128,253 to $60,405. The number of bands and the way grades are assigned to bands can be designed to support the organization's mission, values, and culture.

> Adjusting pay. Once the pay bands are defined, the agency determines how employees move within and across pay bands. The GS system uses longevity (time-in-grade) and quality step increases [incentive pay] to move an employee within a grade, and merit promotion to move . . . to a higher grade. Pay under the GS system also is increased through general, governmentwide pay increases. In pay-banding systems, the amount of pay increase within a band is based on the employee's skills or competencies, job performance, contributions, or similar measures. Monies earmarked in the GS system for within-grade, general, and quality step increases may become "at risk" incentive pay in a pay-banding system. . . . A high-performing employee could move to the top of a pay band much more quickly than is possible in the GS system. . . . These flexibilities allow an agency to manage its workforce by rewarding highly valued behaviors that result in better mission accomplishment. ("Pay banding," 2003, p. 3)

The technique, then, makes it easier to adjust salaries but does little to deal with basic pay problems (indeed, when instituted, it is frequently required to be "budget neutral"). In addition, at least at the national level, there is no evidence that it is cost effective to replace the existing classification system (Blair, 2003). Pay banding, in fact, increases payroll costs, reduces promotion opportunities, and can expose the agency to charges of **Equal Pay Act** (Exhibit 7.5) violations if there are not written plans detailing the method of pay progression within a band. Such problems led one federal agency to abandon its nine-year program. While it offered more horizontal movement and raises, it did not provide career ladders, promotion opportunities, and compensation controls (Rutzick, 2005). Employee satisfaction at agencies with newer systems (e.g., Federal Aviation Administration and Transportation Security Administration), rolled out in 2003, reveal that they were dissatisfied with their raises (Losey, 2008b).

Whereas pay banding implies that job evaluation may be less important in the future, a subject of considerable debate, comparable worth suggests that it will become more significant. That is, job evaluation provides a means not merely to provide equal pay for equal work but also to offer equal pay for jobs of equal worth to the organization (see Exhibit 7.6 on p. 215). Despite these experiments and controversies over job-based compensation plans (and the internal equity they seek to produce), such plans continue to be widely used because few realistic alternatives exist.

Exhibit 7.5   Job Evaluation and Comparable Worth

It is difficult to get a man to understand something when his salary depends upon his not understanding it.

—Upton Sinclair

Job evaluation systems are designed to build an internal equity hierarchy based on comparisons of jobs; compensation systems assume that in setting pay, an organization should evaluate the contribution of each position to the organization. It follows, then, that equal pay should be offered for equal work; indeed, that is mandated by the 1963 Equal Pay Act (which is not always enforced; see AFL-CIO Working Women, n.d.). Job evaluation also, however, provides a way to equate jobs different in content but equal in value. Comparable worth, or **pay equity**, calls for equal pay for jobs of equal value. In concept, comparable worth is gender neutral; in reality, many of its beneficiaries have been women because jobs often held by them pay less than those held by men.

Although seemingly objective, job evaluation can be undermined by the selection of factors, the way they are defined, and how points are assigned to them (Chapter 5). A compensation system, for example, that pays different guards at different base rates in a prison, groundskeepers at a hospital more than nurses, and county dog pound attendants more than childcare workers lacks face validity.

Although the Equal Pay Act and Title VII of the 1964 Civil Rights Act deal with issues of pay equality and sex discrimination, comparable worth claims consistently have been rejected by the courts because existing law does not mandate a job evaluation methodology, is not intended to abrogate market principles, or is relevant only in cases of deliberate discrimination.

The U.S. Supreme Court has yet to hear a comparable worth case. The concept nonetheless has been implemented in state and local government through legislation, collective bargaining, and the development of more valid and reliable evaluation factors. Nearly half of the states and more than 1,500 local governments either have statutory pay equity requirements or have changed their job evaluation and salary practices to reflect comparable worth principles.

Because few argue against the desirability of pay equity (more than 100 nations, but not the United States, have ratified the United Nations' International Labour Organization convention on comparable worth), most of the controversy focuses on its feasibility. Supporters maintain that job evaluation tools—when properly utilized—advance pay equity; opponents argue that these techniques ignore the free market. Advocates counter that markets seldom operate efficiently (e.g., sex and race discrimination); critics say that job evaluation technology is inherently arbitrary. Although the debates of the 1980s have subsided (job security being a higher priority than pay equity in an era of downsizing), many pay equity issues remain unresolved (not the least of which is a legal definition of the term). Indeed, legislation has been proposed in each congressional session since 2001, and by initiatives in state legislatures—where the percentage of women lawmakers is twice as great as it is in Congress. It is unlikely that comparable worth concerns will disappear in the years ahead.

In 2001, the infamous "wage gap" between men and women was 76 cents—for every dollar a male employee earned, a woman worker earned 76 cents, a figure that is approximately 14 cents higher than in 1980 with little change since 1990 (U.S. Bureau of the Census, 2001). Two explanations—human capital factors (e.g., differential experience, education, job longevity, occupational choice, work life views) and sex discrimination—contribute to the disparity. Women with the same experience, education, occupation, and union status as men earn 88% of the male wage (it is generally understood that the public service wage gap is considerably smaller than business).

Some commentators hold that women have different standards for fair pay, expect less than men, and often work for government and nonprofit employers that have less ability to pay than do corporations. Susan Pinker (2008), for instance, argued that women limit the time spent at work as well as the effort to find meaning in it, what Richard Fox and Jennifer Lawless (2008) called the "ambition gap." Even though they work fewer hours for less status and money, Pinker reported—perhaps paradoxically—that women find greater satisfaction in their careers than men. Nonetheless Michele Singletary (2008), summarizing a number of studies, indicated that women experience a "confidence gap." Despite their desire to learn and earn more, they are so overwhelmed by short-term priorities (e.g., child and elder care) that they postpone long-term career and financial planning.

The pay gap may be slowly closing, but it is evident that cultural attitudes, even in the face of lawsuits, are difficult to change. In the meantime, better enforcement of existing laws, as well as use of on-site child care, flextime, and paid family leave policies, may help to address gender-based inequities (Giapponi & McEvoy, 2005–2006). For a compilation of recent data on women in the workforce, with multiple links to original sources, see Heathfield (2008b).

■■ PERSONAL ALLOCATION: INDIVIDUAL CONTRIBUTION

Once job evaluation has established a salary structure and each grade is assigned a range of salaries, attention shifts from internal equity in the agency to **individual equity**—that is, determining the pay level of each employee in the range and, by so doing, the base for subsequent pay adjustments. This requires that rewards be allocated fairly to those doing the same job. Several related approaches are examined here: seniority pay (including **cost-of-living adjustments**), merit pay, **skill pay**, and gainsharing plans (Figure 7.1).

Seniority Pay

Seniority pay or longevity compensation is furnished on the basis that an employee's value to the organization, as a result of continuous training and development (Chapter 8), increases over time. When this occurs, time-in-grade is compatible with merit and skill pay. If a department does not add value to its career employees, then seniority systems can become stagnant and yearly increments an unearned entitlement. Seniority, in any case, is a major determinant of pay progression, even in business incentive programs.

Time-in-grade restrictions were established in the early 1950s as a cost-control measure: during the Korean War, Congress was concerned that federal employees would rapidly progress through pay levels (as they had in World War II). Pay-for-performance programs (see below) typically eliminate time-in-grade requirements; if employees quickly advance, it is likely that overall salaries will rise.

Although conceptually distinct, cost-of-living adjustments, like seniority pay, also are given annually to maintain external equity. The clear difference between the two is that cost-of-living adjustments are merely a way to maintain the compensation system with no developmental dimension. One should recognize, however, that the failure to provide them is the equivalent of a pay reduction. Thus, many employees today are not earning as much on an inflation-adjusted basis as they did earlier in their careers. The attractiveness of seniority systems and inflation adjustments, in sum, is their simplicity, objectivity, predictability, and perceived fairness, as well as their ability to encourage workforce stability.

Nevertheless, many organizations believe that performance should be rewarded and report using some form of pay-for-performance, incentive, or variable pay plans. Such approaches depend on output, personnel, and organizational contingencies (see Exhibit 7.6) and work best in an environment of harmonious labor-management relations characterized by easy-to-understand payouts, high morale, and budgets sufficient enough to provide rewards. For staff personnel to see a link between pay and performance, their work must be evaluated by objective and/or subjective criteria in which they have confidence. Incentive pay also must be clearly distinguished from regular compensation and cost-of-living adjustments.

> In contrast, simplistic notions of pay for performance that reject the concept of seniority tend to discount fundamental notions of fairness and loyalty, and managers who condemn seniority . . . may overlook the virtues of a neutral, wholly objective standard of distributing awards and the advantages of accumulated training and experience. Indeed, it could be argued that if a manager's subordinates do not improve their performance with length of service, the manager should be terminated. Used properly, seniority offers a means of avoiding arbitrary action and the appearance of favoritism. (Hogler, 2004, pp. 161–162)

"The core fallacy of pay for performance," wrote Bob Behn (2004, p. 2) "is that money is a motivator; most people do not work in government for more income."

Merit Pay

Like seniority programs, **merit pay** is an annual increment to base salary, an annuity that compounds for as long as the employee remains with the department. Quite unlike time-in-grade approaches, however, merit programs, which after all are based on achievement, are intuitively attractive because they are supported by conventional wisdom as well as leading motivation theories (economic, need, expectancy): incentives lead to improved performance.

It is not surprising that public and private organizations claim to give great deference to merit; the civil service is even named for it. A substantial discontinuity exists, nevertheless, between rhetoric and reality, as "merit pay may not be as desirable, as easy to implement, or as widely used as commonly believed" (Fisher, Schoenfeldt, & Shaw, 2006, p. 512). In the national government, the results at best are disappointing (Kellough & Lu, 1993). The cardinal paradox is that performance pay is offered as a replacement for traditional pay systems which themselves are supposed to be merit based. That is, there is nothing under those approaches that obligate managers to give time-in-grade raises. Thus, while merit pay is a powerful cultural symbol and a source of control for managers over employees, they are reluctant to use it.

To understand why this happens, preconditions for merit pay—trust in management, a valid job evaluation system, clear performance factors, meaningful and consistent funding, and accurate personnel appraisal (Chapter 10)—must be present. Even if these exist, merit compensation may perversely (a) focus on the short term at the expense of the long term, (b) encourage mediocrity by setting limits on expectations, (c) reduce creativity and risk taking, (d) promote self-interest above other interests, (e) destroy teamwork because it increases dependence on individual accomplishment, (f) generate counterproductive, win-lose

Exhibit 7.6   Pay for Performance: Reality or Illusion?

Pay for performance is a wonderful theory; unfortunately details matter.

—Bob Behn

The idea is so widely accepted that most organizations say they use pay for performance and most employees believe that pay should be tied to performance. An analysis of economic, management, and social psychological research by two Harvard University faculty members, however, demonstrates that what is supposed to occur with these plans in theory seldom occurs in reality. The conditions for success for these programs—(1) the output produced, (2) the people who do the work, and (3) the organization where it is done—"are generally not met in the private sector, and even less so in the public sector" (Bohnet & Eaton, 2003, p. 241).

First, pay for performance runs well if (a) employees have to complete one well-defined task, (b) the output is clearly measurable, and (c) the result can be attributed to one person's efforts. These overlapping and mutually reinforcing factors are difficult to achieve. Most white-collar employees are faced with multitasking problems, hard-to-measure work products, and team-oriented work environments, none of which fit well with individual incentives.

Second, assumptions about human nature and motivation are key to pay-for-performance plans. These programs may be effective if (a) employees work primarily for cash and (b) they care about absolute pay levels. Yet people are interested not only in money but also in job satisfaction and challenge, something not subject to performance pay. Indeed, most research suggests that humans do not want to believe that they work only for money, a finding that is especially true for public servants. Employees can even be offended when treated as if they can be manipulated by transparent monetary incentives.

Furthermore, personnel are less interested in absolute pay than in comparisons relative to some reference point such as others' salaries, the jurisdiction's budget, or the state of the economy, considerations not germane to pay for performance. In fact, although everyone wants to be a winner, incentive plans usually mean that this is not possible. The result is the "silver medal syndrome, based on. . . . Olympic champions, [that] shows the most disappointed people are those that come in second" (Bohnet & Eaton, 2003, p. 248). A system that guarantees that most will be losers is not a useful motivational tool.

Third, institutional factors affect performance pay programs. They operate best when employees know what to do and whom to serve. Knowledge of an organization's objectives, however, is not a given for the rank and file; the absence of clear goals is a result of multiple or changing leaders with different goals. This problem, known as "multiagency," is especially evident in government where staff serve many masters: chief executives, legislators, political appointees, judges, and senior career executives.

The university researchers do not claim that incentives are not effective under the right conditions but only that "ideal conditions are rarely met in empirical reality" (Bohnet & Eaton, 2003, p. 251). They endorse the belief that "the rising and falling tides of interest in the various incentive plans have more to do with changing social, political, and economic fashions than with accumulating scientific evidence on how well the plans work" (Blinder, as cited in Bohnet & Eaton, 2003, p. 241). Nonetheless, most managers, for motivation and cost control reasons, believe that performance should be an important part of the compensation system. More than 80% of the nearly 1,000 private firms surveyed say they "pay for performance," although often for a small part of their workforce (Hewitt Associates, 2003). A meta-study of 39 empirical research projects in the private sector found that financial incentives were not related to performance quality (Jenkins, Mitra, Gupta, & Shaw, 1998). Indeed, Harvard University Press published a book on business

(Continued)

(Continued)

executive compensation entitled *Pay Without Performance* (Bebchuk & Fried, 2004). "There is," wrote Larry Lane (2003, p. 138), "an utter lack of empirical evidence in the private and public sectors that pay for performance has any positive effect on either morale or productivity."

Performance pay programs, in short, are deceptively difficult both technically and politically. They may be good in principle but difficult to do, based on past experience with the federal general pay schedule as well as reform attempts in the 1970s, 1980s, 1990s, and the first decade of this century. First, Gage and Kelly (2003) pointed out that the federal GS is, in fact, a performance-based system that has never been correctly implemented. Supervisors do not take advantage of available incentives—cash awards, within-grade increases, quality-step increases—because there are insufficient funds to do so. When this traditional approach was nonetheless modified to emphasize incentive pay, it had to be repealed as unworkable.

Second, as Risher (2002) noted, the performance compensation was tried, "first for managers under the Civil Service Reform Act of 1978 and then under the Performance Management and Recognition Act starting in 1984. Experience was so bad . . . that [the laws] were allowed to sunset . . . and the idea of pay for performance was all but forgotten" (p. 318). It had led to consternation and delay, paperwork and appeals, and cost more money while still not rewarding the best employees.

Third, in 1996, the Federal Aviation Administration implemented pay for performance. By 2004, it was dubbed "a failure" that led to inequity and poor morale (Kauffman, 2004).

Fourth, in a "best practices" reform program at the U.S. Government Accountability Office, it was reported recently that 81% of employees believed that morale was worse than before-pay restructuring (Ballenstadt, 2008b). In another program once viewed as a model for the rest of government, the four-year-old program for the Senior Executive Service (SES) was found to have little effect on performance while hastening retirements and discouraging midlevel managers from applying to the SES. The U.S. Department of Homeland Security's program produced so many productivity problems, court defeats, and widespread dissatisfaction that it abandoned pay for performance (Tiefer, 2008).

In a triumph of hope over experience, pay for performance, nonetheless, remains as popular in management circles as ever, including state government. Thus, the 16 agencies comprising the intelligence community began implementing performance pay in mid-2008. In addition, an OPM (2008) report claimed success for the federal government's pay incentive plans, lauded over 25 years of successful experiments with all existing alternative pay systems, and later announced a performance pay pilot project at the Veterans Health Administration. A union official, however, noted, "The patchwork of pay programs across government cannot be collectively or individually characterized as a success; the reality is that each is terribly flawed" as they have led to increases in grievances, litigation, attrition rates, and low morale (Walker, 2008). At the Federal Deposit Insurance Corporation, for example, just 12% of employees believed that pay for performance reflected actual performance. Indeed, an arbitrator ruled that the Securities and Exchange Commission performance pay plan discriminated on the basis of sex and race (Ballenstadt, 2008a). Some skeptics, however, were won over by larger-than-expected U.S. Department of Defense performance rewards (Losey, 2008a, 2008b); others found that the payouts were riddled with inequities and doubted that high raises could be sustained in the future.

At best, it remains to be seen if these initiatives will overcome inherent problems typically found in these incentive plans. Even Howard Risher (2004), in an enthusiastic endorsement of performance pay, stated that the technique "may well prove to be the most difficult change any organization has ever attempted" (p. 46). As if to make the point, he offered no fewer than 29 recommendations.

Hays (2004), however, reported two cases in state and local jurisdictions where the approach apparently works. For this to occur, plans must be well designed, meet expectations for pay gains, and be implemented in an atmosphere of high trust and employee morale. As the U.S. Merit Systems Protection Board (2006) stipulated, such systems can only be effective if the following factors are present:

- A supportive organizational culture
- Fair-minded, well-trained supervisors
- A rigorous performance appraisal system
- A system of checks and balances
- An ongoing system of program evaluation

One expert recommends that pay for performance be introduced first for managers. One of the criterion that drives their salary increases is their mastery of the skills needed to manage employee performance.

While an organization's compensation system reinforce good performance, the focus on pay for performance, paradoxically, should not emphasize only money. Incentive compensation is neither quick nor easy. Other factors—public service motivation, good management, importance of work—affect job satisfaction; many professionals do not work for profits, stock values, or commissions. For an account of the unintended consequences, and devastating critique of what happens when physicians are paid for performance see Jauhar (2008).

"The reality is that pay for performance is likely to be of little benefit to organizations with serious performance problems and may actually be harmful" (Perry, 2003, p. 150). If not well implemented, a demoralized, embittered, unmotivated workforce can result. Brown and Heywood (2002, p. 11) noted an official who identified two common attributes of these plans—they involve huge amounts of management time and make everyone unhappy. Indeed, pay for performance can become a substitute for good management. Money can get people to work, but cannot get people to want to work. The evidence suggests that incentives are seen as bribes, thereby reducing self-respect. According to a federal incentive pay consultant, reform-minded officials should look at the culture of the agency, the kind of work it does, and the resources needed to deploy a new program. "Instead of saying, 'we want (it) because everyone else has it,' agencies should ask themselves, 'What are we trying to accomplish?'" (Hewitt Associates, 2003, p. 6).

Sources: Ballenstadt, 2008b; Bohnet & Eaton, 2003; Brown & Heywood, 2002; Gage & Kelly, 2003; Hays, 2004; Hewitt Associates, 2003; Jauhar, 2008; Jenkins et al., 1998; Kauffman, 2004, 2005; Kellough & Selden, 1997; OPM, 2008; Perry, 2003; Risher, 2002, 2004; Tiefer, 2008; Walker, 2008; Zeller, 2004.

competition among employees for merit monies, (g) encourage sycophancy ("do as I say performance pay") and (h) generally politicize the compensation system. Employees may "eventually come to see merit pay as a kind of punishment" (Gabris & Ihrke, 2004, p. 540).

Merit pay, in theory, has the potential to produce high performance, but in practice it is difficult to administer in a way that personnel perceive as fair, as the example below illustrates.

When a municipal government received political pressure to implement a merit pay plan, the city manager and professional staff contracted a consultant to develop a first-rate, by-the-book, technically sophisticated design. . . . This new system should have worked.

Originally, the total money available from the compensation pool was to be divided, with about 60% going for cost-of-living adjustments and automatic pay increases and 40% reserved for merit pay. When the elected officials heard this, they reversed the formula to 75% reserved for merit pay and 25% for cost-of-living increases. These political officials clearly wanted a strong merit message sent to employees.

The city's employees resisted such intense merit pay strategies, and the police department, to avoid the merit program, unionized that same year. After the efforts of cooler heads and the making of various compromises, the merit distribution went back more or less to the original 60–40 split. Why was this so important to the rank-and-file employees? Why did they not want more resources put into the merit pool on the premise that if they performed well, they stood to receive considerable pay increases?

By and large, these employees, like others in the public sector, were more concerned with external and internal equity than with individual equity. Merit raises, although helping, usually do not bring public agency base salaries up to market. What happens instead is that employees find their base salaries compressed in relation to what the market would currently pay someone with their level of skills and experience. This **pay compression** happens when people stay in the same jobs for long durations, receiving generally small base salary increases and only periodic merit raises. Ineluctably, these workers find new hires starting with base salaries not much below, and even in some cases above (pay inversion), their salaries. (Gabris, 1998, p. 649; emphasis added)

Even business admirers like Risher and Fay (1997, pp. 3, 43) concluded,

despite policy statements that make individual merit important, salaries have been managed in a lock step manner. . . . The most aggressive corporate programs rarely give meaningful recognition to outstanding employees. The underlying merit philosophy is solidly entrenched . . . but the typical private sector employee can expect an annual salary increase with almost as much certainty as the typical public sector employee.

Stated differently, merit plans seldom provide enough funds to reward exceptional employees—without unfairly penalizing valued satisfactory ones. It is a major administrative challenge, in brief, for an organization to continuously reevaluate motivation and productivity, to identify the additional level of performance that warrants special recognition, and to provide those incentives on an equitable and timely basis. Merit pay, in short, should never be oversold as a panacea for organizational problems and, if used, should be merely one part of the compensation system (Gabris & Ihrke, 2004, p. 506). It is easy to understand why simpler, "set-it-and-forget-it" compensation systems are so widespread.

In spite of—or perhaps because of—such problems, there is no indication that decision makers are ready to abandon merit pay, an idea that has become a kind of management's "fool's gold."[6] Indeed, OPM, the second National Commission on Public Service (Volcker II), and the National Academy of Public Administration have recommended a new federal government-wide compensation system.[7]

Officials are generally reluctant to admit mistakes, and administrators tend to use merit monies to reward things other than performance (see below and Chapter 10). Merit is simply too oceanic a social myth to reject outright; to do so would suggest that individuals do not make a difference. Instead, Gabris (1998) suggested that because merit plans fixate on individual equity, every effort should be made to ensure that the total compensation system strives to align individual, internal, and external equities. This balance must include attention both to how much people receive (distributive justice) and to the processes used to decide how much (procedural justice). Not to do so exacerbates the vicious, visible, and vital aspects of pay: it is a topic about which few hold neutral feelings.

Skill Pay

Criticisms of merit schemes have triggered a high level of interest in skill (knowledge, competency) pay. Such plans analyze the job knowledge a competent employee will need to possess. As new skills are (a) learned, (b) used, and (c) show results, employees qualify for salary increments.

Skill compensation is consistent with longevity and merit principles and is compatible with pay banding because employees are recognized for gaining additional competencies in a broad array of job practices. Note, however, that it is person centered rather than job centered because, unlike job evaluation, it focuses on how well the individual is doing the job, not on how well the job is defined.

The technique promises to improve productivity: instead of focusing on minimal qualifications, it emphasizes competencies that a fully performing employee is expected to demonstrate. In so doing, it specifies what organizations need (a competent, flexible workforce) and what people want (control over compensation and job success). As an added benefit, it also helps resolve a nettlesome problem for both employers and employees, that of traditional performance appraisal (Chapter 10), as the individual either does or does not progress in skill level.

Although few studies have validated skill-based pay systems, they are growing in popularity, especially in organizations that focus on participatory management and teamwork. Englewood, Colorado, for example, has developed a skill-based pay system that updated all job descriptions, verified each job position's current salary, and formulated career development plans. The strategy was implemented by developing a new pay line (determining the skill base for jobs and assigning monetary values to each skill category), establishing an individualized career development program for employees, and giving employees a choice as to whether or not they would participate in the plan. The program has resulted in higher individual satisfaction, better-defined personal and professional goals, increased employee empowerment, and cost effectiveness (Leonard, 1995).

The Virginia Department of Transportation program, however, failed because it lacked supervisory or union support, compelled all employees to participate (who then complained to legislators), and neglected to redesign human resource systems needed to support the change (e.g., classification and appraisal). A significant factor was the use of business consultants who did not understand the sensitive political milieu in which the agency operated (Shareef, 2002). Between the experiences of Englewood and the Virginia programs are Veterans Benefits Administration, the Federal Aviation Administration, and the North Carolina State Transportation Department, each of which had to undertake major changes in their skill-based initiatives in order to make them work (Thompson & LeHew, 2002).

These plans are not, then, a panacea, for two reasons. First, intrinsic concerns include both the frustration that occurs either when newly achieved skills go unused or when employees "top out" of the program with no further opportunity to earn raises and the complex bureaucratic processes that likely will develop to monitor and certify employee progress. Second, extrinsic impacts include complementary personnel functions that will be affected (short-term training and long-term payroll costs increase) and the dynamic political atmosphere (electoral cycles, employees-voters, unions, rank-and-file vs. managerial pay).[8] Note also it is far more difficult to determine external equity in this approach to pay.

Gainsharing

In a gainsharing type of pay plan, the organization and its employees share greater-than-expected gains in productivity and/or cost reductions. Typically, half of the savings revert to the agency general fund, and the balance is distributed equally among the people involved. In several interesting variations, the provision of funds to city personnel in Loveland, Colorado, depends on the results of citizen satisfaction surveys and the amount of funds left over in the budget. In Blacksburg, Virginia, surplus funds at the end of the year are not shared; instead, public servants decide how the monies will be used to improve operations. Charlotte, North Carolina, has a "competition-based program," which distributes monies either to employees when they competitively bid and win projects or when city departments exceed benchmark performance standards (Jurkiewicz & Bowman, 2002).

Gainsharing, in short, is designed to accomplish the same objective as individual incentives: to link rewards with performance. The difference is that performance is measured as a result of group effort, thereby reinforcing team cohesion, promoting a problem-solving culture, and reducing perceived internal inequities. Individual and group incentives are not mutually exclusive but can be blended by concentrating on individual behavior consistent with gainsharing (i.e., contributions to teamwork). The technique requires a high degree of organizational trust as well as widespread information sharing. Focusing on employee empowerment and quality improvement, a number of experiments in the U.S. Department of Defense since the 1980s have experienced varying degrees of success.

The approach, although not widely used in the public sector, carries genuine potential to create a flexible, proactive, problem-solving workforce (Masternak, 2003). This is one—of many—areas, however, where rhetoric and reality collide. Sanders (1998) ruefully observed that lawmakers may argue that "bureaucrats are already paid (perhaps too much) to efficiently use public funds, and that they should not be offered more money to do what they should be doing anyway" (p. 239).

It comes as no surprise, then, that when incentive plans such as gainsharing or bonuses are attempted, an agency's payroll subsequently may be reduced by the amount of savings generated (see Exhibit 7.7). Successful programs require a cultural change to overcome suspicion and cynicism that permeate incentive plans. Yet, should this occur, these approaches, when used as a partial or complete substitute for other plans, can mean less money for most employees than that provided under other approaches to individual equity.

▪▪ IMPLICATIONS

This discussion has examined the similarities and differences among longevity, merit, skill, and gainsharing pay plans. In the end, the similarities engulf the differences. Any reasonable increase

---

Exhibit 7.7 Employee Bonuses

Money costs too much.

—Ralph Waldo Emerson

A growing compensation trend is the use of bonuses, one-time payments sometimes made instead of awarding more costly permanent pay increases. To encourage high performance, the payouts must be noticeable—at least 10% of salary are common in Europe—because smaller amounts may be demoralizing and counterproductive. For the organization, this technique provides an economical, flexible method to control salary expenditures but nonetheless still reward employees. For the individual, one lump sum may seem like more money than a comparably sized raise spread over an entire year. At least in the short run, then, bonuses appear to resolve the paradox of needs.

Unfortunately, such plans are subject to political processes that frequently undermine them because the politicization of compensation often results in program underfunding. Administrators, then, are faced with two unattractive options: giving a few employees relatively large amounts and other deserving staff nothing, or providing many people with trivial rewards. At the federal level, the average award in 2007 was $577; most believe that their agency's program does not provide incentives to encourage performance (Method, 2008). A similar result can be found at the state level, as the case below illustrates:

Some politicians are fond of blustering about making government run "like a business" and they often stereotype public employees as do-nothing bureaucrats. So when the government does run "like a business," that, one might think, would make them happy.

The Florida Department of Revenue took state lawmakers up on a challenge issued in 1994 when the legislature passed a law allowing monetary rewards—bonuses—to state employees who go above and beyond the call of duty and save the state money. The department saved state taxpayers $9 million. Not bad.

Having accomplished this, the agency's executive director, Larry Fuchs, asked the legislature to appropriate enough to give half of his deserving staff $100 bonuses. Save $9 million. Spend $250,000. But that's when another stereotype came into play: the stereotype of the conniving, forked-tongue, hypocritical politician. The Senate refused to give Fuchs the bonus money.

Some lawmakers say the state should not pay its employees extra for simply doing their jobs. Others have questioned whether the agency met performance standards, but Fuchs says he was never told why the Senate refused to pay the bonuses. If the Senate does not want to offer financial incentives for meeting higher work standards in state government, it should say so. But government leaders have an obligation to keep their promises. Pay the $100 bonuses.

In the same state, many departments paid identical amounts to eligible staff (e.g., $371, although some payouts ranged from $76 to $2,000 for a small number of employees; Cotterell, 2004). For different reasons, most personnel—those receiving and those not receiving the monies—found such bonuses to be demoralizing. In Wyoming, $400 annual performance bonuses were allotted to state agencies for distribution in 12 monthly installments. In some departments, awards were given to a few people who then gave it to others, threw a party, or refused to accept it. In other offices, employees drew straws for the monies (Behn, 2000, p. 4).

Incentive payout schemes, like bonus programs, even if adequately funded should not be used to cover up more fundamental problems in the workplace. There are settings in which bonuses make sense if the work offers no opportunity to find satisfaction. And, yes, there should be a public acknowledgment of extra performance, but the offer of a bonus implies that employees cannot be trusted to do their jobs. The idea that no one will do anything right unless it is required, the more it will become; this is no way to run an organization.

Sources: Behn, 2000; Cotterell, 2004, p. 1B; Lee & Straus, 2004; "State Should Keep Promise," *Tallahassee Democrat,* December 13, 1996, p. 10A. © Copyright 1996 by *Tallahassee Democrat.* Reprinted with permission.

becomes a symbolic lightning rod for criticism. As a result, available resources are often so trivial that managers have little choice but to use the "peanut butter" approach: spread the funds more or less equally among employees to help keep everyone from losing ground to inflation.

This is perhaps most clear when cost-of-living allowances not only are used as a substitute for incentive pay, but also are adjusted below living costs. With little consistent attempt to "keep employees whole" against inflation, the real issue is not a raise (seniority, merit, skill, or gainshare) but the size of the pay reduction. When the economy improves, many lawmakers paradoxically, if predictably, see even less reason to provide raises—to say nothing of furnishing "catch-up" monies.[9] Indeed, they often argue against raises as a way to keep inflation under control.

This strategy serves as an indicator of elected official "toughness" and responsiveness to taxpayers. Thus, equity—external, internal, individual—is simply replaced by the amount of lost purchasing power as the years go by. Nowhere is the dilemma between organizational and individual goals more evident: Employees wish to be treated fairly at the same time that public compensation systems often act to deny that need. The depth of the problem was illustrated in 1999. Rather than pay soldiers salaries sufficient to keep them off public assistance, recruiting standards were again lowered, and some elected officials advocated reinstating the military draft.[10] The value to the public of this conundrum is limited: Employees in an inequitable situation, according to equity theory, seek to reduce the inequity by decreasing performance, increasing absenteeism and tardiness, or simply quitting.

Although it may be true that relative pay levels will not drive government out of business, it is also true that a noncompetitive salary structure has very real consequences for public service. It serves as an impetus to hire peripheral labor—low-paid, often poorly trained, part-time employees, temporary workers, and even volunteers, many of whom are likely to leave as soon as they find full-time positions.[11] It also acts as a stimulus to privatization—the functional equivalent of going out of business—sometimes at a higher cost to the taxpayer.

In this context, then, debates over pay reform plans, although intellectually interesting, are diversionary because they miss the fundamental point: inadequate pay for all employees—women, men, black, brown, yellow, red, and white alike. The actual problem is decidedly not the type of pay technique; rather, the real, substantively rational issue is the amount of pay. It is not unexpected, therefore, that incentive systems often do not produce expected gains. Rather than focus on fundamental problems—insufficient funding, inaccurate evaluations, incomplete feedback, ineffective leadership—incentive pay is thought to be a quick way to increase effort, not the complex, expensive, questionable enterprise that it is.

▪▪ SUMMARY AND CONCLUSION

Pay policies and programs are a significant—and problematic—dimension of management (Zingheim & Schuster, 2000). Pivotal to the employment relationship, compensation decisions can further fulfillment of individual goals as well as organizational goals. Because compensation represents a powerful symbol of an institution's overall beliefs, employees need to know that the organization is looking out for their interests as well as for its own. Without this understanding, pay becomes a target for a wide variety of work-related problems.

This chapter has focused on the elements that influence pay determination. Equity in external competitiveness (labor markets), in internal consistency (job evaluation including pay-banding experiments and comparable-worth debates), and in individual contribution (seniority, merit, skill, and gainsharing compensation) were examined within the context of policy (lead, match, lag) and law (e.g., the 1963 Equal Pay Act and the 1990 Federal Employees Pay Comparability Act). Among the controversies in this important human resource management arena are pay dissatisfaction, the public-private sector pay gap, time and money, and benefits. Reading between the lines, key principles characterize this vital, visible, and vicious topic: (a) Compensation, perhaps more than any other personnel function, is a people problem. (b) Pay is a nonverbal but loud and powerful form of communication. (c) Pertinent strategies are contingent on the culture of the jurisdiction and the vision of its organizations—one size does not fit all. (d) Pay systems must support and be consistent with all other aspects of the agency. (e) Determination of pay is more art than science (also see Flannery, Hofrichter, & Platten, 2002).

Public and nonprofit employers, far more than business employers, need to be able to demonstrate that compensation systems are managed effectively and treat people fairly. Failure to honor competitive pay in law and policy in the name of political expediency does little to foster trust in the democratic process or to ensure productivity. This is dramatically illustrated by the substitution of public employees by contract workers (Exhibit 7.8).

Exhibit 7.8　　Contractors and Compensation: Politics and Policy

Public employees constitute only a fraction of today's government workforce: contractors perform much of government work. While no one has a clear estimate of how many such employees there are, most agree that the number has dramatically expanded in recent years, creating a "silent revolution" in an increasingly hollowed out government. By one 2006 estimate, there now exists a "shadow government": the number of personnel on federal contracts and grants is 10.5 million compared with 1.9 million federal civil servants. The Counterintelligence Field Activity, for example, is staffed 70% by contractors, joining other agencies such as the U.S. Department of Energy and NASA that function as "holding companies" for a consortia of corporations. According to the U.S. Government Accountability Office, 15 of 21 U.S. Department of Defense program offices are staffed primarily by contract workers. Even the government's online database, the Federal Procurement Data System, is contracted out.

To the extent that contracting is based on ideology instead of cost-benefit analysis, it is simply assumed that government should be run like, and increasingly by, business. Yet Paul Light, an expert on the subject, points out, "We have no data to show that contractors are actually more efficient than the government." Every contract, in fact, includes handsome executive salaries, campaign contributions, marketing expenses, and profit margins—monies that could be used to provide goods and services if offered by the public service. Indeed, privatization is often used as a way to outsource problems (e.g., Hurricane Katrina recovery, tax collection, detainee torture, and prison management) to organizations whose actions are frequently unchecked and therefore unaccountable. Simultaneously, the federal government's contract monitoring workforce, now handling a record number of contracts, is experiencing high turnover due to low pay, retirement, and legislative demands for more reports, restrictions, and inspections. Indeed, the Army admitted in 2008 that it turned to contractors, even for inherently governmental work, because it could not fill government employee vacancies. The contracted jobs were paid more than federal positions.

(Continued)

(Continued)

In Iraq and Afghanistan, the U.S. Department of Defense estimates that there are 196,000 contract personnel, more than the number of troops deployed. While they perform a wide variety of tasks, duties parallel combat roles as well as also interrogate prisoners and gather intelligence. The U.S. State Department pays $1,222 per day for private security guards in Iraq compared with the $200 per day that would be paid to a soldier. American military veterans working for a private security company are compensated about $135,000 a year, the same as a U.S. Army two-star general. (Other contractors, often from developing nations, are offered about one-tenth of that amount to perform mundane work.)

The use of contractors has constituted a change in war-fighting capacity without an open debate regarding its potential strategic ramifications. Because contractor injuries and deaths are not counted in casualty reports, for instance, the public does not know the full human cost of the war. Contracting has also had the effect of blunting calls for a military draft. As well, reductions in troop levels may not change the overall American presence in Iraq. With billions of dollars in contracts, companies become a powerful lobbying group whose pursuit of profit may not coincide with the national interest.

In Iraq, allegations of war profiteering, work stoppages, and human rights violations by contracting corporations are so widespread that a nonprofit watchdog group maintains an extensive contractor misconduct database. At home, the U.S. Government Accountability Office found in 2008 that supervisors at the Defense Contract Audit Agency (which oversees all Pentagon vendors) improperly pressured auditors to ensure that poor performance and overbilling were not reported. Furthermore, the head of the federal government's top contracting agency (the General Services Administration) was forced to resign in mid-2008 due to partisan misuse of power and embarrassing exposés. A controversial oversight bill tracking legal proceedings against all contractors, domestic and foreign, passed the U.S. House of Representatives and, as of this writing (late 2008) is being debated in the Senate under the threat of a presidential veto.

The use of contract workers can be effective, however, provided that the overuse and abuse of contracting authority does not undermine the legitimacy and accountability of public institutions. The Acquisition Advisory Panel (appointed by the White House and Congress) concluded in 2007 that the contracting trend "poses a threat to the government's long term ability to perform its mission and could undermine the integrity of the government's decision making." The advantages of contracting, then, are often overstated while disadvantages are understated. In fact, the Pentagon was recently given authority to *in-source* because so many contracts were lent without competition or resulted in poor performance. It is, of course, ironic that a private firm can lure highly trained federal personnel away from public service so it can then sell their services back to the government at a premium.

Sources: "Blackwater's rich contracts," 2007; "Case for insourcing," 2007; Castelli, 2008; Hedgpeth, 2008; Matthews, 2008; Scott & Nixon, 2007; Seahill, 2007; Strivers & Hummel, 2007; Watkins, 2008.

The success or failure of organizations must be supported by the reward system. Fortunately, as this chapter has outlined, there are many compensation techniques available to achieve this end. Unfortunately, none of them is as simple as it may appear. From a technical perspective, the folly is the myth of universal applicability; the ultimate mistake, however, is the failure of political will to provide just salaries so that the public can be faithfully and honorably served.

To put it differently, there is no agreed-upon way to determine compensation; *no job has intrinsic economic worth* simply because human reality is socially constructed. It is certainly not the free market, if for no other reason than there is no such thing. It is possible, however, to suggest criteria that could define an ideal compensation system. Although such standards are neither mutually exclusive nor exhaustive, they do suggest a starting point from which any plan can be assessed.

The criteria, which strive to align employee and employer goals, include the following:

1. *Stakeholder involvement in system design or reevaluation.* Because equity is often in the eye of the beholder, it is vital that all stakeholders—taxpayers, elected officials, nonprofit contributors, managers, and employees—have a meaningful voice in the policy. For example, Kansas commissioned a state pay study that involved 16 focus groups of randomly selected employees, a survey of 3,000 additional employees, and group meetings with legislators and middle managers. It was, no doubt, a difficult process, but responsible democratic governance demands no less.

2. *Simplicity in base pay and diversity in benefits.* As the basis of most people's perception of the entire compensation system, the structure of base pay, which must be competitive, should be readily comprehensible to all. (For instance, Wyoming condensed 37 state pay grades into 11 broad pay bands in 1998.) Although the principle of clarity should also obtain for benefits, given the diversity of the 21st-century workforce, there should be a variety and choice among them. The options must be offered in such a manner that no one can gain advantage or suffer disadvantage, something that occurs with uniform benefit packages.

3. *Salary progression tied to continuous improvement.* Whether through seniority or through merit, skill, or gainsharing pay, people need to be rewarded as they become more valuable to the agency. If these systems, singly or in combination, cannot be properly designed, implemented, or funded, then either (a) cost-of-living adjustments, in the name of fairness, should be seen as an automatic cost of doing business, or (b) the number of hours worked should be reduced (e.g., Pennsylvania, Massachusetts, and South Carolina require 37.5-hour weeks). Employees will then seek promotional opportunities and/or second jobs to increase their income.

4. *Job security.* Precisely because compensation is vital, visible, and vicious, some form of job security, linked to productivity, is necessary to serve the public effectively in the face of political pressure. People must know, as Winston Churchill stated in a speech to the House of Commons on June 18, 1940, "that they are not threatened men, men who are here today and gone tomorrow." The more employees are expected to have creative ideas and solve difficult problems, the less we can afford to manage them with the organizational version of capital punishment. To align the goals of the agency and the individual, managers must be developers—not executioners—of human resources.

Ideally, a compensation system should seek to achieve external, internal, and individual equity. In so doing, it should foster self-managed employees, reward innovation, and focus on citizen service; a successful policy is one that facilitates excellent public service. The above standards (some of which already nominally exist, others are under attack) do not guarantee that every paradoxical problem will be resolved. Their denigration or absence, however, ensures that an equitable system is unlikely.

As the new century unfolds, a number of compensation trends in base pay, salary progression, and employment benefits appear evident. To make base pay more attractive, at least in the short run, pay-banding experiments are likely to continue. Automatic increases in salary probably will be minimized in favor of individual or team incentive and variable pay systems. The doubling of the president's salary in 2000 (to $400,000, a remarkably modest sum compared with the average chief executive salary of more than $13 million) could make it politically easier to lift salary caps that apply to a variety of federal executive and congressional officials. Finally, although more benefits (especially in the arenas of health and family) may become mandatory in the future, what appears to be evolving is a system in which the employee is increasingly responsible not merely for benefit choices, but also for their cost.

Overall, then, low-salary budgets reflect a general trend toward cost containment sparked by global competition for jobs, technological displacement of staff, and increasing use of contingent workers. The traditional social contract at work—hard work justly compensated in exchange for job security and loyalty—has been dramatically eroded as more organizations want less responsibility for their workforces. This portends a turbulent environment for employers, employees, and society in the years ahead. To help navigate this environment, the economic value of a graduate degree in public affairs and administration is discussed in the Appendix for this chapter.

KEY TERMS

Alternative work schedules

Benefits

Bonuses

Comparable worth

Cost-of-living adjustment

Equal Pay Act

External equity

Fair Labor Standards Act of 1938

Federal Employees Pay Comparability Act of 1990

Gainsharing

Herzberg's theory of motivation

Individual equity

Internal equity

Job evaluation

Labor markets

Merit pay

Pay banding

Pay compression

Pay equity

Point factor analysis

Seniority pay

Skill pay

EXERCISES

Class Discussion

1. "We need to pay people based on their value-added contributions to their organization as well as the nation." Discuss, employing da Vinci's "parachute" (Introduction).

2. If teamwork, process improvement, and citizen service are hallmarks of quality management, then discuss the most appropriate pay system for an agency pursuing quality.

3. To what extent do flexible benefit programs resolve individual-organization compensation dilemmas? Would it be better to abolish benefits altogether (Exhibit 7.7)? Identify the conditions necessary for that to occur.

4. At the end of the chapter, it was suggested that the number of work hours be decreased in the name of employee fairness. Actually, European economists have long claimed that organizational productivity increases as hours decrease. Discuss how "less can be more."

5. "As much as it is a disservice not to support the federal workforce, at the end of the day it's a disservice to the public." US Senator Paul Sarbanes. Comment.

Team Activities

6. It was claimed that pay is important because it is vital, visible, and vicious in organizations. Divide into groups and analyze, from the perspective of the paradox of needs (Introduction), at least three strategies to ensure (a) external, (b) internal, and (c) individual equity for employees.

7. Resolved: "If recruitment and placement functions of HRM [human resource management] are done well, then incentive pay plans are irrelevant—even harmful." One team should argue the affirmative position, one the negative.

8. Analyze the importance of and controversies surrounding benefits from the perspective of the employee (one team) and the employer (another team). If some governments use benefit programs to attract and retain employees, is this ethical?

9. Because managers typically lack flexibility to increase employee pay (except to a limited extent in performance appraisal, Chapter 10), they may resort to finding ways to upgrade jobs (Chapter 5) instead. Discuss the ethics of this tactic and whether or not pay banding is a genuine solution to low pay in government.

Individual Assignments

10. There are many paradoxes in the human resource management compensation function. Identify at least three and discuss ways to resolve them. To what extent do they relate to the fundamental paradoxes discussed in the Introduction?

11. Your division has been selected as a demonstration project that will establish a pilot program to ensure individual equity. Top management has created an employee advisory committee to recommend how this can best be established. As its chair, which strategy would you recommend for first committee discussion? Why?

12. Discuss the following paradox: American employees work longer hours than they did a generation ago and work longer hours than employees in most other advanced nations, yet they are among the least protected and often the worst paid. The wages earned by the "working poor," in business and in government, in fact, do not lift them out of poverty.

13. Comparable worth is an important issue in rank-in-job classification systems. Why is it irrelevant in rank-in-person systems (Chapter 5)?

14. In the context of the importance of distributive and procedural justice in pay determination, consider this observation: "We apply rigorous discipline to learn how to earn a living, but not how to live."

APPENDIX

Compensation for Graduate Degrees in Public Affairs and Administration

Although people vary in motivation for pursuing graduate work, when graduation nears most students become interested in using their degree for career advancement. Such advancement is a means to increase income and, at least in the aggregate, higher education is associated with higher incomes.

Of course, no one can guarantee a payoff from higher education. The first step is to get a job that is consistent with the degree—one that would require and reward having a specific degree. Previously, advice has been offered on the importance of networking and on improving interviewing skills and résumés to improve chances of getting a desired position. You should also be able to clearly express what difference you want to make, and how that relates to the needs of a future employer.

But, as a second step, it is also useful to look strategically at compensation as the result of your career choices. Variation exists in compensation among those who have a graduate degree in public affairs, such as a master's of public administration (MPA) or public policy (MPP). In general, there is consensus that this is a propitious time to enter public service. First, the beginning retirement of Baby Boomers will continue to open up numerous career opportunities. Management positions will be available to qualified people at a much earlier time than in the past, though it might take another five years for this to become evident. Second, the link between public service and employment has weakened. People can do service while working for government, nonprofits, and even for-profits. Indeed, careers are no longer tied to any one employer or sector. For example, if a person wants to specialize in environmental regulations, she can work almost anywhere. In a market-based economy, this means ample opportunities for career and salary advancement.

Third, in the public sector the historic gap between the federal, state, and local government salaries has narrowed in recent years. Historically, federal salaries have been greater than those in state government, which have been higher than those in local government. But for some jobs, local government management salaries are now greater than those in state government, and sometimes on par with those in the federal government. The increase found in these salaries is attributed to the high growth of local government and, hence, increased demand for talent. Beyond this, salaries are sometimes greater still in public enterprises, special districts, and other single-purpose public organizations like universities, public hospitals, and transit agencies.

Fourth, competition between the sectors for scarce talent also means that salaries in public organizations are sometimes on par with those of the private sector. In some professions they are higher in government (accountant, librarian, microbiologist), in other professions higher in the private sector (medical doctor, human resource director, chief executive officer). On average, the public and private sectors pay managers about the same, but there is a lot of variation. But while business sometimes pays more (such as in some high-growth, technical firms that offer substantial performance bonuses), job security, benefits, and working hours should also be considered.

With so much change and variation, future graduates would do well to examine data relevant to their specific situation. To learn more about salaries in public administration, visit http://www.naspaa.org/students/careers/salary.asp. A much more thorough look at salaries in public and nonprofit organizations can be found at http://www.bls.gov/oes/current/oessrci.htm (for government, scroll down and select sector 99; for nonprofits, see, for example, under sector 62). For an interesting look at careers, take a look at http://www.naspaa.org/students/careers/careers.asp and especially alumni profiles. There is also a link to job resources. For information on federal jobs, see http://www.calltoserve.org/, which has information about positions and how to find them, as well as links to sites with jobs. For a comparison of public and private salaries, consult http://www.cnn.com/2006/US/Careers/10/11/cb.government/index.html

Figures 7.2 and 7.3 provide available data on these issues. (Federal salaries have increased approximately 3% annually since 2004; in addition, some agencies have pay-for-performance and broadbanding programs that could increase pay beyond the 3% raises.) Many employees earn about

$60,000–$75,000, and managers earn about $70,000–$90,000. City managers can make $80,000–$140,000 per year, and senior federal managers can make $110,000–$165,000. Further analysis shows that there are payoffs from

(a) having technical skills (e.g., budgeting, information technology, evaluation);
(b) working for quasi-government agencies; and
(c) being a manager rather than a senior employee.

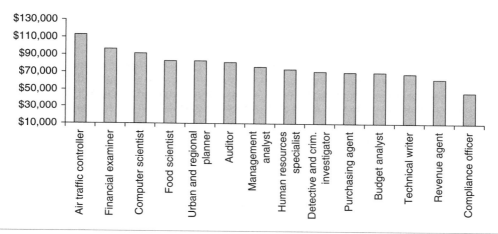

Figure 7.2   Mean Salaries of Selected Occupations in Federal Government (2007)

Source: U.S. Government, BLS, 2008.

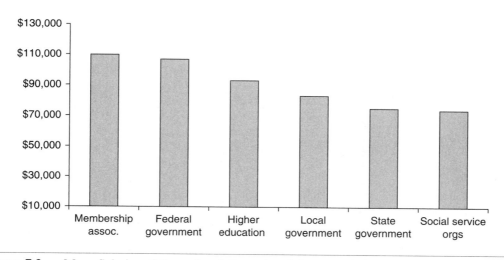

Figure 7.3   Mean Salaries of General and Operations Managers (2007)

Source: U.S. Government, BLS, 2008.

The advantage in each instance may be $10,000 per year; motivated, skilled people are often rewarded. The importance of having additional specialized knowledge, skills, or experience beyond the MPA or MPP degree should not be overlooked. Many graduates who make top salaries worked for several years in entry-level positions; they have paid their dues, and they have developed a positive reputation for success. Others have specialized skills and knowledge in information technology or accounting (both high-demand fields), or a second graduate degree, such as in law or social work. Indeed, some alumni with dual graduate degrees and some professional experience have accepted jobs after graduation with exceptional salaries. In short, top salaries go to those who have made an investment in their careers.

Also, the federal government has a program designed to attract top MPA graduates into federal service. The two-year Presidential Management Fellows program (http://www.pmi.opm.gov) provides salaries, in Washington, D.C., of about $43,000 in the first year and about $52,000 in the second. Upon completion, departments vie for these professionals, who then earn about $57,000–$62,000 per year, depending on location.

Whether just starting out or ready to take advantage of prior experience, opportunities await. It is not advocated that people make career choices solely to maximize their compensation. Rather, it is important to consider as well important factors beyond compensation. In short, know thyself! Set priorities, make a plan, and then work the plan. While there may be no magic bullet, informed choices can be made.

NOTES

1. Furthermore, their tenure in office, in an era of term limits, may be less than that of many career employees. Decision-making horizons, therefore, are likely to differ, and elected officials may be apt to maximize short-term goals at the expense of long-term effectiveness. Nowhere is this more evident than when it comes to compensation policies. Given the substantial funds devoted to payrolls, it might be anticipated that compensation would be one of the most carefully deliberated aspects of government policy, but this is not the case (see Exhibit 7.1).

2. Official pay gap estimates are subject to a variety of technical criticisms (see Kauffman, 2000; U.S. Government Accountability Office, 1995). For a more political interpretation, one that denies the gap exists and claims that the federal workforce has become an "elite island" of highly paid worker, see Edwards (2006). In addition, the magnitude of the gap—and even its existence—is fodder for interest groups as some studies claim the gap is 23% and 17%. Another maintains that federal workers are paid more than business executives. Any such comparisons must recognize that most governmental positions are white-collar professional or technical jobs (relevant comparisons compare governmental positions to those found in large corporations), where public employees generally earn less money.

3. It should be noted that many governments, although committed by law to external equity, actually emphasize an internal labor market strategy in recruitment. That is, except for entry-level positions, most career service job opportunities are filled from within. Governments resort to the outside market when no internal candidates can be found. For data on selected public service salaries, consult GovernmentExecutive.com (n.d.).

4. The importance of these benefits can be seen in employee recruitment and retention. Some seek employment precisely because comprehensive health insurance and retirement programs are offered. Both discourage turnover and thereby provide the opportunity for the employer to recoup training costs (Chapter 8. The best example of this is U.S. military personnel, who benefit from "socialized medicine" and are able to retire at half pay at age 40. In fact by a margin of nearly two to one, Americans prefer a government system of national health care instead of a private-employer-based system (Akst, 2003).

5. Note, however, that legislators, especially at national and state levels, often give themselves very generous benefit programs, as well as substantial perquisites and access to campaign funds.

6. It has been said that the definition of insanity is doing the same thing over and over again—while expecting a different result.

7. One federal official, who worked for five years under a pay-for-performance demonstration project, claimed, "The incentives of the new (DHLS) system are a joke, because they are so small. (T)hey constitute a zero-sum game, in that so little money is available for incentive pay that large increases for some translate into small increases for everyone else, regardless of how they performed" (Kauffman & Ziegler, 2004, p. 4). Most experts suggest an increase of 7–10% in an employee's annual pay is necessary to serve as a motivator. Ironically, the typical "employee likely would earn about the same as under the current system" if the DHLS approach was adapted government-wide (p. 4).

8. These drawbacks may be moderated by a variation of skill pay where one-time, skill-based bonuses are awarded without permanently increasing the pay base.

9. With the end of the postwar social contract at work, there is no doubt that a full-time job with benefits is a precious commodity in today's America. If the logic in the private sector is "business is great—you're fired," then in the public sector it is "expect nothing—you may be the next to be downsized" (see, e.g., Bowman, 2002).

10. Indeed, in 2004, thousands of soldiers were forbidden to return to civilian life when their contracts expired. This was an attempt to stanch the loss of troops from a military stretched thin by the war in Iraq. Some experts found these "stop loss" orders to be inconsistent with the principle of voluntary military service.

11. The Florida Highway Patrol was so strapped for funds in the 1990s that it could not even employ peripheral labor. Instead, one year it purchased department store mannequins, dressed them in uniform, and put them in official vehicles on the roadside. Although this technique may have had some deterrent value, it is not to be mistaken for effective law enforcement in a high-crime state.

REFERENCES

AFL-CIO Working women. (n.d.) www.aflcio.org/women

Associated Press. (2008, March 27). *Fingerprint scanners help companies track workers.* Retrieved March 27, 2008 from http://wcbstv.com

Akst, D. (2003, November 2). Why do employers pay for health insurance anyway? *New York Times,* p. 4BU.

Ballenstadt, B. (2008a, January 31). *OPM touts success of performance-based pay.* Retrieved January 31, 2008, from http://governmentexecutive.com/story_page.cfm?filepath=/dailyfed/0108/013108b1.htm

Ballenstadt, B. (2008b, March 14). *Lawmakers seek remedy for GAO pay reform.* Retrieved March 14, 2008, from http://governmentexecutive.com/story_page.cfm?filepath=/dailyfed/0308/031408b1.htm

Barcellos, D. (2005). The reality and promise of market-based pay. *Employment Relations Today, 32*(1), 1–10.

Bebchuk, L., & Fried, J. (2004). *Pay without performance.* Cambridge, MA: Harvard University Press.

Behn, R. (2000). Performance, people, and pay. *Bob Behn's Public Management Report,* pp.1–6. Retrieved January 13, 2005, from www.ksg.harvard.edu/TheBehnReport/PerformancePeopleAndPay.pdf

Behn, R. (2004, January). Pay for performance. *Bob Behn's Public Management Report, 1*(5), 1–2. Retrieved July 5, 2008, from http://www.hks.harvard.edu/thebehnreport/January2004.pdf

Blackwater's rich contracts. (2007, October 3). *International Herald Tribune.* Retrieved October 3, 2007, from http://www.iht.com/articles/2007/10/03/news/edblack.php

Blair, B. (2003, August 18). Experts debate pay rules for a new personnel system. *Federal Times,* p. 8.

Bohnet, I., & Eaton, S. (2003). Does performance pay perform? Conditions for success in the public sector. In J. Donahue & J. Nye, Jr. (Eds.), *For the people: Can we fix the public service?* (pp. 238–254). Washington, DC: Brookings.

Bowman, J. (2002, Fall). At-will employment in Florida government: A naked formula to corrupt public service. *WorkingUSA,* pp. 90–102.

Brown, M., & Heywood, J. (Eds.). (2002). *Paying for performance: An international comparison.* Armonk, NY: M. E. Sharpe.

Case for insourcing. (2007, October 8). *Federal Times.*

Castelli, E. (2008, June 16). DoD redirects contracting support work. *Federal Times.com.*

Congressional Budget Office (CBO). (2002, November). *Measuring differences between federal and private pay* (CBO Paper). Washington, DC: Author.

Cotterell, B. (2004, July 26). Money talks when handing out bonuses. *Tallahassee Democrat,* p. 1B.

Davidson, J. (2008, August 14). Promises of pay parity—dashed again. *Washington Post,* p. D3.

Edwards, C. (2006, May). Federal pay outpaces private-sector pay. *CATO Institute Tax and Budget Bulletin, 35,* 1–2.

Fisher, C. D., Schoenfeldt, L. F., & Shaw, J. B. (2006). *Human resource management.* Boston: Houghton Mifflin.

Flannery, T. P., Hofrichter, D. A., & Platten, P. E. (2002). *People, performance, and pay: Dynamic compensation for changing organizations.* New York: Free Press.

Fox, R., & Lawless, J. (2008). *Why are women still not running for office?* Washington, DC: Brookings.

Gabris, G. T. (1998). Merit pay mania. In S. E. Condrey (Ed.), *Handbook of human resource management in government* (pp. 627–657). San Francisco: Jossey-Bass.

Gabris, G., & Ihrke, D. (2004). Merit pay and employee performance. In M. Holzer & S. Lee (Eds.), *Public productivity handbook* (pp. 499–514). New York: Dekker.

Gage, J., & Kelly, C. (2003, November 10). Unions support smart performance pay for Homeland. *Federal Times,* p. 21.

Giapponi, C., & McEvoy, S. (2005–2006). The legal, ethical, and strategic implications of gender discrimination in compensation: Can the Fair Pay Act succeed where the Equal Pay Act has failed? *Journal of Individual Employment Rights, 12*(2), 137–150.

GovernmentExecutive.com. (n.d.). Advanced search. Retrieved February 14, 2008, from www.govexec.com/careers.

Hays, S. (2004, September). Trends and best practices in state and local human resource management: Lessons to be learned? *Review of Public Personnel Administration,* 256–275.

Heathfield, S. (2008a). *How to ask for a pay raise.* Retrieved April 14, 2008, from http://human resources.about.com/od/salaryand benefits/a/ask_raise.html

Heathfield, S. (2008b). *Women and work: Then, now, and predicting the future for women in the workplace.* Retrieved October 1, 2008, from http://humanresources.About.com/od/worklifebalance/a/business_women

Hedgpeth, D. (2008, July 24). Pentagon auditors pressured to favor contractors, GAO says. *Washingon Post,* p. D01ff.

Herzberg, F., Mauser, B., & Snoplerman, B. (1959). *Motivation to work.* New York: Wiley.

Hewitt Associates. (2003, September 15). OPM official: Performance pay has staying power. *Federal Times,* p. 6.

Hogler, R. (2004). *Employment relations in the United States: Law, policy and practice.* Thousand Oaks, CA: Sage Publications.

Jauhar, S. (2008, September 9). The pitfalls of linking doctors' pay to performance. *New York Times.*

Jenkins, C., Jr., Mitra, A., Gupta, N., & Shaw, J. (1998). Are financial incentives related to performance? A meta-analytical review of empirical research. *Journal of Applied Psychology, 83,* 777–787.

Jurkiewicz, C., & Bowman, J. (2002, Fall). Charlotte: A model for market-driven public service management. *State and Local Government Review,* pp. 205–213.

Kauffman, T. (2000, April 3). Studies delay pay locality reform. *Federal Times,* pp. 1, 18.

Kauffman, T. (2004, December 13). Pay reform failure: How FAA's bold experiment led to inequity, poor morale. *Federal Times,* p. 1.

Kauffman, T. (2005, January 3). OMB to push performance pay governmentwide in 05. *Federal Times,* p. 11.

Kauffman, T., & Ziegler, M. (2004, May 2). National Academy of Public Administration: Pay reform for all. *Federal Times,* pp. 1, 4–5.

Kellough, J., & Lu, H. (1993, Spring). The paradox of merit pay. *Review of Public Personnel Administration,* pp. 45–63.

Kellough, J., & Selden, S. (1997, Winter). Pay for performance systems in state government: Perceptions of state agency personnel managers. *Review of Public Personnel Administration,* pp. 5–21.

Kelly, E., & Moen, P. (2007). Rethinking the clockwork of work: Why schedule control may pay off at work and at home. *Advances in Developing Human Resources, 9*(4), 487–506.

Kiger, P. (2007, June 19). Throwing out the rules of work. *Workforce Management.*

Lane, L., Wolf, J., & Woodard, C. 2003. Reassessing the human resource crisis in the public service. *American Review of Public Administration 33* (2), 123–145.

Leonard, B. (1995, February). Creating opportunities to excel. *HRMagazine,* pp. 47–51.

Lee, C., & Straus, H. (2004, May 17). Two thirds of federal workers get bonus. *Washington Post,* p. A1.

Losey, S. (2008a, February 4). DOD hands out bigger raisers. *Federal Times,* pp. 1, 19.

Losey, S (2008b, August 25). Better performers net bigger payouts, NSPS numbers show. *Federal Times,* p. 6.

Many workers dissatisfied with pay. (2001, June 30). *HRMazazine,* p. 37.

Masternak, R. (2003). *Gainsharing: A team-based approach to driving organizational change.* Phoenix, AZ: World at Work.

Matthews, W. (2008, March 3). State pays $1,222 per day for contractor security guards. *Federal Times,* p. 8.

Method, J. (2008, June 23). Few bonuses paid to federal employees, survey shows. *Federal Times,* p. 6.

Pay banding in the federal government. (2003, February). Issues of Merit. U.S. Merit Systems Protection Board. Retrieved December 20, 2004 from http://www.mspb.gov/studees/newslettters/03febnws.html

Pay for performance in the federal government. (2008). Subcommittee on oversight of government management, the federal workforce and District of Columbia of the Committee on homeland security and governmental affairs, 110 Cong. (testimony of Linda M. Springer). http:www.opm.gov/NewsEvents/congress/testimony/110Congress

Perry, P. (2003). Compensation, merit pay, and motivation. In S. Hays & R. Kearney (Eds.), *Public personnel administration: Problems and prospects* (pp. 143–153). Englewood Cliffs, NJ: Prentice Hall.

Pinker, S.(2008). *The sexual paradox: Men, women, and the real gender gap.* New York: Scribner.

Risher, H. (2002, Fall). Pay for performance: The key to making it work. *Public Personnel Management,* pp. 317–332.

Risher, H. (2004). *Pay for performance: A guide for federal managers.* Washington, DC: IBM Center for the Business of Government.

Risher, H., & Fay, C. (Eds.). (1997). *New strategies for public pay.* San Francisco: Jossey-Bass.

Risher, H., & Wise, L. R. (1997). Job evaluation: The search for internal equity. In H. Risher & C. Fay (Eds.), *New strategies for public pay* (pp. 98–124). San Francisco: Jossey-Bass.

Rutzick, K. (2005, September 30). *Agency decides pay banding is not the answer.* Govexe.com

Sanders, R. P. (1998). Gainsharing in government. In S. E. Condrey (Ed.), *Handbook of human resource management in government* (pp. 231–252). San Francisco: Jossey-Bass.

Scott, S. and Nixon, R. 2007, February, 4. Washington, contractors take on biggest role ever. *New York Times:* 1, 24.

Seahill, J. (2007, August 13). Flush with profits from the Iraq war, military contractors see a world of business opportunities. *Alternet: The mix is the message.* Retrieved August 13, 2007, from http://www.alternet.org

Shareef, R. (2002). The sad demise of skill-based pay in the Virginia Department of Transportation. *Review of Public Personnel Administration, 22*(3), 233–240.

Singletary, M. (2008, August 24). Despite strides, women still tripped up by confidence gap. *Washington Post,* p. F01.

State should keep promise. (1996, December 12). *Tallahassee Democrat,* p. 10A.

Strivers, C., & Hummel, R. (2007, November/December). Personnel management: Politics, administration, and a passion for anonymity. *Public Administration Review, 67,* 1010–1117.

Thomas, K. W. (2000). *Intrinsic motivation at work.* Williston, UT: Berrett-Kohler.

Thompson, J. R., & LeHew, C. W. (2002). Skill-based pay as an organizational innovation. *Review of Public Personnel Administration, 20*(1), 20–40.

Tiefer, C. (2008, April 4). Re-evaluating pay for performance. *Federal Times,* p. 23.

U.S. Bureau of the Census (Census). (2001). *Statistical abstract of the United States* (121st ed.). Washington, DC: Government Printing Office.

U.S. Government Accountability Office (GAO). (1995). *Federal/private pay comparisons* (OCE- 95–1, pp. 231–252). Washington, DC: Government Printing Office.

U.S. Merit Systems Protection Board (MSPB). (2006). *Designing an effective pay for performance compensation system.* Washington, DC: Author.

U.S. Office of Personnel Management (OPM). (2002). *A white paper. A fresh start for federal pay: The case for modernization.* Washington, DC: Author.

Vroom, V. H. (1964). *Work motivation.* New York: Wiley.

Walker, R. (2008, February 1). *Union disputes OPM claim of success in new pay systems.* FCW.com.

Wamsley, B. S. (1998). Are current programs working? In S. E. Condrey (Ed.), *Handbook of human resource management in government* (pp. 25–39). San Francisco: Jossey-Bass.

Watkins, S. (2008, March 17). An eclipsing shadow. *Federal Times,* p. 2.

Zeller, S. (2004, September 8). *Union's opposition to pay-for-performance systems unrelenting.* Retrieved January 12, 2005, from www.govexec.com/dailyfed/0904/090804sz1.htm

Zingheim, P. K., & Shuster, J. R. (2000). *Pay people right!* San Francisco: Jossey-Bass.

Chapter 8

Employee-Friendly Policies
Fashionable, Flexible, and Fickle

People are assets whose value can be enhanced through investment.

—David Walker

After studying this chapter, you should be able to

- understand the composition of the workforce and trends that drive employee-responsive programs,
- identify different employee-friendly initiatives and their applications,
- determine the relative merits of proposals for resolving work/home conflict,
- develop a telecommuter agreement for use in a public organization,
- assess the impact of employee-friendly policies on agencies and their staff, and
- recognize relevant paradoxes.

Career demands often conflict with personal pressures, and juggling the two poses problems in both settings.[1] Work/life balance is a top career priority for many: 73% of 3,278 U.S. workers "strongly agree" with the statement, "I am willing to take a back seat in my career in order to make time for my family," according to results of a Spherion Corporation survey (Kleiman, 2003, p. 3E). At the same time, though, employees are working longer hours than they ever have in the past: in 2005 both men and women reported working more hours than they were scheduled to work (Bond, Galinsky, Kim, & Brownfield, 2005; Lingle, 2005; Reynolds, 2005; Yates & Leach, 2006). Some employers, responding to employee expectations, especially among younger, **Generation X** (those born between 1960 and 1980) and **New Millennials** (those born after 1980) workers, have introduced employee-friendly policies to reduce home/work conflict and to help people achieve a better balance between work and home. These policies also make the workplace more attractive and help employers to attract and retain younger workers, who are increasingly mobile. Organizations also expect a return on this investment in the form of improved productivity at work. In the past, critics maintain that such organizational initiatives are unjustified, uneven, and extravagant in a period of declining resources, but these employee- and family-friendly policies are increasingly accepted and even expected among today's workers.

Proemployee policies are fashionable (stylish and responsive to trends), flexible (adaptable to the unique needs of a diverse workforce), and fickle (unstable and subject to the fluctuating fortunes of the economy). For example, paternity leave is currently offered to employees at the Federal National Mortgage Association (FNMA, or Fannie Mae), a government-sponsored enterprise. This policy allows fathers to take up to four weeks of paid leave spread out over an extended period to care for their newborn or newly adopted children. The availability of such policies might change with downturns in the economy.

Worker-responsive policies include a variety of initiatives to address employee's needs and to advance organizational interests. Individuals' needs are addressed when agencies introduce work schedules and benefit plans tailored to their age and stage of life. Organizational interests are served if staff performance improves as a result, or if recruitment is enhanced. Experience suggests, however, that "win-win" outcomes are not easy to achieve. Reflecting the paradox of needs (see the Introduction), institutional goals of efficiency and productivity may conflict with employees' goals of a supportive workplace. For instance, **flextime** might be a boon to some, enabling them to care for young children or ailing parents, but in practice it may create problems, such as office coverage and on-time project completion.

This and other paradoxes help explain why employers often hesitate before they undertake large-scale programs of this type and why employee-friendly policies might exist on paper but lack top-management support when people seek to implement them. Organizations may not trust employees who are working in remote locations, or they might resist change that reduces on-site staff and redefines managerial roles. Paradoxes also help explain why personnel may lobby for specific worker-responsive programs but then underutilize them once they are available. This might result from management that does not "walk the talk" of employee-friendly policies. Alternatively, people may like to know the policies exist (e.g., child care, elder care, **wellness programs**, telecommuting), whether or not they use them at the moment. Employees often fear that taking advantage of flexible work options signals to their supervisors that they do not take their careers seriously.

Consistent with the distinction between personnel administration and human resource management, this chapter focuses on the person as a whole by considering the characteristics and use of employee-friendly programs. The social trends that may make such programs popular are summarized. Organizational responses to these trends and the challenges they pose are explored. Several family/work initiatives, health/wellness programs, flexible benefit plans, and relocation assistance efforts are considered. The impacts of such programs on employee and organizational performance are discussed, together with selected implementation issues. Finally, the chapter highlights paradoxes that may be encountered when implementing specific programs.

■■ WORKFORCE AND WORKPLACE TRENDS

Characteristics of the changing American workforce and work-life benefits have been widely discussed (Cayer & Roach, 2008; Reddick & Coggburn, 2008). Projections suggest that coming decades will bring more women, older workers, temporary employees, minorities, and immigrants into positions in both the public and private sectors (Guy & Newman, 1998; West, 2005).[2] For example, 63.7% of women with children under six years old, and 78% of women with children between six and 17 years old participate in the labor force (Bureau of Labor Statistics, 2002). Participation of women in the labor force overall has increased from 33.9% in 1950 to a peak of 60.0% in 1999 (U.S. Department of Labor, 2007). This feminization of the workforce has had numerous ripple effects on life at home and at work. Workforce composition has changed in other ways as well:

- Seven in ten working husbands are married to women in the labor force.
- More than one-eighth of American full- or part-time employees have eldercare responsibilities.
- According to a National Alliance for Caregiving (2004) study, nearly six in ten caregivers (59%) are employed (48% work full-time and 11% work part-time).
- Women (10.4 million) are more than four times as likely as men (2.5 million) to be in charge of single-parent families, but the number of fathers responsible for their children is increasing more rapidly than the numbers of mothers with this responsibility (Leonard, 1996; Levine, 1997; Peterson, 1998; U.S. Bureau of the Census [Census], 2007).

The rise in dual-career couples and in **nontraditional families**, along with the need to consider both work and caregiving for dependent children and elderly parents, adds to the stress of home and career.

As the workforce diversifies, pressures will intensify for policies that address the special needs of these employees. Thus, employer assistance in meeting childcare and eldercare responsibilities will be priority concerns for the **sandwich generation** (those with responsibilities for both children and elderly parents), as will flextime and **parental leave** programs. Telecommuting might have particular appeal for the more technologically sophisticated members of Generation X and New Millennials. Those in nontraditional families (including gay and lesbian couples, unmarried couples in committed relationships, single-parent families, and reconstituted families) will be especially interested in domestic partner benefits.

Alternative work arrangements and cafeteria-style benefit plans (which allow workers to choose among benefits to best suit their needs) will appeal to employees who seek a better balance between job and home life and whose benefit preferences may change over the life cycle of their employment. A recent Bureau of Labor Statistics (2007) survey reported that one-third of state and local governments have access to a flexible benefit plan. Workers who are **downshifting** (scaling back their career ambitions and giving more time and attention to their family and personal needs) may find part-time work or job-sharing options appealing. Those losing their positions because of **downsizing** (e.g., caused by government reductions in force, outsourcing, or base closure) will press employers for employee relocation assistance.

These trends will come up against countervailing pressures in the workplace. There is a need for organizations to consider adopting employee-friendly policies to attract and retain staff. This will help public employers remain competitive with private employers, who may offer a variety of workplace alternatives. To the extent that jurisdictions continue to face resource scarcity, competition, and taxpayer demands that they be lean, mean, and productive, they will avoid expenditures on all but the most essential programs. Indeed, as public organizations are becoming flatter, more nimble, and more automated, they are simultaneously downsizing as well as increasing use of temporary workers and contractors. These trends will lead to lower investments in human capital.[3] Worker-responsive policy proposals, especially absent hard evidence of pending benefits, will be a hard sell in such an atmosphere.

Public officials and managers need to respond to these competing, often contradictory, demands of the workforce and workplace in crafting policies. The menu of options available to promote supportive employee relations is broad, tempting, and rich with possibilities; the options, however, can be costly, and there is a risk that personnel may not come away satisfied. The three sections that follow discuss this array of possibilities: (1) family/work programs; (2) health, safety, and wellness programs; and (3) flexible work arrangements.

▪▪ FAMILY/WORK PROGRAMS

For employees, it is important to know what work/family conflicts might exist and how they can be resolved. For employers, the issues are what programs, if any, to provide and how to implement them. This section briefly examines these questions from both perspectives. Employees with dependent children or elderly parents are concerned about their home/family responsibilities. They want to know about the support and benefits the organizations might provide to reduce conflicts. Employers need to decide how best to respond to work/family conflicts and whether such responses require institution-sponsored services or modifications in benefit packages.

Five programs address these dual employee and employer concerns: (1) child care, (2) elder care, (3) parental and military leave, (4) adoption assistance, and (5) domestic partners coverage. These program types, plus those discussed subsequently, illustrate that one activity (e.g., childcare service) represents a small part of a much broader approach to "holistically" managing employee-responsive policies. Each of these initiatives is discussed in turn below.

Child Care

Former U.S. Representative Pat Schroeder reports a conversation with a colleague early in her career in Congress. She was asked how she would juggle her responsibilities as a mother and a legislator: "I have a brain and a uterus," she answered, "and they both work" (Schroeder, 1998, p. 128). Many women (and men) want what Ms. Schroeder wanted—to use their mental and physical endowments to be both parents *and* employees. This raises the thorny and much-discussed question of what to do about dependent children while parents are working.

The issue touches most people in one way or another. Consider two facts:

1. Of the 23.2 million children under six years of age in the United States, more than half (14.3 million) need child care because both parents work outside the home (Census, 2006).

2. Eighteen thousand preschoolers and 38,000 grade-schoolers need child care, according to the 2000 census (Census, 2003).

Research from the U.S. Government Accountability Office (GAO) indicates that 54% of federal government employees have dependent-care needs, and 19% more expect to have such needs in the future (GAO, 2007). Most parents at one time or another have experienced problems with childcare arrangements that interfered with work. Tardiness, absenteeism, and productivity are all affected. Even if employees arrive on time and work throughout the day, parents may be subject to the **3:00 syndrome**—attention to work-related tasks wanes as they begin thinking about children ready to leave school and return home. Employers can minimize these disruptions and distractions by providing childcare benefits.

The types of benefits employers make available to working parents vary. A small percentage of organizations furnish on-site or near-site childcare centers. A far larger proportion offers financial assistance for off-site child care, and many more provide information and referral services. Paradoxically, a majority of federal agencies offers on-site, near-site, or referral services for child care, but a very small percentage of eligible employees use these facilities. By contrast, only 7% of private employers in a 2002 survey provided direct-cost child care on or near site. The same survey found that 45% of employers provided dependent-care assistance plans, and a third offered referral services for child care (Bond et al., 2005). Specifically, Exhibit 8.1 reports family benefits for full-time employees in private industry as well as in state and local government.

Exhibit 8.1	Eligibility for Specific Family Benefits by Full-Time Employees		
Specific Benefits	*Private Sector* 2007	*State Government* 2007	*Local Government* 2007
Employer resource and referral service for child care	11%	14%	8%
Employer provided funds	3	8	3
On-site and off-site child care	5	17	6
Work-related education assistance	49	85	63
Long-term care insurance	12	43	21
Paid family leave	8	85	14
Unpaid family leave	83	97	92
Adoption assistance	11	19	5
Wellness programs	25	69	46
Fitness center	13	35	19
Employee assistance program	42	87	68

Source: Bureau of Labor Statistics, 2008.

Eligibility for such benefits is greater in state government than in either private industry or local government. President George W. Bush signed a law (P.L. 197–67) in 2001 authorizing the use of appropriated funds by executive agencies to provide childcare services for federal civilian employees. Exhibit 8.2 identifies several types of employer-sponsored childcare options.

Two examples from local governments suggest creative approaches to child care. The city of Westminster, Colorado, formed a public-private partnership with other area employers to provide child care for employees. The local school district and private businesses are members of the partnership consortium. It provides in-home backup care for ill children, subsidizes school vacation childcare programs, and has a resource or referral program for child care. The South Florida Water Management District provides child care for personnel at

---

Exhibit 8.2   Employer-Sponsored Childcare Options

1. Childcare facility
   - On- or near-site center
   - Consortium center
   - Family daycare home or network
   - Expansion of local centers

2. Financial assistance
   - Childcare subsidies
   - Dependent-care assistance plans

3. Resource and referral service
   - Referrals for parents
   - Quality improvements

4. Mildly ill/emergency/special-needs child care
   - "Get well" rooms in childcare program
   - Satellite family daycare homes
   - Home visitor program
   - Special program just for mildly ill children
   - Backup care when school is not in session

5. Flexible benefits
   - Flextime, part-time work
   - Flexplace
   - Job sharing
   - Voluntary reduced time

6. Parental leave

7. Investing in community resources
   - Creating new supply
   - Funding provider training programs

---

no cost to the agency as a result of negotiations with a developer who agreed to build a childcare facility on property owned by the agency. The developer is leasing the land from the district for a nominal fee ($1 a year for 25 years) and rents the building to a childcare operator. The facility will be turned over to the district after 25 years, and will be paid for using the rent paid by the childcare operator.

Another childcare issue—breast-feeding infants in the workplace—has resulted in public policy at the state and federal level and in foreign settings (see Exhibit 8.3).

In Great Britain, a flexible work program has been established that allows employees with children under the age of six to request a change in their work schedules and requires employers to consider the request, at least. The program provides flexibility to employees that may allow them to create a better balance between work and family responsibilities. At the same time, employers may be more able to maintain skilled staff,

---

Exhibit 8.3   Breast-Feeding at Work

The following 14 states have laws protecting breast-feeding in the workplace:

- California
- Connecticut
- Georgia
- Hawaii
- Illinois
- Minnesota
- New Mexico
- New York
- Oklahoma
- Oregon
- Rhode Island
- Tennessee
- Texas
- Washington

There is considerable variation in the content of these state laws. For example, in some states (California, Illinois, Minnesota, and Tennessee) employers are required to provide reasonable break time and to designate a place to pump breast milk, but such breaks should not be unduly disruptive of daily operations. Less-restrictive legislation in Rhode Island merely states that such breaks "may" be provided by employers. Other states (Connecticut and Hawaii) do not mandate breast-feeding breaks, but prohibit employers from refusing to allow women to use existing breaks to breast-feed and from discriminating against such workers. California's is the only state law that authorizes fines for violators of the workplace accommodations law (Oakley, 2008; Vance, 2005). Other state laws protect breast-feeding in any public or private location (39 states), exempt breast-feeding from the public indecency laws (22 states), and exempt breast-feeding mothers from jury duty (12 states; Oakley, 2008).

Breast-feeding in public in a federal building (e.g., museum, courthouse, federal agency) or on federal property (e.g., national park) is protected by a federal law passed in 1999, provided the woman and her child are authorized to be present at the site. Seventy-six other countries protect the right of mothers to breast-feed in the workplace (Oakley, 2008).

Sources: Adapted from Oakley, 2008; Vance, 2005.

---

reduce absenteeism by increasing staff morale, and develop efficient response techniques to changes in market conditions. It is estimated that 25% of employees seeking this option have been successful, without businesses losing any productivity. Due to the program success, as of November 2007 Prime Minister Gordon Brown announced the intent to conduct further research on the possibility of opening the program up to parents of older children (Department for Business Enterprise and Regulatory Reform of U.K., 2008; Obama, 2006). Exhibit 8.4 reports the extent of government support for child care in Denmark.

Exhibit 8.4   Child Care in Denmark

Denmark has granted the right to public child care for all families since 1976, when the Social Assistance Act was put into law, creating a system that recognizes local autonomy and universal concerns for equity. The system allows mothers to work outside the home by providing a mostly publicly funded (parental fees are capped at 30–33% of operation expenses) childcare system that is operated at the local level, providing flexibility which helps communities meet their individual needs.

It is estimated that 70–75% of childcare services in Denmark are provided by local authorities, who set the agenda and framework for the services including facility locations, opening hours, and overall goals. More general guidelines were established in the 1999 Social Services Act, which states that the goals of childcare services should be to provide an environment for good development, well-being, and independence for children.

The childcare system also includes the right to pregnancy leave four weeks before birth, maternity leave for up to 14 weeks after birth, paternity leave for up to two weeks after birth, and another 32 weeks of parental leave to be shared between the father and mother after the first 14 weeks of birth, all with 50% pay. Families are also provided pay allowances and annual childcare allowances paid for by the state until a child reaches 18 years of age.

Sources: Coalition of Child Care Advocates of BC, 2007; Ministry of Science Technology and Innovation, 2008; Walter, 2005.

Elder Care

Caring for elderly relatives is an increasingly common, time-consuming, expensive, and stress-inducing problem. According to a 2002 survey by the Families and Work Institute (2002), 35% of employees report responsibilities for elder care. Employers have responded to this need, with 34% of employers in 2005 providing information to employees about eldercare resources, compared with 23% in 1998.

According to U.S. Office of Personnel Management ([OPM], 2002), 25.8 million Americans spend an average of 18 hours a week caring for a relative. Two studies conducted by MetLife and AARP in 2006 and 2007 (AARP Public Policy Institute, 2007; MetLife, 2006) found that the cost to U.S. business from the lost productivity of employees caring for an elderly family member is more than $33 billion per year. The cost breakdown of the MetLife study is shown in Exhibit 8.5.

Caregivers face additional concerns that take a personal toll. They have reduced time for leisure activities (hobbies, vacations) and are more likely to report physical or mental health problems.

This issue is pervasive and costly to the workplace as well. The 2006 MetLife caregiving study showed that 15% of employees that had care responsibilities left their workplace (6% of whom quit their jobs entirely), 3% retired early, and another 10% reduced their schedules to part-time work (Dobkin, 2006). Similarly, Levine (1997) reported that two-thirds of caregivers are full- or part-time workers. One in 10 caregivers quits her job, a similar proportion take a leave of absence, and six in 10 display sporadic attendance at work. Increased absenteeism, abbreviated workdays, diminished productivity, and excessive turnover linked to caregiving for dependent elderly persons add to costs employers must bear.

Exhibit 8.5   The Costs of Elder Caregiving

Cost factors	Cost per employee	Total cost to U.S. employers
Replacing employees	$413	$6,585,310,888
Absenteeism	$320	$5,096,925,912
Partial absenteeism	$121	$1,923,730,754
Workday interruptions	$394	$6,282,281,750
Elder care	$238	$3,799,217,477
Supervisor time	$113	$1,796,385,842
Unpaid leave	$212	$3,377,082,202
Full-time to part-time	$299	$4,758,135,522
Total	$2,110	$33,619,070,346

Source: Adapted from MetLife, 2006.

Exhibit 8.1 reports the percentage of full-time employees in private, state, and local government who are eligible for long-term care insurance. Once again, state government personnel are more likely to be eligible than those in local government or the private sector.

Eldercare programs address both employees' and employers' needs to reduce work/family conflict by providing staff with some combination of the following: social work counseling, financial assistance, subsidies to service providers, leave policies, information and referral sources, support groups, or other forms of aid. Programs with some of these services or benefits are found in more than half of America's cities and one-third of private corporations (Mercer, 1996; West & Berman, 1996). A 2002 survey found that 79% of employers provide the opportunity for employees to take time off from work to deal with elder care, without risk to their jobs (Bond et al., 2005), The demand for such programs is bound to increase with the continued graying of America's workforce (West, 2005). Among the proposals is one suggesting a wage replacement for family caregivers of the elderly. Giving caregivers time off is another way to address their needs. Resource and referral services for elder care and child care, offered by 8 in 10 federal agencies, actually have been used by a paltry 0.1% of workers (Daniel, 1999).

Parental and Military Leave

The **Family and Medical Leave Act** of 1993 provides eligible workers with up to 12 weeks, during any 12-month period, of *unpaid* leave for childbirth or adoption; for caregiving to a child, elderly parent, or spouse with a serious health problem; or for a personal illness. Six in ten members in the U.S. labor force, including public and private sector employees, work for employers covered by the Family and Medical Leave Act (American Association of University Women [AAUW], 2007).

Thus, it is not surprising that parental leave policies are among the most prevalent of the five items discussed in this section for subnational governments and private sector organizations. Estimates from the Institute for Health and Social Policy at McGill University are that more than 50 million Americans have taken advantage of the program since 1993 (AAUW, 2007). Exhibit 8.1 shows that paid and unpaid leave for full-time employees is more available in state than in local government. Paid leave (maternity and paternity) is much less common in the private sector The International City/County Management Association (ICMA) surveys indicate that 19% of cities offer paid maternity leave, whereas less than 9% offer paid paternity leave. Where paid maternity or paternity leave is available, cities typically make it available to all staff.

Managing parental and family leave programs involves costs of various types at different stages:

- Before leave (absenteeism and productivity impacts)
- During planning (securing and training potential replacements)
- During leave (disability pay and stakeholder impacts)
- While staffing (temps or replacement costs, overtime)
- After leave (retraining, possible turnover costs)

Estimates of the costs associated with parental or family leave, according to five surveys analyzed by Martinez (1993), most frequently ranged between 11% and 20% of annual salary. Employee gains in flexibility and support must be weighed against employer costs in subsidizing parental leave programs.

In 2002, California became the first state to offer paid parental leave, when the state introduced an employee-funded program that allows up to six weeks of paid family leave to care for a child after birth or for a seriously ill family member. The leave is funded by employees who pay $27 a year into the state's disability insurance program, which transfers the funds to the participants. Program benefits include increased employee retention and, as a result, reduced hiring costs; and increased bonding time for parents who may not otherwise be able to afford time off from work, which results in the healthy development of a child (California Employee Development Department, 2008; Equal Rights Advocates, 2008).

Those who serve in the military are also protected by federal and state laws. The Uniformed Services Employment and Reemployment Rights Act of 1994 prohibits discrimination against those in the military or the reserves. Negative job actions against employees because they are in the armed forces or reserves are prohibited. Furthermore, employers are required to reinstate any person who leaves his job to serve in the armed forces so long as certain conditions are met (e.g., advance notice, time limitations, honorable release). Furthermore, most state laws provide additional protections against discrimination against those in the state's militia or National Guard (NOLO, 2003a).

Adoption Assistance

Adoption assistance includes benefits ranging from time off to reimbursement of expenses following adoption of a child. Although employees who give birth to a child typically enjoy paid leave and medical coverage, this may or may not be the case for those adopting a child. Expenses can be substantial, ranging from zero to $40,000 (for, e.g., medical costs, legal fees, travel expenses, etc.; Adoption.com, n.d.). Employers are beginning to recognize that adoptive parents need assistance. Three key issues need to be considered: eligibility, leave time, and reimbursement. Factors related to eligibility are length of employment, age of the child, and whether coverage includes step- or foster-care children. Regarding leave, considerations are the length of time available for unpaid leave; the permissibility of using sick leave, annual leave, or personal leave; and whether those who take leave are guaranteed job reinstatement. Reimbursement issues concern the coverage of legal or medical expenses.

The percentage of private organizations offering adoption assistance ranges from 15% to 32% depending on the survey (e.g., Mercer, 1996; OPM, 2007b). For example, Dow Chemicals USA, Wendy's International, and Campbell Soups provide adoption benefit programs. The city of Philadelphia is a public sector pioneer in making such coverage available. The state of Washington passed a law establishing five weeks of partially paid leave for the adoption of a child (Reddick & Coggburn, 2008). Reimbursement of up to $10,000 for adoption expenses is not unusual in the private sector (*Adoptive Families,* 2008). Local government employees are less likely than either private sector or state government employees to be eligible for assistance (see Exhibit 8.1). The rationale for employers to provide such benefits is linked to equity: if parents giving birth are entitled to benefits, why not adoptive parents? Two other reasons are important: cost factors (adoption benefits are low cost because few use them) and stakeholder loyalty (support for adoptive parents can increase loyalty, morale, and retention). Similar equity, cost, and loyalty issues surround questions of domestic partner benefits.

Domestic Partnership Coverage

Domestic partnership coverage refers to benefits such as health insurance and sick or bereavement leave that may be made available to a person designated as a domestic partner of an employee. Less-encompassing policies might involve little more than public recognition of cohabiting couples; more-encompassing plans include dental and vision benefits, **employee assistance programs**, and posttermination benefits for domestic partners. The need for such coverage has increased in recent years because of changes in the American family and workforce, the importance of benefits as a key component in an employee's total compensation package, and efforts to avoid discrimination against gays and lesbians. According to the 2000 census, 5.5 million couples are living together but are not married, 4.9 million of them households with partners of the opposite sex. One in 9 (594,000) had partners of the same sex (Census, 2003).

Many public and private sector benefit plans have been restructured to add flexibility and take into account these changes. From 2003 to 2007, there was a 61% increase in the number of employers offering health insurance to same-sex domestic partners (Human Rights Campaign Foundation, 2003, 2007). According to the Human Rights Campaign Foundation (2007), employers that offer domestic partner health benefits include the following:

- State governments (13)
- Local governments (211)
- Fortune 500 companies (267)
- Top 125 colleges and universities (75)

New York City provides benefits for domestic partners of employees, and San Francisco goes even farther, requiring private organizations that contract with the city to provide such benefits. In response, the House of Representatives denied federal housing dollars to cities that require organizations doing business with them to provide same-sex domestic partner benefits to the organization's employees. The experience at Disney and the Salvation Army (see Exhibit 8.6) suggests that granting domestic partner coverage is controversial in the private and nonprofit sector as well: it pleases some stakeholders and angers others. Additional obstacles to domestic partner benefits are rising costs of healthcare benefits and reluctance by insurance companies to cover unknown risks. As workforce diversity continues, pressures for such benefits will mount. Vermont's experience with civil unions and the Massachusetts court decision finding gay marriage constitutional in 2004 illustrate the increased salience of this issue.

Exhibit 8.6   Flip-Flops at the Salvation Army

In November of 2001, the Western Branch of the Salvation Army announced it would extend health benefits to same-sex partners of employees. This new policy would affect employees in 13 western states plus Guam, Micronesia, and the Marshall Islands. They said they were acting in compliance with San Francisco's landmark 1998 Equal Benefits Ordinance. Previously the Salvation Army had forfeited $3.5 million in contracts for noncompliance. According to Colonel Phillip Needham, chief secretary for the Salvation Army's Western Corporation, the action "reflects our concern for the health of our employees and those closest to them, and is made on the basis of strong ethical and moral reasoning that reflects the dramatic changes in family structure in recent years" (quoted in People for the American Way [PFAW], 2001).

In response to this action, the national offices of the Salvation Army received 10,000 e-mails and 1,500 phone calls in protest. Groups such as the American Family Association, Focus on the Family, Concerned Women for America, the Traditional Values Coalition, and the Family Research Council loudly decried the act and began protesting. Vociferous negative reactions were also voiced on Christian radio and television and from the evangelical Salvation Army denomination.

Two weeks following the announcement, the policy was rescinded by the national Salvation Army's Commissioners Conference, stating, "We will not sign any government contract or any other funding contracts that contain domestic partner benefit requirements" (quoted in Gordon, 2001).

In response, Parents, Families and Friends of Lesbians and Gays (PFLAG) organized a protest supporting reversal. Opponents to rescinding the policy placed fake money (phony $5 bills), printed from an Internet site, in the Salvation Army collection kettles. They claimed this was more about sending a message than doing harm. The Salvation Army maintains the protest did not hurt their collection efforts.

This issue shows that implementation of domestic partner plans raises complex and contentious political and social issues. National support or opposition is linked to broader gay rights issues.

Sources: Gordon, 2001; Heredia, 2001a, 2001b; King, 2001; People for the American Way, 2001; Price, 2001.

Each of the five work/family programs discussed in this section is likely to appeal to a different group of employees. Jurisdictions that provide a smorgasbord of offerings will be most responsive to a diverse workforce. Some policies have broad appeal; others are important to a narrower clientele. Potential gains in loyalty and productivity may warrant investments in these areas. Health and wellness programs, covered in the next section, promise similar returns on human capital investments.

Family Friendly or Single Hostile?

There are some single employees who harbor resentment against policies designed for their married coworkers. They may feel shortchanged or overburdened when employers expect them to "take up the slack" for their absent coworkers who are given "special help" in dealing with spousal or child-related problems. An example of this sentiment appeared in a published letter to Randy Cohen, author of the popular "The Ethicist" column in the *New York Times Magazine,* with the writer questioning whether his employer's paid "family days" discriminated against single people (Cohen, 2002). If single or childless workers receive fewer benefits, subsidize benefits for which they are ineligible, and are expected to assume more responsibilities than others, friction will likely result. In seeking to achieve work and life balance, it is important for employers to design "lifestyle-friendly" policies that are inclusive, are flexible, and offer choices to workers (Gannon, 1998; Kirkpatrick, 1997; Lynem, 2001).

■■ HEALTH, SAFETY, AND WELLNESS PROGRAMS

As society has become more health conscious, employees have taken greater interest in the health-promoting activities of their employers. Typical personal concerns are accessibility of wellness programs, the range of activities offered, cost-sharing arrangements, convenience, and privacy. Employers are inclined to focus on issues of program demand and productivity returns on whatever funds are invested. Four relevant initiatives are stress reduction, wellness programs, safety initiatives, and employee assistance programs.

Stress Reduction

The causes and consequences of stress at work have been widely discussed, and the human resource management implications are important. Too much stress impedes individual and organizational performance, but too little stress also can be counterproductive. The challenge to managers is to create optimal levels of stress and promote employee well-being while avoiding chronic mental or physical problems that reduce performance. Such "negative stress" is often characterized by high levels of absenteeism and turnover. Because it has been estimated that more than 10 million people in the nation's workforce experience stress-related problems, it is not surprising that some organizations have responded with stress reduction programs.

The prevention, detection, and management of negative stress are beneficial for both employees and employers. Below are ways of reducing stress, linked to human resource management functions:

- Using effective screening devices in recruitment to ensure a good person-environment fit
- Avoiding individual-organization "misfits" in selection by matching the right person with the right job
- Orienting employees in ways to reduce the gap between job expectations and reality
- Providing assessment, observation, feedback, counseling, and coaching in career planning and development
- Offering worker support systems that foster attachments among employees
- Furnishing crisis intervention counseling (including emotional support and problem-solving strategies) to employees who experience difficult moments

- Tracking organizational indicators of stress to identify problem areas
- Training employees with behavioral self-control skills to increase relaxation on the job
- Equipping staff with cognitive problem-solving skills to improve problem solving
- Offering workshops and short courses on time management to reduce stress

Stress reduction programs incorporating some or most of these strategies are found in a majority of local governments (64%) and private sector settings (52%) (Mercer, 1996; West & Berman, 1996). Exhibit 8.7 suggests further stress reduction strategies for managers and employees.

Wellness Programs

The goals of wellness programs are to alter unhealthy personal habits and lifestyles and to promote behaviors conducive to health and well-being. Employers offer such services as health assessment (first aid and emergency), risk appraisals, screenings (blood pressure checks, blood sugar and cholesterol tests), injections (allergy, immunizations), and health and nutrition education or counseling. They may provide exercise equipment and facilities or negotiate health club discounts and reimburse employees for participation. Health promotion activities often focus on physical fitness, weight control, smoking cessation, and health awareness. These activities can be emphasized at brown-bag lunches or wellness fairs. Psychological and physiological benefits and resulting reductions in insurance premiums have been reported for participating employees. Improved morale, organizational commitment, sense of belonging, recruitment or retention, and productivity are potential benefits to organizations that emphasize wellness. Overall, studies have shown that wellness programs are usually successful investments, reducing healthcare costs and providing returns to the employer (Goetzel & Ozminkowski, 2006).

Program availability is greater in state government (92% of states) than in either local governments (65%) or the private sector (46%; Council of State Governments [CSG], 1997; Mercer, 1996; West & Berman, 1996). Nevertheless, benefit eligibility figures for full-time employers are lower than these figures suggest (see Exhibit 8.1). The city of Loveland, Colorado, has an innovative wellness program called Healthsteps. It offers bonus points to those with positive medical history and healthy lifestyle choices. Based on the number of bonus points employees earn, they are eligible for distributions of up to 50% of any annual health plan savings. Attending the annual health fair and undergoing tests there can earn lifestyle points. Lifestyle points also can be earned if employees' test results meet targets for blood pressure, weight, and cholesterol, or if they participate in various fitness activities (walking, jogging, running). Medical points can be awarded for all premium dollars paid for employees and their families (with points subtracted based on the dollar value of claims paid). They are never penalized for heavy use of medical care because point totals do not fall below zero. Some other cities have similar creative, incentive-based initiatives.

Stress reduction and wellness plans promote healthy lifestyles and reduce the likelihood of serious illnesses. Such preventive activities may be buttressed by employee assistance programs designed to address health-related problems when they appear.

Exhibit 8.7	Tips for Managers and Employees on Ways to Reduce Work-Related Stress

What can managers do?

- Follow a consistent management style.
- Avoid actions that erode the competence or confidence of employees.
- Treat all employees fairly.
- Give positive feedback whenever appropriate.
- Support flexible work schedules and job sharing.
- Clarify objectives and communicate them to employees.
- Establish performance targets that are challenging but realistic.
- Make sure tasks are well defined and responsibilities are clear.
- Introduce some variety if jobs are extremely monotonous or boring.
- Establish good two-way communication.
- Increase decision latitude.
- Avoid work overload or underload.
- Decrease role conflict and ambiguity.
- Promote career development and career security.
- Develop job content that avoids narrow, fragmented tasks with little extrinsic meaning.
- Promote participation and control.
- Avoid under- and overpromotion.

What can employees do at work?

- Schedule time realistically.
- Avoid unrealistic expectations for yourself.
- Do one thing at a time.
- Do not depend on your memory to keep track of all tasks.
- Ignore situations you cannot control.
- Get away from your desk at lunchtime.
- Identify sources of stress.
- Mentally rehearse stressful situations.
- Allow extra time when you travel.
- Review your priorities and lifestyle.

What can employees do at home?

- Exercise regularly.
- Explore ways to reduce caregiving and work conflicts.
- Take advantage of community support networks.
- Build fun into your schedule.
- Express your feelings openly.
- Be prepared to wait.
- Begin to rid your life of clutter.
- Spend time each day in relaxing activity.
- Set aside time to eat leisurely, well-balanced meals.

Safety Initiatives

Employees are protected from an unsafe workplace by federal and state laws. Provisions of the Occupational Safety and Health Act provide staff with several rights if they are concerned about unsafe conditions or practices in the workplace (see Exhibit 8.8). State laws typically conform closely to the federal legislation.

Exhibit 8.8	Worker Rights to a Safe Workplace Under the Occupational Safety and Health Act

Workers have the right to the following:

- Receive training from employers on the health and safety standards that the law mandates
- Receive training from employers on any dangerous chemicals workers are exposed to and on ways employees can protect themselves from harm
- Receive training from employers on any other health and safety hazards (e.g., construction hazards, blood-borne pathogens) in the workplace
- Receive information from employers regarding OSHA standards, worker injuries and illnesses, job hazards, and workers' rights
- Make direct requests to employers to cure any hazards or OSHA violations
- File complaints with OSHA
- Make a request that OSHA inspect the workplace
- Find out the results of an OSHA inspection
- File a complaint with OSHA if the employer retaliates for asserting employee rights under the act
- Request the federal government to research possible workplace hazards

Source: NOLO, 2003b.

Employee Assistance Programs

Organizations with employee assistance programs (EAPs) use them to improve employee health and help employees cope with personal problems such as the difficulties resulting from work/family conflict. Such plans usually offer counseling or referral services for people having problems with alcohol, drug abuse, personal debt, domestic abuse, or other problems that impede job-related performance. The objective of EAPs is to improve employees' competence, performance, and well-being. Eligibility for EAP in state and local governments is reported in Exhibit 8.1.

The profile of a comprehensive program includes the following:

- Counseling and referral for employees and their families
- Staff with solid clinical background and knowledge of providers for referral
- Broad health coverage (including mental health) in the benefit package
- Staff familiarity with the health package to ensure that provider services are covered
- Confidential services

- A training component for employees, supervisors, and managers
- Reference checks on all service providers

Many local governments like Ventura County, California; Chesterfield, Missouri; and Middletown, Rhode Island, have EAP programs reflecting several of these "ideal" characteristics. One legal caution: employees and managers need to be aware that information gathered during EAP sessions may belong to the employer, not the employee. Furthermore, decision makers designing EAP programs need to weigh ethical principles and economic imperatives (Exhibit 8.9).

Institutional sponsorship of health and wellness programs signals to individuals that the organization is concerned about their well-being. Another way that agencies can communicate that concern as well as address workforce diversity is by offering more flexible work arrangements, the subject of the next section.

Exhibit 8.9   EAP Programs: Ethical Principles and Economic Imperatives

In weighing ethical principles and economic imperatives, choices can be viewed in terms of their ethical right and wrong and their economic good and bad. Right-good decisions are ethically correct and economically efficient, wrong-bad decisions are ethically incorrect and economically inefficient, right-bad decisions are ethically correct but economically inefficient, and wrong-good decisions are ethically deficient but economically efficient. This fourfold framework can be applied to EAP programs.

Right-good EAP policies provide comprehensive services in recognition of the ethical and economic gains from such an approach. A right-bad strategy (at least without a healthy investment of funds) would not be sustainable, a situation evident in some government jurisdictions. A wrong-good strategy would fail to meet legitimate employee (and arguably organizational) needs given the priority of saving money, a condition characterizing some small firms. A wrong-bad plan would be a lose-lose strategy that is ineffective ethically, yet economically costly.

From a utilitarian perspective, EAP programs would be morally justified if the benefits most clients experience (reduced health expenditures, workers' compensation and disability costs, and reduced risks of workplace violence, sexual harassment, and other behavioral problems) outweigh the costs. Overall, EAPs can promote both utilitarian and altruistic objectives, but ethical dilemmas and fiscal concerns, especially in an era of widespread outsourcing, require adroit juggling to assure individual well-being and organizational productivity.

Source: Adapted from West & Bowman, 2008.

▪▪ FLEXIBLE WORK ARRANGEMENTS

Flexible policies go a long way in reducing work/family conflict. Worker surveys indicate that the overwhelming majority of workers support practices like flextime, **job sharing**, and telecommuting (Goodman, 2003). Employees are interested in the range of options available to them at work that might minimize problems at home: Will they have any control over the hours and location of work? Are there options to leaving home at 8 and returning at 6, Monday through Friday, year-round? Can they work at home? Can they choose their benefits? Can alternatives to full-time work be negotiated? Are job- or leave-sharing arrangements permissible? These are important issues in management. Employers are interested in getting the work done. They have to weigh the pros and cons of flexible arrangements before making such options available to large numbers of employees. This section briefly considers seven alternative work arrangements:

(1) flex options,

(2) telecommuting,

(3) part-time work,

(4) voluntary reduced work time,

(5) temporary work,

(6) leave sharing and pooling, and

(7) job sharing.

Flex Options

Flextime refers to work schedules that allow differential starting and quitting times but specify a required number of hours within a particular period. According to the Bureau of Labor Statistics (2005), about 27 million full-time wage and salary workers (27.5%) had flexible schedules in 2004, down from 29 million in 2001. Only about one in 10 workers is actually enrolled in a formal, employer-sponsored flextime program. In the private sector, flexible schedules are most prevalent in financial activities (37.7%), professional and business services (37.6%), and information (34.9%). In the public sector, flexible schedules are more prevalent at the federal (28.8%) and state level (28.4%) than at the local level of government (13.7%). Formal flextime programs are more prevalent in the public sector than in private industry: more than half the workers in the public service with flexible schedules have a formal program. Nearly three-fourths of federal employees with flextime participated in a formal program, whereas only about one-third of private sector workers with flextime participated in such a program.

Another flex option is the **compressed workweek**, in which the number of hours worked per week is condensed into fewer days. For example, employees work a set 160-hour schedule per month but do it in fewer than 20 workdays by working more than eight hours a day and fewer than five days a week. According to OPM (2003), 357,326 federal personnel use compressed schedules. Compressed workweeks enable employers to extend hours of operation and enable employees to reduce commuting costs and gain leisure time. They may introduce, however, problems of employer supervision and employee fatigue. These two flex options are discussed in Chapter 6 (see Exhibit 7.2), so treatment here is limited. In 2008, Utah became the first state to institute a mandatory four-day workweek for most state employees (Copeland, 2008). Research by Facer and Wadsworth (2008) on the impact of a compressed workweek in a small, growing Utah city found that employees working the four-day, 10-hour (4/10) schedule reported higher levels of job satisfaction, higher perceived productivity, and lower levels of work-family conflict than their non-4/10 coworkers. Other cities (e.g., North Miami and Tamarac, Florida) also have instituted a four-day workweek. Organizations are more likely to offer flextime than compressed workweek options. Overall, it is estimated that 50% of employees are eligible for flextime (Galinsky, Bond, & Hill, 2004; Stockwell, 2006).

Ninety-two percent of federal agencies implement flexible work schedules, and one-third of the federal workforce participates in compressed and flexible work schedules. Only 14% of states (California, Illinois, Maine, Massachusetts, Minnesota, Missouri, and Tennessee), 79% of federal agencies, and 60% of firms offer compressed workweek options. Eight in 10 employees in the U.S. Department of Labor work flexible schedules (Daniel, 1999). In California, air quality regulations provided the impetus for many governments to try alternative schedules as a way to decrease pollution and traffic congestion. A bare majority of cities (52%) nationwide offer flextime to some employees. It may take various forms:

- Core hours (required presence at work)
- Band of flexible hours (typically at the end or beginning of the day)
- Variable lunch hours
- Sliding schedule (variation in the start or stop times daily, weekly, or monthly)
- Bank time (variable length of workday; hours from long days can be banked for short days later on)

The number of employees with the core hours option increased from 29% in 1992 to 43% in 2002.

Clearly, the greatest flexibility is present when a combination of options is available. Implementation problems can result when employees are expected to work as a team, when unions or supervisors resist the move to flextime, and when laws (e.g., maximum hours and overtime requirements) introduce complications. Care needs to be taken to ensure that there is adequate staffing during noncore hours. Compressed schedules may be less successful in smaller governments where staff coverage for leave-taking employees may be inadequate. Telecommuting is another type of flexible benefit.

Telecommuting

Telecommuters are people who work away from the traditional work locale (e.g., at home, at satellite locations, or on the road). It is estimated that 26 million employees in America telecommute (work from home at least one day a week), and their numbers are increasing (Goodman, 2008). An OPM survey (2005) found that more than 140,000 federal employees in 82 agencies were teleworking: 41.4% of the workforce was eligible and 18.7% of eligible employees teleworked. Legislation (P.L. 106–346) requires each executive agency to establish a policy under which eligible employees may participate in telecommuting to the maximum extent possible without impeding employee performance. Four cabinet-level departments reported in 2004 that over 80% of workers were eligible to telecommute, but the percentage of eligible workers actually telecommuting was lower: Labor 50.1%, Treasury 29.2%, Health and Human Services 19.0%, and Energy 10.0% (OPM, 2005). Some members of Congress have considered sponsoring legislation to financially penalize agencies that are not moving aggressively to implement meaningful telecommuting programs, but the Bush administration believes such action is unnecessary at this time (Barr, 2004).

According to an ICMA (1995) survey, approximately 128 cities reported telecommuting arrangements for their employees. Palo Alto, California, has approximately 25 employees telecommuting in a variety of positions. Lombard, Illinois, restricts telecommuting to exempt employees with a personal injury or illness or a workers' compensation injury. Experience with telecommuting in the city of Richmond, Washington, suggests that the tasks most suitable for work at home include writing, reading, telephoning, data analysis or entry, computer programming, and word processing.

A majority of states allow some of their employees to telecommute (Kemp, 1995). Although 37% of private companies offer the same option (World at Work, 2007), only 2% of employees use it (International Public Management Association for Human Resource HR Center, 2007). Kemp's 50-state survey indicates that most states have no formal telecommuting program, but informal arrangements often exist in selected agencies. Nineteen states have telecommuting mentioned on their Web sites. In Arizona, every agency is mandated to implement the state's program with the goal of having 20% of state employees in Maricopa County actively participating in the program. As of 2008, 4,328 employees (more than 20%) were teleworking (Telework Arizona, 2008). Advantages of telecommuting programs include increased productivity, flexibility, economy, and satisfaction. Disadvantages or impediments include loss of management control, inadequate technology, absence of policy guidance, stakeholder resistance, concerns about customer complaints, office coverage, problems scheduling meetings, and insufficient funds. (See Appendix 8A at the end of this chapter.) Subsequent sections of this chapter discuss implementation of telecommuting in detail.

Part-Time Work

Some employees might prefer working a specific number of hours fewer than the traditional 40-hour workweek on a recurring basis. Part-time employment is defined by the federal government as involving fewer than 35 hours per week. The part-time employment rate in the United States is 13%; in Japan it is 25% (Organisation for Economic Co-operation and Development [OECD], 2008). By law (5 U.S.C. 3402), nearly every federal agency is required to have a program for part-time employment. According to OPM (2003), 92% of federal agencies implement part-time work, yet Bureau of Labor Statistics (2008) show that only 5% of workers pursue this option.

In Florida, one-fifth of the state government workforce consists of part-time employees. This might be an attractive option for new parents who want to convert to part-time work temporarily as a transition between family leave and a 40-hour workweek, but these workers receive no benefits despite the fact that many of them work nearly full-time hours.

Voluntary Reduced Work Time

Selected full-time employees want to reduce their work hours and their pay, and some employers prefer this option as a way to reduce labor costs. Such reductions often range from a few hours a week up to 20 hours. Typically, health benefits are prorated. Voluntary reduced time (**V-time**) enables parents to meet caregiving responsibilities, provides an alternative to layoffs or use of part-time replacements, and helps phase workers into retirement. These arrangements are often negotiated.

Temporary Work

The rise of the contingent workforce is tied to employers' need for flexibility and to employees' desires for variable work schedules and employment. For individuals, temporary employment enables them to meet family responsibilities, complete education or training, master new skills, or compete for full-time positions. For organizations, temporary staffing provides a source of specific skills for only the time they are needed, allows for development of a core workforce while supplementing it as budgets fluctuate, and controls labor costs by moving labor from a fixed to a variable expense. The number of temporary workers employed nationwide on an average day in the first quarter of 2002 was 2.1 million (Staffing Stabilized, 2003).

The hiring of "temps" has been a common accompaniment of downsizing in business, and it is becoming more evident in government as belt tightening occurs. For example, the state of Texas has put a legal employment cap on full-time positions to restrain personnel costs. The cap does not cover temporary employees or outside workers. In 1997, Texas had more than 20,000 consultants, contractors, and temps working in state government, a 300% increase from just a decade earlier. This "**hidden workforce**" cost $41 million; of that amount, $24 million was spent on temporary workers (Gamino, 1997). The movement from full-time permanent workers to the "contingent" workforce is likely to continue in both the public and private sectors, and it may raise issues about performance quality, legality, and work alienation. Gains in flexibility should be weighed carefully against potential losses in effectiveness before proceeding with new workplace initiatives.

Leave Sharing and Pooling

Leave sharing and pooling are types of employee-to-employee job benefits whereby healthy workers donate sick time or other benefits to coworkers in crisis. Unlike some employee-friendly policies common in the private sector, leave sharing and pooling are found more often in government. For example, although only 8% of companies nationwide offer such sharing benefits, the federal government, two-thirds of state governments, and many municipal jurisdictions and public school districts allow leave sharing and pooling (Camp, 2006; CSG, 1997; OPM, 2007a; Suttle, 1998). Despite its availability, only 1% of federal employees use it (Daniel, 1999).

Washington State allows employees to pool and share leave days. More than five dozen different agencies, employing 99% of state workers, offer leave sharing programs. More than 800 employees used time donated to them by their coworkers in 1997. The cost of shared leave in that year was about $3 million. Eligibility to use shared leave is contingent on health status: a serious or life-threatening illness is necessary to qualify. The Tacoma School District, for example, further requires that a worker cannot donate more than six days in a 12-month period and cannot reduce his own sick leave account below 60 days. For the donor of sick leave, such programs are a way to give support and express concern for coworkers. For the recipient, it is a way to fill in the gaps not covered by insurance, cope with medical emergencies, and reduce financial hardship (Suttle, 1998). Overall, when organizations offer leave sharing, as when they offer V-time, it is an example of addressing the paradox of needs.

Job Sharing

Job sharing enables two employees to split the responsibilities, hours, salary, and (usually) benefits of a full-time position. A 1997 status report to the president on the federal workplace family-friendly initiatives found that 63% of federal agencies offer job sharing. In 1999, a study conducted by the Human Resources Division (1999) of the Massachusetts government found that 29 states have job-sharing programs. Human Resources Division determined in a survey of 88 state agencies that 344 out of 3,000 total part-time positions were job shares. Earlier studies report favorable experiences in some states (Massachusetts and Michigan), others found limited use (Colorado, Minnesota, and Tennessee), and still others do not allow job sharing (Lord & King, 1991). Colorado's Web site says that it has had job sharing since 1977. Successes are partially attributable to careful planning, supervisory training, and highly motivated workers; problematic results are linked to supervisory resistance and state-imposed restrictions on participation. Examples of positions where job sharing is used include nursing, social work, law, and mental health. Job sharing offers employees the advantages of balancing home/work responsibilities, earning professional wages, and maintaining a career, while cutting back on hours (Lord & King, 1991).

Job sharing is less frequently reported as a benefit in local government (11%), although nonreporting governments may be willing to approve such arrangements in response to specific proposals. The city of Redmond, Washington, uses it to jointly fill secretarial, street maintenance, financial analyst, and recreation coordinator positions. Agencies see potential advantages in job sharing, especially when facing severe financial constraints, possible layoffs, or needs of working mothers. Employers may also see it as a way to reduce absenteeism and turnover and to heighten productivity. However, benefit levels, promotion implications, and seniority issues remain problematic under this arrangement.

To summarize, two factors regarding the employee-friendly and flexible policies discussed so far—employers' attitudes and "the power of peers"—are important determinants of work/family conflict and of whether employees use benefits. The importance of employer attitudes is apparent from research that shows that work/family conflict is greater for employees whose supervisors put work first, regardless of the worker-friendly or flexible benefits provided. The "power of peers" is stressed by research showing that employees more frequently use alternative work schedules when those in their work groups are already using them (Clay, 1998). Contrary to critics' claims that encouraging individuals to use employee-friendly policies will erode employee commitment and loyalty, research by the Families and Work Institute, drawing on a national sample of 2,877 employees, found that support from employers, as demonstrated by flexibility and family-friendly policies, was the most important factor in job satisfaction (Clay, 1998). Clearly, the employment context is crucial.

In addition to employers' attitudes and peer pressures, it is important to consider costs. Although costs may be offset by employee gains in flexibility and support, they can be substantial. This leads to two key problems. First, unlike the private sector, public organizations cannot pass the costs through to the marketplace. Second, managers are, with some exceptions, usually not in a position to authorize these programs; appropriate governing bodies must approve them. That usually means that they become part of negotiations of overall compensation, fringe benefits, and work rules. The complexity of adopting, financing, and implementing such programs requires careful consideration. Furthermore, initiatives can become politically volatile (e.g., domestic partner benefits), suggesting the need to consider intangible in addition to tangible costs.

The preceding sections have highlighted different strategies managers can use to minimize family/work conflict and promote employee well-being. Experimentation to discover the appropriate mix of such plans is necessary as employers search for the best "fit" between employee needs and organizational requirements (see Exhibit 8.10). OPM opened a Family-Friendly Workplace Advocacy Office in 1999 to encourage these programs. Resource scarcity might limit the range of options available for some jurisdictions and agencies, but workforce diversity will provide a counterweight pushing for reform. Jurisdictions will be more likely to respond if the proposed changes meet pressing needs and if payoffs are evident. These issues are considered in the next section.

Exhibit 8.10   Local Government Examples of Employee-Friendly Policies

DuPage County, Illinois: Flexible Scheduling. No formal policy of flexible scheduling is in place; each decision to change a schedule is decided by the department head on a case-by-case basis. In some instances, however, a schedule change may affect an entire department. For the computer operations division, employees work three 12.5-hour days. Because it was often difficult to get weekend coverage, the county's convalescence center implemented a similar schedule for nurse's aides. Any employee can adjust his or her schedule with the approval of the department head (the schedule change must not negatively affect service delivery).

Dane County, Wisconsin: Telecommuting. About a dozen employees are allowed to telecommute a few days a week. Telecommuting is not a systemwide policy; it tends to be limited to management staff whose positions do not involve a great deal of public interaction. Telecommuting is also allowed under special circumstances. For instance, one critically ill department head's chemotherapy treatments make her susceptible to illness. To limit her exposure to germs, she is allowed to work at home.

Most employees supply their own equipment (computers, modems) for their home offices, but in the case of an information systems staff person, the county supplies a special computer that allows him to service the county's 911 system. A portable computer is also available to staff members who do not have their own computer equipment. Supervision of these employees generally is not an issue because most are professional or managerial employees and their performance is judged on the end result of their work.

Birmingham, Alabama: Job Sharing and Subsidized Child Care. There is limited job sharing that tends to be used primarily by library employees because library hours are different from and longer than other city departments' hours. To qualify for benefits, job-sharing employees must work at least three-quarters time; otherwise, they are not eligible for health insurance, sick leave, or vacation. They earn holiday leave based on the percentage of time they work (if they work 75% of the time, they earn 75% of the holiday pay). They can purchase medical insurance, but the locality does not contribute to the payment of premiums.

The city also subsidizes childcare costs for employees with sick children. It is not unusual for an employee to miss a day or several days of work caring for a sick child. Rather than lose an employee, the city encourages employees to take the child to a daycare center that has trained medical staff on hand. The city then reimburses the employee for all childcare costs incurred. Program costs are estimated at about $10,000 annually, but the city gains in productivity.

Kalamazoo, Michigan: Incentive Program. The city offers employees an opportunity to earn extra cash. If a city employee has a spouse who works for another organization and the city employee can be covered under his or her spouse's health insurance policy, the city will offer the employee a yearly $1,500 bonus for dropping city coverage. This provides the employee with extra cash and reduces the city's health insurance expenditures.

Source: Adapted from *International City/County Management Association, Employee Benefits in Local Government* (special data issue), pp. 5, 7. Adapted/Reprinted with permission of the International City/County Management Association, 777 North Capitol Street, NE Suite 500, Washington, DC 20002. All rights reserved.

▪▪ IMPLEMENTATION, ASSESSMENT, AND EVALUATION

Organizations seeking to help workers become more effective, and employees seeking supportive workplace relations have a convergence of goals. The trick is to design a program that meets the objectives of both employers and employees while avoiding the paradoxes described previously. Before embarking on flexible work options or deciding on the mix of employee-responsive policies to pursue, agencies should conduct a needs assessment. Appendix 8B at the end of this chapter lists some of the questions employers should consider as they assess the needs of their agency. At a minimum, data should be gathered on workforce demographics, the range and utilization of existing programs, employee-identified problem areas, satisfaction levels and program preferences, and so forth (data sources include employee personnel records, surveys, interviews, and focus groups). Exhibit 8.11 is a tool for helping to select appropriate programs to meet specific needs. Once the needs, resources, values, and issues have been clarified, the benefits and risks of acting or not acting need to be assessed. Exhibit 8.12 provides an aid for making assessments. Professionals in the human resource office are the most likely candidates to collect, analyze, and interpret relevant data and to present recommendations to officials.

The activities and stages involved in implementing employee-responsive policies (Collins & Magid, 1990; Hall, 1990; Mikalachki & Mikalachki, 1991; Stanger, 1993) can be grouped as follows:

- Set policies and values for the program: task force or advisory committee, values clarification, issue framing, needs and resource assessment, policy formulation and adoption, program management
- Identify options or models: personnel policies, benefit plans, work restructuring, information and referral, parent education and counseling, direct service, career paths, dependent care
- Articulate program objectives: goals, expectations, eligibility, benefits, participation levels, advantages, external factors, planning estimates
- Plan for implementation: involvement of key stakeholders, pilot or phased projects, breadth and depth of change, modified work environments, costs, timetables, communication system, building support, overcoming resistance, training
- Specify outcomes and benefits: benefit or cost projections, impact on key indicators, negative side effects
- Measurement and evaluation: data sources, tracking outcomes, employee surveys, focus groups, cost accounting, program evaluation, data analysis and use

Research by McCurdy, Newman, and Lovrich (2002) on worker-friendly policies in Washington State's local governments notes the paucity of measurement and evaluation efforts. Roberts's (2001) findings from local governments in New Jersey reiterate this concern regarding the need for better documentation. Becerra, Gooden, Dong, Henderson, and Whitfield (2002, p. 315) also stressed the need to assess the "intergroup variations in the worklife needs of their employees."

Exhibit 8.11   Selecting Work/Life Programs Based on Agency Needs

Results	Alternative Work Schedules	Wellness Programs	Telecommuting	Caregiver Programs
Improve productivity	Can double productivity	Significantly improved	Particularly for work requiring intensive blocks of time	Reduce stress that interferes with productivity
Improve recruitment	Most sought-after work/life program	Not applicable	Particularly for information technology jobs	For those needing elder/child care
Reduce attrition	Can cut attrition in half	Fewer employee terminations	Positive impact on retention	For those needing elder/child care
Reduce absenteeism	Can cut absenteeism in half	Significant reductions	Can cut absenteeism in half	Lower rates of unexpected absenteeism
Reduce facility costs	Not applicable	Not applicable	Can cut costs 30–50%	Not applicable
Reduce costs for overtime, recruitment, workers' compensation, travel, relocation	Reduces costs for overtime, recruitment, workers' compensation, travel	Not applicable	Reduces costs for travel, recruitment, relocation	Reduces recruitment costs to replace those with elder/child care needs
Improve customer service	Expands office hours	Not applicable	Permits use of cost-saving technology	Not applicable

Source: Adapted from National Academy of Public Administration, *Work/Life Programs: Helping Managers, Helping Employees,* p. 4. Copyright 1998 by the National Academy of Public Administration. Evidence for generalizations made in cell entries is summarized in this NAPA publication.

Exhibit 8.12	Factors to Consider in Deciding to Act or Not to Act

Benefits	Risks
Acting	
• Improved employee morale • Improved productivity • Reduced absenteeism • Reduced attrition • Improved recruitment • Reduced costs • Improved customer service	• Startup costs • Ongoing costs • Possible negative effect on quality or quantity of work • Potential for unfavorable media or legislative attention • Employee perception of programs as entitlements, creating problems if circumstances later change • Poor program management, leading to reduced productivity
Not Acting	
• Saving funds for other initiatives • Saving staff time needed to set up the program • Keeping options open when the future is uncertain	• Negative effect on employee morale when programs are not available to meet their needs • Continuing decline in productivity resulting from low morale • Increase in attrition when employees leave for employers who offer the programs • Continuing high levels of absenteeism resulting from lack of programs that can help employees meet personal needs

Source: Adapted from National Academy of Public Administration, *Work/Life Programs: Helping Managers, Helping Employees,* p. 46. Copyright 1998 by the National Academy of Public Administration.

■■ AVOIDING AND COPING WITH HOSTILITY AT WORK

Another challenge facing managers is developing and implementing a program dealing with hostility in the workplace. In seeking to create a proemployee environment, it is necessary to remove threats to worker well-being. This includes reducing the likelihood of intimidation, harassment, threats, conflict, or violence. Chapter 2 discusses sexual harassment (in the context of legal requirements prohibiting it) and Chapter 9, Exhibit 9.1, examines workplace violence (especially its causes and some prevention strategies in the context of personnel appraisal). Here it is important to emphasize that managers and officials committed to employee-friendly policies need to consider ways to avoid or cope with hostility. Not to do so is to invite disruption, damage to the lives and health of workers, and loss of productivity. For example, in an average U.S. workweek, violent assaults by current or former coworkers at work result in one employee killed and 25 seriously injured (Armour, 2004). In one 10-day period in 2007, the nation experienced the Virginia Tech mass murders, killings in offices in Troy, Michigan, and killings at the National Aeronautical and Space Administration in Houston. Indeed, workplace violence is so pervasive, according to the U.S. Department of Justice, that the Centers for Disease Control classify it as a national epidemic.

What can be done to prevent these attacks from occurring? It is important to recognize those most at risk, the warning signs or red flags that deserve attention, the various types of workplace violence and rationale, and action steps necessary for appropriate action. First, those most at risk are employees who are in regular contact with the public and strangers coming into the workplace, those working with unstable or volatile persons (e.g., health care, law enforcement), and employees in mobile workplaces (buses, police cruisers). Also employees who may be at risk are those transporting people or goods to unfamiliar locales, working alone or in small groups, exchanging money, and guarding valuable property or possessions. Time of day (late at night or early morning) and place (high crime areas) can also affect the level of risk.

Second, some warning signs of possible workplace violence include poor workplace situations (stress, discrimination); the presence of individual, family, or social problems (finances, illness); aggressive behavior in the workplace (intimidation, bullying); discussion about or presence of a weapon or threat of its use in the workplace; and statements suggesting fascination with violent workplace incidents. Third, where workplace violence occurs, it can occur in various forms: for example, violence by strangers lacking any relationship between the worker and the violent person, by customers or clients (complaints turned violent, prisoner resisting arrest), and by coworkers (response to bullying, response to layoff; International Association of Chiefs of Police [IACP], 1995).

Finally, why and how might organizations best respond to workplace violence? The rationale for action is linked to several concerns, including the costly nature of violent incidents (potential liability suits, reduced productivity); zero tolerance for abusive, threatening, or violent workplace behavior; and anticipated changes in the workplace environment (layoffs, higher workloads). Justification may also be related to research findings indicating the negative impact of workplace violence on employees and employer's desire to ensure a safe workplace for employees, citizens, and visitors.

What form should action take? Here policies, plans, programs, and procedures are needed. Personnel policies stressing thorough preemployment screening and background checks might help to reduce the likelihood of hiring those who would commit violent acts at work. Cooperative relationships can be forged with law enforcement officials to help inform workers on ways to prevent and avoid workplace violence. Security procedures can be reviewed and updated and security devices (silent alarms, metal detectors) can be installed and maintained. Management threat plans can be developed offering guidance on how to respond to workplace threats, and postincident plans can be implemented in the aftermath of a violent event (debriefing, grief counseling; IACP, 2008). The Bureau of Labor Statistics (2005a) conducted a 2005 survey reporting the percentage of state and local government that had a workplace violence prevention program or policy. Results show that most jurisdictions had such a policy or program (58.3%), usually written (52.4%), sometime verbal (16.0%), but that 41.6% had no program or policy.

It is imperative that managers be alerted to these warning signs, violence types, rationales for action, and policy options if they are to better avoid and cope with hostility at work. There is a paradox in implementing both workplace violence and sexual harassment policies, however. Many organizations have policies on these subjects; there is widespread agreement about what constitutes harassing and threatening or violent behavior; and there are numerous instances of such behaviors at work—yet the number of reported violations is low (Duncan, Estabrooks, & Reimer, 2000; McPhaul & Lipscomb, 2004). Implementing the general guidelines and action steps above, with special attention to protecting those who report violators, will help resolve this paradox. Clear policies regarding threats, harassment, and disruptive and dangerous behavior—and specific procedures to follow in case of a critical incident—will reduce the risk of hostility and help to cope with it when it occurs (IACP, 2008). Preventing workplace violence, sexual harassment, and other forms of hostility is consistent with creating a proemployee environment.[4]

▪▪ BEST PLACES TO WORK

Recently, there has been an attempt to identify exemplary workplaces in the federal government. The OPM's 2007 Human Capital Survey collected data from more than 221,000 federal employees (Partnership for Public Service, 2007). Staff ranked agencies according to 10 categories. Two of these categories are work/life balance and family-friendly culture and benefits. Exhibit 8.13 reports these rankings. Among the top in both rankings are the National Regulatory Commission (rank 1, 3), Securities and Exchange Commission (2, 7), General Services Administration (2, 6), NASA (4, 2), and the Federal Deposit Insurance Corporation (5, 1).

▪▪ SUMMARY AND CONCLUSION

Management fads come and go. Are family- or employee-friendly policies just another passing and politically correct fad? This is not an easy question to answer. The subtitle of this chapter refers to proemployee policies as fashionable, flexible, and fickle. The reader may have the impression that most jurisdictions are responding to changes in the workforce with "fashionable" policies that will reduce work/family conflict, promote employee health and wellness, build flexibility into the workplace, and assist in employee relocation. This is not the case. Some public sector environments are more accurately described as family- or employee-unfriendly, in that they do not offer the type and range of programs discussed here to all or most employees. Instead, the experiences highlighted are those of progressive jurisdictions. Many of these experiments are informal, are restricted to a limited number of areas, involve a small number of employees, and may come and go as budgets rise and fall.

Evidence is mounting (although incomplete) that employee-friendly policies can lead to important positive outcomes that "ideally" would catch the attention of public employers—improvements in job satisfaction, absenteeism, productivity, morale, recruitment and retention, and loyalty. On the other hand, some studies show negligible to no effects from such policies because of underutilization or effects that do not benefit the intended groups (Bruce & Reed, 1994; Shuey, 1998). Paradoxes abound and should not be overlooked by employers tempted to undertake such policies or by employees who push for them. Key among the paradoxes is that, once adopted, programs might not be used. When funding for new programs is limited, as is often the situation, a persuasive case must be made to skeptical budget guardians that the returns on investments will be substantial.

Exhibit 8.13 Best Places to Work in the Federal Government in 2007

Agency	Work/Life Balance Ranking	Family-Friendly Culture and Benefits Ranking
Nuclear Regulatory Commission	1	3
Securities and Exchange Commission	2	7
General Services Administration	3	6
National Aeronautics and Space Administration	4	2
Federal Deposit Insurance Corporation	5	1
Department of the Treasury	6	16
Department of Energy	7	13
Department of the Air Force	8	22
Department of the Army	9	23
All Department of Defense	10	20
Environmental Protection Agency	11	4
National Archives and Records Administration	12	18
Department of Commerce	13	8
Department of Health and Human Services	14	12
Social Security Administration	15	15
Department of Education	16	10
Department of the Navy	17	24
Department of Justice	18	25
Department of Labor	19	17
Department of State	20	28
Department of Agriculture	21	9
Office of Personnel Management	22	5
Department of Veteran Affairs	23	26
Department of Housing and Urban Development	24	14
Department of the Interior	25	21
Department of Transportation	26	27
Equal Employment Opportunity Commission	27	11
Small Business Administration	28	19
Department of Homeland Security	29	29
Government Accountability Office	30	30

Source: Adapted from Partnership for Public Service, 2007.

Note: Rankings based on survey data collected by OPM.

It is important to keep in mind, however, that employee-friendly policies refer to a broad range of initiatives, and a holistic view is needed when assessing their value and effectiveness. Failure or underutilization of one should not diminish the value of others. Some plans may appeal to or be relevant to a relatively small segment of the workforce (telecommuting, domestic partner coverage, adoption assistance, leave sharing, job sharing, spousal employment assistance, outplacement services). Others have much broader appeal and relevance (child or elder care; parental leave; wellness, stress reduction, and EAP programs; flex options; cafeteria plans; and other than full-time work options). Some plans are provided in-house, but many (such as EAP services) are often purchased from private and third-sector providers. Furthermore, the use of selected programs (e.g., flextime) differs based on the size of the organization and its service demands. Large organizations that need not address widely varying walk-in service requests have more management flexibility than small organizations in this regard. They can handle leaves of absence better and accommodate flextime more easily than other jurisdictions.

Large, innovative, and resource-rich organizations are more able to provide both the broad and narrow ranges of worker-responsive programs. Unfortunately, this does not characterize most governmental jurisdictions in the United States, which are small or medium size, traditional, and strapped for funds. They may be able to offer a few but not a complete set of these programs. Nevertheless, personnel may want help in reducing work/family conflict and in meeting both individual and organizational obligations. Employers need to explore ways to help them do so.

KEY TERMS

Adoption assistance	Job sharing
Compressed workweek	Leave sharing
Domestic partnership coverage	New Millennials
Downshifting	Nontraditional families
Downsizing	Parental leave
Employee assistance programs (EAPs)	Sandwich generation
Family and Medical Leave Act	Telecommuters
Flextime	Three o'clock (3:00) syndrome
Generation X	V-time
Hidden workforce	Wellness programs

EXERCISES

Class Discussion

1. On an overhead projector or chalkboard, observe two columns: "Buzzwords of Government Success" and "Ideal Friendship and Family Life." Brainstorm words for each topic, one column at a time. Compare and discuss the words in each column. Discuss the reasons that none or only a few words are on both the left and right lists.

2. Form groups and let each group select one of the family-friendly policies discussed in this chapter. Discuss the following: (a) the advantages, (b) the disadvantages, (c) the outcome indicators

you would use to judge program success, (d) the obstacles that you expect to encounter in implementing this program, and (e) the types of employees most likely to benefit from the program. Present a group report on your results to the class.

3. Review examples of employee-friendly policies discussed in this chapter. Identify as many paradoxes related to those policies as you can, and be prepared to discuss ways to resolve them.

Team Activities

4. Separate into four or five different groups. Each group should select three to five of the worker-friendly programs covered in this chapter. Each group member should interview someone who is currently using one of these programs regarding its pros and cons from the user's perspective. Write up the individual interviews in no more than two typed pages and then compile them into an integrated group report for submission to the instructor.

5. Each team member should create a hypothetical employee profile by identifying that individual's personal characteristics on each of the following dimensions: age, gender, dependent children, marital status, sexual preference, distance from work, health status, emotional health, stress level, and job security. The student should then choose three employee-friendly policies that would be most helpful to the hypothetical employee and justify the choices. As a team, compile the personal profile analyses from the individual student papers and add a group analysis section making some generalizations about which policies appeal most to particular types of employees.

Individual Assignments

6. Choose any one of the employee-friendly policies mentioned in this chapter and outline the implementation steps that are most important at each of the six stages from the point of view of the individual public manager or supervisor. Develop your response in a four-page paper and submit it to your instructor.

7. Identify each of the paradoxes mentioned in this chapter and consider various ways to resolve each paradox. Can you identify additional paradoxes related to these topics?

8. Select one of the programs discussed in this chapter and search the World Wide Web to find additional information on this subject. Share the information you find with the class.

9. Review the questions for telecommuters in Appendix 8A and answer either a or b.

   a. Develop a written telecommuter agreement for a particular public organization to be signed by both the employer and the employee. Make sure the agreement adequately addresses each of the questions listed in Appendix 8A.
   b. Obtain a written telecommuter agreement used by a specific organization and write a brief paper showing the degree to which the agreement you have obtained responds to each of the questions in Appendix 8A. Attach a copy of the agreement to your paper.

APPENDIX A

Questions for Employees and Employers Regarding Telecommuting Arrangements

- Has a pilot program been conducted?
- What are the results of the pilot program?
- Who is eligible to telecommute?

- If telecommuting is not to their liking, can employees return to their office work location?
- If the program is terminated, can employees return to their office work location?
- If an employee's performance deteriorates, will he be asked to return to the office work location?
- Will salary, job responsibilities, or benefits be changed because of employee participation in the program?
- Will the total number of work hours change during the program?
- How will employees account for time worked?
- Can employees vary their hours to suit their preferences?
- How can employers be assured that employees are accessible during working hours?
- Will employees divide their time between days at the office location and at the off-site location?
- Will employees be expected to come in to the office as requested when the workload requires it?
- Will employers provide the equipment required for the job?
- Does the employer retain ownership of property provided to telecommuters?
- Who absorbs costs (installation, monthly service) of telephone lines installed for use during the program?
- Who is responsible for off-site-related expenses (e.g., air conditioning, renovation)?
- Who is responsible for travel expenses to and from work on days when employees come into the office?
- Who provides needed office supplies?
- Who absorbs costs of insurance to protect equipment from theft, damage, or misuse?
- How will confidential or proprietary materials be protected?
- Does the employer have the right to visit the off-site location to see if it meets health and safety standards?
- Will the employer provide assistance to ensure the adequacy or safety of the off-site work area?
- Will the employer be liable for injuries resulting directly from off-site work activities?
- Is telecommuting viewed as a substitute for dependent care?
- Will the employer provide income tax guidance to employees who maintain an off-site office area?

Source: Adapted from *Generic Telecommuter's Agreement* from Gil Gordon Associates, Telecommuting/Teleworking Site (www.gilgordon.com). © Copyright 1998 by Gil Gordon Associates.

Note: These are suggested items to include; the actual agreement must be tailored to the needs of each employer and its employees.

APPENDIX B

Some Questions to Answer When
Considering Implementation of Employee-Friendly Policies

- What is the percentage of females employed?
- What is the size of the organization?
- What is the age profile of the employees?
- To what extent are resources available to recruit and train employees?
- What are the education levels required of qualified employees?
- What are current dependent care arrangements, costs, and satisfaction levels?
- What special work/family problems are employees facing?
- How many employees have young children, and how many days have those employees missed work to care for an ill child?
- How many employees care for elderly dependents, and how many days have those employees missed work to provide elder care?

- What is the percentage of employees who currently engage in a variety of wellness-related activities?
- Which employees are more likely to prefer flextime?
- Which employees are more likely to prefer telecommuting?
- What is the percentage of employees who indicate that they experience high levels of work-related stress?
- What are the main sources of work-related stress?
- What is the percentage of employees who have adopted children?
- What is the percentage of employees who are unmarried with domestic partners?
- What is the percentage of employees who are dissatisfied with the current range of employee benefits?
- What is the percentage of employees who are being displaced as a result of downsizing?

APPENDIX C

Family-Friendly Policies

Class Exercise

Background:

The expansion of family-friendly policies has accompanied the redefinition of today's "family." "Family" now means something more than just a married man and woman and their biological off-spring. Today, family responsibilities could include caring for step or foster children, elderly parents, or a domestic partner.

Employees today are often juggling work and family responsibilities. Demands on their time can leave them feeling dissatisfied with the quality of both their work and personal lives.

Faced with the constant struggle to balance work responsibilities with personal commitments, more and more employees are looking for employers that will be supportive of their need for a healthy work/life balance. They are attracted to organizations that offer flexibility in an environment where they can have an interesting career.

Consider:

You are the human resource director of the county Parks and Recreation Department. The organization consists of the following:

- More than 5,000 employees
  - ○ Front line manual labor employees (e.g., landscapers)
  - ○ Transactional-level employees (e.g., credit and collections)
  - ○ Professional-level administration support (e.g., finance, marketing)
  - ○ Management and executive management

You are challenged to develop a business case to support the following premise:

- Organizations that promote family-friendly workplaces have an edge when it comes to recruitment and retention of skilled employees.
- Family-friendly policies are a way to support and recognize the changing needs of employees at different points in their lives and careers.
  - ○ They are good for business.
  - ○ They are good for employees.
  - ○ They are good for families.

Assignment:

- Complete the following outline for this business case proposal.

Family-Friendly Policy Proposal

Objective(s) or Purpose

- Include what you are trying to achieve and why.
- Strategic vision—what will this do for the organization?
- What are the specific objectives of your proposal?
- What are the high-level benefits?
  - ○ To the employee
  - ○ To the organization

Technology Assessment

- What technology improvements or alternatives need to be considered?

Change Analysis

- What implications to the business do you anticipate?
- What business re-engineering issues will arise?

Cost and Benefit Estimate (Nonfinancial)

- What benefits to the employee and employer will result?
- What intangible benefits may change, for better or worse?

Cost and Benefit Estimate (Financial)

- What current costs and cost structures will change?
- What new costs will be incurred?
- Can you estimate? ($10, $100, $1,000, $10,000, etc.)

Risk Assessment

- Identification of organization risks to
  - ○ do nothing
  - ○ move ahead
  - ○ phased approach
- Identification of high-level risk mitigation plans for each potential risk

Measures and Metrics

- Outline how you measure success
  - ○ What would you need?
  - ○ How would you position it?
- What counterarguments would you anticipate?

Example Family-Friendly Initiatives

Flexible Work Arrangements

- Telework—working from home or a remote office
- Flextime—changing the start and end times of the work day
- Job sharing—sharing a full-time position with another employee
- Compressed workweek—working full-time hours in fewer than five days
- Part-time—reducing the number of hours worked each day or week

Employee Assistance Programs

- Counseling support on a range of issues from financial to legal to personal

Childcare and Eldercare Services

- Options range from on-site childcare centers to emergency or back-up child care, to resource materials for new parents.

Health and Wellness Initiatives

- Programs range from health club facilities to smoking cessation initiatives to stress management workshops.

Leaves of Absence

- Regulatory leaves like parental leave and jury duty as well as additional options for time away from work such as educational leave, community service leave, and sabbaticals

NOTES

1. This chapter is titled "Employee-Friendly Policies" instead of "Family-Friendly Policies" because it addresses the needs of single persons as well as those in both traditional and nontraditional families (see Hoyman & Duer, 2004).

2. Although this chapter focuses primarily on the changing workforce in terms of gender, it is important to note that cultural diversity introduces a range of different issues in addition to those covered here. For example, gender stereotypes and familial relationships vary from culture to culture; these differences have important significance for the workforce. The existence of extended families may have changed dramatically over the past four decades for white middle-class families of European heritage, but the situation is quite different for other cultural groups and socioeconomic status categories.

3. Human capital refers to the knowledge, skills, and abilities characterizing a workforce. Investments in human capital (e.g., training, development) are expected to bring improvements in performance and thus to provide a competitive advantage to individual workers and employing organizations. In contrast, human resources traditionally have been viewed primarily as costs to be minimized rather than as assets worthy of investments. Investments have been made in other assets such as land, capital, and raw materials (see West, 2005).

4. Some examples of local governments with innovative workplace violence programs include Phoenix, Arizona; Ventura County, California; Broward County, Florida; Evanston, Illinois; and Cary, North Carolina (ICMA, 1994).

REFERENCES

AARP Public Policy Institute. (2007). *Valuing the invaluable: A new look at the economic value of family caregiving.* Washington, DC: Author.

Adoption.com. (n.d.). *Adoption costs.* http://costs.adoption.com

Adoptive Families. (2008). *Making it work: Top adoption-friendly companies.* http://adoptivefamilies.com/articles.php?aid=832

American Association of University Women (AAUW). (2007). *Family friendly workplaces: Expand family and medical leave and paid sick leave.* Washington, DC: Author.

Armour, S. (2004, July 19). Managers not prepared for workplace violence. *USA Today.* Retrieved February 6, 2008, from http://www.usatoday.com/money/workplace/2004-07-15-workplace-violence2_x.htm

Barr, S. (2004, July 9). Congressmen plan to rev up telecommuting. *Washington Post,* p. B2.

Becerra, R., Gooden, S., Dong, W., Henderson, T., & Whitfield, C. (2002). Child care needs and work-life implications. *Review of Public Personnel Administration, 22*(4), 295–319.

Bond, J. T., Galinsky, E., Kim, S. S., & Brownfield, E. (2005). *National study of employers.* New York: Families and Work Institute.

Bruce, W., & Reed, C. (1994). Preparing supervisors for the future workforce: The dual-income couple and the work-family dichotomy. *Public Administration Review, 54*(1), 36–43.

Bureau of Labor Statistics, U.S. Department of Labor. (2002). *Workforce and workplace trends.* Retrieved January 10, 2005, from http://www.bls.gov/bls/newsrels.htm

Bureau of Labor Statistics, U.S. Department of Labor. (2005a). *Survey of workplace violence prevention.* Retrieved July 1, 2008, from www.bls.gov/iff/osh_wpvs.htm

Bureau of Labor Statistics, U.S. Department of Labor. (2005b). *Workers on flexible and shift schedules in May 2004.* Retrieved June 5, 2008, from http://www.bls.gov/news.release/pdf/flex.pdf

Bureau of Labor Statistics, U.S. Department of Labor. (2007). *National compensation survey: Employee benefits in state and local governments in the United States, September 2007.* Retrieved June 5, 2008, from http://www.bls.gov/ncs/ebs/sp/ebsm0007.pdf

Bureau of Labor Statistics, U.S. Department of Labor. (2008). *Employed persons by class of worker and part-time status.* Retrieved June 5, 2008, from http://www.bls.gov/news.release/empsit.t05.htm

California Employee Development Department. (2008). *Paid family leave.* Retrieved July 7, 2008, from http://www.edd.ca.gov/Disability/Paid_Family_Leave.htm

Camp, S. (2006). The influence of organizational incentives on absenteeism. *Criminal Justice Policy Review, 17*(2), 144–172.

Cayer, N. J., & Roach, C.M.L. (2008). Work-life benefits. In C. Reddick & J. Coggburn (Eds.), *Handbook of employee benefits and administration* (pp. 309–334). Boca Raton, FL: CRC Press.

Clay, R. (1998, July). Many managers frown on use of flexible work options. *APA Monitor,* p. 29.

Coalition of Child Care Advocates of BC. (2007, November 16). *Good governance of child care: What does it mean? What does it look like?* Retrieved July 2, 2008, from http://www.cccabc.bc.ca/cccabcdocs/governance/ggcc_denmark_model.pdf

Cohen, R. (2002, September 8). The ethicist. *New York Times Magazine,* pp. 29–30.

Collins, R., & Magid, R. (1990). Work and family: How managers can make a difference. *Personnel, 67*(7), 14–19.

Copeland, L. (2008, June 30). Most state workers in Utah shifting to 4-day week. *USA Today.* Retrieved August 30, 2008, from www.usatoday.com/news/nation/2008-06-30-four-day_N.htm

Council of State Governments (CSG). (1997). *The book of the states.* Lexington, KY: Author.

Daniel, L. (1999, April). Feds and families. *Government Executive,* pp. 41–46.

Department for Business Enterprise and Regulatory Reform of U.K. (2008). *Flexible working and work-life balance.* Retrieved July 7, 2008, from http://www.berr.gov.uk/employment/workandfamilies/flexible-working/index.html

Dobkin, L. (2006). *The costs of caregiving.* Retrieved June 5, 2008, from http://www.workforce.com/section/09/feature/24/85/10/248516.html

Duncan, S., Estabrooks, C. A., & Reimer, M. (2000). Violence against nurses. *Alta RN, 56*(2), 13–14.

Equal Rights Advocates. (2008). *California paid family leave.* Retrieved July 7, 2008, from http://www.equalrights.rog/professional/fmla.asp

Facer, R., & Wadsworth, L. (2008). Alternative work schedules and work family balance: A research note. *Review of Public Personnel Administration, 28*(2), 166–177.

Families and Work Institute. (2002). *National study of employers.* New York: Author.

Galinsky, E., Bond, J. T., & Hill, E. J. (2004). *Workplace flexibility: What is it? Who has it? Who wants it? Does it make a difference?* New York: Families and Work Institute.

Gamino, D. (1997, December 28). State makes use of "temps" despite job cap. *Austin American-Statesman.* Retrieved January 10, 2005, from http://www.austin360.com/news/12dec/28/temps28.html

Gannon, J. (1998, June 19). Single and childless workers say they're not getting fair share of benefits. *Pittsburgh Post-Gazette.* Retrieved January 10, 2005, from http://www.post-gazette.com/business news/19980619bbenefits1.asp

Gil Gordon Associates. (1998). *Generic telecommuter's agreement.* Telecommuting/teleworking site. Retrieved January 10, 2005, from www.gilgordon.com/downloads/agreement.txt

Goetzel, R. Z., & Ozminkowski, R. J. (2006). What's holding you back: Why should (or shouldn't) employees invest in health promotion programs for their workers? *North Carolina Medical Journal, 67,* 428–430.

Goodman, C. (2003, July 30). New work priority: Flex time. *Miami Herald,* pp. 1C, 8C.

Goodman, C. (2008, June 25). Telecommuting: Driving down the cost of working. *Miami Herald.* Retrieved July 2, 2008, from www.miamiherald.com/business/v-print/story/581847.html

Gordon, R. (2001, November 2). Salvation Army OKs partner benefits: Charity's reversal to allow ties with S.F. *San Francisco Chronicle.* Retrieved January 10, 2005, from http://sfgate.com/cgi-bin/article.cgi?file=/chronicle/archive/2001/11/02/MN128788.DTL

Guy, M. E., & Newman, M. (1998). Toward diversity in the workplace. In S. Condrey (Ed.), *Handbook of human resource management in government* (pp. 75–92). San Francisco: Jossey-Bass.

Hall, D. (1990). Promoting work/family balance: An organization change approach. *Organizational Dynamics, 18*(3), 5–18.

Heredia, C. (2001a, November 14). Salvation Army says no benefits for partners: National panel overturns regional OK. *San Francisco Chronicle.* Retrieved January 10, 2005, from http://sfgate.com/cgi-bin/article.cgi?file=/chronicle/archive/2001/11/14/MN143620.DTL

Heredia, C. (2001b, December 22). Gays spurning Salvation Army: Rights groups protesting benefits policy. *San Francisco Chronicle.* Retrieved January 10, 2005, from http://sfgate.com/cgi-bin/article.cgi?file=/chronicle/archive/2001/12/22/MN200149.DTL

Hoyman, M., & Duer, H. (2004). A typology of workplace policies: Worker friendly vs. family friendly? *Review of Public Personnel Administration, 24*(2), 113–132.

Human Resources Division. (1999). Job sharing information packet. Alternative Work Options Program, Commonwealth of Massachusetts. Retrieved December 18, 2008, from www.mass.gov/Ehrd/docs/policies/files/pol_flextimeguide.doc

Human Rights Campaign Foundation. (2003). Retrieved January 10, 2005, from http://www.hrc.org/content/contentgroups/publications1/state.of.the.family/SoTF.pdf

Human Rights Campaign Foundation. (2007). *The state of the workplace for gay, lesbian, bisexual and transgender Americans.* Retrieved June 5, 2008, from http://www.hrc.org/documents/State_of_the_Workplace.pdf

IACP. (2008). Combating workplace violence. Washington, DC: International Association of Chiefs of Police. Retrieved on July 7, 2008 from www.theiacp.org/documents/pdfs/Publicationscombatingworkplaceviolence.pdf

International Association of Chiefs of Police (IACP). (1995). *Combating workplace violence.* Washington, DC: Author. Retrieved February 4, 2009, from www.theiacp.org/documents/pdfs/Publicationscombatingworkplaceviolence.pdf

International City/County Management Association (ICMA). (1994). Focus on violence. *HR Report, 2*(8), 3–6.

International City/County Management Association (ICMA). (1995). *Employee benefits in local government* (Special Data Issue). Washington, DC: Author.

International Public Management Association for Human Resources HR Center. (2007). *Personnel practices: Telecommuting policies.* Alexandria, VA: Author.

Kemp, D. R. (1995). Telecommuting in the public sector: An overview and a survey of the states. *Review of Public Personnel Administration, 15*(3), 5–14.

King, M. (2001, November 3). Salvation Army allows health-care access for domestic partners. *Seattle Times.* Retrieved January 10, 2005, from http://archives.seattletimes.nwsource.com/cgi-bin/texis.cgi/web/vortex/display?slug=salvation03m&date=20011103&query=%22Salvation+Army%22

Kirkpatrick, D. (1997, April 2). Child-free employees see another side of equation. *Wall Street Journal Interactive Edition.* Retrieved January 10, 2005, from http://lexisnexis.com/

Kleiman, C. (2003, October 8). Workers willing to put family ahead of career advancement. *Tallahassee Democrat,* p. 3E.

Leonard, B. (1996). Dual-income families fast becoming the norm. *HRMagazine, 41*(8), 8.

Levine, S. (1997, March 24). One in four U.S. families cares for aging relatives. *Washington Post,* p. A13.

Lingle, K. (2005). *Workers, workplace and work: Connecting the dots at the speed of change.* Keynote address, Alliance for Work-Life Progress, 9th Annual Conference and Exhibition. Retrieved June 5, 2008, from http://www.awlp.org/library/html/Lingle-A.pdf

Lord, M., & King, M. (1991). *The state reference guide to work-family programs for state employees.* New York: Family and Work Institute.

Lynem, J. (2001, May 13). Family-friendly or single-hostile? Unwed employees feel shortchanged by policies aimed at helping parents. *San Francisco Chronicle.* Retrieved January 10, 2005, from http://sfgate.com/cgi-bin/article.cgi?file=/chronicle/archive/2001/05/13/AW152151.DTL

Martinez, M. (1993). Family support makes business sense. *HR Magazine, 38*(1), 38.

McCurdy, A., Newman, M., & Lovrich, N. (2002). Family-friendly workplace policy adoption in general and special purpose local governments. *Review of Public Personnel Administration, 22*(1), 27–51.

McPhaul, K., & Lipscomb, J. (2004). Workplace violence in health care: Recognized but not regulated. *Online Journal of Issues in Nursing, 9*(3). Retrieved July 23, 2008, from http://www.nursingworld.org/MainMenuCategories/ANAMarketplace/ANAPeriodicals/OJIN/TableofContents/Volume92004/Number3September30/ViolenceinHealthCare.aspx

Mercer, W. M. (1996). *Mercer work/life and diversity initiatives.* Retrieved July 30, 2001, from www.dcclifecare.com/mercer/mercer-1.html

MetLife. (2006). *The Metlife caregiving cost study: Productivity losses to U.S. business.* Westport, CT: MetLife. Retrieved December 19, 2008, from www.caregiving.org/data/CaregiverCostStudy.pdf.

Mikalachki, A., & Mikalachki, D. (1991). Work-family issues: You had better address them! *Business Quarterly, 55*(4), 49–52.

Ministry of Science Technology and Innovation. (2008). *Maternity leave.* Retrieved July 2, 2008, from http://www.workindenmark.dk/Maternity_leave

National Academy of Public Administration. (1998). *Work/life programs: Helping managers, helping employees.* Washington, DC: Author.

NOLO. (2003a). *Providing military leave.* Retrieved January 10, 2005, from www.nolo.com/lawcenter/ency/article.cfm/ObjectID/8077364D-A7D1-4E44-8E88F9B97B187DFB/catID/40338C48-92FD-49FA-93CB1BF16195D519

NOLO. (2003b). *Your health and safety at work FAQ.* Retrieved January 10, 2005, from www.nolo.com/lawcenter/ency/article.cfm/ObjectID/1710112D-A8C2-4DBC-97A3E271E3C8A169/catID/0A323459-4B09-4D32-BB8CD8E6058BE1CF

Oakley, M. (2008, April). *The bottle, the breast, and the state: Breastfeeding rights policy and the role of grassroots and traditional women's rights groups.* Unpublished paper presented at the Midwest Political Science Association annual meeting, Chicago.

Obama, B. (2006). *The audacity of hope: Thoughts on reclaiming the American dream.* New York: Crown.

Organisation for Economic Co-operation and Development (OECD). (2008). *OECD factbook.* Retrieved June 5, 2008, from http://puck.sourceoecd.org/pdf/factbook2008/302008011e-06–01–03.pdf

Partnership for Public Service. (2007). *The best places to work in the federal government, 2007.* Washington, DC: Author. http://bestplacestowork.org/BPTW/about/

People for the American Way. (2001). *Salvation Army rescinds domestic partner benefits after right wing backlash.* Civil Rights and Equal Rights. Retrieved January 10, 2005, from www.pfaw.org/pfaw/general/default.aspx?oid=4162

Peterson, M. (1998, July 18). The short end of long hours. *New York Times,* pp. B1–B2.

Price, J. (2001, December 10). P-FLAG targets Salvation Army: Drops fake money in kettles over repeal of "partner" perks. *Washington Times,* p. A6.

Reddick, C., & Coggburn, J. (Eds.). (2008). *Handbook of employee benefits and administration.* New York: Taylor & Francis.

Reynolds, J. (2005). In the face of conflict: Work-life conflict and desired work hour adjustment. *Journal of Marriage and Family, 67,* 1313–1331.

Roberts, G. (2001). New Jersey local government benefits practices survey. *Review of Public Personnel Administration, 21*(4), 284–307.

Schroeder, P. (1998). *24 years of housework and the place is still a mess.* Kansas City, MO: Andrews & McMeel.

Shuey, P. (1998, October 19). Few use flexible benefits. *Federal Times,* pp. 1, 4.

Staffing stabilized in 2002. (2003, March 10). Staffing today.net. Retrieved January 10, 2005, from www.staffingtoday.net/staffstats/release03–10–03.htm

Stanger, J. (1993). How to do a work/family needs assessment. *Employment Relations Today, 20*(2), 197.

Stockwell, M. (2006). *Flexible work for strong families.* Progressive Policy Institute. Retrieved June 5, 2008, from http://www.ppionline.org/documents/family_agenda_111506.pdf

Suttle, G. (1998, March 8). Solidarity in sickness. *News Tribune,* p. F1.

Telework Arizona. (2008). *Partnering to make a difference.* Retrieved June 5, 2008, from http://www.teleworkarizona.com/mainfiles/visitor/voverview.htm

U.S. Bureau of the Census (Census). (2006). *American community survey 2006.* Washington, DC: Author.

U.S. Bureau of the Census (Census). (2007). *Single-parent households showed little variation since 1994.* Washington, DC: Author.

U.S. Department of Labor. (2007). *Workforce 2007.* Retrieved June 5, 2008, from http://www.dol.gov/asp/media/reports/workforce2007/adw2007.pdf

U.S. Government Accountability Office (GAO). (2007). *An assessment of dependent care needs of federal workers using the U.S. Office of Personnel Management's survey.* Retrieved June 5, 2008, from http://www.gao.gov/docsearch/abstract.php?rptno=GAO-07–43R

U.S. Office of Personnel Management (OPM). (2002, March). *Elder care responsibilities of federal employees and agency programs.* Washington, DC: Author.

U.S. Office of Personnel Management (OPM). (2003). *Part-time employment and job-sharing guide.* Retrieved January 10, 2005, from http://www.opm.gov/pt.employ/pt09.htm

U.S. Office of Personnel Management (OPM). (2005). *The status of telework in the federal government, 2005.* Retrieved June 5, 2008, from http://www.telework.gov/reports_and_studies/tw_rpt05/status-intro.aspx

U.S. Office of Personnel Management (OPM). (2007a). *Leave bank program.* Retrieved June 5, 2008, from www.opm.gov/local/leave/htmllvbank.htm

U.S. Office of Personnel Management (OPM). (2007b). *Work life: Adoption benefits guide.* Retrieved June 5, 2008 from www.opm.gov/employment_and_benefits/worklife/officialdocuments/handbook suides/adoption/index.asp

Vance, M. (2005). *Breastfeeding legislation in the United States: A general overview and implications for helping mothers.* Retrieved June 5, 2008, from www.lalecheleague.org/law

Walter, L. (2005). *Social welfare in Denmark.* The University of Wisconsin-Green Bay SCD senior seminar: Welfare and the welfare state. Retrieved July 23, 2002, from http://www.uwgb.edu/walterl/welfare/denmark.htm

West, J. P. (2005). Managing an aging workforce: Trends, issues, and strategies. In S. Condrey (Ed.), *Handbook of human resource management in government* (2nd ed., pp. 164–188). San Francisco: Jossey-Bass.

West, J. P., & Berman, E. M. (1996). Managerial responses to an aging municipal workforce: A national survey. *Review of Public Personnel Administration, 16*(3), 38–58.

West, J. P., & Bowman, J. (2008). Employee benefits: Weighing ethical principles and economic imperatives. *Handbook of employee benefits and administration* (pp. 29–53). Boca Raton, FL: CRC Press.

World at Work. (2007). *Telework trendlines for 2006.* Scottsdale, AZ: Author.

Yates, C. A., & Leach, B. B. (2006). Why "good" jobs lead to social exclusion. *Economic and Industrial Democracy, 27,* 341–368.

Chapter 9

Training and Development
Creating Learning Organizations

Excellence is an art won by training and habit.

—Aristotle

After studying this chapter, you should be able to

- understand why organizations often underinvest in training and development,
- identify strategic roles of training and development,
- use adult learning theories to improve training and development activities,
- recognize seven relevant strategies and their applications, and
- develop methods for evaluating the effectiveness of this management process.

Employees often begin new jobs with the expectation that they will receive sufficient training and information to learn the ropes and quickly become productive, successful members of their new organizations. If they are fortunate, as many are, their colleagues will assist them, and their employers will provide some training, too. Nevertheless, many new employees believe that they do not receive adequate formal instruction or assistance, and that they are left to learn their jobs through trial and error, adding to their frustration. Why do institutions invest so little in their new members so often?

This chapter examines training and development—not only for new recruits, but also for existing staff, who also must adapt to change: the need for learning and skill development is continuous and for everyone. Training is increasingly mentioned as being the key to retaining young and productive employees who want and need to acquire new, competitive skills as they establish and advance their careers.

Training is defined as the effort to increase the knowledge, skills, and abilities (KSAs) of employees and managers so that they can better do their jobs. New employees frequently need training to help them understand their tasks, technologies, and procedures unique to the organization, and to correctly implement key rules and regulations. Existing personnel periodically need to acquire new abilities, giving real meaning to "lifelong learning." For example, they need to learn new information technology (IT) applications, regulations that affect job performance, criteria of performance appraisal, and patterns of organizational communication.

Whereas training focuses on improving performance in present jobs, **development** is defined as efforts to improve future performance by providing skills to be used in a subsequent assignment. Development increases staff potential, assists in succession planning, and is tied to strategic organizational development, ensuring that agencies have the employees with relevant skills. The distinction between training and development is somewhat inexact because many developmental activities have immediate uses. To illustrate, leadership training for employees can be regarded as a developmental activity. However, these skills are likely to also improve employee teams as such personnel gain new knowledge and insights of group dynamics and processes.

The environment for training and development reveals key paradoxes. The first paradox is that almost everyone from presidents and management gurus to shop stewards and department heads emphasizes the importance of training and development—and agree that it is inadequately provided. Ensuring that people have adequate technical skills has never been more important. As employees are more empowered and cross-trained to do multiple jobs, it is obvious that concerns about their job skills increase. Nevertheless, most observers believe that organizations perennially underinvest in training. To illustrate, the Winter Commission (National Commission on the State and Local Government Public Service, 1993) recommended some years ago that state and local government expenditures for training and development activities be about 3–5% of salaries. Following this report, one estimate placed these federal expenditures at just 1.3% (Kettl & DiIulio, 1995), and an estimate a decade later, in fiscal year 2005, finds a similar percentage (about 1.4%). The reality that training often is a low priority is also reflected in attitudinal data. For example, a 2006 survey of federal workers finds that only 49% agree or strongly agree that their training needs are assessed; hence, many workers do not perceive that their agency makes their training needs a priority (U.S. Office of Personnel Management [OPM], 2006).

It is interesting to speculate about some of the reasons for this situation. One reason is that, although training and development are important, they are less urgent than other budget necessities (salaries must be paid, programs must be implemented). A second reason is that it is very difficult to measure the return on investment of any specific training and development activity (e.g., Russ & Preskill, 2005). The training function may be necessary, but if the impact cannot be measured, then organizations are apt to limit training expenditures to those instances in which it is seen as absolutely necessary (such as ensuring new repair procedures for jet fighters or ensuring that legal rights and responsibilities are met in prison inmate management). A third explanation is that organizations may be reluctant to invest in employees who are viewed as mobile, switching between employers. Some answers to these questions are explored below.

The second paradox is that as training and development become more important to the organization, responsibility for fulfilling these needs is shifted downward to individual employees, supervisors, and units. That is, **decentralization of training** has been occurring. The days of the large training departments are over. Many organizations have cut back or even eliminated training staff in human resource departments. Now, departments and employees must identify, assess, and meet their own needs. Training often is outsourced to take advantage of specialized knowledge. One size does not fit all. Online learning has become increasingly common along with traditional modes of learning, but employees and managers need to be proactive in order to take advantage of these training opportunities. Among federal employees, 75% agree or strongly agree that that they have access to electronic learning and training programs at their desks.

The third paradox is that as responsibilities increase, employees may have less time to focus on training. They may recognize their need for increased KSAs and complain about not getting enough training and development, but that does not mean that they have the time or energy to pursue KSAs. Many people work extra hours, and most have substantial outside obligations. There is only so much that can be done. Still, not all feel this way. Dedicated employees and managers do make the time to pursue career development and strive for high levels of professionalism. Although many organizations do not reward them for doing so, others take notice. Some invite or even require employees and managers to work with higher administrators to formulate a professional development plan in which training and development activities are identified.

These paradoxes reveal the underlying crosscurrents that affect training and development: tight budgets, increased technology, **cross-training**, employee mobility, and overworked staff. Organizations vary in how they respond to these paradoxes. Some recognize the challenges and ensure that training and development are part of the strategic plan that articulates how the organization will meet its present and emerging needs. For others, though, the lack of training and development—often because of the crush of immediate demands—means that these requirements go unmet. The discussion in this chapter begins by examining the strategic role of training. Then specific training and development activities, as well as theories of adult learning, are discussed and applied to the case of ethics training: Can such training reduce the number of ethical transgressions? Finally, examples of needs assessment and evaluation of training are provided.

■■ THE STRATEGIC ROLE OF TRAINING AND DEVELOPMENT

Why do organizations provide training and development? Most agencies and managers are apt to vary in their assessment, but acknowledge that this human resource management function is important. Training and development contributes to

1. assisting new employees to get up to date on the unique procedures, equipment, or standards of the organization;

2. helping existing staff to adapt to new tasks as a result of promotion, restructuring, or other reassignments;

3. confirming that employees are abreast of new laws, procedures, or knowledge pertinent to the organization, the environment, or their jobs;

4. ensuring that personnel in jobs critical to the organization's performance—and which have high costs of failure—perform in satisfactory ways (risk management);

5. using training and development as a tool to ensure that desirable employees and managers stay current and committed to the organization (retention); and

6. ensuring that everyone has the KSAs that are consistent with what is needed to help the organization move forward (planning).

The importance of these responsibilities is readily seen. For example, since 9/11 many law enforcement agencies have increased their concern with terrorism. Training and development is a cost-efficient and effective way to help personnel acquire these new KSAs. Consultants may be brought in to train employees. Such training also allows staff of different agencies to work together and exchange information. Training can be focused on the critical needs of communities (risk management). Indeed, embracing these new law enforcement tasks has resulted in myriad, multimillion-dollar training programs.

How do agencies organize themselves to implement this key human resource management function? Note that Items 1, 2, and 3 above reflect broad organizational needs (all employees have some training requirements, especially recent hires, the newly promoted, or those dealing with new technology or procedures). Given the breadth and diversity of these needs and trends toward empowerment, it is increasingly the employees and their immediate supervisors who are best positioned to assess their own deficits. Different jobs require different KSAs; those doing or overseeing the work are more likely to know what is required. For example, who knows more about the needs of computer maintenance personnel than the personnel themselves, and possibly their supervisors? Certainly not the personnel specialist, city manager, mayor, congressional representative, solid waste director, or health director, unless any of these persons happens to have current training and experience in the field.

Organizations, through their upper management, can do much to ensure that these lower-level assessments of training needs are indeed undertaken. First, they could require that supervisors develop a training plan with each employee, perhaps as part of the annual appraisal process. Such a plan identifies employee skill shortfalls and includes a plan to address these areas. Second, organizations can set aside monies or require that lower units spend a certain amount of their expenditures on training and development. Percentages of 1–2% set aside for training are sometimes reported; such expenditures are typically coupled to some form of heightened accountability—for example, showing that these expenditures support the various strategic aims of the organization.

Third, upper management can arrange for training that cuts across different units, such as (a) generic management training for new supervisors, (b) legal and workplace matters affecting employees (e.g., sexual harassment and discrimination seminars), (c) benefit seminars (e.g., retirement planning, healthcare expenses), and so on. Often the human resource department is responsible for ensuring that these crosscutting training efforts are in fact carried out (International City/County Management Association [ICMA], 2002; Reese & Lindenburg, 2003; Ugori, 1997).

Items 4, 5, and 6 above reflect needs that, in practice, often are less routine special needs. These frequently reflect areas important to senior managers, such as risk management, key personnel (Patton & Pratt, 2002), and organizational development. As previously noted, terrorism emerged as a new or expanded management concern in the wake of the 9/11 attacks.

Many local communities greatly increased their management of threats to their drinking water. Building protection against bomb threats gained increased importance. These new risk management challenges led many top managers to send their staff to seminars designed to address these topics. Initially, this was clearly a nonroutine matter, but the possibility of new and unforeseen threats has made it an ongoing salient issue (Perry & Mankin, 2005).

Line managers are increasingly responsible for knowing where and when they and their staff can acquire new KSAs necessary to address emerging, strategic, or special issues. Training and development often are important parts of employee retention and program implementation strategies. One of many reasons managers often attend professional conferences is to become better informed and to learn where they can acquire new skills. About 75% of top local government managers report that they attend annual meetings of professional organizations (Berman, 1999), and that such attendance assists in their own development as well. Managers send their employees, also, so that they can continue to develop, acquire new KSAs, and provide a motivating and supportive environment to assist in retaining their better employees.

Finally, the broad range of purposes for training and development, coupled with increased demand and tight budgets, is causing agencies to search for cost-effective delivery approaches and to find better ways of assessing training effectiveness. In recent years, online learning is increasingly popular, with ever-improving quality. Video conferencing is also used, especially in specialized training, which allows people from vastly separate locations to participate. The search for cost effectiveness is nothing new; managers should not expect simple answers or an optimal percentage of spending to exist for training and development; more spending does not necessarily make for organizations that are more productive. Rather, it continues to be important that training and development reflect the organization's strategic needs and priorities according to the above-mentioned six points, while also incorporating best practices, discussed in the next section (Bjornberg, 2002; Gorman et al., 2003).

■■ GENERAL PRINCIPLES OF LEARNING

Learning theories provide a foundation for successful training and development and are based on principles gleaned from cognitive psychology, behavioralism, and social learning, which focus, respectively, on the roles of information and understanding, feedback and incentives, and role modeling and tasks (Van Wart, Cayer, & Cook, 1993). The fundamental **principles of learning** are discussed below with an eye to **adult learning theory**. The theory emphasizes the extensive experiences of adults, interest in self-improvement and problem solving, and preferences for active participation and exercise of some control in learning. Consistent with these principles, motivation; relevance and transference; repetition and active participation; underlying principles; and feedback and positive reinforcement are discussed here.

Motivation

A key principle in successful training and development is that people learn better when they are eager to acquire new KSAs, seek out application opportunities, and are not readily discouraged by obstacles. For this reason, training efforts should ensure **motivation in training**. At a minimum, managers should explain the reasons for training, such as the need to meet changed requirements, to master new technology, or to adapt to a more efficient approach to service delivery (ICMA, 2003).

Employees often have concerns about how new approaches will be put into practice, whether they will have the opportunity to use or adjust any training to specific conditions or concerns, and how training might affect their jobs or job security. For instance, will the new procedures interfere with their flextime arrangement or opportunities for career advancement? Because people have such varied concerns, trainers and managers often encourage open discussion prior to training in which employees voice these issues. Some administrators also initiate one-on-one discussions in which employees can privately voice their concerns. The point, of course, is to provide an opportunity for aligning the needs of the organization for training with employees' concerns, thereby ensuring that they are well motivated to put the training into practice and work through whatever adjustments are necessary.

Relevance and Transference

Training relevance and effectiveness are increased when training addresses specific work problems. Trainers must explain how information and skills relate to tasks and how these tasks can be completed. For this reason, it is important that trainers solicit the input of employees and their supervisors in program design. It is also important to acknowledge the relevance of training to many young workers who use it to advance their careers. The problem of **transference** may occur when training is conducted in a setting other than the work environment. Effectiveness requires that new knowledge and skills be readily transferred into the workplace. For example, classroom lectures for customer-employee relations training may not match real-life situations. Training requires illustrative cases. Sometimes, transference is facilitated by breaking complex objectives into smaller modules. Employment law, for example, is best understood by allowing time for addressing problems such as recruitment, discrimination, appraisal, and termination. Each subject should include multiple examples that help staff relate the material to their own workplace issues.

Repetition and Active Participation

Most people do not immediately retain complex information and use new skills. The **rule of three** states that people hear things only after they have been said three times, and the **rule of seven** states that people must practice something seven times to master it. The problem, in part, is that people learn at different speeds. Repetition facilitates the learning process by allowing individuals to process information at their own pace. People also experience **learning plateaus**, or periods during which they must first fully absorb and assimilate material before they are able to learn more. Individuals also vary with regard to the type of material they find easy to comprehend. Repetition helps address this situation, and allows those who readily grasp subject areas to benefit from further honing their knowledge.

Most adults are active learners who prefer to learn through participation in learning processes. Adults prefer to participate in discussions about the meaning of concepts and how they might be correctly applied rather than to sit passively listening to an instructor talk. Repetition and multiple examples increase opportunities for active involvement, especially when applications occur out of class and training is scheduled over multiple sessions, allowing reflection on what was learned.

Overlearning refers to assimilation of material so that it becomes second nature—that is, so that new KSAs are completely integrated into an individual's repertoire. Overlearning is an important aspect of training when high levels of performance mastery are needed. It takes repeated applications before new skills and knowledge become ingrained: "practice makes perfect." Overlearning is particularly important where mistakes would be expensive or dangerous. Overlearning aids performance later when there are time constraints or substantial psychological pressures.

Underlying Principles

Underlying principles help employees deal with situations that they have not previously encountered. Although in some situations immediate goals are straightforward (perhaps how to replace a part in a piece of machinery), learning situations that are more substantial call for a review of general principles such as basic assumptions, physical laws, and legal theories. Matters of computer security, customer relations, and ethical conduct usually require a clear understanding of the principles that give rise to specific protocols and procedures. Such principles not only help employees comprehend the reasons for specific operations, but also provide a context from which new applications can later be developed.

Feedback and Positive Reinforcement

Training impact is enhanced by immediate, direct feedback, which helps reduce errors, enhance motivation, and increase attention to standards. Generally, positive feedback is used to reinforce actions, whereas negative feedback is designed to arrest them. Although negative feedback is important (e.g., pointing out an incorrect application or faulty outcome), it must be constructive in nature to be successful. For many employees, negative feedback must be balanced with **positive reinforcement** lest critical comments decrease motivation and willingness to succeed. Positive reinforcement is key to ensuring staff acceptance. It can involve verbal acknowledgment, certificates of appreciation, or new assignments.

As the saying goes, "What gets measured gets done." Some employees use the extent and nature of feedback as a measure of their organization's commitment. Not surprisingly, effective training outcomes often require that employers demonstrate commitment to follow through and practical results. This is reflected by the frequency of feedback and in other ways, such as when certain efforts are made part of management objectives. Trainees may also be asked to report how the training has benefited their areas of operation.

In sum, the above principles provide important points for ensuring the effectiveness of training and development. Participants need to be motivated to learn and apply that which is taught, and management must address participants' concerns. The material should be relevant to their work and illustrated through multiple examples and opportunities for practice and application. Participants must understand both the specific applications and the underlying principles that may be relevant to future uses. Finally, employers need to follow through by providing feedback and encouragement about the importance and appropriateness of workplace applications. Exhibit 9.1 examines some situations in which these principles are not met.

Exhibit 9.1   Training and Culture

The training principles discussed here reflect learner-centric assumptions that are common in the United States. That is, it is assumed that people want to learn, and that they will use creativity and resourcefulness in applying whatever general and specific knowledge is provided, provided that people are supported and provided with useful information and feedback.

Teachers know well that these assumptions, while key to success, are not correct in every circumstance. Some people do not want to learn, and some have learning deficits, for example, and are unable to master or absorb new material easily. Others have low levels of creativity and imagination, and require specific guidance to apply new knowledge or skills to unique tasks. They need to be told what to do. Still others have low levels of perseverance, and need to be encouraged to "try and try again" when they are not immediately successful.

Yang, Zheng, and Li (2006) suggested that some orientations and limitations may be culture based. They suggested that learners from Mainland China are more instructor-centric: they seek to absorb the expertise and knowledge of the instructor, sometimes through rote memorization, and do not use the information and encouragement of the instructor to develop their own expertise and knowledge. Traditional Mainland Chinese learners may be more likely to focus on providing the right answer rather than providing the answer that reflects their own creativity.

Instructors know well that these orientations are readily found among some U.S. employees and students too, and that they certainly do not describe all Mainland Chinese learners in a modern world. Rather, they point to the need to examine learning assumptions and to work with employees in addressing their limitations such as those that lack creativity, leadership, or perseverance, regardless of their culture.

▪▪ TRAINING STRATEGIES

This section discusses training strategies: on-the-job training approaches, mentoring, in-house seminars, simulation and role-playing, Web-based learning, cross-training, and formal education.

On-the-Job Training

On-the-job training (OJT) is perhaps the most common training technique. OJT is used most often for new hires. It is customized job instruction, either intermittent or continuous, involving detailed monitoring and feedback to achieve rapid improvements in basic skills. The approach involves learning the application of formal knowledge, regulations, and other general principles to actual tasks, as well as the acquisition of often-idiosyncratic information linked to specific jobs, such as evolving technology systems, regulations, or agency procedures. Quality OJT involves the assignment of one or more coaches to the trainee. OJT is not "sink or swim," such as when an employer simply gives an employee a manual and the name of a supervisor to contact if there is a problem. Rather, bona fide OJT involves a thoughtful and guided approach to learning the job as it is performed; it is often supplemented by additional formal instruction. Although associated with employees assuming new positions, OJT also can be used when employees face changes in job responsibilities or new technology (Barron, Black, & Berger, 1997; Wu & Rocheleau, 2001).

Because this training concerns knowledge tied to specific positions, it follows that OJT is often best delivered by those currently or recently in positions that new employees are asked to fill. **Coaching** involves assigning an experienced employee to help other employees to master their job situations. OJT involves one-on-one student-teacher interactions that focus on helping workers apply material in practice, often by working through specific job situations. In this technique, it is important that teachers identify all relevant job situations or problems that may require new skills or knowledge, provide opportunity for application, and provide positive feedback when material is learned. The approach is usually regarded as a cost-effective way of transferring essential job skills and knowledge, although part of the appeal lies in the fact that it seldom requires a separate budget. Existing staff are simply asked to supply it as a temporary, additional duty.

OJT has the potential to meet many of the requirements for effective learning. New employees are often highly motivated, the knowledge is relevant and transference is usually not an issue, there are ample examples that can be repeated as necessary, and employees have opportunities to receive feedback. There are also threats to the success of OJT. It depends heavily on the credibility of the "manager as teacher" as well as the ability to transfer his or her job-specific KSAs to the "employee as student." OJT is best provided by employees who are respected for their abilities in the organization, including the ability to teach. In addition, the "students" must be motivated and able to learn. Finally, OJT is no substitute for formal training. When students lack formal knowledge such as essential accounting or IT skills, OJT will not be successful because teachers cannot build on critical foundations. Also, employees sometimes are not motivated to learn their jobs: for instance, they might have been involuntarily transferred to new assignments.

Although it may seem obvious that managers can improve the effectiveness of OJT by carefully selecting and training experienced employees to fulfill the instructor role, this is not always done. Expert employees do not always make for expert OJT coaches, and it may be useful to send some employees acting as OJT coaches to "train-the-trainer" workshops in which instruction methods are taught. Trainees may request more examples that facilitate their learning, and managers need to ensure that their "teachers" have sufficient time to properly train employees. Administrators must develop a realistic time schedule for acquisition of job skills and develop realistic expectations about the abilities of employees to complete tasks correctly. The success of OJT ultimately is judged by the eventual ability of employees to perform new duties with minimal supervision.

Mentoring

Mentoring is a developmental approach through which inexperienced employees learn and develop their career potential through ongoing, periodic dialogue and coaching from senior managers. Whereas the issues that are dealt with in OJT are usually fairly technical and immediate, mentors often assist in dealing with long-term goals, complex skill development, and professional socialization. Typically, the mentor-employee relationship evolves into one that is both personal and professional. Many officials report having mentors who were key to their career success. Employees and beginning managers, accordingly, are encouraged to reach out and identify mentors. Mentors help shape an employee's career, help the employee to avoid pitfalls, and help expand networks by opening doors and opportunity. Women and minorities report that they find it useful to select mentors who themselves are women or minorities because such people are able to better understand or address their needs. Many personnel prefer to choose their mentors or at least influence the selection of their mentors.

Similar to OJT, mentoring reflects the principles of adult learning. Mentors and coaches provide employees with examples (e.g., making the right career moves or preparing for a job interview), and discussion usually focuses on their application and relevance. Feedback on performance is often used to reinforce important principles; mentoring and coaching assume that employees are motivated to advance their careers and job skills. But the issues of career development and professional development also include those that are somewhat more abstract than the KSAs imparted through OJT, and that thus require more opportunity for reflection, clarification, and feedback through trial and error.

A principal barrier in using mentors is the failure of employees to cultivate relationships with more experienced managers. Individuals need to identify prospective mentors rather than wait for mentors to volunteer. Recognizing this, some organizations take a proactive approach by asking senior administrators to volunteer as mentors. For instance, in some healthcare agencies, nurses are mentored by senior managers as they transition to supervisory positions. But few organizations are proactive in this area, and employees do well to seek their own mentors. Exhibit 9.2 discusses supervisory training, in which good mentoring is important.

Exhibit 9.2   Supervisory Training

Employees frequently are promoted to supervisory positions on the basis of their technical accomplishments, time in service, and perceived ability to get along with others. None of these quali-fications, however, offers much of the know-how and skills that are necessary to succeed as a supervisor. Few employers provide their managers and supervisors with training prior to promotion, and there usually are few persons who are able and willing to help new supervisors learn the ropes of supervision. Promotion to the rank of supervisor is often an exercise in "hitting the ground running."

The main challenges of supervision concern (a) the ability to get work done through staff, in a productive way; (b) dealing with employee discipline, conflict management, and other personnel matters; (c) implementing various policies (e.g., promoting workforce diversity); (d) nuturing a unitwide perspective and efforts to move the unit forward; (e) learning how to develop and administer budgets; (f) ensuring the safety and cleanliness of offices; (g) ensuring adequate information and other technology; (h) ensuring adequate employee training and development; and (i) developing administrative and legal expertise in dealing with employee discipline. Finally, they must continue to develop their interpersonal competencies.

Organizations may assist new supervisors by providing an orientation guide. The problem is that, despite good intentions, such manuals may go unread or be forgotten in the heat of everyday managing. Supervisors need to learn how to learn from employee feedback. Some agencies also provide 1- or 2-day seminars on supervision and leadership. Although these seminars do provide and reinforce important information, "trainees" may be hesitant to share their ignorance with those at similar rank. Selected departments send new supervisors to off-site workshops and seminars. Although the presence of strangers from other organizations ensures some anonymity, such off-site training efforts may lack follow-through.

Perhaps a more effective strategy is the use of mentors. In this approach, new supervisors are asked to identify a mentor, either inside or outside the organization, with whom the supervisor meets on a regular basis. These confidential conversations allow feedback and advice from those who have held similar jobs in the past. Mentors can help deal with a variety of challenges. They also help supervisors respond to employee feedback and prepare themselves for higher functions. Through mentoring, new supervisors get real-time feedback that helps them to quickly progress on the learning curve.

In-House Seminars

In-house **seminars and presentations** are widely used to communicate information such as new developments, expectations, or rules and policies to groups of employees. When limited to small groups, they often include opportunities for clarification, application, and feedback. Indeed, an important trend is seminars tailored to the needs of small work units rather than auditorium-sized groups.

Seminars, though information based, may lack important elements of effective learning. When seminars are mandatory, staff may not be motivated to learn at them. Information taught is often general and not job specific; employees may struggle to see its relevance. Because seminars are often short, there is little time for repetition or hands-on application. For these reasons, seminars are sometimes regarded as inadequate except for strictly one-way communication by management to staff. Their impact is even more problematic when supervisors fail to follow up and ensure that the information is used.

Effectiveness of seminars can be increased, however. To illustrate, managers might gauge employee interest and concern beforehand and address it during seminars. Lecturing can be kept to a minimum; opportunities thereby exist for participants to discuss training materials. Increasingly, training techniques emphasize the development of insight, understanding of principles, and creativity in seeking new applications (Lucas, 2003; Newstrom, Scannell, & Nilson, 1998). Perhaps most important is for trainers and managers to provide follow-up and implementation. Trainers might offer to work with groups of employees to assist in application, and managers can ensure that application is sufficient. Exhibits 9.3 and 9.4 provide suggestions on making presentations and developing writing skills, and Exhibit 9.5 discusses topics of workplace violence training.

Exhibit 9.3   Effective Presentations

Effective oral presentation is key in the delivery of in-house seminars. The following guidelines can help ensure the success of an oral presentation:

- State why the topic is important and how it benefits employees.
- Keep eye contact with the audience.
- Discuss the topic in "bite-size," manageable pieces.
- Use notes to remind oneself of what material must be covered, but do not read verbatim from notes.
- Provide multiple, relevant examples and applications of new concepts or procedures.
- Invite comments at appropriate intervals and provide clarifications as needed.
- Defer tangential comments to the end of the seminar.
- Consider the use of small groups to discuss problems or generate solutions.
- Practice keeping the presentation as short as possible.
- Summarize main points, and discuss implementation or follow-through as appropriate.

Seminars increasingly use overhead slides (typically, PowerPoint) and printed materials that have a professional appearance and that facilitate the communication and dissemination of information. Handouts should help participants focus on the presentation and minimize the need to take notes (Van Kavelaar, 1998).

Exhibit 9.4   Basic Skills Workshops

Training and development is primarily for employees and organizations to upgrade their skills, assuming a basic level of skills. Many organizations, however, are concerned about basic skills, such as writing. Writing is part art, part science, and is essential for grant and proposal writing, for example. Here are some tips that can improve anyone's writing:

- Have a clear picture in mind of the audience.
- Know the audience's preferred writing style, and adopt it.
- Make an outline of the main points.
- Identify the audience's concerns and address them.
- Use third person and active voice whenever possible.
- Write clearly and concisely. Make it easy for people to follow your points.
- State key points in a professional way.
- Refresh familiarity with the rules of grammar.
- Make each paragraph count.
- Quote and attribute, but do not plagiarize.

Basic skills workshops are useful for reintroducing employees and managers to these points, but practice makes perfect. The learning principles of relevance, adequate examples, repetition, and opportunities for reflection and feedback are valid here. Effective training suggests that personnel should also be encouraged to write real-life letters and memos. Training also requires follow-up to ensure that improvements occur and are reinforced in practice. Writing is clearly an important skill and, for some employers, a competitive advantage that prospective employees bring to the table.

Simulation and Role-Playing

Simulation allows managers and employees to replicate on-the-job experiences without disruption of ongoing work processes. It is appropriate when employee learning through OJT could result in unacceptable outcomes. For example, pilots use flight simulators to hone their skills and practice difficult maneuvers. NASA's astronauts simulate entire missions, and firefighters practice blaze control in simulated settings because they cannot risk on-the-job learning. Antiterrorism units practice in mock settings, and technicians use simulation to learn new tools and procedures that would be inappropriate to try out in the real world. Vestibule training is the use of separate areas on which workers practice skills or processes without disrupting ongoing work activities. Budget analysts simulate alternative fiscal scenarios to predict revenue shortfalls, and they use computer simulations in solving a variety of operations and inventory control problems. Finally, managers test staff by simulating real-life examples. The military, for example, simulates attacks without informing personnel that the event is actually a simulation. Such exercises help managers to assess staff performance under real-life conditions (Gillespie, 2002).

Simulation helps employees acquire and perfect skills in ways unavailable through OJT or seminar training, but it can be costly. Although it is obvious that flight simulators are expensive, so too is role-playing. The rule of seven suggests that trainees must have ample opportunity to practice, and they must receive competent feedback if they are to make progress. Thus, simulation often requires employees to be absent from their work for considerable periods. The usefulness of simulation is further affected by transferability—that is, the extent to which simulation reflects actual work conditions. In sum, simulation requires imitation of real-life conditions, sufficient time for trainees to acquire new skills, and follow-up in the workplace.

Exhibit 9.5   Workplace Violence Training

Workplace violence is not new, but it periodically emerges as a priority for organizations, usually in the wake of headline-grabbing incidents. Workplace violence training for employees should cover such topics as

- the employer's zero-tolerance violence policy,
- risk factors associated with violence, and specific risks associated with different jobs,
- ways to recognize and defuse potentially violent situations,
- responsibilities to report suspicious or threatening behavior,
- strategies for protecting oneself and others,
- appropriate ways to obtain medical care for an injured employee, and
- what to during and after incidents of violence.

For managers, additional training topics concern

- how to establish workplace violence policies,
- how much training to give to employees,
- how to encourage employees to report incidents,
- how to perform periodic assessment of potential threats,
- ways to be compassionate to those involved in incidents of violence,
- how to maintain or restore security in the workplace during and after an incident, and
- how to work and coordinate with security and health personnel.

It is clear that workplace violence requires a comprehensive approach, and that training should be recurrent. The federal government, through OSHA, recommends at least annual training. Important for all employees is the prevention of violence by early detection of warning signs of troubled employees and managers:

- excessive absenteeism,
- disrespect for authority,
- increased errors or sloppiness,
- overreaction to criticism,
- inappropriate comments,
- emotional language,
- social isolation,
- change in voice or expression,
- sweating or restlessness,
- avoidance of eye contact, or
- expressions of being victimized.

The challenge is that only few signs may be present. One role of training is to explain these warning signs and help employees react to them appropriately, including when they should inform their superiors.

Some widely used applications are customer service and employee relations. During customer orientation training, staff members are advised of new expectations and are provided an opportunity to discuss how they can best handle service challenges. Role-playing and simulation are part of these efforts. Typical exercises include dealing with irate customers and with contingency situations that upset client expectations. Prison personnel, for example, may have to explain to family members of inmates why they will not be able to visit relatives during scheduled visiting hours. Role-playing is most useful when it closely matches or exceeds the intensity of emotions and behaviors that occur. Experienced trainers rather than coworkers often play these roles, since coworkers may hesitate to be as aggressive to their colleagues as they are to clients. Video recordings are also used so that trainees can watch and learn from their own reactions. Through repeated interactions until they "get it right," employees increase their skills without risking the adverse consequences of the workplace.

Whatever the virtues of simulation and role-playing techniques may be, it should be noted that they have important limitations. For instance in the largest such exercise ever held, 13,000 troops accompanied by sophisticated computer simulations pitted U.S. military forces against a Middle Eastern enemy. When the radicals inflicted serious damage during the ensuing attacks, the American "dead" were ordered back to life, the sunk fleet was refloated, and the enemy was ordered to stand down while the Marines performed a victorious amphibious landing (Borger, 2002; Peters, 2007). In another case, Louisiana emergency management planners did not simulate mass civilian evacuations and did not include levee breaches for Category 4 or 5 hurricanes in their training exercises due to lack of funding. Finally, FBI's Critical Incidence Response Group developed a computer-based training program because commanders resisted simulations conducted by real people. The reason? A poor performance in simulations would damage careers.

Web-Based Learning

Web-based learning is increasingly used in employee training. While some people still prefer traditional face-to-face instruction, many younger employees are familiar with Web-based learning, either alone or in combination with other methods. The main advantages of Web-based learning in employment are remote access (thereby reducing travel time and costs), convenient participation times for employees, and access to information through the Internet, downloads, and other modules. The main disadvantages are the lack of immediate instructor feedback, some advanced content subject areas that are not yet well developed, and the need for considerable self-discipline by learners. Online learning is here to stay, and it is likely to become more important in coming years (e.g., U.S Government Accountability Office [GAO], 2003).

Formal Education

Advanced academic degrees are increasingly a prerequisite for management positions, so many employees return to universities. **Education** prepares people for the future. It differs from training in that it is concerned with broad principles of knowledge and practice rather than the technical details of work. Training makes people more alike because they learn the same skills. Education, because it involves self-discovery, makes them more different; it emphasizes not merely information, but also formation. This includes better understanding of the context of personal choices, a perspective on human affairs, and ideas about what is important—a passion for living well. The master's in public administration (MPA) is the degree of choice for those in the field of human resources because it provides students with telling viewpoints on the role of agencies as democratic institutions, the structure of public budgeting and personnel systems, the role of leadership, and many other vital topics. Employees who receive the MPA are assumed to have the appropriate background to quickly apply their education. Education has become accessible through distance learning and outreach efforts (branch campuses, off-site education) as well as the growing trend toward certificate programs that involve a set of courses from graduate or undergraduate curricula.

At least two contrasting views exist about the use of education as a training and development strategy. Some organizations view education benefits as excessively expensive and uncertain in their returns. Current graduate fees range from several hundred to more than $1,200 per credit hour at private universities; employees who receive tuition benefits usually pay only a share of the cost of these tuition bills. Organizations cannot be wholly certain how education will benefit their agencies, as some employees may fail to be promoted and others may leave. To avoid the latter, some agencies require staff to continue working with the agency for up to three years on program completion. Some other agencies view education as a useful instrument to attract and retain highly qualified personnel. Motivated employees are likely to stay for the duration of their education (often pursued on a part-time basis over many years), and it gives employers a first crack at retaining them on graduation, even if competitive, market-based salary increases are required. It also motivates employees to know that their agencies offer education benefits, thereby contributing to creating a favorable work climate.

■■ APPLICATION: ETHICS TRAINING

In recent years, concern with ethics has prompted many organizations to provide ethics training for their employees and managers. Negative reports of personnel being caught up in unethical conduct tarnish the image of organizations. Agencies now believe that an emphasis on values and ethics is consistent with building up a modern and desirable workplace. Training is seen as a means for reducing wrongdoing and increasing desirable behaviors and attitudes. But ethics is obviously difficult to shape, let alone control. What can organizations realistically expect from ethics training?

The six strategic purposes of training and development are well applied to ethics training. Ethics training can be used to ensure that both new and existing employees are aware of important laws and practices—say, gift taking, conflict of interest, fraud, or harassment—can be made mandatory, either through in-person attendance at workshops or completion of online training. Organizations can hope to reduce their legal exposure and improve their risk management by ensuring that all personnel have been made duly aware of critical laws and policies.

Beyond general topics, employers can also tailor some ethics training to special circumstances or tasks of their employees. For example, law enforcement involves concerns for the rights of alleged offenders and their victims. Those in police custody deserve to be treated with respect and dignity, regardless of race or alleged crime, and this aspect has certainly received heightened interest in recent years. Law enforcement also raises concern about bribery and criminal wrongdoing by officers themselves. Prolonged exposure to criminal activity can have a corrupting influence on those who come in contact with it. Thus, ethics implementation in law enforcement requires ethical standards that address these specific problems (Berman, 2008). Other areas have their own unique ethics challenges, such as those relating to health care or fund-raising for nonprofits.

Ethics training also reinforces retention and performance strategies by emphasizing the "value basis" of the modern workplace—specifically, efforts to create heightened emphasis on objectivity, equality, and concern for stakeholders and the environment. For instance, ethics training can be used to raise awareness of and promote discussion about the impact of a unit on the environment. What is the ethical obligation of an agency toward the environment? How well is it meeting its environmental obligations? These types of discussions further awareness that may resonate with workers.

While the above purposes support the strategic aims mentioned earlier, the general principles of learning and specific training strategies suggest that ethics training is more likely to be effective when it is part of a broader effort to instill awareness and reinforce behavior; one-time, isolated training events are likely to have less effect. For example, the rule of three discussed above suggests that employees will likely need to hear several times from managers that a new ethics policy or practice is now important, especially if it is very different from existing policies or practices. Repetition might be needed to overcome a certain skepticism. Also, the complexity of many ethical dilemmas suggests that decision making and application may not always be as self-evident as training scenarios suggest. It is not always easy to recognize or to resolve ethical issues (e.g., when should residents be forewarned of street closures?). The rule of seven discussed above suggests that employees and managers may need some practice, trial and error, and discussion before they have well ingrained the new practices.

Looking a bit further, though, how is such practice to occur? Feedback and positive reinforcement are important principles of behavioral change, and employees need feedback and positive reinforcement from the people around them—including their supervisors. The best practices of ethics training include repeated and open discussions—some as part of training with exercises and discussion, others as part of ongoing department operations. Rather than looking to ethics training as a panacea or silver bullet, it is more appropriate to view ethics training as one of several tools that managers use—along with role modeling, appraisals, and feedback—to instill or change ethical conduct. Training alone is not enough.

Some organizations use a multifaceted approach. In this regard, the well-known acronym POSDCORB (Planning, Organizing, Staffing, Directing, Coordinating, Reporting, and Budgeting) can be applied to ethics, as well, and some organizations are increasingly beginning to do so. Managers can plan for ethics ("What behaviors do we expect?" "What behaviors do we discourage?"), organize for ethics ("How are offices to be made responsible for implementing ethics objectives?"), staff for ethics (making ethics a criterion in hiring and promotion, assigning responsibilities for ethics objectives), budget for ethics (resources for training), and report on ethics accomplishments and violations. Many organizations are now putting elements of this in place, supported by training (Menzel, 2006; Svara, 2007; West & Berman, 2007). Ethics leadership means that not only do managers now bring new ethics to their employees, but also that changes in ethical awareness start with managers themselves. Not surprisingly, some agency heads have made ethics reforms a top priority for all of their managers. Training can make use of videos and role-playing scenarios. At the end of the day, though, ethics training is likely to be more effective when it is integrated with how the organization is run (van Blijswijk, van Breukelen, Franklin, Raadschelders, & Slump, 2004; Williams, 2007).

Research is providing evidence for the above propositions. In an award-winning article, West and Berman (2004) researched the use of ethics training in U.S. cities. They found that about two-thirds of cities with populations over 50,000 use some form of ethics training, and that such training is mandatory in about one-third of cities. However, the mean duration of such training is only about one-half day per year. In a sophisticated empirical analysis, West and Berman showed "targeted" ethics training (i.e., training oriented toward specific applications and practices rather than toward general awareness) is integrated with broader management efforts, and as such has a positive impact on the organizational culture and perceptions of employee performance. The complex relationship among training, leadership, and performance is shown in Exhibit 9.6. In the words of the authors, "Training is part of a jurisdiction's ethics management practices, and the results indicate that it provides managers with leverage as they seek to attain their ethics goals" (p. 202). Note also that Exhibit 9.6 shows that the source of organizational improvement begins with "moral leadership by senior managers," which is shown to affect or even drive all other ethics activities. Exhibit 9.7 shows a broad range of ethics training methods that cities report.

Exhibit 9.6 Methods of Instruction for Ethics Training	
Ethics training . . .	*Yes (percent)*
Is offered in the form of live instruction	94.6
Occurs at different points in time	84.1
Includes hypothetical scenarios	82.5
Is delivered with class sizes of 30 or fewer trainees	81.7
Is designed so that time away from the job is minimized	81.6
Includes materials for later reference	81.4
Includes realistic case materials	80.9
Is specifically tailored to the needs of our jurisdiction	79.6
Includes in-class evaluation of training	72.3
Includes role-plays or short exercises	67.8
Involves the use of a professional trainer or outside consultant	64.3
Is delivered primarily in lecture format	61.4
Has a decision-based focus	57.5
Is part of our new employee initiation program	56.6
Is one of a series of training modules for all employees	53.1
Includes self-assessment instruments	42.9
Includes a powerful message from the city manager or Chief Administrative Officer	42.5
Includes a "how to" checklist for ethical decision making	42.5
Includes follow-up communications	34.2
Includes separate courses for compliance areas	28.3
Uses Web-based or other electronic means	9.6
Includes an ethics audit survey	8.8

Source: J. West and E. Berman (2004). Ethics training efforts in U.S. cities: Content and impact. *Public Integrity, 6*(3), 189–206. Used with permission.

Exhibit 9.7   Structural Equation Model of Ethics Training, Leadership, and Outcomes

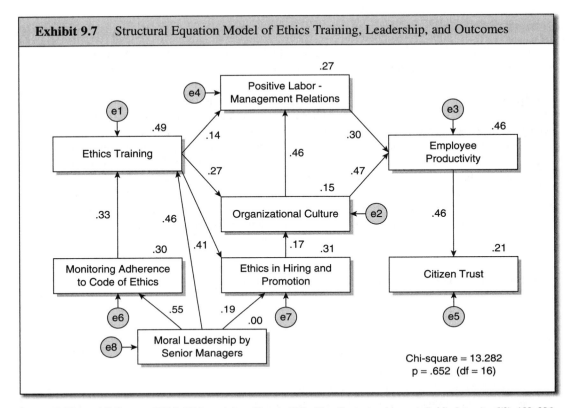

Source: J. West and E. Berman (2004). Ethics training efforts in U.S. cities: Content and impact. *Public Integrity, 6*(3), 189–206. Used with permission.

Finally, while an important purpose of ethics training in many jurisdictions is to reduce wrongdoing and reduce legal liability, no amount of training can eliminate human folly and misconduct. Who among us has not done something best left unspoken? "There but for the grace of God go I," is a shared sentiment. The human mind is subject to finding itself in a fog and beset by misjudgment. Yet, the fact that human error cannot be avoided does not mean that managers should not seek to minimize it—indeed, they should do so. Training reinforces the message that ethical conduct matters, and it tells employees what to do and what not to do. Ethics training, in some form or practice, is likely here to stay. Nevertheless, it does not replace the need for vigilance by managers; appraisal and discipline are necessary as well. After all, the next ethical misstep is just a step away.

■■ NEEDS ASSESSMENT AND EVALUATION FOR TRAINING

Needs assessments are systematic efforts used to identify organizational and personnel strengths and weakness; they can also be used for assessing training needs. Although some assessments are little more than impromptu managerial assertions ("We need more employees who can do X"), systematic approaches can use **surveys**, too. Whereas assessments are prospective, **evaluation** is largely retrospective. It is used to ensure that training activities have achieved their aims. Evaluation is used not only to justify current training, but also to obtain user input in designing future programs.

Needs Assessment

Needs assessments are undertaken to determine training requirements that are (a) organization- and unit-wide, (b) related to improving specific work processes, and (c) concerned with the training needs of individual employees (Brown, 2002; Jacobson, Rubin, & Selden, 2002). At the organizational level, assessments can reflect a variety of different purposes from which training and development needs are inferred. Van Wart (2004) discussed seven types: (1) ethics assessments; (2) mission, values, vision, and planning reviews; (3) customer and citizen assessments; (4) employee assessments; (5) performance reviews; (6) benchmarking; and (7) quality assessments. Each of these areas may suggest different needs for employee training. Organizations vary in the extent to which they perform these assessments, if they do them at all. In some organizations, such assessments are little more than discussion items in top management leadership meetings ("I have heard several complaints that involve our employees. Does anyone think that training might help?"). Other organizations conduct discussions in a more systematic way, such as by conducting focus groups at different levels of the organization.

Many organizations conduct comprehensive employee surveys, involving 50–100 items that address working conditions; supervisory relations and collegiality; access to technology, policies, and procedures; salary and benefits; availability of training and development; and many other areas. To ensure that employees complete the survey, they can be instructed to complete it during work hours; to ensure confidentiality, employees do not include their names on the surveys. Exhibit 9.8 shows a sample of a survey. Low ratings in any area are obviously cause for concern, and may prompt further inquiry and future training. Although local governments do not always use surveys, state and federal agencies often conduct them on a (bi-) annual basis. The development and implementation often is led by the human resource staff; results are disseminated to managers and employees through a succession of meetings.

Needs assessments are sometimes also conducted prior to undertaking work process improvements. In recent years, many organizations have reengineered their service delivery processes to make them more citizen oriented and to take advantage of new IT capabilities. Top managers sometimes require lower units to rigorously assess their performance by collecting performance data and by evaluating their delivery processes to detect shortfalls or bottlenecks. In addition, they may also require units to increase performance. Such improvement processes may require skills that employees currently do not have.

As this discussion shows, justification for training and development usually follows from the context in which the assessment is made: concern for general workforce development, strategic concern for retention and development, future needs of departments, or efforts to ensure or improve organizational processes and functions. These justifications can be augmented by the following efficiency-focused, analytical techniques: comparing the cost of training and follow-up to that of recruiting new employees or using consultants, the cost of continuing to use outdated technology, and the cost of dealing with resulting errors. Managers

---

Exhibit 9.8   Selected Survey Questions for Needs Assessment

Please note your level of agreement with the following statements, using the following letter codes:

SA   = Strongly Agree
A   = Agree
DK/CS = Don't Know, Can't Say
D   = Disagree
SD   = Strongly Disagree

A. Rules and Regulations

    I am familiar with the laws and policies concerning workplace discrimination.
    I am familiar with the laws and policies concerning workplace harassment.
    I am familiar with workplace leave policies.
    I am familiar with my benefit options.
    I am familiar with the workplace safety rules of my unit.
    I am familiar with ethics requirements and expectations.

B. Workplace Relations

    My unit needs to improve its teamwork.
    My supervisor is considerate and supportive.
    I can approach my supervisor to discuss almost any work-related issue.
    In our unit, we conduct ourselves in ethical ways.
    Colleagues support one another in carrying out their duties.

C. Training Needs

    I would like to learn more about conflict management skills.
    I would like to improve my spreadsheet skills.
    I would like to learn how to better use PowerPoint for presentations.
    I would like to improve my report-writing skills.
    I would like to improve my public speaking skills.
    I would like to improve my time management skills.
    I would like to improve my basic computer skills.
    I would like to learn how to use the following equipment: please identify _____.
    I would like to learn new skills so that I can contribute to a broader range of tasks.

D. Performance Management

    I know the vision and mission of my department.
    We maintain high standards of customer satisfaction.
    We regularly survey our customers about their needs.
    We regularly compare our performance to that of similar organizations.
    We regularly measure and discuss our performance.
    My supervisor tells me what is expected from me.
    My supervisor provides adequate, ongoing feedback about my performance.
    Colleagues discuss new or better approaches for improving operations.
    My coworkers are solid professionals.

can also compare the cost of different training methods to further justify a preferred training approach. Such analyses can help to further bolster the case for using training (Fitz-Enz & Davison, 2001).

Evaluation

Different evaluation approaches can be distinguished based on the nature of the process and the type of information collected. These are (a) subjective assessments of training seminars (obtained immediately after completion), (b) controlled pre- and postevaluations, and (c) subsequent assessments about on-the-job improvements (obtained some period, usually one to three months, after completion). **Training evaluation** involves approaches that aim to assess the effectiveness of training, typically involving feedback from employees and managers.

It is common to obtain employees' perceptions about training immediately afterward. Exhibit 9.9 shows a sample evaluation instrument that can readily be adapted for organizational use. Human resource departments sometimes use such forms for soliciting

---

Exhibit 9.9   Questions for Evaluating Training Seminars

Please note your level of agreement with the following statements, using the following 5-point scale:

5 = Strongly Agree
4 = Agree
3 = Don't Know, Can't Say
2 = Disagree
1 = Strongly Disagree

The training accomplished the stated objectives.	[ ]
The training was useful.	[ ]
The level of difficulty was about right.	[ ]
The material was presented in a way that facilitated learning.	[ ]
The training included practical examples.	[ ]
The training material was up to date.	[ ]
The trainer tried to address our needs.	[ ]
The trainer was approachable.	[ ]
The supplemental materials were relevant and useful.	[ ]
Overall, I am satisfied with the training I received.	[ ]

. . . and please answer the following questions, too:

What was the most helpful thing that you learned today?

Would you like a follow-up session? If so, when?

What suggestions do you have for improving this session?

input about their service from other departments. The advantages of student perceptions are that they are easy to obtain. Although low levels of satisfaction indicate that training has not met the employees' needs, high satisfaction levels do not necessarily imply that the training has met their needs. Management may fail to follow up, and there may be problems of transference that obstruct application. Furthermore, in some settings employees generally give positive ratings to trainers, reducing the effectiveness of this approach. A final problem is that some evaluations focus on delivery style rather than on the content and usefulness of the material; the former information is useful to trainers rather than to managers.

Evaluations also take place after employees have had an opportunity to apply the training material. Such evaluations emphasize changes in on-the-job behaviors as well as results obtained through training (Kirkpatrick & Kirkpatrick, 2007). For example, training on hazardous materials should include behaviors associated with safe handling, such as the use of protective devices or the consultation of handbooks to better familiarize the employee with properties of chemicals. In recent years, considerable effort has been made to evaluate the effectiveness of training for health professionals who are involved in terrorism response efforts (e.g., Benson & Westphal, 2005; Markenson, Reilly, & DiMaggio, 2005).

Discussion of evaluation frequently conjures up images of carefully controlled, scientific approaches. However, it is seldom feasible to find equivalent groups for evaluation purposes in training, and measurement of pre- and posttraining capabilities cannot conclusively prove that skill increases are caused by training: they could be affected by other learning that is not part of formal training. Still, many examples show how evaluation can be used to improve training initiatives and program performance. In one instance, a county jail faced numerous complaints from families about inmate visitation and release procedures. The jail director suspected that part of the problem was inadequate client orientation. A client satisfaction survey was conducted among inmates' family members before a customer service training improvement effort, and a second survey was conducted shortly thereafter. By comparing the scores, the effect of training on satisfaction could be determined. Such cases show how training evaluation is used for program decision making and improving future training (Fitz-Enz & Davison, 2001; Phillips, 1997).

■■ SUMMARY AND CONCLUSION

Training and development are essential for personnel to acquire and maintain up-to-date skills as well as knowledge about procedures of the organization. As training and development activities have become decentralized, managers are encouraged to develop a **strategic focus**, one that relates training and development to the objectives and strategies of their units. Although managers can often count on central human resource personnel to provide general training (such as for word processing or ADA compliance), they must develop their own training resources to provide for their unit's needs.

As the new century unfolds, several contemporary trends have become evident. First, the need for basic skills remains important, such as those relating to writing, public speaking, and teamwork. Second, employees and managers are expected to take an active role in ensuring their own needs for training and development. Organizations help by providing opportunities, but it is up to individuals to take advantage of them. Third, training is increasingly used to ensure legal compliance; as the legal environment of public management evolves, it is in the interest of all personnel to stay abreast. Fourth, training in such areas as management of information systems and contract management are key in today's public service. The upshot is that "mindware" will be at least as important as hardware and software in the years ahead.

At the same time, training can be improved. Effective training and development builds on the principles of adult learning, ensuring that participants are motivated, that material is relevant and transferable to the specific problems and settings at hand, that training includes numerous examples and opportunities for practice and application, that training addresses the underlying principles of whatever material is being taught, and finally that participants receive sufficient feedback to encourage correct application and use of the material. Application of these principles should guide how different training approaches are used. In short, if training is to be effective, then managers and employees would do well to heed the rule of three and the rule of seven.

Public service is based on knowledge residing in employees. The traditional tendency to roll along needs to be replaced by training and development that extends and stretches human resources to better serve citizens. In many forward-looking organizations, this is the new reality. For instance, in early 2009 there was bipartisan congressional support for creation of a National Public Service Academy, a type of "civilian West Point" to highlight importance of public service and help meet the challenges in the new century.

KEY TERMS

Adult learning theory	Overlearning
Coaching	Positive reinforcement
Cross-training	Principles of learning
Decentralization of training	Rule of seven
Development	Rule of three
Education	Seminars and presentations
Evaluation	Simulation
Learning plateaus	Strategic focus
Mentoring	Surveys
Motivation in training	Training
Needs assessment	Training evaluation
On-the-job training	Transference

EXERCISES

Class Discussion

1. Discuss how the principles of learning apply to a training program to improve the effectiveness of (a) agency trainers, (b) frontline customer service personnel, and (c) supervisors.

2. How many agencies require supervisors to develop a skills development plan for individual employees? How can agencies go about doing that, and what should be some elements of such a plan?

3. Examine how the paradoxes and trends discussed in the Introduction to this book are present in the agencies where students in the class are employed.

4. "You will always find some Eskimos ready to instruct the Congolese on how to cope with heat waves" (Stanislaw Lec, Polish writer). Discuss.

Team Activities

5. Identify three objectives of a training program for new police officers. Focus on what participants should be able to do on completion. What should be the relative emphasis of OJT, in-house seminars, cross-training, simulation, and formal education? Why?

6. Analyze a training program for first-time supervisors. Identify some competencies for which overlearning is relevant. Develop a needs assessment.

7. Many employees complain about a lack of positive reinforcement. Design a training program to increase its use. Why don't managers use positive reinforcement, and how does the program address this problem?

8. "We don't want to invest money in training because it is lost when employees leave." Explore the paradoxes in this statement.

9. Consider this statement in the context of the paradox of needs: "Never let your professional development be governed by our organization."

Individual Assignments

10. Identify job-related skills and knowledge that your employer should provide. How likely is it that your employer will actually help you acquire these skills? How will not acquiring these skills or knowledge affect your job performance and career? What can you do to acquire these KSAs?

11. Consider how small organizations might differ from large organizations in their training approaches. Consider how training might differ between different types of employees: old versus young, technical versus managerial, supervisory versus senior management, for example.

12. You have been appointed the training director in a large state agency university to develop and implement programs for staff personnel. Paradoxically, no monies are budgeted for this training. Can this dilemma be resolved? How?

13. Develop a skills acquisition plan for yourself. Identify specific skills that you would like to acquire and when you will be acquiring them over the next 24 months. Try to identify at least one additional skill every six months.

REFERENCES

Barron, J., Black, D., & Berger, M. (1997). *On-the job training*. Kalamazoo, MI: Upjohn.

Benson, L., & Westphal, R. (2005). Emergency department preparedness trainings in New York State: A needs assessment. *Journal of Public Health Management & Practice, 11*(Supplement Nov/Dec), 135–137.

Berman, E. (1999). Professionalism among public and nonprofit managers. *American Review of Public Administration, 29*(2), 149–166.

Berman, E. (2008). Implementing ethics. In E. Berman & J. Rabin, et al. (Eds.), *Encyclopedia of public administration and public policy* (2nd ed., pp. 461–464). New York: Marcel Dekker.

Bjornberg, L. (2002). Training and development: Best practices. *Public Personnel Management, 31*(4), 507–516.

Borger, J. (2002, Sept. 6). War game was fixed to ensure American victory, claims general. *Guardian.*co.uk. Retrieved January 9, 2009, from http://www.guardian.co.uk/world/2002/aug/21/usa.julianborger

Brown, J. (2002). Training needs assessment: A must for developing an effective training program. *Public Personnel Management, 31*(4), 569–578.

Fitz-Enz, J., & Davison, B. (2001). *How to measure human resource management* (3rd ed.). New York: McGraw-Hill.

Gillespie, G. (2002). High tech training for military air traffic control. *Summit, 5*(4), 25.

Gorman, P., McDonald, B., Moore, R., Glassman, A., Takeuchi, L., & Henry, M. (2003). Strategic HR training: Custom needs assessment for strategic HR training: The Los Angeles County experience. *Public Personnel Management, 32*(4), 475–495.

International City/County Management Association (ICMA). (2002). *Supervisory skills for improving employee performance* (training package). Washington, DC: Author.

International City/County Management Association (ICMA). (2003). *So, now you're a trainer!* Washington, DC: Author. Complete text available at http://bookstore.icma.org/freedocs/NowYoureATrainer.pdf

Jacobson, W., Rubin, E., & Selden, S. (2002). Examining training in large municipalities: Linking individual and organizational training needs. *Public Personnel Management, 31*(4), 485–506.

Kettl, D., & DiIulio, J. (1995). *Inside the reinvention machine: Appraising governmental reform.* Washington, DC: Brookings.

Kirkpatrick, D., & Kirkpatrick, S. (2007). *Implementing the four levels: A practical guide for effective evaluation of training programs.* San Francisco: Berrett-Koehler.

Lucas, R. (2003). *The creative training idea book: Inspired tips and techniques for engaging and effective learning.* New York: AMACOM.

Markenson, D., Reilly, M., & DiMaggio, C. (2005). Public Health Department training of emergency medical technicians for bioterrorism and public health emergencies: Results of a national assessment. *Journal of Public Health Management & Practice, 11*(Supplement Nov/Dec), 68–74.

Menzel, D. (2006). *Ethics management for public administrators: Building organizations of integrity.* New York: M. E. Sharpe.

National Commission on the State and Local Government Public Service (Winter Commission). (1993). *Hard truths/tough choices: An agenda for state and local reform.* Albany, NY: Rockefeller Institute of Government.

Newstrom, J., Scannell, E., & Nilson, C. (1998). *The complete games trainers play: Vol. 1.* New York: McGraw-Hill.

Patton, D., & Pratt, C. (2002). Assessing the training needs of high-potential managers. *Public Personnel Management, 31*(4), 465–485.

Perry, J., & Mankin, L. (2005). Preparing for the unthinkable. *Public Personnel Management, 34*(2), 195–214.

Peters, K. M. (2007). Testing their mettle. *GovernmentExecutive.com.* Retrieved January 9, 2009, from http://www.govexec.com/story_page.cfm?filepath=/features/1105–01/1105–01s2.htm

Phillips, J. (1997). *Handbook of training evaluation and measurement methods.* Houston, TX: Gulf.

Reese, L., & Lindenburg, K. (2003). The importance of training on sexual harassment policy outcomes. *Review of Public Personnel Administration, 24*(3), 175–191.

Russ, D., & Preskill, H. (2005). In search of the Holy Grail: Return on investment evaluation in human resource development. *Advances in Developing Human Resources, 7*(1), 71–85.

Svara, J. (2007). *The ethics primer for public administrators in government and nonprofit organizations.* Sudbury, MA: Jones & Bartlett.

Ugori, U. (1997). Career-impending supervisory behaviors. *Public Administration Review, 57*(3), 250–255.

U.S. Government Accountability Office (GAO). (2003). *Strategic planning and distributive learning could benefit the special operations forces foreign language program.* Washington, DC: Author.

U.S. Office of Personnel Management (OPM). (2006). Federal Human Capital Survey. Washington, DC: Author.

van Blijswijk, J., van Breukelen, J. R., Franklin, R. A., Raadschelders, J., & Slump, P. (2004). Beyond ethical codes: The management of integrity in the Netherlands Tax and Customs Administration. *Public Administration Review, 64*(6), 718–727.

Van Kavelaar, E. (1998). *Conducting training workshops: A crash course for beginners.* San Francisco: Jossey-Bass.

Van Wart, M. (2004). Organizational investment in employee development. In S. Condrey (Ed.), *Handbook of human resource management in government* (2nd ed.). San Francisco: Jossey-Bass.

Van Wart, M., Cayer, N., & Cook, S. (1993). *Handbook of training and development for the public sector.* San Francisco: Jossey-Bass.

West, J., & Berman, E. (2004). Ethics training efforts in U.S. cities: Content and impact. *Public Integrity, 6*(3), 189–206.

West, J., & Berman, E. (Eds.). (2007). *The ethics edge* (2nd ed.). Washington, DC: International City/County Management Association.

Williams, R. (2007). Ethics management for public administrators: Building organizations of integrity. *Public Integrity, 9*(4), 389–391.

Whitcomb, C. (2007, April 20). Building a better lockdown. *New York Times.*

Wu, L., & Rocheleau, B. (2001). Formal versus informal end user training in public and private organizations. *Public Performance & Management Review, 24*(4), 312–321.

Yang, B., Zheng, W., & Li, M. (2006). Confucian view of learning and implications for developing human resources. *Advances in Developing Human Resources, 8*(3), 346–354.

Chapter 10

Appraisal

A Process in Search of a Technique

If anyone can solve the performance evaluation problem, he should be entitled to the Nobel, the Pulitzer, and the Heisman in the same year.

—Federal personnel official

After studying this chapter,[1] you should be able to

- learn why personnel appraisal is at once important and paradoxical,
- weigh the advantages and drawbacks of typical types of appraisal,
- understand that appraisal accuracy may not be an important goal,
- value why the root problem is not technical in nature,
- demonstrate and apply appraisal interview skills in a self-study exercise,
- know that an annual formal evaluation may be the least important component in an effective appraisal system,
- recognize the value of an exit interview,
- consider ways to improve the appraisal process,
- assess alternative approaches to employee discipline,
- evaluate an appraisal system, through fieldwork, in the light of the characteristics of a "litigation-proof" process, and
- explore future trends in this arena.

After having been hired, classified, paid, and trained, an employee will have his work reviewed to assess the extent to which individual and collective needs coincide—or conflict. The process may be valued by employees for both intrinsic reasons (as a validation of one's workplace efficacy) and extrinsic factors (recognition and rewards). Because many decisions can hinge on these ratings, the process is central to human resource management. Playing key functions in employee compliance, performance improvement, and system validation, reviews are mechanisms to reinforce organizational values. They provide data on the effectiveness of recruitment, position management, training, and compensation (where such information is most frequently used). In the absence of this feedback, supervisors may have difficulty in understanding how well other management functions are working. Likewise, judgments about individual conduct may be needed if performance-contingent decisions in such areas are to have a rational basis.

Clearly, then, employee evaluation is a chief activity of management. It is also a complex topic that includes administrative decisions (e.g., pay), developmental recommendations (e.g., training), technical issues (system design), and interpersonal skills (superior-subordinate appraisal interviews). Although a well-designed process can benefit an agency, creating, implementing, and maintaining it is not easy. Programs serving multiple purposes, in fact, may serve none of them particularly well.

An emotional, inexact, human process, it is a complicated, difficult task—one that is not done well by most organizations. In business, for instance, a 2004 survey found that just a third of employees believed that performance appraisal accomplished its goal (www .watsonwyatt.com). Furthermore, less than 10% of organizations judge their appraisal systems to be effective (Grensing-Pophal, 2001). There is no reason to believe, as discussed below, that the situation is any different in government. Indeed, only 20% of federal employees indicate that the appraisal system motivates them to do a better job (U.S. Merit Systems Protection Board [MSPB], 2003). Donna D. Beecher (2003), a founding member of the federal Senior Executive Service, wrote that "performance management systems are rarely effective in communicating specific expectations, providing helpful feedback, engaging and energizing the workforce and raising levels of employee satisfaction" (pp. 463–464). It is highly ineffective for organizations to conduct individual appraisals if the system is problematic. It is premature, for instance, to install pay for performance if there is not a sound appraisal system in place.

Personnel appraisal, in short, is one of an administrator's most difficult issues, precisely because it is both important and problematic. Few managerial functions have attracted more attention and so successfully resisted solution than employee evaluation (Halachmi, 1995, p. 322). Personnel systems predicated on rewarding merit are undermined when questionable appraisal practices take place. What these widely used and intensely disliked systems reveal is that instead of being a solution, they are often part of the problem; in point of fact, many authorities agree that appraisal contributes to Enron-style corruption (Meisler, 2003; Spector, 2003) or workplace violence (Exhibit 10.1).

Not surprisingly, paradoxes abound:

- People are often less certain about "where they stand" after than before the assessment.
- The higher one rises in a department, the lower the likelihood that quality feedback will be received; most employees perceive little connection between performance and pay.
- Although the communication of negative information is difficult, not communicating it can be much worse.
- Although many authorities (e.g., DelPo, 2007) recommend that appraisal be kept separate from salary decisions (appraisal is supposed to be a developmental function), most organizations link them tightly.

Exhibit 10.1   Preventing the "Ultimate" Evaluation Solution

The work site definitely has become leaner and meaner in the last generation. The traditional social contract between employers and their minions has been broken: organizations downsize, management turns over, employees wonder if they are "next," pay stagnates, benefits become more expensive, and computers monitor humans (see discussion later in this chapter). Beginning in the 1970s (with blue-collar employees) and continuing since the 1980s (with white-collar personnel), organizations have regarded employees not as valuable assets but rather as a flexible cost to be excreted as necessary. It is perhaps no coincidence that violence at work has become an important issue in recent years.

About half of workplace violence is employee on employee; the balance is citizens or family members entering offices. One in four employees has been harassed, threatened, or assaulted. Homicide is the leading cause of occupational death for women, the second for men. The costs of abuse to personal well-being, organizational productivity, and American society as a whole are substantial in terms of counseling, turnover, litigation, security measures, insurance premiums, and the social fabric of the nation.

Although many people—incorrectly—feel safe at work, offices, courts, schools, and hospitals are no longer safe havens; occupational violence is a serious and underreported public health problem. Indeed, defense mechanisms such as denial ("it can't happen here") actually put employees at risk and impede preventive measures.

Management policies, including personnel practices, can both provoke and help prevent violence in organizations. Factors such as poor job design, inadequate space, outdated equipment, demanding schedules and workload, and weak interpersonal skills can lead to aggressive behavior. A key critical incident provoking danger, for instance, is performance appraisal and its possible consequences: close supervision, layoffs, and terminations.

In 2007, a negative performance review led a National Aeronautics and Space Administration employee to shoot his supervisor and take another employee hostage before killing himself. In an already tense workplace, the evaluation method used, how it is employed, and the way people learn about its results can produce paroxysms of shock and sorrow, anger, and rage. For example, not long ago a newly elected speaker of a southern state house of representatives distributed Christmas cards to all house employees on December 24. If the card came in a green envelope, then the employee still had a job; if it was in a red envelope, the person was told to clear out her desk by 5:00 P.M. Similarly (albeit without the Christmas cheer), a private corporation called the police to secure the premises, then asked 200 employees to go to the auditorium. They were told to turn in their building keys and were escorted from the company property. Neither case, luckily, resulted in further violence, but abandoned employees sometimes return to the workplace months or years later to exact retribution. Although it is not possible to prevent violence entirely in American culture, its probability in organizations can be lowered by proactive and reactive planning such as these:

- Establishing a violence prevention team to conduct a needs assessment that includes a review of personnel recruitment, training, and appraisal practices, as well as employee assistance programs (see Chapter 8).
- Training managers to identify risks and how to defuse problem that can precipitate an incident. (Perpetrators often evidence early warning signs such as talking about retribution, threatening supervisors, and showing weapons to other employees.)

(Continued)

(Continued)

- Developing a plan comprising a clear agency policy on workplace violence, a penalty schedule for violations, a mechanism to report incidents, and employee training on topics such as stress management, problem solving, and negotiation.
- Forming a crisis management group, to be mobilized when needed, with defined procedures and role definitions in key areas such as employee communication (e.g., rumor hotlines), media relations, and counseling (see, e.g., Minor, 1995).

As an official in a security firm observed, "A written plan may not work but an unwritten plan never works." A carefully designed approach, then, can mean the difference between acting decisively to cope with and defuse incidents and reacting haphazardly in a manner that may exacerbate a difficult situation. Yet prevention is a low priority in many organizations, as many employers remain unprepared to deal with violent episodes. Likely to increase in the years ahead, trauma at work is related to management practices as well as all experiences employees bring to the organization. Still effective human resource management makes it easier to contain than violence in the streets. It is the agency's responsibility to provide a safe working environment—and the Americans with Disabilities Act (Chapter 2) specifies that reasonable accommodations be made for those who exhibit stress-related symptoms that may lead to aggressive conduct. Is this duty being fulfilled in your jurisdiction? To help answer this and other questions, see Bates (2007) for a comprehensive prevention and response strategy. Also see Kelloway, Barling, and Harrell (2006), Lewis (2006), and Chapter 8, this volume.

Contrary to popular perceptions, the U.S. Postal Service—a very large, visible, hierarchical, and high-pressure organization—does not have a greater rate of incidents than other workplaces. Indeed, it has an effective prevention program that has reduced the amount of violence in recent years (Trimble, 1998, p. 12).

- The more appraisal systems are made objective, the more it is evident that there is no way to avoid their inherent subjectivity.
- If a manager does not effectively address employee behavioral problem, the manager herself may be regarded as a problem.

Despite—or perhaps because of—the vexing, intractable nature of personnel appraisal, political pressures to "just do it and get it over with" are substantial. Although members of the general public know appraisal problems from their own work experiences, they nevertheless make an odd assumption: because evaluations are done successfully (somewhere) in business bureaucracies, they should especially be used in government agencies. For this human resource function, myth is not merely more important than reality: it often seems to be reality. The chapter begins with the evolution, as eerie as it is, of the appraisal function. Common types of appraisal, who does them, and typical—if robust—rating errors are then examined. That section climaxes with a discussion of the fundamental and beguiling reason for these problems. Diagnosis completed, attention then shifts to ways to design and improve evaluation programs, including an examination of disciplinary systems. This leads to a specification of the characteristics of a system that could withstand legal scrutiny. The chapter closes by sketching future trends in this administrative function. The overall objective is to describe the processes, problems, and paradoxes, as well as to critique the premises on which many appraisal systems are built.

▪▪ EVOLUTION

The paradoxical nature of service ratings—rarely do they deliver in practice what is promised in theory—stems from the legacy of the spoils system (Chapter 1). Aghast at widespread looting, plunder, and corruption during the spoils system era, good-government groups, armed with scientific management techniques such as job analysis (Chapter 5), sought to guarantee competence by insulating employees from political influence. Reformers established merit systems, closely monitored by nonpartisan civil service commissions. As these systems evolved, the emphasis was on recruiting meritorious people (Chapter 3) and protecting them from partisan entanglements. Less attention was devoted to divining ways to evaluate their work; after all, the system was designed to select competent workers in the first place.

It should not be surprising, then, that although concern for appraisal has existed for a long time (Congress mandated evaluations as early as 1842), the topic for decades was a stepchild slighted by both academicians and managers. The dramatic growth of government during the Great Depression and World War II, however, culminated in considerable interest in appraisal programs so that by the 1950s many jurisdictions had adopted them.

Characteristic of the times, an underlying faith in science to control, direct, and measure human performance resulted in the continuing search for—if not the perfect evaluative scheme—then at least ways to improve existing technology. Thus, many of the early systems, based on personal traits (discussed in the next section), were widely criticized for failing to differentiate between employees: virtually everyone received a "satisfactory" rating.

Aiming to correct this problem, the 1978 Civil Service Reform Act sought to evaluate employees, not on subjective characteristics but on objective, job-related performance standards. This effort, in turn, produced its own set of problems so that the National Performance Review (NPR, 1993, p. 36) declared it to be dysfunctional and detrimental to the success of governmental programs. For its part, in calling for simplified, decentralized, team-based evaluation, the NPR deemphasized the need for results-oriented appraisals. This approach, as discussed below, has not been any more successful than it has been in business. Today, service ratings remain as the most criticized area of human resource management and seem to be endured only because realistic alternatives are not currently in wide use. Abandoning the function altogether may not be a solution, however, because human beings have always made informal or formal evaluations of others. The challenge is to decide what to appraise in a manner that meets the needs of the organization and the individual. Ironically, "the primary problem supervisors encounter is not *knowing* who are the best performers, but rather *measuring* and *documenting* performance differentials" (Perry, 2003, p. 147; emphasis in original).

▪▪ COMMON TYPES OF APPRAISAL

Because there are few jobs with clear, comprehensive, objective output measures that eliminate the need for judgment, the most widely used evaluation methods are judgmental in nature.[2] What differentiates them is the degree of subjectivity that is likely in the judgments made. The approaches can be readily grouped as trait-, behavior-, and **results-based systems**. Recognize, however, that there is considerable variety in available techniques. Not only are they frequently combined with one another, but also different systems may be used for various types of employees.[3] Only the most familiar are examined here, and even these, albeit in differing degrees, produce evaluations that are either **deficient** (not all pertinent factors are considered) or **contaminated** (irrelevant considerations are included).

Trait-Based Systems

Trait-based systems require assessments on the degree to which someone possesses certain desired personal characteristics deemed important for the job (Exhibit 10.2). Despite the inherent subjectivity of this format, it continues to be practiced because human beings frequently make trait judgments about others in daily life. The approach, although often inscrutable, seems intuitively sensible as a result.

Exhibit 10.2	Examples of Trait Appraisal, a Behaviorally Anchored Rating Scale, and Management by Objectives

Trait Appraisal

	Excellent	Good	Fair	Poor	Failure
Loyalty					
Manner					
Attitude					
Drive					
Adaptability					
Knowledge					
Decisiveness					

Behaviorally Anchored Rating Scale

Dimension: Communication Skills

Far exceeds requirements	Talks with God
Exceeds requirements	Talks with angels
Meets requirements	Talks with himself
Needs improvement	Argues with himself
Lacks minimum requirements	Loses those arguments

Management by Objectives*

Objectives for This Evaluation Period	Percent of Job	Present Status	Types of Measures (how objectives will be measured)	Results Achieved	Rating*
Objective One					
Objective Two					
Objective Three					

Employee Signature	Supervisor Signature

Note: *Exceeded, met, or not met objectives.

There are colorful iterations of such graphic rating scales based on the characteristics chosen, their definitions (if any), and the number of categories (adjective or numeric) used. None, however, overcomes serious validity and reliability questions. Thus, because it is difficult to define personality characteristics (much less the extent to which someone has them), subordinates may become suspicious, if not resentful, especially because this technique has little value for the purpose of performance improvement. Human traits, after all, are relatively stable aspects of individuals.

This is not to suggest that vivid personal characteristics are unimportant in job performance; individuals can hardly perform without them. And people routinely make trait judgments about one another because they can be a powerful way to describe someone, so powerful that recalling something about a person typically elicits a personal trait. Indeed, the use of flexible, subjective criteria seems inevitable, especially for ambiguous managerial jobs. The problem is valid measurement. When used with accurate job descriptions and trained evaluators, such ratings may become more credible. Even when the traits measured are job related (e.g., job knowledge, dependability), however, a landmark court opinion (*Brito v. Zia Co.,* 1973) criticized their subjective nature because the results were not anchored in or related to actual work behavior.[4]

Just as trait rating is no longer likely to be used alone, neither is the narrative essay technique; in fact, in one form or another written descriptions often supplement most appraisal formats. Because individuals are unique, a thoughtful commentary can provide personal, intimate, and detailed information. Done well, such an essay includes an employee's strengths and weaknesses, developmental needs, and potential for advancement. The premise of the approach is that a candid statement is at least as useful as more-complicated techniques. Or maybe not.

The "anything goes" nature of these essays lends them to rater idiosyncrasies, subjectivity, and pop psychology. Their interesting, sometimes ambiguous, statements (e.g., "When it comes to self-improvement, Van Westman has great potential") make comparisons virtually impossible. Subject to a wide variety of rater errors (see discussion in a later section), essay-type appraisals are often deficient and contaminated, thereby unreliable and invalid. Although they may be of value to the employee, such reviews are of limited use to anyone else. In their pure, stand-alone form, then, narratives are rarely used.

Behavior-Based Systems

Unlike trait-focused methods, which emphasize who a person is, **behavior-based evaluation systems** attempt to discern what someone actually does. The relatively tangible, objective nature of these systems makes them more legally defensible than personality scales. In point of fact, civil rights legislation from the middle of the last century led to the development of a number of tools that concentrate on behavioral data, two of which are considered here.

The **critical incident technique** is used to record behaviors that are unusually superior or inferior. It can be implemented in a responsive and flexible manner; supervisors can be trained to pay more attention to incidents of an exceptional behavior in some performance areas at certain times and in other areas in different periods (Halachmi, 1995, p. 326). A critical incident log may be helpful in supporting other appraisal methods.

Important drawbacks, however, include its "micro management" feature: supervisors keep a "book" on people; mistakes, rather than achievements, may be more likely to be recorded because employees are supposed to be competent. Another concern is that subordinates may engage in easily documented activities while hiding errors and neglecting tasks not readily observed. In addition, valuable, steady performers, not generally involved in spectacular events, may be overlooked. Halachmi (1995) also noted that the record could be incomplete or unreliable because of the rater's knowledge or the nature of the appraisee's job—either one of which makes comparisons between individuals problematic. The anecdotal nature of the method, in short, is both its strength and its weakness.

The **behaviorally anchored rating system** (BARS) builds on the incident method as well as the graphic rating scales discussed in the previous section. It defines the dimensions to be evaluated in behavioral terms and uses critical events to anchor or describe different performance levels (Exhibit 10.2). When introduced in the 1960s, BARS was claimed to be a breakthrough technology because raters could match observed activity on a scale instead of judging it as desired or undesired (Halachmi, 1995, p. 330). Because the scales are developed from the experience of employees, it was also thought that user acceptance was likely. As a job-related system, it remains relatively invulnerable to legal challenge.

Yet the method is often not practical because each job category requires its own BARS; either for economic reasons or the lack of employees in a specific job, the approach is often infeasible. Second, Gomez-Mejia, Balkin, and Cardy (2007, p. 215) argued that if personal attributes are a more natural way to think about other people, then requiring supervisors to use BARS (or for that matter, any nontrait technique) is merely a sleight of hand that introduces psychometric errors (discussed in Rating Errors section below). Indeed, they cited research findings that both employers and employees prefer trait systems. Other studies demonstrate that managers and staff personnel do not make much of a distinction between BARS and trait scales (e.g., Wiersma & Latham, 1986). Not surprisingly, there is little evidence to support the superiority of this technique over other approaches.

Finally, most experts do not find that the potential gains in using BARS warrant the substantial investment required in time and resources. Thus, where this technique is used, it often plays a residual role, limited to either a small number of selected job categories or to the developmental function of personnel appraisal. Overall, then, whatever else trait- and behavior-based systems may do, they are largely silent on the question of what an employee is to accomplish.

Results-Based Systems

As measures of neither personal characteristics nor employee behaviors, results-based systems or outcome-oriented approaches attempt to calibrate one's contribution to the success of the organization. Although "results" have always been of keen interest to administrators, **management by objectives** (MBO)[5] promises to achieve substantial organization-individual goal congruence. Introduced in the 1950s, this most common results-focused approach establishes agency objectives, followed in cascading fashion by derivative objectives for every department, all managers, and each employee. These systems require specific, realistic objectives, mutually agreed-upon goals, interim progress reviews, and comparison between actual and expected accomplishments at the end of the rating period (Exhibit 10.2).

Despite its rationality and evidence of effectiveness, MBO, like other appraisal techniques, has serious drawbacks:

- Although development of objectives may not be as technically demanding as BARS, the process nevertheless is quite time consuming; an effective program takes three to five years to implement. (Accordingly, few agencies adopt the formal hierarchical process to ensure organization-department-manager-employee linkage.)

- There likely will be conflicting objectives, differing views on the appropriateness of the objectives, and disagreements about the extent to which objectives are mutually agreed upon—and fulfilled.
- Because it focuses on short-term goals, a compulsive "results-no-matter-what" mentality can produce predictable quality and ethical problems, as anything that gets in the way of the objective gets shunted aside. (How a job is done often is as critical as its output.)
- Not only is establishing equally challenging objectives for all people difficult, but also expectations that they will invariably improve (an MBO-induced "treadmill") also can lead to user acceptance problems.
- The technique can stifle creativity because employees may define their job narrowly (as they "work to quota"), leaving some problems undetected and unresolved.
- Teamwork is likely to suffer if people become preoccupied with personal objectives at the expense of collegiality. (They may fulfill their goals but not be good all-around performers.)
- The method may not assist in the employee development function because performance outcomes do not indicate how to change.

In short, results-oriented approaches are susceptible to contamination errors when results are affected by factors beyond employee control and deficiency problems: when results are emphasized, important "organizational citizenship" behaviors may be discouraged. And supervisors must devote considerable effort to such result-based performance schemes, which provokes comments like this one from a federal manager: "I don't have time to do evaluations, now, so how would I have the time to do this?" (Ziegler, 2004, p. 6). The sort of rational planning embodied in MBO is seldom effective; human condition is too complicated and human reason too frail. "MBO works," Peter F. Drucker, the founder of the technique, wrote, "if you know the objective; 90 percent of the time you don't" (cited in Gilson, 2007); the law of unintended consequences likely will prevail. Treating people like the responsible professionals that they are, instead of rational robots, is likely to produce superior results. "You can be totally rational with a machine," wrote Akio Moriata, founder of Sony. "But, if you work with people, sometimes logic has to take a back seat to understanding." Nevertheless, MBO, in particular, remains a popular technique to appraise managers because their roles are often ambiguous; it does provide a measure of accomplishment against predetermined objectives.

Commentary: "Man plans, God laughs" (Yiddish Proverb)

To summarize, Exhibit 10.3 specifies the promise, problems, and prospects of the three categories of appraisal. Although the intuitive appeal of trait rating is considerable, it is highly susceptible to both contamination and deficiency errors. Its future potential, accordingly, is limited to a supplemental role in the review process because of subjectivity and vulnerability to court challenge. Systems based on employee behavior also hold substantial promise because they are job related—something most judges expect. They, too, are likely to play a modest role in the years ahead, however, largely because of their susceptibility to deficiency errors and, in the case of BARS, high technical demands coupled with limited applicability. Results-derived approaches, like the others, have face validity but often suffer from a host of

Exhibit 10.3	Promise, Problems, and Prospects of Person-Centered Appraisal Systems		
System	*Promise*	*Characteristic Problems*	*Prospects*
Trait based	high (intuitive appeal)	high (contamination and deficiency errors)	low (supplemental role)
Behavior based	high (job related)	average (susceptible to deficiency errors)	average (high technical demands)
Results based	high (face validity)	average (deficiency problems)	average (emphasizes accomplishments)

deficiency and implementation problems. Still, they do emphasize actual accomplishments, as opposed to personalities or behaviors, and therefore may survive litigation.

Although combined techniques can offer advantages, available research does not support a clear choice among methods. Because each has its own strengths and weaknesses, selecting one to cure a problem likely will cause a new problem; there is no foolproof approach. Notice, too, that all three systems are backward looking. Because there is no systematic continuous improvement process, they may be self-defeating as they perpetuate the organizational status quo. The better traditional appraisals are done, paradoxically, the more likely it is that the organization will remain the same. Hauser and Fay (1997, p. 193) wistfully argued that the search for the perfect instrument—a goal that has eluded industrial psychologists for more than 60 years—is now largely regarded as futile. Instead, they suggested, efforts to improve the overall process likely will provide much larger returns than developing (and redeveloping) seemingly better rating forms every time a new high official takes office. The technique used, then, is decidedly not the central issue in personnel appraisal because the type of tool does not seem to make much difference (Cardy & Dobbins, 1994). A National Research Council study report found no conclusive evidence to support claims that distinguishing between behaviors and traits has much effect on rating. Psychologically, supervisors form broad opinions that affect evaluation of actual work behaviors. There is little research data that rating systems based on job-specific factors produce results much different from those using general dimensions (Milkovich & Wigdor, 1991).

That is, available evidence indicates that judgments about performance are not necessarily correlated with results (Murphy & Cleveland, 1995) precisely because these decisions rely on cognitive abilities that are notoriously prone to error (see Rating Errors below). Compromised evaluations are common. Not surprisingly, the choice of a tool is less significant than the fact the employees often have little confidence in the abilities of managers to implement the tools effectively. It is not the assessment technique that fails to yield accurate evaluations; it is managers. The NPR (1993, p. 32) found, for instance, that "performance ratings are unevenly distributed by grade, gender, occupation, geographic location, ethnic group, and agency" (although shoe size was not mentioned). That is, technically sophisticated and well-designed systems do not operate in a vacuum; organizational culture, leadership credibility, employer-employee relations, and levels of trust affect the efficacy of appraisal processes. Stated differently, it is important to ensure that there is an alignment between organizational performance and individual performance (Riccucci & Lurie, 2001). The exact evaluation method used is less relevant than building a goal-oriented organization where people have productive attitudes toward work and each other (Palguta, 2001).

Appraisal software programs nonetheless promise to (a) enable managers to select predigested forms (or to design their own), (b) walk them through form completion (including tips and hints, provision of preprogrammed phrases and prompts for examples, and even reminders when appraisals are due), and (c) verify their work with arithmetical, logical consistency and legal checks before printing out a professional looking report. Prospective customers are assured that an automated system is "a snap" by one enthusiastic vendor. A balanced review of these programs, however, reveals that they run on algorithms with no knowledge of the organizational culture, job standards, or individual performance—problems likely to intensify in a virtual workplace. Indeed, they make the process too easy; managers should devote real thought to appraisals, and not simply point and click. The software contributes nothing to the most important part of service ratings: the manager-employee interview (discussed in a subsequent section).

∷ RATERS

Given that common appraisal methods are judgmental in character, an important question is, "Who makes this judgment?" Traditionally, there was one answer: the subordinate's immediate supervisor. Other knowledgeable information sources include the ratee, peers, computers, and outsiders.

Self-appraisals, based on the belief that the employee has important insights about how the job should be done, can provide valuable data, particularly when the supervisor and employee engage in joint goal setting. These evaluations are, however, subject to distortions including self-congratulation or, less likely, self-incrimination. (See Kunreuther, 2008, for a devastating critique of the technique.) People tend to be inadequate judges of their own performance. Inept individuals are often self-assured because they lack self-monitoring skills; their incompetence robs them of the ability to realize their own incompetence. It is well established, for instance, that many people attribute good performance to their own efforts and blame poor performance on other factors. These biases can be moderated if objective standards exist and the ratee is regularly provided candid feedback. Still, because these evaluations tend to focus on personal growth and motivation, they are best used for developmental rather than administrative purposes.

As work in some organizations has changed from a stable set of tasks done by one person to a more fluid ensemble of changing requirements done by groups of employees, **peer** or **team evaluation** becomes appropriate. In an agency culture high in trust where coworkers develop rating scales and have access to relevant information, such assessments can be accurate. When these conditions do not exist, supervisors likely will be reluctant to give up control, and subordinates will often see these techniques as a disruptive competition that can easily be sabotaged by lenient ratings or converted into "popularity contests." Thus, these reviews are often most useful when done anonymously and for developmental reasons.

The objective of **electronic monitoring** (via email and video surveillance, Web site blocking, GPS tracking) is to increase productivity, improve quality, and reduce costs. It does so by continuously collecting performance data, pinpointing problems, and providing immediate feedback (Flynn, 2008). When such monitoring provides objective performance appraisals, employee satisfaction and improved morale may result. Today, computer-generated statistics are the basis for evaluations of millions of office workers engaged in clerical, repetitive tasks. The virtual work site of the future is almost certainly going to expand the collection and use of such information. Indeed, as software becomes more sophisticated, a wide variety of occupations (e.g., medicine, engineering, accounting) are likely to undergo electronic scrutiny. When implemented without reasonable safeguards (e.g., employee access to data, rights to challenge erroneous records, rating decisions made on the basis of nonelectronic as well as electronic information), these programs can create an "electronic sweatshop" environment damaging creativity, morale, and health. If employees feel helpless, manipulated, and exploited, then most techniques eventually will be circumvented.[6]

Finally, multirater or **360° evaluation systems**—those that gather information from superiors, subordinates, peers, and citizens—by definition provide more data than other approaches. More data may produce more-reliable, but not necessarily more-valid, information. The administratively complex and time-consuming nature of these systems is compounded by distrust among peers and a lack of convergence among the different information sources. That is, managers may be confronted with a host of seemingly conflicting opinions—all of which may be accurate from their respective viewpoints. Systems that assure respondent anonymity and encourage participant responsibility, nevertheless, no doubt supply some useful feedback for improving both management processes and employee development. The value of the method reveals itself, paradoxically, when used as a developmental—not an evaluation—technique, an approach that reduces fear and encourages honesty. Organizations that use it this way foster a "development culture" that, in turn, results in higher performance (Carson, 2006). In short, although one's immediate supervisor is apt to play an important role in the rating process, feedback from other sources is increasingly seen as a way to obtain a more holistic understanding of performance (Society for Human Resource Management, 2000) since a third of American organizations use multirater systems. An effective program is one that is developed in a participatory manner, is pilot tested, and provides adequate training to both managers and employees. There has been little critical evaluation of 360° appraisal systems.

■ RATING ERRORS

The use of ratings assumes, rather naïvely, that the definition of job performance is clear, that direct measures are available to assess the employee—and that evaluators are reasonably objective and precise. Regardless of the appraisal instrument used, though, a large number of well-known errors, to be examined below, occur in the process. These result from

- cognitive limitations,
- intentional manipulation,
- organization influences, and
- human nature.

When they happen—and they are difficult to prevent—not only is the rater's judgment called into question, but also the resulting evaluation may leave the ratee unable to accurately judge her own performance.

Cognitive limitations. When confronted with large amounts of information, people generally seek ways to simplify that information. **Cognitive information processing theory** maintains that appraisal is a complex memory task involving data acquisition, storage, retrieval, and analysis. To process data, subjective categories are employed that in turn produce no less than five problems. Thus, **compatibility** ("similarity" or liking) **error** is potent because both compatibility and ratings are person focused. Indeed, most employees believe their supervisor's liking of them influences evaluations (Cardy & Dobbins, 1994).[7] When the Wei dynasty in China rated the performance of its household members in the third century, the philosopher Sin Yu noted, "An imperial rater of nine grades seldom rates men according to their merits, but always according to his likes and dislikes." This error may be tempered, however, to the extent that managers like good performers. In other words, flaws in rating can represent, paradoxically, "true" performance levels, and removing such errors may not improve accuracy! (Hauenstein, 1998). The next mental shortcut is the **spillover effect** (halo effect or black mark effect): that is, if the ratee does one thing exceptionally well (halo) or poorly (black mark), then that unfairly reflects on everything else. Third, the **recency effect** takes place when a major event occurs just prior to the time of the evaluation and overshadows all other incidents. **Contrast error** exists when people are rated relative to other people instead of against performance standards. Finally, **actor/observer bias** (partially alluded to earlier) occurs when subordinates, as actors, often point to external factors, whereas supervisors, as observers, attribute weak performance to employees. Ratings, in short, are as much a reflection of raters as they are of those being evaluated.

Intentional manipulation. The second general source of rating problems is that appraisals in many organizations are adroitly seen as a political, not necessarily a rational, exercise. Results are deliberately manipulated, higher or lower, than the employee deserves. The goal is not measurement accuracy but rather management discretion and organizational effectiveness. The Nuclear Regulatory Commission, for instance, "made a conscious decision to be more generous with its *performance* ratings" (Losey, 2008, p. 1; emphasis added) in order to boost retention, acknowledge increased workloads, and be more competitive with private industry. As stated by one expert, "It would be naïve to think of performance appraisal as anything other than a political process. Rating accurately is not always the goal of evaluators and there are many situations when providing *inaccurate* appraisal data is sound management" (Hauenstein, 1998, p. 428, emphasis added; also see Tziner, Murphy, & Cleveland, 2005).

Accordingly, **leniency** or friendliness **error** (the "Santa Claus" effect) is the consequence of a desire to maintain good working relationships, maximize the size of a merit raise, encourage a marginal employee, show empathy for someone with personal problems, or avoid confrontations (and appeals) with an aggressive worker.[8] This error is exacerbated when raters think that other supervisors are inflating their employees' evaluations. There is a consensus that when done for administrative purposes (as opposed to being done for developmental reasons) reviews tend toward leniency (Curtis, Harvey, & Ravden, 2005).

Fair appraisals, in short, are not necessarily accurate. Indeed, **severity error** (the "horns" effect) may be emphasized as a way either to send a message to a good performer that some aspect of his work needs improvement or to shock an average employee into higher performance. More than 70% of managers in one survey (Longenecker & Ludwig, 1990) reported that they deliberately inflated or deflated evaluations for such reasons. Note that the inherent conflict of interest present in supervisory evaluations is a powerful political reason likely to make the leniency effect prevail over other psychometric errors. That is, if all (or most) subordinate evaluations are inflated, then the supervisor may look like an effective manager; if the appraisals are not so inflated, then her management abilities may be called into question.[9] The employer, however, has an obligation to conduct appraisals with due care. This duty may be violated (as a result of the Santa Claus effect) when a poor performer receives satisfactory ratings and subsequently is subjected to attempts at termination.

Organizational influences. This leads to examination of a set of organizational influences that causes a variety of problems. The first is insufficient management commitment to performance appraisal. In light of the difficulties with various evaluation schemes, much skepticism, a sense of futility, and even doubts about the possibility of performance appraisal exist (Nigro, Nigro, & Kellough, 2007, p. 170). Investing heavily in these systems, then, does not make a lot of sense for some administrators. The daily press of business makes them a peripheral, not central, responsibility. Appraisals are often isolated not only from getting the job done, but also from organizational planning and budget strategies. There are few incentives—and sometimes genuine disincentives—to use appraisal as a management tool. Why convert an acceptable employee into a hostile one when it can be reported that he meets expectations? Employee reviews, then, are done for the sake of evaluation: an irrelevant, once-a-year formality to complain about, complete, and forget in the service of administrative rules. Such programs quickly become "organizational wallpaper" that exist in the background, but are not expected to add value.

Such an attitude can produce the **error of central tendency** (if not leniency), where nearly all employees are rated satisfactorily—if for no other reason than that higher or lower scores may require time-consuming documentation. This "error," in turn, is reinforced by the **no money effect**—that is, either there are insufficient funds to distribute or they are awarded on an across-the-board basis (see also Chapter 7). All of these problems are exacerbated if reviews are tied, as they often are, to salary decisions. When mandated by organizational policy, appraisals tend to be less accurate and helpful for developmental purposes as employees and managers focus on monetary rewards. Performance pay plans (Chapter 7) raise the stakes in appraisal, making the already-existing problems more severe. Evaluations, in fact, may be done to support a decision to offer a raise, rather than the other way around.

Human nature. Overall, cognitive, political, and organizational limitations help explain the reasons for rater error. Although some of these constraints can be addressed in training (see Improving the Process, below), something more fundamental lies at the root of personnel appraisal difficulties: human nature. Its pertinent aspects are revealed by risk aversion, **implicit personality theory**, conflicting role expectations, and personal reluctance.

Defending one's judgment in open court is not something most relish; as a result, it is natural that supervisors reduce risk by being aware of all possible pitfalls in the appraisal process. Because reviews are often tied to pay, the well-known tendency to avoid supplying negative feedback is exacerbated (especially in performance pay programs) if it means inflicting financial harm on employees. When negative information must be conveyed, managers have three options: avoid giving it, delay giving it, or distorting it. The latter option is often the most viable, if inaccurate (Curtis et al., 2005, p. 45). A paradox arises, however, when playing safe through leniency may invite a legal challenge on the grounds that appraisals do not differentiate employees by performance (Halachmi, 1995, p. 325).

Second, implicit personality theory suggests that people generally judge the "whole person" based on limited data (stereotyping based on first impressions, or the spillover effect); ratings then tend to justify these global opinions rather than accurately gauge performance. Conflicting role expectations, third, are inherent in the appraisal process because evaluators must reconcile being a helpful coach with acting as a critical judge. In playing these roles, administrators (as noted earlier) also, in effect, evaluate themselves. Human nature suggests that better-than-deserved ratings will occur because one's own managerial skills may be called into question should employees receive poor evaluations.

Last, appraisal systems are complicated by the understandable distaste that people have for formally evaluating others. Because there is no such thing as infallible judgment, when administrators must take responsibility for judging the worth of others, "it is dangerously close to a violation of the integrity of the person" (McGregor, 1957, p. 90). Most people, especially in light of all the other questions about the reliability and validity of personnel appraisal, are as reluctant to judge others as they are to be judged themselves. It is onerous, in other words, to "play God."

It is little wonder, then, that the sentiment expressed in this aphorism is shared by many: "Appraisal is given by someone who does not want to give it to someone who does not want to get it." More formally, "Employees and supervisors alike dread the end-of-the-year annual performance appraisal cycle, when productivity plummets for several weeks and hard feelings translate into grievances. The paperwork, damage to self-esteem, and drops in productivity are simply not worth [it]" (Beecher, 2003, p. 464).[10] Such problems are not confined to American institutions, as the Chinese experience suggests (Exhibit 10.4). Lest one think that human nature in its various forms inevitably makes personnel appraisal a hopeless task, one veteran county manager provides a balanced defense of this human resource function (see Exhibit 10.5, and McElveen, 2000).

To summarize, because many jobs are not amenable to objective assessment and quantification, ratings typically incorporate nonperformance factors—for all the reasons discussed above. When this occurs, of course, it leads to a violation of the most revered principle of the human resource management field: Appraisals evaluate performance, not the person.[11] Verisimilitude trumps veracity. When this happens, issues of law and liability arise (see key legal principles and their relationship to appraisals identified in Exhibit 10.6). Suggestions for limiting liability in the personnel evaluation process based on selected problems include the following:

- Harassment or constructive discharge. Require employees to notify employer of any conditions related to job, job performance, or appraisals (e.g., supervisor bias or improper conduct) that allegedly are so severe as to require quitting. Establish and consistently follow procedures to promptly investigate and eliminate any such offending conditions or conduct by supervisors or other employees to avoid claim that employer tacitly accepted or approved of harassment.
- Age discrimination. Train supervisors to avoid age-loaded comments in verbal or written appraisals. Update performance criteria as technology changes to avoid pretext claims when older workers are laid off for lack of newer skills.
- Disability discrimination. Review recommendations and appraisal results for evidence of perceived ("regarded as") discrimination. Ensure that only essential functions are evaluated. Train supervisors to identify reasonable accommodations in performance criteria and appraisal procedures on an interactive basis in a discrete and confidential manner.

Exhibit 10.4   Personnel Appraisal in Chinese Public Service

As a result of the economic boom during the last generation, China is seen as an important model in a globalizing world economy. Reforms in government, accordingly, have sought to more appropriately fit a market economy. Key factors animating change include these:

- Hierarchical loyalty is a highly prized cultural value.
- The Chinese Communist Party (CCP) plays a leading role in the management of the civil service, including maintenance of complete personnel files on each public servant.
- Decentralization of personnel management decision making, following international trends, has taken place, but the hegemonic role of the CCP ensures that the civil service remains more centralized than in many other nations.

Reforms have been problematic because employees tend to be rewarded on the basis of organizational loyalty and political reliability, at the expense of technical competence. A gap exists between national policy makers (who look to increase economic gains) and agency managers (who emphasize organizational harmony, a cultural factor threatened by use of foreign personnel techniques). Indeed, China as a whole may be understood as a conflict and convergence of Confucianism, socialism, and capitalism, with the former having the most enduring effect.

In 1993, the State Council launched civil service reform aimed specifically at personnel evaluation to improve administrative efficiency, enhance government capacity, and reduce corruption. The ministry of personnel directed that appraisals should be based on merit (work ability and accomplishments) and political integrity (support and understanding of party ideology). The linkage of salary to rank and years of service indicates that seniority is a significant factor as well. The goal of good relations with superiors and coworkers in Chinese culture suggests that personal loyalty complements these criteria.

The changes included appraisal committees, self-reviews, and supervisory evaluations in an attempt to institutionalize openness, fairness, and participation. Employee reviews soon experienced many of the problems discussed in this chapter. The system was rife with inaccurate data, and supervisors were not held responsible for falsifying records. Exacerbating the situation was that government found it difficult to retain and motivate personnel when more lucrative careers were available in China's surging business sector.

Although the importance of performance appraisal is understood by leaders, the changes underestimated the importance of maintaining organizational harmony in a collectivistic culture. The prevailing system is characterized by authority networks composed of reciprocal relations and mutual obligations. Managers reward loyal followers with career opportunities, raises, training, and moral support, while subordinates aid superiors during occasions such as performance ratings or political strife. To maintain goodwill, harmony is critical. In an environment valuing interpersonal associations and personal trust, people tend to avoid confrontation and to save face. Social accord and stability is seen as a priority, one that is more important than individual rights; individuals are regarded as a part of a network of social connections (*guanxi*) where personal interests are subordinated to the group.

This conflicts with more-discriminating evaluation techniques used in Western societies, notably the United States. Because both managers and employees in China find the cost of revealing each other's performance weaknesses too high (i.e., the disruption of comity), foreign systems that assess performance by pointing out weaknesses have not been used effectively. The impact of the reform is undermined when managers cover up deficiencies of subordinates and manipulate appraisal results. In return, workers overlook the faults of managers. Nearly all civil servants are rated excellent or satisfactory and receive merit awards because pointing out each other's problems risks deep resentment and, in the end, conflict. When systems are attempted that require that some employees be rated as less than satisfactory, then in practice it is newcomers who receive poor ratings. If there are no junior employees, then everyone in the office takes turns getting a low score.

In countries that focus on harmony, appraisal systems might be designed to bring out the importance of each person to the organization by treating each one as a stakeholder. Perhaps gainsharing systems (Chapter 7) would be beneficial so that the gains derived from department productivity could be distributed among the managers and staff. An approach that emphasizes the positive aspects of employee performance, in any case, likely will be more efficacious than one that damages agency well-being and interpersonal relationships. While it may be true that as the market economy expands the importance of personal relations may diminish, it is also true that a nation's cultural heritage cannot be easily transformed; reforms can only be adapted to that heritage.

Source: Benson, Debroux, Yuasa, & Zhu, 2000; Black, Gregersen, & Mendenhall, 1992; Burns, 1999; Chou, 2008; Gregersen, Hite, & Black, 1996; Muñoz, 2006; Yang & Zheng, 2003; Yang, Zheng, & Li, 2006; Zhao, 1994.

- Defamation or misrepresentation. Establish procedures to control or avoid providing false performance information (favorable or unfavorable).
- Negligence. Keep employees advised if performance is poor so they cannot contest discharge by claiming performance would have improved but for faulty evaluation process. (Adapted from Smither, 1998, p. 78.)

If these problems are successfully confronted, and the evaluation and discipline process improved as discussed below, then it may be more realistic to take such steps to reduce potential problems than to abolish personnel reviews entirely.

■■ IMPROVING THE PROCESS

How would you like a job where every time you make a mistake, a big red light goes off and 18,000 people boo?

—Jacques Plante, hockey player

Designing an appraisal system requires not only establishing policies and procedures, but also obtaining the support of the entire workforce and its union or unions. Top officials need to publicly commit to the program by devoting sufficient resources to it and by modeling appropriate behavior. Managers, in turn, need to be convinced that the system is relevant and operational. Employees likewise should see it as in their interest to take it seriously. A profile (or "slice") task force, representing all these groups from different parts of the department, can then conduct a needs assessment by collecting agency archival and employee attitudinal data. It should then revise an existing system (or create a new one) based on the findings and test that system on a trial basis. This could be done in jurisdictions that allow customization to agency needs (more than half of state governments, for example) or as part of a government-sponsored pilot program.

| **Exhibit 10.5** | A Manager's View of Performance Appraisal: Theory in Practice |

Mary L. Maguire

Administrative Manager/Public Information Officer

Department of Fire and Rescue Services

Loudoun County, Virginia

Having nearly 30 years' experience with city and county government agencies, I have been on the giving and receiving ends of a wide array of evaluation methods. From early forms where we were judged on appearance to the more modern ones where we are judged on contributions to the organization, each has had its merits. The one that seems to be the most promising is our current performance management system. It is a multifaceted tool aimed at improving individual employee job performance. It is anticipated that through the effective use of this system managers and supervisors will be better equipped to help with the enhancement, motivation, and retention of employees (the county's most valuable resource), while achieving the goals of the organization.

From the minute a new employee sets foot through the door, they are provided instructions on the finer points of the system. Through classes and written guidelines, managers and subordinates are told that emphasis on the following skill sets is essential to be successful:

- Performance planning
- Coaching
- Counseling
- Documenting
- Recognizing and motivating employees
- Handling unsatisfactory employee performance
- Assessing performance

Although each piece is equally important, the attention focuses heavily on the beginning and end components: planning and assessment. This, so to speak, is where the "rubber meets the road"—where the employees believe they will be rewarded for their efforts. As one of many tools in the managerial toolbox, the planning and assessment components provide opportunities for the organization to show its commitment to its employees, while recognizing them for their contributions. The system is designed to ensure that all parties involved know up front what is expected. Through the other components—coaching, counseling, documenting, recognizing and motivating employees, and addressing unsatisfactory performance—supervisors are provided with additional tools for guiding and evaluating their employees. By effectively outlining expectations, maintaining open dialogues between manager and subordinate, keeping employees apprised of their progress, and redirecting them when improvement is needed, everyone knows what to expect when it comes time for the year-end evaluation.

All this looks good on paper, but how does it really work? Annually, employees outline their goals as they relate to the department's mission and that of the county. The goals are then weighted based on relative importance. Both the employee and the supervisor develop and sign this plan; it can be modified as the person's duties evolve. In this way, there will be no surprises by the end of the evaluation cycle.

As the year draws to a close, the subordinate is asked to prepare a self-evaluation, while the manager develops his assessment. When they meet, an open dialogue helps clarify areas where the supervisor may have some concern. If consensus is reached and the employee has met the goals and objectives, she may receive a merit increase. If expectations were exceeded, then she may be nominated for a performance bonus. (If she is not in agreement with the evaluation, then she can make an appeal. It is interesting to note that employees are also afforded the opportunity to anonymously evaluate their supervisor.) During the meeting, a development of the upcoming year's plan will begin. Although this process can be quite time consuming and cumbersome, it is effective.

I was a bit dismayed, however, when I actually began comparing this process with a list of common appraisal defects. For every effort made to fight these defects, I could find example after example where the defects still exist. For instance, the system was designed so that we would not be evaluating for evaluation's sake. Although great pains were taken to eliminate this problem, many agencies find themselves scrambling at the end of the year to get the paperwork done. In addition, while the system was set up so that it can be modified at any time, this does not really occur. Employees continually find themselves being evaluated with respect to the goals found in outdated plans.

Managers also continue to pit people against one another and have a tendency to grade everyone the same, whether positively or negatively. And employees, not only supervisors, become victims of the halo effect. Employees might do a bang-up job on one little project: because they were recognized for their work on that assignment, the employee believes that he has exceeded the expectations on every other aspect of his evaluation, which can lead to great disappointment during the evaluation phase.

Furthermore, during economic downturns there is often little to nothing left to reward employees. Bonuses for exceptional performance are thrown out the window in an effort to cut taxes. Employees are given miniscule or no increases in salary for cost of living and even less for performance. Therefore, the exceptional performer who strives to do her best may receive the same increase as the average employee who is just meeting expectations. There is no incentive for doing well. Even more devastating is the fact that one of the organization's core values of recognizing its personnel as the primary resource for service delivery is compromised. The entire process, as a result, becomes suspect.

Despite its faults, there are benefits to this process. It provides guidance for future performance and is used to help further develop our staff. People at all levels have been involved in its design. Furthermore, they play an active role in the actual development of individual plans. The approach tries to use valid and reliable standards that are usually based on past performance. In addition, the standards are often measured against criteria established in the county. For instance, there are specific criteria for processing purchase orders. If met, then the employee would be rated fully successful. If able to complete the purchase order accurately in less time than allocated, thereby reducing costs, then the employee may be seen as exceeding the criteria. Supervisors are also provided ample opportunity to conduct the evaluation, and they are trained so that they are capable of doing it. Finally, the process provides for continual feedback. When properly documented this would, I believe, stand up in court. Although far from perfect, the performance management system still exceeds many of the subjective alternatives based on perception not performance. In light of the problems, why even bother with appraisal systems? We take the time because, when done correctly, they will provide an effective mechanism that can recognize and reward employees while providing the necessary documentation that shows the organization is successfully meeting its goals.

Exhibit 10.6	Selected Legal Principles and Laws Relating to Performance Appraisal	
Legal Principle or Law	Summary	Relationship to Appraisals and the Employment Relationship
Employment at will	Status under which the employer or employee may end an employment relationship at any time	Allows the employer considerable latitude in determining whether and how to appraise
Implied contract	Nonexplicit agreement that affects some aspect of the employment relationship	May restrict manner in which employer can use results (e.g., may prevent termination unless for cause)
Violation of public policy	Determination that given action is adverse to the public welfare and is therefore prohibited	May restrict manner in which employer can use appraisal results (e.g., may prevent retaliation for reporting illegal conduct by employer)
Negligence	Breach of duty to conduct performance appraisals with due care	Potential liability may require employer to inform employee of poor performance and provide opportunity to improve
Defamation	Disclosure of untrue information that damages an employee's reputation	Potential liability may restrict manner in which negative performance information can be communicated to others
Misrepresentation	Disclosure of untrue favorable performance information that causes risk of harm to others	Potential liability may restrict willingness of employer to provide references altogether, even for good former employees
Fair Labor Standards Act (FLSA)	Imposes (among other things) obligation to pay overtime to nonexempt (nonmanagerial) employees	Fact that employee appraisals may influence determination that employee functions as supervisor or manager and is therefore exempt
Family and Medical Leave Act (FMLA)	Imposes (among other things) obligation to reinstate employee returning from leave to similar position	Subjecting employee to new or tougher appraisal procedures upon return may suggest that employee has not been given similar position of employment

Source: Adapted from J. W. Smither (Ed.), *Performance Appraisal: State of the Art in Practice* (San Francisco: Jossey-Bass, 1998), p. 52. © Copyright 1998 by Jossey-Bass. Adapted with permission.

It is, of course, possible to marginalize formal requirements entirely. In one major unit of a large hospital, a charismatic department manager decided that whatever the administration of the hospital did, he was going to run his facilities department on the basis of total quality management. Well in advance of the hospital's annual tedious performance appraisal drill, he gathered his troops together, reviewed the hospital's sorry form, and told them that what it represented was the starting point for them to practice their *kaizen*—continuous improvement—skills.

"What do we need to do, given the fact that this basic form is mandated, in order to complete it well enough to keep the personnel monkeys off our backs but also get some good out of the process for ourselves?" he asked his team. He funded a series of weekly pizza meetings for a task force of facilities employees who were charged with developing an answer to his question that everyone supported enthusiastically (Grote, 1996, p. 351).

Finessing the system may be faster, more flexible, and just as effective as formally reforming it. The design chosen involves numerous key technical questions, many of which were discussed earlier. These include selection of the most useful tool(s), as well as raters, based on system objective, practicality, and cost. Training is needed in an effort to minimize the various kinds of errors previously examined. Yet it is generally acknowledged, however, that mere awareness of these problems is unlikely to affect behavior. Instead, raters must engage in and receive feedback from role-plays, simulations, and videotaped exercises. Evaluators also need training in interpersonal skills to conduct appraisal interviews effectively.

Monitoring performance in the period between plan approval and formal appraisal includes frequent positive or corrective feedback based on performance, not personality. When performance is monitored conscientiously throughout the year, the actual evaluation will then simply confirm what has already been discussed.[12] Stated differently, the process of performance management is a continuous one involving coaching, development, accountability, and—both last and least—assessment. In fact, the traditional competitive approach to personnel appraisal is misplaced if the goal is to develop people and promote strong working relationships among managers and employees. Bersin (2007) identified seven elements that should constitute appraisal (goal setting, alignment of individual and organizational goals, self-assessment, 360 reviews, managerial appraisal, competency assessment, development planning), six of which emphasize coaching and development and only one (managerial appraisal) that does not. The job of the manager is to identify strengths in people and move them into the right job. A coaching-based, goal-centric, employee-engaged approach can change the way one thinks about performance management and the role of appraisal.

Finally, the evaluation process culminates in the appraisal interview. In preparing for the meeting, the employee may do a self-assessment, and managers should collect necessary information and complete, in draft form, the rating instrument. Although a collaborative problem-solving approach is effective, most managers use a one-way "tell-and-sell" technique in which they inform subordinates how they were rated and then justify the decision (Wexley, 1986). No matter the approach, supervisors should use the event to support the policies and practices of the entire system and be trained in goal setting, communication skills, and positive reinforcement.

Thus, before the interview, communicate frequently with subordinates, get training in appraisal interviewing, and use a problem-solving approach. During the session, judge specific performance (not personality), be an active listener, avoid destructive criticism, and set mutually agreeable future objectives. Afterward, periodically assess progress toward goals, and make rewards contingent on performance (Cascio, 2006, pp. 357–360). Although conducting a good interview requires a great deal of skill and effort, many managers say that having an honest exchange is the hardest part of the entire process. Most do not do it (Pickett, 2001), and those who do see little or no value in doing such interviews (London, 1995). Yet, as Amy DelPo (2007, pp. 121–122) pointed out, constructive criticism is exactly that: a positive force for change. Straightforward, specific, balanced, and encouraging feedback fulfills the developmental function of performance appraisal. Employees must be reassured that they are valued and that the rater believes in them. Indeed, this interview could be the last one (see Exhibit 10.7).

Like appraisal, employee discipline and discharge (discussed in Disciplinary Systems below) can be awkward and difficult. Indeed, secondary only to personnel appraisal, managers dislike taking disciplinary actions, generally for many of the same reasons (cognitive limitations, intentional manipulation, organizational influences, human nature). The process can be excruciating because administrators

- may not have kept good records needed as a basis of discipline,
- do not want to spend any more valuable time dealing with poor performers than they already do,
- prefer to avoid putting the office climate at risk by taking action,
- might believe that disciplinary actions will not be effective—partly because the employee likely has years of satisfactory evaluations, and
- may have been corrupted by the subordinate who could have evidence of inappropriate or wrongful managerial behavior most often involving money, power, and/or sex.[13]

Not surprisingly, officials prefer to avoid taking adverse action. That is both understandable and unacceptable. The goal, accordingly, should be to reduce the need for adverse action, and when it is necessary, make it as easy as possible to use.

◼◼ DISCIPLINARY SYSTEMS

For the most part, employees discipline themselves by conforming to what is considered acceptable behavior simply because it is the sensible thing to do. Self-discipline can be encouraged when people are treated like adults—i.e., the organization uses an "open book" management style, offers opportunities for input into decisions, and makes employees comfortable when "speaking truth to power." Yet mistakes are made that require attention, and the test of a well-managed agency "is not how many personnel problems arise, but how effectively" they are addressed (Wise, Clemow, Murray, Boston, & Bingham, 2005, p. 181). The need for managers to use best practices in the disciplinary process is illustrated by the availability of professional liability insurance to safeguard one's livelihood and career. That is, the manager—not the agency's human resource or legal office—is the one accountable for the decision.

The term "discipline" is best understood as orderly conduct at work achieved by self-control and respect for agency rules. When performance problems (failure to satisfactorily complete assignments) or misconduct issues (insubordination, document falsification, loafing, carelessness, fighting, drug use) occur, the personnel appraisal and/or discipline systems may be utilized to improve performance. Factors to consider when using these systems include problem severity, duration, frequency, extenuating circumstances, organizational policies and employee training, agency past practice, and management support.

Exhibit 10.7   Final Interview: Exit and Termination Sessions

Nothing happens until it happens to you.

—Anonymous

The best time to obtain an employee's opinions is when he is fully committed to the agency. It is also true, however, that **exit interview**s and termination sessions are a unique opportunity to receive feedback on a wide variety of issues such as employee recruitment, training, evaluation, and retention. Such interviews, when supplemented with employee satisfaction surveys, can yield interesting information.

Many organizations do not conduct exit interviews; others may use online questionnaires or have the human resources department conduct interviews. Either of these two options suggests that the employee is not important enough to be worth the line manager's time. In contrast, virtually all agencies use **termination interviews**, as discussed in the section.

Whether the individual is leaving voluntarily or not, it is well documented that the emotions involved in job change are comparable to those found in divorce or death of a loved one. Indeed, people experience a five-stage cycle of grief: shock, resistance, acceptance, exploration of other opportunities, and commitment to a new future. Thus, the Golden Rule is key—i.e., how would you feel if you were in the situation? What would you expect your superiors to say? (Selden, 2008).

Possible interview questions, which should be adjusted depending on the reason for the session, include these:

- What do you value about the agency? What do you dislike?
- What would you tell the next person who does your job?
- Did you receive adequate feedback while you were here?
- Describe the characteristics of a person most likely to succeed here.
- Do you have any recommendations for agency human resource policies?
- Was there a single factor in the decision to leave?
- If you were asked to consider working here again, what would you say?

The decision to quit a job, or the reaction to being fired, is personal and often complex, so receiving clear answers to such questions may not be a given. The emotional stress of leaving, under even the best circumstances, can produce unreliable statements.

Some things an employee should consider before participating in a voluntary exit interview are:

- Is the interview anonymous or does a document (such as a questionnaire) need to be signed?
- Is the reason for leaving any of the agency's business or could it be an invasion of your privacy?
- Why did the employer wait until now to ask your opinion?
- Will the organization really use comments for improvements or are they just trying to find out the "real" reason you are leaving?
- Might an exit interview result in "burning bridges," thereby putting future references at risk?

If the purpose of the meeting is termination, then the situation should be presented in a concise, considerate, final manner that avoids arguments about past behavior; explains outplacement services and how references will be handled; and includes delivery of a paycheck (Coleman, 2001). Discharges are best done at the end of the day when other staff have left, and the employee is allowed to return to his desk. All dismissal activities must preserve the person's dignity and privacy (also see Gentry, 2005, and Scott, 2007). Discussion of the adverse action with others should be restricted to those who have a legitimate need to know.

Not to be overlooked is how the final session is done can impact the people who remain in the agency. How well this event is managed provides insight into the manager's interpersonal skills when under the strain of losing an employee.

Sources: Adapted from Heathfield, 2007; Selden, 2008.

Given the nature of the issues involved, taking action is indispensable to ensure a productive workforce. Yet, paradoxically, officials may tolerate poor performers because they lack an understanding of agency rules, documentation, and top management support—to say nothing of fearing onerous employee grievances and/or false accusations of discriminatory behavior (MSPB, 1995). Indeed, managers may sidestep discipline procedures and write acceptable personnel reviews for marginal employees to avoid unpleasantness, something that may haunt them if there is a subsequent attempt to discharge someone for sustained inadequate performance.[14]

Simply demanding that managers "get tough" is not an efficacious approach because "a supervisor who is very effective at removing someone can nevertheless be ineffective at selecting good employees in the first place or at motivating superior performance from that majority of employees who are capable of doing good work" ("Firing Poor Performers," 2003). Critics also ignore that unsatisfactory performance needs to be addressed in a larger context comprising societal and organizational culture, compensation levels, and training. Those who focus on the difficulty of terminating workers overlook the utility of existing procedures that result in more than 10,000 separations per year in federal service—not counting those who resign first or those removed through layoffs ("Firing Poor Performers," 2003). They also overlook that performance improvement plans are often successful in rehabilitating employees. In short, although termination affects a small percentage of personnel, this is how it should be when human resource functions like selection and training operate effectively (Daley, 2008).

To protect both the individual and the institution, the use of appraisal and discipline must be for justifiable reasons. To ensure fair treatment, actions must be derived from written guidelines; be corrective not punitive; be based on the act, not personality; and be timely, consistent with previous cases, and proportionate to the problem. The evaluation will be only as good as the evidence on which it is based. Documentation is the cornerstone, and it commences with a prompt and thorough investigation. Records should include the date, location, and nature of any incident; the effects on the organization; prior actions by the person and agency; the decisions made and improvement anticipated; and the employee's reaction. Recognize that a manager's complaint about an employee is only an allegation until proven true; the burden of proof is on the agency to show how the employee's behavior negatively affected operations and the supervisor's actions were neither arbitrary nor capricious. If the administrator has performed his responsibility to train the worker and the worker fails, then appropriate adverse action is in the best interest of the organization.

Progressive punishment (or discipline) and **positive discipline** are two approaches used by organizations. For either to be productive, workers must know what the problem is, what change is expected, and the consequences of inaction. Progressive punishment, the most common policy, is the application of coercive measures by increasing degrees of severity: informal counseling, verbal warning or reprimand, written warning or reprimand, minor suspension, major suspension, and separation.

Because this approach can be autocratic, adversarial, and intimidating, some jurisdictions have replaced it with positive, nonpunishment discipline based on the premise that adults must assume responsibility for their own conduct (also see MSPB, 2008). Rather than treating people "worse and worse and expecting them to get better and better," affirmative discipline uses reminders instead of reprimands. More participative than punitive, the technique utilizes these steps:

- A conference to find a solution to the problem, with an oral agreement to improve
- A subsequent meeting, if reform is not accomplished, to determine why the agreed-upon solution did not work, with a written reminder that the solution is the responsibility of the individual as a condition of employment

- Paid leave time (a "day of decision"), if change is not forthcoming, wherein the employee is expected to return the next day either with a "last chance" specific written commitment or a decision to leave the agency.

In brief, the employee, not the employer, is the decision maker.

The principle underlying both approaches is a "just cause" standard: Was the investigation done properly? Was the employee aware of the rule violation? Was the standard reasonable? Was the rule in question violated? What mitigating circumstances merit consideration? Finally, have comparable cases occurred and how were they addressed? The premise is that a just procedure should help ensure a fair outcome.

The purpose of the system is not to win battles but to provide feedback and training to foster responsible employees. Many of the problems that managers experience during the discipline process can be reduced through training, establishing clear work rules, following procedures, and documenting actions taken (DelPo & Guerin, 2003; Guffey & Helms, 2001). The key is to understand the scope of one's administrative authority, focus on behavior (not the person), avoid decisions based on hearsay, use appropriate penalties, and follow through on the judgments made.

Although the objective of personnel appraisal and disciplinary systems is to ensure employee development and rehabilitation, the documentation they provide—including past personnel reviews—can be used to support termination decisions. Unlike much of the private sector, where employees can be arbitrarily dismissed for no reason or for any reason not contrary to law, public servants have constitutional rights as citizens to due process.[15]

There may be good grounds for action (deficient performance or egregious misconduct such as theft), but managers nonetheless can create serious problems if the process is not handled well (Wise et al., 2005). An adverse action is aimed at not only the employee, but also at any judge who may review it. It is imperative, therefore, that administrators, in consultation with the human resources department, follow established procedures, to avoid mistakes that could lead to organizational liability as well as to assist employees whose rights might have been violated.

While it is true that there are appeal processes available to fight termination—it is not supposed to be easy to fire employees for political or other illegitimate reasons—some 10,000 federal workers are discharged each year (Holan, 2007). It is also true that only 3% of workers win their jobs back using appeal and grievance systems (Gilson, 2007). Stated differently, poor performers are not a serious problem in government. The MSPB study (1999) determined that the conventional wisdom about the number of these employees, and the disposition of their cases, not only distracts consideration from developing additional approaches to them, but also diverts attention from other, more important workforce issues.

Because discharge is a painful event for both the individual and the organization, it is critical that it be done with care and deliberation. This means that it must be approached in a humane, confidential, professional, nonaccusatory, factual way, and that it be based on substantiated, legitimate business reasons consistent with similar cases (see Exhibit 10.7.). When people are treated fairly, wrongful discharge suits are unlikely to withstand legal scrutiny.[16] Employee termination is part of a manager's job: Doing it well is an opportunity to learn how to improve other human resource management functions such as recruitment, training, and appraisal. Officials, in brief, have the responsibility to address unacceptable behavior in a timely manner. Failing to demand even minimal competence implies that performance does not matter. This negatively affects the morale of contributing employees and can damage the reputation of the agency as a whole.

▪▪ SUMMARY AND CONCLUSION

The two hardest things in life to handle are success and failure.

—Anonymous

As an aid to distill this chapter, the characteristics a personnel appraisal system should contain to satisfy both employers and employees—and to survive a court challenge—are specified below. As discussed, however, implementing this human resource management function is fraught with paradoxes. Indeed, readers are invited to evaluate the extent to which the following standards are met by agencies in their jurisdictions:

1. The rating instruments, which should strive for simplicity rather than complexity, are derived from job analysis (Chapter 5).

2. Training is provided to all employees about the systems and to all managers in the use of the systems.

3. The appraisal is grounded in accurate job descriptions, and the actual ratings are based on observable performance.

4. Evaluations are completed under standardized conditions and are free of adverse impact (Chapter 2).

5. Preliminary results are shared with the ratee.

6. Some form of upper-level review, including an appeal process, exists that prevents a single manager from controlling an employee's career.

7. Performance counseling and corrective guidance services exist.

Although many systems may not compare favorably to such standards, recall that the crux of the appraisal problem is not system design. Instead, because evaluation is a matter of human judgment, the conundrum is how the plan and the information it generates are used. Typical barriers to effective appraisal include the absence of trust in the organization, supervisory training and top management support, rater accountability, and overall evaluation of the system itself (Roberts, 2003). Ways to overcome such barriers are providing constructive, nonthreatening feedback and coaching; avoiding numeric rating scales that pigeonhole employees and pit them against each other; ensuring multiple sources of data through use of peer reviews; and utilizing group evaluations. It might be argued, however, that if employees are given an important mission, provided training, and offered competitive salaries, then appraisal becomes epiphenomenal and redundant.

The perennial, melancholy search for the best "genuine fake" technique, nonetheless, relentlessly (sometimes shamelessly) continues. Peering into the century ahead, personnel appraisal will become—either more or less—complex. Should the long-standing preference for person-centered evaluations persist, then both organizational downsizing and workforce changes will likely complicate appraisals. The virtual workplace—unbound by time and space—is likely to exacerbate this situation.

Downsizing has been a one-two punch. Personnel offices have shrunk, placing more responsibilities on line managers. At the same time, the numbers of supervisors have been reduced, requiring the remaining ones to evaluate more subordinates. The potential for both system design and implementation problems, as a result, has increased. Several changes in the composition of the workforce also imply a more challenging climate for appraisals. Employees are becoming increasingly diverse, and evaluating people of all colors and cultures is surely more arduous than assessing a homogenous staff. Also, the fastest-growing part of the working population is contingent employees—temporaries, short-term contract workers, volunteers—who, by definition, present evaluation challenges.

Alternatively, should institutions begin to shift away from person-centered appraisal and toward **organization-centered** or process-centered appraisals, individual evaluations may be less complex in the years ahead—or perhaps abolished altogether (see Exhibit 10.8, and Coens & Jenkins, 2000). For example, one organization stopped doing the orthodox top-down appraisals and instituted APOP—the Annual Piece of Paper. The one-page, bottom-up review form simply summarizes ongoing daily feedback (there are no scores or future goals) by focusing on what the manager can do to make employee tasks easier and what gets in the way of accomplishing the job. Whether the appraisal function becomes more or less difficult in the 21st century, it is worth doing only if it is an integral part of the management system and if it helps both the institution and the individual develop to full potential.

Exhibit 10.8   Evaluating Organizations, Not Individuals

> *Body swayed to the music, O brightening glance, How can we know the dancer from the dance?*

> —William Butler Yeats, *Among School Children*

As this chapter shows, individual appraisal is a complex issue. Even when done with great care, it can be devastating to people and destructive to organizations. Although it may be true that management practices are seldom discarded merely because they are dysfunctional, it is also true that the reinventing government movement (Chapter 1) provides an opportunity to reexamine orthodox approaches to appraisal.

The premise of organization-centered evaluation is that quality services are a function of the system in which they are produced. Systems consist of people, policies, technology, supplies, and a sociopolitical environment within which all operate. Note that these parameters are beyond appraisee control; indeed, the employees themselves are hired, tasked, and trained by the organization. A person-only assessment, stated differently, is deficient if the goal is to comprehend all factors affecting performance. In a well-designed management system, virtually all employees will perform properly; a weak system will frustrate even the finest people.

Traditional, person-centered appraisal methods are based on a faulty, unrealistic assumption: that individual employees are responsible for outcomes derived from a complex system. Because an organization is a group of people working to achieve a common goal, the managerial role is to foster that collaboration. If the result is inadequate, then it is management's responsibility—and no one else's.

From a systems perspective, the causes of good or bad performance are spread throughout the organization and its processes. Many results in the workplace are outside the power of employees traditionally made responsible for those outcomes. When more than 90% of performance problems are the consequence of the management system (Deming, 1992), holding low-level minions accountable is a way of evading responsibility; the cause of most performance problems lies not within the individual employee but within the organization divined by its leaders.

(Continued)

(Continued)

Because employees have little authority over organizational systems, relevant appraisals should provide two kinds of feedback:

- System performance data automatically generated from statistical process controls (i.e., evaluation is built into the work process itself)
- Individual performance data—used primarily for developmental purposes—derived from anonymous multirater 360° evaluations (focusing on attributes such as teamwork, customer satisfaction, timeliness, communication skills, and attendance)

The key is to listen to customers of the process and emphasize continuous improvement. By making the system as transparent as possible, the focus can be kept on nonthreatening analyses of work processes and people's contributions to those processes. Such an approach would be organizationally valid, socially acceptable, and administratively convenient—key criteria for any appraisal method. Importantly, it would change the process from an often adversarial one to a more constructive collaborative effort.

Reflecting American individualism,[1] the field of human resource management has focused on people rather than systems. It is politically unlikely, therefore, that organizational appraisals will supplant individual ratings (indeed, when performance appraisals were abolished at one well-known federal government demonstration project in California, the project was terminated, partly because productivity improved). A number of public agencies (National Oceanic and Atmospheric Administration, Internal Revenue Service, Social Security Administration) and private companies (Motorola, Merrill Lynch, Procter & Gamble) have modified their approach to appraisals. To better reflect a systems perspective, they have incorporated teamwork (in addition to individual achievements), citizen/customer feedback (in addition to supervisory opinions), and process improvement (in addition to results) dimensions into their evaluations.

A more complete reform would be to clearly state a performance standard and then assume that most employees will do the job for which they were hired. Greg Boudreaux (1994), a manager at the National Rural Electric Cooperative, continued by saying that for the small number who do not do their jobs, "Investigate why. Some will need further training or management counseling. Some may be an actual problem. But deal with those problems on a case-by-case, and not through a generic, faculty performance appraisal system" (p. 24; also see Eckes, 1994).

Indeed, the approach described here is partly consistent with the most recent appraisal fad: performance management (Cedarblom & Permerl, 2002). This strategy emphasizes that managing performance (not merely appraisal but also planning, accountability, compensation, training) is key to institutional goal setting. Thus, performance management is a continuing cycle of goal setting, coaching, development, and assessment. From a systems perspective, however, it exemplifies the "wrong-problem problem." Yet it tries to solve the wrong problem precisely by emphasizing the individual, not the organization. The same criticism can be levied at multirater 360° evaluation systems, discussed earlier in this chapter.

Note:

1. This is an area where our myths may be more dangerous than our lies. The lone frontiersman and the outlaw gunslinger—largely products of Hollywood—were far less important in the American West than farmers raising barns together and shopkeepers settling in small towns. The myth also does not explain the wild popularity of team sports in contemporary life.

KEY TERMS

Actor/observer bias

Behaviorally anchored rating system (BARS)

Behavior-based evaluation systems

Cognitive information processing theory

Compatibility, "similarity," or liking error

Contaminated (evaluations)

Contrast error

Critical incident technique

Deficient (evaluations)

Electronic monitoring

Error of central tendency

Exit interview

Implicit personality theory

Leniency error (Santa Claus effect)

Management by objectives (MBO)

No money effect

Organization-centered evaluations

Peer (team) evaluations

Positive discipline

Progressive punishment

Recency effect

Results-based systems

Self-appraisals

Severity error

Spillover (halo, black mark) effect

Termination interview

360° evaluation systems (multirater systems)

Trait-based systems

EXERCISES

Class Discussion

1. "Inaccurate appraisals are often sound management." Discuss.

2. "You were hired to make our organization succeed and to make your boss look successful." Do you agree with this claim? Why or why not?

3. What would be the most appropriate rating instrument for a middle manager? Staff assistant? Telecommuter? Intern? Why?

4. Visit a local agency to determine why, how, and by whom appraisals are done there. Analyze the rating form used. Is it legally defensible? Report the findings to the class.

5. In theory, personnel appraisal can provide feedback on management processes such as selection, position management, training, and compensation. Given the many problems with appraisal, however, it often does not supply this information. Accordingly, appraisal has been called the "missing link" in human resource management. Comment.

Team Activities

6. "Performance appraisal seldom improves performance." Debate, with one team taking the affirmative and one team the negative position.

7. Using the "25 in 10" technique (Exhibit 0.3), discuss this statement: "The root problem in performance rating is not technical in nature."

8. David is a star performer who frequently irritates his coworkers and managers. The city's appraisal includes an interpersonal relations category, and his supervisor rates him low in this category as well as in other categories. Discuss this situation in the context of the paradoxes of freedom and needs (Introduction).

9. Does traditional performance appraisal help or hinder other personnel functions and their paradoxes?

Individual Assignments

10. Identify three of the most difficult rater errors. How can they be dealt with?

11. Most people, including supervisors, like to be liked. Discuss.

12. Whenever a rating is less than the best, or less than what the employee perceives her contribution to be, the manager is seen as punitive. Use examples to support your agreement or disagreement with this claim.

13. Use the last examination you took in any class to discuss the reasons for using performance appraisals—and their limitations.

14. Consider the tips for conducting a performance appraisal interview. Would they have helped you—either as a manager or employee—the last time you were involved in this situation?

15. "Regardless of the reason, when an employee is terminated the employer should assist the person to find other employment." Evaluate this claim.

16. Take an "imagination break" (Exhibit 0.3) and speculate about alternative futures for personnel appraisal.

NOTES

1. The chapter subtitle is purloined from Tyer (1983).

2. Whether or not such decisions should be relative (based on comparisons between employees) or absolute (based on performance standards) is largely settled because ranking is not the equivalent of rating employees. That is, relative judgments do not reveal how well someone actually performed; thus, they are not job related. The 1978 Civil Service Reform Act, as a result, does not permit ranking methods (e.g., simple rankings from best to worst or forced-distribution techniques such as the bell-shaped curve) for evaluation of federal employees. Relative approaches, however, may be used for other, related administrative matters such as promotions, pay, and layoffs. Most jurisdictions traditionally make these judgments annually to coincide with the fiscal year, although more-frequent informal assessments tied to project completion are quite valuable.

3. It is neither feasible nor desirable, therefore, to discuss all these instruments. To do so would be to encourage the notion that the problem of performance measurement is merely one of technique; it is, rather, a process, not a form.

4. Despite all these problems, the technique has obvious intuitive appeal because traits may simply be a shorthand way of describing a person's behavior. This may explain why some psychologists

contend not only that personality rating scales are reasonably valid and reliable, but also that they are more acceptable to evaluators (Cascio & Aguinis, 2005).

5. Fondly known in the trade as "massive bowel obstruction," precisely because such a bureaucratic hyperrationalism system could, in the view of critics, never work with human beings. Indeed, Dan Ariely (2008) made a similar point: people are less rational than they think they are; in fact their "irrational behaviors are neither random nor senseless—they are systematic and predictable" (p. 239). Just as people are tricked by visual illusions, they are fooled by illusions about how they make decisions.

6. Early examples include (a) data entry personnel who, when evaluated by the number of keystrokes, pressed the space bar while making personal calls, and (b) telephone operators who, when expected to fulfill a quota in a given time period, would hang up on people with complex problems. The National Institute of Occupational Safety and Health estimates that two-thirds of all video display terminals are electronically monitored (Ambrose, Alder, & Noel, 1998, p. 70). The American Management Association, who conducts annual electronic monitoring and surveillance surveys, recently found that more than three-fourths of private firms use routine monitoring of their employees' activities, a figure that doubled since 1997.

7. Several comprehensive studies have found that racial and sex discrimination, once common in evaluations, are no longer pervasive (Pulakos, Oppler, White, & Borman, 1989; Waldman & Avolio, 1991).

8. According to Bernardin, Cooke, and Villanova (2000), raters who score high on "agreeableness" (trust, sympathy, cooperation, politeness) are more lenient than those characterized as "conscientious" (excellence, high performance, ability to achieve difficult goals). Leniency (or "grade inflation," in academe) is "the refusal by faculty members to behave like adults, that is, like people with enough integrity to disappoint other people. It is as though some professors want to believe that everybody deserves to be first. Everybody doesn't" (Carter, 1996, p. 79). This may conflict with Generation Y expectations who critics see as having gotten trophies for 7th place when growing up.

9. The saying. "When you point your finger at me, remember that your other fingers are pointing back at you," is appropriate here.

10. It should be noted that those who are "high self-monitors" are more adept at deciphering cues in the environment and are more capable of adjusting their behavior to fit the context than "low self-monitors" (Jawahar, 2005).

11. The pervasiveness of this problem accounts for the use of the term "personnel appraisal," not "performance appraisal," in this chapter.

12. In the private sector, those companies that emphasized frequent feedback outperformed those that did not in all financial and productivity measures (Campbell & Garfinkel, 1996).

13. For a useful discussion on "thinking about poor performers," see Maranto (2008).

14. For example, no high-ranking officials were dismissed for their failures in Iraq; in fact, the only one to lose his position was the Army chief of staff who testified before the war that hundreds of thousands of troops would be needed to secure the country. Indeed the Presidential Medal of Freedom was awarded to the CIA director who said Saddam Hussein had weapons of mass destruction, the general who failed to secure Iraq, and the head of the Coalition Provisional Authority whose decisions, in effect, encouraged insurgency. Promotions, rather than punishment, were the fate of most torture-tainted officers in the Abu Ghraib prison scandal.

15. While social norms in public and business bureaucracies generally discourage discharge, private sector layoffs and terminations are significantly higher than those in government (Bureau of Labor Statistics, 2005).

16. Treating employees fairly includes avoiding attempts at (a) constructive discharge (deliberately creating intolerable working conditions that compel employees to resign), and (b) retaliatory discharge (actions taken against personnel, such as demotions or denial of pay raises, when they exercise their rights under employment laws such as the Civil Rights Act of 1964).

REFERENCES

Ambrose, M. L., Alder, G. S., & Noel, T. W. (1998). Electronic performance monitoring: A consideration of rights. In M. Schminke (Ed.), *Managerial ethics: Moral management of people and processes* (pp. 61–80). Mahwah, NJ: Lawrence Erlbaum.

Ariely, D. (2008). *Predictable irrationality.* New York: Harper.

Bates, G. (2007). *It could happen here.* Retrieved December 1, 2005, from www.workforce.com/archive/feature/25/00/14/index.php?ht=

Beecher, D. (2003, Winter). The next wave of civil service reform. *Public Personnel Management,* pp. 457–474.

Benson, J., Debroux, P., Yuasa, M., & Zhu, Y. (2000). Flexibility and labour management: Chinese manufacturing enterprises in the 1990s. *International Journal of Human Resource Management, 11*(2), 183–196.

Bernardin, L., Cooke, M., & Villanova, P. (2000). Conscientiousness and agreeableness as predictors of rater leniency. *Journal of Applied Psychology, 85,* 232–234.

Bersin, J. (2007). *Performance management: Taking aim at performance appraisal.* Retrieved February 2, 2008, from http://www.talentmgt.com/performance_management/2007/December

Black, J. S., Gregersen, H. B., & Mendenhall, M. E. (1992). Evaluating the performance of global managers. *Journal of International Compensation and Benefits 1,* 35–40.

Boudreaux, G. (1994, May/June). What TQM says about performance appraisal. *Compensation and Benefits Review,* pp. 20–24.

Brito v. Zia Co. 1973 478 F.2d 1200, 1205–06 (10th Cir.).

Bureau of Labor Statistics, U.S. Department of Labor. (2005). *Job opening and labor turnover survey.* Retrieved from December 1, 2005, http://data.blsulov/PDQ/servlet/Surveyoutput Servlet

Burns, J. (1999). Changing environmental impacts on civil service systems: The cases of China and Hong Kong. In H. Wong & H. Chan (Eds.), *Handbook of comparative public administration in the Asia-Pacific basin* (pp. 179–218). New York: Marcel Dekker.

Campbell, R. B., & Garfinkel, L. M. (1996, June). Strategies for success in measuring performance. *HRMagazine,* pp. 98–104.

Cardy, R. L., & Dobbins, G. H. (1994). *Performance appraisal: Alternative perspectives.* Cincinnati, OH: South-Western.

Carson, M. (2006). Saying it like it isn't: The pros and cons of 360-degree feedback. *Business Horizons, 49,* 395–402.

Carter, S. (1996). *Integrity.* New York: Basic Books.

Cascio, W. F. (2006). *Managing human resources* (7th ed.). Boston: Irwin.

Cascio, W. F., & Aguinis, H. (2005). *Applied psychology in human resource management* (6th ed.). Upper Saddle River, NJ: Prentice Hall.

Cederblom, D., & Permerl, D. (2002). From performance appraisal to performance management: One agency's experience. *Public Personnel Management, 31*(2), 131–140.

Chou, B. (2008). Implementing reform of performance appraisal in China's civil service. *China Information, 19*(1), 39–45.

Coens, T., & Jenkins, M. (2000). *Abolishing performance appraisals: Why they backfire and what to do instead.* San Francisco: Berrett-Koehler.

Coleman, F. (2001). *Ending the employment relationship without ending up in court.* Alexandria, VA: Society for Human Resource Management.

Curtis, A., Harvey, R., & Ravden, D. (2005). Sources of political distortions in performance appraisals. *Group and Organizational Management, 30*(1), 42–60.

Daley, D. (2008). The burden of dealing with poor performers: Wear and tear on supervisory organizational engagement. *Review of Public Personnel Administration, 28*(1), 44–59.

DelPo, A. (2007). *The performance appraisal handbook: Legal and practical rules for managers* (2nd ed.). Berkeley, CA: Nolo Press.

DelPo, A., & Guerin, L. (2003). *Dealing with problem employees: A legal guide.* Berkeley, CA: Nolo Press.

Firing poor performers. (2003, June). *Issues of Merit,* p. 4.

Deming, W. E. (1992). *The new economics.* Cambridge: MIT/CAES.

Eckes, G. (1994, November). Practical alternatives to performance appraisal. *Quality Progress,* 57–60.

Flynn, N. (2008). *The epolicy handbook* (2nd ed.). New York: AMACOM.

Gentry, J. (2005). *HR how-to: Discipline.* Chicago: CCH, Inc.

Gilson, B. (2007, May 21). *Avoid getting fired.* FedSmith.com. Retrieved May 21, 2008 from http://www.fedsmith.com/article/1255/

Gomez-Mejia, L. R., Balkin, D. B., & Cardy, R. L. (2007). *Managing human resources* (4th ed.). Upper Saddle River, NJ: Prentice Hall.

Gregersen, H. B., Hite, J. M., & Black, J. S. (1996). Expatriate performance appraisal in US multinational firms. *Journal of International Business Studies, 27*(4), 711–752.

Grensing-Pophal, L. (2001, March). Motivate managers to review performance. *HRMagazine,* pp. 44–48.

Grote, A. (1996). *The complete guide to performance appraisal.* New York: AMACOM.

Guffey, C., & Helms, M. (2001). Effective employees: A case of the Internal Revenue Service. *Public Personnel Management, 30*(1), 111–127.

Halachmi, A. (1995). The practice of performance appraisal. In J. Rabin, T. Vocino, W. Hildreth, & G. Miller (Eds.), *Handbook of public personnel administration* (pp. 321–355). New York: Marcel Dekker.

Hauenstein, N. (1998). Training raters to increase accuracy and usefulness of appraisals. In J. W. Smither (Ed.), *Performance appraisal: State of the art in practice* (pp. 404–442). San Francisco: Jossey-Bass.

Hauser, J. D., & Fay, C. H. (1997). Managing and assessing employee performance. In H. Risher & C. H. Fay (Eds.), *New strategies for public pay* (pp. 185–206). San Francisco: Jossey-Bass.

Heathfield, S. (2007). *Perform exit interviews.* Retrieved June 7, 2008, from http://humanresources.about.com/od/whenemploymentends/a/exit_interview.htm

Holan, A. (2007, September 5). Firing federal workers is difficult. *St Pete Times.*

Jawahar, I. (2005). Do raters consider the influence of situation factors on observed performance when evaluating performance? *Group & Organizational Management, 30*(1), 6–41.

Kelloway, E., Barling, J., & Harrell, J. (2006). *Handbook on workplace violence.* Thousand Oaks, CA: Sage.

Kunreuther, R. (2008, June 23). *Let us praise . . . ourselves.* Fedsmith.com. Retrieved June 23, 2008, from http://www.fedsmith.com/article/1634/

Lewis, G. (2006). *Organizational crisis management: The human factor.* Boca Raton, FL: Auerbach Publications.

London, D. (1995). Giving feedback: Source-centered antecedents and consequences of constructive and destructive feedback. *Human Resource Management Review, 5,* 159–188.

Longenecker, C. O., & Ludwig, D. (1990). Ethical dilemmas in performance appraisals revisited. *Journal of Business Ethics, 9,* 961–969.

Losey, S. (2008, September 1). More exes get top performance ratings. *Federal Times,* pp. 1, 20.

Maranto, R. (2008, August). Thinking about low performers. *PATimes,* pp. 10–11.

McElveen, R. (2000, March 6). Rewards for employees reap reward for agency. *Federal Times,* pp. 1, 10.

McGregor, D. (1957, May/June). An uneasy look at performance appraisal. *Harvard Business Review,* pp. 89–94.

Meisler, A. (2003, July). Dead man's curve. *Workforce Management,* pp. 44–49.

Milkovich, C. T., & Wigdor, A. K. (1991). *Pay for performance: Evaluating performance appraisal and merit pay.* Washington, DC: National Academy Press.

Minor, M. (1995). *Preventing workplace violence.* Menlo Park, CA: Crisp.

Muñoz, V. (2006, November 27). *An examination of the failures of performance appraisal reform attempts in China's public service system.* University of Miami presentation.

Murphy, K. R., & Cleveland, J. N. (1995). *Understanding performance appraisal: Social, organizational and goal-based perspectives.* Thousand Oaks, CA: Sage.

National Performance Review. (1993). *From red tape to results: Creating a government that works better and costs less.* Washington, DC: Government Printing Office.

Nigro, L., Nigro, F., & Kellough, J. (2007). *The new public personnel administration* (6th ed.). Belmont, CA: Thomson Wadsworth.

Palguta, J. (2001, October 1). Go beyond performance appraisal for good performance. *Federal Times,* p. 15.

Perry, J. (2003). Compensation, merit pay, and motivation. In S. Hays & R. Kearney (Eds.), *Public personnel administration: Problems and prospects* (pp. 143–153). Englewood Cliffs, NJ: Prentice Hall.

Pickett, L. (2001, January 1). *Annual fiasco.* ARDTO (Melbourne, Australia: Asia-Pacific HRD Center).

Pulakos, E. D., Oppler, S. H., White, L. A., & Borman, W. C. (1989). Examination of race and sex effects on performance ratings. *Journal of Applied Psychology, 74,* 770–780.

Riccucci, N., & Lurie, I. (2001, Spring). Employee performance evaluation in social welfare offices. *Review of Public Personnel Administration,* pp. 27–37.

Roberts, G. (2003). Employee performance appraisal system participation: A technique that works. *Public Personnel Management, 32*(2), 89–97.

Scott, G. (2007). *A survival guide to managing employees from Hell.* New York: AMACOM.

Selden, B. (2008). *Employee termination: Does it have to be painful, for them and you?* Retrieved March 15, 2008, from www.employer-employee.com/Nopainfiring.html

Smither, J. W. (Ed.). (1998). *Performance appraisal: State of the art in practice.* San Francisco: Jossey-Bass.

Society for Human Resource Management. (2000). *Performance management survey.* Alexandria, VA: Author.

Spector, B. (2003). Human resource management at Enron: The unindicted co-conspirator. *Organizational Dynamics, 32*(2), 207–219.

Trimble, S. (1998, June 8). The postal scene: Workplace violence hits a five-year low. *Federal Times,* p. 12.

Tyer, C. B. (1983). Employee performance appraisal: A process in search of a technique. In S. W. Hays & R. C. Kearney (Eds.), *Public personnel administration* (pp. 118–136). Englewood Cliffs, NJ: Prentice Hall.

Tziner, A., Murphy, K., & Cleveland, J. (2005). Contextual and rater factors affecting rating behavior. *Group and Organizational Management, 30*(1), 89–98.

U.S. Merit Systems Protection Board (MSPB). (1995). *Removing poor performers in the federal service.* Washington, DC: Author.

U.S. Merit Systems Protection Board (MSPB). (1999). *Poor performers in government: A quest for the true story.* Washington, DC: Author.

U.S. Merit Systems Protection Board (MSPB). (2003). *Federal workforce for the 21st century: Results from the merit principles survey 2000.* Washington, DC: Author.

U.S. Merit Systems Protection Board (MSPB). (2008). *Alternative discipline: Creative solutions for agencies to effectively address employee misconduct.* Washington, DC: Author.

Waldman, D. A., & Avolio, B. J. (1991). Race effects in performance evaluations: Controlling for ability, education, and experience. *Journal of Applied Psychology, 76,* 897–911.

Wexley, K. (1986). Appraisal interview. In R. A. Berk (Ed.), *Performance assessment* (pp. 167–185). Baltimore: Johns Hopkins University Press.

Wiersma, U., & Latham, G. (1986). Practicality of behavioral observation scales, behavioral expectation scales, and trait scales. *Personnel Psychology, 39,* 619–628.

Wise, C., Clemow, B., Murray, S., Boston, S., & Bingham, L. (2005). When things go wrong. In S. Freyss (Ed.), *Human resource management in local government.* Washington, DC: International City/County Management Association.

Yang, B., & Zheng, D. (2003). A theoretical comparison of U.S. and Chinese culture: Implications for human resource theory and practice. *International Journal of Human Resources Development and Management, 3*(4), 338–358.

Yang, B., Zheng, W., & Li, M. (2006). Confucian view of learning and implications for developing human resources. *Advances in Developing Human Resources, 8*(3), 346–354.

Zhao, S. M. (1994). Human resource management in China. *Asia-Pacific Journal of Human Resources, 32*(2), 3–12.

Ziegler, M. (2004, March 1). Merit pay anxiety. *Federal Times,* pp. 1, 6.

Chapter 11

Unions and the Government

Protectors, Partners, and Punishers

The best union organizer? Bad management.

—Anonymous

After studying this chapter, you should be able to

- appreciate the mixed views of unions held by employees and managers;
- identify differences in orientation and behavior between unions and management;
- understand paradoxes, contradictions, trends, and variations in labor-management relations;
- determine key bargaining issues that require resolution before, during, and after negotiations;
- distinguish between positive and negative behaviors at the bargaining table; and
- recognize differences between the doctrine of hostility and the doctrine of harmony, as well as between traditional bargaining and cooperative problem solving.

Organized labor flexed its political muscle to help defeat a controversial California ballot initiative in 2005. The proposal, Proposition 75, would have prohibited public employee unions from using dues or fees for political contributions unless the employee provides annual written permission on a specified form. Defeat of the proposal (53.5% to 46.5%) was a come-from-behind victory for labor. A similar result on this issue occurred in 1998 when Proposition 226 was defeated 53.3% to 46.7%. In 2005, labor's vigorous $43 million, no-holds-barred campaign helped to overcome a 23% deficit in public support for the proposal that existed a few months prior to the election. Union staffing helped as well: thousands of union members made phone calls and knocked on doors. The battle identified as "mortal political combat" by the media (Richardson, 2005) resulted in the unions' victory, illustrating the political power of organized labor to mobilize members and leverage public policy.

Visible opposition to Proposition 75 came from the AFL-CIO, State Democratic Party, state public employee associations, and other unions. Union leaders, concerned about the declining economic power of unions in recent years and weakened by a schism in the national AFL-CIO, were anxious about preserving their political clout, which depended in large measure on their ability to obtain dues from their members. They detected a not-so-hidden agenda on the part of business to silence the political voice of working families. Supporters of Proposition 75 called the measure a "paycheck protection" plan (Steinberg, 2005). They argued that it would be fair to workers who disagreed with their union's stance on political issues and candidate endorsements. Governor Arnold Schwarzenegger put his weight behind this and three other ballot measures as part of his sweeping "reform agenda." Other prominent supporters included members of the National Tax Limitation Committee, the California Republican Party, the Small Business Action Committee, and the Citizens to Save California (Institute of Government Studies [IGS], 2006).

Union leaders were concerned that a victory by antilabor forces in California would propel "paycheck protection" onto the national agenda. Such laws have been passed in six states. Ohio's law was enjoined by the courts and never implemented, however. Three states (Michigan, Washington, and Wyoming) adopted paycheck protection laws that applied to all unionized workers in those states, and two states (Idaho and Utah) approved paycheck protection laws that applied only to public sector unions (Sherk, 2006). At the national level, Congress has been unable to pass a paycheck protection bill, despite repeated attempts to do so (Crampton, Hodge, & Mishra, 2002).

Protecting the political clout of unions was deemed essential in California to safeguard members' interests in the future. To succeed in defeating Proposition 75, unions had to "partner" with other concerned parties (public employee groups, including teachers, firefighters, nurses, and police). The defeat of Proposition 75 highlights another role of unions. They are "punishers" of those whose interests run counter to those of labor. Business typically outspends unions by a large margin on politics, so unions battled valiantly to avoid restrictions on union political spending. They succeeded in punishing the "enemies of labor" who supported the proposal by engineering a public and embarrassing defeat of the proposition.

As this case shows, unions are adept at hardball politics: They act as protectors (defending employees' rights and interests), partners (with prolabor stakeholders), and punishers (against those perceived to be antilabor). These three roles help explain union behavior both internally (within the workplace) and externally (outside the workplace).

The defeat of Proposition 75, along with some union victories in the private sector, may signal a resurgence of union strength. Improved union prospects may be linked to the national trend toward an "hourglass" economy with high-wage, high-skill jobs on one end, low-wage service jobs on the other, and a shrinking middle class in between. The case also may give the mistaken impression, however, that public sector unions are currently very strong. Although some unions in selected locales exercise considerable clout, the trend has been in the opposite direction, notwithstanding the numbers of employees who belong to unions. This chapter examines union roles in governmental labor-management relations (LMRs). It explores the mixed perspectives of employees and managers toward unions. Key paradoxes, contradictions, trends, and variations in LMRs are highlighted. Issues linked to representation and **collective bargaining** in government are discussed. The doctrines of hostility and harmony are contrasted, as are the practices of **traditional bargaining** and **cooperative**

problem solving. In short, LMRs are critical to both the foundations and functions of human resource management, now and in the future.

■■ DIFFERING VIEWS OF UNIONS

Most public employees and managers have definite opinions about unions—some favorable, some unfavorable. On the positive side, employees dissatisfied with their job or working conditions might see unions as a way to salve their smoldering discontent by championing workplace reforms. Unions might protect vulnerable workers and enable them to seek redress against arbitrary or capricious actions by employers. Workers may also think union membership would amplify their voice in the workplace and increase their influence with management. Vigilant unions can help keep management honest and ensure fair dealings with personnel. Collective action, especially in the labor-intensive public sector, sometimes yields results unattainable through concerted individual efforts. For example, unions have assumed leadership in supporting employee-friendly initiatives (Chapter 8) and in helping workers' stagnant salaries (Chapter 7) become more competitive. Indeed, a recent public sector survey finds that professional employees in collective bargaining states have weighted mean salaries nearly 20% higher than those in states without collective bargaining (American Federation of Teachers, 2004). Employees might also enjoy the feelings of solidarity as well as the perks (discounts, legal aid, loans, credit cards, insurance) that accompany union membership.

Negative views might dwell on union dues, unresponsive labor leaders, unflattering stereotypes associated with unions, and questionable benefits. Additional objections could include distaste at the defense unions may give to nonproductive workers, their tendency to support "one-size-fits-all" solutions, and a belief that unions are unnecessary to accomplish workers' aims. Furthermore, some might prefer to be represented by a professional association than by a union.

Administrators have negative or positive views toward unions as well. Some see unions as spiking up costs, pushing down productivity, impeding organizational change, and concentrating more on advancing employee interests than on serving citizen interests. Others oppose union organizing efforts fearing that rigid, binding labor contracts alter or erode managerial rights and decrease administrative discretion and flexibility. Managers may view unions as introducing conflict, distraction, and disruption into the workplace, thus inhibiting cooperative working relationships. Unions may be viewed as reflexively proemployee and antimanagement. Also, unions may be seen to complicate or delay policy implementation. Some managers, especially those in **right-to-work states** (where mandatory union membership is outlawed), believe that current organizational policies and procedures are fair to employees. Such managers may believe that there is no need for **meet-and-confer rights** (i.e., laws requiring agency heads to discuss, but not to settle, grievances) or bargaining rights with unions on employment matters. Those opposed to unions often combine their criticisms with proposals to privatize public services. Managers may try to inoculate employees against union appeals by quickly responding to morale concerns, establishing grievance procedures, and empowering workers. Some officials think that union organizing efforts result from management's unfair treatment of employees. Actually, proper treatment could be the best impediment to organizing. This is the view taken by the AFL-CIO, which has identified five factors that reduce the chances for union organizing: (1) bosses not taking advantage of employees, (2) employee pride in their work, (3) agency records of good employee performance, (4) avoidance of favoritism and high-handed treatment, and (5) good supervisor-subordinate relations ("What to Do," 1966). Appendix 11A at the end of the chapter provides a list of tips for managers when dealing with unions; Appendix 11B provides a list of tips for unions when dealing with managers.

Employers with positive attitudes see unions as contributing to a form of workplace democracy, enabling labor and management to join in improving conditions of employment. Such managers may want to tap employee preferences, prefer one-stop bargaining, and see unions as a way to ensure a level playing field for workers. They prefer to work with member-supported union representatives rather than disparate groups purporting to reflect worker sentiments but lacking the legitimacy of a **representation election**.

Managers and employees can have either positive or negative perceptions about each other. In some cases, this is most evident in relations between the chief executive officer and her union leader counterpart. When stereotypes threaten to poison such relationships, they are often based on negative perceptions each participant has of the other party (see Benest & Grijalva, 2002). Exhibits 11.1 and 11.2 show some of the stereotypes that might get in the way of effective relations between labor union leaders and city managers, as well as some steps that might be taken by each to enhance the relationship.

It is not surprising, then, that employees and managers react differently to unions. Working in a unionized environment prods both parties to consider how their jobs are affected by the presence of organized labor. Exhibit 11.3 lists some questions that public employees and administrators are likely to ask as they sort out their thoughts on unions, labor relations, and collective bargaining. Answers to these questions will change from one work environment to another because of the complicated nature of public sector LMRs and existing trends. These complications are discussed below.

Exhibit 11.1 Overcoming Stereotypes and Enhancing the Chief Executive Officer-Union

Union Leaders' Perceptions of Managers	Managers' Perception of Union Leaders
Managers "don't get it."	Leadership is not management oriented.
They are "political" animals.	They are insulated, isolated.
They have no backbone in the face of political controversy.	Leaders have a high need to be liked by their members.
Managers have no ethics.	They "don't do much."
Administrators have a short attention span and are "frenetic."	Union leaders are not politically savvy.
They are shortsighted regarding labor relations.	They lack a big picture perspective.
They are too concerned about quantity, not quality.	Leaders are change resistant.
They are "cheap."	They do not promote diversity.
	Leadership knows more about their service than managing people.
	They are poor collaborators.

Exhibit 11.2   Fifteen Ideas to Enhance the Relationship

Fifteen Ideas to Enhance the Relationship:

Ideas for both partners:

- Acknowledge difference in roles
- Put aside negative perceptions
- Get to know each other
- Look at the relationship as a partnership

Suggestions for chief executive officers:

- Acknowledge the benefit of improved public services
- Support the advocacy of union leaders
- Do not demonize the union
- Appreciate the union leader's relationship to an active union
- Reach out to public employees
- Insist that union leaders develop wider perspectives

Suggestions for the union leader:

- Educate the manager
- Pick your battles
- Distinguish between facts and perception
- Proactively become an asset to the larger organization
- Broaden the perspective of union members

Source: Adapted from Benest & Grijalva, 2002.

▪▪ PARADOXES AND CONTRADICTIONS

Like other areas of human resource management, paradoxes are plentiful and contradictions are unavoidable in LMRs. Some examples include the following:

- High-performance work organizations require high levels of trust and cooperative activity, but zero-sum bargaining, where one side's gain is another side's loss, makes this difficult.
- Collective bargaining arrangements are crucial but may be incompatible with efficient merit system operations.
- Union and management might profess support for productivity improvement efforts, but that support might drop off when job security is threatened.
- Dispute resolution mechanisms add stability to LMRs, but such provisions in collective bargaining laws empower unelected arbitrators, which may diminish democratic accountability to citizens.

- Unions claim to compete on a level playing field with other interest groups (e.g., taxpayer associations, privatization advocates) seeking to influence government. They have a distinct advantage over these groups, however, given the union's right to bargain on wages, hours, and working conditions, as well as to lobby the legislative body for special benefits.
- Managers are held accountable for making decisions and taking actions in the public interest, but the extent of unionization and the provisions of a management-approved labor contract may limit their discretion.
- Administrators frequently profess support for employee participation in program design and implementation, but they often prefer that such participation be conducted through nonunion channels.

Three other paradoxes and problems deserve mention. First, LMRs in government are based on old-style, private sector conflict resolution where both sides stake out adversarial positions before negotiations commence. The traditional framework underlying the labor-management relationship actually undermines it. A new style for managing conflict would turn this old

---

Exhibit 11.3   Questions for Employees and Employers Regarding Unions, Labor-Management Relations, and Collective Bargaining

Employee

- Should I join a union?
- What do unions do?
- Will I have a voice in a union?
- Will unions act on my complaints?
- Will unions protect my rights?
- Will unions affect my relationship with management?
- What is the downside of a union?
- Does collective bargaining affect me?
- Will unions effectively represent my interests?
- What should unions push for in negotiations?
- Should I participate in a work stoppage?

Employer

- How will a union affect my organization?
- How do unions affect the way employees work?
- Should I support or resist unionization?
- Will relationships with unions be cooperative or adversarial?
- Can I work effectively with union leaders?
- Do I have confidence in management's negotiating team?
- What should management seek to have in a contract?
- Will management prerogatives be protected in negotiations?
- Will contract provisions limit my managerial discretion?
- How will employee grievances be handled?
- How will contract or grievance disputes be resolved?

process on its head and put greater emphasis on cooperation, with labor and management representatives talking first and drafting specific policies last. Experiments in LMRs using this approach show promising results (Fretz & Walsh, 1998; Parsons, Belcher, & Jackson, 1998).

Second is the **free rider** problem that is based on the distinction between union membership and union representation: employees may benefit from unions without being members. Membership figures are often much smaller than representation figures (i.e., employees belong to bargaining units but fail to join the union). For example, in 2003 the American Federation of Government Employees had 222,000 dues-paying members, but it represented approximately 600,000 employees. This represents a free rider rate of 64%. Thus, in many **open shop** governmental settings, workers may be the beneficiaries of union-sponsored initiatives without joining the union or paying dues.[1] Free riders avoid the pain but receive the gain from union efforts.[2] Overall trends in union membership and representation in the federal, state, and local government sectors are shown in Exhibit 11.4. The two columns represent membership versus the number of employees represented by the unions (these data reflect a less pronounced free rider problem than the example above from the American Federation of Government Employees).

Third is the paradox relating to the inherent value differences between unions and management. Although there was some movement toward greater cooperation, a number of incompatibilities still existed between organized labor and management in the 1990s (see Exhibit 11.5).

Exhibit 11.4	Government Union Membership and Representation, 2005, 2006 (in thousands)				
	Total Employed	*Members of Unions*		*Represented by Unions*	
		Total	*Percentage*	*Total*	*Percentage*
2006 gov workers	20,392	7,378	36.2	8,172	40.1
Federal	3,381	960	28.4	1,139	33.7
State	6,102	1,843	30.2	2,049	33.6
Local	10,908	4,575	41.9	4,984	45.7
2005 gov workers	20,381	7,430	36.5	8,262	40.5
Federal	3,427	954	27.8	1,134	33.1
State	5,874	1,838	31.3	2,056	35.0
Local	11,080	4,638	41.9	5,071	45.8
2006 private	107,846	7,981	7.4	8,688	8.1
2005 private	105,508	8,255	7.8	8,962	8.5

Source: Bureau of Labor Statistics, 2007b.

Exhibit 11.5	Union-Management Value Differences

Union	Management
Egalitarian—few distinctions between members, all are treated the same	Hierarchical—more distinctions between people, levels of control, chain of command
Democratic decision making by members	Decision making by few
Security through mutual protection, "an injury to one is an injury to all"	Security based on competition, each gets what each deserves, individualism
Seniority is basis for deciding among members	Performance is basis for deciding among members
Goals: job security, quality of work life, safety, better wages and benefits	Goals: productivity, approval from voters, low tax rates, customer satisfaction
Past practice and precedent control actions and decisions	Pragmatic—what works best now

As noted in Exhibit 11.5, unions and management differ in the distinctions between organization members, involvement in decision making, the basis for security, allocation of rewards, goals, and the grounds for action. (These differences will become more apparent below.) The next section fleshes out the context of public sector labor relations and highlights some of the trends and variations that distinguish it from the private sector—patterns in LMRs that evolved in the business sphere were later adapted to the government arena.

Trends and Variations

Union membership has been steadily declining since the 1950s in business and industry, despite fluctuating growth spurts in public sector union membership. Overall, organized labor's share of the workforce dropped from 14.5% in 1996 to 12.0% in 2006, down considerably from 1954 when unions represented 35% of the nation's workers. However, in 2007 union membership grew for the first time since 1983 to 12.1%, representing an increase of 311,000 employees. This change reflects a slight increase in the private sector union membership rate, from 7.4% to 7.5%, even though public union membership dropped from a rate of 36.2% to 35.9%. Still, public sector workers were nearly five times more likely to be a union member; it is not yet known whether the gap will continue to close. Exhibit 11.6 reports the percentage of union membership in the private and public spheres for the period from 1990 to 2007; total union membership was 15.7 million in 2007. Note that in 2007, 35.9% of government employees belonged to unions, contrasted with only 7.5% of business employees (Bureau of Labor Statistics, 2004). Thus, nearly four in ten government workers are union members, compared with fewer than one in ten corporate personnel. The unionization rate among government workers has varied little since 1983. Currently, they account for 48% of union membership in the United States. Exhibit 11.7 reports membership in selected public arena unions in 1997 and 2007 and provides their Web sites.

Exhibit 11.6	Union Membership in Public and Private Sectors, 1994–2007	
Year	*Public (all levels)*	*Private*
1994	38.7	10.8
1995	37.7	10.3
1996	37.6	10.0
1997	37.2	9.8
1998	37.5	9.5
1999	37.0	9.4
2000	37.5	9.0
2001	37.2	8.9
2002	37.5	8.5
2003	35.9	8.29
2004	36.4	7.9
2005	36.5	7.8
2006	36.2	7.4
2007	35.9	7.5

Source: Hirsch & Macpherson, 2007.

There are several reasons for the drop in private sector union membership. Among the most frequently mentioned is the growth of high-tech industries (where unions are harder to organize), geographic shifts (from Frostbelt to Sunbelt), changes in the workforce (from blue collar to pink collar; greater representation of Hispanics, Asians, and African Americans), and changes in the workplace (downsizing, outsourcing). Other factors include management opposition in representation elections, replacement of striking workers, and reluctance by unions to push organizing drives in an era when gains in union jobs can be erased by losses. Stanley Aronowitz (1998) attributed declining rolls to the tendency of unions to cater to the least needy (steel and auto workers) rather than the neediest (farm and hotel workers), the self-interested parochialism of union leaders, and misplaced attention on bargaining and grievance processing rather than on organizing. Thomas J. Donahue, president of the U.S. Chamber of Commerce, puts a different spin on the reasons for falling membership: "Improved employer-employee relationships, the fading appeal of labor's 'big government' politics, and persistent tales of union corruption" ("U.S. Labor," 1998, p. 7A). Whatever the explanation, public sector unions have done a better job of maintaining membership than their private sector counterparts.

The rise in public arena union membership has occurred in the past five decades with the largest growth spurt in the 1960s and 1970s, moderate growth in the 1980s, and flat growth in the 1990s and 2000s. In 1960, there were 900,000 public sector union members (penetration of 10.8%). By 1980, government unions were the largest department in the AFL-CIO, and two out of five employees had union representation. The overwhelming majority of all public sector union members are currently at the state and local level (87.9%), not at the federal level (1.21%; Bureau of Labor Statistics, 2007b). This represents a remarkable "flip-flop" from 1950 when more members were federal (69%) than state and local government

Exhibit 11.7   U.S. Membership in Selected Public Sector Unions, 2003–2007 (in thousands)

Labor Organizations	2003	2007	Web Site
American Federation of Government Employees	222	NA	www.afge.org
American Federation of State, County & Municipal Employees	1,400	NA	www.afscme.org
American Federation of Teachers	1,200	1,400	www.aft.org
American Postal Workers Union	366	332	www.apwu.org
International Association of Firefighters	260	280	www.iaff.org
International Union of Police Officers	NA	100	www.iupa.org
National Association of Letter Carriers	304.7	300	www.nalc.org
National Association of Postal Supervisors	36	35	www.naps.org
National Education Association	2,700	3,000	www.nea.org
National Federation of Federal Employees	NA	90	www.nffe.org
National Fraternal Order of Police	308	324	www.grandlodgefop.org
National Rural Letter Carriers Association	96	104	www.nrlca.org
National Treasury Employees Union	155	150	www.nteu.org
Service Employees' International Union	1,500	1,800	www.seiu.org

Source: Bureau of Labor Statistics, AFL-CIO, and individual unions (personal communication).

employees (Orzechowski & Marlow, 1995). The following are some of the reasons for subnational growth:

- Changes in public policy (executive orders, statutory laws)
- Vigorous union organizing efforts
- The rise of social movements (civil rights, antiwar, feminism)
- The success of various job actions (slowdowns, strikes)
- Lagging wages
- Rising public sector employment
- Inexperience of government employers in resisting early union organizing campaigns
- Increasing threats to employee job security

An example of efforts to organize and represent younger public employees is found in Exhibit 11.8. Many younger workers are in entry-level jobs making relatively low salaries, sometimes close to minimum wage.

Not only do membership trends vary between the two sectors, but labor law also varies. Public sector labor law has lagged behind developments in the private arena, but it draws on several concepts first codified in private sector legislation, so some familiarity with the earlier legislation (summarized in Exhibit 11.9) is important as a foundation. Although public sector labor relations are an adaptation from the business model, there are significant differences that need clarification (Exhibit 11.10) before introducing public sector policy developments in LMRs.

Turning to policy at the local government level, New York City Mayor Robert F. Wagner, Jr., issued Executive Order 49 in 1958 recognizing collective bargaining with unions, establishing grievance procedures, and setting procedures for **bargaining unit determination** and exclusive representation (see Aronowitz, 1998). The evolution of public policy dealing with federal public sector legislation began four years later with a series of executive orders in the Kennedy (EO 10988), Nixon (EO 11491), and Ford (EO 11838) administrations. These were then brought together and amplified with the passage of Title VII in the **Civil Service Reform Act of 1978** during the Carter presidency.

This law gives federal employees (General Schedule and wage grade) the right to form unions and bargain collectively. It created the **Federal Labor Relations Authority (FLRA)** to oversee federal LMRs, disallowed union security arrangements, restricted the scope of bargaining (e.g., excludes wages and benefits), and banned strikes. In recent years, the FLRA has been subject to criticism by the courts and other observers (Exhibit 11.11). The U.S. Office of Personnel Management's Office of Labor-Management Relations assists federal agencies with contract administration and technical advice.

President Bill Clinton issued an executive order in 1993 establishing a National Partnership Council to further empower federal employee unions to work cooperatively with management in identifying problems and designing solutions to improve service delivery. President George W. Bush revoked the order and dissolved the council in early 2001, reflecting his administration's more promanagement, proagency philosophy.

Exhibit 11.8   Organizing Younger Workers: Teaching Assistants

The Lion Tamer School of Management: Keep them well fed and never let them know that all you've got is a chair and a whip.

—Anonymous

Organized labor has targeted younger workers in recent membership drives. Labor-sponsored surveys of young workers' concerns reveal that they focus on wage rates, health care, and retirement security (Brackey, 1999). They worry about the cost of living, high debt levels, job discrimination, and availability of affordable housing. The difficulty involved in gaining union victories with these workers is illustrated in the efforts to win union recognition and bargaining rights for graduate students who work as teaching assistants (TAs) in public universities. The 16-year battle on behalf of TAs in California is one recent example.

In March 1999, the University of California (UC) reluctantly recognized the results of graduate student union elections. This occurred only after a four-day strike on all eight teaching campuses simultaneously. Representation elections were held on UC campuses such as UCLA and UC Berkeley, resulting in local affiliates of the United Auto Workers representing TAs. The Coalition of Graduate Employee Unions estimates that 20,000 of the nation's 100,000 graduate assistants are part of a union. Opposition to union representation is based on contentions that TAs are more like apprentices than employees, that unionization drives would raise the cost of higher education, and that graduate students are not eligible to organize. Opponents further argue that unionization would replace a flexible and collegial system with an industrial and adversarial one, and that TAs have no legal rights to bargain. Others opposed to unionization fear that it would result in pay stagnation, rigid working hours, corruption of the faculty-student mentoring relationship, and strikes. The California Public Employees Relations Board (PERB) rejected these claims and concerns. Supporters of bargaining rights for TAs argue that they carry a heavy portion of the teaching load (an estimated 60% of undergraduate instruction in the UC system) as a result of university downsizing and cost cutting, and that they are like unprotected corporate "temp" workers. TAs maintain that unions will help them achieve reduced workloads or fees; increased salary or stipends; improved health benefits, working conditions, and job security; and more-effective grievance procedures.

Although some successes have been achieved in organizing younger workers such as TAs (graduate assistants on 20 campuses were unionized between 2000 and 2007), union victories are matched by union losses. When victories do occur, they are hard fought and follow prolonged struggles. It took 16 years, numerous work stoppages, intervention by influential state legislators, and considerable agitation to achieve labor peace, recognition, and bargaining rights for UC's TAs. Nevertheless, it is easier for public university TAs to unionize because state labor laws govern public universities, whereas private universities fall under the jurisdiction of the National Labor Relations Board (NLRB). The NLRB has ruled in the past that students who work as part of their education do not meet the definition of "employees" under prevailing law and therefore lack the right to organize. Graduate students at several private universities have waged a bitter, decade-long battle challenging this interpretation, but it was upheld in a 2004 NLRB decision. This NLRB decision stated, "[T]here is a significant risk, even a strong likelihood, that the collective bargaining process will be detrimental to the educational process."

Sources: Bacon, 1999; Bernstein, 1998; Brackey, 1999; Folmar, 1999; Greenhouse & Arenson, 2004; Palmaffy, 1999; Sanchez, 1996; Shenk, 2007.

Exhibit 11.9   Five Major Pieces of Private Sector Labor Legislation, 1926–1959

1926: Railway Labor Act—grants rail workers unionization and bargaining rights. Also covers resolution of disputes with, and interpretations of, any negotiated contract.

1932: Norris-LaGuardia Act—restricts injunctions and repudiates "yellow-dog" contracts.

1935: Wagner Act—also known as National Labor Relations Act, or NLRA, gives all workers the right to unionize and collectively bargain, lists unfair labor practices, describes union certification elections, and creates the National Labor Relations Board to watch over it all.

1947: Taft-Hartley Act—amended the NLRA and created the Federal Mediation and Conciliation Service to aid in dispute resolution; provides emergency procedures, lists unfair union labor practices, and gives states the right to pass right-to-work laws.

1959: Landrum-Griffin Act—also known as the Labor-Management Reporting and Disclosure Act; requires unions to file financial and trusteeship reports and to set employee rights, including the ability of union members to attend meetings and nominate/vote for candidates.

Exhibit 11.10   Public and Private Sector Differences

1. Benefits

   - *Public sector.* Many nonbargained benefits are provided via civil service statutes (e.g., employee grievance procedures, health/life insurance, sick leave, holidays), and the scope of negotiations is narrow (e.g., pay and benefits for federal employees are excluded as bargaining topics).
   - *Private sector.* The scope of negotiations is broad, with most terms and conditions of employment open for negotiation.

2. Multilateral Bargaining

   - *Public sector.* Dispersed authority means bargaining involves more players (e.g., negotiators, public/taxpayers/media, elected officials, courts, other third parties) and more complex approval processes.
   - *Private sector.* Bargaining is a two-party process resulting in agreements that each party's policy body ratifies.

3. Monopoly Versus Competition

   - *Public sector.* Government is a monopoly and generally not subject to market forces, making product/service (e.g., police, fire) substitution difficult.
   - *Private sector.* Businesses are subject to market forces, and consumers can shop for price/availability of desired goods/services.

(Continued)

(Continued)

4. The Strike

- *Public sector.* Strikes occur, but they are often illegal and strikers/unions can be punished.
- *Private sector.* Strikes are legal and a legitimate tool when negotiations reach impasse.

5. Sovereign Versus Free Contract

- *Public sector.* The **doctrine of sovereignty** maintains that government has responsibility to protect all societal interests; therefore, it is inappropriate to require it to share power with interest groups (e.g., unions in negotiations) or dilute managerial rights. Similarly, the **special responsibility theory** maintains that public employees hold critical positions in society and therefore should not be permitted to strike.
- *Private sector.* The sovereignty doctrine does not apply.

6. Political Versus Economic

- *Public sector.* Decisions have economic impacts but are based on political criteria.
- *Private sector.* Decisions can have political impacts, but they are economic decisions.

Sources: Adapted from Coleman (1990, pp. 8–12); Denholm (1997, pp. 32–33).

Exhibit 11.11   Political Influences on Regulatory Decision Making

Public Administration is often influenced by partisan politics.

Up to mid-2001, the Federal Labor Relations Authority (FLRA) was meeting many of its goals, including increasing productivity and improving labor-management relationships. However, by 2007, FLRA had faced many court defeats and failed to adequately complete its mission. Defeats along the way included the rejection of 13 out of 25 FLRA decisions between January 2004 and December 2006 by U.S. courts, and the inability of the three-member FLRA to meet any of its performance goals in 2006. Judicial decisions criticized FLRA saying, among other things, "analysis fundamentally misapplies the Statute, reasoning would yield 'bizarre results' or lead to an 'absurd situation,'" "standards are being deliberately changed, not casually ignored," and "the Authority's decision . . . is premised on an entirely untenable interpretation."

The defeats are partly a result of the "scuttling" of the FLRA. In mid-2001, Republicans established a majority of the FLRA and appointed Dale Cabaniss as chair. Since Cabaniss took control, staff has been reduced by 25% and the same amount of annual appropriations has not been used. Cabaniss also reduced transparency in the agency by deleting data presumed to be embarrassing for FLRA—for example case process times that were deemed to take too long. The professionals on the Federal Service Impasses Panel were cut by 60%: Cabaniss replaced them with a political appointee with no history in labor relations. President Bush nominated her for another term in 2007.

Source: Adapted from Ferris, 2008.

Bush's action, together with civil service reforms in the departments of Defense and Homeland Security (Exhibit 11.12), outsourcing initiatives, cutbacks, pay-for-performance plans, and concern about reducing the scope of bargaining and employee appeal rights (Exhibit 1.12), had at least one federal union leader claiming, "This administration is attacking the civil service, period" ("AFGE's 'Fighting Spirit,'" 2003). George Nesterczuk, vice president of Global USA, a consulting firm, supported the Bush initiative claiming that, under Clinton's partnership policy, "Unions had the power to run around management to get what they wanted" (Young, 2001, p. 17). Management and labor are still seeking a new footing in their relationship following the dissolution of the National Partnership Council and have had to recognize the leeway given to agencies in establishing their own labor relations philosophies.

Exhibit 11.12   Civil Service Reform and Unions in the U.S. Department of Defense

Congress passed the 2004 National Defense Authorization Act, which enabled the U.S. Department of Defense to rewrite personnel policies and labor management rules. The changes included the following:

- Reducing the number of workers eligible to be in a bargaining unit
- Creating a pay-for-performance system
- Removing seniority and veterans' preference in layoff decisions
- Removing prohibitions against unfair labor practices
- Allowing unions to "consult" on personnel changes, but—absent agreement—authorizing management to act unilaterally
- Substituting in-house review of employee appeals and union grievances in place of third-party reviews
- Barring from collective bargaining all employees who must be certified to work (i.e., those in professional occupations)
- Changing the criteria for employees to join or leave unions
- Instituting national collective bargaining in place of local bargaining

Supporters of the changes argue that management currently negotiates with an unwieldy number of recognized bargaining units (1,300), that it is difficult to achieve its objective of converting tens of thousands of jobs from military to civilian status, that the intent is not to rescind collective bargaining rights, and that a more agile, flexible, and responsive system is needed.

A 30-union coalition mobilized to oppose new U.S. Department of Defense personnel rules that affect hundreds of thousands of civilian defense workers, reduce union influence, and modify the structure of labor-management relations in existence for 45 years. Union leaders view the proposed changes as union busting that would reduce workplace protections for employees, harbor mistrust, replace bilateralism with top-down decision making, and set the precedent for dismantling collective bargaining rights in other agencies. Indeed, two weeks after DOD proposed its rules, the U.S. Department of Homeland Security announced a similar set of proposals.

Sources: Adapted from International Brotherhood of Electrical Workers, 2004; Kaufman, 2004; Losey, 2004.

A bewildering array of federal, state, and local laws, regulations, court decisions, ordinances, and attorneys' general opinions shape governmental LMRs. The federal system for LMRs is different from the state or local system, and the local arrangements are different, in many instances, from the state. Local-level developments reflect considerable variation. The vast majority of serious labor issues, however, arise in a relatively narrow range of local government unions associated with police, fire, sanitation, and education. At the state and local levels, public policy dealing with public employee labor relations is difficult to summarize. Nevertheless, some key features of state public employee labor relations laws include responsibility to bargain, the bargaining team, bargaining relationships, the agreement, union rights, civil rights, and government obligations.

Another trend deals with LMRs themselves. The legal right of public employees to strike is hotly debated (see Exhibit 11.13). In recent years, there has been a decrease in **work stoppages** (strikes) and an increase in the use of third-party mediators. There were 21 major work stoppages in 2007: 17 in the private sector and four in the public sector (Bureau of Labor Statistics, 2007a).[3] The decline in government work stoppages may be attributable to growing antitax, antiunion, and antigovernment public sentiments; the discharge of air traffic controllers by President Reagan in 1981 (Exhibit 11.14); employer practice of hiring permanent replacements for striking workers; and increased use of alternative dispute resolution mechanisms. Nonetheless, strike rights for some state employees have been established in 13 states. In four other states, judicial rulings have upheld strike rights for public workers (Kearney, 2003). Use of alternative dispute resolution mechanisms has occurred at all levels of government (e.g., Dibble, 1997). Public sector strikes in European countries are common. For example, France has had major work stoppages in response to President Nicolas Sarkozy's recent reform agenda (Exhibit 11.15).

Exhibit 11.13   Arguments Opposing and Supporting Public Sector Strikes

Opponents to public sector strikes argue the following:

- Sovereignty rests with the American people, and public workers should not be entitled to strike because it would violate the public's will and undercut governmental authority.
- Strikes pervert the policy process by bestowing special privileges on unions that other interest groups do not have.
- Public services are monopolistic, and labor market constraints to hold down labor costs are absent where strikes are allowed.
- Essential services are curtailed in strikes, posing a threat to public health and safety.

Supporters of the legal right of public employees to strike contend the following:

- Not all public services are essential, and the disruption of government services seldom seriously threatens public health and safety.
- Alternatives to government services are frequently available from the private sector.
- Denying the right to strike to public employees but allowing it for private sector workers performing identical work is inequitable.
- Work stoppages will occur regardless of legal strike bans.
- The incidence of strikes is no greater in states that permit work stoppages than it is in those that prohibit them.

Sources: Adapted from Kearney, 1998a, 1998b.

Exhibit 11.14   PATCO Strike: Misguided and Overreaching Strategy

The Professional Air Traffic Controllers Organization (PATCO) strike was a watershed development in federal labor-management relations in the 1980s. The strike resulted in 11,400 air traffic controllers losing their jobs, PATCO's decertification and eventual dissolution, and Ronald Reagan's signaling to public employers that they should stand firm and take a hard line against unions.

The union had been involved in rocky, bitter bargaining with the Federal Aviation Administration (FAA) from the late 1960s to the early 1980s. These negotiations took place on a range of issues despite restrictions on the scope of negotiations under Executive Order 10988. PATCO demands included substantial salary hikes, improved overtime pay rates, better night shift differentials, and more generous severance pay. Other demands were for greater union involvement in determining operational/safety policies, a shorter workweek, and lucrative early retirement plans. The FAA resisted union proposals. After unsuccessful haggling with the FAA, union members voted overwhelmingly in favor of an illegal strike in 1981.

President Reagan gave strikers an ultimatum: Return to work within 48 hours or lose your jobs. PATCO did not comply. The president then delivered on his threat, dismissing and ultimately establishing a process for replacing strikers. In the end, union leadership and strategy was faulted for failing to garner public sympathy, framing the issues too narrowly, discounting the public interest, overreaching, and making insufficient effort to shore up support for the strike from AFL-CIO affiliates.

Sources: Coleman, 1990, pp. 52–53; Devinatz, 1997, pp. 105–106; Northrup, 1984.

Exhibit 11.15   Public Sector Strikes in France, 2007 and 2008

In late 2007, in France, public sector strikes broke out in response to President Nicolas Sarkozy's attempts to reform pension plans, reduce jobs in education, and privatize funding in previously public sector–funded establishments, including the university system. The strikes have put a test to the clout of the relatively strong unions in France for the first time since 1995, when government unions defeated similar reform plans.

Sarkozy has claimed the cuts and reductions in benefits are necessary to meet European Union budget deficit guidelines, which require deficits to remain under 3% GDP, but the unions have said Sarkozy's plans are unnecessary and are actually designed to dismantle the public sector.

At the top of concerns is France's special pensions system, which allows some workers to retire after only 37.5 years of public employment, compared with the normal 40 or more years. The program accounts for 6% of total state pension payments, benefiting 1.6 million workers and 1.1 million retirees, many of whom are employed in the rail and utility sectors. Sarkozy has sought to end the special pensions program, which would eliminate retirement benefits for 500,000 public employees.

As a result of his plans, in November 2007, rail and metro workers and employees of public electric utilities began striking, reducing TGV (train à grande vitesse, or high-speed) train service to about 15%, metro and bus services to 20% and 15% capacity, respectively, and electricity

(Continued)

(Continued)

production by about 10%. The strikes had mostly ended by November when the government agreed to negotiate with the participating unions.

Strikes in other sectors followed, however, including teachers who opposed an expected cut of 23,000 jobs in education, newspaper printers unions who opposed reorganization plans, and students who opposed attempts to allow private funding for universities. In May 2008, postal workers, hospital employees, customs officials, and other civil servants went on strike in objection to plans for 58,000 public sector job cuts by 2009. In total, it was estimated that up to 60,000 workers in Paris alone participated in a 24-hour strike in May. The feud is ongoing and the results may indicate whether unions maintain political power and if Sarkozy's reform agenda is possible.

Sources: BBC News, 2007a, 2007b, 2007c; Bennhold, 2007; M&C Business, n.d.

Appendix 11C contains a role-play exercise based on a Mock Disciplinary Appeal Board Hearing where additional issues are raised regarding LMRs and the legal and ethical issues that can arise.

■ REPRESENTATION AND COLLECTIVE BARGAINING

National labor laws that govern collective bargaining and representation rights for federal and private sector employees do not pertain to state and local government employees. State and local public employees' bargaining and representational rights are enumerated wherever authorized by state law and, less frequently, by local ordinance or executive order. Currently, many states authorize collective bargaining for public employees. Some states restrict coverage to certain occupational groups (e.g., public safety, teachers). Other states lack collective bargaining statutes for their state and local government employees. In some instances, however, executive orders or local ordinances confer rights to bargain or have representation.

Collective bargaining is the process whereby labor and management representatives meet to set terms and conditions of employment for personnel in a bargaining unit. Certain legal factors help to frame bargaining and union-management relationships. These factors are also influenced by and help to determine the strength of public unions. Identification of such factors is a necessary prelude to painting a portrait of the bargaining process. These include the nature of the bilateral relationship, the type of union security provisions, the kind of administrative arrangements, the range of **unfair labor practices**, and the existence of dispute resolution or **impasse procedures**. These legal distinctions are clarified in Exhibit 11.16.

The bargaining process itself is shaped by these factors. It typically unfolds in three phases: (1) organizing to bargain, (2) bargaining, and (3) administering the contract. Each stage is characterized by distinct activities, discussed in turn as follows.

Exhibit 11.16	Selected Legal or Contextual Factors Regarding Unions

Relationship Between the Parties

Meet-and-Confer—characterized by inequality between partners (labor and management); employer selects agenda items and is not obligated to bargain; management retains virtually all rights and exercises ultimate authority; and outcomes are nonbinding and typically skewed to management's perspective.

Collective Bargaining—the rights of employees to form and join unions for bargaining purposes are recognized; an administrative agency oversees bargaining unit determination and establishes administrative procedures; unions with majority support become exclusive bargaining agents; employers are obligated to bargain; selected management rights are protected; and provisions provide for union security, impasse procedures, and unfair labor practices.

Union Security Provisions

Union Shop—Employee must join the representing union after a certain number of days (e.g., 30–90 days) specified in the collective bargaining agreement. This is rare in government.

Agency Shop—Employee is not required to join the union, but most contribute a service charge to cover collective bargaining, the grievance process, and arbitration costs. Nonpayment can result in job loss. Such arrangements are infrequent in the public sector.

Maintenance of Membership—Employee is obligated to maintain union membership in the representing union once affiliated during the life of the contract. Withdrawal may lead to forfeiture of job.

Dues Check-off—Employee may select payroll deduction option to pay union dues to representing union.

Administrative Arrangements

Public Employee Relations Boards (PERBs)—state administrative agencies typically charged with determining appropriate bargaining units, overseeing certification elections, and resolving unfair labor practices. At the federal level, the three-member Federal Labor Relations Authority (FLRA) performs PERB functions. In the private sector, administrative responsibilities rest with the National Labor Relations Board (NLRB).

Unfair Labor Practices (ULPs)

Unfair Employer Practices—interfering with a public employee's right to form or join a union, discriminating against public employees because of union membership, dominating a labor organization, or violating a collective bargaining agreement.

Unfair Union Practices (UUPs)—denying union membership because of race, color, creed, and so forth; interfering with, restraining, or coercing (a) employees in exercising their statutory rights or (b) employers regarding the exercise of employee rights; refusing to meet with the public employer and to bargain in good faith; or interfering with the work performance or productivity of a public employee.

Impasse Procedures

Mediation—a dispute resolution procedure that relies on a neutral third party who attempts to facilitate communication and bring the parties together to reach an agreement.

(Continued)

(Continued)

Fact-Finding—a dispute resolution procedure that relies on a neutral third party who conducts hearings, researches contentious issues, and makes nonbinding recommendations for consideration.

Arbitration—a dispute resolution procedure that relies on a neutral third party who reviews the facts and makes determinations that are binding on both sides.

Arbitration takes many forms:

- **Interest arbitration**—refers to arbitration dealing with the terms of the negotiated contract; it can be voluntary or compulsory.
- **Grievance arbitration**—or rights arbitration, to resolve outstanding disputes regarding employee grievances.
- **Final-offer arbitration**—the arbitrator's decision is restricted to the position taken by one or the other of the parties—this can include selection of a position taken by one side or the other on all issues taken together (by package) or selection on an issue-by-issue basis.
- **Med-arb**—requires an arbitrator to begin with mediation, settle as many disputes as feasible, and move to arbitration only on items that remain contentious.

Organizing to Bargain

Collective bargaining, as traditionally practiced, does not occur until (a) an appropriate bargaining unit is determined, (b) a representation election is held, (c) an exclusive bargaining agent is certified, and (d) a bargaining team is selected. Each step is necessary to determine who will engage in negotiations. Bargaining unit determination identifies whom a union or other association in negotiation sessions will represent. An administrative agency, a statute, a union, or an arbitrator makes such determinations. Specifically, the FLRA makes unit determinations at the federal level, and **Public Employee Relations Boards (PERBs)** do so in many states. The criteria used in determining the composition of the bargaining unit vary state by state, but the following National Labor Relations Board (NLRB) guidelines are typically followed:

- Community of interest: Common job factors, for example, are similar position classifications, duties, skills, working conditions, kinds of work, or geographic locations.
- Bargaining history: This includes such things as prior patterns of negotiation, representation, or LMRs.
- Unit size: Units that are too small can absorb too much of bargaining representatives' time, create unwieldy fragmentation, and create a **whipsaw effect** (gains by one union might be used to justify benefits for another); those that are too large may lack cohesion and a community of interest.
- Efficiency of operations: Bargaining structures may impede efficiency if they are a poor "fit" with existing human resource policies and procedures.
- Exclusion of supervisory or confidential employees: This is predicated on the idea that there is a potential conflict of interest in a unit that combines supervisors (management) with employees.

Election is the next step in this phase of the process. Identification of who is to represent the union in negotiations need not involve an election; the employer may choose to voluntarily recognize a union for this purpose. More typically, a *representation election* is held. Although either the employer or the union may request such an election, the union usually must "make a showing" that a certain percentage (e.g., 30%) of workers in the unit want representation. As the unfair labor practices in Exhibit 11.16 indicate, certain management tactics (intimidation, force, coercion) are prohibited during a representation election. Unions must receive a majority vote in a secret ballot election to achieve recognition as the exclusive bargaining agent for workers in the unit. State laws vary regarding the definition of "majority vote" in a representation election. It can mean either a majority of votes cast (most common) or an absolute majority of eligible bargaining unit members without regard to the number of votes actually cast.

The actual certification as the appropriately constituted exclusive bargaining agent for the unit is done by the relevant administrative agency (FLRA, PERB, or equivalent). **Certification of the bargaining agent** may be rescinded if workers become sufficiently dissatisfied, if the agent violates the bargaining law (e.g., decertification of the Professional Air Traffic Controllers by the FLRA in 1981), or if another union "makes sufficient showing" of support to challenge the exclusive bargaining agent. In such cases, a decertification election (modeled on the same procedures described above) is held to determine who, if anyone, should represent employees in the unit.

Selection of the bargaining team is a crucial task. There is considerable variation in team composition depending on the level of government in question, the extent of professionalism existing within the labor relations office (if such an office exists), and the preferences of the labor and management leadership groups. Each side designates a chief negotiator. This may be a professional labor negotiator, a labor lawyer, or a savvy manager or union leader. In local government, the management team may include the chief administrative officer (city or county manager), someone from the legal office, or a human resource or budget professional, among others. Top union leaders often handpick their most rhetorically gifted and politically astute spokespersons as negotiators. Other stakeholders (public, media) may attend or comment on negotiations in some states (e.g., Florida, Minnesota, and North Dakota), but this is more the exception than the rule.

Bargaining

Once the stage has been set and the cast determined, the curtain goes up on bargaining, although the audience is often restricted to the key participants. The great drama is usually reserved for the final scene, when negotiations become most heated. In the beginning, the more mundane preparations occupy center stage. Getting prepared involves studying the lines of the existing contract, collecting and analyzing relevant comparative data (wages, salaries, benefits), and sorting through bargaining priorities. Bargaining strategy needs to be clarified. Opening gambits need to be scripted and choreographed differently from the compelling scenes in the last act. The costs and benefits of alternative bargaining proposals need to be weighed carefully. The logistical details of where, when, how, and how long to conduct bargaining sessions require attention, as does the agenda for each meeting.

Legal and behavioral considerations come into play here. Two legal requirements in particular require attention: bargaining must be conducted in good faith, and the scope of negotiations is often prescribed. Although the term "good faith" is subject to multiple interpretations, the public sector has relied heavily on NLRB rulings and private sector case law to determine its meaning. Good faith is perhaps best understood by considering examples of its opposite. Employer negotiators who reject union proposals but advance no counter-proposals, undermine or bypass the union, schedule meetings arbitrarily, or fail to respond to a union request for a bargaining session are not dealing in good faith (Baker, 1996). A bargaining checklist and behavior observation sheet is presented in Appendix 11D.[4]

The scope of negotiations is often addressed in the law but contentious in practice. Conflict arises because unions want more perquisites (perks) and want to haggle over a broad range of issues. "What does labor want?" When the press asked this question of Samuel Gompers, the first president of the American Federation of Labor, he began by responding, "More . . ." and since then, his entire comment has been edited down to that single word. Gompers's unabridged response was, "We want *more schoolhouses* and less jails, *more books* and less arsenals, *more learning* and less vice, *more constant work* and less crime, *more leisure* and less greed, *more justice* and less revenge" (emphasis added). If unions want "more," management, intent on preserving its prerogatives, often wants to give "less" and takes a more restrictive, narrow view of what is negotiable. Vague statutory language frequently specifying the scope to include "wages, hours and conditions of employment" fuels the debate over the legitimate array of discussable items. Issues fall (not always neatly) into three categories:

1. Mandatory issues. "Must do" matters that fall within the porous language of "wages, hours and terms, or other terms and conditions of employment." Wages and hours of federal employees are excluded from bargaining, however.

2. Permissive. "May do" subjects about which the negotiating team may bargain if they opt to (i.e., they are neither mandatory nor prohibited), but disagreements are especially heated regarding the phrase "other terms and conditions of employment."

3. Prohibited. "Can't do" topics that authorizing statutes, administrative agencies (PERBs or FLRA), or the courts have determined are not subject to bargaining or beyond the employer's authority to bargain (e.g., civil service laws, organizational mission).

Mandatory subjects can be pushed to an impasse: neither team is required to concede. One novel "permissive" topic from the private sector that Briggs and Siegele (1994) urged on public sector bargainers is a 13-point "ethics standards clause" for inclusion in collective bargaining agreements that would formalize a commitment to ethical behavior and discourage attempts to pursue unethical agendas incompatible with employee or organizational interests.

Principled negotiations, or integrated bargaining, sometimes characterize proceedings at the bargaining table; other times distributive bargaining prevails. In distributive bargaining, hostility is high, relationships are conflictual, bargaining parties are viewed as adversaries, and one side's gain is another side's loss. Principled bargaining is less prevalent and more consensus oriented. It stresses identification of common ground, focuses on cooperative problem solving, and thrives in an open trusting environment (Walton & McKersie, 1965). Fisher and Ury's (1981) well-known version of integrative bargaining (or principled negotiations) lays out a list of suggested guidelines:

- Separate the people from the problem.
- Focus on interests, not positions.
- Invent options for mutual gain.
- Insist on use of objective criteria.

Where both parties to negotiations are committed to pursuing partnership strategies, such approaches find fertile ground to take root; where more abrasive and conflictual relations prevail, principled bargaining may lack the nurturance necessary to bear fruit.

Prevailing economic conditions influence bargaining strategy. In recent years, belt tightening, downsizing, and privatizing have led to two related trends: concession bargaining and **productivity bargaining**. Negotiators on the management team are responding to taxpayer concerns that sometimes require "give-backs" from unions or promises to "do more with less" (heightened worker productivity in the future). Unions in such environments have had to switch adroitly from offense to defense, fighting a rear-guard action to preserve past bargaining victories or to protect their flanks from onerous threats (e.g., reductions in force, two-tier wage structures, benefit copayments). Management may demand greater productivity (e.g., incentive-based plans) or changes in performance-impeding work rules (e.g., staffing ratios). Unions may agree with such changes to avoid concessions on less-palatable alternatives. Organized labor's productivity-related demands might include worker autonomy, flextime, or gainsharing. As labor relations have become more formalized, there has been greater reliance on written agreements and less on verbal understandings or symbolic handshakes. Indeed, state bargaining statutes specify that written contracts must be drawn up on the mandatory issues of wages, hours, and working conditions; most agreements go beyond these topics, covering a broad range of additional matters. Verbal agreements are too easy to squeeze out of and are subject to (sometimes intentional) misinterpretation. Legal contracts are written to minimize this problem. Skillful lawyers can be contortionists who may use legalese to obscure meaning and preserve "wiggle room" or loopholes to slip through when formal contracts contain objectionable provisions.

Written contract provisions may create inflexibility. This may occur with a policy like pattern bargaining, in which every union receives the same percentage raise. Such a policy has been contentious in some cities. For example, in New York City certain unions (e.g., police, teachers) have called for an end to pattern bargaining, arguing for more flexibility in job categories like theirs, where noncompetitive salaries make it difficult to attract enough qualified personnel (Greenhouse, 1998). Scrapping the pattern-bargaining approach to union contracts, they argue, would help put salaries on par with those in adjacent communities. In the New York City case, however, eliminating pattern bargaining would likely sour relations between city hall and other municipal unions, and among the unions themselves.

Once the parties have reached agreement on key sticking points and contractual language has been approved, both sides must seek ratification of the contract. Members of the union bargaining team must convince their membership that the final product of negotiation deserves their consent; managers seek ratification from the relevant governing body (e.g., city or county council, state legislature). If negotiators have assiduously maintained open lines of communication with their respective constituencies, ratification is likely to be pro forma. Where information sharing has been more sporadic, negotiators could be told that their work product was deficient and be told to reopen negotiations. When dealing with an intractable problem, leaders and managers often have to take creative steps to avert an impasse or salvage negotiations. William Ury (1991, Chap. 3) suggested one approach is to reframe the problem in order to get one's negotiating counterpart to "buy in" to a mutually beneficial outcome, as a partner rather than an opponent. The following open-ended, problem-solving-type questions are among those that Ury suggested in "reframing" contentious bargaining issues: "Why?" "Why not?" "What if?" "What makes that fair?"

Impasse procedures are triggered when bilateral negotiations come to a standstill. If contract disagreements cannot be resolved in the course of normal bargaining, mechanisms of "first resort" or "last resort" may be necessary. Most states use **mediation** as a first step in dispute resolution. Neutral third-party mediators seek to serve as catalysts to keep the parties talking and suggest alternative proposals to reach voluntary agreement on outstanding issues. If mediation fails, the next step is **fact-finding**. Appointed by the FLRA or the PERB, fact finders hold hearings, sift through arguments, and issue advisory opinions laying out proposed grounds for settlement.

If these "first resort" options do not succeed, "last resort" alternatives include **interest arbitration** (distinct from **grievance arbitration** or rights arbitration) or strikes, where available. Because strikes are prohibited in most public sector jurisdictions (and declining where permitted, as noted earlier), binding arbitration (conventional arbitration and **final-offer arbitration**) is the most common means of achieving final resolution. Exhibit 11.16 defines **arbitration** and lists the various forms it can take. Nearly half of all public sector arbitration cases from 1985 to 1992 dealt with discharge, wages, suspensions, and benefits (Mesch & Shamayeva, 1996). Critics express reservations about binding arbitration, contending that (a) settlements are imposed by outsiders, which runs counter to voluntary two-party contract bargaining; (b) arbitrators lack political accountability (neither directly nor indirectly accountable to the electorate); and (c) parties may drag their feet in negotiations or "first resort" stages of dispute resolution in hopes of succeeding with favorable arbitration decisions (Tomkins, 1995).

Administering the Contract

Contract administration is the third phase of the bargaining process. The principal mechanism here is a grievance procedure, typically provided for in the negotiated agreement. Grievance procedures lay out the available steps or levels to resolve disputes about contract interpretation or implementation. Binding arbitration typically is the last step in this process.

Two key players in contract administration are the union steward and the first line supervisor. Both must be intimately familiar with the provisions in the contract and well trained in interpersonal skills and cooperative problem solving if contract administration is to proceed smoothly. Despite the knowledge, skills, and best intentions of stewards and supervisors, there are bound to be disagreements that lead to the filing of grievances. Grievance mechanisms provide a peaceful and fair way to address these contentious issues with minimal disruption of the workplace. It is important to observe due process and to resolve issues definitively. Binding arbitration of grievances provides finality to the resolution of disputes. Although some writers portray arbitration as a low-cost and impartial alternative to litigation, others contend that arbitration is more costly, tilts in favor of defendants, and yields lower monetary awards to plaintiffs (Vinson, 2002).

■■ HOSTILITY VERSUS HARMONY

Ideas shape institutions. The ideas undergirding public sector collective bargaining are borrowed from models previously designed for the private sector. A critical view of public unionism and collective bargaining was put forward by David Denholm (1997), the publisher of the journal *Government Union Review*. He contends that key LMR concepts drawn from the private sector are inappropriate when applied in government because of differences between the two sectors. Concepts such as competition, market economy, and free contracts are defining characteristics in the private sector, whereas government is characterized by monopoly, politics, and sovereignty. The **doctrine of hostility** between parties is fundamental to traditional collective bargaining (adversarial, conflictual, confrontational). Critics argue that the **doctrine of harmony** offers a more appropriate set of ideas and behaviors to guide public sector LMRs (cooperation, service orientation, participation) and advance the public interest, as discussed in the Wye River Conference (Exhibit 1.6). Denholm posits that the public interest in public employment includes

- maintaining a peaceful, stable employer-employee relationship;
- safeguarding the rights of all public employees;
- protecting the right of the citizenry to control government policy and costs through their elected representatives; and
- providing services in the most efficient and orderly manner possible.

Denholm (1997) argued that collective bargaining is ill suited to government and that the common interest is ill served by it. His conclusion: "It is time to move beyond the failed nostrums of the past into a better future for public employees and the public they serve" (p. 52).

Cardinal distinctions between these two approaches are outlined in Exhibit 11.17. Exciting recent developments in LMRs are those guided by the doctrine of harmony. They take the form of collaborative problem solving, participative decision making, and partnerships (Fretz & Walsh, 1998; Parsons et al., 1998; U.S. Department of Labor, 1996). Instructive examples of such creative experiments are found at all levels of government. Those profiled in Exhibit 11.18 are drawn from state and local jurisdictions. Cooperative problem solving is more likely to succeed when there is mutual trust, commitment, and leadership from all participants as well as from flexible, adaptive organizational structures (Levine, 1997; Rubin & Rubin, 2001). Among the improvements attributed to partnerships of this kind are better service, lower costs, improved quality of work life, fewer grievances, speedier dispute settlement, increased use of gainsharing, more-effective discipline, and more-flexible negotiated agreements (Lane, 1996). Although it is important not to oversell win-win bargaining and harmony-based solutions or to undervalue the merits of traditional bargaining (see Lobel, 1994), these examples suggest that public unions and managers should explore diverse paths and think strategically about ways to improve LMRs and citizen services in the future.

Exhibit 11.17   Traditional Bargaining Versus Problem-Solving Bargaining

Traditional bargaining: Opposing bargaining teams engage in zero-sum posturing and demands.

Problem-solving bargaining: Discussion is resolution oriented, leading to mutually agreeable and beneficial answers to common problems.

Traditional bargaining: Each side has but one goal—to wring the maximum number of concessions from the other side in exchange for the minimum amount of effort, focusing on short-term gains over long-term benefits.

There are several key avenues to reaching that goal:

- Emphasizing form over substance
- Using highly legalistic language

(Continued)

(Continued)

- Obscuring real wants and needs
- Using a hierarchy to limit communication

Although traditional bargaining can be functional, it is rarely efficient, as the process itself necessitates repetition every few years.

Problem-solving bargaining repudiates the antagonistic stance of the traditional model and seeks to forge long-lasting agreements based on the needs of all stakeholders.
There are several courses of action that accomplish this:

- Honestly appraise what needs to be changed.
- Inform other stakeholders of these basic needs.
- Encourage exchange of possible solutions.
- Reach agreements on specific solutions.

Problem-solving bargaining creates real, self-sustaining solutions to problems that benefit all stakeholders.

Exhibit 11.18	Five Examples of State and Local Governments Engaged With Unions in Cooperative Problem Solving

- A labor-management committee in Connecticut's Department of Mental Retardation with District 1199 of the SEIU tackled the issue of how to improve employee safety. In 1 year, the committee's recommendations produced a 40% reduction in injuries and a 23% reduction in what had been an annual $25 million worker's compensation expenditure.
- Healthcare costs in Peoria, Illinois, were climbing annually at 9–14%, while city revenues were declining. With the cooperation of all city unions, Peoria took health care off the table and placed it in its own joint labor-management committee. The result was a 20% reduction in healthcare costs and a 100% decline in healthcare decision arbitration.
- As part of citywide planning in Madison, Wisconsin, labor-management cooperation dramatically improved a contentious relationship between city building inspectors, represented by AFSCME Local 60, and private electrical contractors. Management, employees, and their union worked together with contractors to develop a compliance effort that emphasizes education instead of punishment and a program that enhances safety, savings, and results.
- In Phoenix, Arizona, a long-standing dispute between management and the Firefighters Local 493 was ended by using joint annual plans to address problems and seek improvements. As a result, arbitration has not been used in more than 10 years.
- In Indianapolis, Indiana, the mayor and the AFSCME union initially came to loggerheads over privatization of 25% of the city workers, but when the union was allowed to bid for work projects and share in the cost reductions below the bid, unionized departments frequently won, and not a single union job was lost.

Sources: Fretz & Walsh, 1998; Osborne & Plastrik, 1998; Parsons et al., 1998; U.S. Department of Labor, 1996.

This move from unilateral to consensus decision making is still in its infancy, but some experiences with cooperative partnerships have been encouraging. For example, at the federal level the U.S. Department of Commerce's Patent and Trademark Office is partnering with the National Treasury Employees Union to implement a telecommuting program. A similar partnership between the U.S. Department of Housing and Urban Development and the American Federation of Government Employees in 1999 supported pilot projects that include telecommuting but go beyond it to cover a wide range of family-friendly workplace initiatives. Germany provides a European example of consensus decision making (Exhibit 11.19).

Exhibit 11.19   Labor-Management Relations in Germany: Codetermination

Germany developed a consensual model of labor-management relations after World War II based on a system of "democratic corporatism," whereby labor, management, and the state work together to prevent and solve conflicts.

Since the 1950s, the system of "codetermination" (*Mitbestimmung*) stipulates that workers participate, in some form, in both strategic corporate decisions and workplace conditions. Codetermination takes place in two forms. (1) Workers are directly represented on supervisory boards in large companies, and (2) employees can (but do not always) elect workers councils (*Betreibsräte*) in every company with 10 or more employees. As part of a democratic corporatist model of labor-management relations, the workers' councils are charged with representing workers' concerns in the context of the interests of the company as a whole. Workers' councils are distinct from trade unions, though there is a close relationship between them. The codetermination system is oriented toward enhancing personnel management by giving workers a voice in everything from training to improving workplace culture.

Codetermination gives workers a say in the following areas:

- job cuts and compensation packages
- conditions for bonuses
- productivity targets
- training programs
- the introduction of new technologies
- vacation schedules
- workplace discrimination
- the scheduling of breaks
- the monitoring of worker activity
- the hiring of apprentices
- the transfers of employees
- the shutting down of plants (Albach, 1993; Fulton, 2007; "Germany: Mitbestimmungsrechte," 2007; Library of Congress, 1995; Simon, 2007)

This is only a small part of the wide-ranging scope of worker participation in German workplaces. Trade unions are still responsible for collective bargaining and for the representation of workers along industry lines, though they are heavily involved with most workers' councils in

(Continued)

(Continued)

facilitating training sessions and sharing of information. Contentious issues between workers' councils and management that cannot be resolved within the workplace are settled in special labor courts that are distinct from the civil law system.

The motivation for codetermination initially revolved around a concern for the right of workers to participate in the workplace. A second motivation slowly developed as some employers, despite initial opposition, discovered that meaningful worker participation in workplace activities actually serves the long-term interests of their companies (Girnt, 1998; Patriarca & Welz, 2008, pp. 345–346). Codetermination has long been criticized by free market economists and some German employers as reducing the flexibility, and therefore the competitiveness, of German industry and of imposing undue costs on German firms. Employers must pay all the costs of workers' councils, including the paid work time lost to council activities, copying and telephone costs, and even staff support for large councils in big firms (Fulton, 2007). On the other hand, Germany loses far fewer days to strikes than countries with contentious labor-management relations and its workers have enjoyed a more stable workplace environment with a sense that their voice in personnel management really matters on a day-to-day basis (Simon, 2007).

Codetermination is currently being buffeted by the strong winds of economic change. The increasing number of start-up companies based on new technologies, company bankruptcies, foreign buy-outs, outsourcing of production abroad, and the general impact of globalization are all making stable workplace participation increasingly problematic. Contemporary German workers must now face the problems that their counterparts in other countries have long been used to: fear of job loss, reduction in benefits and pay bonuses, and uncertainties about the future of their companies. Despite the economic pressures against worker participation, codetermination has become a fact of life in the German economy and, more recently, in the European Union as a whole, so that it is likely to remain a feature of personnel management even at the cost of the quantitative bottom line (European Commission, 2008; Girnt, 1998).

One way to think about LMRs that was proposed by James Flint (2002) is to visualize a relationship continuum. This continuum is depicted in stages that vary based on dimensions of control and effectiveness (most to least). Exhibit 11.20 maps the stages across the relationship continuum with Stage 1 (Healthy Workplace Environment) at one end, with most control and greatest effectiveness, and Stage 5 (Resort to Litigation) at the other end, with least control and least effectiveness. The continuum is both a diagnostic tool to isolate where LMRs are in a jurisdiction at a given point in time and a prescriptive device that helps participants see what is necessary to move from where they are (e.g., acrimony) to where they want to be (e.g., cooperation).

▪▪ SUMMARY AND CONCLUSION

Unions have played an important role in government for the past five decades. As signaled in the subtitle and opening vignette of this chapter, unions function as protectors, partners, and punishers. Reactions to unions are far from uniform. Employees and managers both have "love-hate" relationships with unions. One fundamental paradox in LMRs is that the doctrine

Exhibit 11.20	Effectiveness and Control on the Relationship Continuum

Most Effective   Least Effective

<-->

| Healthy Workplace Stage 1 | Need for Problem Solving Stage 2 | Need for Mediation Stage 3 | Arbitration Required Stage 4 | Resort to Litigation Stage 5 |

Most Control   Least Control

<-->

Stage 1 Healthy Workplace Environment: Commitment to leadership by both management and labor; commitment by both to build a positive, trusting relationship; collaboration; creating an organizational infrastructure to ensure accountability and employee development.

Stage 2 Need for Problem Solving: Training in problem-solving skills; investment in employees and the organization; selection of problem-solving tools; recognition of inevitable conflict and decisions on proactive responses.

Stage 3 Need for Mediation: Incurring moderate expenses; reliance on external problem solving; expending additional time to reach agreement; recognizing that an acceptable result may not occur; damaging labor-management relationship.

Stage 4 Arbitration Required: Absorbing increasing expenses; accepting arbitrator's decision without appeal; relinquishing control for resolution to arbitrator; creating a more confrontational environment; producing a result that may be unsatisfactory to one or both parties; altering labor-management relationship; reducing effective communication.

Stage 5 Resort to Litigation: Requiring the often expensive process of rebuilding the labor-management relationship; heightening of adversarial relations; relying on experts who lack knowledge of in-house relationships; creating win/lose decisions; injuring labor-management relations; blocking effective communication.

Source: Adapted from Flint, 2002.

of hostility from the private sector was adapted with minor modifications by the public sector, thereby inhibiting emergence of a competing model built on the doctrine of harmony. The legal structures underlying public LMRs ensure the continued dominance of the adversarial approach of traditional bargaining. Recent experiments, however, point the way to promising experiences with cooperative problem solving.

Dealing with unions is a way of life for many managers as they struggle to cope with thorny human resource problems. Difficulties are inevitable if administrators fail to understand the (actual or potential) role of organized labor and to heed requirements spelled out in the negotiated contract or mutual agreement. Public managers need to track trends and variations in labor relations. The activities associated with each phase and stage of the collective bargaining process requires careful monitoring if managers are to do their job properly. At the same time, officials should be aware that alternatives to traditional bargaining exist.

Where LMRs are extremely adversarial and hostile, both workers and managers are likely to fail former Secretary of Labor Robert Reich's (1998) "pronoun test". He assessed employees' feelings toward their employers by listening carefully to the way they responded to questions about their work. If they use "they" and "them" in referring to the organization instead of "we" and "us," they fail Reich's pronoun test of collective commitment. Similarly, "we-they, us-them" characterizations of LMRs suggest an ingrained adversarial environment, making principled negotiations (win-win) and cooperative problem solving less likely. In workplaces predominantly peopled by those who pass the pronoun test, strategies built on the doctrine of harmony and incorporating participative decision making are more likely to succeed.

Heeding the tips and avoiding the traps below can provide a lubricant to reduce unnecessary friction in labor management relations.

Tips

- Be willing to share power to solve problems.
- Be patient and acknowledge mistakes.
- Invest time and effort in building relationships and in resolving differences.
- Cooperate where the interests of both sides converge.

Traps

- Be unwilling to fix deteriorating relationships.
- Fail to recognize the inevitability of conflict.
- Be inattentive to cultivating a harmonious work atmosphere.
- Provide tardy and unfair response to complaints.

Given entrenchment of existing legal structures and behavior patterns built on five decades of experience with traditional union-management relations, movement from institutional patterns built on the doctrine of hostility to those grounded in the doctrine of harmony will be slow and incremental. Government managers must carefully assess the organizational cultures and institutional arrangements in their jurisdiction and decide whether they should press for change in LMRs or work through existing human resource and LMRs mechanisms to achieve public purposes.

KEY TERMS

Agency shop	Civil Service Reform Act of 1978
Arbitration	Collective bargaining
Bargaining unit determination	Cooperative problem solving
Certification of the bargaining agent	Doctrine of harmony

Doctrine of hostility	Meet-and-confer rights
Doctrine of sovereignty	Open shop
Dues check-off	Principled negotiations
Fact-finding	Problem-solving bargaining
Federal Labor Relations Authority (FLRA)	Productivity bargaining
Final-offer arbitration	Public Employee Relations Boards (PERBs)
Free rider	Representation election
Grievance arbitration	Right-to-work state
Impasse procedures	Special responsibility theory
Interest arbitration	Traditional bargaining
Maintenance of membership	Unfair labor practices
Med-arb	Union shop
Mediation	Whipsaw effect

EXERCISES

Class Discussion

1. What are the key implications of (a) the doctrine of hostility and (b) the doctrine of harmony as they pertain to public sector LMRs?

2. Which is preferable: traditional bargaining or cooperative problem solving? Why?

3. Based on past trends in public and private labor relations, what do you predict the future will hold?

4. What important obstacles are likely to be encountered in each of the three phases of collective bargaining? How can each be resolved? How is this like a chess game?

5. Invite someone who is involved on a collective bargaining team to visit your class. Ask the visitor to discuss his experiences involving some of the negative and positive bargaining behaviors listed in Appendix D.

Team Activities

6. Divide into four groups: (1) an aggrieved employee, (2) a mediator, (3) a fact finder, and (4) an arbitrator. Group 1 defines the nature of the grievance, and each of the third-party neutrals indicate how they would go about resolving the grievance.

7. Divide into four groups, each one representing a different type of arbitration (see Exhibit 11.16). Within the group, discuss the pros and cons of the type of arbitration. Report back to the class as a whole.

8. Should public employees have the right to strike? Is this preferable to binding arbitration? Why?

9. What is the case against collective bargaining in the public sector?

10. Divide into two groups. One team will develop arguments in favor of Prop. 226 and the other will develop arguments against. Discuss both with the full class.

Individual Assignments

11. Why do some employees join public sector unions? Why do some employees fail to join?

12. What are the special challenges of managing in (a) a union environment and (b) a nonunion environment?

13. Why are there so many paradoxes and contradictions in public sector labor relations? Select five important paradoxes and consider how they can be resolved.

14. How is collective bargaining similar and different in the public and private sectors?

15. Why have private sector unions lost members, whereas public sector unions have gained members?

    a. Where an open shop exists, a union can represent workers, but nonunion members have no financial obligations to the union. Workers who join a union under an open-shop arrangement have a financial obligation to the union.

    b. A free rider, in this context, is a worker in a bargaining unit who acquires a benefit from union representation without the effort or costs that accompany membership.

    c. Federal employees do not have the right to strike. In most states, it is illegal for state employees to strike. Some states give employees a limited right to strike.

APPENDIX A

Tips for Managers When Dealing With Unions

- Reach out to all employees and let them know that their work is valued.
- Survey employee attitudes on working conditions.
- Provide a healthy and safe work environment.
- Examine pay rates and benefit packages to maintain them at or above "market" levels.
- Maintain close contact with first-line supervisors on employee-relations matters.
- Develop a cordial and personalized relationship with union officers.
- Work with union representatives in communicating policies to employees.
- Build trust between unions and management.
- Foster transparency in labor-management relations (LMRs).
- Avoid arbitrariness in personnel and management decisions.
- Give employees a voice in their own working conditions.
- Respect employees' right to self-organization.
- Involve labor when implementing privatization plans.
- Respond promptly and fairly to grievances.
- Seek to resolve complaints about unfair labor practices informally.
- Consult with lawyers on a case-by-case basis as needed.
- Tailor your approach to unions depending on their ideology, political organization, and leaders' personalities.
- Recognize that it takes time to negotiate separately with every recognized bargaining agent.
- Accept negotiators as equals; do not underestimate them.
- Document each meeting with labor representatives by taking careful notes.
- Keep negotiators focused on giving customers (taxpayers, clients, citizens) what they want.
- Make effective use of third parties in resolving collective bargaining deadlocks.
- Develop a crisis management plan.
- Prepare a media and public relations plan.

- Create labor-management committees to discuss short- and long-term objectives of the organization.
- Agree only to those terms that are likely to be ratified by decision makers on both sides.

APPENDIX B

Tips for Unions When Dealing With Managers

- Always be honest. Never lie to or mislead anyone for any reason. Once you compromise your integrity, you cannot get it back.
- Never tell a union member to lie or intentionally mislead any authority. There is no excuse for lying.
- Always act in a professional, business-like manner. Conducting union business is just that: business.
- Always be aware of a possible conflict of interest.
- If a member asks you a question and you are unsure of the answer, be honest. Tell her that you will find the right answer.
- Do not place your trust blindly. Trustworthiness must be earned through consistent follow-through on commitments.
- Take advantage of the knowledgeable, experienced people in the union. They are very familiar with many of the situations you will encounter, and can save you the pains and troubles that often result from reinvention.
- Surround yourself with all types of people, including those who disagree with your views. The consideration of different points of view is an important part of the decision-making process.
- Confide only in those you feel you can trust. Remember that anything you say can come back to haunt you.
- Do not make decisions in anger. Always seek a second opinion.
- Be suspicious of but respectful of management. Thoroughly analyze their possible motivation.
- Remind employees that their statements and memos are frequently used against them. Remind them to constantly be on their guard in their dealings with management.
- Keep a copy of all correspondence that you generate and receive.
- Copy all policy memoranda that the agency issues, and keep them in your filing system.
- Never meet with management by yourself. The recollections of two or more witnesses are far more persuasive than that of an individual.
- Regardless of your personal feelings, remember that you represent the interests of the entire bargaining unit.
- Pay attention to everyone who speaks up at a union meeting. Most people are there only to listen. Those who speak up may be willing to get involved.
- Delegate. Ask for help. The natural tendency is to let someone else handle the work. Do not be shy about admitting that there is too much work for one person.
- Recognize those who assist. All of us are volunteers. Praise and encouragement are often the only motivational tools we can offer. Dispense them liberally.
- Keep meticulous records of all of your dealings with management and of internal union business.
- Do not be afraid to ask questions.
- Do not be intimidated by management's fear tactics.
- If you are not sure about whether management's actions violate the contract or law, ask someone who knows.
- Beware of divide-and-conquer tactics.
- The local president should also coordinate all of the bargaining in the sector.
- Record and keep contemporaneous notes of all conversations or encounters with management.

- Do not be afraid to request sufficient official time to perform representational functions. If the agency refuses to grant the requests, coordinate the filing of a grievance with your local.
- Do not abuse official time. If you are done using official time, you should return to work.
- Do not be afraid to call the local union president.

Source: Adapted from Gilson, 2008. ©BobGilson. Reprinted from FedSmith.com.

APPENDIX C

Mock Disciplinary Appeal Board Hearing[5]

Cast of Characters

Wilson Worker	Appellant
Loren Lawyer	Appellant's attorney
Estimate Value	Tax assessor
Guy Noir	Security director for tax assessor
Chris Counselor	Tax assessor's attorney
Fred Fair	Hearing examiner

Fred Fair: The parties will come to order. The hearing is now open and on the record before the appeal board. Let the record show that the presiding officer for the hearing is Fred Fair. The hearing will take up the matter of the appeal from Wilson Worker, appeal number 100010, of the appellant's dismissal, effective November 1, 2010, from a supervisor's position with the Office of the County Tax Assessor. The parties will state their appearances.

Chris Counselor: For the tax assessor's office, appearing are Estimate Value, the county tax assessor; Guy Noir, security director for the assessor's office; and Chris Counselor, legal counsel for the office.

Loren Lawyer: The appellant, Wilson Worker, appears in person and by counsel Loren Lawyer.

Fred Fair: Do the parties have any stipulations in this matter?

Loren Lawyer: Yes, the appellant stipulates that notice of the dismissal and opportunity to discuss the matter prior to becoming effective followed established county rules and regulation. The appellant does not appeal the procedures followed in the dismissal but appeals the reasonableness of the tax assessor in dismissing the appellant.

Chris Counselor: The tax assessor also stipulates that the process it followed in dismissing the appellant was in compliance with its disciplinary policies set forth under county rules.

Fred Fair: The process followed in the dismissal of the appellant has been stipulated to by both parties and is uncontested for this hearing. Does the tax assessor wish to enter any exhibits into evidence at this time?

Chris Counselor:	Yes, we have prefiled the tax assessor's Exhibits 1 through 5. The appellant was served with copies of these exhibits in compliance with the hearing examiner's orders. The exhibits are a copy of the tax assessor's policy on the confidentiality of records, copy of the investigative report of this incident made by the tax assessor's security department, letters proposing and finalizing the dismissal, and a notarized statement from a former employee.
Fred Fair:	Does the appellant have any objections?
Loren Lawyer:	The appellant has none.
Fred Fair:	Thank you. The tax assessor's Exhibits 1 through 5 are admitted and made part of the record in this matter. Does the appellant wish to enter any exhibits?
Loren Lawyer:	The appellant has no exhibits to enter at this time but reserves the right to enter exhibits as appropriate at a later time during the hearing.
Fred Fair:	Does the tax assessor have any objection?
Chris Counselor:	The tax assessor has no objection but also reserves the right to raise objections to any appellant's exhibits as may later be introduced.
Fred Fair:	Thank you. The hearing will proceed with the presentation of evidence and testimony. The tax assessor's office will present its case first. The tax assessor may call the first witness.
Chris Counselor:	We call Estimate Value to the stand.

(Estimate Value takes the stand. Fred Fair, the hearing examiner, swears the witness in.)

Fred Fair:	Stand and raise your right hand. Do you swear or affirm that the testimony you are about to give is the truth, the whole truth, and nothing but the truth?
Estimate Value:	I do.
Fred Fair:	You may sit down.
Chris Counselor:	Please state your name for the record and where you are employed.
Estimate Value:	My name is Estimate Value. I am the county tax assessor. I was elected to office in 2000 and have been reelected to the office since then. My education includes a bachelor's degree in accounting and a master's degree in public administration.
Chris Counselor:	Are you acquainted with the appellant, Wilson Worker?
Estimate Value:	Yes, Wilson was employed in my office as a supervisor of our data entry and records processing team. Wilson supervised a team of seven data entry clerks and three file clerks. Up until this incident, Wilson had a clean record in my office and was a hard-working and trusted employee.
Chris Counselor:	What are the facts in the matter that led you to dismiss the appellant?
Estimate Value:	We received an anonymous tip on the "hot line" that Wilson Worker's home was listed substantially under value for tax purposes. The "hot line" allows persons to report allegations of wrong-doing, inappropriate and unethical behavior, or illegal activities involving tax assessments. I ordered the security director to investigate the allegation. I am dedicated to the integrity of tax records in my office. The public must be able to trust the accuracy of records processed by this department.

Chris Counselor: What happened next?

Estimate Value: The security director completed the investigation and gave me a copy. The security director found that the assessed property value listed on official records of the tax assessor's office for Wilson Worker's residence was approximately half of that for comparable residents in the same neighborhood with comparable homestead exemption histories.

Chris Counselor: What was the impact on Wilson Worker's tax liability?

Estimate Value: Property taxes for Wilson's residence were underassessed in 2006. Wilson's property taxes prior to 2009 were correctly assessed and paid. The report concluded that Wilson underpaid property taxes by $3,000 last year.

Chris Counselor: Did the investigation determine how the undervaluing and underassessment of Wilson's liability for property taxes could have occurred?

Estimate Value: Yes, the security director reviewed the computer records affecting Wilson's tax records during his entire tenure with the tax assessor's office, interviewed employees in the computer department, members of Wilson's work team, and Wilson. The investigative report concluded that official tax assessment records were altered under Wilson's security access password. The changes gave Wilson an illegal reduction of property taxes.

Chris Counselor: Did the investigative report conclude that Wilson acted alone or with the help of any coconspirators?

Estimate Value: The report concluded that Wilson acted alone. The security director said no other employees were incriminated.

Chris Counselor: Did the report identify who the anonymous caller was who identified Wilson's taxable property value was grossly underreported?

Estimate Value: Yes, he was identified as Tom Tenure, a former employee.

Chris Counselor: Did you confront Wilson Worker with the evidence of the investigation?

Estimate Value: Yes. I met with Wilson and gave him a copy of the investigative report.

Chris Counselor: What did Wilson say?

Estimate Value: Wilson denied any culpability. Wilson claimed to have been practicing on the software we were installing during 2009 to upgrade our computer system.

Chris Counselor: How would that have changed tax records?

Estimate Value: During installation of the new software, a parallel system was available for staff to practice with. Wilson claimed to have entered a lower tax assessment on the parallel system for 123 SW 57th Avenue, the address where Wilson resides. Wilson realized immediately the entry was not made on the parallel system but on the real system, and lowered the property tax liability.

Chris Counselor: Did Wilson attempt to correct the incorrect data entry? What did Wilson say about that?

Loren Lawyer: Your honor, I object to the form of the question. Chris Counselor asked the witness two questions and I won't be able to determine to which question the witness is responding.

Chris Counselor:	Your honor, I believe I asked one question using a two-question format. However, the intent of the question is clear and I respectfully request you overrule the objection of my worthy opponent and permit the witness to proceed.
Fred Fair:	The objection is overruled. The witness may respond to the question.
Estimate Value:	By now I've forgotten the question.
Chris Counselor:	Did Wilson try to change the incorrect data entry?
Estimate Value:	Wilson spoke with another team supervisor about the incident. Wilson said that the supervisor's advice was not to worry because record changes made during the trial period would not alter official records.
Chris Counselor:	From whom did Wilson get that advice?
Estimate Value:	Wilson said the advice was from Tom Tenure, a long-time supervisor in the tax assessor's office. Mr. Tenure retired and moved out of the area before the incorrect property value on Wilson's home was discovered.
Chris Counselor:	Did you question Mr. Tenure?
Estimate Value:	Since Mr. Tenure's testimony was so critical, we spoke to him by phone. Mr. Tenure did not recall the conversation Wilson claims they had. Mr. Tenure could not be here for today's hearing but provided his notarized statement.
Chris Counselor:	What happened next?
Estimate Value:	That left me with no other course of action than to dismiss Wilson for cause and terminate his employment with the tax assessor's office. I advised Wilson of my final decision by letter that same day. The letter also advised Wilson when he would receive his last paycheck. Information from the human resources office would follow, regarding eligibility to continue healthcare benefits under COBRA. I also told Wilson of the opportunity under County Employee Relations policies to appeal the dismissal within 30 days for a hearing before the appeal board.
Chris Counselor:	This concludes the direct examination of this witness. Thank you.
Fred Fair:	Does counsel for the appellant want to cross-examine this witness?
Loren Lawyer:	Yes, thank you. Estimate Value, you said that neither the investigation report nor the security director concluded that anyone other than Wilson Worker altered computer records to lower Wilson's tax liability. Correct?
Estimate Value:	That is my testimony.
Loren Lawyer:	Does that mean that only Wilson could have altered the records to obtain lower taxes?
Estimate Value:	That is what I believe.
Loren Lawyer:	And you are sure that happened in this case?
Estimate Value:	That was the conclusion reached by the security director after a thorough investigation.
Loren Lawyer:	What consideration did you give Wilson for the many years of faithful work for the tax assessor's office?

Estimate Value: Up until this incident, Wilson had earned a reputation as a faithful, hard-working employee with at least satisfactory performance evaluations. However, I could not overlook my conclusion that Wilson breached the trust we have in employees to respect and guard the accuracy of our records. Wilson was dishonest with me and violated that trust. That is why I fired Wilson.

Loren Lawyer: I have no further questions of this witness.

Fred Fair: Thank you. You may return to your seat. The tax assessor's office may call the next witness.

(Estimate Value steps down from the witness stand.)

Chris Counselor: The tax assessor's office calls Guy Noir to the stand.

(Guy Noir takes the stand. Fred Fair, the hearing examiner, swears the witness in.)

Fred Fair: Stand and raise your right hand. Do you swear or affirm that the testimony you are about to give is the truth, the whole truth, and nothing but the truth?

Guy Noir: I do.

Fred Fair: You may take your seat.

Chris Counselor: Please state your name and where you work, for the record.

Guy Noir: My name is Guy Noir and I am responsible for internal investigations in the tax assessor's office. I am a graduate of the Private Eye Institute, located on the 12th floor of the Acme Building in downtown Minneapolis.

Chris Counselor: How are you acquainted with the appellant in this matter?

Guy Noir: Wilson Worker was the supervisor of the data entry and records processing team. I became personally acquainted with Wilson when the tax assessor asked me to investigate a case of fraudulent tax assessment involving Wilson's residence.

Chris Counselor: Please tell the appeal board about your investigation.

Guy Noir: I asked the manager of the management information systems—the MIS computer whiz—to determine who made the alterations to Wilson's tax records. The MIS manager said that the changes to Wilson's tax records were made under Wilson's password on Wilson's office computer.

Chris Counselor: What else did you learn?

Guy Noir: The MIS manager said that during the installation period of the new software system entries on the system were "live" while entries on the parallel system were not. The manager thought that was made clear to all employees during the installation period.

Chris Counselor: Whom else did you interview?

Guy Noir: I interviewed Wilson. He admitted making the entry lowering the residential tax liability but said a long-time employee in office advised that no entries made during the trial period would take effect. Wilson denied willfully lowering the tax liability. When I asked Wilson who said that entries during the trial period would not become effective, Wilson identified Tom Tenure, a former employee, now retired and living out of the area.

Chris Counselor: Did you contact Mr. Tenure?

Guy Noir:	Yes. He could not recall the conversation with Wilson. In fact, I got the impression that Mr. Tenure and Wilson were not the best of friends and had difficulties working together at the tax assessor's office.
Chris Counselor:	Why is Mr. Tenure not present today to offer his testimony?
Guy Noir:	He refused to travel back here because of the expense. A subpoena would be invalid because he lives out of state. He cooperated by providing a notarized statement of his testimony.
Chris Counselor:	The tax assessor's office calls your attention to its Exhibit 5, the statement by former employee Tom Tenure. I have no further questions of this witness.
Fred Fair:	Counselor Loren Lawyer, do you have any cross-examination of this witness?
Loren Lawyer:	Yes.
Fred Fair:	Thank you. I remind the witness you are still under oath. Counselor, you may proceed.
Loren Lawyer:	You testified that the tax records for Wilson's residence were fraudulent. Are you a criminal law expert?
Guy Noir:	No.
Loren Lawyer:	Did you report the incident to the county attorney or seek the assistance of the state's attorney?
Guy Noir:	No.
Loren Lawyer:	Why, then, do you testify that Wilson committed an illegal act?
Guy Noir:	I did not say it was illegal, just fraudulent.
Loren Lawyer:	What's the difference?
Guy Noir:	That's a question you should address to an attorney.
Loren Lawyer:	Then why didn't you ask an attorney before recommending the tax assessor fire Wilson?
Guy Noir:	That was the tax assessor's call, not mine.
Loren Lawyer:	Passing the buck!
Chris Counselor:	I object!
Fred Fair:	Sustained. The comment will be stricken from the record.
Loren Lawyer:	Are you sure that all employees knew that records changed during the trial period could become final at the end of the trial?
Guy Noir:	The MIS manager said there was a general distribution of a note advising employees to be careful with data entries during the trial period.
Loren Lawyer:	Did the MIS manager say he had personal knowledge that Wilson received and understood the importance of entries made during the trial?
Guy Noir:	No.
Loren Lawyer:	So you can't be sure that Wilson understood the consequence of the entry?

Guy Noir:	Well, no, but Wilson should have known.
Loren Lawyer:	What was the relationship between Mr. Tenure and Wilson when they worked together?
Guy Noir:	I gather it was not friendly. Tenure said that he and Wilson had serious disagreements at work. Tenure complained that his retirement pension was lowered because Wilson got more overtime work than he did. There was bad blood between the two over the issue.
Loren Lawyer:	I have no further questions for this witness.
Fred Fair:	Thank you. The witness may step down from the witness stand.

(Guy Noir steps down from the witness stand.)

Fred Fair:	Does the tax assessor have any further evidence or witnesses?
Chris Counselor:	No, your honor. The tax assessor rests.
Fred Fair:	Wilson Worker may now present evidence.
Loren Lawyer:	I would like to call Wilson Worker to the stand.

(Wilson Worker takes the stand and is sworn in.)

Fred Fair:	Stand and raise your right hand to be sworn in. Do you swear or affirm that the testimony you are about to give is the truth, the whole truth, and nothing but the truth?
Wilson Worker:	I do.
Fred Fair:	You may be seated.
Loren Lawyer:	Please state your name and where you were employed.
Wilson Worker:	My name is Wilson Worker and I was employed as the supervisor of the data entry and records processing team at the county tax assessor's office.
Loren Lawyer:	Tell the appeal board about your qualifications.
Wilson Worker:	I was employed by the tax assessor's office for 15 years. I rose from a data entry clerk to team supervisor after completing the associate's degree in computer operations and supervision management from County Community College in 2000.
Loren Lawyer:	Let's get right to the heart of this matter. Did you change the tax records for your residence and lower the tax liability?
Wilson Worker:	Yes.
Loren Lawyer:	Why?
Wilson Worker:	I was practicing on a new software system being installed in the office on what I thought was a parallel version of the software. After I entered a taxable value for my property that cut it in half, I discovered that I had mistakenly made the change in the real version, not the parallel. I was horrified.
Loren Lawyer:	Then what did you do?
Wilson Worker:	I asked my coworker, Tom Tenure, if I should report this to the tax assessor. Tom said "no" because all record changes made during the practice period would not change any permanent records. "Don't worry," he said to me.
Loren Lawyer:	What about your relationship with Mr. Tenure?

Wilson Worker:	It wasn't good but I trusted him in this case because of his many years of experience in the office and his reputation for honesty. Later, I learned that he had given me very bad advice, advice that he knew was false. I had no idea he would deceive me, threaten my employment, and ruin my reputation.
Loren Lawyer:	Were you aware of the memo from the MIS manager that changes made to the tax database during the trial period would be converted into official records later?
Wilson Worker:	I remembered the memo but understood it to say that no record changes made during the trial period would convert into the official database afterwards. Besides, I thought I changed my records in the parallel system. Anyway, Mr. Tenure certainly did not warn me of it when we spoke about the incident.
Loren Lawyer:	Were you surprised to learn that Tom Tenure was the "anonymous" person who reported you had falsely altered your own tax records?
Wilson Worker:	No, we never got along. Tom retired and left the area knowing that I inadvertently changed my records. The "anonymous" informant knew that I would not realize my taxes were undercalculated until the tax payment information arrived from the mortgage company. Tom had the motivation and opportunity to do me in.
Loren Lawyer:	So, you deny any wrong-doing in this case?
Wilson Worker:	Absolutely and emphatically, yes. I deny doing anything wrong or illegal.
Loren Lawyer:	What do you ask the appeal board to do for you in this appeal?
Wilson Worker:	I believe I did nothing wrong and should not have been fired. However, if the appeal board finds that my actions violated any policy, then I will accept a suspension without pay and then be returned to my supervisor's position.
Loren Lawyer:	Thank you. I have no further questions of the appellant.
Fred Fair:	Does counsel for the tax assessor's office wish to cross-examine the appellant?
Chris Counselor:	No, your honor.
Fred Fair:	Does counsel for the appellant have any additional testimony or evidence to present?
Loren Lawyer:	No, your honor. Wilson Worker rests.
Fred Fair:	The appellant may step down from the witness stand.

(Wilson Worker returns to the appellant's seat.)

Fred Fair:	The tax assessor may make a closing statement.
Chris Counselor:	Thank you. Members of the board, Wilson Worker breached the trust the tax assessor places on employees. The public must be able to rely on the accuracy of tax records to accept the property tax bills we all receive yearly. The public may be unhappy with the amount of their taxes but never question its accuracy. Wilson Worker falsified tax records for personal gain and deserves to be fired. We ask that you affirm the decision of the tax assessor to dismiss Wilson Worker and restore public trust in the property tax assessment process.
Fred Fair:	Thank you. The appellant may make a closing statement.
Loren Lawyer:	Thank you. Honorable board members, Wilson Worker is an honest person. The deceitful action of a coworker made Wilson appear a liar and possibly a criminal. A terrible wrong was committed against my client. At worst, Wilson may have

stumbled in following office procedures when trying to learn a new computer system. That's not a crime. Wilson does not deserve the punishment that was given. I implore this board to restore Wilson to the supervisor position. The evidence in this case justifies your decision to do just that. Thank you.

Fred Fair: The appeal board thanks both parties for their conduct throughout this proceeding. The Board will now recess to discuss the matter and try to reach a decision.[5]

APPENDIX D

Bargaining Checklist and Observation Sheet

Observed Behavior	*Management*		*Union*	
A. Negative Behaviors				
Did the bargaining team . . .				
Underestimate the other party?	Y	N	Y	N
Overestimate the strength of their case?	Y	N	Y	N
Seem unprepared?	Y	N	Y	N
Advance vague proposals?	Y	N	Y	N
Argue among themselves?	Y	N	Y	N
Lose their temper?	Y	N	Y	N
Make assumptions about the other party's priorities?	Y	N	Y	N
Escalate demands unrealistically?	Y	N	Y	N
Oversell?	Y	N	Y	N
Compromise too readily?	Y	N	Y	N
Act defensive?	Y	N	Y	N
Interrupt the other parties?	Y	N	Y	N
Rush the proceedings?	Y	N	Y	N
React prematurely to the other party's proposals?	Y	N	Y	N
End the meeting on a negative note?	Y	N	Y	N
Make promises they could not keep?	Y	N	Y	N
Lie?	Y	N	Y	N
Break confidences?	Y	N	Y	N

Observed Behavior	Management		Union	
B. Positive Behaviors				
Did the bargaining team . . .				
Act calm and cool?	Y	N	Y	N
Show respect to the other party?	Y	N	Y	N
Demonstrate flexibilty?	Y	N	Y	N
Act reasonably?	Y	N	Y	N
Listen carefully?	Y	N	Y	N
Focus on relevant issue?	Y	N	Y	N
Study alternatives and new information?	Y	N	Y	N
Caucus when needed?	Y	N	Y	N
Avoid intimidation?	Y	N	Y	N
Respect confidentiality?	Y	N	Y	N
Negotiate in good faith?	Y	N	Y	N
Exhibit careful planning?	Y	N	Y	N
Heed mutually agreed-upon deadlines?	Y	N	Y	N
Tell the truth?	Y	N	Y	N

Source: Adapted from Colosi, 1985.

NOTES

1. Open shop refers to workplaces with unions but where union membership is not a condition of employment.

2. Free riders are those who do not belong to a union, but who nonetheless benefit from its activities.

3. Federal employees do not have the right to strike. In most states, it is illegal for state employees to strike. Some states give state employees a limited right to strike.

4. The negative behaviors by bargaining team members shown in section A are contrasted with the positive behaviors listed in section B. Although some of the section A examples may be "bargaining as usual" rather than legal violations of the "good faith" requirement, they are likely to be off-putting to the other side, and the temptation might be for the opposite team to respond in kind, thereby escalating the hostility.

5. Conceived by Jeff J. Montague, Human Resources Manager, Kansas Department of Commerce, and adapted by John T. Collins, Office of Civil Rights and Labor Relations, Miami-Dade Transit. Used with permission, 2008.

REFERENCES

AFGE's "fighting spirit": Gage outlines challenges. (2003, December 1). *Federal Times,* p. 8.

Albach, H. (1993, December). *Culture and technical innovation: A cross-cultural analysis and policy recommendations.* Berlin: Akademie der Wissenschaften zu Berlin, Forschungsbericht 9, Walter de Gruyter.

American Federation of Teachers. (2004, June). *AFT public employee compensation survey.* New York: Author. Retrieved July 23, 2008, from www.aft.org/salary/2004/download/aftpe04survey.pdf

Aronowitz, S. (1998). *From the ashes of the old.* New York: Houghton Mifflin.

Bacon, D. (1999, January 10). UC buckles under grad student strike. *In These Times,* p. 7.

Baker, J. G. (1996, April). Negotiating a collective bargaining agreement: Law and strategy. *Labor Law Journal,* pp. 253–266.

BBC News. (2007a, November 14). *French strike brings travel chaos.* Retrieved July 3, 2008, from http://news.bbc.co.uk/2/hi/europe/7093373.stm

BBC News. (2007b, November 20). *France gripped by massive strike.* Retrieved July 3, 2008, from http://news.bbc.co.uk/2/hi/europe/7093373.stm

BBC News. (2007c, November 22). *France's rail strike "nears end."* Retrieved July 3, 2008, from http://news.bbc.co.uk/2/hi/europe/7106764.stm

Benest, F., & Grijalva, R. (2002, January/February). Enhancing the manager/fire chief relationship. *Public Management.* Retrieved October 25, 2003, from www.icma.org/upload/library/IQ/500632.htm

Bennhold, K. (2007, November 13). France: Strike to challenge Sarkozy. *New York Times.* Retrieved July 3, 2008, from http://www.nytimes.com/2007/11/13/world/europe/13BRIEFS-FRANCE.html?_r=1&fta=y&oref=slogin

Bernstein, A. (1998, December 14). Grad students vs. California. *BusinessWeek,* p. 6.

Brackey, H. (1999, September 6). Economy passes by younger workers. *Miami Herald,* pp. A1, A17.

Briggs, S., & Siegele, M. H. (1994). The ethical standards clause: A lesson from the private sector for the public sector. *Journal of Collective Negotiations, 23*(3), 181–186.

Bureau of Labor Statistics, U.S. Department of Labor. (2004). *Union member summary.* Retrieved February 3, 2004, from http://bls.gov/news.release/union2.nro.htm

Bureau of Labor Statistics, U.S. Department of Labor. (2007a). *Major work stoppages in 2007.* Retrieved June 5, 2008, from http://www.bls.gov/news.release/wkstp.nr0.htm

Bureau of Labor Statistics, U.S. Department of Labor. (2007b). *Union members in 2006.* Retrieved June 5, 2008, from http://www.bls.gov/news.release/archives/union2_01252007.pdf

Coleman, C. (1990). *Managing labor relations in the public sector.* San Francisco: Jossey-Bass.

Colosi, T. R. (1985). The negotiating process. In R. Helsby, J. Tener, & J. Lefkowitz (Eds.), *The evolving process: Collective negotiations in public employment* (pp. 217–232). Fort Washington, PA: Labor Relations Press.

Crampton, S., Hodge, J., & Mishra, J. (2002). The use of union dues for political activity: Current status. *Public Personnel Management, 31*(1), 121–129.

Denholm, D. Y. (1997). The case against public sector unionism and collective bargaining. *Government Union Review, 18*(1), 31–52.

Devinatz, V. G. (1997). Testing the Johnston "public sector union strike success" hypothesis: A qualitative analysis. *Journal of Collective Negotiations, 26*(2), 99–112.

Dibble, R. E. (1997). Alternative dispute resolution of employment conflicts: The search for standards. *Journal of Collective Negotiations, 26*(1), 73–84.

European Commission. (2008). European Works Councils: Consultation of the European Social Partners on the revision of Council Directive 94/45/EC of 22 September 1994 on the establishment of a European Works Council or a procedure in Community-scale undertakings for the purposes of informing and consulting employees. Brussels. Retrieved July 23, 2008, from http://ec.europa.eu/employment_social/labour_law/docs/2008/ewc_consultation2_en.pdf

Ferris, F. (2008, June 08). Scuttling the federal labor relations authority. *Fedsmith.com*. Retrieved June 16, 2008, from http://www.fedsmith.com/article/1621/

Fisher, R., & Ury, W. (1981). *Getting to yes*. New York: Penguin.

Flint, J. (2002, August). Mending labor-management relationships. *Public Management*. Retrieved October 25, 2003, from www.icma.org/upload/library/IQ/500289.htm

Folmar, K. (1999, June 18). UCI teaching assistants vote to unionize. *Los Angeles Times*, p. B10.

Fretz, G. E., & Walsh, D. E. (1998). Aggression, peaceful coexistence, mutual cooperation—it's up to us. *Public Personnel Management, 27*(2), 69–76.

Fulton, L. (2007). Germany: Workplace Representation. European Union, National Industrial Relations, European Trade Union Institute (ETUI). Retrieved July 23, 2008, from http://www.workeparticipation.eu/layout/set/print/national_industrial_relations/countries/germany/workplace_representation

Germany: Mitbestimmungsrechte des Betriebsrats (Co-Determination Rights of the Works Council). (2007, October 31). European Foundation for the Improvement of Living and Working Conditions. Retrieved July 23, 2008, from http://www.eurofound.europa.eu/emire/germany/codetermination rightsoftheworkscouncil-de.htm

Gilson, R. J. (2008). Retrieved June 3, 2008, from www.fedsmith.com/article/authors/5.html

Girnt, C. (1998). A sense of reality and pragmatism: An interview with industrial relations guru Wolfgang Streeck. *Mitbestimmung* International edition, Hans Boeckler Stiftung. Retrieved July 23, 2008, from http://www.boeckler.de/164_29131.html

Greenhouse, S. (1998, October 12). Friction seen in future talks on city labor. *New York Times*, p. B1.

Greenhouse, S., & Arenson, K. (2004). Labor board says graduate students at private universities have no right to unionize. *New York Times*. Retrieved August 8, 2004, from www.nytimes.com/2004/07/16/education/16union.html

Hirsch, B., & Macpherson, D. (2007). *Union membership and coverage database from the CPS (Unionstats.com)*. http://www.unionstats.com/

Institute of Governmental Studies (IGS). (2006, January). *Proposition 75: Use of union dues for political purposes*. Berkeley, CA: Institute of Governmental Studies. Retrieved February 4, 2008, from www.igs.berkeley.edu/library/htlUnionDues.html

International Brotherhood of Electrical Workers. (2004, June). IBEW, unions fight new defense rules. *IBEW Journal*. Retrieved June 30, 2004, from www.ibew.org/stories/04journal/0406/p9.htm

Kaufman, T. (2004, February 16). Union-busting DOD style. *Federal Times*, pp. 1, 6, 7.

Kearney, R. C. (1998a). Labor law. In J. Shafritz (Ed.), *International encyclopedia of public policy and administration* (pp. 1241–1244). Boulder, CO: Westview Press.

Kearney, R. C. (1998b). Strike. In J. Shafritz (Ed.), *International encyclopedia of public policy and administration* (pp. 2180–2182). Boulder, CO: Westview Press.

Kearney, R. C. (2003). Problems and prospects for public employee unions and public managers. In S. Hays & R. Kearney (Eds.), *Public personnel administration: Problems and prospects* (4th ed., pp. 310–333). Upper Saddle River, NJ: Prentice Hall.

Lane, C. M. (1996, February). Unions and management are finding common ground, but cultural change is slow and difficult for these former adversaries. *Government Executive*, p. 41.

Levine, M. (1997). The union role in labor-management cooperation. *Journal of Collective Negotiations, 26*(3), 203–222.

Library of Congress. (1995, August). *Germany: Co-determination*. Federal Research Division, Country Studies Series. Retrieved July 23, 2008, from http://www.country-data.com/cgi-bin/query/r-4945.html

Lobel, I. B. (1994, December). Realities of interest-based (win-win) bargaining. *Labor Law Journal, 7*, 1–777.

Losey, S. (2004, April 12). Why weaker unions worry managers. *Federal Times*, pp. 1, 8.

M&C Business. (n.d.). *Thousands protest as French public sector workers strike* (Roundup). Retrieved July 3, 2008, from http://www.monstersandcritics.com/news/business/news/article_1405653.php/Thousands_protest_as_French_public_sector_workers_strike_Roundup_

Mesch, D., & Shamayeva, O. (1996). Arbitration in practice: A profile of public sector arbitration cases. *Public Personnel Management, 25*(1), 119–131.

Northrup, H. (1984). The rise and demise of PATCO. *Industrial & Labor Relations Review, 37*(2), 167–184.

Orzechowski, W., & Marlow, M. (1995). Political participation, public sector labor unions and public spending. *Government Union Review, 16*(2), 1–25.

Osborne, D., & Plastrik, P. (1998, March/April). Empowerment in the public sector. *New Democrat,* p. 21.

Palmaffy, T. (1999, June 7). Class struggle. *New Republic,* pp. 20–24.

Parsons, P. A., Belcher, J., & Jackson, T. (1998). A labor-management approach to health care cost savings: The Peoria experience. *Public Personnel Management, 27*(2), 23–38.

Patriarca, M., & Welz, C. (2008, March 20). *European Works Council in practice: Key research findings.* European Foundation for the Improvement of Living and Working Conditions. Retrieved July 23, 2008, from http://www.eurofound.europa.eu/pubdocs/2008/28/en/1/ef0828en.pdf

Reich, R. (1998). *Locked in the cabinet.* New York: Vintage.

Richardson, V. (2005, October 17). For Arnold, stakes are high; Special election "a huge gamble." *Washington Times,* Nation.

Rubin, B., & Rubin, R. (2001). *Labor-management partnerships: A new approach to collaborative management.* Arlington, VA: IBM Endowment for the Business of Government. www.business ofgovernment.org

Sanchez, R. (1996, February 4). Graduate teaching assistants press their call for equity in academia. *Washington Post,* p. A3.

Shenk, T. (2007). *The effects of graduate-student unionization.* Unpublished master's thesis, Iowa State University, Ames.

Sherk, J. (2006). *What do union members want? What paycheck protection laws show about how well unions reflect their members priorities.* Center for Data Analysis Report #06–08. Washington, DC: The Heritage Foundation.

Simon, P. (2007, April). *Germany: Freedom of association and labour law.* Organization for Security and Cooperation in Europe. Office for Democratic Institutions and Human Rights. Legislation Online. Retrieved July 23, 2008, from http://www.legislationline.org/?tid=221&jid=21&less=false

Steinberg, A. (2005, November 10). A not-so-special election; Schwarzenegger comes up empty in California. *The Washington Times,* p. A21.

Tomkins, J. (1995). *Human resource management in government.* New York: HarperCollins.

Ury, W. (1991). *Getting past no: Negotiating your way from confrontation to cooperation.* New York: Bantam.

U.S. Department of Labor. (1996). *Working together for public service.* Washington, DC: Author.

U.S. Labor struggles to regain clout. (1998, September 7). *Miami Herald,* p. 7A.

Vinson, J. (2002, May/June). Report debunks arbitration's low-cost myth. *Public Citizen, 1,* 5.

Walton, R. E., & McKersie, R. B. (1965). *A behavioral theory of labor negotiations.* New York: McGraw-Hill.

What to do when the union knocks. (1966, November). *Nation's Business,* p. 107.

Young, I. (2001, March 12). Partnership directive bewilders unions, agencies. *Federal Times,* pp. 4, 17.

Conclusion

The Future as Opportunity, Not Destiny

There are costs and risks to a program of action, but they are far less than the long-range risks and costs of comfortable action.

—John F. Kennedy

Peering into the 21st century, it is clear that the future is already here. At the beginning of the 20th century, the public service was dramatically transformed by the merit system (Chapter 1) undergirded by bureaucratic structures and the scientific management principles of the Machine Age. In the context of spending cuts and demands for better service delivery, contemporary times have witnessed fundamental challenges to these ideas—privatization (provision of public services by business), devolution (transfer of federal functions to subnational jurisdictions), and personnel reform (human resource management innovation)—in the name of smaller, more flexible, and more efficient government. What is needed is a systemic approach to such initiatives that deals with the overall role of government, the place of civil and military servants in that role, and the root causes of workforce problems. Strategies that focus on citizen needs, process improvement, and employee involvement likely will generate appropriate approaches, thereby enhancing the quality and productivity of government.

One hundred years ago, the public sector in all its size and diversity was an ideal laboratory for merit system innovations; in developing best practices, it became a model employer for the nation. Although remnants of such practices remain, notably in areas such as equal employment opportunity and employee-friendly policies, it has largely ceded its leadership position in the last several generations. How or whether that proud heritage is restored depends on its response to at least two major societal changes now under way: (1) rapidly expanding technologies, and (2) the demand for human competency.

■■ NEW TECHNOLOGIES
AND HUMAN COMPETENCIES

Most obvious is the explosion of office technology. What was once seen as merely a productivity measure is now affecting the definition of work and how it is organized: Tasks done by a room full of personnel in an earlier era can be handled by one person—anytime, anywhere. These technologies have only begun to be tapped, but the "death" of time and distance in a virtual work environment has already substantially altered the flexibility and speed of policy making—and who may be involved in decisions. These developments have affected a wide range of human resource functions with the advent of virtual recruitment centers, online job analysis systems, just-in-time computer-based training, and personnel appraisal software. Although information technologies may advance faster than human capacities to use them responsibly, they can foster broad participation on the part of the workforce. To the extent that this occurs, pathways through the paradoxes of competing needs and democracy may be discovered.

As technologies become widely accessible, requirements for human competency expands. These range from technical know-how such as client server technologies, virtual teaming, and Web-based videoconferencing to personal qualities such as genuine trust and sincere service. Indeed, in a high-tech atmosphere the only way that public agencies may be able to distinguish themselves from competing private providers is by the performance of their employees. Downsizing and disrespect have made it clear that individuals must anticipate change and add value and be responsive to reform. Unless or until they are seen as an asset worthy of investment, beginning with their selection, it is difficult to see how the public interest will be served effectively. When labor is regarded as a cost to be reduced rather than an asset to be enhanced, quality, productivity, and citizen service usually are sacrificed.

▌▌ TAKING INDIVIDUAL
RESPONSIBILITY FOR PARADOXES

The scope and diversity of these technological and human capacity changes mandate that there is no one best way to manage people. Management is a highly individualized art, as one must discover what works in difficult circumstances. Any number of techniques can succeed when aligned with the needs and goals of an agency, its employees, the populace they serve, and the manager's own natural style. Readers having come this far have ideas about what to do and why, but only those who have a strong desire to influence the performance of others and get real satisfaction in doing so will learn how to manage effectively.

Tom Morris (1997) examined what might happen if four key dimensions of the human experience were used to run a modern organization. He urged conscious recognition of the four philosophical transcendentals that enrich life: intellectual (truth), aesthetic (beauty), moral (goodness), and spiritual (unity). Each dimension produces individual and organizational excellence.

Truth is the foundation of all relationships; one must be true to self and in interactions with others. (There is no greater source of waste than speculation, gossip, and rumor that arise in the absence of truth.) People cannot flourish without ideas; without truth, they intellectually perish. The world is too dangerous for anything except the truth.

While essential, truth is not enough for fulfillment since humans are not mere intellects. They must also have something attractive to motivate them—beauty. The aesthetic dimension includes not only external observational beauty (e.g., flowers), but also internal performance beauty (e.g., quality work). Beauty liberates, refreshes, inspires, and thereby increases productivity; in contrast, ugliness depresses the spirit.

Doing true, beautiful things, though, is incomplete, Morris argues. Leaders must be convinced of the essential morality of what they are doing. Indeed, goodness might be considered a special kind of truth and beauty. People are at their best when engaged in a worthy task, one in which they can make a genuine difference. As Emerson said, "I pass this way but once; any good that I can do, let me do it now."

Truth, beauty, and goodness are still not sufficient: humans also must perceive a sense of wholeness, that they are a part of something greater than themselves. Matters of spirit are connected to truth, beauty, goodness—the worth of person and the collectivity to which she belongs. The Athenian Oath from ancient Greece, taken by all 17-year old citizens, captures the idea:

> We will ever strive for the ideals and sacred things of the city, both alone and with many; we will unceasingly seek to quicken the sense of public duty; we will revere and obey the city's laws; we will transmit this city not only not less, but greater, better and more beautiful than it was transmitted to us.

If Aristotle had run GM, he would have created strength and integrity throughout the company by nourishing a culture based on the four transcendental values. Living life centered on truth, beauty, goodness, and unity is ideal for the resolution of the signature paradoxes that have animated this book: organizations need the brains, bodies, and hearts of each individual—and vice versa. Transforming the organization—internalizing and institutionalizing the four dimensions—is anyone and everyone's job, but one that must be assumed by leaders. The keys to excellence lie before us.

Turning this page marks the end of the beginning for the keen student of the management of human resources. As an introduction to the subject, the book represents an invitation to be both an informed participant and a critical observer of the field. Common and surprising, confusing and understandable, the paradoxes, processes, and problems pondered here will continue to animate theory and practice throughout your career. "The art of progress," wrote Alfred North Whitehead, "is to preserve order amid change and to preserve change amid order." It is only fitting, then, that the book stops where it started, with the paradoxes of democracy and needs.

Striving for excellence means dealing with conflicting organizational and individual needs, and that may be done by emphasizing democratic values at work. The workplace is in transformation as agencies are doing everything to maximize use of technology and human capacities by revamping hiring strategies, refiguring job designs, broadening employee skill bases, and redesigning reward systems. A troubled example of this is the federal departments of Homeland Security and Defense, which other agencies and jurisdictions nonetheless may emulate. Such changes can be assessed and used to build on the key recruitment, compensation, training, and evaluation functions discussed in earlier chapters.

Indeed, Barack Obama's presidential administration confronts many problems and prospects as the first decade of the new century comes to a close and the second begins. The widely anticipated retirement tsunami of Baby Boomers from the workforce offers an opportunity to rethink the nature and character of public service, as a whole new generation of talented employees will be needed. Will the administration take a predominately bottom-up reform approach similar to the Clinton-Gore years, a top-down strategy like the Bush-Cheney era, or something different? What does the president, as chief public manager, think of the nation's largest workforce—government employees? Will he encourage American citizens—both at the beginning and end of their careers—to see the civil service as an opportunity to make a genuine difference? Does he perceive the increase in contract workers and political appointees in the last generation as healthy for the country? What does he think of recent human resource administration reforms? Is the proposed Public Service Academy worthy of political support? In the end, will there be a renaissance in public service in response to a call to serve and sacrifice for the common good?

Answers to such questions are important for both policy and management reasons. Thus, among the key stakeholders who will deal with the numerous policy issues in the years ahead—war, record deficits, alternative energy sources, the subprime mortgage debacle, health care, education, global warming—are public employees. Nothing happens in government without people. How they are managed, then, will determine investments in new technologies and human capital that drive the future. When people are treated as ends for which government exists rather than as means to be manipulated, the quality and productivity of public service can only improve in the years ahead. If so, look for more initiatives and innovations in human resource management. Some of these programs will be successful, and some will not. Those with the greatest value are likely to be management driven and cognizant of past experience and research data. Changes that seek partisan advantage with little interest in or knowledge of the complexities of governance can do a great deal of damage, and ultimately can become self-defeating (Bowman & West, 2007).

■■ ENVOI: "DREAM WHILE AWAKE"

As you close this textbook, dear reader, you may not be the same person that you were at the beginning of the term. Because of your studies, your understanding, compassion, and ability to engage others in informed discussion of human resource management has grown. The challenge is not to "tell it like it is," but instead to "tell it as it may become"—to eliminate hypocrisy and live up to cherished values. Unless the disconnect between autocratic organizational values and societal democratic values is bridged, human resource problems will only intensify. The entire range of an agency's human resource functions—selection, recruitment, position management, compensation, training, appraisal, and labor-management relations—must be aligned with the norms of democratic culture if the dilemmas and contradictions discussed in this volume are to be resolved. The alternatives are either to accept the status quo as fate or to abandon ideals for the security of authoritarian institutions. Either way, life will surely be a series of collisions with the future.

Dr. Jonas Salk, discoverer of the first vaccine against polio over a half century ago, reflected on his achievement:

> Ideas came to me as they do to all of us. The difference is I took them seriously. I didn't get discouraged that others didn't see what I saw. I had trust and confidence in my perceptions, rather than listening to dogma and what other people thought, I didn't allow anyone to discourage me—and everyone tried. But life is not a popularity contest.

This book, too, has sought to provoke new ideas and to encourage readers to create their own futures. In so doing, few facile solutions have been offered, for to do so would defeat the purpose. Instead, general principles and specific propositions have been suggested, leaving the discerning individual to align, adapt, and apply them to make the public service, in the words of John F. Kennedy, "a proud and lively career."

REFERENCES

Bowman, J., & West, J. (2007). *American public service: Radical civil service reform and the merit system.* New York: Taylor and Francis.

Morris, T. (1997). *If Aristotle ran General Motors.* New York: Holt.

GLOSSARY

3:00 syndrome. Attention to work-related tasks wanes as employees begin to think about children ready to leave school and return home.

80% rule. A standard for determining discrimination. Any selection process that results in qualification rates of protected groups that are less than 80% of the highest group.

360° evaluation. Superiors, peers, subordinates, and sometimes people outside the organization rate one another.

Actor/observer bias. An actor sees his behavior as blameless; when observing the same behavior by another, however, he sees it as blameworthy.

Adoption assistance. Includes benefits ranging from time off to reimbursement of expenses following adoption of a child.

Adult learning. A theory of employee training that integrates employee experience, active participation, motivation for self-improvement, problem solving, and control over the learning material.

Adverse action. Employer's sanction against an employee for unsatisfactory performance or misconduct.

Affirmative action. A strategy that aims to overcome barriers to equal employment opportunities or remedy the effects of past discrimination. See also *Quotas*.

Age Discrimination in Employment Act of 1967 (ADEA). Prohibits discrimination in employment decisions based on age. Applies to workers 40 years and older.

Agency shop. Employee is not required to join the union but must contribute a service charge to cover collective bargaining, grievance processes, and arbitration costs.

Alternative work schedules. The arrangement of hours of the day, days of the week, and place of work that differs from the traditional 8-to-5 hours, Monday-through-Friday days, and the in-office work site.

Americans with Disabilities Act of 1990 (ADA). Prohibits discrimination in employment decisions based on disability and requires employers to provide reasonable accommodations.

Arbitration. A dispute resolution procedure that relies on a neutral third party who conducts hearings, researches contentious issues, and makes nonbinding recommendations for consideration.

Assembled tests. When the selection process requires one or more tests in addition to experience and education such as a typing exam, psychological test, or work sample.

Assessment center. A location where employees and job applicants take job-related tests and exercises in order to assess their skills, competencies, and character traits.

At-will employment. A doctrine by which both employers and employees can sever their relations at a moment's notice. The bulk of the public sector provides tenure rights that require a demonstration of appropriate cause, due process proceedings, and internal and external appeals processes.

Authorized salary range. The range of pay stipulated in the pay plan of the jurisdiction. The range is generally provided in a series of step increments. In the past, new employees were required to start at the first step of the range. They generally moved along it according to time in position. Today there is more willingness to grant exceptions to experienced employees or where employee shortages exist. Broadbanding essentially increases the authorized salary range to include several positions.

Banding. When numerous job applicants within a certain range are treated as having identical test scores.

Bargaining unit determination. Identifies whom a union or other association in negotiation sessions will represent.

Behaviorally anchored rating system (BARS). Behavioral approach to appraisal, consisting of a series of scales based on key dimensions of performance.

Behavior-based evaluation systems. The evaluation of performance based on specific behaviors.

Benchmark jobs. In a comprehensive pay study, a portion of the total number of positions is compared with jobs outside the organization to ensure external equity. That is, these positions become pay benchmarks for the entire compensation system. These positions are anchored to general market salary ranges as indicated by reliable compensation information gathered directly, either by those conducting the pay study or organizations that periodically provide compensation survey information.

Benefits. All indirect payments provided to employees as part of their membership in the organization.

Bonus. A one-time payment made as a supplement or replacement for a raise that is added to base pay.

Broadbanding. When several grades are combined, creating a broader salary range for a position. Formal promotions are not required for substantial pay movement (as is the case with more traditional—and narrow—classification series that limit pay movement). Broadbanding has the effect of allowing greater discretion at the agency level, offering more organizational flexibility, and providing incentives for long-term development. It may increase total employee costs to the organization over time.

Certification of the bargaining agent. Action by the appropriate administrative agency (Federal Labor Relations Authority, Public Employees Relations Board, or equivalent) recognizing that an exclusive bargaining agent for a unit is appropriately constituted.

Certified lists. Lists of technically qualified individuals from whom a hiring authority may officially select. Certified lists in the past were limited to the top three candidates when civil service commissions ranked all candidates. Today, it is more common for human resource departments and hiring departments to assemble a list of all eligible candidates, and then pull from the top of the list as needed.

Civil law system. A scheme in which the law is based primarily on a code of laws that is applied by judges.

Civil Rights Act of 1964. A broad law which prohibits employers from discriminating against employees in hiring, promotion, and termination decisions, based on their race, color, religion, national origin, or gender.

Civil service. Refers to the branches of public service excluding legislative, judicial, or military, and in which positions are typically filled based on competitive examinations and a professional career public service exists with protections against political influence and patronage.

Civil service commission. The governing body authorized to oversee the civil service employment system. Originally, civil service commissions administered all competitive examinations, reviewed qualifications for technical merits, provided certified lists, and acted as a judicial review board for hiring abuses. Today, most selection functions have been moved to human resource departments in the executive branch or to the line agencies themselves. Where they continue to exist, civil service commissions tend to be policy and review boards.

Civil service reform. Efforts to modify the structures, process, and functions of the civil service system, such as the Pendleton Act of 1883, the Civil Service Reform Act of 1978, and the New Public Management movement of the 1990s.

Civil Service Reform Act of 1978 (CSRA). Federal law replacing the Civil Service Commission with two agencies: the U.S. Office of Personnel Management as the staff arm of the chief executive, and the U.S. Merit Systems Protection Board to adjudicate employee appeals. It also created the Federal Labor Relations Authority to oversee federal labor-management policies.

Class series. Refers to job classifications that are linked developmentally, such as Secretary I, II, III, and IV.

Climate for motivation. A relatively enduring set of perceived conditions at work that affect workers' motivation and behaviors.

Closed personnel system. Typical in rank-in-person systems in which few opportunities exist for lateral entry for those outside the organization. Ideally, such systems encourage employee development through job rotation and foster employee loyalty. See also *Open personnel system.*

Coaching. The training practice of assigning an experienced employee to help other employees master various job situations.

Cognitive information processing theory. Maintains that appraisal is a complex memory task involving data acquisition, storage, retrieval, and analysis. To process data, subjective categories are employed that in turn can produce rating errors.

Collective bargaining. A process whereby labor and management representatives meet to set terms and conditions of employment for employees in a bargaining unit.

Common law system. A scheme in which the law is developed primarily by decisions of courts rather than by codifications of legislatures or by executive actions.

Comparable worth. The theory that different jobs, equal in value to the organization, should be paid the same.

Compatibility, "similarity," or liking error. Appraisals may reflect the evaluator's tendency to rate highly those he or she likes or who are compatible with him or her.

Compressed workweek. A flex option where the number of hours worked per week is condensed into fewer days.

Contamination. Occurs when evaluations include factors unrelated to actual performance.

Contingent hiring. A preliminary hiring status that can be procedurally overturned if certain contingencies intervene. Appropriate contingencies include a postselection physical examination or drug test, funding availability, job freezes, and completion of specialized training programs. Where contingencies such as these exist, it is important to inform the selected candidate in the letter of intent.

Contrast error. Tendency to rate people relative to others instead of to performance criteria.

Cooperative problem solving. A form of labor management relations characterized by joint deliberations and planning to address pressing workplace problems.

Cost-of-living adjustment. Across-the-board pay change based on economic conditions, not performance.

Critical incident technique. Records key acts assumed to make the difference between effective and ineffective performance.

Cross-training. The practice of training employees to fill multiple job functions.

Dealing with difficult people. The basic strategy for dealing with problem employees is to arrest patterns of interaction with the difficult person through avoidance, setting boundaries, and confronting each untoward behavior in appropriate and controlling ways.

Decentralization of training. The shifting of responsibilities for training from the central human resource department to operating departments and line managers.

Defamation. A false statement, oral or written, that injures an individual's work reputation.

Deficiency. Occurs when evaluations fail to include all essential elements of performance.

Development. Preparing employees for assuming future responsibilities. See also *Training*.

Dialectic. Systematic reasoning that juxtaposes contradictory, competing ideas (theses, antitheses) and seeks to resolve them by creating a new synthesis.

Direct evidence. In a discrimination or retaliation case, proof of statements made by the decision maker that show unlawful bias against the employee at the time of an adverse decision.

Disparate impact. Also known as "adverse impact discrimination," it is a theory of liability in which plaintiffs claim that a facially neutral practice has a harmful effect on a class of employees characterized by race, gender, or other protected conditions. Disparate impact is generally defined as a selection rate of less than 80% of the group with the highest selection rate. See also *Disparate treatment discrimination*.

Disparate treatment discrimination. Discrimination in which plaintiffs claim that adverse personnel actions are based on race, gender, or other protected conditions. See also *Adverse impact discrimination.*

Diversity policies. Employers' policies which promote an environment that allows all employees to contribute to organizational goals and experience personal growth, regardless of individual ethnic or other differences.

Doctrine of harmony. Relationship between labor and management in which both sides emphasize cooperation, service orientation, participation, and the public interest.

Doctrine of hostility. Relationship between labor and management under traditional collective bargaining (adversarial, conflictual, confrontational).

Doctrine of sovereignty. Maintains that government has a responsibility to protect all societal interests. Therefore, it is inappropriate to require it to share power with interest groups (e.g., unions in negotiations) or dilute managerial rights.

Domestic partnership coverage. Refers to benefits such as health insurance and sick or bereavement leave that may be made available to a person designated as a domestic partner of an employee.

Downshifting. Process of scaling back career ambitions and giving more time and attention to family and personal needs.

Downsizing. Reducing the number of employees, often caused by actions such as reductions in force, outsourcing, or base closures.

Dress codes. Employer standards for employee appearance including clothing, grooming, and body ornamentation.

Due process rights. Pertains to public employees' right to a hearing when faced with adverse action.

Dues check-off. Employee may select payroll deduction option to pay union dues to representing union.

Education. Prepares people for the future by helping them to acquire necessary KSAs as well as value orientations. In the context of training and development, education differs from training in that it is concerned with broad principles of knowledge and practice rather than the technical details of work.

Education and experience evaluations. Includes application forms as well as requests for information about specific job competencies, which can be addressed in skill inventories (such as checklists), cover letters, and/or résumés.

Electoral popularity selection. The basis for representative democracy. As a selection method, it is good for the selection of major policy makers but ineffective as a method for selecting those who primarily fill administrative functions.

Electronic monitoring. Via email and video surveillance, Web site blocking, GPS tracking, this form of monitoring is used in attempt to increase productivity, improve quality, and reduce costs. It does so by continuously collecting performance data, pinpointing problems, and providing mediate feedback.

Electronic posting: Listing jobs on agency Web sites or Web sites exclusively dedicated to job seekers.

Ellerth/Faragher affirmative defense. A legal doctrine in hostile environment harassment claims which provides that if an employer can prove that it exercised reasonable care to prevent and correct the harassment and that the employee failed to use its remedial procedures, the employer may avoid liability.

Employee assistance programs (EAPs). Programs usually offering counseling or referral services for people having problems with alcohol, drug abuse, personal debt, domestic abuse, or other problems that impede job-related performance.

Equal Employment Opportunity Commission (EEOC). Federal agency that processes complaints of discrimination and reviews affirmative action plans.

Equal Pay Act of 1963. Prohibits sex discrimination in compensating people doing substantially the same jobs.

Error of central tendency. All staff receive average ratings or all dimensions of performance are rated average.

Essential function. The contemporary term for the major job duties of a position. The term was ushered in by the Americans with Disabilities Act, which prohibits discrimination of "an individual with a disability who, with or without reasonable accommodation, can perform the essential functions of the employment position."

Ethics Reform Act of 1989. Federal law establishing uniform financial disclosure requirements, prohibiting lobbying of former departments, and raising pay for executive, legislative, and judicial officials.

Evaluation. In the context of training, approaches that aim to assess the effectiveness of training, typically involving feedback from employees and managers.

Exit interview. A session conducted by the supervisor or human resource department in an attempt to learn why an employee is leaving.

External equity. The comparison of the pay of employees with the pay of those performing similar jobs in other organizations. Generally implemented in pay plans through occasional pay studies that compare a sample of positions (benchmark positions) to anchor the entire wage scale.

Fact finding. A dispute resolution procedure that relies on a neutral third party who conducts hearings, researches contentious issues, and makes nonbinding recommendations for consideration.

Fair Labor Standards Act of 1938 (FLSA). Basic federal statute that established the minimum wage and hours of work.

Family and Medical Leave Act (FMLA). Provides eligible workers with up to 12 weeks of unpaid leave during any 12-month period for childbirth or adoption; for caregiving to a child, elderly parent, or spouse with a serious health problem; or for a personal illness.

Fast-track positions. This informal term refers to positions that offer rapid career opportunities for training, management, exposure to a variety of techniques, and ultimately, promotion and increased salary levels. The Presidential Management Fellows program is an illustration at the federal level; placement as a managerial analyst in a city manager's office is an example at the local level.

Federal Labor Relations Authority (FLRA). The federal administrative unit charged with overseeing, investigating, and enforcing rules pertaining to labor-management relations.

Federal Employees Pay Comparability Act of 1990. Mandated that the 30% public-private sector pay gap be closed gradually by the end of the century.

Feedback. Evaluative information given to employees about their performance or behavior; purpose is to influence future performance or behavior.

Final-offer arbitration. The arbitrator's decision is restricted to the position taken by one or the other of the parties. This can include selection of a position taken by one side or the other on all issues taken together (by package) or selection on an issue-by-issue basis.

Flextime. Work schedules that allow flexible starting and quitting times but specify a required number of hours within a particular time period.

Free rider. In the context of labor-management relations, one who is a worker in a bargaining unit who acquires a benefit from union representation without the effort or costs that accompany union membership.

Free speech rights. The rights that public employees have to speak out as citizens in matters of public debate. These rights, however, do not protect them from adverse action when speaking out disrupts the efficiency of their workplace.

Gainsharing. Financial gains as a result of organization-wide performance are shared with employees.

General skills test. Provides information about abilities or aptitudes in areas such as reading, math, abstract thinking, spelling, language usage, general problem solving, judgment, proofreading, and memory.

Generation X. Those born between 1960 and 1980.

Grievance arbitration. Also called rights arbitration. Used to resolve outstanding disputes regarding employee grievances.

Halo effect. See *Spillover effect.*

Harassment. The subjection of an employee to unwelcome conduct that is so severe and pervasive it creates a hostile work environment. The unwelcome conduct must be because of a criterion protected by discrimination laws. In the case of sexual harassment, it may be the subjection of an employee to tangible employment action because of the employee's gender.

Hatch Act of 1939. Law prohibiting political activities by public employees. Some restrictions of this law were relaxed under the Federal Employees Political Activities Act of 1993.

Headhunting. Also known as external recruitment, occurs when the staffing function is farmed out to a third party that makes the initial contact or even provides the hiring contract.

Herzberg's theory of motivation. Determinants of job satisfaction, such as recognition, relate to job content. Determinants of job dissatisfaction are associated with job context, such as physical facilities.

Hidden workforce. Temporary employees or outside workers (consultants, contractors). Their numbers and costs are increasing.

Horns effect. See *Spillover effect.*

Hostile environment. The situation that results when an employee is subjected to severe and pervasive abuse at the workplace because of a criterion protected by discrimination laws. This is a type of unlawful harassment.

Human capital. Productive human capabilities (knowledge, skills, abilities, attributes) that can be acquired and used to yield income and improved performance in the workplace.

Human resource management. A perspective that recognizes that human resources are important assets that must be managed strategically and proactively to improve organizational performance. Development of processes for the effective utilization of people in an organization. Comparable to, but largely replaced, the term "personnel administration."

Impasse procedures. Procedures, typically involving third parties, established to reconcile differences between labor and management.

Implicit personality theory. Suggests that people generally judge the "whole person" based on limited data (stereotyping based on first impressions, or the spillover effect); ratings then tend to justify these global opinions rather than accurately gauge performance.

Indirect evidence. In a discrimination or retaliation case, proof of actions taken by the employer that support an inference of unlawful bias against the employee.

Individual equity. Perceived fairness of individual pay decisions.

Individual vs. "pool" hiring. Broad, entry-level classifications in moderately large organizations generally are filled using pool hiring in which many positions are advertised simultaneously or in which advertising for a job classification is continuous. All other positions generally hire on an individual basis.

Inside (internal) vs. outside (external) recruitment. Refers to whether recruitment and hiring is limited to organizational members. Generally, this decision is a matter of organizational tradition. Those organizations that are rank based hire internally, whereas those that are position based hire from outside as well.

Institutional recruitment. Similar to hiring from a "pool" (see *Individual vs. "pool" hiring*).

Interest arbitration. Refers to arbitration dealing with the terms of the negotiated contract; it can be voluntary or compulsory.

Internal equity. Comparison of what employees are paid doing similar jobs in an organization.

Internally based hiring. When selection is limited to the agency or department, or sometimes the governmental body. Frequently, internally based hiring simply opens positions to internal candidates first, and then to external candidates if no suitable internal candidates are found. Internally based hiring is most common in nonentry hires (with the major exception of converting interns to permanent employees). Although internally based hiring limits the merit principle, it is done in the name of increasing hiring assurance (because hires are known), improving initial hiring with better long-term promotional opportunities, and increasing employee morale.

Internship recruitment. The practice of using internship programs as a source of recruitment. Often used to attract high-quality management and professional candidates.

Job analysis. A systematic process of collecting data for determining the knowledge, skills, abilities, and other characteristics required to successfully perform a job and to make numerous judgments about the job.

Job announcements. Generally tailored to the specific purpose to which they are being addressed. A full job announcement generally includes the job title and agency or organization affiliation, salary range, description of the job duties and responsibilities, minimum qualifications, special conditions, application procedures, and notice of equal employment opportunity and AA. May also include classification, career potential, and special benefits.

Job classification. Clusters of individual positions with similar characteristics that are organized in groups for classification purposes. Other terms often used as synonyms are *job, classification, job class,* or simply *class.*

Job description. Written statements that describe or list the typical or average duties (sometimes by using work examples), levels of responsibility, and general competencies and requirements of a job classification.

Job design. Specification of job features, primarily the duties, the quantity of work expected, and the level of responsibility.

Job duties. The term most frequently used in the past to refer to the major functional responsibilities of a position. The more common term today, because of the Americans with Disabilities Act, is *essential function.* Job duties can be further divided into job tasks in job analysis.

Job enlargement. Increases the scope of a job by extending the range of job duties and responsibilities. It can sometimes be an antidote to jobs that are perceived as too narrow, stifling, or in which the work is too fragmented from either a worker or client perspective.

Job enrichment. Attempts to motivate employees by giving them more authority or independence for organizing their work and solving problems.

Job evaluation. Systematic determination of the value of each job in relation to others in an organization.

Job posting. Posting was originally placing a job announcement on walls in prominent places. Many civil service systems require posting in a minimum number of public places. Today, it also refers to listing jobs with in-house job bulletins, newspapers, or communications such as Intranet or email.

Job rotation. A means of developing employees at all levels so that they understand the "big picture" and become cross-trained.

Job sharing. Enables two employees to split the responsibilities, hours, salary, and (usually) the benefits of a full-time position.

Job specialization. Narrowing job responsibilities to just a few. Tends to promote higher levels of task mastery and thus speed, less training, and simpler incumbent replacement. In many situations, job specialization leads to more-manageable jobs and greater professionalization. In other situations, however, it can be perceived as treating employees like replaceable parts who are in deadening assembly-line-type jobs.

Job tasks. Elements of job duties. See also *Job duties* and *Essential function.*

Labor market. A geographical area or occupational field within which the forces of supply and demand, often constrained by political factors, interact to affect the size of the workforce and its pay level.

Labor market survey. A critical source of information about long-term staffing trends.

Lateral entry. When non-entry-level positions can be filled from outside the organization. Lateral entry exists in rank-in-job systems, which tend to encourage competition based on technical qualifications.

Learning plateau. A period during which employees must first fully absorb and assimilate the training material before they learn more.

Leave sharing. A type of employee-to-employee job benefit whereby healthy workers donate sick time or other benefits to coworkers in crisis.

Leniency error. All individuals or all performance dimensions are rated favorably.

Letter of intent. A letter that confirms the offer of a specific position and may stipulate major work conditions such as starting date, salary, or hiring contingencies (if any).

Liberation management. A reform tide with the goal of higher performance characterized by implementation strategies such as standards, evaluations, and outcomes and typified by laws such as the Government Performance and Results Act of 1993.

Mail recruitment. A highly personalized approach in which individuals are encouraged by letter to apply for positions. Today it may include email recruitment as well.

Maintenance of membership. Employee is obligated to maintain union membership in the representative union once affiliated during the life of the contract.

Management by objectives (MBO). Results-oriented rating system based on how well managers achieve predetermined goals.

***McDonnell Douglas* burden-shifting approach.** In discrimination and retaliation claims, this is a framework that explains how a plaintiff may prove that discrimination or retaliation occurred.

Med-arb. Requires an arbitrator to begin with mediation, settle as many disputes as feasible, and move to arbitration only on items that remain contentious.

Mediation. A dispute resolution procedure that relies on a neutral third party who attempts to facilitate communication and bring the parties together to reach an agreement.

Meet-and-confer rights. Laws requiring agency heads to discuss, but not to settle, grievances.

Mentoring. A development approach through which employees develop their career potential through ongoing, periodic dialogue with more-experienced personnel.

Merit pay. System under which permanent increases in base pay are based on performance.

Merit selection. Emphasizes technical qualifications using processes that analyze job competencies and require open application procedures.

Merit system. A fair and orderly process for recruitment, promotion, rewards, and punishments on the basis of qualifications, performance, and competitive selection as judged by experts.

Motivation. The drive or energy that compels people to act, with energy and persistence, toward some goal.

Motivational needs (groups). This book identifies eight groups of needs that provide motivation: (1) physical security, (2) acknowledgement and recognition, (3) achievement, (4) power, (5) employee relationship needs, (6) nonwork needs, (7) predictability and control, and (8) the need to minimize demotivators.

National Partnership for Reinventing Government. Initiative by the Clinton administration that sought to cut red tape, improve government performance, and hold public employees responsible for program results.

Needs assessment. A strategy related to training that involves surveying employees and managers about their training needs.

Negligent hiring. When employers are deemed not to have used satisfactory screening through reference checks, background investigations, and thorough selection processes for positions that have a public safety dimension. Examples include driving, law enforcement, corrections, elder care, and those working with children.

Neutral competence. A standard or value that early civil service reformers thought should be applied in selecting and retaining civil servants, as opposed to patronage.

New Millennials. Those born after 1980.

No money effect. Occurs when either there are insufficient funds to distribute or they are awarded on an across-the-board basis.

Noncompetitive recruitment. A single official completes the hiring process with a formal comparison of candidates. Sometimes immediate hiring is allowed if candidates meet certain standards. At other times, *noncompetitive recruitment* means that the decision maker has the authority to select those people deemed appropriate, for whatever reason.

Nontraditional families. Includes gay and lesbian couples, unmarried couples in committed relationships, single-parent families, and reconstituted families.

Occupational families. The grouping of class series (or positions that are not in a class series) into large clusters. Examples include firefighters, administrative support staff, corrections personnel, and human service personnel. Occupational families are sometimes based primarily on job function (law enforcement regardless of agency affiliation) and sometimes on job mission (law enforcement related to drug enforcement).

Official immunity. A legal doctrine that prevents government employees from being held individually liable for actions within the scope of their duty.

Onboarding. The process of preparing for and supporting a new employee. It includes workplace preparation, initial training, provision of a mentor, and any other assistance a new person needs to make a successful transition into the organization and to increase the likelihood of a positive long-term appreciation of the position and agency.

On-the-job training. Learning that employees undergo as they master the unique requirements of their specific jobs.

Open personnel system. Typical in rank-in-job systems in which opportunities exist for lateral entry for those outside the organization. Ideally, such systems foster high technical qualifications, foster healthy competition, and prevent organization "inbreeding" and "groupthink." See also *Closed personnel system.*

Open shop. A union can represent workers, but the nonunion workers have no financial obligations to the union.

Organization-centered evaluation. Organizational processes are monitored and evaluated on the premise that employees will work effectively within the system if it is well designed by management.

Overlearning. The assimilation of material so that it becomes second nature.

Paradox. Seemingly incompatible ideas. Clashes between apparent truths.

Paradox of democracy. People as citizens have many civil rights, but as employees of organizations they surrender those rights.

Paradox of needs. Individuals and organizations need one another, but their respective needs are as likely to conflict as they are to coincide because people are dynamic and organic, whereas many organizations are static and mechanical.

Parental leave. Provides leave from work for the employee to care for needy family members.

Patronage. Selection decisions in which a single person is responsible for designating officials or employees without a requirement for a formalized application process. Those deciding patronage appointments may balance party loyalty, personal acquaintance, and technical competence. Such appointments may or may not be subject to a confirmation process. Although *patronage* and *spoils* are frequently used interchangeably, they are not identical. *Spoils* refers to the use of patronage appointments primarily as a means of reward and where technical qualifications are noticeably lacking. *Spoils* also refers to handling positions in the career service as patronage appointments. See also *Spoils system.*

Pay banding. See *Broadbanding.*

Pay compression. The narrowing of differentials between pay grades in an agency.

Pay equity. The perception that the compensation received is equal in value to the work performed.

Pay plan. A pay schedule in which the grades, steps, and related pay is determined. In reality, most jurisdictions have numerous schedules as a part of their pay plan for different occupational clusters, often based on union representation of different occupational groups.

Peer evaluation. Method of appraisal in which employees at the same level in the organization rate each other.

Pendleton Act of 1883. Established a system of open competition for government jobs via examinations, prohibiting firing of civil servants for partisan reasons, authorizing creation of a civil service commission, and empowering the president to alter the extent of civil service coverage.

Performance tests in selection. Directly assesses the skills necessary for specific jobs. Can apply to physical skills, knowledge tests of job aspects, or work samples (or assessment centers). In all performance tests, the connection between the test and some aspect of the job should be direct, unlike aptitude and skill tests in which the connection may be indirect.

Personal contact recruitment. Occurs when recruiters, managers, or search panel members attend job fairs, conduct on-campus recruiting, or personally contact top candidates for positions.

Personnel administration. A series of activities—recruitment, compensation, discipline—directed at enhancing productivity of the people who work within an organization. Synonymous with human resource management.

Piecemeal personnel system. One that lacks grades or ranks and assigns salaries on an ad hoc basis. Only common in very small jurisdictions.

Point factor analysis. Job evaluation method that assigns points to compensable factors, which are summed to determine pay.

Point factor method. Starts with the assumption that factors should be broad enough to apply consistently to all jobs in an organization or schedule. Differs from job factor systems that may only use those factors directly related to specific positions.

POSDCORB. Acronym for *planning, organizing, staffing, directing, coordinating, reporting,* and *budgeting.* Originated by Frederick Taylor during the scientific management "tide" in an effort to provide the "one best way" to administer government programs.

Position. The job of a single individual, as well as the specific duties and responsibilities.

Position announcements. See *Job announcements.*

Position classification system. Provides grades or ranks for all merit positions as well as for nonmerit positions. Position classification systems can provide both the basis for position evaluation and management, on the one hand, and job support and design on the other.

Position description. Written statement that defines the exact duties, level of responsibility, and organizational placement of a single position.

Position management system. Generally refers to the allocation of positions for budgetary purposes.

Positive discipline. A step-by-step participatory procedure that encourages employees to take responsibility for correcting problems.

Positive reinforcement. Feedback that helps employees reduce errors and meet standards; enhances their motivation to excel.

Preemployment investigations. Various procedures used to validate applicant-provided information and to otherwise determine the suitability of candidates.

Principle of motivation. A principle which statses that people are motivated to pursue and satisfy their needs.

Principled negotiations. Negotiation process that stresses identification of common ground between labor and management, focuses on cooperative problem solving, and thrives in an open, trusting environment.

Principles of learning. Tenets for the effectiveness of training that involve increasing employee motivation, relevance, transference, attention to general principles, repetition, feedback, and positive reinforcement.

Problem-solving bargaining. Resolution-oriented discussion leading to mutually agreeable and beneficial answers to common problems.

Proceduralism. Connotes processes that have become excessively detailed, complicated, protracted, or impersonal.

Process management. Ensuring that the flow of work among individuals and units is as rational (smooth and optimal) as possible.

Process reengineering (process management). Ensuring that the flow of work among individuals and units is as rational (smooth and optimal) as possible.

Productivity bargaining. Labor-management negotiations on matters affecting the efficiency and effectiveness of government operations.

Progressive punishment. An adverse-action approach that uses penalties with increasing severity and provides opportunities to correct problems prior to termination (or *progressive discipline*).

Psychological contract. An unwritten understanding about mutual needs, goals, expectations, and procedures

Psychological tests in selection. Examines the personality traits of the individual and compares them to the job requirements. Although psychological tests can include general intelligence tests and motivation tests, these have generally not met the rigorous validity standards expected in the public sector. Tests, however, that measure the ability to handle stress, the inclination toward aggressiveness, and the disposition toward high standards of moral integrity have been used in the public sector.

Public Employee Relations Boards (PERBs). State administrative agencies typically charged with determining appropriate bargaining units, overseeing certification elections, and resolving unfair labor practices.

Race norming. The practice of adjusting test scores of minority groups to ensure that a sufficient number of candidates can be hired. Race norming is disallowed by the Civil Rights Act of 1991.

Rank-in-job. A personnel strategy in which rank and salary are determined by the job one holds. Substantial salary increases and higher status are attained only through a better job (promotion or reclassification), but multiple promotions within an organization are uncommon beyond predetermined job series.

Rank-in-person. A personnel strategy that emphasizes the development of incumbents over time within the organization through the use of closed systems and movement through ranks. No matter what the assignment of the individual, they are generally paid according to their rank. Tends to encourage the development of generalists (except in academic settings). Often has an "up-or-out" philosophy in which those passed over for promotion are encouraged or required to leave the organization.

Reasonable accommodation. An employer's obligation under the ADA to modify the workplace to make it possible for disabled persons to work there. It also refers to an employer's obligation under Title VII to make workplace modifications to allow employees to observe religious beliefs and practices.

Recency effect. Gives undue weight to recent occurrences when evaluations are done.

Recruitment process. Generally includes three major steps: planning and approval of the position, preparation of the position announcement, and selection and use of specific recruitment strategies.

Recruitment strategies. Include (1) posting, (2) newspapers, (3) trade journals, (4) mail, (5) other mass communications, (6) personal contacts, (7) internships, (8) external recruitment (use of a third party), and (9) noncompetitive.

Representation election. An election to determine whether a union will be recognized as the exclusive bargaining agent for workers in the unit.

Representativeness in selection. Can be interpreted in numerous ways such as by geography, social class, gender, racial or ethnic groups, prior military service, and disability.

Results-based systems. Rating format that emphasizes what employees produce.

Retaliation. Adverse action by an employer against an employee because of the employee's opposition to a prohibited employment practice or participation in an investigation, proceeding or hearing.

Right-to-work state. A state where mandatory union membership is outlawed.

Rule of seven. States that people must practice something seven times in order to master it.

Rule of three (hiring). Originally promulgated by civil service commissions. Restricted hiring to the top three candidates on the certified list. Recent trends have been to allow the hiring authority as much latitude as possible among those technically qualified.

Rule of three (training). States that people only hear things that have been said three times.

Sandwich generation. Workers who are sandwiched between responsibilities for young children and elderly parents.

Scientific management. A reform tide with the goal of efficiency, characterized by the use of implementation strategies such as structure, rules, and experts and typified by laws such as the Reorganization Act of 1939.

Self-appraisal. A rating completed by the employee herself.

Seminars and presentations. Common training strategies for conveying information.

Senior Executive Service (SES). Top-level administrators. Mostly career civil servants and a lesser number of political appointees.

Seniority. Seniority principles assert that those already employed in the agency (a) have already been through the merit process once, (b) have been screened in probationary periods and evaluation processes, and (c) have superior organizational insight and loyalty because of their history of employment.

Seniority pay. Pay determined by length of service.

Seniority-based selection. Uses time in the hiring organization as a primary or exclusive factor for promotion. Philosophically, it asserts that those already employed in the organization have been through the merit process once, have been screened in probationary and evaluation processes, and have superior organizational insight and loyalty because of their employment.

Severity error. All individuals or performance dimensions are given an unfavorable rating.

Sham recruitment. When a candidate, usually internal, has implicitly been selected for the position, even though the position is posted as open. Also know as a "wired" position.

Simulation. A training strategy whereby job conditions and situations are simulated, such as responses to natural disasters and the like.

Skill pay. Compensation for skills that employees have, develop, and use in a multiple-task environment.

Social class selection. Generally illegal as an explicit selection philosophy in the United States. It does indirectly operate, however, through proxies such as educational institutions and the subtle imposition of dominant-culture values on minorities in the selection process.

Special responsibility theory. Maintains that public employees hold critical positions in society and therefore should not be permitted to strike.

Spillover effect. An unusually good or poor trait or performance affects the entire rating, or *halo effect* or *horns effect.*

Spoils system. A special type of patronage in which appointment of jobs is viewed as spoils of office (similar to spoils of war) to those active in the victorious campaign. Can also refer to political nepotism (appointment of the family members and friends to salaried positions) and assignment of contracts based on personal contacts rather than on technical qualifications. See also *Patronage.*

Staffing. A term that incorporates both the recruitment and selection processes.

Strategic focus. In the context of training, an approach that encourages managers to relates training and development to the objectives and strategies of their units. See also page 277–278.

Strategy for feedback. Series of specific activities through which feedback is given to workers in ways that enhance performance and which minimze demotivating effects. See page 193.

Structured interviews. Interviews in which the questions are organized and refined in advance, as opposed to unstructured interviews which tend to allow the candidate to discuss past work experiences. Structured interviews emphasize job competencies by matching past experiences to current job needs through behavioral anchoring, or probe the potential of candidates by asking situational judgment questions of job-related hypothetical issues or problems.

Succession planning. Refers to an organization's ability to replace its executive and senior management ranks with high-quality talent. When there is not sufficient in-house talent to ensure an adequate pool to complement the external pool, organizational succession planning provides additional training and rotational experiences to high-potential employees, or employees who have been fast-tracked.

Surveys. A method of collecting information, often involving the perceptions of a target population or sample about some topic. In the context of training, an approach to getting information about perceived training needs, as well as information about the perceived effectiveness of training, often involving perceptions of employees or managers.

Tangible employment action. A significant change in an individual's employment status (such as a hiring, firing, failing to promote, reassignment with significantly different responsibilities, or a significant change in benefits) based on unwelcome sexual conduct. This is unlawful sexual harassment, a type of gender discrimination.

Telecommuters. People who work away from the traditional work locale (e.g., at home, at satellite locations, or on the road) by means of an electronic linkup with the workplace.

Temporary employees. Those without tenure rights and usually without benefits. A recent IRS ruling has enhanced the benefits rights of many formally considered temporary employees, creating a new class of term employees. See also *Term employees.*

Term employees. Those without tenure rights but usually with full benefits. Term employees generally have contracts for set periods of time. This is a rapidly increasing category in the public sector in which governments seem to be seeking more flexibility for long-term position management. Increasingly used by the federal government for multiple-year contracts (two to four years) and state governments, reducing the civil service protections for job classes such as managers in Maryland (see Exhibit 4.1) or whole systems of employees such as in Georgia (see Exhibit 5.3).

Termination interview. A session conducted by the supervisor or human resource department informing the employee that she is dismissed from employment at the organization.

Test validity. A psychometric concept that addresses the question of whether the test or selection instrument measures what it is intended to measure. The three types of validity allowed by the *Uniform Guidelines to Employee Selection Procedures* are content, criterion, and construct. *Content validity* requires demonstrating a direct relationship of the test to actual job duties or responsibilities. *Criterion validity* involves correlating high test scores (the predictor) with good job performance (the criterion) by those taking the test. It generally examines aptitudes or cognitive skills for learning and performing well in a given environment (e.g., the aptitude to learn a language, remember key data, or use logical reasoning). *Construct validity* documents the relationship of select abstract personal traits and characteristics (e.g., intelligence, integrity, creativity, and aggressiveness) to job performance.

The 25–50–25 rule. An heuristic rule which states that 25% of employees are highly motivated, 50% are "fence sitters," and 25% are withdrawn or cynical.

Theory X. People are inherently lazy, and therefore need a "stick and carrot" approach in order to be motivated.

Theory Y. People are inherently motivated to learn and grow. The manager's job, therefore, is to provide developmental opportunities for workers.

Tides of reform. Four reform philosophies identified by P. C. Light (1997, *Tides of Reform: Making Government Work 1945–1995,* Yale University Press, New Haven, CT)—*scientific management, war on waste, watchful eye, and liberation management*—each of which has its own goals, implementation efforts, and outcomes.

Traditional bargaining. Two bargaining teams opposing each other across the table, each side engaging in zero-sum posturing and demands.

Training. Efforts to increase knowledge, skills, and abilities to better meet the requirements of present jobs. See also *Development*.

Training evaluation. Assessments of the effectiveness-of-training efforts that usually focus on both behavioral changes and results.

Trait-based systems. Systems to examine employees for selected personal characteristics believed to be important in working effectively.

Transference. The extent to which training material is relevant in actual job situations.

Unassembled tests. The selection processes when the initial selection is primarily based on education and experience evaluation.

Unemployment compensation. A mandatory federal-state insurance program created by law that is funded by employers through a tax on payrolls. Individuals who are unemployed through no fault of their own and who are actively seeking work are eligible for partial, temporary replacement wages.

Unfair labor practices (UFLPs). Practices by unions or employers that are unfair and legally prohibited.

Union shop. New employees must join the representative union after a certain number of days (e.g., 30–90 days) specified in the collective bargaining agreement.

Unreasonable search. An inspection by government officials that violates the Fourth Amendment to the U.S. Constitution.

Up-or-out philosophy. Those who are not promoted in rank-in-person systems may eventually be forced to leave the organization. For example, assistant professors who are not promoted to associate after six years are generally given terminal contracts.

U.S. Office of Personnel Management (OPM). The federal agency charged with the "doing" side of public human resource management—coordinating the federal government's personnel program. OPM's director is appointed or removed by the president and functions as the president's principal advisor on personnel matters.

U.S. Merit Systems Protection Board (MSPB). Established by the **Civil Service Reform Act** of 1978 with responsibility to hear appeals from employees who allege that their rights under the civil service system laws and regulations have been violated.

Veterans' points. Typically, veterans serving during wars are eligible for 5 points and wounded veterans are eligible for 10 points, which increases their ratings as job candidates, although practice varies among the states and federal government.

V-time. Voluntary reduced time. Enables parents to meet their caregiving responsibilities, provides an alternative to layoffs or the use of part-time replacements, and helps phase workers into retirement.

War on waste. A reform tide with the goal of economy, characterized by use of implementation strategies such as generally accepted practices, audits, and investigations and typified by laws such as the Inspector General Act of 1978.

Watchful eye. A reform tide with the goal of fairness, characterized by use of implementation strategies such as whistleblowers, interest groups, and media, and typified by laws such as the Administrative Procedure Act of 1946.

Wellness programs. Programs with a goal of altering unhealthy personal habits and lifestyles and promoting behaviors more conducive to health and well-being.

Whipsaw effect. In the context of labor-management relations, gains by one union might be used to justify benefits for another.

Whistleblower Protection Act of 1989. Law protecting federal employee whistleblowers from unfair retaliation, specifying burden-of-proof requirements regarding retaliation, and outlining appeals channels.

Whistleblower statutes. Laws that protect employees who disclose wrong-doing by their employers from retaliation by their employers.

Whole job analysis. Does not systematically break down a job into its constituent parts for purposes of grade and classification, but instead relies on past experience and intuition.

Whole job evaluation. Does not systematically break a job down into its constituent parts for purposes of compensation, but instead relies on past experience and intuition.

Workers' compensation. A mandatory insurance program created by federal and state laws that is funded by employers. Workers who are injured on the job are compensated for medical bills and lost earnings, but they give up the right to sue for negligence.

Work samples. When performance tests simulate actual aspects of the job, they are called *work samples*. For example, having a trainer provide a demonstration is a work sample, as is having a lawyer provide examples of former legal briefs. When a variety of work samples is constructed to test the range of abilities of an applicant over an extended period (such as a full day), it is generally called an *assessment center*.

Work stoppages. Strikes.

AUTHOR INDEX

Subject Index

ABOUT THE AUTHORS

Evan M. Berman is Distinguished University Professor at National Chengchi University in Taipei (Taiwan). He is Editor-in-Chief of the American Society for Public Administration's Book Series in Public Administration and Public Policy, Senior Editor of Public Performance and Management Review, a Distinguished Fulbright Scholar, and past chair of the ASPA's Section of Personnel and Labor Relations. His areas of expertise include human resource management, public performance, local government and, after spending a career in U.S. settings, his further international interests have now taken him to East Asia. Berman is a prolific author in the discipline who has over 100 publications and 10 books, including *Public Administration in East Asia: China, South Korea, Japan and Taiwan* (forthcoming), *Encyclopedia of Public Administration and Public Policy* (2007, third edition), *Essential Statistics for Public Managers and Policy Analysts* (2006, second edition), and *Performance and Productivity for Public and Nonprofit Organizations* (2006, second edition). Berman was previously a policy analyst with the National Science Foundation and the Huey McElveen Distinguished Professor at Louisiana State University. He has also assisted local jurisdictions on matters of team building, performance measurement, and citizen participation.

James S. Bowman is professor of public administration at Florida State University. His primary area is human resource management, complemented by work in ethics and quality management. He is author of more than 100 journal articles and book chapters, as well as editor of six anthologies. He is coauthor of *Achieving Competencies in Public Service: The Professional Edge* (second edition, 2010). He is editor in chief of *Public Integrity,* a journal of the American Society for Public Administration, and serves on the editorial boards of three other professional journals. A Kellogg Foundation Fellow and a past Fellow of the National Association of Schools of Public Affairs and Administration, he has a background in business as well as experience in both the military and civil service.

Jonathan P. West is professor of political science and director of the Graduate Public Administration Program at the University of Miami. His research interests include human resource management, productivity, local government, and ethics. He has published eight books and more than 100 scholarly articles and book chapters. *American Public Service: Radical Reform of the Merit System* (2007), *The Ethics Edge* (second edition, 2006), and the *Achieving Competencies in Public Service: The Professional Edge* (second edition, 2010) are his most recent coauthored or coedited books. His coauthored book titled *American Politics* *and the Environment* was published in 2002. He is managing editor of *Public Integrity* and a member of the editorial board of two other professional journals. He has experience as a management analyst working for the Office of the Surgeon General, Department of the Army.

Montgomery R. Van Wart is professor and chair of the Public Administration Department at California State University, San Bernardino. His publications include eight books and a substantial number of articles in the leading journals in his field. *Dynamics of Leadership in Public Service: Theory and Practice* (2005) was awarded "Outstanding Academic Title" by *Choice.* His research areas are administrative leadership, human resource management, training and development, administrative values and ethics, organization behavior, and general management. He also serves on numerous editorial boards and as the associate editor for *Public Productivity & Management Review.* As an instructor, he has spent as much time teaching and facilitating programs for executives and managers in public agencies as he has teaching graduate students. His training programs have been offered to individuals in all levels of government in the United States, and to executives and elected officials from other countries.

Supporting researchers for more than 40 years

Research methods have always been at the core of SAGE's publishing program. Founder Sara Miller McCune published SAGE's first methods book, *Public Policy Evaluation*, in 1970. Soon after, she launched the *Quantitative Applications in the Social Sciences* series—affectionately known as the "little green books."

Always at the forefront of developing and supporting new approaches in methods, SAGE published early groundbreaking texts and journals in the fields of qualitative methods and evaluation.

Today, more than 40 years and two million little green books later, SAGE continues to push the boundaries with a growing list of more than 1,200 research methods books, journals, and reference works across the social, behavioral, and health sciences. Its imprints—Pine Forge Press, home of innovative textbooks in sociology, and Corwin, publisher of PreK–12 resources for teachers and administrators—broaden SAGE's range of offerings in methods. SAGE further extended its impact in 2008 when it acquired CQ Press and its best-selling and highly respected political science research methods list.

From qualitative, quantitative, and mixed methods to evaluation, SAGE is the essential resource for academics and practitioners looking for the latest methods by leading scholars.

For more information, visit **www.sagepub.com**.